MENU DESIGN

MERCHANDISING AND MARKETING

MENU DESIGN

MERCHANDISING AND MARKETING

FOURTH EDITION

Albin G. Seaberg

VAN NOSTRAND REINHOLD
New York

Library of Congress Catalog Card Number 89-33712
ISBN 0-442-31958-4

I(T)P Van Nostrand Reinhold is an International Thomson Publishing company.
ITP logo is a trademark under license.

Printed in the United States of America

Van Nostrand Reinhold
115 Fifth Avenue
New York, NY 10003

International Thomson Publishing GmbH
Königswinterer Str. 418
53227 Bonn
Germany

International Thomson Publishing
Berkshire House,168-173
High Holborn, London WC1V 7AA
England

International Thomson Publishing Asia
221 Henderson Bldg. #05-10
Singapore 0315

Thomas Nelson Australia
102 Dodds Street
South Melbourne 3205
Victoria, Australia

International Thomson Publishing Japan
Kyowa Building, 3F
2-2-1 Hirakawacho
Chiyoda-Ku, Tokyo 102
Japan

Nelson Canada
1120 Birchmount Road
Scarborough, Ontario
M1K 5G4, Canada

16 15 14 13 12 11 10 9 8 7 6 5 4 3

Library of Congress Cataloging-in-Publication Data

Seaberg, Albin G.
Menu design—merchandising and marketing / Albin G. Seaberg.—4th ed.
p. cm.
Includes index.
ISBN 0-442-31958-4
1. Menus. I. Title.
TX911.3.M45S4 1990
642'.5—dc20
89-33712
CIP

Contents

Preface

When customers are seated at a table in your restaurant, they are given a menu—the primary communications, sales, and public relations tool of your restaurant. Your wait staff may be trained to tell the customer about daily specials or items for which the restaurant is famous, but the main selling and communicating are the job of the menu. It may not bring your customers into the restaurant, but once they are there, the menu determines what they will order and how much they will spend. Thus, the menu is important to running a successful and profitable restaurant.

A menu is a piece of paper on which words and illustrations are printed. It should be colorful, attractive, clean, and reflective of the quality, appearance, and style of the restaurant. A dirty, poorly printed, hard-to-read menu creates a negative first impression. An attractive, colorful, well-written menu, on the other hand, puts the customer in an ordering mood.

The average customer does not always come to your restaurant knowing exactly what he or she wants, unless yours is a very limited fast-food operation. Instead, the menu guides the decision of what to order, and the right words and pictures appropriately arranged determine both what and how much the customer orders.

This book will help you produce a better, more effective menu that will increase profits. It has often been demonstrated that, by changing nothing in a restaurant's operation but the menu, sales and profits can be increased. The examples shown in this book, therefore, are those of successful, creative restaurant operators and the people who have helped them produce their menus.

THE MENU AS A MARKETING TOOL

The menu reflects all of the decisions concerning what to serve, how to serve it, and what to charge for it. The actual food and drink items listed may have been selected by the chef or the proprietor, but how they are sold on the menu is decided by the menu designer. This book attempts to help you choose what to serve and how to sell it on the menu.

The menu can also act as a marketing scorecard. That is, a record can be kept of weekly or monthly changes on the menu—the listing of different items, or the different ways of listing dishes—which will indicate the item's popularity. Some large chains and hotel groups check monthly computer-generated consumption figures based on their menus to ensure that items the public wants are being served throughout their foodservice operations.

Since different kinds of foodservice operations require different kinds of menus, this book presents information useful to every type of operation, from fast food to elegant and expensive dining. Besides presenting the basic rules of advertising, publicity, and merchandising as they apply to the restaurant business, we have also attempted to show what is being served in restaurants across America and abroad. In this sense every menu is a result of the market research done by a particular restaurant or, in the case of larger group operations, by hundreds of food outlets.

HELP IN CREATING A MENU

Some larger, big-city restaurants or multiple-outlet organizations have access to sophisticated suppliers, including advertising agencies that can help them write, design, and organize their menus. Other, smaller restaurant operators may be limited to only the help of a printer. This book is designed to help both groups.

A foodservice operator must fill many roles, including those of chef, accountant, public relations person, personnel and labor consultant, tax collector, and even psychologist. He or she cannot know everything and must rely on outside experts. In producing menus, the restaurateur may use artists, writers, designers, and advertising agencies. In the final analysis, it is the restaurateur who decides if an idea is "go" or "no-go." The material in this book should help that person make the right decisions.

THE CHANGING MENU

The foodservice industry changes along with the rest of the American economy. Indeed, change is the reason for this new, revised fourth edition of *Menu Design*, whose purpose is to keep restaurant people aware of changes in food and drink preferences, as well as the more constant aspects of the menu. The trick is to know what to keep and when and what to change. The guidelines provided in this book will help menu planners make effective decisions.

1

Producing a Menu

The menu begins in the kitchen with the chef, who prepares the food to be served. The general style and kind of restaurant, the market, and the hours and meals served also influence the thought and marketing study that must go into the items that are to appear on the menu before the actual production begins. The size of the menu, the number of items to be offered, and the range of items, from appetizers to desserts, also must be determined. Another major decision is whether to offer a fixed-price dinner or luncheon or to list everything à la carte. Of course, any complete dinner must describe the complete "package," which may include vegetables, rolls, salad (or soup), beverage, and dessert, or some variation of extras.

Not all menus are new, of course; often they are revisions of old menus, given a new look and character to meet changing trends. In any case, when you have made your marketing decisions to fit your clientele and your kitchen, you next need to turn those decisions into a menu.

COMPILING MENU DATA

The following table should help you compile your data. You can use it for all the various categories of the menu: appetizers, soups, salads, sandwiches, entrées, side orders, desserts, and beverages—both alcoholic and nonalcoholic. You can organize your menu planning by filling in the six columns in the table—item number, description, cost, price, profit, and popularity—for every entrée, appetizer, dessert, salad, and sandwich on a menu. This information helps the restaurant operator and the menu designer decide which items to feature in each category. For example, an item may be popular but not profitable. Unless it is used as a "loss leader," its price should be raised. Conversely, if an item is profitable but not popular, it should be given more prominence on the menu and presented in a way that will win more consumer acceptance. Once a table for each category has been filled out, the menu designer and writer can devise an effective menu that should increase profits. The following paragraphs cover the most common menu categories.

Appetizers. Six appetizers is the average number for a fairly large menu. Their final description should be more complete and more persuasive than their simple identification on the table of data.

Soups. A soup du jour (soup of the day) can be listed in the menu or on a daily supplement, which makes the soup list more flexible.

Salads. There are two types of salads: the entrée salad and the salad that accompanies dinner, either included or à la carte. The two should be differentiated on the menu.

Sandwiches. Not every restaurant offers sandwiches. For example, an expensive French restaurant with a fixed-price dinner for $65 will not serve sandwiches. But many restaurants that serve both lunch and dinner have a broader customer base and offer a sandwich selection.

Entrées. The entrée section generally can be divided into the categories of meat—beef, pork, lamb, and veal; seafood—fish and shellfish, such as shrimp, crab, and lobster; and poultry, including chicken, turkey, and Cornish game hen.

Side Orders. Side orders or extras may accompany a complete dinner or luncheon or be served as à la carte items. The latter can include vegetables; french-fried potatoes, onion rings, or mushrooms; chili; and pizza. The type and number of these side orders depend on the kind of restaurant. A separate ice-cream menu—malts, shakes, and sundaes—can be included in this category.

Desserts. Desserts can be listed on the entrée menu or separately on a dessert menu. They also can be presented on a tray or dessert cart.

TABLE 1.1 Data for Items Appearing on the Menu

Item #	Description	Cost	Price	Profit	Popularity

Children's menu. The "family" restaurant should offer some items for children, consisting of smaller portions at a lower price. They can be included on the regular menu or listed on a separate children's menu.

Beverages. Nonalcoholic beverages include coffee, tea, milk, soft drinks, and mineral water. Nonalcoholic cocktails, wines, and beers should probably be listed along with the alcoholic beverages under a separate heading.

Alcoholic beverages may include cocktails, beer, brandy, and cognac in addition to wine. If desired, after-dinner drinks, including dessert wines, can be listed on a separate menu.

Many restaurants have a separate wine list. The table for wines should contain a column for bin number. Identifying each wine's location with a bin number enables the server to find the correct bottle easily. This is especially important when the wine list is long.

Besides the standard classifications—red, white, sparkling, rosé, dessert—and "by the glass," wines may be designated as imported or American, and the imported wines may be further identified as French, German, Italian, and so forth. The longer the list, the more important it will be to use these subclassifications. Indeed, a big wine cellar can contain up to fifteen hundred bottles, which would require a great amount of identification.

Breakfast items. Breakfast menus have several categories—juices, egg dishes, cereals, breakfast meats, and bread or pastry. Juices can include orange, grapefruit, tomato, apple, prune, and vegetable juices. Fresh fruits vary with the season. This category may also include yogurt, plain or flavored.

The cereal category should include both hot and cold cereals.

Many egg combinations are possible: one, two, or three eggs with bacon or sausage and hash browns, eggs Benedict, eggs and corned beef hash, and steak and eggs. The omelette list can include standard options such as cheese and bacon or Spanish omelette, or a variety of other combinations.

Breakfast side orders may include ham, bacon, sausage, hash brown potatoes, toast, muffins, rolls, pastry, corned beef hash, pancakes, waffles, and French toast. These all may appear on one table of data.

The breakfast beverages category includes coffee, tea, hot chocolate, and whole or skim milk.

Specials are an important part of the menu; they provide variety, spice, and flexibility to an otherwise stable bill of fare. Menus are usually changed every month, every three months (seasonally), or every year rather than daily. It is thus important to devise a way to display daily or weekly specials.

European chefs usually shop at the local markets in the morning, buying fresh fruits and vegetables, fish, meat, and poultry, which determine their menu for the day. This is the most flexible of all menus. But American restaurants tend to have less changeable menus, and thus specials are even more important. The designer of your menu need not know what all of your specials will be but should allow for them on the standard menu. Some typical specials are

- *Seasonal specials.* Examples are fruits in season, fish or other seafood available that day, or vegetables flown in from overseas.
- *"For two" combinations.* These can be either occasional additions or part of the regular menu.
- *Ethnic specials.* Italian, German, Greek, or Asian items may be mixed into an otherwise American menu.
- *Special Sunday or other buffets.* An example is a Scandinavian smörgåsbord.

Specials are indicated by means of tip-ons in a box, by table tents, by special menus (for a holiday, for example), and by the server, who should recite the daily specials when presenting the menu.

DESIGNING AND PRINTING THE MENU

The selection of a designer, writer, and producer of a menu depends in part on the size and location of your restaurant. The following list offers several possibilities.

An advertising agency. If you are currently using an ad agency for your restaurant's publicity, you can ask them to write and design your menu as well. You may want to arrange for the actual printing of the menu yourself, in order to establish an ongoing relationship with a printer.

A menu printer. Some printing companies specialize in producing menus. The best of them have a complete staff to serve you—writers, artists, and experienced production people—and can show you menus that they have produced for other restaurants so that you can see their capabilities. A menu printer will have printing presses and typesetting equipment suitable for producing menus as well as experience in the problems of producing a menu.

An artist-designer. A commercial artist or graphic designer can give you an attractive menu plus a functional layout. But you still must write the menu yourself or hire a writer.

A writer. An advertising copywriter can help you organize your menu and add creative sparkle to the descriptions of your food and drink. The writer must also work with the designer to ensure that text and graphics are compatible.

A printer. Most printers can produce a menu after the artwork and typesetting have been finished, although most printers are not specially equipped for menu printing. The size of the menu, kind of paper, and coating that you choose may determine the printer to be selected. In addition, most menus are short-run printing jobs, whereas some printers are equipped only for longer runs. Large restaurant chains with larger runs of menus, of course, use a printer with the appropriate equipment. And if your menu is to be printed in two or more colors, your printer must have suitable presses and plate-making capabilities.

Typesetting, or composition, facilities also are needed to produce a menu or wine list. Today, nearly all typesetting is cold phototypesetting. The days of hot metal are long gone. You can of course go to a type house, but some printers and design studios offer composition services as well. Whichever you choose should have a wide selection of typefaces.

A word processor or computer and a laser printer are most useful in the production of a menu. Most word processors offer many type styles and sizes, so that the finished result will look like type set by the phototypesetting process. Since the paper used is lightweight, it usually has to be put into a clear plastic folder.

Computer-generated copy is particularly suited to wine lists. For example, The 95th restaurant, the ARA flagship eatery on the ninety-fifth floor of the John Hancock Building in Chicago, has a wine list produced on a word processor. Because the restaurant offers eight hundred different wines, the list is constantly changing, with some wines removed and others added. Storing the entire list in the computer makes it easy to add and delete items and to keep the list current. The wine list itself is a book containing clear plastic pages into which the laser printouts are inserted.

PRICING

In addition to deciding what to serve, the restaurant operator must decide what to charge for each item. Pricing is determined by cost, what the market will bear—and what the competition will allow.

Pricing varies from restaurant to restaurant, city to city, and among neighborhoods in cities and suburbs. A baseline to start from is a 1985–1986 Gallup poll showing an average check of $7.10 for the American diner. Table 1.2 shows the average price paid for meals eaten out in 1985.

TABLE 1.2 Average Price of Meals, 1985

Type of Restaurant	Breakfast ($)	Lunch ($)	Dinner ($)
Adult-oriented	5.33	7.93	14.47
Family style	3.45	5.16	7.63
Fast food	2.27	3.11	3.55
Cafeteria	2.17	2.84	3.99

Inflation has already pushed these prices higher and will continue to do so, but the ratios between the type of restaurant and the meals—breakfast, lunch, and dinner—will probably remain the same.

TARGETING THE MARKET

The restaurant market is so varied that not every segment can be covered by one restaurant or even a whole restaurant chain. For example, fast-food restaurants aim at a mass market but not a class market. A family-style restaurant usually offers a children's menu, but a bistro does not. Obviously, it is important to decide on the type of customer to be targeted before producing the menu, the restaurant decor, and the cuisine.

In the United States, forty cents of every food dollar is spent eating out. A 1987 Gallup poll found that 33 percent of women dined out at least once a day. In fact, women make up the majority of diners in cafeterias at lunch (54 percent) and dinner (52 percent), but men lead in other categories. Of the total eating-out population, women comprise 47 percent and men 53 percent.

Women working full time increased their frequency of eating out from 35 percent in 1978 to 42 percent in 1985, a trend that is likely to continue. Unmarried people under the age of fifty are more likely than is the population as a whole to eat each meal out, with fast-food restaurants their top choice. Household income plays an important part in the frequency of eating out: Around 47 percent of those with incomes over $30,000 dine out often.

In regard to healthful eating, 50 percent of adults surveyed in 1985 said they were likely to order a low-salt meal. In all cases, women were much more concerned about health and diet than were men. For example, 55 percent of the women ordered low-salt meals, but only 45 percent of the men did so. Women are also apt to order smaller portions than men are (66 percent to 41 percent). In addition, the likelihood of ordering low-calorie entrées remained constant through the 1980s: One of every two consumers is fairly likely or very likely to choose a lower-calorie menu item if the restaurant offers it. The restaurateur needs to be aware of trends such as these if menu planning is to be effective.

2

Type and Paper for a Better Menu

IMPORTANCE OF THE TYPEFACE

Some people may think that the menu's typeface is an unimportant detail in the operation of a restaurant, but because verbal communication between the server and the served is limited and patrons are generally reluctant to ask questions, written communication becomes very important. Remember that the purpose of a restaurant menu is to describe to the customer the food items being served and their prices. An effective menu is one that is printed in a readable and attractive typeface.

A study of thousands of menus showed that many were printed in a typeface too small for easy reading, had lines set so close together they caused confusion, or listed entrées, appetizers, salads, sandwiches, desserts, and beverages in such an illogical manner that selection became a chore instead of a pleasure.

Many typefaces are available, and your printer will have a book from which you can select one. The varieties that we will discuss here are Roman, Modern, and Script (see Figure 2.1).

Roman. Roman typefaces are patterned after engraved Roman inscriptions. The letters have both thick and thin elements and are extremely readable. Most books, magazines, and newspapers are set in some version of a Roman typeface such as Bodoni, Garamond, Caslon, and Century Schoolbook.

Modern. Modern typefaces are newer and do not have the thick–thin character of Roman faces. They are cleaner looking, do not have serifs (the flourishes at the ends of the strokes), and are more regular in shape. Examples of Modern typefaces are Futura, Twentieth Century, Spartan, and Venus.

Script. Script typefaces are an imitation of handwriting or lettering. They generally should be used only for headings and subheads, as script typefaces may be hard to read. However, their occasional use adds variety and beauty to a menu. Some script typefaces are Commercial Script, Lydian Cursive, and Brush.

Each of the typefaces can be set in either uppercase (A, B, C, D, E) or lowercase letters (a, b, c, d, e). When composing a menu, remember that it is easier to read lowercase letters than uppercase, or "all caps." The irregular appearance of lowercase letters catches the eye as it moves along. Evidence of the easier readability of lowercase type is the fact that books, magazines, and newspapers are always set mainly in lowercase type. This emphasis does not mean that uppercase letters should not be used; indeed, caps are most effective for headings, subheads, and emphasis. They provide a change from the lowercase letters and often are used to establish categories and breaks in the menu, the body of which is generally in lowercase letters.

In addition to lowercase and uppercase letters, most typefaces can be set in italics. Like uppercase letters, italics should be used sparingly for emphasis; large amounts of italic type are tiring to the eye and hard to read.

The size of the type is as important as the style. Type is measured by points. Usually starting with a 6-point type, the size increases to 8, 10, 12, 14, 16, 18, 24, 48, and 72 points. When composing a menu, never set any part smaller than 12-point type. Your menu will be read by people with a variety of visual problems. For example, many older people have trouble reading small type, and many people who wear glasses only for reading are reluctant to take them out in a public place such as a restaurant. To be considerate of all your customers, set your menu in a large, easy-to-read type.

The next consideration is the space between the lines of type or, as it is called in the printing trade, the *leading*. Leading, like type, is measured in points. Type set without any leading between the lines is set "solid." As a rule of thumb, three points of leading should be the

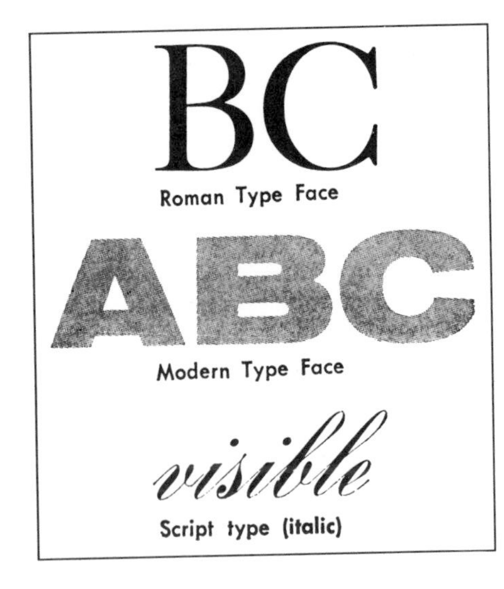

FIGURE 2.1 Different typefaces for menus.

SOLID

The main purpose of letters is the practical one
of making thoughts visible. RUSKIN says that "al
l letters are frightful things, and to be endured o
nly upon occasion, that is to say, in places wher
The main purpose of letters is the practical one
of making thoughts visible. Ruskin says that "all
THE MAIN PURPOSE OF LETTERS IS THE PRACTICAL O
THE MAIN PURPOSE OF LETTERS IS TH

Type set solid—no leading.

3 PT. LEADED

The main purpose of letters is the practical one
of making thoughts visible. RUSKIN says that "al
l letters are frightful things, and to be endured o
nly upon occasion, that is to say, in places wher
e the sense of the inscription is of more importa
The main purpose of letters is the practical one
of making thoughts visible. Ruskin says that "all

Same type set with 3 points of leading.

minimum on a menu. Leading gives air, or white space, around the type so that it is easy to read and easy on the eyes.

So far, we have emphasized readability, as communication is the primary purpose of a menu. Other considerations, such as design, character, or color, though important, are secondary to communication.

Of secondary consideration, however, is the type style. First you must consider the character of your restaurant, which should be reflected in the appearance of your menu and thus the type style(s) you choose. For instance, if your restaurant has a modern design—concrete, lots of glass, and clean, simple lines and decor—then the type style for your menu should be modern, and set in a clean, simple manner to complement your decor. But if your restaurant has a different character—Old English, Rathskeller, Chinese, Italian, Greek—you should choose a type style that will match its character and cuisine. With the wide selection of type styles available, you are sure to find one that is appropriate. A word of warning, however. Strange, exotic, and unusual type styles are usually difficult to read and therefore should be used sparingly. Just as seasoning is used to add flavor to food, unusual type is used to add flavor to a menu. But as you well know, seasoning must be used with care.

When discussing typefaces, typesetters refer to "color," even when they are talking about black type on white paper. What they are referring to is the type's weight, lightness, grayness, or open or closed character. That is, some types are heavy, thick, or very black because of their bold design, whereas others are open, light, and airy. Selecting a type for its character is important to your restaurant menu. If the type is bold and heavy, shouting in a loud voice, while your restaurant is a quiet, elegant place that caters to the "carriage trade," the result will be a sour note.

Type is most readable when printed black on white or light-tinted paper (cream, tan, ivory, gray), but it may be printed in colored ink on white or colored paper. If your type is printed in green, blue, or brown, for example, be sure it is a very dark green, blue, or brown. The key, again, is readability. Copy printed in a light color on a gray or dark paper is hard to read. Section headings such as Sandwiches, Salads, Appetizers, Beverages, and Complete Dinners may be printed in a second color to distinguish them from the dominant black or dark-colored type. As a rule, reverse type (white type on a black background) is very hard to read and should be avoided.

The following general rules should be used when composing a menu:

1. Do not use a typeface smaller than 12 points.
2. Use lowercase type for most of the menu, for maximum readability.
3. Use uppercase letters for heads and subheads.
4. Use at least three points of leading between the lines.
5. Select typefaces that match the character of your restaurant.
6. Use strange, exotic typefaces sparingly.
7. If the type is in color, be sure it is a dark one.
8. Avoid reverse type.

COMPUTER TYPESETTING

The computer has now become a general-purpose tool for restaurant personnel, and one of its uses is to set type and print it on a printer. Unlike a typewriter, a personal computer usually has a variety of typefaces, which can be printed in a variety of sizes. This means that the inside pages of a menu or wine list can be typeset and printed in-house.

Using a computer is less expensive than printing a menu and it gives the menu builder flexibility. For example, the menu or wine list can be changed daily to meet market and supply conditions. Such changes can also be made quickly. A Macintosh personal computer, for example, offers a range of typefaces (see Figure 2.2), which can be printed in various sizes (see Figure 2.3). A simple rule for setting menu type on a computer is to set the item in bolder, bigger type or in caps. Then the descriptions can be set in a lighter typeface, and if a wine is suggested to go with the listing (an entrée), it may be set in italic.

Nonetheless, using a computer to create a menu has some limitations. The main drawback is that the user of a computer usually has no design experience, and often the result is a menu that looks as though it

Athens	This is a sample of Athens
Charlotte	This is a sample of Charlotte
Chicago	This is a sample of Chicago
Courier	This is a sample of Courier
Geneva	This is a sample of Geneva
Helvetica	This is a sample of Helvetica
London	This is a sample of London
Los Angeles	This is a sample of Los Angeles
Monaco	This is a sample of Monaco
New York	This is a sample of New York
San Francisco	This is a sampleof San Francisco
Times	This is a sample of Times
Toronto	This is a sample of Toronto
Venice	This is a sample of Venice
Zapf Chan	This is a sample of Zapf Chan

FIGURE 2.2 The fifteen typefaces shown here are available on the Macintosh Plus computer.

If you SERVE it, SELL it, on the Menu

If you SERVE it, SELL it, on the Menu

If you SERVE it, SELL it, on the Menu

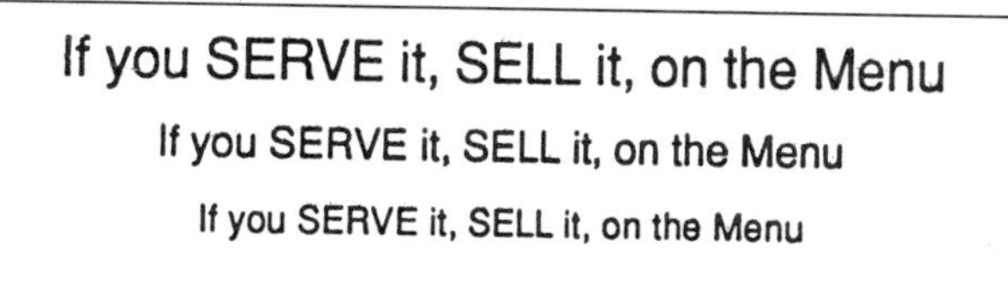

If you SERVE it, SELL it, on the Menu

If you SERVE it, SELL it, on the Menu

If you SERVE it, SELL it, on the Menu

FIGURE 2.3 Variety of computer typefaces. The size as well as the style of computer-set type can be varied.

were composed on a typewriter instead of on a computer. One way to get around this problem is to have a designer set a sample listing using the computer that the menu maker will use. This model can then be used for changes, additions, and deletions.

Another drawback to using a computer to produce the menu actually handed to customers is the paper; that is, computers print on a lightweight white paper that cannot be used by itself in a menu. Instead, it must fit into or be attached to a heavy paper menu cover, or it must be inserted into clear plastic holders. (If you are having the menu printed, of course, this output can be your camera-ready copy.) Given these limitations, much can still be done with a computer to make a menu.

CHOOSING APPROPRIATE PAPER

Your menu will last longer and look better if you take the time to select a good paper. Indeed, the design of a menu should begin with the selection of the paper on which it will be printed. The paper is as important to the menu's design as the copy, type style, and art. The paper also represents about one-third of the menu's printing cost (exclusive of art and copy).

What is paper? One answer may be that paper is the ideal printing surface, and of course, nearly all menus are printed on some kind of paper. Until the Industrial Revolution, paper was made almost completely by hand, from rags. But with the invention of papermaking machinery and advances in chemistry, modern papermaking processes were developed. Most paper used today is made by machine, from wood pulp.

The restaurateur selects paper for a menu according to how the menu is to be used and whether immediate obsolescence or maximum permanence is desired.

A menu that changes every day can be printed on lightweight, noncoated paper, as it will be used for only one day and then thrown away. A light, inexpensive paper, however, can still have color, texture, and good tactile qualities that will enhance the menu's design. But one need not consider, for this type of menu, the paper's resistance to stain, handling, and rough usage, as the menu is as impermanent as the daily newspaper. In fact, some menus of this type are printed on newsprint.

The menu designed for maximum permanence is usually printed on a heavy, durable, coated paper that will last a long time despite much handling by the customer. It should probably be a water-resistant paper that can be wiped clean with a damp cloth. Such paper is usually a heavy cover, bristol, or tag stock that is coated or treated with clay, pigment, varnish, or plastic to make the paper water and grease resistant and give it a longer life, even with constant handling.

Compromise Solutions That Work

There are variations on or combinations of these two approaches to constructing menus. For instance, a menu does not have to be printed entirely on one kind of paper. A common solution to the immediate-versus-the-permanent-menu problem is to use a heavy, coated paper for the cover of the menu and a lighter, less permanent (and less expensive) paper for the inside pages. This division can also apply to the permanent and daily items on the menu. That is, the permanent items on the menu—beverages, sandwiches, salads, house specialties—are printed on heavy paper and the items that change daily are printed on lighter paper on an insert or inserted pages. The use of different kinds of paper in the same menu can also have a design and functional purpose. Papers of different texture, thickness, and color can emphasize a particular part of the menu that the restaurateur wishes to give an extra sales push.

Selecting the right paper for a menu is the same as selecting the right silverware, dishwasher, or china. First are the physical and aesthetic qualities of paper such as strength, dimensional stability, opacity, ink receptivity, smoothness, and whiteness. Then there is texture, which varies from very coarse to very smooth. Because the menu is held in the customer's hand, as well as read, its texture or "feel" can be important.

Color can be added to the menu through the paper, from the purest white, to the softest pastels, to the richest solids. In addition, paper can be folded in many different ways to create interesting configurations, and it can be die-cut into unusual shapes other than the conventional square or rectangular form. These two characteristics of paper—foldability and the fact that it can be cut into almost any shape—should be used to advantage to create interesting menus.

MCDUFFY'S MENU: A MODEL

The menu from McDuffy's (Figure 2.4), a sports-oriented bar and dining emporium in Tempe, Arizona, is a good example of both good typesetting and a creative use of paper. Folded, the menu is 11 × 11 inches. Opened, it is twice as big, 22 × 22 inches. It is printed in brown and green on lightweight, uncoated, white paper.

The front cover has a large McDuffy's logo. When the cover is opened, the customer is presented with a two-page spread listing beers. Seven domestic and nine imported brands are listed under the Draft heading, and fourteen domestic and eleven imported beers appear under the heading of Cans. No prices are given.

The inside design and headings are creative. The listings are printed diagonally from corner to corner like a baseball diamond, with a drawing of McDuffy himself and the heading All*Star Program on second base.

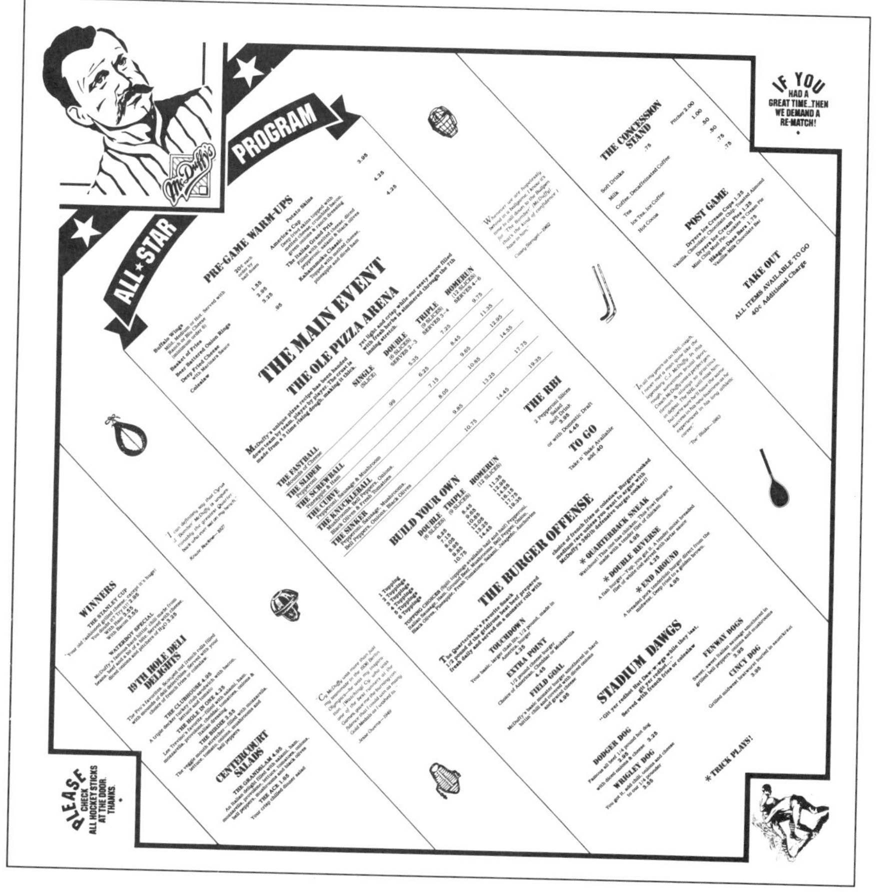

FIGURE 2.4 Creativity in a menu from McDuffy's. (Reproduced by permission.)

Pre-Game Warm-Ups include eight appetizers; three potato skins appetizers are of special interest: America's Cup (deep-fried skins topped with melted cheese, crumbled bacon, green onions, and ranch dressing); Italian Grand Prix (filled with melted cheese, diced pepperoni, salami, and black olives); and Kahanumoka Classic (topped with melted cheese, pineapple, and diced ham).

The Main Event concentrates on pizza, burgers, and hot dogs. The Old Pizza Arena offers six different pizzas in Single (one slice), Double (six slices), Triple (nine slices), and Homerun (twelve slices). A Build-Your-Own listing has from one to six toppings. A somewhat different pizza is the Screwball with pineapple and ham.

The pizza list is followed by The Burger Offense—six different selections including chicken, white cod, and pork tenderloin burgers. After the burgers come four Stadium Dawgs—the Dodger Dog, the Wrigley Dog (with chili, onions, and cheese), the Fenway Dog (Italian sausage), and the Cincy Dog (bratwurst).

In left field in McDuffy's menu, under the headings Winners, 19th-Hole Deli Delights, and Centercourt Salads, are more sandwiches, chili, and salads. In right field, under the headings The Concession Stand, Post Game, and Take Out, appear beverages other than beer, desserts, and take-out copy.

As you can see, the headings on this menu are all in bold caps, and the listings are in bold caps and lowercase, set in type that is large enough for easy reading.

Some of the printing and design techniques that can be used for paper and menu design are as follows:

1. Opaque and transparent inks on colored and white paper.
2. Embossing.
3. Light inks on dark paper.
4. Tints and metallics on tinted paper.
5. Three-dimensional use of paper.
6. Printing on transparent (cellophane) or semitransparent paper.
7. Textural, tactile, and other sensory effects.
8. Varieties of paper within the same menu.

Although the printing process dictates the kind of paper to be used, the quality of the paper itself largely determines the success of the finished product. The following glossary defines some of the kinds of paper used in menus.

TYPES OF PAPER

Antique paper. Paper with a rough, textured surface.

Bond. Paper for letterheads, forms, and business uses.

Book paper. Paper having characteristics suitable for books, magazines, and brochures.

Bristol. Cardboard that is .006 of an inch or more in thickness (index, mill, and wedding are types of bristol).

Coated. Refers to the treatment of paper or paperboard with clay or some other pigment.

Cover stock. A variety of papers used for the outside covers of menus, catalogs, booklets, and magazines.

Deckle edge. A rough edge on paper formed by pulp flowing against the frame (deckle), creating a feathered, uneven edge when the paper is left untrimmed.

Dull-coated. A low-gloss coated surface on paper.

Eggshell. Paper with a semirough surface similar to the surface texture of an egg.

Enameled. Any coated paper.

English finish. A machine finish and uniform surface.

Grain. A weakness along one dimension of the paper (paper should be folded with the grain).

Machine finish. A medium finish, rougher than English finish but smoother than eggshell.

Offset paper. Coated or uncoated paper suitable for offset lithography printing.

Vellum finish. A finish similar to eggshell but from harder stock and with a finer-grained surface.

3

Menu Copy

There is no need to be stingy with words on a menu. They are cheap, can work hard, and can make the customer spend more. Suppose a customer went to a car agency to buy a new car and the dealer would not show the car or let it be driven, and described the car in only a couple of sentences. Such obvious poor salesmanship is what usually happens in a restaurant: The customer does not see, taste, or even smell the food in advance, and often the description is too limited to be meaningful.

Now a $10, $20, or even $65 meal is not a major purchase like that of an automobile costing thousands of dollars. But the principle is the same. When the customer is seated in your restaurant, he or she is already "sold" on eating your food and is enjoying the restaurant's atmosphere. And the customer has some knowledge of what to expect when the meal is served, but you can do more to capture that diner's interest.

> What does cookery mean? It means the knowledge of Medea and of Circe, and of Calypso, and of Helen, and of Rebekah, and of the Queen of Sheba. It means knowledge of all herbs, and fruits, and balms, and spices, and of all that is healing and sweet in groves and savory in meat. It means carefulness and inventiveness, watchfulness, willingness, and readiness of appliance. It means the economy of your great-grandmother and the science of modern chemistry, and French art and Arabian hospitality. It means, in fine, that you are to see imperatively that everyone has something nice to eat *(John Ruskin)*.

If cookery is indeed all that Ruskin says, it will take a lot of words to describe it. Everything new, different, better, or more exciting in the items listed can be put into words. The rule should be: If you serve it, sell it—with words.

COMMUNICATING THROUGH THE MENU

Every menu is a written communication. Some menus are just a list, a bill of fare. Others list the items for sale with only a cursory description. The best menus describe, idealize, and sell what is being served. A menu is like an advertisement in a national magazine, and as much time and effort should go into the writing of a menu as into a four-color ad. In addition, the menu is an ideal place to sell the unique character and cuisine of your operation, and thereby help to create atmosphere and the sort of publicity that leads to repeat business.

The copy in a menu can be broken down into three categories: (1) listing of food items, (2) description of these items, and (3) institutional copy about the restaurant, its service, and its cuisine.

Just listing the food is not as simple as it might seem at first. For example, consider a common item such as potatoes. Is a potato merely a potato? The following is a sample listing:

Hash Brown Potatoes
Brabant Potatoes
French-fried Potatoes
Lyonnaise Potatoes
Parsley Potatoes
Baked Idaho Potatoes
Au Gratin Potatoes
Whipped and Creamed Potatoes
Parisienne Potatoes
Escalloped Potatoes
Country-fried Potatoes
Potato du Jour
Boiled Potatoes
Mashed Potatoes
Cottage-fried Potatoes
Potato Salad

We can make several observations from this list. First, the name of the food item is important. A rose by any other name may smell the same, but the name *rose* conjures up a definite mental picture; the same is true of the name of a food item. Every item on the bill of fare, therefore, must be named with care and precision. Second, the name of a food item is not a scientific label. From our list of potatoes, for example, how many people could describe exactly what they would get if they ordered Brabant Potatoes or Parisienne Potatoes? A short survey in your own dining room would probably reveal more than one word on your menu that the general public does not understand. For instance, how many customers know that *au jus* means "served in gravy" or "juice of the meat"? Or how many people know that *lyonnaise* means "cooked with flaked or sliced fried onions"?

All these terms are well known to a chef or an experienced restaurateur. Unless the customers are familiar with such uncommon words, they will need help. The alternative is a Berlitz course in foreign languages used in menus. The glossary following defines some common foreign and other culinary terms.

GLOSSARY OF SELECTED MENU TERMS

À la. In the fashion of.

À la Mode. (1) Topped with ice cream or (2) marinated and braised with vegetables (roast beef à la mode).

Aperitif. A beverage served as an appetizer.

Aspic. A savory meat jelly, with or without gelatin and containing bits of meat, fish, egg, or vegetables.

Au Gratin. Baked with bread crumbs or cheese.

Au Jus. Served in its natural juices (roast prime ribs of beef au jus).

Au Lait. Made and served with milk (café au lait).

Bar-le-Duc. A special type of fruit preserve made from currants.

Barbecue. To roast slowly on a spit or grid over slow-burning coals or under a broiler, usually while being basted with a sauce.

Baste. To moisten (meat or other foods) while cooking, to prevent drying and to add flavor.

Blanch. To cook briefly in boiling water or steam.

Blend. To combine two or more ingredients thoroughly.

Boil. To cook food in boiling liquid, usually water.

Bouillon. A clear soup made from a brown beef stock.

Braise. To brown (meat or vegetable) in a small amount of hot fat and then to cover it and cook it slowly in the food's own juices.

Bread. To cover or coat with bread crumbs.

Brochette. Cut-up pieces (meat and vegetables) threaded on skewers and cooked over an open fire.

Broil. To cook directly under the heating unit.

Brush. To coat the surface with melted butter, oil, milk, cream, or beaten egg white.

Candy. (1) To cook (fruit) in a heavy sugar syrup until transparent or (2) to cook (vegetables or fruits) with sugar or syrup to give them a glaze.

Caramelize. To melt sugar over medium-low heat until it develops a characteristic caramel flavor and color.

Chop. To cut into small pieces with a sharp knife.

Coat. To roll food in flour, crumbs, sugar, chopped nuts, and the like until uniformly covered.

Coddle. To cook slowly in water just below the boiling point.

Compote. Fruits in sugar syrup.

Conserve. Fruit preserve made with fruits, nuts, or raisins.

Consommé. A clear soup made from a combination of meat stocks.

Court Bouillon. A stock made from fish.

Cracklings. The crisp pieces left after rendering the fat from pork.

Cream. To mix shortening until it is smooth and creamy by rubbing it against the side of the bowl.

Crepe. A thin, rich pancake rolled with a filling and served with a sauce. Crepes suzette are made with grated orange rind and liqueurs. Crepes gruyère have a cheese filling.

Croutons. Small cubes of fried or toasted bread.

Cube. To cut into small pieces.

Demitasse. A small cup of strong black coffee.

Devein. To remove the veins (as from shrimp).

Devil. To mix with hot seasonings, such as pepper or mustard.

Dice. To cut into cubes.

Drippings. Fat or juice that cooks out of meat or poultry.

Fillet. Boneless strips of meat or fish.

Flake. To break into small pieces.

Flambé. To cover warm food with brandy, rum, or a liqueur with a high alcohol content, then ignite it and serve it flaming.

Flan. Custard that is baked and coated with caramel.

Fold. To combine ingredients by cutting vertically through the mixture and gently turning it under and over until thoroughly blended.

Fondue. (1) A baked dish similar to cheese souffle or (2) Swiss cheese melted with wine in a chafing dish.

Forcemeat. Finely chopped meat or fish.

Fricassee. To cook meat or fowl, cut into pieces, by braising.

Fry, Deep Fat. To cook in a deep layer of fat preheated to the desired temperature. The result should be food with a golden, crisp crust and a thoroughly cooked center.

Garnish. To decorate a dish with parsley, fruit slices, and the like.

Glacé. To coat with a sugar syrup cooked to the cracking stage.

Glaze. To make a smooth, glossy surface by coating with a thin layer of aspic, melted jelly, sugar syrup, or fruit juice sweetened and thickened with cornstarch.

Goulash. A thick meat stew with vegetables and paprika.

Julienne. To cut into thin strips.

Lyonnaise. Cooked with chopped onions.

Macedoine. A mixture of cut-up fruits or vegetables.

Marinate. To let food stand several hours in a seasoned oil–acid mixture to improve flavor and tenderness.

Plank. To broil or bake meat or fish on a wooden plank.

Pot Roast. To cook by braising (moist heat).

Precook. To partially cook food in liquid below the boiling point.

Preheat. To heat the oven to a given temperature before the food is inserted.

Render. To free fat from connective tissue by melting over low heat.

Rissole. Minced meat, fish, or potatoes, covered in pastry and fried in deep fat.

Roast. To cook by means of dry heat in an oven.

Roux. Cooked mixture of flour and butter used to thicken soups and sauces.

Sauté. To fry food in a small amount of fat.

Scald. To heat milk or other food to just below the boiling point.

Scallop. To arrange food in layers in a casserole with sauce.

Score. To cut shallow gashes or slits in the fat of meat before cooking.

Sear. To brown the surface (of meat) over high heat or in a very hot oven.

Shir. To break eggs into a dish with cream and crumbs and bake.

Simmer. To cook in liquid just below the boiling point.

Skewer. Metal or wooden rod to hold meat, poultry, fish, or vegetables in place while barbecuing or broiling.

Sliver. To cut (meat or vegetables) into thin, narrow strips.

Steep. To extract the essence by standing in liquid.

Stew. To cook in a small quantity of liquid over gentle heat.

Stock. Liquid in which meat, poultry, fish, or vegetables have been cooked.

Torte. A rich cake, usually in layers, topped with fruit and whipped cream.

Toss. To mix with a light, quick motion without crushing the ingredients.

Whip. To beat rapidly to incorporate air and increase volume.

The next consideration is the descriptions of the individual menu items. They can be simple or elaborate, but they usually should add interest and sales value to a menu. For example, bread and butter can be described better as "oven-fresh rolls and creamery butter," a short but mouth-watering description. Following are some other descriptions that enhance the customer's mental picture.

Tender Thick Pork Chops . . . *cut from the loin of the finest homegrown pork and broiled to perfection. A unique experience that will long be remembered.*

Danish Brook Trout . . . *from cold Scandinavian waters by way of the gentle savory heat of the hearth coals to you . . . truly the perfect fish. Served with lemon butter.*

Oysters and Bacon en Brochette . . . *ten of the most delicious, salty, fresh Gulf oysters we can find, skewered with bacon, brushed with butter, and broiled. Served with crisp brabant potatoes, a baked tomato, and mushrooms.*

Boneless Fried Chicken . . . *Transocean Airlines. Something to remember Hawaii by. Tender halves of chicken, all of whose bones have been carefully replaced with pineapple sticks, then dipped in fresh coconut cream and rolled in grated coconut. Baked to a golden crunchy brown and sauced with coconut cream giblet gravy. Served with baked bananas.*

Advertisers and semanticists have studied many of the words appearing on menus and found that they often mean different things to different people. The word *homemade,* for example, means to most people "made at home from scratch." On a menu, therefore, the word *homemade* should be qualified to indicate that it is made in the restaurant's kitchen from scratch or fresh ingredients.

Spicy is also a word to be used carefully. Most people associate it with Italian and Mexican foods. Because many do not like spicy foods, the degree of hotness should be explained. Phrases such as "delicate flavoring" or "slightly spicy" may be used only if true of the food served.

Four words with good associations are *natural, nutritious, light,* and *lean. Natural* means, in reference to food, unadulterated with no evidence of mass production or the addition of chemicals, additives, and preservatives. *Nutritious* refers to the meal as a whole, that is, a balanced meal with vitamins, minerals, protein, complex carbohydrates, and little cholesterol. *Light* means fewer calories and indicates something that is not filling. And *lean* means with little or no fat.

The definition of the restaurant itself can also be important. The phrase "family restaurant," for example, means suited to everyone. It also means generous portions of food at reasonable prices and with many people around. Definitions such as "casual dining," "fast food," "supper club," and "bistro" often vary and so should be used carefully.

A third broad copy category is institutional copy. Just as a company has a "corporate image," so a foodservice operation has a public image. The menu is one of the best places to create this image. The approach varies with every establishment because each has its own feature, character, service, or history.

One institutional approach is the "Our Philosophy—Our Creed—The Tradition of This Restaurant" approach. This is a good general method of presenting the restaurateur as a serious student of the customer's gastronomic needs. Vic's Tally Ho restaurant in Des Moines, Iowa, begins its story with "You're on the board of directors," then leads into an explanation of the restaurant's goals and ideals.

EXAMPLES OF MENU COPY

The Manor Restaurant

The Manor Restaurant in West Orange, New Jersey, begins its elegant menu with the following words:

> Probably the Most Beautiful Restaurant in America. The Manor is the result of restaurateur Harry Knowles' determined efforts toward gracious elegance in dining. The goal was a replica of a palatial estate where guests can enjoy a return to the era of elegance and where gracious dining was a way of life. The Manor takes pride in carrying on this tradition of gracious elegance and offers lavish hospitality in an atmosphere of charm. At the Manor luxurious service becomes commonplace in an all-pervading aura of grace and refinement devoted to prestige dining.
>
> The classic excellence of the Manor has been reflected in its receipt of consecutive *Holiday Magazine* awards for dining distinction, *Institution Magazine's* coveted international award, and highest honors for elegant and colorful service in *Hospitality Magazine's* "Top of the Table" program.
>
> Please know that all our efforts and countless awards are of no significance unless you, our customer, can enjoy this return to elegance through attentive service, quality food, and leisurely dining.

Ojai Inn

A short statement on the first page of the Ojai Inn menu (Figure 3.1) by the executive chef is a good introduction:

> Our name and concept mark several new beginnings . . . the renewal of the legend of the Ojai Valley Inn, my introduction to the outstanding variety of California products and tastes, the pioneering experience of Hilton International in the West, and of course your rediscovery of "Lost Horizons." Wishing you Bon Appetit.

Quaglino's

The following copy on Quaglino's menu cover gives a little history of the restaurant's name and adds charm and sophistication (Figure 3.2):

> WELCOME TO QUAGLINO'S
>
> Italy's premier restaurateur Ernesto "Tino" Fontana is responsible for Quaglino's spirit, casual elegance, and most of all, its remarkable cuisine. His internationally acclaimed culinary style is modern Northern Italian cuisine, with highly individual creative touches in taste and presentation. His hallmark is insistence on the very freshest ingredients and attention to every detail.
>
> Our original Quaglino's in London was a sophisticated rendezvous of the haut monde, before and after World War

OUR NAME AND CONCEPT MARK SEVERAL NEW BEGINNINGS . . . THE RENEWAL OF THE LEGEND OF THE OJAI VALLEY INN, MY INTRODUCTION TO THE OUTSTANDING VARIETY OF CALIFORNIA PRODUCTS AND TASTES, THE PIONEERING EXPERIENCE OF HILTON INTERNATIONAL IN THE WEST, AND OF COURSE YOUR REDISCOVERY OF "LOST HORIZONS."

WISHING YOU BON APPETIT

YVES BLONDEAU

EXECUTIVE CHEF

OJAI VALLEY INN & COUNTRY CLUB

A VISTA INTERNATIONAL RESORT

FIGURE 3.1 Menu from Ojai Valley Inn & Country Club, a Vista International Resort. (Reproduced by permission.)

II. Its fashionable yet relaxed elegance is the style of the New York Quaglino's which is as much attuned to the New York scene as London's is to London.

From these examples of institutional copy we can see that there is great variety in merchandising and publicizing the quality, flavor, or specialty of almost any restaurant.

The best advice for a foodservice operator (unless he or she is actually a writer) is to use a professional, whether you hire an advertising agency or a free-lance writer. The writing of a menu is too important to be left to an amateur.

Beside the Pointe

Beside the Pointe, a restaurant in Phoenix, Arizona, has a creatively written menu (Figure 3.3). One section begins, "Each of these items are named after birds who *can't* fly and who have one other thing in common, they *lay* eggs!"

RHEA (SOUTH AMERICA) EGGS BENEDICT

An English muffin topped with Canadian bacon, lettuce leaf, slice of tomato and poached eggs, then smothered with Hollandaise sauce and topped with a ripe olive. Fruit garnish.

DODO (MAURITIUS: EXTINCT) CRAB BENEDICT

Another favorite combination. An English muffin with crab, sliced tomato and our own Hollandaise sauce.

CORMORANT (GALAPAGOS) STEAK AND EGGS

A New York strip, two eggs (any style), Hash Browns, refried beans or grits. Served with bolillo bread.

OSTRICH (AFRICA, YOU THOUGHT AUSTRALIA, RIGHT?)

Eggs (any style) served with Hash Browns, refried beans or grits and your choice of bacon, ham, sausage. One egg, two eggs, three eggs. With machaca or chorizo instead of bacon, ham or sausage.

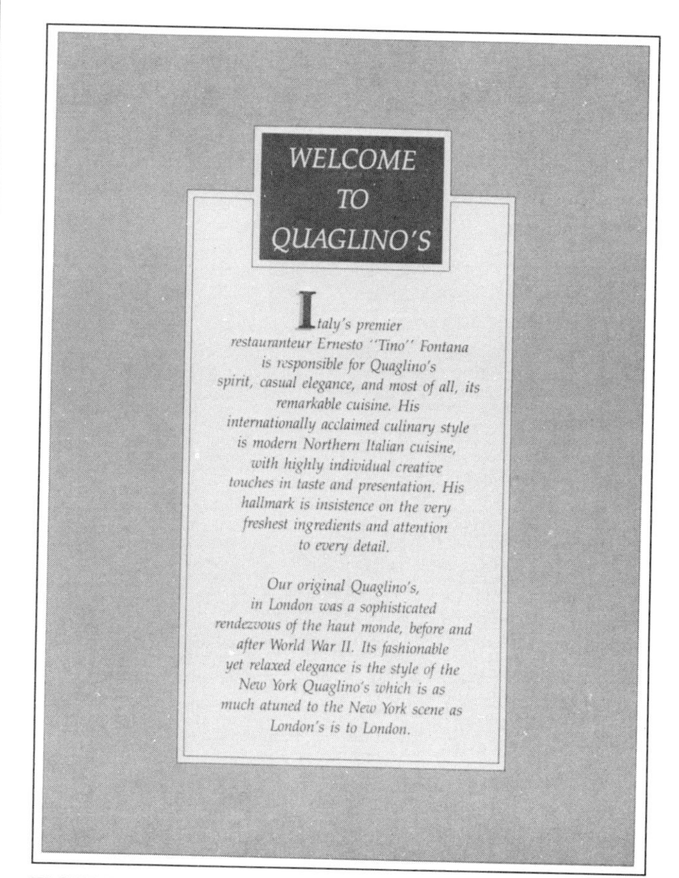

FIGURE 3.2 Cover from menu of Quaglino's Restaurant. (Reproduced by permission.)

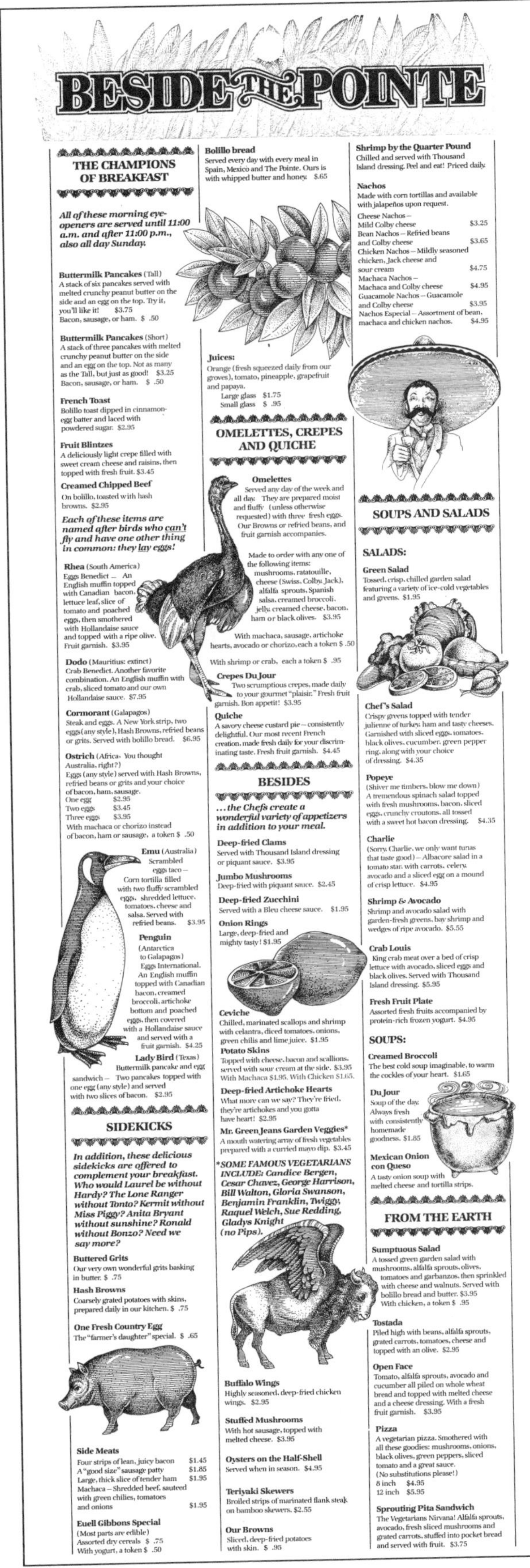

BESIDE THE POINTE

THE CHAMPIONS OF BREAKFAST

All of these morning eye-openers are served until 11:00 a.m. and after 11:00 p.m., also all day Sunday.

Buttermilk Pancakes (Tall)
A stack of six pancakes served with melted crunchy peanut butter on the side and an egg on the top. Try it, you'll like it! $3.75
Bacon, sausage, or ham. $ .50

Buttermilk Pancakes (Short)
A stack of three pancakes with melted crunchy peanut butter on the side and an egg on the top. Not as many as the Tall, but just as good! $3.25
Bacon, sausage, or ham. $ .50

French Toast
Bolillo toast dipped in cinnamon-egg batter and laced with powdered sugar. $2.95

Fruit Blintzes
A deliciously light crepe filled with sweet cream cheese and raisins, then topped with fresh fruit. $3.45

Creamed Chipped Beef
On bolillo, toasted with hash browns. $2.95

Each of these items are named after birds who can't fly and have one other thing in common: they lay eggs!

Rhea (South America)
Eggs Benedict – An English muffin topped with Canadian bacon, lettuce leaf, slice of tomato and poached eggs, then smothered with Hollandaise sauce and topped with a ripe olive. Fruit garnish. $3.95

Dodo (Mauritius: extinct)
Crab Benedict. Another favorite combination. An English muffin with crab, sliced tomato and our own Hollandaise sauce. $7.95

Cormorant (Galapagos)
Steak and eggs. A New York strip, two eggs (any style), Hash Browns, refried beans or grits. Served with bolillo bread. $6.95

Ostrich (Africa. You thought Australia, right?)
Eggs (any style) served with Hash Browns, refried beans or grits and your choice of bacon, ham, sausage.
One egg $2.95
Two eggs $3.45
Three eggs $3.95
With machaca or chorizo instead of bacon, ham or sausage, a token $ .50

Emu (Australia)
Scrambled eggs taco – Corn tortilla filled with two fluffy scrambled eggs, shredded lettuce, tomatoes, cheese and salsa. Served with refried beans. $3.95

Penguin (Antarctica to Galapagos)
Eggs International. An English muffin topped with Canadian bacon, creamed broccoli, artichoke bottom and poached eggs, then covered with a Hollandaise sauce and served with a fruit garnish. $4.25

Lady Bird (Texas)
Buttermilk pancake and egg sandwich – Two pancakes topped with one egg (any style) and served with two slices of bacon. $2.95

SIDEKICKS

In addition, these delicious sidekicks are offered to complement your breakfast. Who would Laurel be without Hardy? The Lone Ranger without Tonto? Kermit without Miss Piggy? Anita Bryant without sunshine? Ronald without Bonzo? Need we say more?

Buttered Grits
Our very own wonderful grits basking in butter. $ .75

Hash Browns
Coarsely grated potatoes with skins, prepared daily in our kitchen. $ .75

One Fresh Country Egg
The "farmer's daughter" special. $ .65

Side Meats
Four strips of lean, juicy bacon $1.45
A "good size" sausage patty $1.85
Large, thick slice of tender ham $1.95
Machaca – Shredded beef, sauteed with green chilies, tomatoes and onions $1.95

Euell Gibbons Special
(Most parts are edible)
Assorted dry cereals $ .75
With yogurt, a token $ .50

Bolillo bread
Served every day with every meal in Spain, Mexico and The Pointe. Ours is with whipped butter and honey. $.65

Juices:
Orange (fresh squeezed daily from our groves), tomato, pineapple, grapefruit and papaya.
Large glass $1.75
Small glass $ .95

OMELETTES, CREPES AND QUICHE

Omelettes
Served any day of the week and all day. They are prepared moist and fluffy (unless otherwise requested) with three fresh eggs. Our Browns or refried beans, and fruit garnish accompanies.

Made to order with any one of the following items: mushrooms, ratatouille, cheese (Swiss, Colby, Jack), alfalfa sprouts, Spanish salsa, creamed broccoli, jelly, creamed cheese, bacon, ham or black olives. $3.95

With machaca, sausage, artichoke hearts, avocado or chorizo, each a token $ .50

With shrimp or crab, each a token $ .95

Crepes Du Jour
Two scrumptious crepes, made daily to your gourmet "plaisir." Fresh fruit garnish. Bon appetit! $3.95

Quiche
A savory cheese custard pie – consistently delightful. Our most recent French creation, made fresh daily for your discriminating taste. Fresh fruit garnish. $4.45

BESIDES

...the Chefs create a wonderful variety of appetizers in addition to your meal.

Deep-fried Clams
Served with Thousand Island dressing or piquant sauce. $3.95

Jumbo Mushrooms
Deep-fried with piquant sauce. $2.45

Deep-fried Zucchini
Served with a Bleu cheese sauce. $1.95

Onion Rings
Large, deep-fried and mighty tasty! $1.95

Ceviche
Chilled, marinated scallops and shrimp with celantra, diced tomatoes, onions, green chilis and lime juice. $1.95

Potato Skins
Topped with cheese, bacon and scallions, served with sour cream at the side. $3.95
With Machaca $1.95. With Chicken $1.65.

Deep-fried Artichoke Hearts
What more can we say? They're fried, they're artichokes and you gotta have heart! $2.95

Mr. Green Jeans Garden Veggies*
A mouth watering array of fresh vegetables prepared with a curried mayo dip. $3.45

**SOME FAMOUS VEGETARIANS INCLUDE: Candice Bergen, Cesar Chavez, George Harrison, Bill Walton, Gloria Swanson, Benjamin Franklin, Twiggy, Raquel Welch, Sue Redding, Gladys Knight (no Pips).*

Buffalo Wings
Highly seasoned, deep-fried chicken wings. $2.95

Stuffed Mushrooms
With hot sausage, topped with melted cheese. $3.95

Oysters on the Half-Shell
Served when in season. $4.95

Teriyaki Skewers
Broiled strips of marinated flank steak on bamboo skewers. $2.55

Our Browns
Sliced, deep-fried potatoes with skin. $ .95

Shrimp by the Quarter Pound
Chilled and served with Thousand Island dressing. Peel and eat! Priced daily.

Nachos
Made with corn tortillas and available with jalapeños upon request.
Cheese Nachos – Mild Colby cheese $3.25
Bean Nachos – Refried beans and Colby cheese $3.65
Chicken Nachos – Mildly seasoned chicken, Jack cheese and sour cream $4.75
Machaca Nachos – Machaca and Colby cheese $4.95
Guacamole Nachos – Guacamole and Colby cheese $3.95
Nachos Especial – Assortment of bean, machaca and chicken nachos. $4.95

SOUPS AND SALADS

SALADS:

Green Salad
Tossed, crisp, chilled garden salad featuring a variety of ice-cold vegetables and greens. $1.95

Chef's Salad
Crispy greens topped with tender julienne of turkey, ham and tasty cheeses. Garnished with sliced eggs, tomatoes, black olives, cucumber, green pepper ring, along with your choice of dressing. $4.35

Popeye
(Shiver me timbers, blow me down)
A tremendous spinach salad topped with fresh mushrooms, bacon, sliced eggs, crunchy croutons, all tossed with a sweet hot bacon dressing. $4.35

Charlie
(Sorry, Charlie, we only want tunas that taste good) – Albacore salad in a tomato star, with carrots, celery, avocado and a sliced egg on a mound of crisp lettuce. $4.95

Shrimp & Avocado
Shrimp and avocado salad with garden-fresh greens, bay shrimp and wedges of ripe avocado. $5.55

Crab Louis
King crab meat over a bed of crisp lettuce with avocado, sliced eggs and black olives. Served with Thousand Island dressing. $5.95

Fresh Fruit Plate
Assorted fresh fruits accompanied by protein-rich frozen yogurt. $4.95

SOUPS:

Creamed Broccoli
The best cold soup imaginable, to warm the cockles of your heart. $1.65

Du Jour
Soup of the day. Always fresh with consistently homemade goodness. $1.85

Mexican Onion con Queso
A tasty onion soup with melted cheese and tortilla strips.

FROM THE EARTH

Sumptuous Salad
A tossed green garden salad with mushrooms, alfalfa sprouts, olives, tomatoes and garbanzos, then sprinkled with cheese and walnuts. Served with bolillo bread and butter. $3.95
With chicken, a token $ .95

Tostada
Piled high with beans, alfalfa sprouts, grated carrots, tomatoes, cheese and topped with an olive. $2.95

Open Face
Tomato, alfalfa sprouts, avocado and cucumber all piled on whole wheat bread and topped with melted cheese and a cheese dressing. With a fresh fruit garnish. $3.95

Pizza
A vegetarian pizza. Smothered with all these goodies: mushrooms, onions, black olives, green peppers, sliced tomato and a great sauce.
(No substitutions please!)
8 inch $4.95
12 inch $5.95

Sprouting Pita Sandwich
The Vegetarians Nirvana! Alfalfa sprouts, avocado, fresh sliced mushrooms and grated carrots, stuffed into pocket bread and served with fruit. $3.75

FIGURE 3.3 Menu from Beside the Pointe. (Reproduced by permission.)

EMU (AUSTRALIA)

Scrambled eggs taco—corn tortilla filled with two fluffy scrambled eggs, shredded lettuce, tomatoes, cheese and salsa. Served with refried beans.

PENGUIN (ANTARCTICA TO GALAPAGOS)

Eggs International. An English muffin topped with Canadian bacon, creamed broccoli, artichoke bottom and poached eggs, then covered with a Hollandaise sauce and served with a fruit garnish.

LADY BIRD (TEXAS)

Buttermilk pancake and egg sandwich—two pancakes topped with one egg (any style) and served with two slices of bacon.

This menu also has the following copy under the heading of Sidekicks:

> In addition, these delicious sidekicks are offered to complement your breakfast. Who would Laurel be without Hardy? The Lone Ranger without Tonto? Kermit without Miss Piggy? Anita Bryant without sunshine? Ronald without Bonzo? Need we say more?

The Seafood listing for Beside the Pointe:

> Straight from the pages of Jules Verne's *20,000 Leagues Under the Sea*, we present our three fantastic seafood entrees:

BAKED OYSTERS

Oysters on the half shell with Hollandaise sauce, served only in season with a vegetable, wild rice and boiillo bread.

MICKEY ROONEY*

"Fresh shrimp" stuffed with Jack cheese and bacon. Served with wild rice, a vegetable, bolillo bread and salsa.
**Mickey Rooney had eight wives, that's a "fresh shrimp."*

ALASKAN KING CRAB

Steaming hot and served with melted butter. Wild rice, bolillo bread and a vegetable.

The Boston Subway

Humor is always welcome on the menu, and if the humorous copy ties in with the restaurant's name, so much the better. The Boston Subway (see Figure 22.2) uses a poem about a famous Boston subway rider, Charlie of the M.T.A. (Words and music by Bess Hawes and Jacqueline Steiner, 1948.)

THE M.T.A. SONG

Well, let me tell you a story of the man named Charlie on a tragic and fateful day.
He put $.10 in his pocket, kissed his wife and family, went to ride on the M.T.A.

CHORUS:

Well, did he ever return, no, he never returned and his fate is still unlearned.
He may ride forever 'neath the streets of Boston, he's the man who never returned.

Charlie handed in his dime at the Kendall Square Station and changed at Jamaica Plain.
But when he got there the conductor told him one more nickel, Charlie couldn't get off of that train.

CHORUS

Now all night long Charlie rides through the tunnel, crying what will become of me?
How can I afford to see my sister in Chelsea or my cousin in Roxbury?

CHORUS

Charlie's wife goes down to the Scollay Square Station every day at a quarter past two
And through the open window, she hands Charlie a sandwich as the train comes rumblin' thru.

CHORUS

Now you citizens of Boston, don't you think it's a scandal how the people have to pay and pay?
Fight the fare increase; vote for whoever's running and get Charlie off the M.T.A.

Most people think Charlie rode the subway because he wouldn't pay the extra nickel. Yes, it's true Charlie was a shrewd Yankee who knew a good value. But it was that sandwich that Charlie's wife handed him every day at a quarter past two that made him decide to stay on the train. What kind of sandwich was it? Why, a Boston Subway Sandwich, of course. That's what the Boston Subway is all about: GREAT SANDWICHES served on time at the right price.

Everyone of us on the crew at the Boston Subway is committed to providing you with the best food and service. If you do not like something we serve you, please let us know. On the other hand, as much as we enjoy accepting compliments if you are pleased with our product and service, tell someone else.

4

The Menu Cover

The menu cover is the symbol of a restaurant's identity. A well-designed, attractive, and clean menu cover is one indication to the customer of a good restaurant. The cover should be the last part of the menu to be designed. A good menu should be put together from the inside out; that is, the items inside—their sequence and the importance given to them—should come first. Only after all of the inside problems have been solved should the cover be designed.

After the size of the menu, number of pages, and number of items to be listed have been chosen, attention can be given to the cover. This means that a preprinted menu cover should not determine the menu's size, form, or number of panels or pages.

Several things should be considered when designing the menu cover, including color (or colors), paper, and the relationship of the cover design to the restaurant's decor. Also, if the cover is to be long lasting and easy to keep clean, coatings (plastic or varnish) may be necessary. The use of color is also related to cost: The more colors that are used on a cover, the more expensive it will be.

The selection of paper can also help make a menu cover attractive and functional. Leather or simulated leather with the restaurant's name and logo embossed in gold is appropriate for certain types of restaurants. Color photographs of the food and drinks served have become popular. These kinds of covers, however, though attractive, tend to be expensive. They are used mostly by multiple operations or hotel chains that can spread the cost of photography and printing over a larger run.

Black-and-white photos are less expensive to reproduce and can make very effective menu covers. The addition of a second color on the logo can help with a basic black and white cover, and the use of colored paper is another method of adding color at minimum expense. Also, the cover may be made out of heavy, durable, and easy-to-keep-clean material, and the inside—a four- or eight-page insert—may be of lighter material. This allows for changing the inside while keeping the cover more or less permanent.

By using an independent artist/designer, the restaurant operator can be sure of getting an attractive menu cover. An advertising or public relations agency also has designers available, as do menu houses (printers who specialize in producing menus).

An inexpensive source of art for menu covers is old prints, woodcuts, or engravings. They are usually black-and-white line drawings and are therefore easy to reproduce. Etchings and lithographs by talented artists are usually less expensive than original drawings and paintings and often make an attractive menu cover. Art fairs are also a good source of artwork for a cover. Or an artist can be commissioned to make a painting or drawing of the restaurant itself if the architecture outside or inside lends itself to illustration.

The cover design as well as the general look and "feel" of the restaurant's menu should fit its decor and style. For example, a fast-food, family-style, or casual dining restaurant tends to have a brightly colored menu on plastic-coated stock, whereas a more expensive French restaurant uses white or pastel colors to reflect its more elegant or quieter decor. This type of restaurant (expensive, white tablecloth) generally uses quality uncoated paper and replaces the menu when it gets soiled.

Regarding copy on the menu cover, the name of the restaurant is enough. Other information such as address, phone number, credit card acceptance, and reservation policy can be printed inside or on the back cover.

Even though the design and appearance of the menu cover should be carefully considered, remember that the customer usually spends only a few seconds glancing at the cover and spends much more time reading the inside. Figures 4.1 through 4.7 illustrate a variety of cover concepts.

FIGURE 4.1a Menu cover for United Airlines. The airline often uses paintings by well-known artists. (Reproduced by permission.)

FIGURE 4.1b A second United Airlines menu by the same artist.

FIGURE 4.2 Menu cover for the restaurant at Roosevelt Raceway. (Reproduced by permission of Harry M. Stevens, Inc.)

FIGURE 4.3 Cover for the Pinnacle. This restaurant at Lake Shore Holiday Inn in Chicago uses a photograph from the 1890s on the cover of its menu. (Reproduced by permission.)

FIGURE 4.4 Air Canada menu cover. The airline uses a space illustration on one of its menu covers. (Reproduced by permission of Air Canada.)

FIGURE 4.5 Menu cover for The 95th. This restaurant on the ninety-fifth floor of the John Hancock Center in Chicago uses an illustration of its view on the menu cover. (Courtesy The 95th. Operated by the Dining Division of ARA Services. Reproduced by permission.)

FIGURE 4.6 Menu cover for Green Frog Restaurant. This excellent illustration in black, orange, and green makes an attractive cover. (Reproduced by permission.)

FIGURE 4.7 If you have a clever name like Al E. Gator, feature it on your cover. (Reproduced by permission.)

5

Menu Strategy

A strategy is a plan or technique for achieving some end. In military terms, it is the science and art of conducting a military campaign; in business, the purpose of a strategy is to meet and overcome the competition, to be profitable, and to expand. Every business has some strategy, even if it is not stated explicitly. As a business venture, every successful restaurant is the result of certain marketing decisions regarding where to locate, what kind of cuisine to serve, what market to target, what prices to charge, and what overhead to carry.

CAMS: COMPUTER-AIDED MENU STRATEGY

The acronym CAD/CAM stands for computer-aided design and computer-aided manufacturing. Restaurants or their accountants already use computers to manage costs, payrolls, taxes, and other financial matters. CAMS, or computer-aided menu strategy, is just another use of computers: But a complex computer is not required, as the restaurant's cash register and checks provide a great deal of information about what is happening in regard to its menu. Even a hand calculator plus paper and pencil can do the job. An efficient restaurant operator uses records of its sales, including the menu, to determine profitability. The menu is not only a communications and selling tool but also a research and experimentation device that can be studied to increase restaurant profits.

Which items are offered on a menu—appetizers, soups, salads, sandwiches, entrées, and desserts—depends on the type of restaurant and its market. These items are either popular and good sellers or unpopular and slow movers. This is the first information to find out. Second, the restaurant's profitability can be calculated for each item on the menu by noting the price and the food cost. Each item must be graded according to gross profit and the number sold as a percentage of total sales. Its "grade" is a good indication of the item's value to the restaurant.

Popularity and profitability are thus the two key factors to keep in mind when analyzing a menu over a period of time—weeks, months, a year. The menu items fit into the following broad categories:

1. Items that are both popular and profitable
2. Items that are popular but not profitable
3. Items that are profitable but not popular
4. Items that are both unpopular and unprofitable

After the information concerning popularity and profitability has been gathered and perhaps graphed or charted, a strategy can be planned. Obviously, items that are both unprofitable and unpopular should be dropped from the menu, but the other three categories require more complicated action.

Items that are both profitable and popular should generally be left alone, although if they are very popular, their price may be raised a bit. Items that are popular but not profitable need to stay on the menu, but their profitability must be increased, either by raising the price or by "tinkering" with the items to convince the customer to continue buying them, albeit at a higher price. An item that is profitable but not popular must be changed to make it sell.

Raising prices is relatively easy and is the usual way to increase profitability. But prices must be raised cautiously. The selling price of each item should be compared with the total number of items sold. By plotting sales on a bar chart the restaurant operator can see at what point the item's popularity drops as the price increases. The cutoff point may be $8 for one restaurant and $16 for another. This procedure, along with using the menu price profile (see Chapter 7), may show the operator any areas or gaps between low-priced and high-priced items that can be closed.

After the information on profitability and popularity has been gathered, the next question is what should be done. Consider the following:

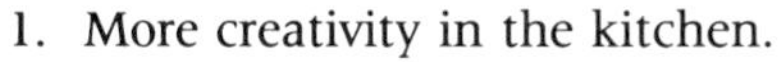

1. More creativity in the kitchen.
2. More and better copy that sells and idealizes the items (see Chapter 3).
3. Menu layout—changing the sequence and location of listings.
4. Price changes.
5. A more flexible menu.
6. More menus.
7. Specials as an R&D tool.
8. Color in the menu.
9. Atmosphere.

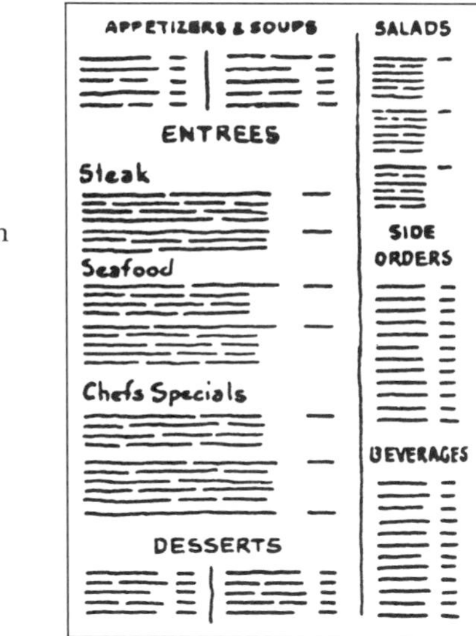

FIGURE 5.1
Sequence of items in a one-panel menu.

MENU LOCATION AND SEQUENCE

How you organize your menu and where you place various items make a difference. Locating certain items in a particular place can increase profitability. For example, the first place that most people look when reading a single-fold menu is the area just above and to the right of the center point, and so this would be the best place to list the restaurant's most profitable item.

Eye motion patterns, however, vary according to graphics, layout, number of pages or panels, and other factors. National advertisers generally do not pay much attention to eye motion studies, as they already know that a big, bold heading and an interesting illustration catch the eye. There are many ways for menus to catch the eye and many ways to organize menus.

Like a novel or a symphony, a meal has a beginning, a middle, and an end, and this sequence indicates how a menu should be designed. Regardless of the size of the menu, the fold of the pages, and the number of pages, the menu layout should follow the meal sequence. The usual order of reading a menu is from the outside to the inside pages, from top to bottom, and from left to right.

A meal progresses from appetizers, to soups and entrées, and ends with desserts. Within this sequence are side orders, salads, sandwiches, beverages, and the children's menu. The location of the salads and sandwiches depends on how the establishment wants to treat or sell them. For instance, when salads and sandwiches are considered entrée items, they should be listed as such. Side orders (à la carte) should be placed near the entrées. The problem of the children's menu is best solved by a separate menu.

Figure 5.1 is an example of this straightforward sequence. On this menu the time sequence is followed by placing the appetizers and soups at the top, the entrées at the center, and the desserts at the bottom. Salads and side orders are placed on the panel to the right. Furthermore, even the sequence or order in which you list your entrées is important. The top item on any entrée listing has the best chance of being ordered, and likewise the top group—steaks, seafood, or whatever—has the best chance of being ordered.

An example of the time sequence layout for a somewhat larger menu is shown in Figure 5.2, a four-page insert in a four-page cover. Page 1 of this insert lists the appetizers and the soups and salads. They are given enough room to have a large listing with good descriptive copy, which is important if they are big, expensive items. The entrées are listed by groups—steaks, fowl, seafood, and chef's specials—on pages 2 and 3. In all cases, the entrées should be given top billing—best position, largest and boldest type, and most descriptive copy. Desserts and beverages are listed on page 4. Side orders appear at the bottom of pages 2 and 3 under the entrées. A separate page or, even better, a dessert menu enables the wait staff to present this information to the customers without asking them whether they want a dessert—positive instead of negative selling.

The four-page cover (Figure 5.2) is used for the items and services that fall outside the time sequence. For instance, sandwiches and the children's menu can be listed on the inside back cover. The inside front cover can also be used to sell your party-banquet-meeting facilities, which may be illustrated with a photo.

The foodservice operation that serves alcoholic beverages has another menu layout problem, but the sequence formula works here as well. Some drinks are before-dinner drinks (cocktails), some are beverages consumed with dinner (wines, beers), and some are after-dinner drinks (brandies, cordials, dessert wines, some cocktails). The aim is to list the beverage item in its proper order so that it will sell itself at the proper time. The cocktail list should be what the customers see first when they pick up the menu, as this is what you want them to order first. The beer and wine list should be next to the entrée list, as they will order these items

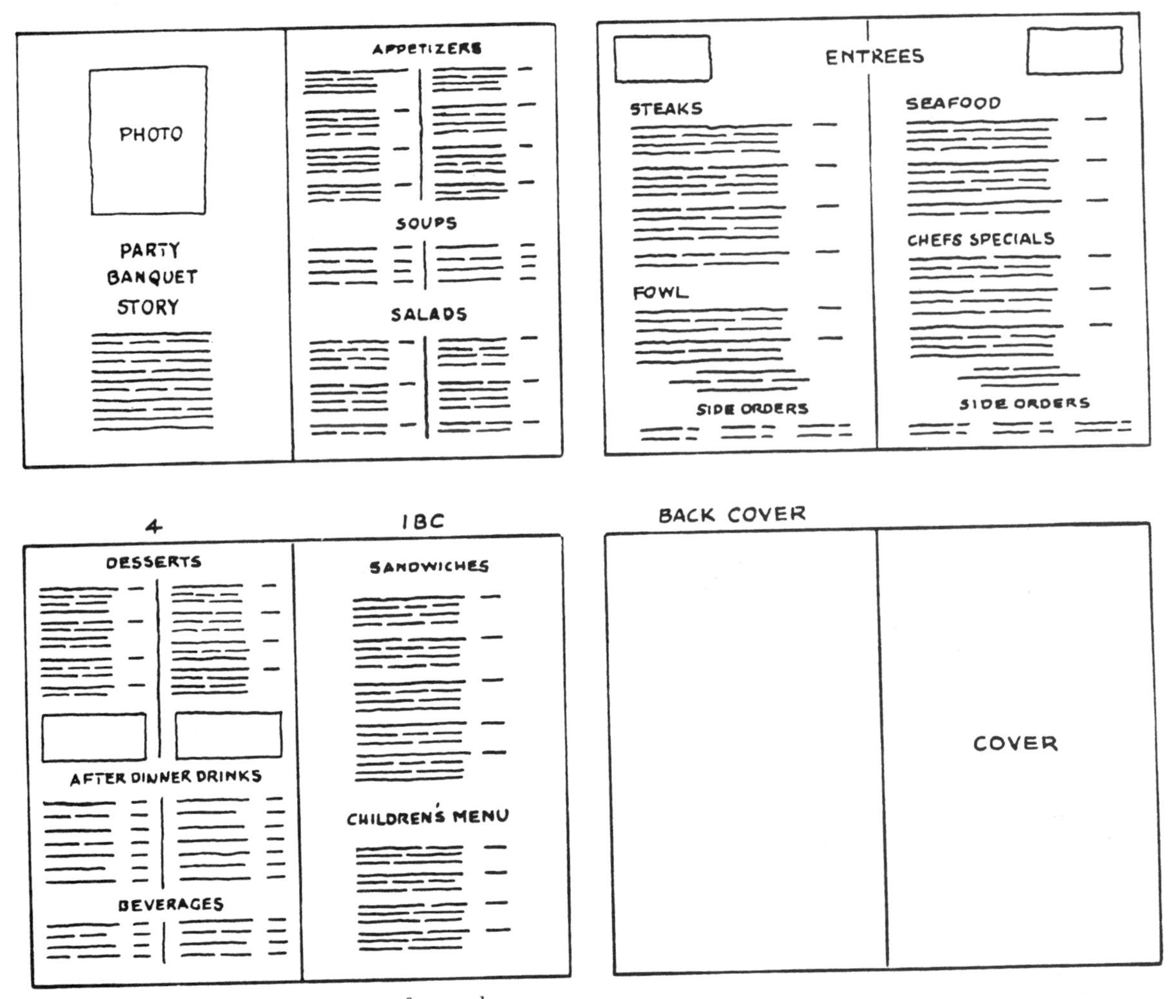

FIGURE 5.2 Sequence in a menu of several pages.

to be drunk with their meal. And the after-dinner drinks list should accompany the dessert listing.

Figure 5.3 shows one solution to the drink sequence listings. This menu folds as shown in the diagram in Figure 5.3. The first panel the customer sees after the cover thus is panel 8, which is the listing of cocktails and other "before" drinks. The wine list is printed on panel 1 next to the entrée listing, and beer is listed on panel 4, also next to the food selection. Finally, the after-dinner drink selection is printed on panel 6 with the dessert selection.

Another way to list bar selections on the menu, following the sequence pattern, is shown in Figure 5.4. This menu is a four-page insert in a four-page cover with a smaller wine list in the center. A complete before-dinner drink listing, From Our Bar, is printed on the inside front cover and includes cocktails, bourbon, scotch, vodka, gin, rum, and the like. The wine list is a smaller, four-page insert in the center of the menu between pages 2 and 3. Notice that it is right in the middle of the entrée listing. This location solves the problem of the separate wine list. Customers often do not ask for such a list, and the waiter or waitress cannot be depended on to present it to them. Finally, the after-dinner drinks are listed on page 4 with the desserts.

The important thing to remember, when arranging the sequence and position of items on your menu, is to give the best position to your profit leaders, that is, your best sellers. Placing such items in boxes or panels, listing them in heavier type, and adding descriptions of them all are ways of attracting the customers' attention.

MULTIPLE MENUS

Another menu strategy is multiple menus. Just as a company has more than one salesperson, a restaurant can have more than one menu. One advantage of multiple menus (for example, a separate dessert menu and wine list) is that the server can present each one individually to the customer and thereby draw attention to a part of the restaurant's offerings that might otherwise be overlooked on the regular, combined menu.

Every foodservice operation has different menu needs, depending on the number of meals it serves and

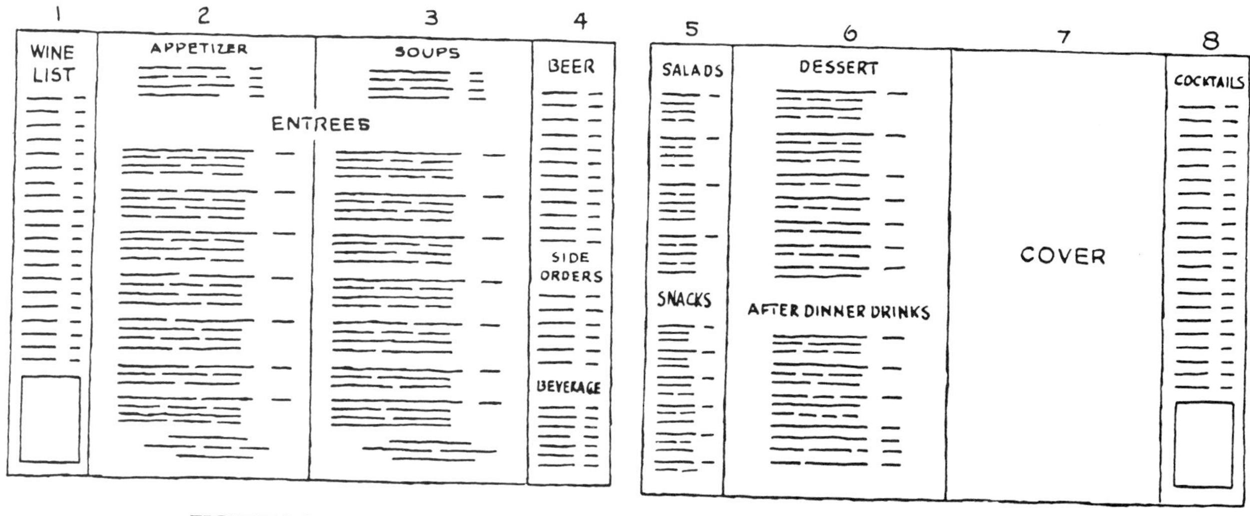

FIGURE 5.3 Sequence in a folded menu.

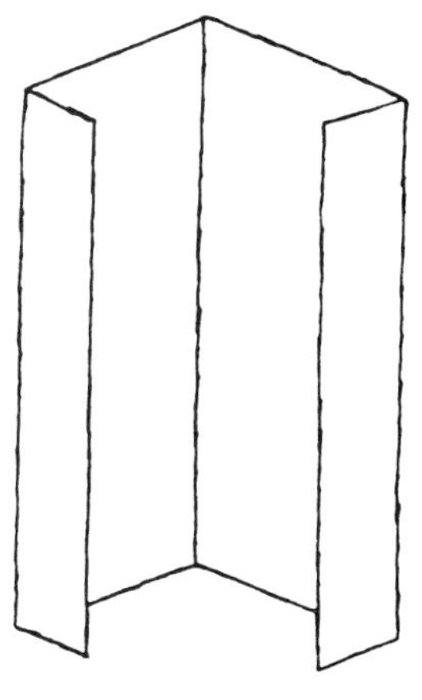

FIGURE 5.4 Menu combining meal offerings and drinks.

the type of operation it is. Besides the basic separation into breakfast, lunch, and dinner menus, there are the following:

Breakfast menu
Luncheon menu
Dinner menu
Late evening snack menu
Sunday brunch menu
Children's menu
Dessert or after-dinner menu
Room service menu
Poolside menu
Banquet menu
Takeout menu
Wine list
Drink list

No restaurant and hardly any hotel or motel would create and print thirteen menus, but the fact that it is possible to print and use thirteen different menus for thirteen different purposes shows the menu's scope and importance. Instead of multiple menus you might have only one menu that covers all thirteen subjects. But that extreme may combine too many subjects. Let us examine the problem.

First, there is the breakfast, lunch, and dinner problem. An establishment that serves all three meals can print three separate menus, one menu that combines all three, or some combination such as a separate breakfast menu and a combination luncheon and dinner menu.

Figure 5.5 shows both a separate breakfast menu and a combination luncheon and dinner menu. If you have a cutoff time for serving breakfast, it is almost mandatory that you have a separate breakfast menu; otherwise your customers will continue to order the breakfast items after you have stopped serving them. On the other hand, it is advisable to give the hours the breakfast menu is served, even if it is served twenty-four hours a day.

The key to combining the luncheon and dinner menu is the tip-on, which enables you to remove the luncheon menu and replace it with the dinner menu. But this means that the luncheon and dinner (or complete dinner or dinner specials for the day) listing must be small enough to fit into the space allowed. Thus if you have a big, varied, and complicated luncheon or dinner listing, a separate menu for each is recommended. The menu should fit what you serve, not the other way around. Also, because the tip-on is the key to the efficiency of this type of menu, it should be carefully prepared and printed. The typesetting should be as good as that of the rest of the menu, and the printing and

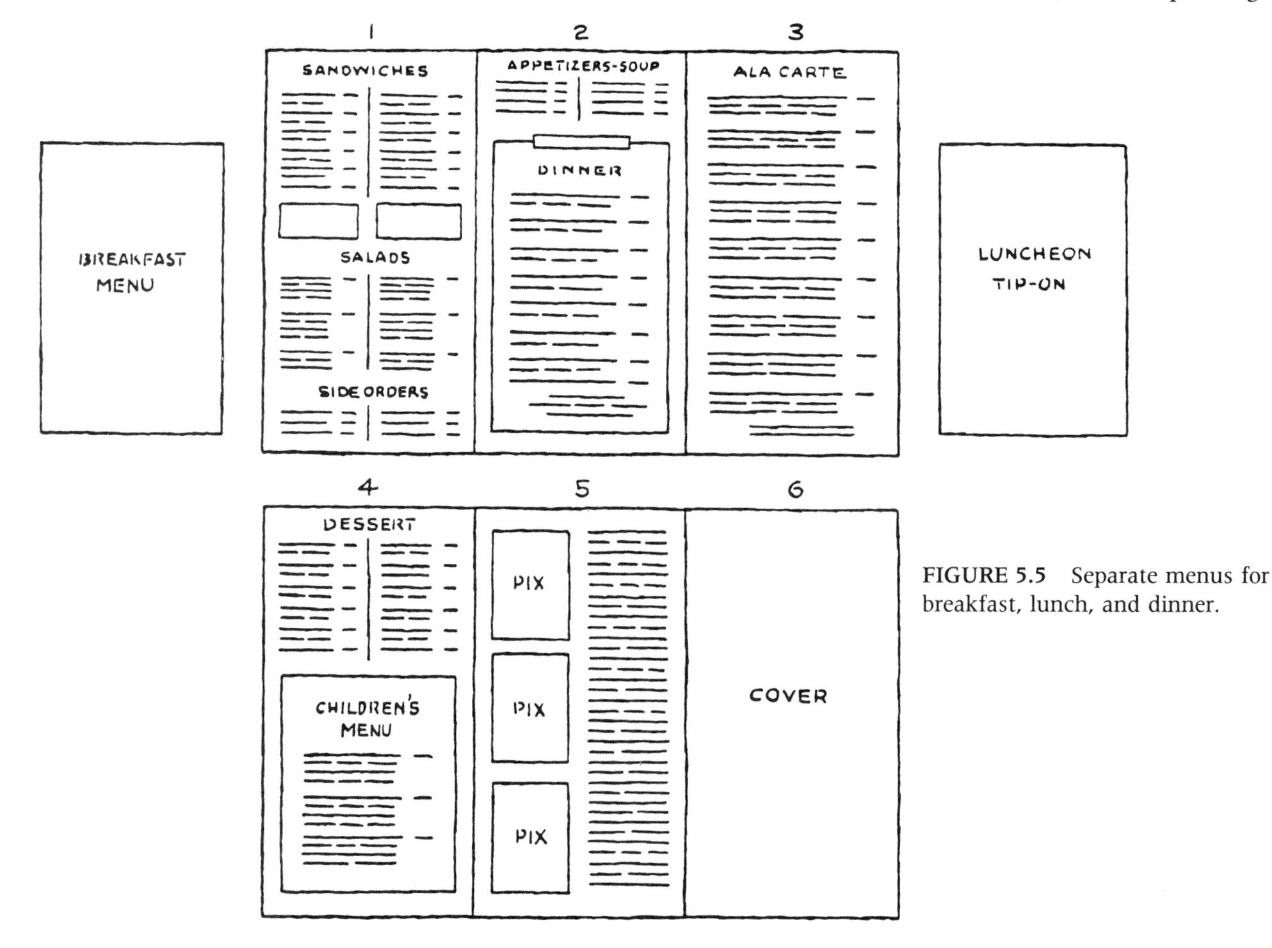

FIGURE 5.5 Separate menus for breakfast, lunch, and dinner.

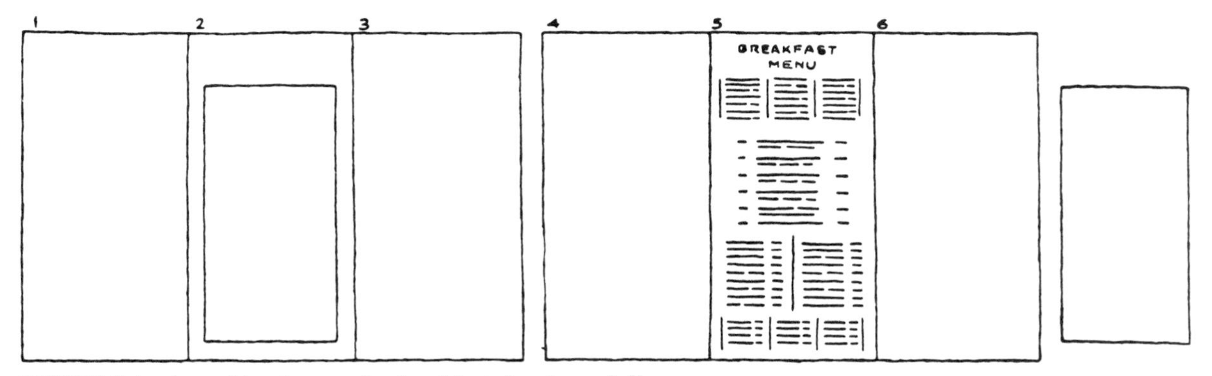

FIGURE 5.6 A combined menu for breakfast, lunch, and dinner.

paper should be of the same good quality.

Figure 5.6 illustrates one possible combination of all three meals—breakfast, luncheon, and dinner—on one menu. The dinner-luncheon combination is the same as that in Figure 5.5, but the breakfast menu is printed on panel 5 (the back) of this two-fold, three-panel menu. When the menu is folded, the breakfast part can be presented to the customer without exposing the rest of the menu. Combining all three meal listings on one menu and using tip-ons can save you money in printing, but the menu must be designed with care so that each part can function separately.

A combination menu also presents problems if you want to change your menu in the future. If all three menus are combined into one, the only change that you can make without reprinting the entire menu will be the tip-ons. And there is a limit to the number of tip-ons that can be put on a menu.

Another menu possibility that works for the three-meal problem is shown in Figure 5.7. This type of menu requires a permanent cover into which you insert the listings as needed—luncheon, dinner, or even breakfast. The main advantage of this type of menu, besides its flexibility, is that the cover (four pages) can be of heavier, more expensive, coated paper, whereas the inserts, which change more often, can be of lighter, less expensive paper. Also, the expensive two-, three-, or four-color printing can be on the cover, and the run can be larger to bring the unit cost down.

When using a semipermanent cover, you should remember to use all four pages (front cover, back cover, inside front cover, and inside back cover). Often only the front cover is used, and the other three pages are left blank, which is a waste of valuable advertising/selling space. Some of the possible uses for these three pages are

Bar list
Wine list
Party–banquet story
Late evening snacks
Weekly menu
Takeouts
History of establishment

If you are worried about making price changes on this semipermanent part of the menu (liquor list, wine list, takeouts, late evening snacks) you can use a tip-on.

Children's menus are often separate menus, and a great variety of these entertainment types of menus are available: Any menu house or printer can show you samples. If you have a big, or desire a bigger, "family" business, a separate children's menu that entertains as well as itemizes the food for children is a good idea. But if your service to children is small, a small listing on the regular menu is enough or, in some cases, merely the statement "Children's portions available at half price." Your emphasis on this part of the menu depends on your market and type of restaurant.

In the case of desserts and after-dinner drinks, a separate menu can do a better job; its effectiveness is in how it is used. The menu must be presented to the customers after they have finished their meal or entrée, without asking whether they want dessert or an after-

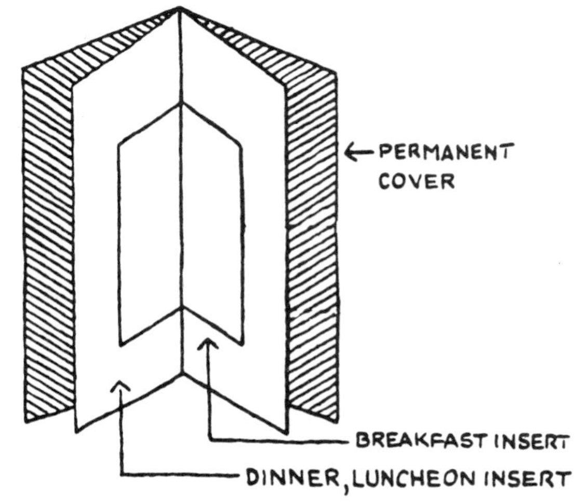

FIGURE 5.7 Insert menus for breakfast, lunch, and dinner.

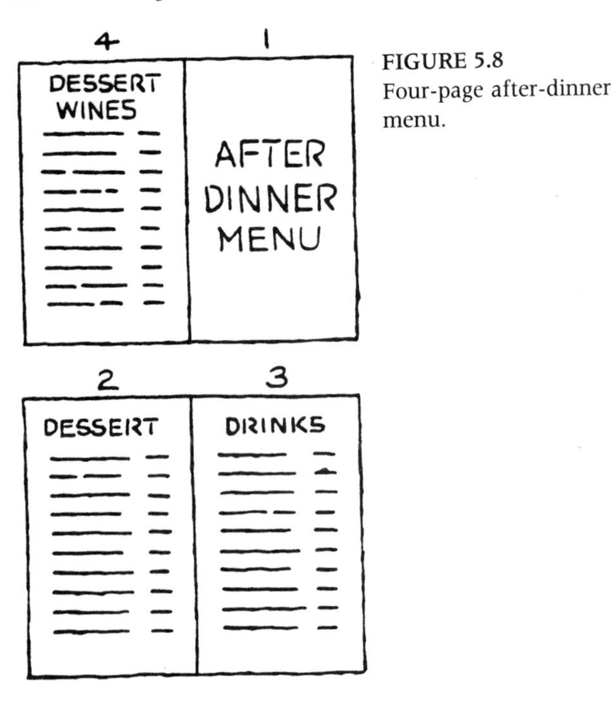

FIGURE 5.8 Four-page after-dinner menu.

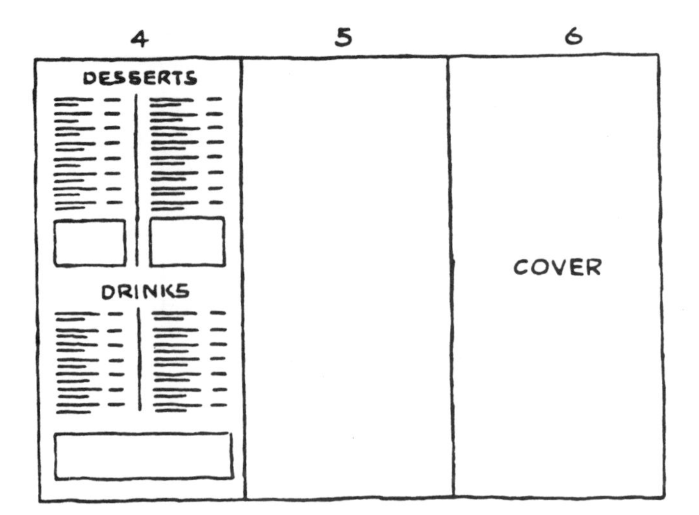

FIGURE 5.9 Folded after-dinner menu.

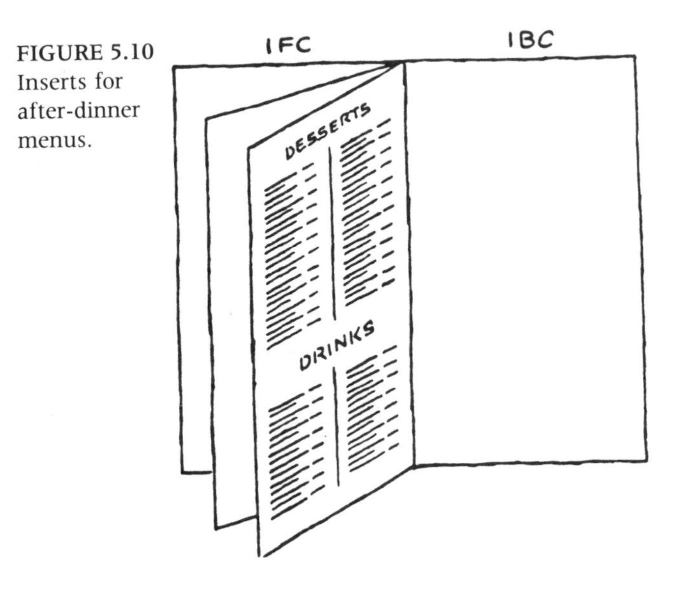

FIGURE 5.10 Inserts for after-dinner menus.

dinner drink. Only after they have had time to look at the menu should the question be asked.

The desserts and after-dinner drinks listing can be part of the total integrated menu as well as a separate menu. Figures 5.8, 5.9, and 5.10 show three ways of listing the "after" portion of a menu:

Figure 5.8 is a separate after-dinner menu with the desserts listed on page 2, the after-dinner drinks on page 3, and the dessert wines on page 4. Figure 5.9 is a three-panel, two-fold menu, with the desserts and after-dinner drinks printed on panel 4. Figure 5.10 is a four-page insert in a four-page cover, with the desserts and after-dinner drinks on page 4. The two menus illustrated in Figures 5.9 and 5.10 should be used in the same way that the separate after-dinner menu is used; that is, it should be presented to the customers after they have finished their entrées. Another advantage of a separate dessert and after-dinner menu is that the prices and items can be changed separately.

Specialty menus can be used for banquets, room service, poolside, takeout, Sunday brunch, and late evening snacks. In most cases, if you want to highlight a part of your menu, a separate menu or a separate treatment on your regular menu is the answer. This means presenting information, items, prices, and so on with good copy, good art (illustrations), and good printing. Any items or services that you sell as part of your foodservice should be described either somewhere on the regular menu or on a separate menu.

Major menu changes should be restricted to two or three a year, but a flexible menu allows for minor changes, specials, and price changes to be made more often. Figure 5.11 shows the use of a menu insert to make changes without redoing the entire menu. This menu has a four-page cover, which is usually made of heavier, coated paper with a four-page insert of lighter, less expensive paper. The bar items can be printed on the inside front cover, and the wine list, on the inside back cover. Alcoholic beverage prices generally change more slowly than do food prices. But even here, these items and their prices could be a tip-on that could be changed without throwing away the expensive covers.

The four-page insert contains the main food listing. Appetizers, soups, and salads are on page 1, entrées on pages 2 and 3, and desserts and after-dinner drinks on page 4, all in the usual sequence. The fastest-changing items (the entrées) should be on pages 2 and 3. Desserts, appetizers, and soups do not change as often, so this side of the insert (pages 1 and 4) can be preprinted and still allow for a quick change on pages 2 and 3.

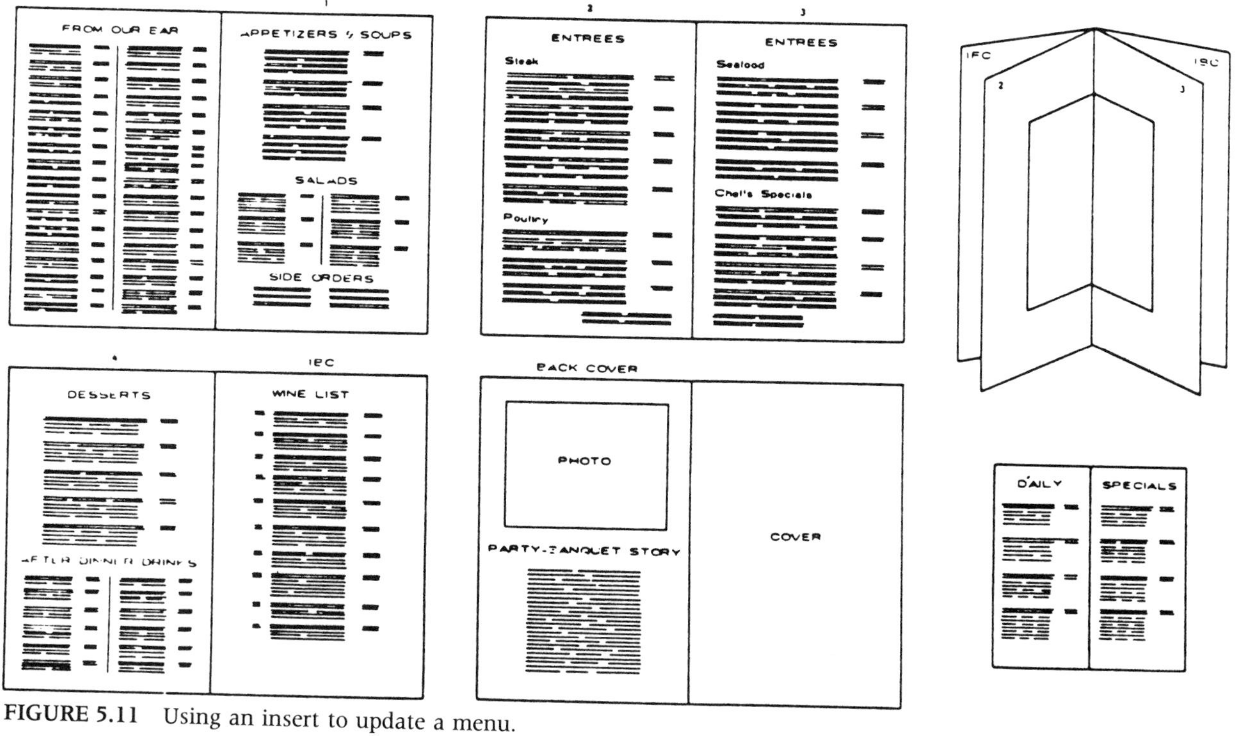

FIGURE 5.11 Using an insert to update a menu.

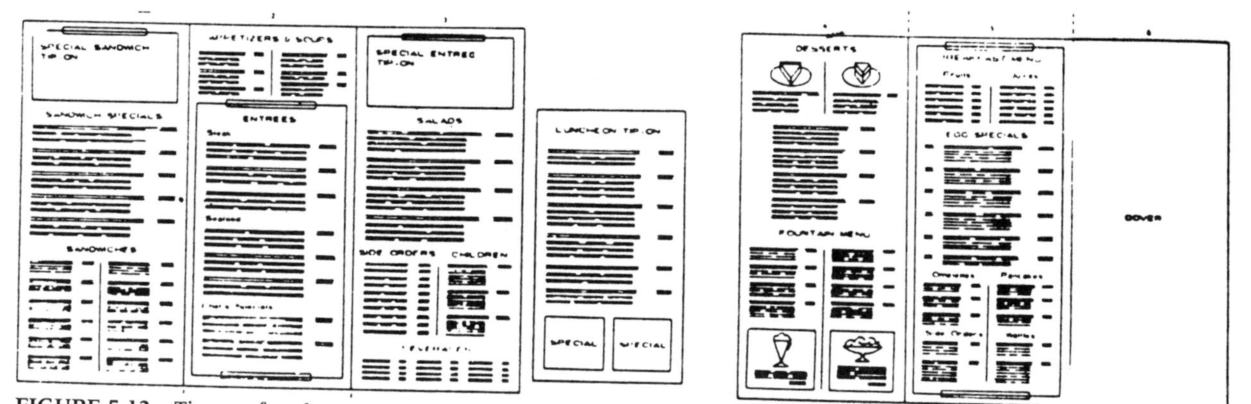

FIGURE 5.12 Tip-ons for changing menu items.

In addition, a daily special insert can be printed and placed in the center of the menu, thus allowing for even more flexibility in changes of price and items.

Figure 5.12 is a three-panel, two-fold menu with five tip-ons. Sandwiches are listed on panel 1, and space is allowed for a tip-on (sandwich special, steak sandwich, and so on). Soups and appetizers are listed at the top of panel 2, and space is allowed on the main portion of the menu for an entrée tip-on, thus permitting a daily or weekly change in the prices and items. The luncheon entrée tip-on can be substituted for the dinner entrée tip-on, so this menu can serve as both a lunch and dinner menu.

A variety of items can be listed on panel 3—salads, side orders, children's menu, and so on. Here also, a tip-on can be used for another entrée or salad special. Page 4 can be used for desserts and the fountain menu. These items can be on the permanent part of the menu, as their prices do not change as often as do those on the other parts of the menu.

Page 5 can be used for the breakfast menu and can be printed either permanently on the menu or on a tip-on, depending on the amount of change anticipated in the cost of these items.

The three-panel, two-fold menu is popular because a number of items can be listed in a logical way on only one menu. Figure 5.13 is another layout for the three-panel menu. Note, however, that the menu design should fit what the restaurant wants to feature and sell; that is, the food and drink items should not be made to fit a proposed menu layout.

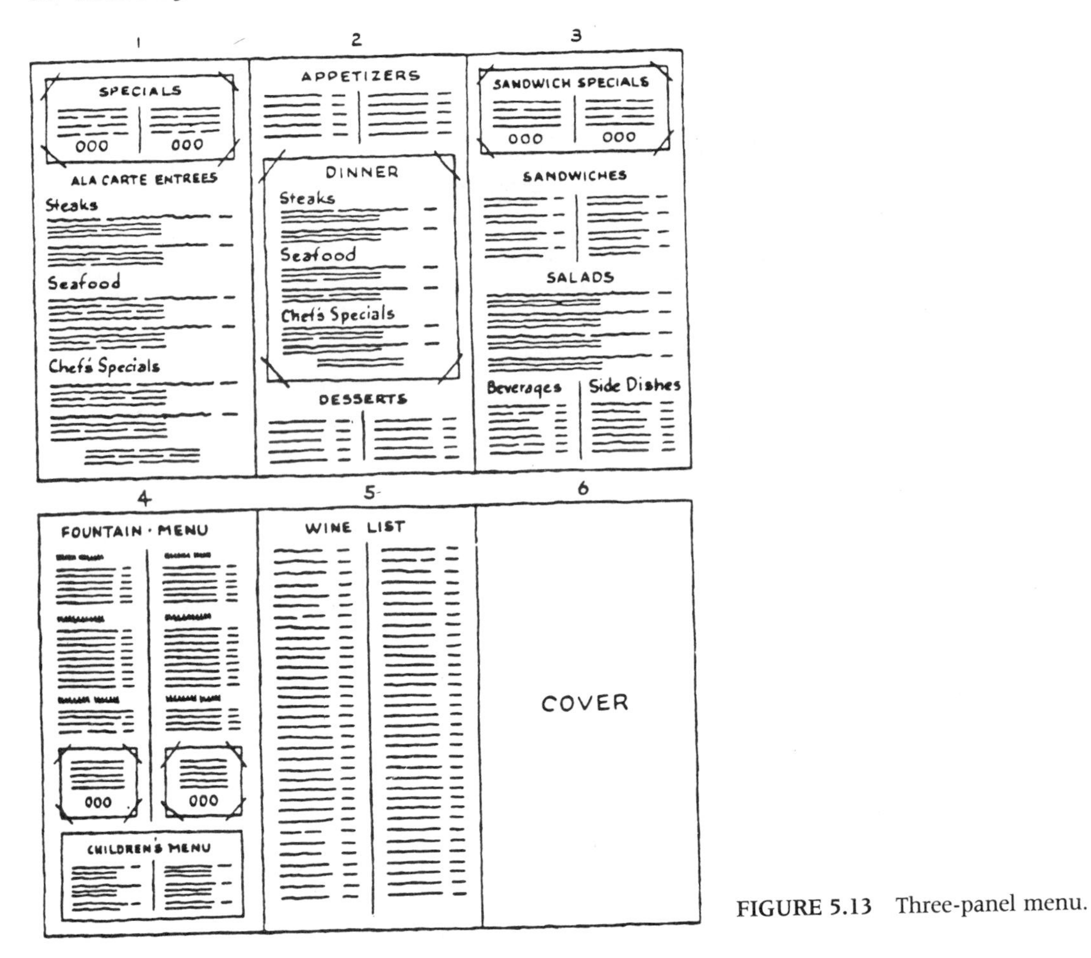

FIGURE 5.13 Three-panel menu.

SPECIALS

The words that retail outlets use most often to advertise special merchandising promotions are *new, sale,* and sometimes *free*. Such promotions on the menu allow the restaurant manager to have a sale, present something new, or create "packages," part of which can be labeled *free*. With a flexible menu that allows for changes, specials can be offered regularly (see Figure 5.14). The word *special* may be used to head the item, but the word *new* is just as effective.

The "special department" of the menu can also be considered as market research. That is, if a new special item proves to be popular (and profitable), it can then become a permanent part of the menu. Such specials are important, because American diners are changing their eating and drinking habits. A 1985 Gallup survey shows that of those people who eat out, 59 percent are concerned most with nutrition, 53 percent are eating smaller portions, and 28 percent are eating meals without traditional entrées.

Few, if any, foodservice operators consider every item on the menu—whether appetizers, soups, salads, entrées, or desserts—to be equal to every other item in the same category. Some items deserve special treatment. From the operator's point of view, there are two types of specials: the items for which the establishment is famous (if it is famous at all) and the items that the operator would especially like to sell, for example, high-profit, easy-to-prepare items.

The menu planner must decide which items will receive special treatment and then make sure that they are getting it. To do this, the menu planner should

1. List the specials in larger, bolder type than that of the rest of the menu.
2. Give the specials a longer description and more "advertising."
3. Place the specials in boxes, panels, or some kind of graphic device to make them stand out from the rest of the layout.
4. Use more color and illustrations for specials.

Some interesting specials that have been featured on menus of successful restaurants are as follows:

The Country Greens Restaurant near Lancaster, Pennsylvania (see Figure 15.2), has several unusual specials on its breakfast menu:

COUNTRY STYLE FRENCH TOAST

Slices of raisin bread layered with cream cheese and strawberry preserves, then egg-dipped and grilled to perfection. Served with maple flavored syrup.

On its dinner menu the restaurant has another interesting special featured on a color panel:

CHICKEN AND WAFFLES

The original dish that started Mr. & Mrs. Miller in the restaurant business over 50 years ago. Chicken and vegetables simmered in gravy over a fresh baked waffle. Coleslaw, rolls & butter.

The Bowery Restaurant in Traverse City, Michigan (see Figure 19.1), is a casual restaurant built in the

FIGURE 5.14 Menu from José Babushka's. This menu is made flexible by combining American and Mexican cuisine and having extra and replaceable panels. (Courtesy Joe Babushka's, Schelde Enterprises, Inc. Reproduced by permission.)

servants' quarters behind Bowers Harbor Inn. During the summer season the restaurant features fresh beef, chicken, Great Lakes whitefish, and award-winning BBQ ribs. During the off-season (spring and fall), the restaurant offers four special items on the front cover of the menu:

CHICKEN MARSALA

A tender chicken breast sautéed with marsala wine and mushrooms—served on a bed of linguine in pesto sauce.

BROILED RAINBOW TROUT

A generous broiled fillet laced with pecan butter. Fresh from neighboring Mancelona, Michigan!

TENDERLOIN BROCHETTE

Grilled, marinated tenderloin, skewered with fresh vegetables. Served on a bed of wild rice.

CAJUN CHICKEN & BOWERY RIBS

A fresh chicken breast char-grilled with bayou spices and the Bowery's award winning pork ribs.

The Chancery

What to serve and how many different items to serve (as well as what to charge) are the big questions for the restaurant operator who is creating a menu. The menu for the Chancery in Wauwatosa, Wisconsin, is a creative and extensive menu that solves the problems in an interesting way (Figure 5.15).

Each panel of the three-panel menu measures 10 by 13 inches and is printed in full color with eye-catching illustrations on heavy, plastic-coated paper. The inside spread (three panels) is organized in an unusual way. Each panel has three columns; the listing begins with snacks and appetizers at the far left column and continues to Refreshments (beverages and desserts) at the bottom of the ninth column. Each heading is illustrated by a line-drawing, and new items are flagged by a small black triangle with the word NEW in it.

FIGURE 5.15 Menu for the Chancery. (Reproduced by permission.)

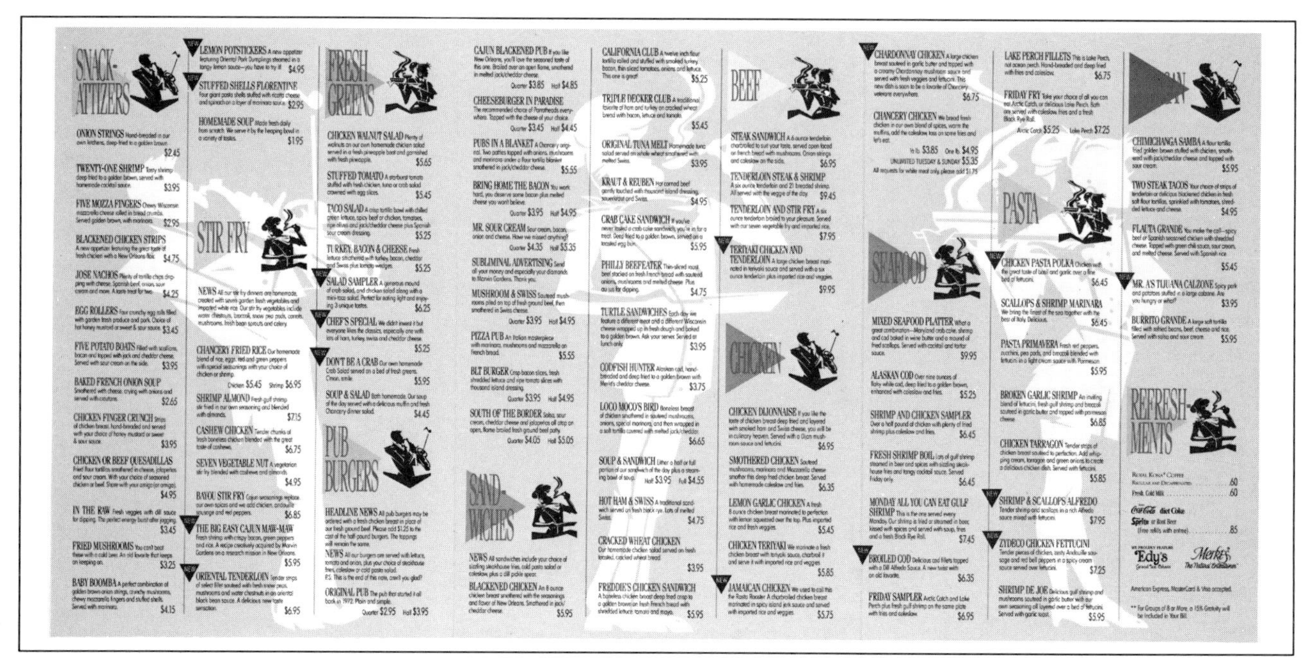

Among the sixteen items under the heading Snack-Attizers are:

FIVE MOZZA FINGERS

Chewy Wisconsin mozzarella cheese rolled in bread crumbs. Served golden brown, with marinara.

EGG ROLLERS

Four crunchy egg rolls filled with garden fresh produce and pork. Choice of hot honey mustard or sweet and sour sauce.

FIVE POTATO BOATS

Filled with scallions, bacon and topped with jack and cheddar cheese. Served with sour cream on the side.

STUFFED SHELLS FLORENTINE

Four giant pasta shells stuffed with ricotta cheese and spinach on a layer of marinara sauce.

Under the heading Stir Fry are Chancery Fried Rice, Shrimp Almond, Cashew Chicken, Seven Vegetable Nut Bayou, Stir Fry, the Big Easy Cajun Maw-Maw (fresh shrimp with crispy bacon, green peppers and rice), and Oriental Tenderloin.

Seven salads plus soup and salad are listed under Fresh Greens. Next come Pub Burgers, which include:

PUBS IN A BLANKET

A Chancery original. Two patties topped with onions, mushrooms and marinara under a flour tortilla blanket smothered in jack/cheddar cheese.

SOUTH OF THE BORDER

Salsa, sour cream, cheddar cheese and jalapeños all atop an open, flame broiled fresh ground beef patty.

The fourteen different sandwich creations include Blackened Chicken, California Club, Triple Decker Club, Original Tuna Melt, Kraut & Reuben, Crab Cake Sandwich, Philly Beefeater, Turtle Sandwiches, Codfish Hunter, Loco Moco's Bird, Hot Ham & Swiss, Cracked Wheat Chicken, Freddie's Chicken Sandwich, and a Soup & Sandwich Combination.

The entrées begin with beef items—Steak Sandwich, Tenderloin Steak & Shrimp, Tenderloin and Stir Fry, and Teriyaki Chicken and Tenderloin. Seven chicken and nine seafood entrées follow, including:

CHICKEN DIJONNAISE

Chicken breast deep fried and layered with smoked ham and Swiss cheese. Served with a Dijon mushroom sauce and fettucini.

The seafood specials include Monday All You Can Eat Gulf Shrimp, Friday Sampler, Friday Fry (Arctic Catch), and Lake Perch.

Next come pasta items—Chicken Pasta Polka, Scallops & Shrimp Marinara, Pasta Primavera, Broken Garlic Shrimp, Chicken Tarragon, Shrimp & Scallops Alfredo, Zydeco Chicken Fettucini, and Shrimp De Joe. The Mexican entrées are Chimichanga Samba, Two Steak Tacos, Flauta Grande, Mr. A's Tijuana Calzone, and Burrito Grande.

The final heading, Refreshments, lists coffee, soft drinks, and ice cream for dessert.

The Aux Deux Magots restaurant in Paris, known as Le Café Litteraire, features two specials under the heading Plates, which combine a food-and-drink package.

Norwegian Smoked Salmon and toasts, with a glass of Vodka.

Duck foie gras from the Landes and toasts, with a glass of Sauternes.

The Ivy Barn restaurants in San Diego, California, and West Palm Beach, Florida (see Figure 22.1), list their food and beverages in two seed packages (sweet peas). Each package has three separate listings. The first panel in the food package, Home Cookin', offers six weekly specials which are also food and beverage packages. Under the heading of Country Sippin' the customer is offered a free drink with each special entrée of the week.

MONDAY

ITALIAN COOKING

Enjoy it with a glass of chianti, beer, wine or a hi-ball

TUESDAY

ORIENTAL DELIGHTS

served with a Tokyo Rosé, a glass of beer or wine

WEDNESDAY

DOWNHOME COOKING

with apple cider or chilled beer

THURSDAY

MEXICAN COOKING

with a margarita or glass of sangria or beer

FRIDAY

GERMAN CUISINE

served with a glass of light or dark beer or wine

SATURDAY

POT LUCK, WHO KNOWS

with a hi-ball, glass of wine or beer

ADDING COLOR

Advertising in America vividly illustrates the effectiveness of color as a sales and merchandising tool for products of all kinds. Because people respond to it, color fills our magazines, books, newspapers, and television. Color photography plus modern methods of color reproduction have made color illustration commonplace in printed media, and the trend to colorful menus is accelerating.

Color on the menu can function in many ways. First, it can act as decoration, making the menu more attractive and interesting. Second, color photography accurately portrays your food and drink, and third, color can set the mood and style for your restaurant.

Color as decoration or design on your menu can be done simply by adding one color plus black, or it can be complex, using all the colors of the rainbow. Color can also be added to the menu through the use of colored paper.

Lum's

A menu that is absolutely tops in color is Lum's eight-page food and drink listing with full color photography (Figure 5.16). A large menu, 10 by 13 inches, it has correspondingly large illustrations. The hamburgers, for example, are shown bigger than life-size. Besides the Beautiful Batch of Burgers and Ollie's Greatest Creations (ten hamburgers and cheeseburgers), customers may order Deep Sea Delights, Steak Dinners, Lumberjack Sandwiches, and Desserts, Beverages, and Side Orders. A complimentary Lum's Breakfast Menu also uses large, colorful life-size photos.

Bobby McGee's

Special means of a kind different from others, distinctive, or unique, according to the dictionary. The menu for Bobby McGee's (Figure 5.17) not only meets this

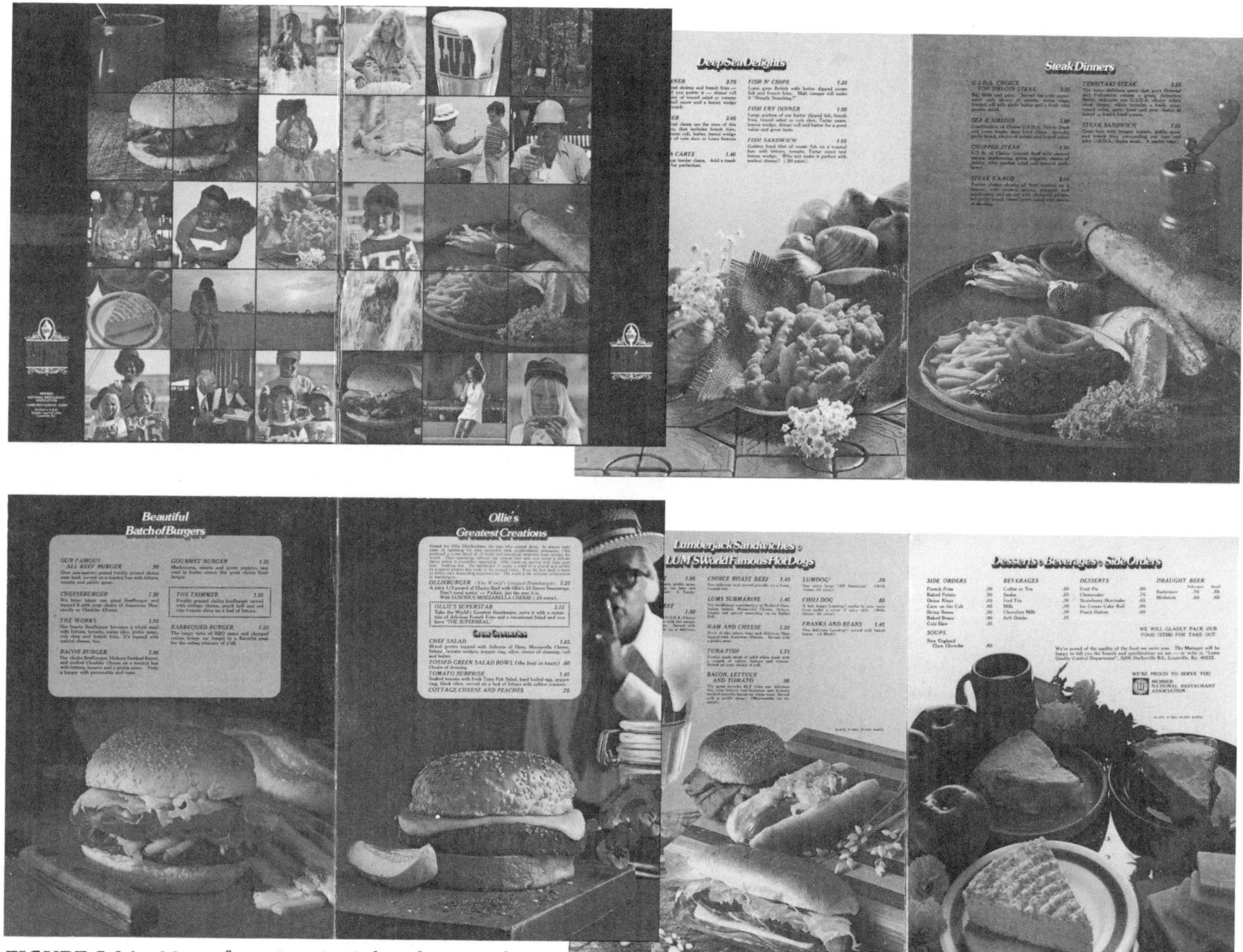

FIGURE 5.16 Menu from Lum's. Color photographs whet the appetite and facilitate ordering. (Lum's Restaurant Corporation. Reproduced by permission.)

FIGURE 5.17 Menu from Bobby McGee's, U.S.A., Inc. (Reproduced by permission.)

definition, it also shows how specials can attract notice through graphic devices and illustrations.

The three-panel menu measuring 8 by 15 inches is printed in full color on heavy, white, glossy paper. The first panel features appetizers, favorites, entrées, and a special.

The nine appetizers range from a Party Platter at $7.95 to Spicy Onion Rings, $2.75. Our Favorites include Mahi Mahi Macadamia, Chicken Parmigiana, Oriental Shrimp, BBQ Chicken, Chicken Stir Fry, Lasagna, Orange Roughy, and Top Sirloin, with prices ranging from $6.95 to $8.25. The special on this page is "Dem Bones, Dem Bones: Slow smoked meaty back ribs taken from the prime rib, $7.95. Monday Night—All You Can Eat."

Panels 2 and 3 are outlined and headed in bold type with the words Soup and Salad Bar—All You Can Eat. Panel 2 is headed by the main special, Prime Rib of Beef, in a yellow box with an illustration, which is offered in three sizes at $10.75, $13.75, and $15.75. Next come Fresh Fish items, Traditional Steaks (five), a small special (Sautéed Mushrooms), and the Hickory Smoker, which has three items. At the bottom in a smaller panel is a Wednesday night offering of All You Can Eat, Dem Bones, Dem Bones, and BBQ Chicken, $10.95.

The third panel begins with combination plates:

COMBOS & COMBINATIONS

MIX AND MATCH YOUR OWN PERSONAL FAVORITES.

Fried Shrimp	*Shrimp Scampi*	*Sautéed Scallops*
Fried Scallops	*Lasagna*	*Island Chicken*
Fried Clam Strips	*Top Sirloin*	*Deviled Crab*

Pick any two for $13.95; pick any three for $15.95; for each additional add $3.95.

Next are four chicken dishes (Fowl Play) followed by Classic Shellfish (six items ranging from $12.95 to $21.95).

The back panel begins with a Kids Menu of six items. A Desserts heading follows, but no list. Instead, the diner is told to save room, as the server will describe the house specialty desserts. This is followed by a Specialty Drinks listing (six items) plus information on the brand of coffee served (Kozana) and a message from the founder/owner. The back center cover contains the Wine List.

Velvet Turtle

On most menus the appetizers, salads, entrées, and desserts offered are listed in columns in descending order, which tends to give top importance to the first item listed and less importance to those following. Eye studies have shown that the menu reader tends to look at the first one or two items, then jump to the last item on the list, before exploring the rest.

One way to avoid this "order of importance" is shown in the Velvet Turtle restaurant menu (Figure 5.18). The entrées—Specialties of the Chef, Beef and Combinations—are listed across the page with plenty of space around each entrée listed. This treatment gives each item its own "stage"; its story stands alone. Each item thus gets the customer's attention, and choice is less dependent on where the item is listed.

Specialties of the Chef lists three entrées—From the Chef (daily special), New Zealand Rack of Lamb Bouquetiere, and Beef Wellington. The type selection is very good, with the items in uppercase letters and the descriptive copy in upper- and lowercase italic. The description is short but well done:

BEEF WELLINGTON

Filet mignon baked in light pastry crust, served with bordelaise sauce. Wine suggestion: Cabernet Sauvignon, Bin No. 22.

Served with your choice of Soup du Jour or Gazpacho a la Seville or Chilled Cucumber Soup or mixed green salad. Served with fresh vegetable and warm sourdough bread.

Specialties of the Chef

FROM THE CHEF
In addition to the selections below, each evening we take pride in featuring a specialty of the Chef. We will be pleased to describe tonight's selection.

NEW ZEALAND RACK OF LAMB, BOUQUETIERE
Young and tender lamb served with duchess potatoes. Wine suggestion: Beaujolais, Bin. No. 25.
14.50

BEEF WELLINGTON
Filet mignon baked in light pastry crust, served with bordelaise sauce. Wine suggestion: Cabernet Sauvignon, Bin No. 22.
14.50

Beef and Combinations

Served with your choice of Soup du Jour or Gazpacho a la Seville or Chilled Cucumber Soup or mixed green salad. Served with fresh vegetable and warm sourdough bread.

ROAST PRIME RIB OF BEEF
Velvet Turtle Cut 13.95
Regular Cut 12.95
Choice beef served with creamed horseradish and baked potato. Wine suggestion: A robust red wine, Cabernet Sauvignon, Bin No. 27.

BEEF & SEAFOOD BROCHETTE
Tender pieces of beef sirloin, served with shrimp, medallions of lobster tail and scallops broiled on a skewer. Wine suggestion: Rose of Cabernet Sauvignon, Bin No. 33.
9.95

PEPPER STEAK GOURMET
New York cut steak with cracked peppercorns. Topped with fresh mushrooms, crisp bacon and green onions. Served with baked potato. Wine suggestion: Zinfandel, Bin No. 24.
12.50

PETITE FILET MIGNON
Served with baked potato. Wine suggestion: Petite Sirah, Bin No. 20.
12.95

TOURNEDOS BEARNAISE
Two small filets topped with bearnaise sauce and garnished with mushroom caps. Wine suggestion: Cabernet Sauvignon, Bin No. 27.
11.75

NEW YORK CUT STEAK
Served with baked potato. Enjoy your steak with a fine Pinot Noir, Bin No. 21.
13.95

TOURNEDOS ROSSINI
Two small filets garnished with pate and mushroom caps. Topped with bordelaise sauce. Wine suggestion: Cabernet Sauvignon, Bin No. 27
11.75

LOBSTER COMBINATION
Your choice of filet mignon or roast prime rib of beef and lobster tail. Wine suggestion: Mateus Rose, Bin No. 12.
16.95

Accompaniments

FRESH MUSHROOMS SAUTÉ
2.50

FRENCH FRIED ZUCCHINI
Served with mustard sauce.
2.50

BAKED POTATO
Served with butter or sour cream, bacon and chives.
1.00

FIGURE 5.18 Menu of the Velvet Turtle. (© 1989 Velvet Turtle Restaurants. Reproduced by permission.)

Listing a wine suggestion right next to the entrée is good menu merchandising strategy.

The heading Beef and Combinations offers eight more entrées—Roast Prime Rib of Beef, Beef and Seafood Brochette, Pepper Steak Gourmet, Petite Filet Mignon, Tournedos Bearnaise, New York Cut Steak, Tournedos Rossini, and Lobster Combination. Included with the entrées are

Choice of Soup du Jour, Gazpacho à la Seville, Chilled Cucumber Soup, or mixed green salad. Served with fresh vegetable and warm sourdough bread.

An additional Accompaniments listing includes Fresh Mushrooms Sauté, French Fried Zucchini, and Baked Potato. These à la carte extras are given the same billing in size and importance as the entrées—a good idea since they are check builders.

MENU STRATEGIES FOR THE 1990s

According to *The Wall Street Journal*, October 1989, most American consumers have modest expectations. Reports from the nation's marketers indicate that the majority of Americans are happy to stay at a Holiday Inn, drink Budweiser beer, and eat ice cream at Baskin-Robbins. This information is the result of a *WSJ* survey of the aspirations and attitudes of more than four thousand consumers from all walks of life.

While the public is generally satisfied, people still complain about high prices, mediocre quality, and poor service. Although an upper-level group in America is interested in high-end products, the largest consumer group consists of average middle-of-the-roaders, and marketers are not paying much attention to them.

This groups hates poor service, waiting in line, and failure to respond to requests and seeks new dining experiences. Smart restaurant operators like Denny's, Red Lobster, and Domino's have met their complaints by providing quick service and quick delivery programs. Other restaurateurs, aware of the desire for something *new* on the menu, are giving the customer new dining experiences.

The *WSJ* survey also showed how consumers react to restaurants that offer discount coupons. The fast-food chains in particular recently have been couponing and discounting heavily, and nearly every pizza chain is offering a two-for-one pizza deal. Price wars among the fast-food giants like McDonald's, Burger King, and Wendy's have hurt franchisees, since the buyer tends to choose the coupon offer regardless of past loyalties.

The pizza market, according to *Pizza Today*, is divided among Pizza Hut ($3.2 billion), Domino's ($2.3 billion), others ($2.2 billion), and independent pizza vendors ($6.3 billion). Thus, when the chains are issuing coupons and reducing prices, the independent operator can offer a different product at possibly a higher price. Nevertheless, the price cutting of the chains still has an impact.

The number of fast-food outlets increased dramatically in the 1980s. According to the National Restaurant Association, quick service restaurant units in the United States rose 131,146, a total of 14 percent between 1983 and 1987, the last year for which figures are available.

Why all the interest in quick service, fast food, and time saving? According to the *WSJ*, the microwave is the most favored household product, just behind the smoke alarm. The microwave is both a symptom and a symbol of American's new attitude toward time. Between 75 and 80 percent of American homes have microwaves, and if the appliance satisfies people's urge to save time, it has also changed the sense of how fast is fast. It has made even fast-food restaurants seem not fast because at home the diner doesn't have to wait in line.

If quick service and fast food are the trend in quick service restaurants, the definition of service in better, upscale restaurants is different. Here the customer expects to spend time instead of save it. This type of dining is an enjoyable and often rare experience. The *WSJ* survey in some respects contradicts itself. On the one hand people want new experiences; on the other, they are happy with good old Holiday Inn and Budweiser beer.

The enormous variety of American restaurants provides plenty of new eating experiences. This desire for the new along with the old, tried, and true has led to combination cuisines—seafood and pasta or Chinese and deli, for example. Many restaurants have menus with a mixed offering—some pasta, some Mexican foods, plus standard chicken, seafood, and beef entrées.

Alert marketers are also aware of demographic changes. As the American population becomes older, marketers seek the business of the senior citizen crowd. Another trend is the increasing emphasis on health and nutrition. The baby boomers are not only jogging and working out, they are looking for low-fat, low-cholesterol foods and staying away from alcohol. Many restaurants are aware of this trend and are using the menu to tell customers how they are cooking with healthier oils and serving healthier foods.

Many restaurants also use their menus to encourage the loyal customer (or even the occasional customer) to return. The weekly menu with a different entrée for every day of the week and special all-you-can-eat nights or Sunday buffets are used to draw repeat customers. Some restaurants serving a big beer selection have formed beer clubs, where the customer who has ordered and drunk every beer on the drink list gets a special reward of some kind.

Peter Drucker, the grand old guru of corporate economics, believes that the 1990s will bring far-reaching changes in the social and economic environment and in the strategies, structure, and management of business. Several of Drucker's observations are of interest to the restaurant industry. He predicts that business in the 1990s will move work to where people are rather than people to where the work is. He also believes businesses will farm out activities such as clerical work, maintenance, and corporate catering, which do not offer opportunities for advancement and professional positions. The trend toward farming out is already under way in America. Most hospitals are cleaned by outside maintenance companies, and some hospitals have contracted out their foodservice. The reason for this trend is the growing need for productivity in service work that is done largely by people without much education or skill. This need almost requires that the work be done by outside organizations with their own career ladders.

The contracting out trend means the continued growth of catering. Creative Gourmets, a catering company headquartered in Boston, did $25 million worth of business in 1988 with sixty foodservice accounts ranging from Harvard's Kennedy School of Government to the Dana-Farber Cancer Institute. In addition, the movement of populations and businesses from the center city to the suburbs and beyond may also stimulate the catering and take-out business. The delivery of pizzas to the home and the workplace may be just the beginning of moving food to where the people are instead of moving people to where the food is.

6

Menu Demographics

According to the U.S. Bureau of the Census, in 1987 the population of the United States was 242,712,000, and by the year 2000 it will be 267,498,000, an increase of 24,786,000. In addition, the number of Americans seventeen years and younger was 63,475,000 in 1987 and is projected to reach 65,713,000 by the year 2000. The group of eighteen- to fifty-four-year-olds totalled 128,516,000 in 1987, is expected to reach 143,514,000 by the year 2000. The group fifty-five years and older numbered 51,836,000 in 1987 and is projected to reach 59,040,000 by the year 2000.

POPULATION CHARACTERISTICS

These figures tell us that the U.S. population is generally growing older. Although the younger population will increase slightly, the number of people over fifty-five will increase significantly. How will these projections affect the restaurant business? According to the U.S. Bureau of Labor Statistics, Americans spend the following dollar amounts weekly for food that is eaten away from home:

25 and under: $17.62
26 to 54: $26.22
55 and older: $14.22

As expected, people who are in the middle age bracket (twenty-six to fifty-four years) spend the most on eating out, and older persons spend the least. But the older group is expected to grow larger, and many older people will have both the numbers and the money to constitute a significant eating-out group, as they tend to have more disposable income. They usually are not paying off mortgages and sending their children to college.

The restaurant industry has not developed this market as well as it probably could, although there is some movement in this direction. Some restaurants do offer discounts to people dining from 4:00 to 6:00 P.M., which are aimed at older people, who often dine earlier. Other restaurants give senior citizens discounts on their regular prices.

Although restaurants provide children's menus—smaller amounts and entertainment (games and puzzles)—they have given less thought to senior menus, written in larger type, the portions sized for smaller appetites, and with lower prices and food that is easy to eat. Restaurants should identify the size of their older market and adjust their menus accordingly. One factor that is often ignored is that older people do not appreciate loud rock music and avoid dining in restaurants that play it.

Restaurants pay more attention to senior needs where there are pockets of older, retired people—mainly where the weather is warm all year round, as in Florida, southern California, Arizona, and New Mexico. Other areas also have concentrations of older people. For example, in the following states 12.5 percent or more of the population is sixty-five or older: Oregon, South Dakota, Nebraska, Arkansas, New York, Iowa, Missouri, Kansas, Maine, and Massachusetts. This distribution shows that many older, retired people do not move to warm retirement areas but stay where they have lived most of their lives.

Turning to the younger sector of the population, U.S. Census Bureau figures show that in 1987 there were 18,198,000 children aged five years and under. This figure should stay the same for about a decade and then it is predicted to decline in the year 2000 to 16,898,000. For those aged five to seventeen, the figure for 1987 is 45,277,000 and will increase by the year 2000 to 48,815,000. Assuming these projections are accurate, it is obvious that the youth market will remain large for at least a decade.

What does this mean to the menu builder, the restaurant operator? First, the operator must decide whether or not to target the youth market. A good example of a restaurant conglomerate that has been youth oriented since it began and has a record of success that is far beyond that of all its competitors is McDonald's.

McDonald's is more than just an American fast-food success story; it is also an international phenomenon. Today the "golden arches" can be found in Andorra, Belgrade, Kuala Lumpur, and Moscow. Early in 1988 the company opened its ten thousandth restaurant and announced plans to open twenty more in the Soviet Union. In the entire world more people eat at McDonald's every day than live in Australia and New Zealand!

There are many reasons for McDonald's success, a story that began in 1955 and continues today. The corporate creed of "quality, service, cleanliness and value" tells part of the story, but a more relevant factor is that when the restaurant chain began, there was a population explosion, known as the post–World War II baby boom. From the beginning, McDonald's aimed its product and its promotions at children and the family.

By taking direct aim at the youth market, McDonald's not only secured a big part of that market, it also created a habit among the population of eating its Big Mac hamburgers and french fries. As the baby boomers grew up, married, and had their own children, this habit continued, which kept the market strong for McDonald's products.

McDonald's spends more than $1 million a day on TV commercials, most of them targeted at children or families. Some of these commercials say nothing about food, price, convenience, or service. For example, a "Little Sister" commercial has a big brother recalling his times at Mac's with his sister from childhood to prom night.

McDonald's promotions extend beyond the restaurant world. Ronald McDonald, the company spokesman, is really a clown who entertains children. Ronald McDonald Houses have been established to help the families of seriously ill children.

Does all this "kid stuff" pay off? Well, last year McDonald's restaurants—mostly franchises—grossed more than $14.3 billion, and the corporation made a profit of $4.9 billion. Through the first two quarters of 1988 the company had logged ninety-two quarters of record earnings. McDonald's is the biggest owner of commercial real estate in America and is the biggest foodservice corporation in the world—not exactly kid stuff.

The youth market can be classified into three or four categories: preschool, grade school, high school, and a quasi-adult category of college-aged youths. The preschool and grade school children can be reached in a restaurant by a children's menu. The high school youth are a different problem. A teen menu might offer hamburgers, pizza, malts, soft drinks, and, of course, rock music.

POPULATION MOVEMENTS

The population of the United States is not only growing and changing its mix of old, young, and middle-aged components, it is also on the move. Americans have been moving west and south and from the countryside to the cities. The U.S. Bureau of the Census' 1986 *State and Metropolitan Area Data Book* lists the populations of the four major areas of the United States as follows:

Northeast: 50,140,000
Midwest: 59,450,000
South: 84,658,060
West: 49,658,000

By the year 2010, the U.S. population distribution is projected to be

Northeast: 52,496,000
Midwest: 59,018,000
South: 104,919,000
West: 65,622,000

The Northeast will grow slightly, the Midwest will lose population, and the West and South will continue to grow. States such as California are expected to grow from 27,531,000 to 37,347,000 and Florida will grow from 11,962,000 to 17,530,000. Assuming that these projections are correct, they indicate economic, social, and even political changes in the areas affected. Such population shifts present both problems and opportunities.

At the time of the 1980 census, the center of the United States' population was one mile west of the small town of DeSoto, Missouri and forty miles south of St. Louis. Today this center has shifted to Oklahoma and is continuing to move south and west. Another population movement in the United States that is important to restaurant operators and all business is that the population and commerce in every region have broken through the suburbs of large cities and are establishing new low-density settlements independent of the urban centers that once held outlying areas within their orbit.

This new growth and population movement is occurring so far out from the cities and is accompanied by so much economic development that traditional ties to cities and suburbs are no longer as strong as they used to be. The cities of America seem to be breaking apart, and the pieces are moving out across the countryside without a center of direction. The population is also becoming scattered around small towns, in retirement communities, and along lakes and seashores. This new low-density development, which is neither suburban nor rural but a mixture of the two, is a new form of American community.

An example of this trend is Mohave County, Arizona, which is a stretch of desert divided from California by the Colorado River. In 1960 this county had a population of 7,786; by 1986 it had grown to 76,700. Of this total, 21,000 people arrived after 1980. The area grew first as a retirement and recreation community, with the inhabitants—mostly from the East—settling in Lake Havasu City. Then light industry and younger people came to the area.

Another example of the trend is Jefferson County, south of St. Louis, which is in the path of the population movement out of St. Louis. It is a good example of what is happening across the nation. In 1950 its population reached a peak of 857,000 and then began to decline. Middle-class whites began to move to the suburbs, and blacks and poor whites moved into the city, but in smaller numbers than the outflow. Small suburban municipalities began to spread out into St. Louis County and beyond. By 1980 the population of St. Louis had dropped to 453,000, and it has fallen even further since then.

In the St. Louis metropolitan area, as in other cities, old neighborhoods have been restored by professionals, with new construction downtown and along the riverfront. These new buildings serve as financial, legal, entertainment, and tourist centers, but most of the people who use these facilities live outside the city or are visitors.

A different kind of development is taking place fifteen miles northwest of St. Louis. St. Charles County has so much commerce and industry that it is largely independent of the city and its suburbs. The growth has clustered around the small city of St. Charles, with a population of 41,000. In 1980 the U.S. government recognized it as an area with its own population and economic base. The movement of people, however, went beyond the city of St. Charles, following an interstate highway corridor that runs west through farm towns and villages. In the 1970s nearly half of the new settlers built homes outside the municipalities.

A similar pattern of outward growth has occurred in metropolitan areas such as Atlanta and Phoenix. The movement is so strong that employers in the outer areas are having trouble finding workers, as often no public transportation exists from the inner city, where the unemployed live, to these outer regions, which can be reached only by car.

To give you an idea of the population spread across the United States, consider Nashville, Tennessee. Its metropolitan area, with a population of less than a million, is spread over eight counties and four thousand square miles. The spread is facilitated by three interstate highways that intersect in the city, sending out spokes in six different directions. The terrain also helps. The meandering Cumberland River plus lakes, state parks, wildlife areas, and wooded hills all help to attract people to live outside the city.

Although North Carolina pioneered scattered growth away from city and suburbs, it has retained much of its old landscape in the process of industrialization and economic growth. With a population of six million, North Carolina is now the tenth largest state in the country. A larger percentage of its work force—about 35 percent—is engaged in manufacturing than that of any other state. Yet it has no city comparable in size to those in other industrial states. Charlotte, the largest, has a population of 350,000, but no other North Carolina city has more than 200,000.

North Carolina has many square miles of suburbs; yet these, too, are less massive than those in other states. Rather, they tend to give way to scattered development that has left many farms, villages, forests, and old buildings intact. Some sociologists and urbanologists believe that the pattern in North Carolina is the blueprint of the future for the rest of the country.

The forces that have brought about the dispersal of people from cities to suburbs to outlying areas even farther away are strong, and there is no reason to believe that the trend will stop. Some of the reasons are the advance of technology centered on light industry (even small steel mills), the change from a manufacturing to a service- and information-based economy, and the accumulation of private wealth. These factors and American political freedom have made it possible for people and commerce to settle anywhere they please. And the inner cities seem not to be where they please.

For the restaurant operator these trends are something to watch. Is the restaurant market area population growing or shrinking? Are the population changes affecting the popularity of items on the menu? Are there new foodservice opportunities in outlying areas? If you ask a real estate agent what the three most important factors are in judging the value of real estate, the answer is most likely to be "location, location, and location." This also probably applies to the location of any foodservice outlet.

They say that if you build a better mousetrap, the public will beat a path to your door. That may be true, but advertising and marketing help. A small restaurant in Lockport, Illinois—an hour's drive from Chicago—manages to draw customers from a fifty-mile radius because the food is that good.

Called The Tall Grass, this country restaurant seats only thirty-six, but it has been successful since 1981. The menu is not fancy (see Figures 6.1 and 6.2); in fact, it is written by hand by chef/owner Robert Burcenski. It is changed seasonally (four times a year) as well as weekly, to fit the market availability of certain items.

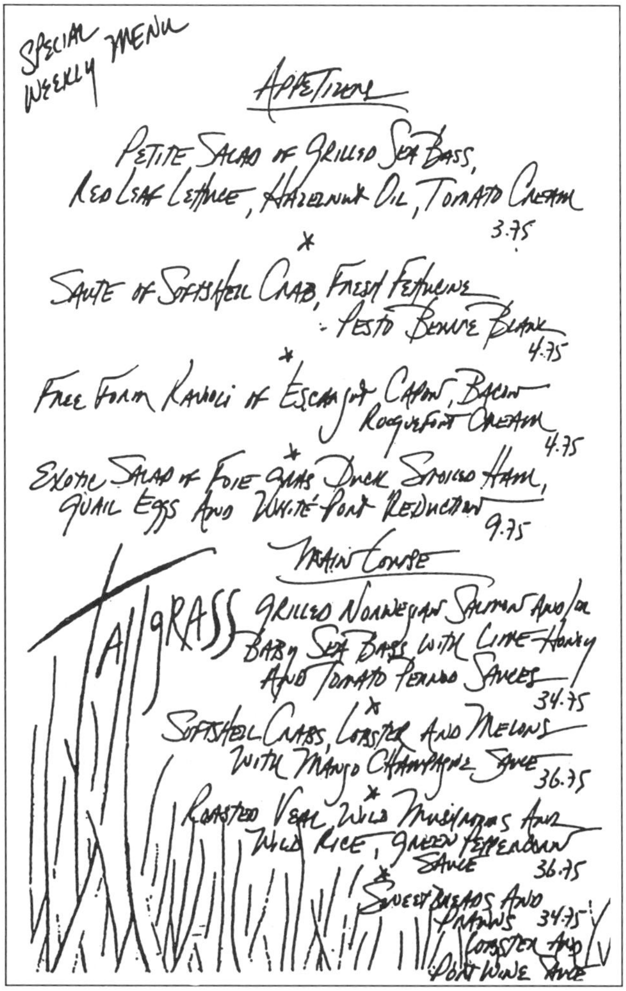
SPECIAL WEEKLY MENU
APPETIZERS
PETITE SALAD OF GRILLED SEA BASS,
RED LEAF LETTUCE, HAZELNUT OIL, TOMATO CREAM
3.75
*
SAUTE OF SOFTSHELL CRAB, FRESH FETTUCINE
- PESTO BEURRE BLANC
4.75
*
FREE FORM RAVIOLI OF ESCARGOT, CAPON, BACON
ROQUEFORT CREAM
4.75
*
EXOTIC SALAD OF FOIE GRAS, DUCK, SMOKED HAM,
QUAIL EGGS AND WHITE PORT REDUCTION
9.75
MAIN COURSE
TALL GRASS
GRILLED NORWEGIAN SALMON AND/OR
BABY SEA BASS WITH LIME-HONEY
AND TOMATO PERNOD SAUCES
34.75
*
SOFTSHELL CRABS, LOBSTER AND MELONS
WITH MANGO CHAMPAGNE SAUCE 36.75
*
ROASTED VEAL, WILD MUSHROOMS AND
WILD RICE, GREEN PEPPERCORN
SAUCE 36.75
*
SWEETBREADS AND
PRAWNS 34.75
LOBSTER AND
PORT WINE SAUCE

FIGURE 6.1 Weekly menu at The Tall Grass. (Courtesy Tall Grass Restaurant. Reproduced by permission.)

MENUS TO MEET POPULATION CHANGES

Denny's

Denny's is a family-style restaurant chain with over twelve hundred outlets and sales of $1,300 million in 1988 (Figure 6.3). Its menu has eight pages, each measuring 6 by 14 inches. It is printed in full color on heavy, white cover paper and is plastic-coated for easy maintenance. The cover has a large Denny's logo as its design.

Each panel of the menu, except the cover, has a 4½- by 3-inch color photo of a specific menu item. The various categories of listings, on six pages, are Salads, Weekday Lunch Combinations, Appetizers, Sandwiches, Sides, Beverages, Classic Burgers, Desserts, Distinctive Dinners, Breakfast Favorites, Hot Off The Griddle, Senior Citizens' Breakfasts, Denny's Grand Slam Breakfasts, Three-Egg Omelettes, Breakfast Sides, and Beverages.

On the back panel of the menu are listed the Senior Citizens' Specials and Senior Citizens' Breakfast. The

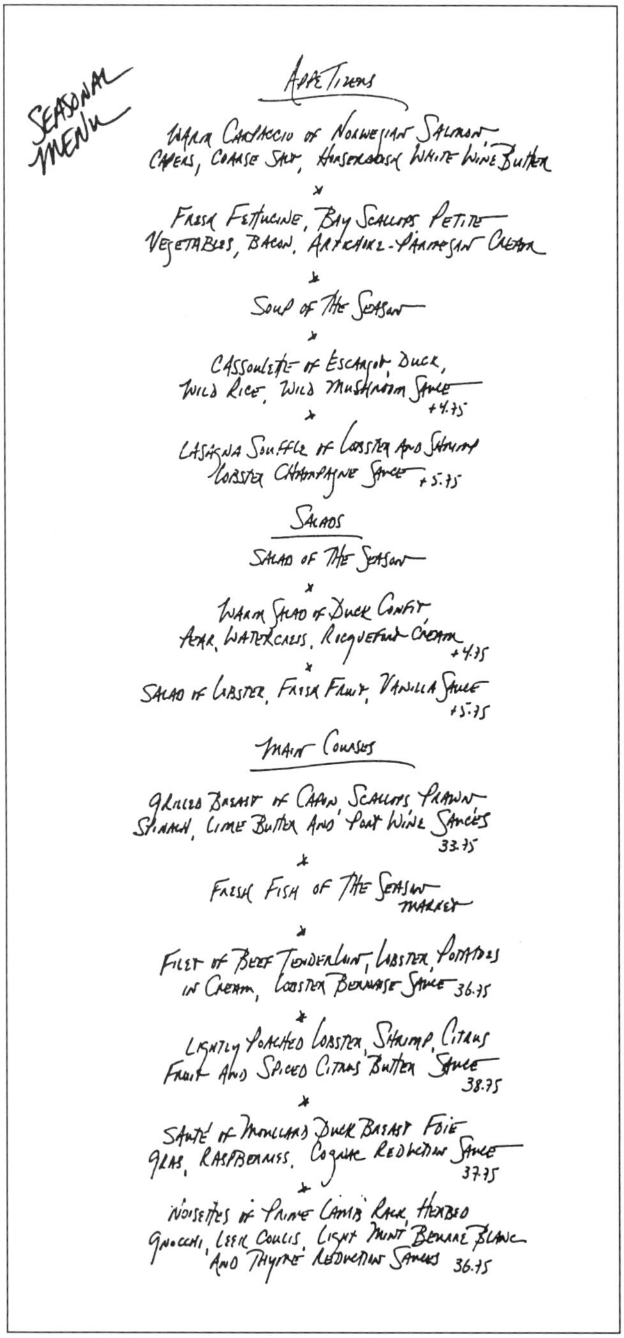
SEASONAL MENU
APPETIZERS
WARM CARPACCIO OF NORWEGIAN SALMON,
CAPERS, COARSE SALT, HORSERADISH WHITE WINE BUTTER
*
FRESH FETTUCINE, BAY SCALLOPS, PETITE
VEGETABLES, BACON, ARTICHOKE-PARMESAN CREAM
*
SOUP OF THE SEASON
*
CASSOULETTE OF ESCARGOT, DUCK,
WILD RICE, WILD MUSHROOM SAUCE
+4.75
*
LASAGNA SOUFFLE OF LOBSTER AND SHRIMP
LOBSTER CHAMPAGNE SAUCE +5.75
SALADS
SALAD OF THE SEASON
*
WARM SALAD OF DUCK CONFIT,
PEAR, WATERCRESS, ROQUEFORT CREAM
+4.75
*
SALAD OF LOBSTER, FRESH FRUIT, VANILLA SAUCE
+5.75
MAIN COURSES
GRILLED BREAST OF CAPON, SCALLOPS, PRAWN,
SPINACH, LIME BUTTER AND PORT WINE SAUCES
33.75
*
FRESH FISH OF THE SEASON
MARKET
*
FILET OF BEEF TENDERLOIN, LOBSTER, POTATOES
IN CREAM, LOBSTER BEARNAISE SAUCE 36.75
*
LIGHTLY POACHED LOBSTER, SHRIMP, CITRUS
FRUIT AND SPICED CITRUS BUTTER SAUCE
38.75
*
SAUTE OF MOULARD DUCK BREAST, FOIE
GRAS, RASPBERRIES, COGNAC REDUCTION SAUCE
37.75
*
NOISETTES OF PRIME LAMB RACK, HERBED
GNOCCHI, LEEK COULIS, LIGHT MINT BEURRE BLANC
AND THYME REDUCTION SAUCES 36.75

FIGURE 6.2 Seasonal menu at The Tall Grass. (Courtesy Tall Grass Restaurant. Reproduced by permission.)

menu therefore functions as a combination breakfast, lunch, and dinner menu for a group of restaurants open twenty-four hours a day, seven days a week.

Denny's is not afraid to use the word *new* on its menu, just to the left of several items on the menu. Under Appetizers, for example, *New* is listed beside Chicken Strips—a basket of breaded, deep-fried chicken strips, served with barbecue sauce.

Served under the heading of Distinctive Dinners are New York steak, steak and shrimp, halibut steak,

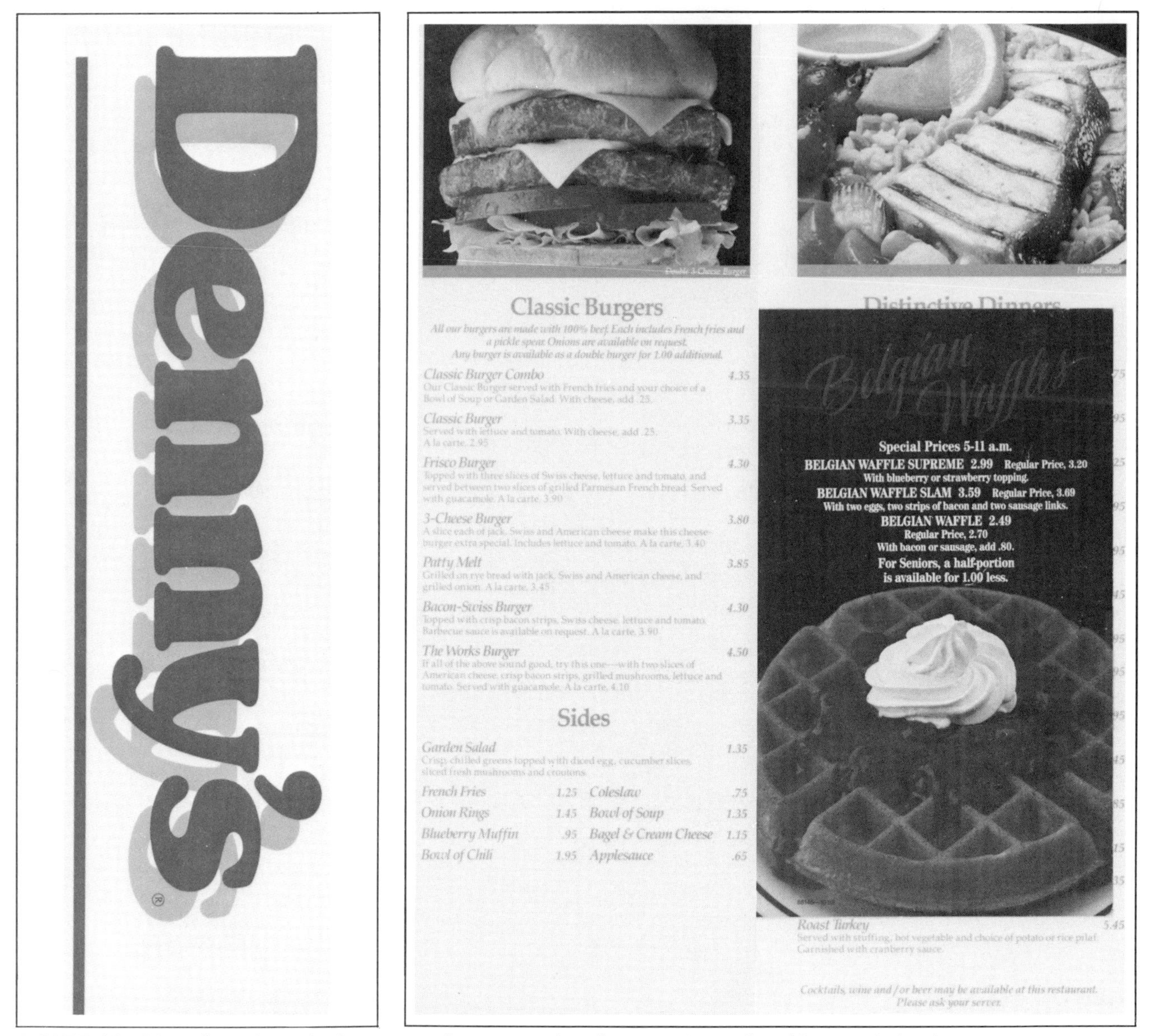

FIGURE 6.3 Menu from Denny's. So many outlets mean a lot of menus. (Reproduced by permission.)

grilled breast of chicken, sirloin tips and mushrooms, fried chicken, stir-fry chicken and vegetables, shrimp, fish-in-a-basket, pork chops, spaghetti, chicken fried steak, and roast turkey.

Another interesting and successful category on this menu is Denny's Grand Slam Breakfasts:

GRAND SLAM®

Two large pancakes, two eggs, two bacon strips, and two sausage links;

SOUTHERN SLAM

Two biscuit halves with sausage gravy, two eggs, two bacon strips, and two sausage links;

FRENCH SLAM

Two slices of french toast, two eggs, two bacon strips, and two sausage links.

Denny's Over-55 Menu

The age classification for senior citizens keeps falling: One can now join AARP (American Association of Retired Persons) at age fifty-five. Accordingly, Denny's has lowered the age limit for its senior citizen menu. For four years, the La Mirada, California–based chain offered twelve menu items at a discount to people over sixty-five. Then in 1986 the age limit was lowered to fifty-five. The idea was to attract customers and keep them as they grew older.

The promotion for younger seniors began in 1987 with a print-advertising campaign depicting people such as Frank Lloyd Wright, Grandma Moses, and Winston Churchill, who accomplished great things later in life. The objective was to convey the message that Denny's understood the life-style and needs of older people. The campaign also introduced the senior citizen menu, which has twenty-two breakfast, lunch, and dinner items that have smaller portions, lower prices, and lowered fat and sodium. Variations in the regular menu include smaller entrée salads and soup with half a sandwich.

The introduction to the Senior Citizens' Specials reads: "A selection of special entrées for persons 55 years and over. Each is served with your choice of a bowl of soup or tossed greens, and Italian-herb toast or dinner roll." The Senior Citizens' Specials entrées are halibut steak, grilled breast of chicken, sirloin tips and mushrooms, chicken-fried steak, pork chop, roast turkey and stuffing, fried chicken, grilled ham, and deep-fried cod. Daily specials are offered from 4 P.M. to 7 P.M..

The American Heart Association has approved seven items on this senior menu: entrée salads, halibut, roast beef dip, tip stuffer, roast beef dinner, grilled ham dinner, and pork chop dinner.

The price for entrées on the senior menu range from $2.99 to $4.99. There is no senior discount for the regular menu items, although Denny's occasionally hands out coupons at special events to encourage trial visits. It does not, however, offer coupons on a regular basis.

The introduction to the Senior Citizens' Breakfasts reads: "For persons 55 years and over. You may substitute Egg Beaters® (Fleischmann's cholesterol-free egg substitute) on any breakfast." The items included in the Senior Citizens' Breakfast are Senior Citizens' Omelette, Senior Starter, and Senior Grand Slam Breakfast™. This last breakfast contains one large pancake, one large egg, one bacon strip, and one sausage link.

THE CHILDREN'S MENU

According to the U.S. Bureau of the Census, in 1988 63,613,000 persons in the United States were between the ages of one and seventeen. In the year 2000 this number is estimated to reach 65,713,000, a large market whose size will evidently stay constant over the next decade. The U.S. Bureau of the Census also reported that in 1985 the under-twenty-five age group spent $17.62 per week on food away from home. This is less than what they will spend when they reach middle age, but it is still a considerable amount, and it does not take into account the eating-out money spent by their parents on their behalf.

Family restaurants usually pay some attention to children on their menu, usually a corner in which three or four items are offered in smaller portions at a lower price. The alternative is a separate children's menu that has some entertainment value, such as a game or a puzzle. Fast-food operators know that children look for more than food. *The Wall Street Journal* has noted that fast-food restaurants throw hundreds of millions of dollars into advertising their burgers, pizza, and fried chicken. The paper suggested that, "Instead, they might consider spending all that money on free toys for kids." The reason for this observation was a study by Wendy's International, Inc. that found that, in 83 percent of families, children play a major role in restaurant decisions. The study also found that, for half of the parents surveyed, toy promotions affect their fast-food choices.

McDonald's is the children's favorite fast-food restaurant, and it is the kids who are making McDonald's the number one chain. A recent survey by R. H. Bruskin Associates, a consumer research firm, showed that adults prefer other fast-food restaurants: Burger King leads at 28 percent, ahead of Wendy's at 25 percent and McDonald's at 21 percent.

With 1.7 million children under the age of six eating at the fast-food chains every day, this market segment is obviously worth pursuing. Wendy's is trying to increase its appeal by offering more and better-quality toys. In the past, chains offered toys that cost them about a dime apiece. After Wendy's began spending from $.50 to $.75 per toy, the sales of its Kids Meals, which include toys, rose by 50 percent over the previous year.

There is a battle in the fast-food business between the "kid image" and the "adult image," which is important not only to present but also to future sales. That is, if children become accustomed to eating at a certain restaurant, they will tend to eat there as adults.

The "get 'em young" slogan is also the marketing strategy of the beer industry. The hearts and thirsts of the young drinkers are worth fighting for, because once they pick their brands, they are difficult to change. What the beer industry calls "entry-level" drinkers seem to have an unquenchable thirst. According to Stroh's estimates, drinkers twenty-one to twenty-four years old drink an average of sixty-three gallons of beer annually, whereas those twenty-six to forty-four years old drink only about forty gallons of beer a year.

Likewise, the children's menu represents entry-level dining. The Stouffer Restaurant Company, with sixty-seven restaurants around the United States and growing, has an interesting series of children's menus (Figures 6.4). They measure 7 by 8 inches folded and open up to 7 by 16 inches. Three animals are featured on the covers, a panda, a hippo, and an elephant, and various games and puzzles are printed on the menus. The food and drink listing is as follows:

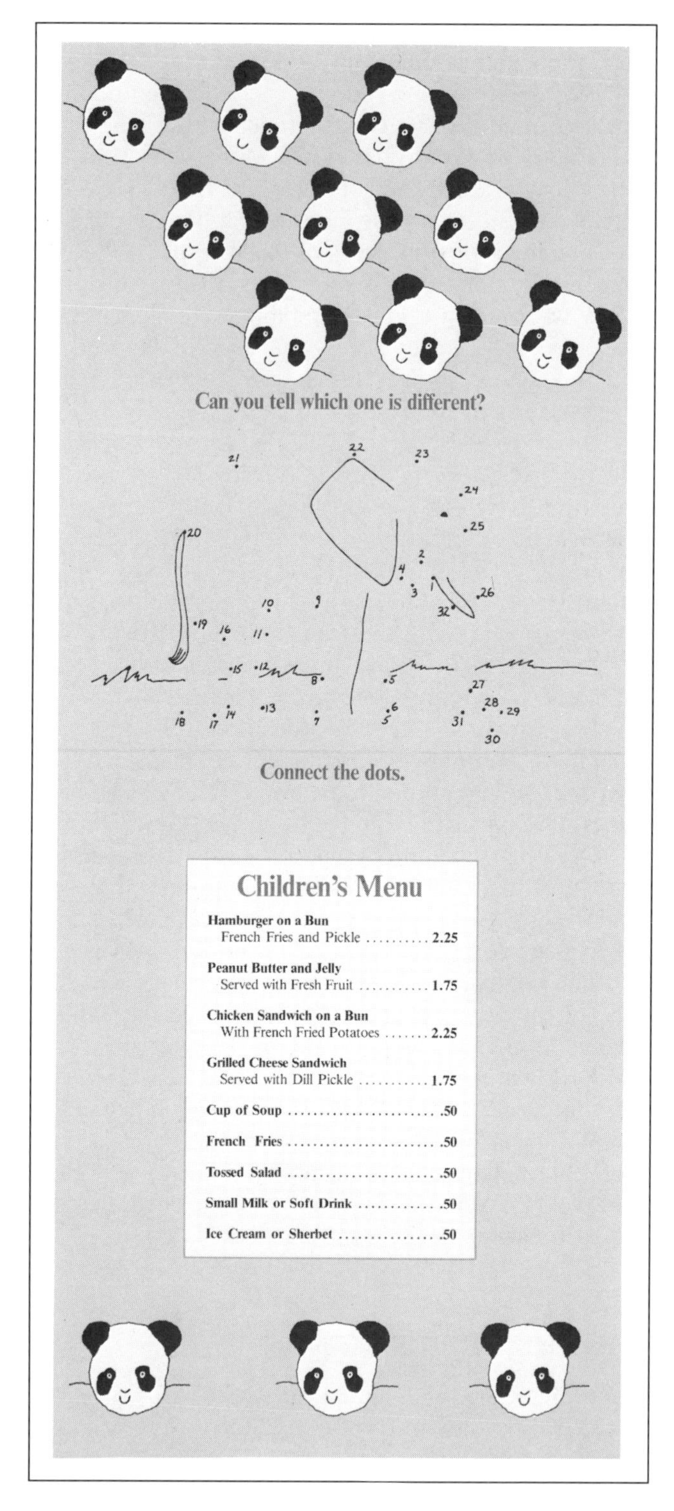

FIGURE 6.4a Three children's menus from Stouffer's. These menus provide fun and games as well as food. (Reproduced by permission.)

Hamburger on a Bun
French Fries and Pickle......2.25
Peanut Butter and Jelly
Served with Fresh Fruit......1.75
Chicken Sandwich on a Bun
with French Fried Potatoes......2.25
Grilled Cheese Sandwich
Served with Dill Pickle......1.75
Cup of Soup......50
French Fries......50
Tossed Salad......50
Small Milk or Soft Drink......50
Ice Cream or Sherbet......50

The Terrace Garden Inn has a children's menu called The Jolly Old Roger (Figure 6.5). It measures 7½ by 9 inches and is printed in green and orange on white stock. Parts of the menu are die-cut to come apart, and they then can be put together to form a cardboard ship. The menu features four items:

Roger's Toothful: Jello and whipped cream, ice cream, or sherbet, and milk or small Coke

Roger's Fin: Fresh fish fingers, tartar sauce with french fries, vegetables, dessert, and beverage

Roger's Bite: Small hamburger on roll, potato chips, peanut butter and jelly sandwich, and tuna salad on bun

Roger's Munch: Beef patty or sliced turkey with whipped potatoes, vegetables, dessert, and beverage.

Howard Johnson's Amuse-a-Menu is an eight-page menu measuring 7 by 11 inches (Figure 6.6), and printed in full color in comic book style. It contains a coupon to be filled out for those who want to join the HoJo Birthday Club, which promotes a birthday party at

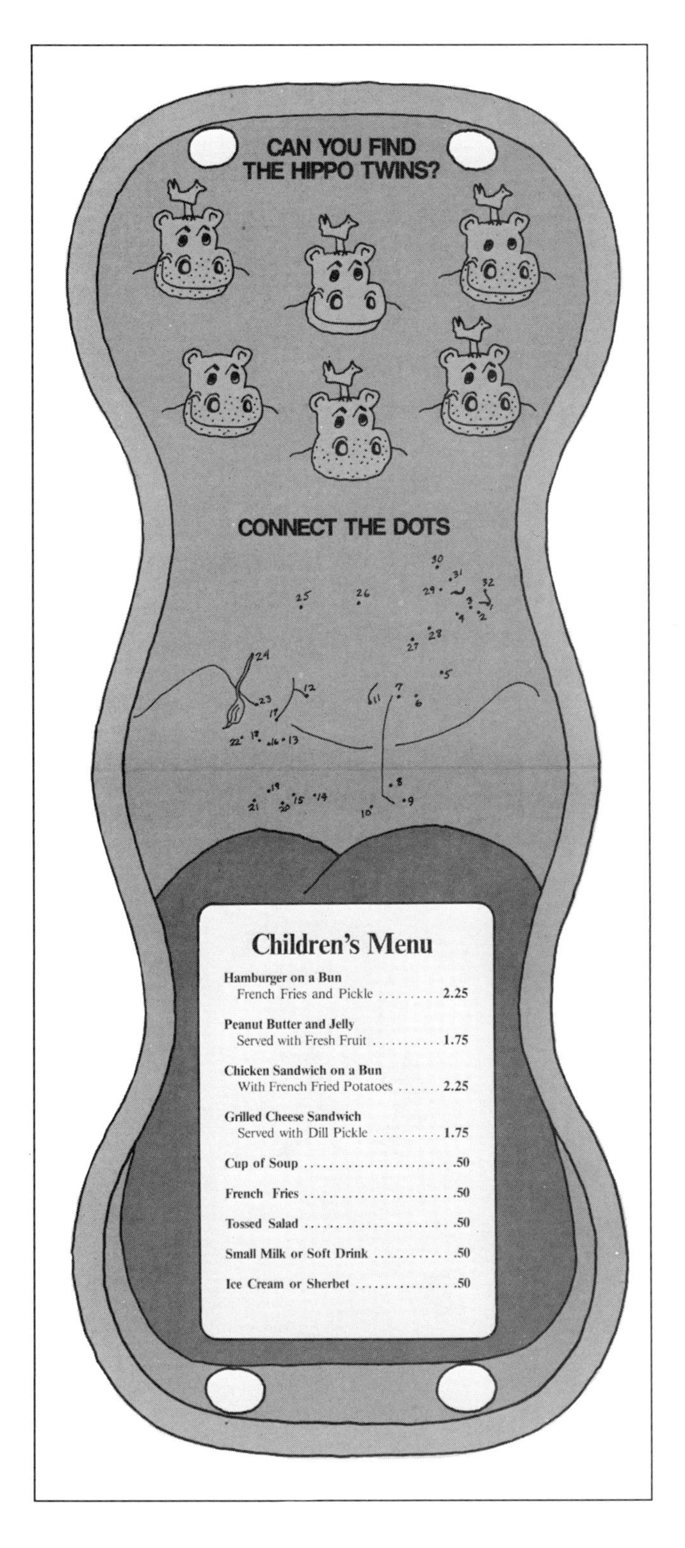

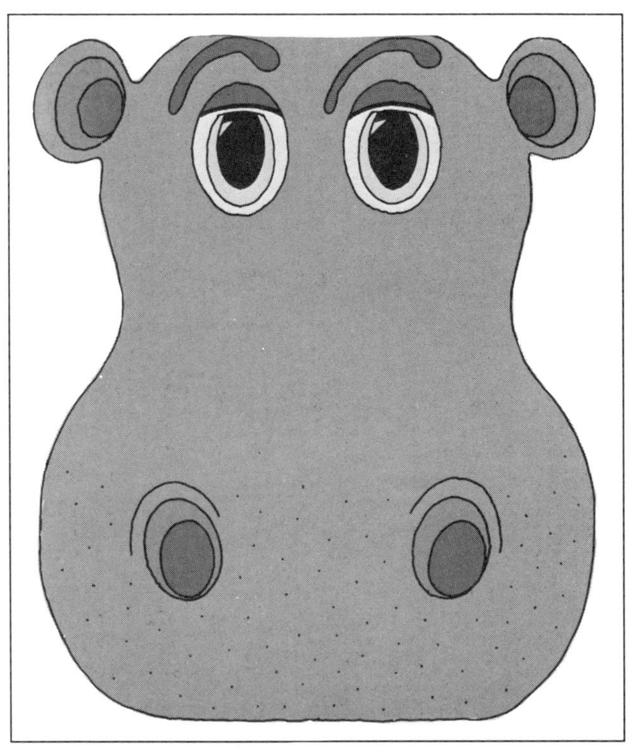

FIGURE 6.4b

the restaurant with a free birthday cake thrown in as an extra. Good promotion. Listed on the back of this menu are the entrées.

Junior Hamburger: on Toasted roll with French Fries

London Bridge: Grilled Frankfort in Toasted Roll with French Fries, Ice Cream, Sherbet, or Jello and Beverage

Tommy Tucker: Sliced Roast Turkey, Potato, Vegetable, Roll and Butter, Ice Cream, Sherbet, or Jello, and Beverage

Little Boy Blue: Grilled Hamburger Patty, Potato, Vegetable, Roll and Butter, Ice Cream, Sherbet, or Jello, and Beverage

Small Fry: Fried Clams with French Fries, Roll and Butter, Ice Cream, Sherbet, or Jello, and Beverage

Jack Horner: Peanut Butter and Jelly Sandwich, Ice Cream, Sherbet, or Jello, and Beverage

The Happy Clown: Spaghetti Italian Style, Tomato Sauce, Roll and Butter, Ice Cream, Sherbet, or Jello, and Beverage

One way to build family business is to let children eat free, for a promotion period, that is. The Acapulco and Los Arcos Mexican Restaurants helped reduce the cost of going back to school in September by inviting all children under twelve to dine free when accompanied by an adult, a way of encouraging children to take their parents out to lunch or dinner. The promotion helped build a customer base by emphasizing the Acapulco and Los Arcos restaurants' friendly family atmosphere and dining value. The menu lists thirty adult meals that cost less than $5. The "free kids" promotion lasted for three weeks, during which time the children's business doubled; it has stayed at this new level since. A children's coloring place-mat menu was also introduced with the promotion. One side had pictures for coloring, the other side, puzzles and games. The restaurant already had a family image, and the promotion reinforced it.

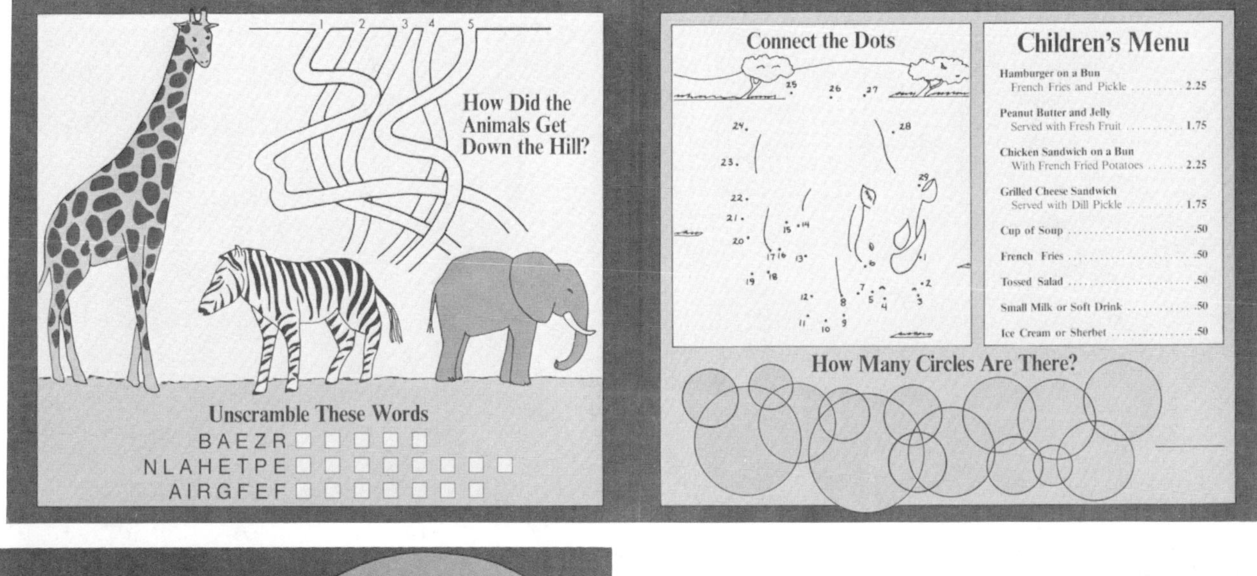

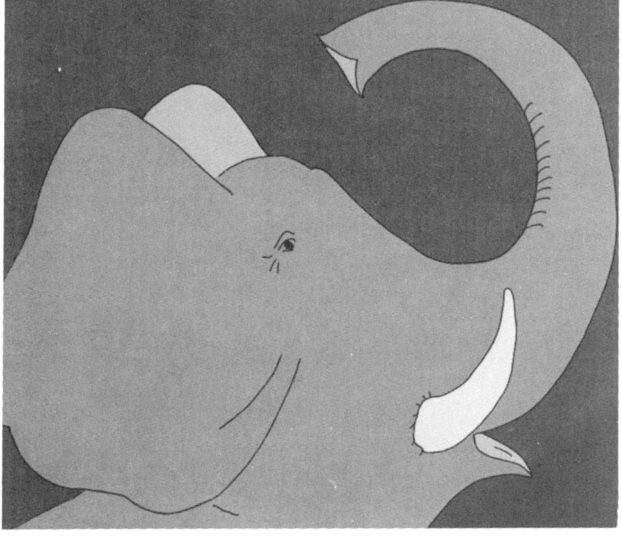

FIGURE 6.4c

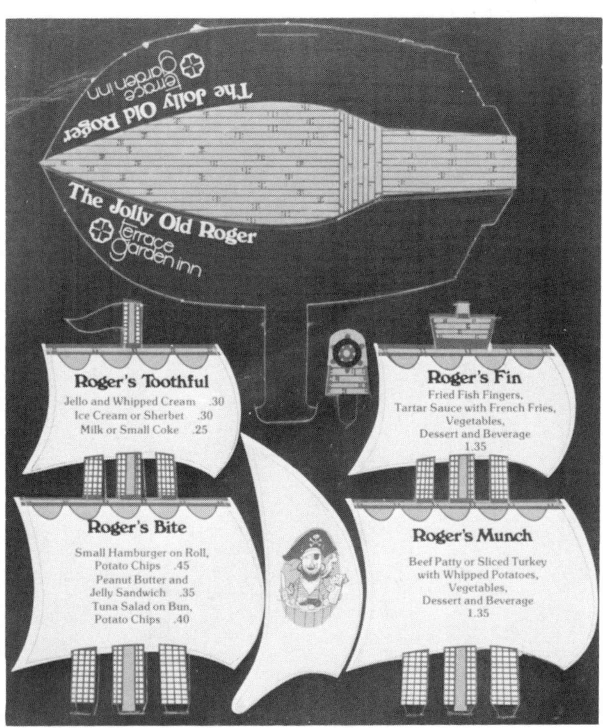

FIGURE 6.5 Children's menu from Terrace Garden Inn. The cut-out menu becomes a paper sailboat. (Reproduced by permission.)

Checkers Café welcomes children with special party plans and souvenir menus (Figure 6.7). At this restaurant, children's birthday parties take center stage, especially on Saturday and Sunday afternoons between noon and 6 P.M. The party ingredients that can be provided include clowns, jugglers, puppets, and a magician or two. Checkers' special party package includes a sketch of the birthday child or a photo of the party group and balloon bouquets. The party menu features a luncheon snack and a specialty dessert. But children are welcome at any time at this café where the emphasis is on family dining during the day and on rock and roll dancing and fun by night. In keeping with this welcoming approach to families and children, the restaurant has a special souvenir menu for youngsters to take home and play. It is a pint-sized, actual 33⅓ rpm record contained in an 8-by-8 inch folder menu.

The record contains five songs with safety messages that were specially recorded for Checkers Café by the "singing policeman," Carl Mittelhammer. Among his helpful advice are songs about looking both ways before crossing streets and not talking to strangers.

FIGURE 6.6 Children's menu from Howard Johnson's. It shows the restaurant recognizes the importance of the children's market. (Reproduced by permission.)

These educational songs were recorded by special arrangement with the National Child Safety Council.

The children's menu lists Starters—soup, fresh fruit cocktail, and kiddie chili; Between Breads—six sandwiches plus chips and a pickle spear; Junior Burgers and the Doggers; Kiddie Entrées—deep-fried shrimp, chopped sirloin steak, crisp chicken, and sliced roast turkey; and Tasty Treats—malts, ice cream, soda pop, sundaes, and milk and chocolate milk.

Brigham's

This Kid's Menu of Brigham's restaurant in Maine (Figure 6.8) is a clever board game as well as a listing of five children's entrées and a junior sundae. The opened menu measures 11 by 14 inches and is printed on heavy, white, coated stock in red and blue. Directions for the game appear at the top right-hand corner.

FIGURE 6.7 Souvenir children's menu from Checkers Café. The menu is printed on a record. (Courtesy Checkers Café, Treadway Inns Corporation. Menu Album Designed/Produced by Ron Carlucci Advertising, Inc. Reproduced by permission.)

You can play the game alone or with someone else at your table. Take a coin and place it on START. Answer a riddle correctly and move ahead the number of spaces written in red. If more than one person is playing, take turns answering the riddles. See how far you can get without being stumped. You can find the answers along the blue border.

The riddles are:

1. Using the letters C and Y can you spell a 5-letter word that's sweet to eat?
2. Which is better—and old one-hundred dollar bill or a new one?
3. What four-letter Midwest State is high in the middle and round on the ends?
4. Which is heavier—a pound of bricks or a pound of feathers?
5. What has eight wheels and carries only one passenger?
6. One word is mispelled in this box. Can you find this incorrect word?
7. What word is always pronounced wrong?
8. What stays hot even in the refrigerator?

The five Kid's Meals offered at $2.39 each are macaroni and cheese, hamburger and french fries, grilled cheese and french fries, frankfurter and french fries, and chicken fingers and french fries. Children's-size milk and Coca Cola are offered at $.35, and a junior sundae is also listed for $.95.

Besides the game described above, the back cover of this menu offers Tongue Twisters, Illusion Tricks, and How Long Is It? This last game asks the junior diner to estimate the length of things on the table—fork, spoon, napkin, plate—in both inches and centimeters. An inch and centimeter ruler is printed on the bottom of the menu.

FIGURE 6.8 Game menu from Brigham's. Games help entertain the young customer. (Reproduced by permission.)

7
Menu Economics

Economics is the study of the production, distribution, and consumption of wealth. For the restaurateur, there are macroeconomics, microeconomics, and menu economics. Macroeconomics refers to the world economy. According to a Kraft Foods study, $.41 of every U.S. food dollar is spent on eating out. The study also predicted that the amount of the food dollar spent eating away from home will reach $.60 by the end of the century. If that is true, the outlook for the foodservice business is good.

But except for restaurant chains, all foodservice business is local, or microeconomics. In the United States as a whole, the South Atlantic states generate more foodservice sales than does any other region, nearly one-fifth of the total. The top-grossing states, however, are spread across the country. California, Texas, and New York together account for nearly 25 percent of all sales. And in each town or city, the percentage of restaurant sales varies from restaurant to restaurant.

EFFECT OF ECONOMIC CHANGE

The increase in food prices (in 1987, fruits and vegetables rose by 7 percent) has had a major impact on menus. The decline or leveling off of alcoholic beverage sales has also affected restaurant profits. Even so, gross restaurant sales rose from $170.9 billion in 1985 to $206.8 billion in 1988. Even alcoholic beverage sales increased from $21.5 billion in 1985 to $25.7 billion in 1988, although part of this increase is due to population growth.

If food prices increase and alcoholic beverage sales continue to decline or not grow, the menu should probably be changed more often. This refers not just to price changes but also to item changes and different item emphases. One method used by many successful restaurants is to devise seasonal menus, or four different menus a year, reflecting different seasonal foods and different customer tastes.

During the 1980s, unemployment was low—around 6 percent, the lowest since 1974. Real wages, however, slipped after 1980 and are now about 10 percent below their peak in 1972. Thus, although average family incomes are higher, it is only because most families have a second wage earner in the work force. The prospect for an end to this wage stagnation is not bright because productivity gains, which largely determine wage increases, slowed to a crawl in the last two decades. Moreover, America's rapidly accumulating debt is sure to become a drag on domestic purchasing power.

Family incomes fared fairly well into the 1980s. According to the U.S. Census Bureau, average household income before taxes in 1986 was $30,759, about 10 percent more in real terms than in 1980. Households did well in after-tax terms, too. Increases in state income taxes and social security payroll taxes were principally offset by the reduction in federal income taxes. Most families, however, were forced to work harder to realize and enjoy the gain. Between 1980 and 1987, average real wages fell by 2 percent.

The tough question for the future is why anticipated gains in productivity have not materialized. Output per hour worked in private business grew by 1.4 percent annually between 1979 and 1986, which was better than the record from peak to peak in the previous business cycle but less than between 1948 and 1965. Unless things get better, there will be little in the way of productivity dividends to finance higher living standards. But even if the economy does manage to return to the healthy productivity-growth rate of the postwar years, the burden of current and past borrowing from foreign countries to finance the trade and federal deficits is bound to weigh heavily on future incomes. By the end of 1988, the external debt exceeded $500 billion. Eliminating the current $150 billion annual trade deficit and paying off the accumulated debt could cost a full percentage point of annual productivity improvements over a decade.

For the restaurant operator, location is all-important, as it determines the kind of restaurant and the prices on

TABLE 7.1 Top Ten States in Economic Output

State	1986 Gross State Product ($ billions)	% of 1986 U.S. Gross National Product
California	533.8	12.59
New York	362.7	8.55
Texas	303.5	7.16
Illinois	209.7	4.95
Pennsylvania	183.6	4.33
Florida	177.7	4.19
Ohio	176.1	4.15
New Jersey	154.8	3.65
Michigan	153.2	3.61
Massachusetts	115.5	2.72

the menu. Food and other costs can easily be determined. The amount of markup—what the market will bear, or pay—is harder to determine. First, the state in which the restaurant is located makes a difference. According to the Commerce Department's Bureau of Economic Analysis, some states are both bigger and wealthier than others. Vermont's 1986 output, for example, was less than 2 percent of California's gross state product (see Table 7.1).

Only 6.2 percent of all U.S. households have annual incomes of $75,000 or more, according to U.S. Census Bureau survey data. That comes to 5.7 million households. And where are most of these households located? Mainly (two-thirds) in the suburbs of large cities. A restaurant located in one of these areas or within an hour's drive can therefore consider this a prime market area.

The income of the average person living in the area, or passing by, determines what a restaurant can charge. A fast-food operation generally aims at the lower-income market, whereas the upscale restaurants aim at the lower-middle, middle, and upper-middle income markets. Most restaurant operators have learned what their market population is willing to pay.

A way of looking at your menu prices to see whether your customers are buying at the low, high, or middle end of the price spread is to construct a menu price profile. The Carlton restaurant in Pittsburgh, for example, has five listings (Figure 7.1): Soups & Appetizers, Salads, Luncheon Specialties, Traditional Favorites, and Signature Pastas. The menu price profile plus the average price for each of these listing sections is as follows:

Soups & Appetizers			
2.25	2.95		6.95
2.25	2.95	4.95	6.95
Average Price $4.18			

Salads		
	7.95	
	7.95	11.95
6.95	7.95	11.95
Average Price $9.11		

Luncheon Specialties				
6.95	7.95			
6.95	7.95	8.95	9.95	10.95
Average Price $8.52				

Traditional Favorites				
			14.95	
		12.95	14.95	
	11.95	12.95	14.95	
10.95	11.95	12.95	14.95	15.95
Average Price $13.59				

Signature Pastas		
8.95		
8.95	9.95	11.95
Average Price $9.45		

Listing the prices in this way makes it easier to get an overall picture of the menu's price structure. Using this base and the record of sales from the cash register or computer, you also can calculate the popularity of the items. If the top-priced items move too slowly compared with the medium-priced items, they may be priced too high. And if the low-priced items are very popular, their prices probably can be raised.

Notice that on this menu the highest-priced items—Traditional Favorites—have the best and dominant position; there also are more of them, and they probably are the most profitable items on this menu.

The Carlton has a separate dessert menu (Figure 7.2), whose menu price profile is as follows:

Desserts			
	2.95		
	2.95		
	2.95		
2.75	2.95	3.25	3.95
Average Price $3.11			

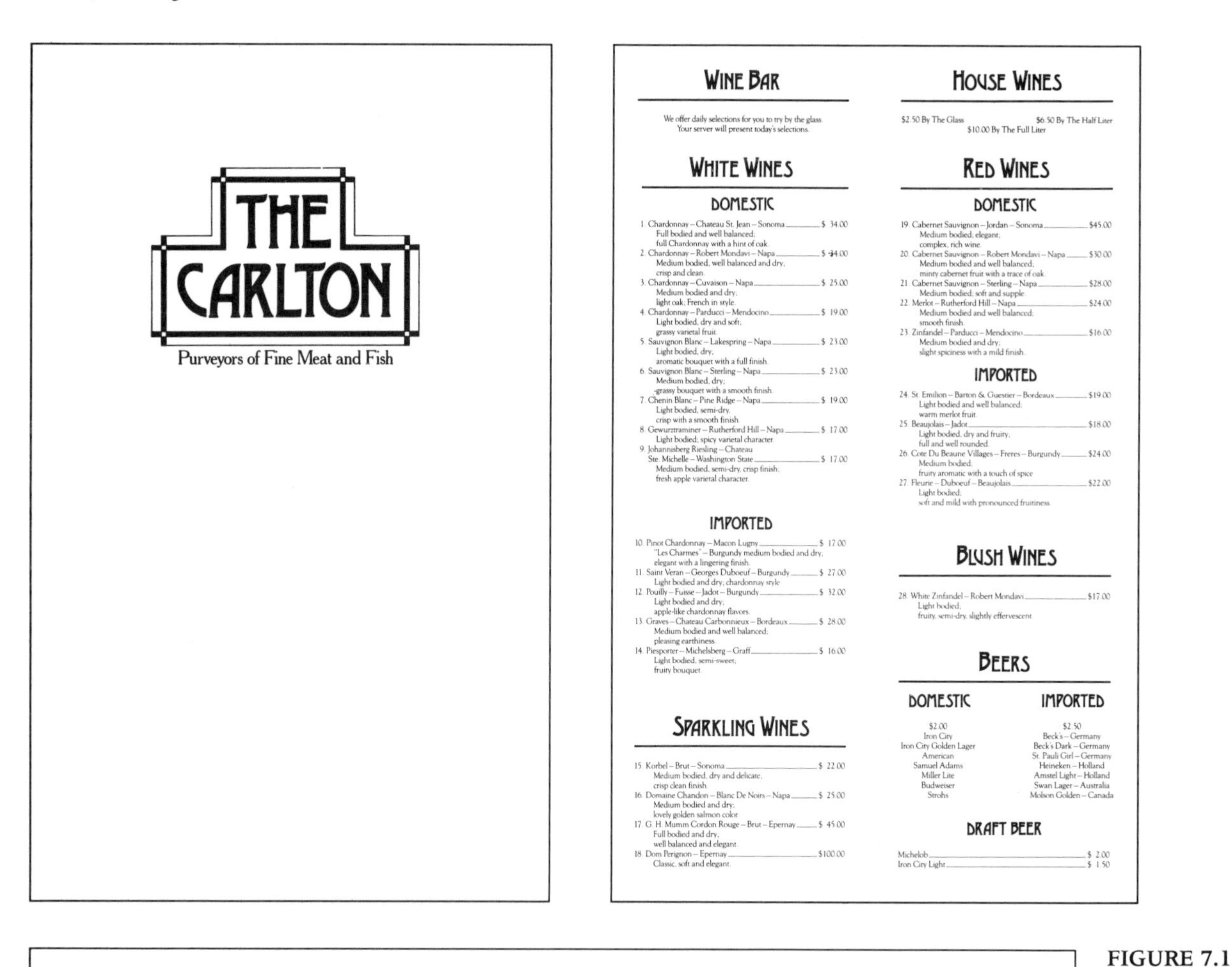

THE CARLTON

Purveyors of Fine Meat and Fish

WINE BAR

We offer daily selections for you to try by the glass.
Your server will present today's selections.

WHITE WINES

DOMESTIC

1. Chardonnay – Chateau St. Jean – Sonoma .... $ 34.00
   Full bodied and well balanced;
   full Chardonnay with a hint of oak.
2. Chardonnay – Robert Mondavi – Napa .... $ 34.00
   Medium bodied, well balanced and dry;
   crisp and clean.
3. Chardonnay – Cuvaison – Napa .... $ 25.00
   Medium bodied and dry;
   light oak; French in style.
4. Chardonnay – Parducci – Mendocino .... $ 19.00
   Light bodied, dry and soft;
   grassy varietal fruit.
5. Sauvignon Blanc – Lakespring – Napa .... $ 23.00
   Light bodied, dry;
   aromatic bouquet with a full finish.
6. Sauvignon Blanc – Sterling – Napa .... $ 23.00
   Medium bodied, dry;
   grassy bouquet with a smooth finish.
7. Chenin Blanc – Pine Ridge – Napa .... $ 19.00
   Light bodied, semi-dry,
   crisp with a smooth finish.
8. Gewurztraminer – Rutherford Hill – Napa .... $ 17.00
   Light bodied; spicy varietal character.
9. Johannisberg Riesling – Chateau Ste. Michelle – Washington State .... $ 17.00
   Medium bodied, semi-dry, crisp finish;
   fresh apple varietal character.

IMPORTED

10. Pinot Chardonnay – Macon Lugny .... $ 17.00
    "Les Charmes" – Burgundy medium bodied and dry;
    elegant with a lingering finish.
11. Saint Veran – Georges Duboeuf – Burgundy .... $ 27.00
    Light bodied and dry; chardonnay style
12. Pouilly – Fuisse – Jadot – Burgundy .... $ 32.00
    Light bodied and dry;
    apple-like chardonnay flavors.
13. Graves – Chateau Carbonnieux – Bordeaux .... $ 28.00
    Medium bodied and well balanced;
    pleasing earthiness.
14. Piesporter – Michelsberg – Graff .... $ 16.00
    Light bodied, semi-sweet;
    fruity bouquet.

SPARKLING WINES

15. Korbel – Brut – Sonoma .... $ 22.00
    Medium bodied, dry and delicate,
    crisp clean finish.
16. Domaine Chandon – Blanc De Noirs – Napa .... $ 25.00
    Medium bodied and dry;
    lovely golden salmon color.
17. G. H. Mumm Cordon Rouge – Brut – Epernay .... $ 45.00
    Full bodied and dry,
    well balanced and elegant.
18. Dom Perignon – Epernay $100.00
    Classic, soft and elegant.

HOUSE WINES

$2.50 By The Glass $6.50 By The Half Liter
$10.00 By The Full Liter

RED WINES

DOMESTIC

19. Cabernet Sauvignon – Jordan – Sonoma $45.00
    Medium bodied; elegant;
    complex, rich wine.
20. Cabernet Sauvignon – Robert Mondavi – Napa $30.00
    Medium bodied and well balanced;
    minty cabernet fruit with a trace of oak.
21. Cabernet Sauvignon – Sterling – Napa $28.00
    Medium bodied; soft and supple.
22. Merlot – Rutherford Hill – Napa $24.00
    Medium bodied and well balanced;
    smooth finish.
23. Zinfandel – Parducci – Mendocino $16.00
    Medium bodied and dry;
    slight spiciness with a mild finish.

IMPORTED

24. St. Emilion – Barton & Guestier – Bordeaux $19.00
    Light bodied and well balanced;
    warm merlot fruit.
25. Beaujolais – Jadot $18.00
    Light bodied, dry and fruity;
    full and well rounded.
26. Cote Du Beaune Villages – Freres – Burgundy $24.00
    Medium bodied,
    fruity aromatic with a touch of spice
27. Fleurie – Duboeuf – Beaujolais $22.00
    Light bodied;
    soft and mild with pronounced fruitiness.

BLUSH WINES

28. White Zinfandel – Robert Mondavi $17.00
    Light bodied;
    fruity, semi-dry, slightly effervescent.

BEERS

DOMESTIC	IMPORTED
$2.00	$2.50
Iron City	Beck's – Germany
Iron City Golden Lager	Beck's Dark – Germany
American	St. Pauli Girl – Germany
Samuel Adams	Heineken – Holland
Miller Lite	Amstel Light – Holland
Budweiser	Swan Lager – Australia
Strohs	Molson Golden – Canada

DRAFT BEER

Michelob .... $ 2.00
Iron City Light .... $ 1.50

·Soups & Appetizers·

NEW ENGLAND SEAFOOD CHOWDER Bowl $2.95 Cup $2.25
SOUP OF THE DAY Bowl $2.95 Cup $2.25

FRIED CALAMARI $4.95
SHRIMP COCKTAIL $6.95
COMBINATION APPETIZER
Fried Calamari, Stuffed Mushrooms and a Chesapeake Bay Crab Cake. $6.95

·Salads·

SEAFOOD COBB SALAD
Freshly chopped vegetables, crabmeat, baby shrimp and cheddar cheese.
Choice of dressing. $11.95

ROASTED CHICKEN SALAD
Boneless breast of chicken, roasted and served on a bed of radicchio, bibb and romaine lettuce with onions and bean sprouts. Served with a soy vinaigrette dressing. $11.95

CARLTON WALDORF SALAD
Grilled chicken, apples, oranges, chopped walnuts and celery tossed in classic waldorf dressing and served on bibb lettuce. $7.95

SPINACH SALAD
Hickory smoked bacon, water chestnuts, bean sprouts, red onions and fresh spinach tossed in our raspberry vinaigrette. $6.95

COBB SALAD
Freshly chopped vegetables, smoked breast of turkey, bacon, chicken and cheddar cheese.
Choice of dressing. $7.95

SHRIMP AND BAY SCALLOP SALAD
Sliced tomatoes, red onion, vinaigrette dressing and crumbled blue cheese. $7.95

·Luncheon Specialties·

PRIME RIB SANDWICH AU JUS
A tender cut of roasted prime rib served open faced on San Francisco sourdough bread with whipped cream horseradish sauce. $10.95

PESTO STEAK SANDWICH
6 oz. New York strip steak, broiled with fresh pesto, served open faced on San Francisco sourdough bread with tomatoes and watercress. $9.95

DEEP DISH QUICHE
Cheddar and Swiss cheese with scallops, baby shrimp and asparagus in a flaky deep-dish pie crust. $7.95

CRABMEAT BENEDICT
Poached eggs and crabmeat served on an English muffin with hollandaise sauce. $7.95

CLUBHOUSE CHOPPED STEAK
Half pound of freshly ground sirloin, charcoal grilled to order with a mild burgundy-mushroom wine sauce. $6.95

SMOKED TURKEY CLUB SANDWICH
Triple decker sandwich of smoked breast of turkey, hickory smoked bacon, lettuce and tomato, on thick sliced whole wheat toast. $6.95

SMOKED TURKEY DEVONSHIRE
Smoked breast of turkey, hickory smoked bacon and tomato slices served open faced on toasted wheat with sharp cheddar cheese sauce. $7.95

THE CARLTON PRIME RIB HASH
A traditional dish of prime rib, potatoes, onions and gravy, topped with a poached egg and shredded cheddar cheese. $8.95

Above served with shoestring potatoes.

·Traditional Favorites·

HERBED CHICKEN
Boneless breast of chicken marinated in seasoned herbs, lemon and white wine, charcoal grilled. $11.95

CHESAPEAKE BAY CRAB CAKES
Two traditional crab cakes with red chili pepper mayonnaise. $11.95

SAUTEED LEMON SOLE
Fresh filets of sole sauteed in a sweet lemon caper sauce. $14.95

CENTER CUT SWORDFISH STEAK
Charcoal grilled and served with a beurre blanc sauce. $15.95

CHICKEN SALTIMBOCCA
Prosciutto ham, asiago cheese and fresh sage, rolled in a boneless chicken breast. Served in a white wine sauce. $12.95

FILET MIGNON (8 oz.)
Aged tenderloin, served with shallot butter. $14.95

BROOK TROUT
Fresh Idaho brook trout, charcoal grilled over hardwood coals. $10.95

BEEF TENDERLOIN ZINFANDEL
Medallions of tenderloin, grilled medium-rare, served with a mushroom and zinfandel wine sauce. $12.95

VEAL PICCATA
Medallions of provimi veal sauteed with lemon, butter and capers. $14.95

GRILLED LAMB STEAK (8 oz.)
Marinated center cut leg of lamb steak served on a bed of onions with mint sauce. $12.95

CAJUN BARBECUED SHRIMP
Prepared New Orleans style, with a spicy paprika and pepper butter sauce. $14.95

The above entrées are served with The Carlton Salad (romaine lettuce, tomato, bacon, egg and mushrooms, tossed in our house dressing) plus your choice of twice-baked potato, seasoned rice pilaf or shoestring potatoes.

·Signature Pastas·

LOBSTER RAVIOLI
Semolina pasta filled with lobster and ricotta cheese served in a lobster cream sauce. $11.95

ANGEL HAIR PASTA WITH SCALLOPS
Scallops and fresh tomato basil sauce served over angel hair pasta. $9.95

FETTUCCINE CARBONARA
Fettuccine with prosciutto ham, bacon, fresh basil, spinach and chives tossed in a cream sauce with asiago cheese. $8.95

FETTUCCINE CARLTON
Fettuccine with shrimp and julienne vegetables in an Alfredo sauce, topped with freshly grated parmesan cheese. $8.95

Above served with The Carlton Salad (romaine lettuce, tomato, bacon, egg and mushrooms, tossed in our house dressing).

DAILY SPECIALS
Your server will present today's selections

FIGURE 7.1 Menu for The Carlton. The prices on this menu reflect good menu strategy; they are placed so they do not stand out by themselves. The customer reads the descriptions first and then the price. (Reproduced by permission of The Carlton. A Signature of The Levy Restaurants.)

This separate dessert menu not only gives the server a chance to sell the desserts, it also prevents the "adding machine" customer from referring the dessert prices to the prices on the "big" menu. The customer's decision to order a dessert is thus based more on appetite and desire than on cost.

Notice also that this menu lists the prices in the same typeface right after the last word in the description. Many menus list the prices to the right of the item name, in boldface type:

Herbed Chicken **$11.95**
Crab Cakes **$11.95**
Sautéed Lemon Sole........... **$14.95**
Filet Mignon **$14.95**

This method draws attention to the price, and the customer's eye tends to go up and down the row of prices. This in turn encourages the tendency to order by price without even reading the description. The next method is much better:

VEAL PICCATA

Medallions of provimi veal sautéed with lemon, butter, and capers. $14.95

THE CARLTON

· DESSERTS ·

TOLLHOUSE COOKIE SUNDAE
Two scoops of French vanilla ice cream atop a tollhouse cookie, covered with hot fudge sauce. $3.95

CHEESECAKE
Smooth, creamy cheesecake in a graham cracker crust. $2.95

PRALINE ICE CREAM
Rich French vanilla ice cream laced with crunchy glazed pecans. $2.95

CREME BRULÉE
Custard baked and topped with a brown sugar glaze. $2.75

WHISKEY BREAD PUDDING
Raisin bread pudding served with warm whiskey sauce. $2.95

CAPPUCCINO ICE CREAM
A rich blend of chocolate and coffee ice cream with bits of toffee. $3.25

PECAN PIE
Rich buttery pecan filling in a flaky pie crust. $2.95

FRESH BAKED PASTRIES
Choose from our pastry tray which offers a variety of homemade pastries, baked daily on premise by our own pastry chef. Market Price

FIGURE 7.2 Dessert menu for The Carlton. A separate dessert menu is always good merchandising. (Reproduced by permission of The Carlton. A Signature of The Levy Restaurants.)

Located in downtown Pittsburgh, The Carlton has downtown businesspeople and shoppers for its market base. A restaurant with a different market base is Carlos', a "three star" French restaurant located in Highland Park, Illinois, about 30 miles north of the Chicago Loop and sandwiched between two affluent North Shore suburbs. (See Figure 7.3.) Carlos' is an expensive place to dine; yet its tables are full every night. Its menu price profile follows.

Appetizers—Hot and Cold			
7.50			
7.50	8.00	10.00	16.00
Average Price $10.00			

Soups and Salads		
4.75	5.00	5.75
Average Price $5.17		

CARLOS' RESTAURANT

Carlos and Deborah Nieto, Hosts
Roland Liccioni, Chef de Cuisine

Hot Appetizers

Ravioles de pigeon à l'ail 7.50
Raviolis of squab with garlic sauce

Brioche d'escargots au roquefort et ciboulette 7.50
Snails in brioche with roquefort sauce and chives

Feuilletté surprise 8.00
Chef's selection in puff pastry shell

Cold Appetizers

Salade tiède de foie gras aux champignons 16.00
Fresh duck liver with warm mushroom salad

Assiette de saumon fumé et caviar 10.00
Fresh smoked salmon with caviar

Potages

Soupe a l'oignon 4.75
Onion soup

Soupe de homard 5.75
Lobster soup

Salades

Salade Maison .... *with entree*
House salad

Salade gourmande au roquefort et pignons 5.00
Special salad garnished with roquefort and pinenuts

Sorbet 3.00

Entrées

Caneton grillé a l'Armagnac 19.50
Duckling with Armagnac sauce

Petits tournedos en rosace 20.00
Sliced filet of beef with 3 mustard sauce

Médaillons de veau au romarin 20.00
Veal medallions with rosemary sauce

Whitefish grillé aux légumes du marché 19.00
Grilled Whitefish lightly seasoned with fresh vegetables

Saumon sauté marinière 19.50
Sauteed salmon with aromatic herbs

Ris de veau sautés meunière 20.00
Sweetbreads sauteed

Homard à la nage .... *Market Price*
Succulent lobster with sauce a la nage

Patisseries du jour .... Desserts on Cart

Coffee, tea, decaffeinated coffee 2.25
Espresso 2.25
Cappuccino 2.75
Water served on request

We respectfully request at least one entree per guest.

Because cigar and pipe smoke may interfere with the comfort of others, we respectfully request your cooperation.

Artwork is courtesy of the Merrill Chase Galleries

429 Temple Avenue, Highland Park, Illinois 60035
(312) 432-0770

FIGURE 7.3 Menu from Carlos' French restaurant. With everything listed à la carte and coffee costing $2.25, the check quickly adds up. (Reproduced by permission.)

Entrées		
		20.00
	19.50	20.00
19.00	19.50	20.00
Average Price $19.66		

A cup of coffee at this restaurant costs $2.25, or $2.75 for cappuccino.

The Country Inn restaurant in Addison, Illinois, another suburb of Chicago, serves a different customer base (Figure 7.4). Under the heading Soups, Stews, and Starters are both appetizers and items that can serve as entrées. The entrées are headed Country Skillet Dinners (four items) and Country Inn à la Carte (four items).Two of these, Steak of the Day and Lobster Scampi, have no prices. The menu price profile is as follows:

Soups, Stews, and Starters				
2.25				
2.25	4.75	5.00	5.25	5.95
Average Price $4.24				

Entrées				
		6.50		
5.50	6.25	6.50	9.00	10.95
Average Price $7.45				

Desserts	
2.00	2.25
2.00	2.25
Average Price $2.12	

The price of a cup of coffee at this restaurant is $.85.

One source of menu pricing is the menu price surveys made by *Restaurants & Institutions* magazine (see Table 7.2).

These surveys are valuable to restaurant operators because they indicate trends and establish a standard of comparison. But because foodservice business is local, menu prices must fit the local market. In addition, average prices do not indicate highs and lows.

Another source of nationwide economic data is the *Monthly Labor Review*, published by the U.S. Department

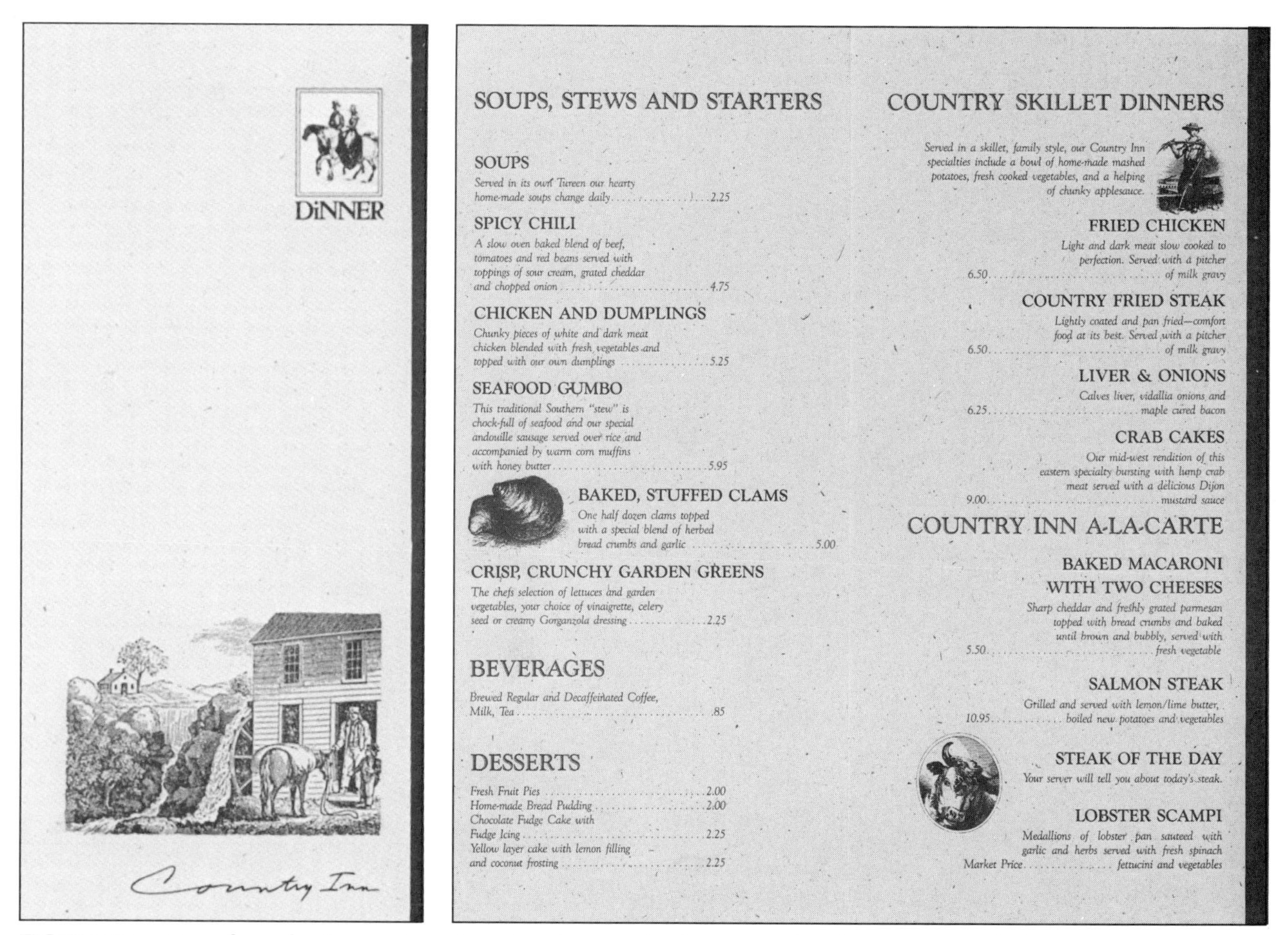

FIGURE 7.4 Menu from the Country Inn. Complete dinners plus à la carte give the customer a choice. (Reproduced by permission of Country Inn at Oak Meadow.)

TABLE 7.2 Menu Price Survey of Beverages

Item	Full Service	Fast Food	Hotel/motel	Northeast	South	North Central	West
Beverages							
Coffee	$ .66	$ .53	$ .73	$ .63	$ .70	$ .61	$ .64
Iced tea	.70	.61	.73	.72	.69	.68	.68
Soft drinks	.77	.64	.90	.82	.75	.76	.76
Beer	1.71	1.18	1.75	1.46	1.63	1.70	1.70
Wine (glass)	1.75	1.33	2.68	3.34	1.78	2.15	1.68

Source: *Restaurants & Institutions*, May 1987.

of Labor. In the Current Labor Statistics section, data on the following categories are reported each month:

- Comparison
- Labor force
- Labor compensation
- Price
- Productivity
- International comparisons
- Injury and illness

The price data show changes in food costs and food prices both at home and away.

Other price information and trends relevant to restaurant operators are published by trade groups such as the National Restaurant Association and state and regional restaurant associations. General economic information is published daily in *The Wall Street Journal* and the business sections of local newspapers. Weekly and monthly publications such as *Business Week*, *Forbes*, and *Fortune* give more detailed economic news.

CREDIT CARDS

According to *The Wall Street Journal* (1988), "The retailers' predicament illustrates the extent to which they have become hostages of the credit card industry." One restaurant owner commented, "I'm paying for allowing my customer to use the card."

The major credit card companies tend to raise their fees to restaurants. Some restaurants may consequently refuse to honor the card, but most will either absorb the higher fees or pass them on to the customer. The problem is that credit cards are the basis of business today. Because fees are rising, some large retailers are pushing their own credit cards, but this is not practical for a small restaurant, and the major credit cards are too popular to ignore.

The problem is that credit cards have become a habit of American consumers. Credit card companies are taking advantage of the cards' greater popularity. The card companies like American Express and Sears, with its Discover card, are financial giants, and both Visa and Mastercard are controlled by a handful of big banks that issue millions of cards. Recent fee increases are just another move by the credit card companies to protect a very profitable business. Rises may reflect higher costs, but retailers have noted that when these costs fell, the banks kept the savings for themselves.

Credit card fees are established through a multistep process. To illustrate, this is what happens to a $100 Visa or Mastercard transaction: Under the current fee structure, a processing bank buys the credit card slip from a restaurant for $97.80, collecting a 2.2 percent fee. Then the bank, acting through the Visa or Mastercard clearing association, sells, for about $98.60, the slip to the bank that issued the credit card. The remaining $1.40 discount in the $100 face amount is called the *interchange fee*, which is what the processing bank passes along to the issuing bank. When the processing banks pass the increase along to restaurants and other businesses, the average so-called merchant discount is expected to jump from 2.2 percent to about 2.56 percent. That will raise the total amount of fees charged on a $100 purchase by $.36, to $2.56. This increase means that the consumer will probably pay higher prices.

The major credit cards besides Visa and Mastercard are American Express and the Sears Discover card, plus the new Optima card issued by American Express. A restaurant should indicate whether it honors credit cards by posting decals on the door and the same information on the menu, clearly and boldly. Likewise, if the restaurant does not honor credit cards, it should say so on the menu. The customer should not be surprised by the server's saying, "Sorry, we do not accept credit cards."

Surveys have shown that retailers (including restaurants) lose sales if they fail to display signs showing that they accept certain cards. These studies also show that many consumers are embarrassed to ask whether they can use their card to make a purchase or order a meal. Thus they may leave the store without buying anything or not even enter a restaurant if the acceptance signs are not posted.

Is there a way out of the credit card bind? Yes, and it is the oil companies who have found the way. When the customer (driver) comes to a self-service gas station and drives up to the pump, he or she can push one of two buttons on the pump, one marked *credit card* and the other marked *cash*. Buying gas with a credit card is more expensive than paying cash.

The *Fortune* 400 oil companies prefer cash to credit, and the public may be willing to pay the extra charge to use their credit card, or they may decide to pay cash and get the gasoline for less. So why can't restaurants, which also prefer cash, tell the customer on the menu that there is a charge for using a credit card? This is only fair to the cash customer who now pays part of the costs of using credit cards. If the oil companies—who have their own credit cards—can promote cash sales, why can't restaurants do likewise?

SERVICE CHARGE

The latest change in menu economics, which is just appearing on the American restaurant scene, is including a service charge on the check instead of relying on the traditional tip. This practice has been standard in Europe for many years. If this trend becomes common in the United States, it is another bit of information that should be clearly printed on the menu.

TABLE 7.3 Annual Inflation Rate, 1968 to 1986

Year	% Increase
1968	4.2
1969	5.4
1970	5.9
1971	4.3
1972	3.3
1973	6.2
1974	11.0
1975	8.9
1976	5.8
1977	6.5
1978	7.7
1979	11.3
1980	13.5
1981	10.4
1982	6.1
1983	3.2
1984	4.3
1985	3.6
1986	2.0

Source: Consumer Price Index, U.S. Dept. of Labor, 1986.

INFLATION AND THE MENU

The restaurant operator will continue to live with and operate a business in an inflationary environment. Only the rate will change, most likely upwards. There are as many explanations for the cause of and cure for inflation as there are economists, bankers, politicians, and professors. The result is confusion and continued inflation. What is inflation? It is a general increase in prices caused largely by unsound government fiscal and monetary policies. Under noninflationary economic conditions, prices continually change. Some go up while others go down. This change is the result of free-market mechanisms, which encourage investment in some sectors and discourage it in others. When inflation prevails, however, all prices rise.

Price increases in some sectors of the economy lag behind those of other sectors in the earlier stages of inflation. Such delays work to the advantage of those who receive their increase first. But as inflation strikes more segments of the economy, the interval between price increases grows shorter, until few benefit.

Inflation affects wages as well as prices. Employees receive higher wages, generally proportionate to the rise in price levels. Wage increases may lag behind increases in prices, but this situation is temporary and will yield no significant long-term advantages to either employees or employers.

As businesspeople and entrepreneurs, restaurateurs have more freedom to maneuver in an inflationary environment than do employees on a payroll. Restaurateurs can invest profits in durable goods, such as real estate (a bigger restaurant), valuable decor (paintings or sculptures), or even a larger wine cellar whose contents, if properly selected, will increase in value in a few years. But restaurateurs cannot avoid the continually rising costs of doing business. Food costs keep going up, and the cost of utilities—heat, lighting, and air conditioning—keeps increasing.

Note that in 1979, 1980, and 1981 the United States experienced double-digit inflation (see Table 7.3). Then, in 1982, as a result of actions taken by the Federal Reserve, the inflation rate began to fall. By 1986, the rate had fallen to 2.0 percent. For bondholders, the decline in the inflation rate was good. But for farmers, who had bought land at high prices and who saw the prices of their commodities fall, the drop in the inflation rate often led to financial disaster. In 1988 the inflation rate was holding steady at around 4.5 percent.

What happened to menu prices over these twenty-three years? Following are prices for 1965 and 1988 for five restaurants in New York, Chicago, New Orleans, and Los Angeles. These are expensive, top-quality restaurants that have been in business for a long time, so their pricing policies and operating methods must be suitable for the markets they serve. The comparisons show the considerable price increases that have occurred over the past twenty years.

To meet these increasing costs and operate at a profit, the foodservice operator must constantly monitor and change prices, which means more attention to the menu, more menu changes, and a menu that will

Whitehall Club, Chicago		
Appetizers	*1965*	*1988*
Shrimp Cocktail	$1.50	$16.00
Soups		
Onion Soup	.75	4.50
Entrées		
Dover Sole	4.00	25.00
Steak Diane	6.50	24.00
Filet Mignon	6.25	22.00
Prime Sirloin	6.25	21.00
Breast of Chicken	4.00	17.00

Four Seasons, New York		
Appetizers	*1965*	*1988*
Shrimp	$2.25	$15.50
Clams	1.65	10.50
Entrées		
Lobster	6.50	40.00
Lamb Chops	5.95(3)	38.00(2)
Sirloin Steak	7.50	38.00
Filet Mignon	7.50	38.00
Grilled Quails	6.75	37.50

Gage & Tollner, Brooklyn		
Appetizers	*1965*	*1988*
Shrimp Cocktail	$1.85	$ 7.00
Crabmeat Cocktail	1.90	8.50
Seafood Cocktail	2.25	8.00
Soups and Bisques		
Clam Chowder	.60	3.00
Lobster Bisque	3.25	7.00
Oysters		
Steamed	2.25	12.50
Baltimore Fry	2.25	12.50
Celery Cream Broil	2.75	12.50
Fresh Fish (in season)		
Bluefish, boned	2.50	10.00
Filet of Sole	2.25	12.00
Seafood à la Newburg	4.00	18.00
Bay Scallops		
À la Newburg	3.75	12.50
Seasoned Broil	3.25	12.00
Steaks, Chops, and Other Meats		
Sirloin Steak	6.00	18.00
Single English Mutton Chop	3.00	10.00
Calf's Liver and Bacon	2.75	14.00
Chicken		
Fried with Bacon and Corn Fritters	3.00	9.00
Broiled or Fried	2.50	8.00
Lobsters		
Cream Stew	3.50	16.50
Thermidor	4.50	17.00
À la Newburg	5.00	17.00

Scandia Restaurant, Los Angeles		
Appetizers	*1965*	*1988*
Shrimp Cocktail	$1.65	$10.75
Lobster Cocktail	1.75	14.75
Salads		
Scandia Salad	1.35	4.50
Soups		
Swedish Pea Soup	.65	3.50
Entrées		
Veal Oskar	4.85	22.50
Filet Mignon	5.75	21.50
Lake Superior Whitefish	4.25	17.75
Biff Lindstrom	3.25	13.75

Restaurant Antoine, New Orleans		
Nous Recommandons	*1965*	*1988*
Huitres Nature	$ .90	5.75
Crevette Cardinal	1.25	6.75
Avocat Crabmeat Garibaldi	1.25	7.75
Canapé St. Antoine	1.25	7.25
Potages		
Gumbo Creole	.75	4.50
Consomme Froid en Tasse	.60	3.50
Poissons		
Pompano Grille	3.00	20.25
Filet de Truite Amandine	2.50	15.50
Crevettes à la Creole	2.25	15.75
Bouillabaisse à la Marseilles	3.50	22.75
Oeufs		
Omelette Española	1.50	10.75
Ouefs Benedict	1.25	10.75
Omelette au Fromage	1.50	9.75
Entrées		
Poulet aux Champignones	2.75	15.75
Poulet Sauce Rochambeau	2.75	16.25
Poulet Sauté Demi-Bordelaise	2.50	15.25

"work" better in inflationary times. Several factors may be considered.

First, an expensive menu can be expensive to change. One way of getting around this is by having an expensive, four-color or two-color cover printed on heavy, coated stock with four, eight, or twelve inside pages printed on lighter stock in only one color. The inside pages can then be changed less expensively, and the cover does not have to be changed at all.

Another way to make the menu flexible for easy price changes is to use a computer-generated menu. The entire menu can be programmed and then printed. With all of the information, including prices, stored in the computer, any changes can be easily made. A new menu can therefore be printed daily in the restaurant. This method is also used to keep wine lists current.

Another popular way of reducing menu reprinting and revision costs is to use a newspaper format, printed on cheap newsprint. Beall's 1860 Recorder of Beall's restaurant in Macon, Georgia is an example of this type of menu (Figure 7.5). Printed in one color (dark brown) on newsprint (page size 11½ by 17 inches), the front and back covers have old stories and ads from 1860. The inside spread has more old ads plus the food listing: Beall's 1860 Midday Provisions, Beall's 1860 Extras, and Beall's 1860 Potables. Thirteen food items and twelve wines and liqueurs are offered. One dessert—Proprietor's Crowning Provision—a rich, tempting dessert freshly made in Beall's own kitchen—has no price, just the word *ask*. A side benefit of this type of menu is that because of its low cost, it can be given away, for more advertising mileage. In a box at the top of the front cover is the note: "Feel free to take our menu home as a souvenir of your visit to Beall's 1860."

Another way of handling price changes in an inflationary environment is to have a limited menu. The fewer items that you offer, the fewer price changes you will have to worry about. Some restaurateurs meet the price change challenge by writing in the prices on preprinted menus that have no prices on them. New prices can then be written in as desired or, in some cases, removed with a special solvent and changed.

The drawback to this method is that the customer's attention is drawn to the prices, which stand out because they are written in with a heavy, dark pen. The first thing the customer notices when picking up the menu is the price of everything, whereas this should be the last thing noticed. This method also signals to the customer that this is a restaurant in which prices change often. Prices thus should be changed in a way that does not make the increase obvious.

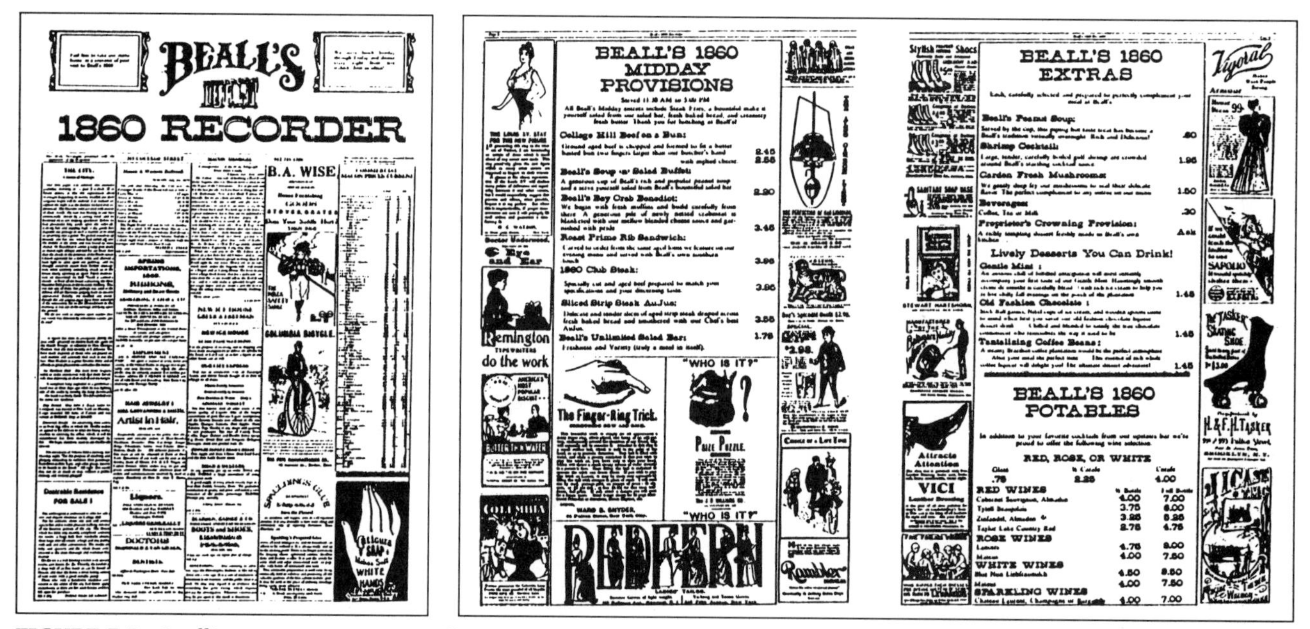

BEALL'S 1860 RECORDER

BEALL'S 1860 MIDDAY PROVISIONS

College Hill Beef on a Bun: 2.45 / 2.55

Beall's Soup 'n' Salad Buffet: 2.20

Beall's Bay Crab Benedict: 3.45

Roast Prime Rib Sandwich: 3.95

1860 Club Steak: 3.95

Sliced Strip Steak Au Jus: 3.55

Beall's Unlimited Salad Bar: 1.75

BEALL'S 1860 EXTRAS

Beall's Peanut Soup: .60

Shrimp Cocktail: 1.95

Garden Fresh Mushrooms: 1.50

Beverages: .30

Coffee, Tea or Milk

Proprietor's Crowning Provision: Ask

Lively Desserts You Can Drink!

Gentle Mint: 1.45

Old Fashion Chocolate: 1.45

Tantalizing Coffee Beans: 1.45

BEALL'S 1860 POTABLES

RED, ROSE, OR WHITE

Glass	½ Carafe	Carafe
.75	2.25	4.00

	½ Bottle	Full Bottle
RED WINES		
	4.00	7.00
	3.75	6.00
	3.25	5.25
	2.75	4.75
ROSE WINES		
	4.75	9.00
	4.00	7.50
WHITE WINES		
	4.50	8.50
	4.00	7.50
SPARKLING WINES		
	4.00	7.00

FIGURE 7.5 Beall's menu. (Courtesy Beall's 1860. Reproduced by permission.)

8

Appetizers and Desserts

Appetizers and desserts are the before and after of the menu and thus tend to play second fiddle to the more important entrées. These two ends of the meal, however, are important to both the restaurant operator and the diner. Along with the appropriate wines, each part of a memorable meal should include an interesting before—the appetizer—and a pleasant ending—the dessert. Thus, just as much attention should be given to creating these items as to merchandising them.

For the restaurant operator, appetizers and desserts are important for several reasons. First, an attractive and creative selection of appetizers and desserts takes the restaurant out of the ordinary and makes the meal a memorable experience. The most effective form of restaurant advertising is WOMA—word of mouth advertising. An interesting and unusual appetizer or dessert can make a meal so memorable that the customer may recommend the restaurant to his or her friends.

Second, and just as important, on an à la carte menu the appetizers and desserts ordered build the check and increase the restaurant's profits. The appetizers and desserts thus must tempt the diner to order them. There are several ways to do this, on or off the menu.

APPETIZERS

Appetizers are the prelude to the meal. They should be light so that they whet the appetite without satisfying it. And they should be fun. The French call them *hors d'oeuvres,* literally, "outside of the works." They can have a lot of calories, and people have come to expect them with cocktails. The French picked up the habit of predinner snacking from the Russians, who call these tidbits *zakuskis.* The Italians offer trays of *antipasti* as the introduction to dinner. And the Scandinavians serve a variety of spicy and pickled foods at the *smörgåsbord,* sometimes making a whole meal out of appetizers. The challenge for the restaurant chef is to stimulate the diner's appetite but not to spoil it for the rest of the meal. When the restaurant has a comprehensive appetizer listing, hot and cold appetizers should be headed separately. Seafood, especially shrimp cocktail, is a favorite appetizer, as are clams and oysters. Other popular appetizers are chicken and seafood nuggets, chicken wings, chilled melon, and salsa with chips.

Following are some interesting appetizers served by successful restaurants.

OYSTERS ROCKEFELLER

Baked on the half-shell with spinach, bacon, onions, cayenne, and a hint of pernod and topped with hollandaise sauce.

OYSTERS CASINO

Freshly shucked oysters baked on the half-shell with chopped chives, wine seasonings, and topped with mornay sauce and sprinkled with bacon.

CLAMS BORDELAISE

A bucket of fresh clams steamed in vermouth and served with drawn butter and clam nectar.

STUFFED MUSHROOMS HOLLANDAISE

Six large mushrooms stuffed with crab and shrimp and topped with hollandaise.

AVOCADO STUFFED WITH CRABMEAT

Half an avocado filled with crabmeat and topped with thousand island dressing.

ESCARGOTS

Six large snails baked in garlic butter and crowned with puff pastry.

FRENCH-FRIED ZUCCHINI

Strips of fresh zucchini, french fried and served with mustard sauce.

DEEP-FRIED CALAMARI

Strips of calamari deep fried and served with cocktail and tartar sauce.

FILET OF SMOKED TROUT

Served with whipped horseradish.

CHAMPIGNONS FRITS À LA VIENNOISE

Delicately fried white mushrooms served with tartar sauce. A favorite dish in old Vienna.

QUICHE LORRAINE

Petite custard pie with Gruyère cheese and bacon.

LOBSTER CREPONETTE

Petite French pancake filled with bite-sized chunks of lobster meat in a delightful Newburg sauce and glazed.

TORTELLINI ALLA PARMA

Delicate pasta rings filled with a mousse of seasoned chicken and served in a sauce of heavy cream and Parmesan cheese.

MAINE LOBSTER CLAWS À LA MAISON

This delicate gem of the sea is lightly sautéed and served on a bed of cucumber slices, covered with a white wine sauce and then glazed.

SPICY CHILI

A slow, oven-baked blend of beef, tomatoes, and red beans served with toppings of sour cream, grated cheddar, and chopped onions.

CHICKEN AND DUMPLINGS

Chunky pieces of white and dark meat blended with fresh vegetables and topped with our own dumplings.

FROGS' LEGS "POULETTE"

Frogs' legs poached in white wine and herbs.

MENU STRATEGY

It is easy for the diner to ignore the appetizer listing and move directly to the entrée or soup and salad. This can be avoided by listing the appetizers on a separate page. Or a separate appetizer menu could be given first to the diner (see Figure 8.1). Many motels print separate appetizer menus to be used in the cocktail lounge, to sell these items along with cocktails.

After a menu survey has been made to determine the appetizers' popularity in relation to food cost and profit, several options are possible. If the item is a low-profit one and not moving, it might be eliminated. If the item is a high-profit one but not moving, it might be given special treatment, for example, a better position on the menu, larger type, or more and better descriptive copy.

If the customers are not ordering the entire appetizer listing à la carte, perhaps the appetizers should be included in the meal and the price of the appetizer included in the complete dinner price. This assumes that the diner will buy the more expensive complete package. Finally, if a dessert cart helps sell desserts, why not an appetizer cart to sell appetizers?

DESSERTS

Dessert is the end of the meal. It may be gooey, creamy, chewy, baked, frozen, or flaming. Surveys have shown that, despite their devotion to dieting, most Americans have a sweet tooth and love dessert. According to the *Restaurants & Institutions* 1987 menu census, dessert consumption has increased by 18 percent since 1978. Yet, many restaurants—judging by their menus—do not give this check-building item the treatment it deserves.

The objective is to serve popular and creative desserts and to sell them both on the menu and through the server.

Mai-Kai Appetizers

Egg Roll 2.75
The most famous of all Cantonese specialties — one of our most prideful achievements.

Crab Rangoon 3.25
Won Ton stuffed with Alaskan King crab meat and a blend of imported cheeses, a hint of curry and deep fried.

Fried Won Ton 2.25
Crisped Won Ton chips served with a tantalizing green pepper, onion and tomato sauce for dipping.

Cha Siu 3.25
Tender slices of pork tenderloin barbecued in our Chinese ovens.

Tahitian Cheese Tangs 2.50
Imported cheeses with diced ham and mushrooms, breaded and deep fried.

Javanesian Beef 4.35
Prime strip sirloin marinated, charcoal broiled and served bite size.

Cantonese Fried Shrimp 3.95
Large imported white shrimps dipped in a delectable batter and fried in peanut oil.

Shanghai Chicken 2.50
Tender chunks of marinated chicken breasts and Chinese parsley, wrapped in bacon and deep fried.

Maki-Maki 2.25
Spiced chicken livers and water chestnut wrapped in bacon and crisp fried.

Polynesian Chicken 2.95
Marinated half chicken, with our own special seasonings, crisped in bubbling peanut oil and cut into easily handled pieces.

Scampi Singapore 3.50
Patties of diced shrimp blended with Oriental spices and fried to a golden brown.

Barbecued Baby Back Ribs 4.35
Selected tiny Canadian pork ribs, marinated and slowly barbecued over our oak log fires.

Pupu Platter 4.95
A combination of Shanghai Chicken, Scampi Singapore, Crab Rangoon and Tahitian Cheese Tangs. (Serves two)

FIGURE 8.1 Mai-Kai restaurant menu. Chinese and South Seas appetizers. (Reproduced by permission.)

Among the classic desserts, good old-fashioned apple pie still heads the list. Cheesecake is a close second, and chocolate cheesecake is a fast-growing dessert in nearly every foodservice operation. Among pies, lemon, custard, and chocolate have shown the greatest growth in the last few years. And America's love affair with chocolate makes chocolate cake a favorite.

Ice cream continues to be a popular dessert that appears on most menus, but often it is not merchandised. This includes soft-serve, plain or gourmet, or sundaes. Soft-serve ice cream is popular in fast-food chains. Plain ice cream is popular in hospitals and contract operations, whereas sundaes are ordered more often in family restaurants. The gourmet ice creams are also making an impact, especially in fine dining establishments. Even alcoholic ice-cream drinks are appearing at some bars.

For those customers interested in their health and their weight, there are ice-cream alternatives. Yogurt, for example, is finding a strong following. Other popular desserts are fresh fruit, cookies, and brownies. Light desserts are important. Most diners who refuse a dessert do so because they are already too "full" or feel that desserts are fattening. Low-calorie desserts can overcome this objection. The restaurant menu thereby joins the food and beverage industries that advertise "lite" beer and wine.

According to the *Restaurants & Institutions* 1987 survey, the best-selling pies in order of preference are apple, chocolate, berry, cherry, and pecan.

Other, more interesting and creative desserts are being sold and described on the menus of fine dining establishments.

PEACH MELBA

Yellow cling peach halves arranged around vanilla ice cream and covered with melba sauce and topped with freshly whipped cream.

CHOCOLATE MOUSSE

A soft and light blend of cream and chocolate with a hint of crème de cacao and bits of bittersweet chocolate.

ICE CREAM JAMAICAN

Light vanilla ice cream flavored with Jamaican rum.

FUZZY NAVEL PIE

José's original ice-cream version of the Fuzzy Navel cocktail. Peach schnapps ice cream packed into a graham cracker crust topped with creamy orange sherbet and a dash of whipped cream.

COUNTRY APPLE PIE

Deep-dish, double-crusted, our "secret ingredients" are the pecans, raisins, and cranberries sprinkled through this old-fashioned pie. Served warm with a scoop of ice cream.

CHOCOLATE PECAN PIE

Chocolate chunks and lots of pecans in every slice. Served warm with a scoop of ice cream.

CHOCOLATE MOUSSE CHEESECAKE

When you can't decide between cheesecake or chocolate, this fabulous dessert can give you both!

PENNSYLVANIA DUTCH SHOOFLY PIE

This local treat is a "Dutch-cross" between a cake and a pie. Special dark syrups bake to form the gooey wet bottom in the pie crust while the spice cake layer forms on the top. Vanilla ice cream and whipped cream are traditional with warm shoofly pie. First-time visitors cannot leave without trying this local trademark. Seasoned travelers often find themselves longing for its unique flavor.

JUDY'S MUD PIE

A chocolate cookie pie shell filled with rich coffee ice cream and covered with chocolate fudge.

BELGIAN WAFFLE

The incredible dessert—a scoop of ice cream, topped with hot fudge and our own whipped cream, or smothered with fresh fruit.

TABLE 8.1 Dessert Preferences

Overall	Commercial	Institutional
Apple pie	Apple pie	Cookies
Cookies	Cream-style cheesecake	Brownies
Chocolate cake	New York–style cheesecake	Chocolate cake
Cream-style cheesecake	Soft-serve ice cream	Apple pie
Soft-serve ice cream	Chocolate pie	Soft-serve ice cream
New York–style cheesecake	Chocolate cake	Cream-style cheesecake
Chocolate pie	Any berry pie	Chocolate pie
Brownies	Gourmet ice cream	Sundaes
Fresh fruit	Fresh fruit	Fresh fruit
Plain ice cream	Plain ice cream	Plain ice cream

Source: Restaurants & Institutions 1987 menu survey.

FLAMBÉ FOR TWO

Crepes Suzette—Delicate French pancakes served with a flair!

Cherries Jubilee—Bing cherries and ice cream . . . festive as the Mardi Gras.

Bananas Foster—With coffee ice cream and Jamaican rum.

PINEAPPLE PUKA

Fresh pineapple chunks simmered in flaming rum sauce and served over vanilla ice cream.

FLAMING BAKED ALASKA

Regally served on a silver tray with sweet black cherries flamed in brandy—serves two.

EXOTIC ICE CREAMS

Crème de Menthe and vanilla-bean ice cream.

Kahlua and vanilla-bean ice cream.

Amaretto and vanilla-bean ice cream.

Frangelica Wild Hazelnut and vanilla-bean ice cream.

ZUPPA INGLESE

Italian traditional dessert—spongecake with custard, syrup, meringue, and amaretto liqueur.

ZABAGLIONE

Our famous egg dessert served with marsala wine and served over fruit.

GELATO DI NOCE DI COCO CON LIQUORE AMARETTO

Coconut ice cream with amaretto liqueur.

BLACK FOREST CAKE

German chocolate cake soaked in brandy and smothered in whipped cream, bing cherries, and sliced almonds.

Figure 8.2 illustrates a tropical dessert menu.

MENU STRATEGY

If the consumption of desserts has increased 18 percent since 1978, then every restaurant should participate in this market. The favorites are a beginning. Then, studies should be made over a period of a month to determine (1) popularity, (2) profit, and (3) the relationship among food cost, popularity, and profit.

Items with poor profit and poor popularity should be dropped. Items with high profit and high popularity should be retained. Items that are popular but not very profitable should be worked on. Just raising their price would affect their popularity, and so they might be kept as is, functioning as loss leaders. Or, an unusual element may be added, a brandy sauce or a more spectacularway of serving, for example, to allow for a higher price while maintaining popularity.

But the entire dessert listing may be sick. What if very few customers are ordering desserts? The merchandising tools used by many good dessert-conscious restaurants are (1) a dessert cart, (2) a separate dessert menu, and (3) a better listing on the menu in the form of more space (a separate page) or better copy, possibly with a dessert special.

Although the dessert cart or tray is good merchandising—it makes sure that the diner will at least look at the desserts—it limits the dessert items to baked goods. A separate dessert menu given to the customers, without asking whether they want desserts, combined with the dessert cart makes sure that every possibility is covered.

FIGURE 8.2 The Mai-Kai dessert menu. After-dinner drinks and desserts are listed together on this smaller menu. (Reproduced by permission.)

A common remark of diners when presented the dessert menu is, "I'm too full to eat any dessert" or "I couldn't eat any more, thank you." The Hoffman House menu addresses this problem up front. The first page of its menu does not list appetizers or any other "before" item. Instead, this first page is headed Save Room For . . . . Below this heading desserts are listed: Hoffman House Dessert Tray, New York–Style Cheesecake, Pecan Pie, Fresh Fruit and Cheese, Goblets of Goodies, Bananas Foster Sundae, Ice Cream Fruit Cup, and Bread Pudding with Whiskey Sauce.

On the last page of this menu, the same dessert listing is repeated. If the customer has saved room as a result of this early introduction to the desserts offered, or if the entrée portions are not gigantic (that is, controlled), the customer is more likely to order dessert. The other alternative is to offer light desserts—light in substance and low in calories but satisfying to the sweet tooth.

The City Tavern

The City Tavern restaurant (Figure 8.3) in Chicago, Illinois, lists the following seven appetizers on both its luncheon and dinner menus.

THE ORIGINAL NACHOS $4.95

Corn tortillas covered with refried beans, red peppers, green chiles, salsa, Monterey Jack and cheddar cheeses. Served with sour cream and jalapeño peppers.

CHESAPEAKE BAY CRAB FRITTERS $5.50

A basket of specially seasoned, deep-fried crab fritters, with chili-pepper mayonnaise.

CHICKEN WINGS $4.50

Original Hot or Sweet & Spicy (1/2 doz.)

SPICY POPCORN SHRIMP..$5.95

Cajun battered shrimp, deep fried, with a zesty dipping sauce.

SHRIMP COCKTAIL $6.50

Five jumbo shrimp served on ice with cocktail sauce and lemon.

FRIED ONION LOAF $3.95

Thinly sliced onions, lightly battered and deep fried to a crispy, golden brown.

COMBINATION APPETIZER $6.95

Chesapeake Bay crab fritters, spicy popcorn shrimp and original hot chicken wings.

Appetizers

The Original Nachos — $4.95
Corn tortillas covered with refried beans, red peppers, green chiles, salsa, Monterey Jack and cheddar cheeses. Served with sour cream and jalapeño peppers.

Chesapeake Bay Crab Fritters — $5.50
A basket of specially seasoned, deep-fried crab fritters, with chili-pepper mayonnaise.

Chicken Wings – Original Hot or Sweet & Spicy — ½ dozen $4.50 / dozen $6.95
Served with blue cheese dipping sauce.

Spicy Popcorn Shrimp — $5.95
Cajun battered shrimp, deep fried, with a zesty dipping sauce.

Shrimp Cocktail — $6.50
Five jumbo shrimp served on ice with cocktail sauce and lemon.

Fried Onion Loaf — $3.95
Thinly sliced onions, lightly battered and deep fried to a crispy, golden brown.

Combination Appetizer — $6.95
Chesapeake Bay Crab Fritters, Spicy Popcorn Shrimp and Original Hot Chicken Wings.

Homemade Soups & Chili

New England Clam Chowder — Cup $1.95 Bowl $2.95

Tavern Soup of the Day — Cup $1.95 Bowl $2.95
City Tavern's kettles of home-style soups, made fresh every day with the finest ingredients.

Texas Panhandle Chili-served in a mini skillet. — $3.95
Our all-meat, hot and spicy, Texas chili, with cheddar cheese, onions, sour cream, kidney beans and Texas Toast.

City Tavern Skillets

Individual Pan Omelettes — $5.50
Made-to-order with three farm fresh, extra-large eggs and your choice of cheese, green peppers, onions, mushrooms, spinach, ham or bacon. Served with thick-cut Texas Toast, Tavern hash browns and fresh fruit.

Classic Eggs Benedict — $6.50
Two poached eggs with Canadian bacon on a toasted English muffin, topped with Hollandaise and served with Tavern hash browns and fresh fruit.

Skillet Corned Beef Hash & Eggs — $5.50
Home-style corned beef hash, topped with two farm fresh eggs, served any style, and Texas Toast.

Tavern Prime Rib Hash — $6.95
A hearty hash with diced pieces of prime rib, potatoes and special seasonings served with two farm fresh eggs, any style, and Texas Toast.

Texas Panhandle Chili — $6.95
An entree-sized skillet of spicy, all-meat Texas chili, with cheddar cheese, onions, sour cream, kidney beans and Texas Toast.

Smoked Turkey Devonshire — $6.95
Smoked breast of turkey, hickory smoked bacon and tomatoes served open face on toasted, thick-cut challah bread topped with melted cheddar cheese sauce. Served with steak fries and cole slaw.

FIGURE 8.3 Dessert menu of The City Tavern. A country-style dessert menu with some "All-American" desserts. (A signature of The Levy Restaurants. Reproduced by permission.)

Beside the Pointe

This hotel restaurant in Phoenix, Arizona, has some unusual appetizers and desserts (see Figure 3.3). Under the heading *Besides*, the following appetizers are listed.

DEEP-FRIED CLAMS

Served with Thousand Island dressing or piquant sauce.

JUMBO MUSHROOMS

Deep-fried with piquant sauce.

DEEP-FRIED ZUCCHINI

Served with a bleu cheese sauce.

CEVICHE

Chilled, marinated scallops and shrimp with cilantro, diced tomatoes, onions, green chilis and lime juice.

POTATO SKINS

Topped with cheese, bacon and scallions, served with sour cream on the side.
With Machaca.
With Chicken.

DEEP-FRIED ARTICHOKE HEARTS

What more can we say? They're fried, they're artichokes and you gotta have heart!

BUFFALO WINGS

Highly seasoned, deep-fried chicken wings.

STUFFED MUSHROOMS

With hot sausage, topped with melted cheese.

OYSTERS ON THE HALF-SHELL

Served when in season.

TERIYAKI SKEWERS

Broiled strips of marinated flank steak on bamboo skewers.

SHRIMP BY THE QUARTER POUND

Chilled and served with Thousand Island dressing. Peel and eat! Priced daily.

Under the heading Grand Finale, this menu lists some different desserts and dessert drinks such as:

MUD PIE

In your eye.

CANNONBALL WITH RUM HARD SAUCE

You eat a dozen and your party of four is on us.

The dessert drinks include:

PEACHES AND CREAM

Peach flavored liqueur, white creme de cacao and cream garnished with a peach.

RANGOON RUBY

Pineapple/Coconut, vodka and cherry brandy.

Scottsdale Princess

The Scottsdale Princess resort in Scottsdale, Arizona, has a separate dessert menu (Figure 8.4). A four-panel, 7½-inch square menu, it is a small version of the dinner menu of the La Hacienda restaurant in the resort. The paper is a white coated stock. The cover design is in full color. The inside spread features a color border.

The left panel begins with Cafes, which may be served "on the rocks" in summer—Cafe Mexicano, Cafe Isla de Mujeres, Cafe Hacienda, Acapulco Princess Cafe, Cafe Keoke, and Cafe Español. Next come Ports and Sherries—Imperial Corregidor, Sandeman Founders Reserve, Sibarita, Nieport, Rebello Valente, and Venerable.

The right-hand panel lists the desserts—Postres—Flan De Naranja (orange custard with caramel sauce), Pastel De Chocolate (chocolate cake with Kahlua), Helados y Sorbets (ice creams and sorbets), Platanos Fritos (fried bananas in a natural honey glaze with powdered sugar), Crepas Con Cajeta (custard cream folded in hot crepes with caramel sauce), Fruta de Temporada (fresh fruit of the season served with hot chocolate sauce), Sombrero de Chocolate (a sombrero of white chocolate surrounded with tropical fruit sorbet).

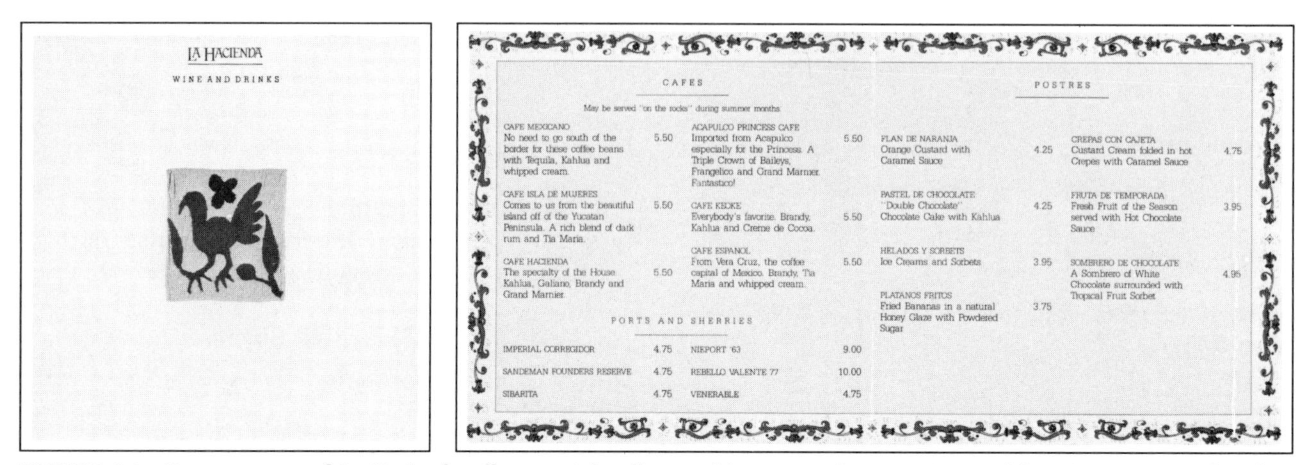

LA HACIENDA
WINE AND DRINKS

CAFES

May be served "on the rocks" during summer months

CAFE MEXICANO
No need to go south of the border for these coffee beans with Tequila, Kahlua and whipped cream. 5.50

CAFE ISLA DE MUJERES
Comes to us from the beautiful island off of the Yucatan Peninsula. A rich blend of dark rum and Tia Maria. 5.50

CAFE HACIENDA
The specialty of the House. Kahlua, Galiano, Brandy and Grand Marnier. 5.50

ACAPULCO PRINCESS CAFE
Imported from Acapulco especially for the Princess. A Triple Crown of Baileys, Frangelico and Grand Marnier. Fantastico! 5.50

CAFE KEOKE
Everybody's favorite. Brandy, Kahlua and Creme de Cocoa. 5.50

CAFE ESPANOL
From Vera Cruz, the coffee capital of Mexico. Brandy, Tia Maria and whipped cream. 5.50

PORTS AND SHERRIES

IMPERIAL CORREGIDOR	4.75	NIEPORT '63	9.00
SANDEMAN FOUNDERS RESERVE	4.75	REBELLO VALENTE 77	10.00
SIBARITA	4.75	VENERABLE	4.75

POSTRES

FLAN DE NARANJA
Orange Custard with Caramel Sauce 4.25

PASTEL DE CHOCOLATE
"Double Chocolate" Chocolate Cake with Kahlua 4.25

HELADOS Y SORBETS
Ice Creams and Sorbets 3.95

PLATANOS FRITOS
Fried Bananas in a natural Honey Glaze with Powdered Sugar 3.75

CREPAS CON CAJETA
Custard Cream folded in hot Crepes with Caramel Sauce 4.75

FRUTA DE TEMPORADA
Fresh Fruit of the Season served with Hot Chocolate Sauce 3.95

SOMBRERO DE CHOCOLATE
A Sombrero of White Chocolate surrounded with Tropical Fruit Sorbet 4.95

FIGURE 8.4 Dessert menu of La Hacienda offers special coffees and ice-cream desserts. (Scottsdale Princess. Reproduced by permission.)

9

Soups, Salads, Sandwiches, and Side Orders

SOUPS

Lewis Carroll, in *Alice's Adventures in Wonderland*, wrote:

> *Beautiful Soup! Who cares for fish,*
> *game or any other dish?*
> *Who would not give all else for two*
> *pennyworth only of Beautiful Soup?*
> *Beau-ootiful Soup!*
> *Beau-ootiful Soup!*
> *Soo-oop of the e-e-evening,*
> *Beautiful, beautiFUL Soup!*

Soup has historically been a basis for nourishment and survival. The cauldron was the original stockpot, and it provided an ever-changing broth enriched daily with whatever meats or vegetables were available. But soup can be gourmet food as well as basic fare.

The early peasant cauldron gave birth to many national soups. These have survived, and today there is a national soup for virtually every country. Their preparation is often similar, but they differ in ingredients, which tend to reflect the ingredients available and regional and national tastes. Some of these national soups are the pot-au-feu of France, the minestrone of Italy, borscht from Russia, gazpacho from Spain, and erwtensoep from Holland.

The first cookbook of soups is *Le Viandier*, written in 1375 by a French chef known as Taillevent. The soup recipes in this book are strange combinations. Some were based on thick meat juice or stock, others on milk flavored with honey, saffron, and wine. A soup from Germany was composed of sliced onions fried in oil, crushed ginger, cinnamon, cloves, saffron marinated in vinegar, crushed blanched almonds, hot water, and beaten eggs. *Soup au pain*, or bread soup, was made with a base of sugar and white wine ornamented with egg yolks, perfumed with rose water to which were added thick slices of bread soaked in broth, fried in oil, and sprinkled with sugar and saffron.

On the average restaurant menu today, however, only a few soups are listed, usually with or after the appetizers. Yet, according to a 1987 *Restaurants & Institutions* survey, "Soups are growing in popularity on nearly every menu in the country." This should be no surprise. In the average supermarket the Campbell Soup Company usually takes up at least six square feet on the shelves. This company, with $4.5 billion in annual sales, is marketing much more than soups today, but soup remains the cornerstone of its business.

(In the annals of successful restaurants there is also a soup success story, Pea Soup Andersen's in Buellton, California. According to the menu, "Carefully selected peas for Andersen's pea soup are split personally by chefs Hap-Pea and Pea-Wee." Andersen's soups are also available in cans and sold in grocery stores.)

A surprise in the 1987 *Restaurants & Institutions* survey was the number of fast-food operations serving soup. More than one-third of the fast-food restaurants surveyed served chicken soup or chili, and 25 percent offered beef soup, split pea, or cream of broccoli. Of the fast-food operations offering soup, 89 percent listed vegetable soup; 87 percent listed chicken soup; and 85 percent listed New England clam chowder.

The soup that is growing fastest in popularity is cream of broccoli. Beef and vegetable soups also are very popular. In terms of popularity, the leader is beef soup, followed by cream of broccoli, vegetable, potato, cheese, and seafood soups. Of the two popular seafood chowders, New England clam chowder is more popular than Manhattan-style chowder, a preference that seems to hold throughout the nation.

Apparently there is no sector of the restaurant industry that does not serve soup, and although the preferences may vary somewhat from a hospital or cafeteria to a fine dining restaurant, soups tend to have the same basic appeal.

More creative—and more expensive—fine dining restaurants are not confined to the standard soups. Their more interesting soups are usually made "from scratch" and reflect the talent and creativity of the restaurant's chef. The following listings were taken from a variety of successful restaurants.

TORTUE LADY CURZON

Clear turtle consommé with a touch of curry and glazed with cream.

FRENCH ONION SOUP AU GRATIN

Rich beef stock with browned onions, croutons, and Parmesan cheese.

MARYLAND CRAB BISQUE

A base of Maryland crab is enhanced with carrots, onions, celery, cognac, and white wine and finished with egg yolk and heavy cream.

GAZPACHO À LA SEVILLE

Chilled Spanish-style soup, a blend of bell peppers, cucumbers, onions, diced tomatoes, chopped jalapeños, tomato juice, and a wisp of garlic.

CHILLED CUCUMBER SOUP

Delicately seasoned and topped with sour cream.

LA BISQUE DE HOMARD

Lobster cream soup flavored with whiskey.

LA TEXAN PEPPER POT

An original soup prepared with green and red peppers, onions, tomatoes, and cubed potatoes. Very hot!

CHILLED BUTTERNUT SQUASH AND APPLE BISQUE

A new taste sensation . . . worth a try!

WEST COAST SEAFOOD CHOWDER

Served with a plankton fritter.

GUMBO YA YA

A New Orleans tradition. A mix of chicken and andouille sausage in rich gumbo stock.

PACIFIC OYSTER STEW

A tureen of whole baby Pacific Oysters simmered in a rich cream stock, accented with chopped onions and a float of country butter.

ELLIOTT BAY BOUILLABAISSE

Whitefish, clams and crab in the shell, whole prawns, lobster, scallops, salmon, and tomatoes in a hearty stew simmered with cloves of garlic and served with French bread for dipping.

SENATE BEAN SOUP

A thick spicy bean soup surrounding a mound of steamed rice.

PORTUGUESE BEAN SOUP

Laced with sherry or a dip of sour cream.

The most popular soup on any menu is the soup of the day or its French twin, soup du jour. If asked, the server will tell the customer or, if better trained, will inform the customer without being asked. The best answer to this problem is to have a tip-on that describes the soup of the day. Remember, a soup worth serving is a soup worth selling!

SALADS

Salads are usually served as accompaniments to the main meal. Although they still are an important part of dinner, they now have become entrée items as well. Chefs are using their talents to create new ones, and the old favorites, like Caesar salad, remain popular. The popularity of salads is probably linked to the growing concern with nutrition. Salads provide the vegetables and fruits recommended by nutritionists and usually contain seafood and chicken, rather than beef and pork.

TABLE 9.1 Best-Selling Soups

Overall	Commercial	Institutional
Vegetable	Vegetable	Chicken
Chicken	Chicken	Vegetable
Beef	New England clam chowder	Beef
New England clam chowder	Cream of broccoli	Chili
Cream of broccoli	Beef	New England clam chowder
Chili	Cheese	Cream of broccoli
Cheese	Seafood	Minestrone
Potato	Chili	Cheese
Seafood	Potato	Potato
Minestrone	Manhattan clam chowder	Tomato

Source: Restaurants & Institutions, 1987 survey.

Salads are usually listed on the menu after the soups and appetizers. According to the 1987 *Restaurants & Institutions* menu survey, salads, especially the old favorites, are selling better than ever. The entrée salad, which usually costs as much as a seafood or meat entrée, must be given equal billing on the menu. This means large, readable type and a good description. The older salads may be familiar to the customer, but the newer taco and pasta salads may not be as well known.

Many menus fail to list the salad dressings offered, and usually the server has to recite the list of those available, including the house dressing, which then has to be described. These dressings should be listed on the menu and described as necessary.

A new development in better, more creative restaurants is to offer a special dressing with a special salad. The most popular dressings are house dressings, blue cheese and roquefort, Italian, and thousand island. Across the entire foodservice industry the most popular salads, according to the *Restaurants & Institutions* survey are tossed green, house salad, taco salad, chef's salad, fruit salad, potato salad, coleslaw, cottage cheese and fruit, spinach salad, and pasta salad.

The hottest new salad seems to be the pasta salad, which is most popular with customers who want a quick, filling meal. Other interesting salads, such as those listed next, were taken from the menus of creative and successful restaurants.

SPINACH SALAD

Chilled raw spinach, chopped egg, fresh mushrooms, real bacon bits, and shrimp, topped with hot bacon sherry dressing.

SEAFOOD SALAD SUPREME

An array of Dungeness crab, bay shrimp, chilled salmon, sole, and prawns with assorted vegetables, avocado, and cheese.

RIPE OLIVE AND TUNA

Refreshing as a stroll through the park. Flaked tuna combined with chunks of cheddar cheese, celery, pickles, and ripe olives.

CREATION SALAD

Chunks of tender oven-roasted turkey, blue cheese crumbles, tomatoes, cucumbers, avocados, ripe olives, egg slices, crisp bacon, and croutons.

CARCIOFINI

Artichoke hearts and limestone lettuce.

CUORE DI PALMA, BRAZILIANA

Brazilian palm hearts with sauce vinaigrette.

ESQUIRE SALAD

French endive, bibb lettuce, watercress, tomatoes, and avocado tossed with lemon and walnut oil dressing, with sprinkles of bleu cheese.

PINEAPPLE BOAT

Fresh pineapple and a combination of fruits served with cottage cheese and date-nut bread.

SHRIMP LOUIS

Jumbo Gulf shrimps served on shredded iceberg lettuce, garnished with hard-boiled eggs, asparagus, tomato wedges, and Russian dressing, and sprinkled with capers.

CALCUTTA SALAD

Whole breast of chicken, sliced and presented on fresh tossed greens and served with a delicate curry and chutney dressing.

LOBSTER SALAD

Half Maine lobster with green asparagus and sour cream potato salad.

COLD PRIME BEEF AND FIVE-BEAN SALAD

With horseradish mustard remoulade.

SMOKED CHICKEN

A unique combination of fruits, curry, and vegetables served in a fresh pineapple.

2350

Rows of smoked chicken, bacon, tomatoes, chopped egg, avocado, scallions, and Swiss Gruyère on a bed of mixed greens, with sweet-sour poppy seed dressing.

CHINESE CHICKEN

Mixed greens tossed with mushrooms, water chestnuts, scallions, red peppers, celery, and mandarin oranges, topped with chow mein noodles, almonds, and chicken and served with Oriental dressing.

PASTA TUNA SALAD

White tuna, chopped egg, and mayonnaise tossed in tricolor pasta. Garnished with lemon wheels.

JOSE'S TACO SALAD

A fresh light combination of lettuce, tomatoes, ground beef, guacamole, and cheddar cheese served with a special taco dressing.

CHICKEN AND SPINACH SALAD

Broiled breast of chicken marinated in honey-mustard sauce and sliced over a bed of fresh spinach. Served with hot bacon dressing.

SOMBRERO STEAK SALAD

Tender strips of marinated broiled sirloin sliced over a bed of mixed greens, tomatoes, black olives, and jack cheese. Served on a crisp tortilla shell accompanied by poppy seed dressing.

A new twist to the selling of salads in restaurants is the premade salad sold in fast-food chains. Hardee's,

Jack-in-the-Box, and McDonald's now offer packaged salads to their drive-through customers, who account for about 60 percent of the fast-food business. Included are chef's, garden, and shrimp salad, complete with croutons and dressing.

SANDWICHES

Do Americans eat anything other than sandwiches? Consider first the ubiquitous hamburger. According to *Restaurants & Institutions* magazine, in 1988, McDonald's sales were $16,100 million; Burger King's sales were $5,400 million; and Wendy's International sales were $2,902 million. It is not hard, therefore, to answer the question "Where's the beef?" It is primarily in hamburgers. There are other sandwich chains. In 1988, the sales of just the leading sandwich chains were as follows: Arby's Inc., $1,160 million; Roy Rogers, $630.2 million; Subway, $600 million; and Rax Restaurants, $366.7 million (*Restaurants & Institutions*). Obviously, the American appetite for the sandwich goes on and on.

The burger itself has many creative variations. And even though the large chains like McDonald's consider themselves "limited menu" operations, they constantly experiment with new items to find winners. Arby's, for example, has recently come out with a chicken-and-ham Cordon Bleu Sandwich, and Dunkin' Donuts is selling croissant sandwiches as well as doughnuts.

Besides hamburgers, cheeseburgers, and various gourmet burgers, the old favorites that appear on most menus are still the club sandwich and the bacon, lettuce, and tomato sandwich. The latest trendsetter is the croissant sandwich, and the steak sandwich continues to be popular. The chicken patty sandwich has also become a good seller, as are roast beef, sliced turkey, and tuna salad sandwiches.

American delicatessens also have contributed to the sandwich world, as the following list demonstrates.

REUBEN

Corned beef, Swiss cheese, and Russian dressing grilled together on rye bread.

GRILLED CORNED BEEF AND CHEDDAR

A good combination of corned beef, melted cheddar cheese, and rye bread, with a special, well-seasoned dressing.

CHOPPED CHICKEN LIVER COMBINATIONS

. . . with Romanian pastrami; with corned beef; with hard-boiled egg, onion, and tomato; and with roasted breast of turkey.

PIZZA–OLA BURGER

Italian sausage patty, spicy tomato sauce, and mozzarella cheese.

PICKLE IN A PACKAGE

Slices of tender corned beef, pastrami, bacon bits, dark mustard, and kosher dills, all wrapped in pumpernickel.

D.B. Kaplan's Delicatessen

The ultimate sandwich menu of D.B. Kaplan's Delicatessen begins, "Never before has a restaurant delicatessen risen to such great heights (7th floor Water Tower Place). Nowhere on earth will you find a sandwich more mountainous than at D.B. Kaplan's Delicatessen" (Figure 9.1).

The menu lives up to this claim. It measures 11½ by 30 inches and accordion-folds down to 11½ by 6 inches. It is printed in full color on both sides, with drawings of the sandwiches and drinks served. The listings are set in three columns that extend the full length of the menu.

Beginning at the top of the left-hand column is the heading Fresh Features, which lists five sandwiches: The Californian, Sprouts of This World, Perky Turkey,

TABLE 9.2 The Most Popular Sandwiches

Overall	Commercial	Institutional
Cheeseburger	Cheeseburger	Cheeseburger
Hamburger	Hamburger	Hamburger
Gourmet hamburger	Gourmet hamburger	Gourmet hamburger
Club sandwich	Club sandwich	Chicken patty
Bacon cheeseburger	Sliced turkey	Bacon, lettuce, and tomato
Roast beef sandwich	Bacon cheeseburger	Ham and cheese
Chicken patty	Roast beef	Bacon cheeseburger
Bacon, lettuce, and tomato	Tuna salad	Thin-sliced steak
Sliced turkey	Bacon, lettuce, and tomato	Grilled cheese
Thin-sliced steak	Thin-sliced steak	Roast beef

Source: Restaurants & Institutions, 1987 survey.

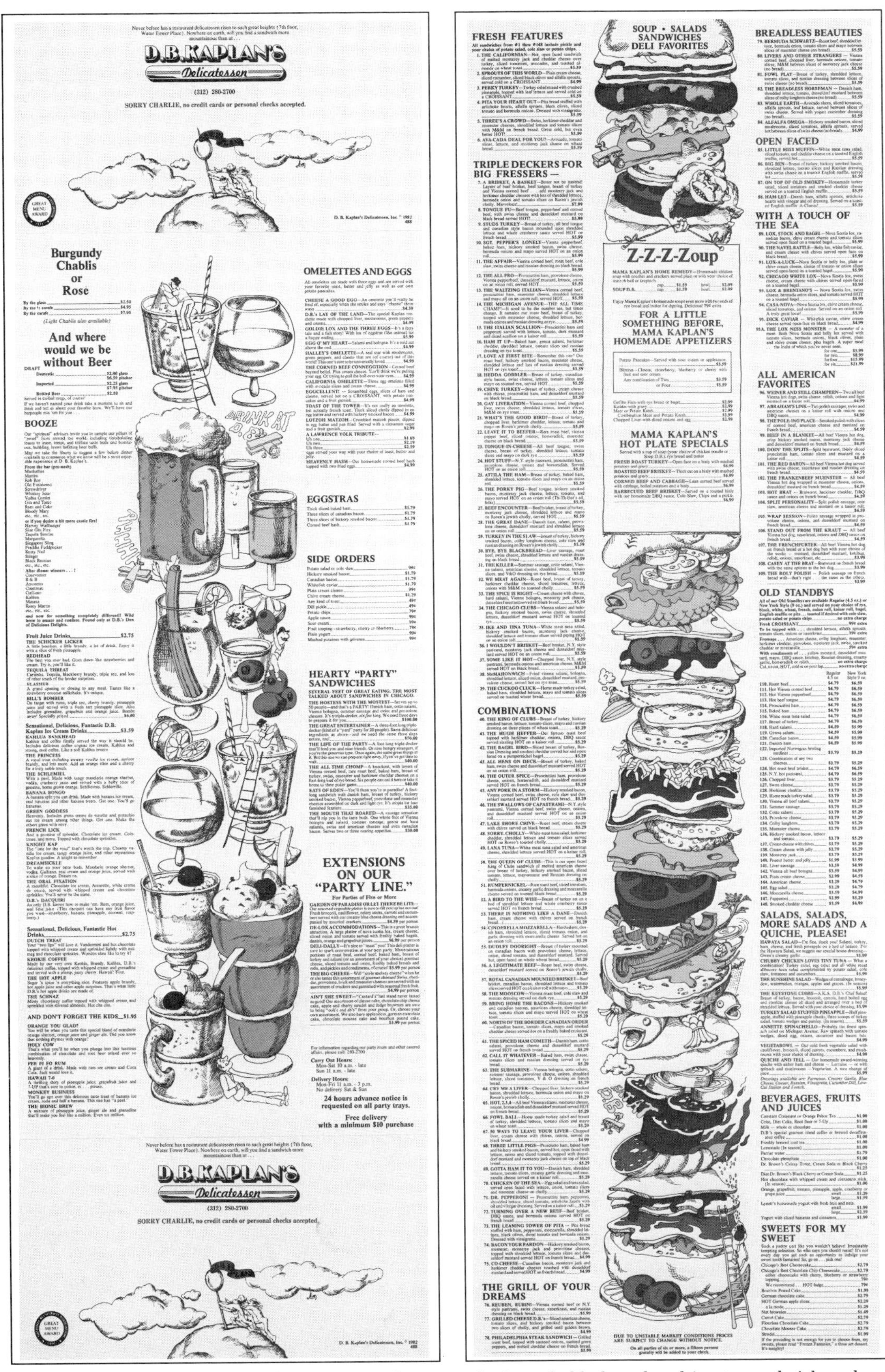

FIGURE 9.1 Sandwich menu from D.B. Kaplan's. Kaplan's probably has the ultimate sandwich and deli menu. (Courtesy D.B. Kaplan's Delicatessen, Inc. A Signature of The Levy Restaurants. Reproduced by permission.)

Pita Your Heart Out, and Three's a Crowd. Prices range from $4.99 to $5.59.

The next heading is Triple Deckers for Big Fressers, with thirty-two sandwiches such as the following:

THE ITALIAN SCALLION

Prosciuttini ham and pepperoni served with lettuce, tomato, dark mustard, and diced scallions on a kaiser roll.

HEDDA GOBBLER

Breast of turkey, Canadian-style bacon, lettuce, Swiss cheese, tomato slice, and mayonnaise on toasted rye, served HOT.

THE SPICE IS RIGHT

Cream cheese with chives, hard salami, Vienna bologna, Monterey Jack cheese, and Dusseldorf mustard, served on black bread.

The price of these sandwiches is $5.59 except for the lead item, Brisket a Basket, which is $7.99.

The next list in the left-hand column is Combinations, thirty-five sandwiches priced from $4.99 to $5.29.

ALL HENS ON DECK

Breast of turkey, baked ham, Swiss cheese and Dusseldorf mustard, served HOT on an onion roll.

THE MOOSCOW

Vienna roast beef, coleslaw, and Russian dressing served on dark rye.

HOT, 2, 3, 4

All-beef Vienna salami, Muenster cheese, onions, horseradish, and Dusseldorf mustard served HOT on French bread.

The final listing on the left-hand panel, entitled The Grill of Your Dreams, has three items: Reuben, Rubin; Grilled Cheese D.B.'s; and Philadelphia Steak Sandwich. These are priced at $4.99 and $5.99.

On the center panel between the illustrations are the soup, appetizers, and four hot plate specials. The soup is Mama's Chicken Noodle, and the appetizers are Gefilte Fish, Kishke with Gravy, and Meat or Potato Knish. Two other appetizers—Potato Pancakes and Blintzes—are featured in a box. Appetizer prices vary from $2.99 to $3.99. The hot plate specials are Fresh Roast Turkey, Roasted Beef Brisket, Corned Beef and Cabbage, and Barbecued Beef Brisket, priced at $6.99.

The right-hand column begins with Breadless Beauties, mainly salads composed of sandwich ingredients on lettuce without the bread. The six items are priced at $5.59, with one at $4.99. They are followed by four open-faced sandwiches priced at $5.59. Next, in the same column, are eight seafood sandwiches headed A Touch of the Sea. They are basically lox and bagel sandwich variations with caviar and other ingredients added. One of them provides an excuse for nonstop puns:

THE LOX NESS MONSTER

A monster of a meal. Both Nova Scotia and belly lox served with tomato slices, bermuda onions, black olives, plain and chive cream cheese, plus bagels. A super meal . . . the lochs of which you've never seen.

For one $5.99
For two $8.99
For four $15.99
For six $21.99

The next sandwich listing in this column, All-American Favorites, consists of fourteen sandwiches. Prices range from $3.99 to $4.99. Examples are:

THE POLE-ING PLACE

Smoked Polish sausage with slices of corned beef, American cheese, and mustard on French bread.

HOT BRAT

Bratwurst, herkimer cheddar, DBQ sauce, and onions on French bread.

Next come the Old Standbys, which are basically a "build your own" listing with various breads and rolls, plus cheeses, condiments, vegetables, and dressings, plus forty meats or other special fillings. These "put-together" sandwiches are offered in two sizes, regular and New York style.

The next listing is Salads, Salads, More Salads, and a Quiche, Please!—seven salads and one quiche—whose prices range from $4.99 to $5.99. The last two listings in the right-hand column are Beverages, Fruits and Juices, and Sweets for My Sweet, and include some unusual items.

Dr. Brown's Celery Tonic, Cream Soda, or Black Cherry
Yogurt with Sliced Bananas and Cinnamon
Chocolate Chip Cheesecake with Cherry, Blueberry, or Strawberry Topping
HOT German Apple Slices
Flourless Chocolate Cake

In the left-hand column of D.B. Kaplan's Delicatessen's menu is the drink list. First are burgundy, chablis, and rosé, then And Where Would We Be Without

Beer, followed by Booze. Finally, there is And Don't Forget the Kids. In the right-hand column, beginning at the top, is Omelettes and Eggs, with fourteen items, ranging in price from $1.69 to $4.99. This is followed by Eggstras and Side Orders.

The last two listings on this comprehensive menu refer to takeouts and catering. First are Hearty Party Sandwiches, six "party sandwich packages." Here are three examples:

THE HOSTESS WITH THE MOSTEST

Serves up to 50 people—and that's a PARTY! Danish ham, cotto salami, Vienna bologna, summer sausage, and Swiss and provolone cheeses. It's a triple-decker six feet long. We need three days to prepare it for you $100.00

THE LIFE OF THE PARTY

A foot-long triple-decker that'll feed you and nine friends. Or nine hungry strangers if you're the generous type. Once again the same great things in it. But this one we can prepare right away if you've got the time to wait. $40.00

THE MOUTH THAT ROARED

A sausage sensation that'll nip you in the taste buds. One whole foot of Vienna bologna and salami, summer sausage, genoa and hard salami, Swiss and American cheeses, and even Canadian bacon. Serves two or three roaring appetites. $30.00

Five more party platters are advertised on this menu, under the heading Extensions on Our Party Line. They serve parties of five or more and range from $3.99 to $6.99 per person. The advantage of listing and selling takeouts on the regular menu is that the regular customers see the offerings and may remember this service later when having an office or home party. Also, the complete descriptions are better than "Try Our Takeouts" or "Party Platters Available."

Ordinarily, D.B. Kaplan's menu would be much too long and contain too many items; the average luncheon or dinner menu should not contain over thirty or forty items. Indeed, a menu with several hundred items usually has a great number of "dead" items that are never ordered or confuse the kitchen when they are ordered. Sandwiches, however, are different. On D.B. Kaplan's menu they are basically entrée items and present no problem to the kitchen. Although there may be over a hundred individual sandwiches, there are not that many ingredients. The number of breads and rolls, meats, cheeses, and other condiments is limited. What makes the list long is the combinations. The sandwiches, with similar ingredients, can also be open-face, double-decker, or triple-decker. So, what the D.B. Kaplan's menu does is give the impression of being enormous, without actually being that big. In the process, it impresses the customer.

Limit Up! Fast Market

The Fast Market menu is much smaller than D.B. Kaplan's, but packs a lot of humor, as well as a varied menu, into the small magazine-cover format. The "table of contents" offers Italian entrées as well as several salads, soups, burgers, and hot and cold sandwiches (see Figure 9.2).

SIDE ORDERS

On most menus, the side orders probably get the least attention. A few standard items appear on many menus, but some offer creative side orders that attract the customers' attention and tell them that this is not an ordinary, run-of-the-menu restaurant.

Potatoes are the most popular side orders, from French and American fries to baked and mashed. Baby vegetables—small, tender new potatoes, carrots, squash, or beans, for example—are a trend in side orders. Egg noodles, fettuccini, and vermicelli plus broccoli, green beans, cauliflower, rice pilaf, onion rings, carrots, and asparagus also are popular side orders. The following list includes some less common offerings.

Sweet Potato: baked or mashed
Creamed Spinach
Corn Fritters with Maple Syrup
Mashed Potatoes Colcannon: with scallions, onions, and black peppercorns
Potato Skins: baked, scooped, and golden fried
Bacon Cheddar Skins: real bacon bits and melted cheese with sour cream for dipping
New York Potato Salad
Homecooked Baked Beans
Hot Flemish Sauerkraut
Whipped Potatoes and Carrots

MENU STRATEGY

If you serve soup, salads, sandwiches, and side orders, what are their popularity, food cost, and profitability? Are these items profit builders or loss leaders? Menu research should give you the answers. Some may have a low food cost and a high profit. Others may be popular but have a high food cost and a low profit. Should you raise prices? Will your customers buy the item at a higher price?

FREE DELIVERY PHONE 207-1402
Open 6:30 AM to 4:00 PM
Minimum Delivery Order $10
Ask about our "Late Nite"
Delivery—4:00 PM to 8:00 PM

Table of Contents

Table of Contents

Limit Up! Fast Market™
Chicago Mercantile Exchange Center
30 South Wacker
Chicago, Illinois 60606

PASTA & SAUCE

Each day we offer a selection of pasta made with either "Semolina" flour, "whole wheat" flour, "spinach," or "tomato basil." Our Pasta & Sauces change daily. Call us!

Marinara Sauce 3.00
Tangy tomato sauce
Carne Sauce 4.00
Tomato sauce with meat
Zucchini Sauce 3.75
Spicy zucchini and tomatoes
Clam Sauce 4.25
White, thick clam sauce
Alfredo Sauce 4.00
Cream, butter & parmesan cheese
Shrimp Tosca Sauce 4.50
Baby shrimp, sauteed with peppers, garlic in fresh marinara sauce.
Meatballs .... 1.00 Sausage 1.00
Garlic Bread .... .45

ITALIAN SPECIALS

Our Specials change daily. Call us!

Lasagne 4.50
Homemade with thick layers of ricotta, mozarella, and parmesan cheese. The "best" in the city.
Eggplant Parmesan 4.50
Battered and fried slices of eggplant layered and baked with plenty of mozzarella cheese. Served with linguini.
Meat Ravioli 4.50
Jumbo meat filled ravioli. Covered with our marinara sauce.
Veal Parmesan 4.50
Breaded Provimi veal, baked with parmesan cheese, marinara sauce and fresh grated mozzarella. Served with pasta.
Chicken Parmesan 4.50
Breaded chicken breast, baked with parmesan and mozzarella cheese, topped with our Marinara sauce and served with pasta.

ITALIAN SALADS

Green Salad 2.50
Julienne Salad 3.50
above with French, 1000 Island, Lo-Cal Italian, Bacon Dressing
Stuffed Tomatoes (chicken or tuna salad) 3.00
small large
Artichoke Pasta Salad 1.75/3.50
Pasta Verde 1.50/3.00
Pasta Tonnato 2.00/4.00
Tortellini 2.50/5.00

BEVERAGES

"16 oz" Coke, Diet Coke, Sprite, Cherry Coke .... .75
Iced Tea .... .75
Lemonade .... .75
"Pellegrino" Italian Sparkling Water 1.25
"Jolt" Cola .... .75

BURGERS & FRIES

Burger 2.75
1/3 Pound 100% Pure Beef Pattie on a sesame seed bun, topped with lettuce, tomato, and a Kosher pickle!
With a slice of American cheese 2.95
Burger with Fries 3.50
Cheeseburger with Fries 3.75
French Fries .... .85

HOMEMADE SOUPS

Our homemade soups change daily.

Minestrone 1.00/1.50
Lentil 1.00/1.50
Chicken Rice 1.00/1.50
Split Pea 1.00/1.50
Cream of Tomato 1.00/1.50
Beef Vegetable 1.00/1.50
Clam Bisque 1.00/1.50

HOT SANDWICHES

Sausage 3.50
Meatball 3.50
Italian Beef 3.50
Combo-Beef & Sausage 3.95
add .30 for shredded mozzarella
Corned Beef 3.50
Chicago Style Hot Dog 1.62
Ham & Cheese Croissant 1.85
Submarine 3.50
add .20 for either "Hot" or "Sweet" Peppers on any sandwich

COLD SANDWICHES

BREADS: whole wheat, white or rye

Roast Beef on Kaiser 3.50
Chicken Salad 3.00
Tuna Salad 3.00
Submarine 3.50
Ham 'n' Cheese 3.00
Potato Chips .... .45

DESSERTS

"Dove" Bar 1.85
"Silverland" Gourmet Brownies 1.10
"Fresh Baked Cookies" by "Cookies Chicago" .... .69
"Rice Krispie" Marshmallow Treats .... .79

BREAKFAST

Assorted Doughnuts .... .60/.75
Fresh Muffins .... .75
Fresh Jumbo Muffins 1.35
Fresh Bagels .... .75
with cream cheese 1.10
with vegetable cream cheese 1.25
Ham & Cheese Croissant 1.85
Assorted Filled Croissant 1.15
Fresh Orange Juice 1.25
"Rich 'N' Pure" Juices .... .89
Coffee, Tea .... .60
Milk .... .60

FIGURE 9.2 Menu from Limit Up! Fast Market. This restaurant provides a big soup, salad, and sandwich menu. (Reproduced by permission.)

One method of increasing the profit on a popular but low-profit item is through add-ons or packaging. In the case of soups, salads, and sandwiches this is easy. A soup and sandwich combination can ask a higher price without the customer's objecting. In the case of salads, if they are listed with the entrées, their price will be compared with those of the other entrées and thus considered to be in line with the entrées.

If side orders are unusual, the customer may be willing to pay extra. (A side order like coleslaw is considered nothing by the average customer.) Many operators add interesting side orders to their sandwiches to make a more appealing—and more profitable—combination.

10

Meats and Poultry

MEAT

America is still a nation of meat eaters—think of those millions of hamburgers eaten daily. Then there are the fancier favorites, steaks and ribs. But the worry about cholesterol and fat may have reduced meat consumption. Do Americans still like beef? According to a May 13, 1987, article in *Restaurants & Institutions*, "Given a choice between prime ribs of aged Texas beef and Southern fried chicken, which will the average customer choose? With 28 percent of the vote compared to chicken's 12 percent, beef won hands down as the most popular entrée in a recent Gallup report on eating out." The popularity of meat on the menu, in descending order, is as follows:

Prime rib/roast beef
Steak
BBQ spare ribs
Veal Parmesan
Chopped steak
Pot roast
Meatballs
London broil
Swiss steak
Pork chops
Roast pork
Veal Oskar
Lamb chops

Beef

Meat from a steer or a cow is referred to as beef. This most popular meat is generally the most expensive one, although prices vary according to quality and cut. Most expensive are the rib roast, tenderloin, and all steaks except the full and bottom round, arm, and flank, which are medium priced. Also in the moderate price range are the boneless rump, standing rump, heel of round, blade roast, arm roast, boneless stew, eye round, boneless chuck, sweetbreads, and brisket. The rest are low-priced cuts.

Pork

The consumption of pork has dropped in the past decade. But owing to consumer demand, hogs have been bred (streamlined) to produce more meat and less fat per animal. As the national income increases, the consumption of beef rises and that of pork declines. The most costly cuts of pork are the loin roast, tenderloin, chops, boneless ham roast, baked ham, center ham slice, and ham butt double slices. Medium priced are the shoulder butt, picnic shoulder, shoulder slice, and bacon. The least expensive are spareribs and pork shoulder cuts.

Lamb

Lamb, the smallest of the meat animals, is most popular on Greek or Middle Eastern menus. It is a tender, juicy meat with an unusual, almost gamelike flavor and is usually served roasted or broiled. Most of the lamb eaten in this country is brought to the market up to a year old, weighing between thirty and fifty pounds. Beyond a year in age the meat from sheep is called mutton, which has never been as popular in America as it is in England. Around 93 percent of the sheep raised for meat in the United States is sold as lamb.

The most expensive cuts of lamb are the leg, rib, and loin chops, leg and crown roasts, leg steaks, and the loin end of the leg. Medium-priced cuts are the boneless rolled shoulder and Saratoga chops. The economy cuts are neck slices, boneless rolled breast, shoulder, and shank.

Veal

Baby beef or calf brought to market at six weeks to two months old is known as veal. The texture and flavor of this meat is totally different from that of full-grown beef. This younger animal yields smaller and fewer cuts. Because it comes from a young animal, veal is always tender, but it requires long, slow cooking with fat added. Veal is seldom broiled. When cooked with delicacy and subtlety as in French, Italian, and German cuisine, it is appreciated by gourmets. Veal comes in six wholesale cuts: leg (round), loin, breast, rib, shoulder, and shank.

Even though beef consumption has lost ground to chicken in the last decade, the popularity of beef continues; in fact, what beef has in its favor is flavor. For the customer who wants the taste of well-marbled, aged steaks, the traditional cuts are available at most fine restaurants. These range in size from a dainty 3-ounce portion to a Texas-sized 16-ounce steak. Leaner cuts such as top round and flank steak are also in demand.

The reduction in beef consumption can be traced to worries about levels of fat and cholesterol. The beef industry, however, points out such facts as a three-ounce serving of beef has only 76 milligrams of cholesterol; half the fat is mono- or polyunsaturated; and beef is rich in protein, iron, zinc, and niacin.

A larger product line has made beef more popular; in fact, beef may be on the verge of a comeback. Growers are concentrating on breeds with a higher natural proportion of lean to fat and slaughtering cattle younger to produce leaner beef. Some growers are also resorting to dietary supplements, including beer, yams, and garlic to add more flavor to lean beef. Organically grown beef comes from cattle that have not yet been given antibiotics and whose feed is free of pesticides. Advertising "organically grown beef" on the menu is good merchandising.

The U.S. Department of Agriculture has reacted to these changes with two new designations. Beef is labeled *light* when the carcass averages 25 percent less fat or 25 percent fewer calories than standard beef, and *natural* when it is organically grown. The industry calls these products *designer beef*. Also, once on the cutting board, beef is getting a closer trim. Industry surveys show that when customers demand lean beef, they mean the near absence of external fat. Thus, many restaurants are demanding that beef fat be limited to one-quarter inch. Doing away with the fat on cuts such as strip steak also pleases customers.

Restaurants featuring beef also are becoming careful about the beef they buy and are choosing the beef that is right for their customers. For example, Morton's, a steak house based in Chicago, selects and ages prime cuts in Chicago and then ships them to its restaurants in other cities. Another restaurant group gets its beef from only grain-fed animals. Precut, low-grade beef that is loaded with chemicals is not for the customers of this restaurant group.

Restaurants are now promoting specially chosen beef. The menu of the Embassy Suites Hotel O'Hare in Rosemont, Illinois, proudly points out that it serves only certified Angus beef. The servers are trained to explain this designation to customers. Also, during the cocktail hour, a chef carves a steak in the lounge and serves the pieces as complimentary appetizers to customers, who are then encouraged to make dinner reservations in the restaurant. This Black Angus program is also featured in the room service menus.

The Harris Ranch restaurant in Coalinga, California, has an effective method of promoting beef. They do it "up front" in the glass cases of the restaurant's retail meat market. The restaurant's brochures explain the nutritional value of the beef offered to customers. Besides featuring individual brands of beef, restaurants are also describing their steaks as "dry aged for 21 days" or "biologically farmed."

The Omni International Hotel's Rotisserie in St. Louis serves beef in the form of prime ribs and other tender cuts, cooked on an elaborate French rotisserie. Butler's Restaurant in Mill Valley, California, serves an antipasto misto that combines rare, thinly-sliced beef with shiitake mushrooms, celery root and caper salad, and a marinated crookneck squash salad. Another entrée is soft tacos with grilled skirt steak, black beans, guacamole, and salsa.

A new item at Jackies in Chicago is a fillet-of-beef cassoulet. It contains grilled beef strips with exotic mushrooms, green peppercorn sauce, and chunks of red, green, and yellow peppers. Another different beef menu item is beef for breakfast in the form of paper-thin slices of beef with melon, which makes both a nutritious and an interesting breakfast.

Much beef comes from the West, and beef is the favorite food of many Westerners. So it is not surprising that a restaurant in Frontier Town, fifteen miles west of Helena, Montana, specializes in beef. The principal offerings are the Squaw (an 8-ounce filet mignon) and the Cowboy (a 16-ounce New York steak served with Belgian candied carrots, saffron rice, and cowboy beans mixed with brown sugar, mustard, ketchup, and ham base). The price is $12.95 each.

The star attraction of this restaurant, however, is its Cow Camp Buffet, featuring a 40-pound baron of beef. During the season the restaurant prepares 8.2 tons of baron of beef, of which 4.6 tons is served during the three-month summer period.

The restaurant, built forty years ago, is located on twenty steep acres high atop the eastern slope of the Continental Divide. Open from April 1 to October 31, it does 60 percent of its annual $300,000 business during June, July, and August. More than half of its customers are local, from a population of fifty thousand within a 20-mile radius. During the peak months the restaurant averages two hundred dinners a night. The food costs run just above 38 percent, labor is 26 percent, and overhead is 27 percent. The profit has been a steady 9 percent.

No restaurant need be ashamed of serving meat. Since the time that people lived by hunting to the era of the astronauts, meat has been a favorite food. It is highly nutritious and can contribute to a healthy diet, and it can be described and sold as such on the menu. An average 3.5-ounce (100-gram) serving supplies 52 percent of the daily protein requirements of the average adult male, a substantial amount of vitamins, 31 percent of the thiamine requirements, 26 percent of the niacin RDA, 22 percent of the riboflavin RDA, 36 percent of the iron RDA, and significant amounts of additional minerals. Lean meat is also low in calories.

Beef, veal, and lamb are graded from Prime, the highest grade, to Canner or Cull, the lowest grade. There also are federal grades for pork, but they are not widely used. The government's grades for beef, veal, lamb, and pork are shown in Table 10.1.

If your restaurant serves Prime aged steak, it is important to say so on the menu. Don't just list your steaks; sell them with informative copy. Expensive items deserve top billing on any restaurant menu.

Most restaurants list steaks on their menu, but in too many cases it is only a listing. The assumption is probably that everybody knows what a steak is, so why describe it? This, however, is not the case. There are many kinds and grades of steaks. These two factors alone call for an explanation, and when they are combined with the steak's size, weight, and type of preparation, there is plenty to talk about. The following is "steak copy" that can be used by any restaurant to increase its steak business, which, considering prices, is an important part of any restaurant.

Steak Descriptions

1. *Porterhouse.* Considered by some to be the finest, greatest steak of all, it is a combination of two steaks in one divided by the bone, a fillet and a strip steak.
2. *Filet Mignon.* The tenderest steak of all; it cuts like butter and melts in your mouth! Selected from heavy U.S. Choice tenderloins; selection, aging, and trimming make this steak especially flavorful.
3. *T-Bone.* The steak that is almost two steaks in one: a U.S. Prime center-cut strip plus a small fillet.
4. *Tenderloin.* A large cut of U.S. Choice tenderloin with a slight trace of sweet fat for flavor makes this choice cut an all-time favorite.
5. *Bone-in-Strip.* Sometimes called Kansas City sirloin, this is the same strip as the sirloin, tender, flavorful, and succulent. The bone, however, is not trimmed away. Broiling with the bone in helps retain flavor and juice.
6. *Strip Sirloin.* Often called New York strip or New York sirloin, this is a tender fillet. The sweet, prime fat on the sides of this cut should be eaten with the meat to make it even tastier.
7. *Butterfly Fillet.* This is the same piece of U.S. Choice as filet mignon but sliced lengthwise before cooking. The chef suggests this steak for those who order steaks medium well to well done.
8. *Tip Butt Sirloin.* A solid, generous cut of top U.S. Prime beef that is easy on the budget and will satisfy the biggest appetite. Also called Club or Chef's Special, this steak has the taste of Prime beef.
9. *Chateaubriand.* The royalty of steak, prepared and served for two or more, the chateaubriand is a king-sized cut of tenderloin broiled, with the grain running horizontally. This produces a succulent, crisp, tender crust with a warm pink center. The chateaubriand is an "occasion" steak that should be sliced across the grain, served with a good wine, and enjoyed with good company.
10. *Chopped Steak.* A tasty meat using only U.S. Choice and Prime beef.

Although steak descriptions are probably the most important words on your steak menu, how your customers like their steak is also important. In order that everyone follows the same definitions, we recommend that you print the descriptions in the adjoining column and also tell your guests what grade you serve.

How Do You Like Your Steak?

1. *Rare.* Brown, seared crust with a cool red center.
2. *Medium Rare.* Brown, seared crust, steak warmed through with a warm red center.
3. *Medium.* Outside of steak is well done, dark brown with a hot pink center.
4. *Medium Well.* Outside is dark brown, inside is done through; steak has little juice left.
5. *Well Done.* Outside is black-brown, inside is dried out.

MEAT MENU COPY

The Manor Restaurant in West Orange, New Jersey, has a very fine meat entrée selection which is described in a few well-chosen words:

TWIN LAMB CHOPS

Two double chops from prime lamb seared on the outside, juicy tender inside.

DOUBLE PRIME BLUE RIBBON SIRLOIN STEAK

A specially selected and aged double steak broiled to luscious perfection and supreme flavor. Served with a bouquet of vegetables.

CHATEAUBRIAND BOUQUETIÈRE

The ultimate in superior steaks, thick and generous. This rich prime tenderloin is recognized the world over as an epicurean masterpiece, lovingly surrounded by a dazzling necklace of garden-fresh vegetables.

TABLE 10.1 U.S. Government Grades of Meat

USDA Beef	USDA Veal	USDA Lamb	Pork
USDA Prime	USDA Prime	USDA Prime	U.S. No. 1
USDA Choice	USDA Choice	USDA Choice	U.S. No. 2
USDA Good	USDA Good	USDA Good	U.S. No. 3
USDA Standard	USDA Standard	USDA Utility	U.S. No. 4
USDA Commercial	USDA Utility	USDA Cull	Utility
USDA Utility	USDA Cull		
USDA Cutter			
USDA Canner			

Source: USDA.

RACK OF LAMB PERSILLE

The whole rack of baby lamb is broiled, encrusted with parsley, garlic, and breadcrumbs, and then baked. A gourmet's dream.

MEDALLIONS OF VEAL OSKAR

Medallions of veal Oskar, tender veal cutlet, artichoke bottoms, and king crab legs glazed with a delicate bearnaise sauce.

FILET DE BOEUF À LA WELLINGTON

(Filet of Beef Wellington.) Individual filet mignon covered with mushrooms duxelles and then enveloped in puff pastry and baked.

FILET MIGNON AU CHAMPIGNONS

Extratender heart of beef with all the savory juices sealed in.

PETIT FILET MIGNON

Dainty prime filet mignon—a favorite with the ladies.

GOURMET SLICES OF PRIME BEEF TENDERLOIN

Generous slices of tenderloin, sautéed in butter and served with a sauce made with a delicate Madeira wine, shallots, and mushrooms.

THE BEEFEATER'S DELIGHT

The monarch of sirloin steak designed for the robust appetite.

SIRLOIN STEAK MAÎTRE D'HÔTEL

A splendid sirloin beautifully broiled to your taste. Served with herb butter.

MINUTE STEAK MAÎTRE D'HÔTEL

A smaller steak for those with a light appetite. Served with herb butter.

PRIME RIB OF BEEF AU JUS

A thick slice of carefully aged and roasted prime rib. Served with its own natural juice.

POULTRY

Poultry includes chicken, turkey, duck, and goose. The categories of chicken are rock Cornish hen—not over 2 pounds; broiler/fryer—¾ to 3½ pounds; roaster—2½ to over 5 pounds; capon—4 to 8 pounds; and stewing chicken—2½ to over 5 pounds. The categories of turkey are fryer or roaster—4 to 8 pounds; young turkey—8 to over 24 pounds; and mature turkey—8 to over 24 pounds. Ducks are classified as broiler or fryer duckling—3 to over 5 pounds; roaster duckling—3 to over 5 pounds; and mature duck—3 to over 5 pounds.

Chicken and turkey are the two most popular items on the menu. The forms they can take include roast turkey, fried chicken, turkey breast, chicken tenders, turkey slices, chicken nuggets, chicken patties, and roast chicken.

Chicken is big business. According to the *Restaurants & Institutions* "400" issue, in the fast-food category, Kentucky Fried Chicken has 7,761 units and annual sales of over $5 billion. And the number-two chicken chain, Church's Fried Chicken, has 1,422 units and annual sales of $534 million. Despite the trend toward low-fat foods, fried chicken continues to be very popular. Chicken nuggets and tenders were introduced by the fast-food chains, but these items and chicken patties are now appearing all over the country.

Other poultry dishes such as chicken Kiev, turkey or chicken Parmigiana, duck, and rock Cornish hen are also found on many menus. Light and healthful, chicken and turkey appear in many salads and sandwiches, and chicken *cordon bleu* is no longer just for expensive French or continental restaurants.

Clucker's

The fast-food chicken outlets have been around for a long time, but a sit-down restaurant featuring only chicken is something new. The first Clucker's Restaurant was opened in Chicago in 1984, and a second

R.D. Clucker's
IN WHEELING

Clucker's Breakfast

Saturday & Sunday opened to 2:30 p.m.

French French Toast 4.25
Croissant dipped in an orange batter, topped with fresh strawberries and pecans with warm syrup

The Natural 3.95
Buttermilk pancakes in a healthy combination of grains and nuts

Pumpkin Waffle 4.50
A Clucker's original, topped with raisins, pumpkin seeds, sour cream and honey

Lox Platter 6.50
All of the fixings, bagel, lox, tomato, onions, cucumber and cream cheese

Omelettes

All of our omelettes are made with 3 large fresh eggs

The Veggie 4.95
Fresh seasonal vegetables

Goldie Lox 5.50
With sauteed onions and lox

Three Cheese 4.50
Monterey Jack, cheddar and swiss gruyere

The Works 6.25
Sausage, onion and cheese

Apple Omelette 4.75
Fresh apples and apple butter

Chorizo Omelette 5.95
Mexican hot spicy sausage and green salsa with Monterey Jack cheese

Eggs-Traordinary

Chicken Benedict 6.95
Two poached eggs served with fresh grilled boneless breast of chicken on english muffin, topped with hollandaise

Chicken Bialy 6.95
Two poached eggs and chicken hash on toasted bialy bagel served open face with hollandaise

Moo & Peep 8.25
8 oz. Grilled skirt steak served with eggs, your way

Chicken Hash 6.95
Combination of red and green peppers, chicken pieces and potatoes topped with two poached eggs and melted cheese

Egg-Ceptional 5.75
Layers of country potatoes, fresh diced vegetables and melted cheese, topped with two basted eggs

Eggs Ole 6.95
Two flour tortillas filled with a combination of scrambled eggs, sausage and avocado. Topped with melted Monterey Jack cheese, sour cream and salsa on the side

Above items served with choice of: Country style potatoes or apple pan dowdy and croissant, fresh muffin or bagel. All egg dishes available with egg beaters.

Extra Touches

Fresh Squeezed Juices 1.25
Orange, grapefruit, apple,
Potatoes 1.25
Oatmeal 1.50
Fried Matzo 2.75
Croissant 1.25
Muffin or Bagel 1.25

Bacon 1.75
Sausage 1.75
Fresh Berries with Cream 1.50
Extra Egg .... .95
Cream Cheese .... .75
Additional Omelette Ingredients .... .50

Appetizers & Soups

Redfish Beignets 3.75
Redfish marinated in cajun heat and deep fried, served with remoulade sauce

Chicken Beignets 3.50
Redfishes' cousin!!
Try a Combo of Both 3.95

Chicken Cluster 3.95
Strips of chicken and vegetables marinated in oriental seasonings. Fried in a light tempura butter, served with honey apricot sauce

Skewered Chicken 3.50
Marinated and grilled, served with a zesty peanut sauce

Eggplant Caviar 1.95
Our Signature!

Peasant Picnic 3.95
Baked brie cheese topped with apricot butter, toasted almonds, served with fresh fruit
With Soup & Loaf of Bread 5.95

Chicken Matzo Ball Soup .... Cup 1.50 Bowl 2.25

Soup of the Day .... Cup 1.50 Bowl 2.25

Gumbo Ya Ya .... Cup 1.75 Bowl 2.75
A New Orleans tradition. A mix of chicken, andouille sausage in a rich gumbo stock.

Chicken Chili .... Cup 1.75
Soon to be famous! .... Bowl 2.50

Clucker's Taster 2.75
A mini portion of your favorite 3 soups

Entrees

Chicken Luncheons .... 1/4 6.95 1/2 7.95 Whole 10.95
Clucker's chicken originates from the southwestern style of outdoor charbroiled chicken. We start only with the freshest, plumpest chicken available. Our chicken is slowly marinated in our special recipe of fresh fruit juices and zesty herbs. Then charbroiled over open flames while you watch.

Clucker's Style
honey, chutney, curry sauce

Cancun Style
If you like it hot!
Served with salsa

Jerk
Jamaican style -hot-hot!

Italian Style
fresh pesto

Bar-B-Que
brushed with our own chunky sauce

Peasant Chicken 6.75
A half chicken, fresh vegetable and matzo balls cooked in a rich chicken broth. Whipped horseradish sauce accompanies, with house salad

Herb Chicken 6.25
Skinless, salt free, boneless breast marinated in lemon, basil, and other fresh herbs. Served with steamed vegetables.

Boneless Chicken Breast 6.25
Grilled in a choice of 3 mustards or fresh herbs. With julienne of fresh veggies

Blackened Chicken Breast 6.50
Creole style boneless chicken brushed with Cajun seasoning and charred in a cast iron skillet with traditional red beans and rice & julienne of fresh veggies. We suggest mustard or BBQ sauce

Cajun Crispy 6.50
Boneless breast marinated in Cajun heat, rolled in Creole flour and pan fried, served with homemade mashed potatoes & gravy & julienne of fresh veggies

Chicken Fajitas .... For One 6.95 For Two 9.95
Strips of boneless breast of chicken, sauteed, fresh vegetables seasoned in garlic and fresh herbs, served on a sizzling skillet. Accompanied with flour tortillas, garnished with all the fixins'

Chopped Steak 6.95
Fresh ground chuck filled with mushrooms, onions and seasonings, Served with homemade mashed potatoes

Blackened Fish .... Market Price
Prepared from market fresh fish, brushed with Cajun seasonings and charred in a cast iron skillet with traditional red beans and rice & julienne of fresh veggies

Catch of the Day .... Market Price
Prepared from market fresh fish

All of the above entrees served with our house salad, country style potato, shoestring potatoes, or red beans and rice

Salads

Smoked Chicken 5.75
A unique combination of fruits, curry and vegetables served in a fresh pineapple

2350 .... 6.25
Rows of smoked chicken, bacon, tomatoes, chopped egg, avocado, scallions and swiss gruyere on a bed of mixed greens, sweet sour poppy seed dressing

Cashew Chicken 6.25
Boneless breast pieces of chicken and fresh vegetables steeped in a sesame soy broth. Served on a bed of a cellophane noodles. Topped with cashews

Chinese Chicken 6.25
Mixed greens tossed with mushrooms, water chestnuts, scallions, red peppers, celery, mandarin oranges, topped with chow mein noodles, almonds, Clucker's chicken, served with Oriental dressing

Pasta Tuna Salad 5.95
White tuna, chopped egg, mayonnaise tossed in a fresh tricolor pasta. Garnished with lemon wheels

All salads served with fresh baked carrot cake.

Sandwiches

Clucker Salad 4.95
Our original house salad. A melange of fresh vegetables

Crispy Sandwich 5.95
Boneless breast marinated in Cajun heat, rolled in flour with Creole seasoning, pan fried, served with remoulade sauce on a homemade sesame seed bun. Topped with cheddar cheese

Clucker Burger 4.95
For the health conscious, ground turkey, shredded zucchini, carrots and scallions with our own BBQ sauce. Topped with choice of cheese

R.D. Burger 4.95
The burger with green peppers, onions and Cajun heat, choice of cheese: cheddar, swiss, gruyere or monterey jack. Available without heat

Grilled Chicken Breast 5.25
Grilled boneless breast of chicken broiled with a lemon and fresh herbs, served with dill mayo sauce

Clucker Club 5.50
Smoked chicken breast, gruyere cheese, bacon, lettuce, tomato and remoulade sauce on a croissant

Blackened Chix 5.95
Creole style: lettuce, tomato and remoulade sauce on a homemade bun

SANDWICHES SERVED WITH FRENCH FRIED SHOESTRING POTATOES

SOUP & SALAD
Choose from a smaller version of any salads-Chicken, Tuna, Cashew 2350, Chinese or Clucker's-and a cup of our homemade soup
5.95

OMELETTE OF THE DAY
Served with potatoes and fresh baked carrot cake
(Available with egg beaters)
5.50

FARMER'S PIZZA
Homemade parmesan crust layered with onion, mushrooms, tomatoes, artichokes, topped with goat and gruyere cheese
5.95

The Final Touch

Custard Bar .... With Entree 2.25 Without 3.25
A selection of two flavors of custard and many kinds of candies and a special selection of fruit

Homemade Cheese Cake 2.50
Brownie 1.50
A La Mode 2.75
Louisiana Bread Pudding 2.95
Fresh Fruit Plate 2.50
Chocolate Chickory Cake 3.50
Carrot Cake 2.50

With respect to the comfort of others, cigar and pipe smoking is limited to the lounge
Plate sharing charge on entrees - 1.50

FIGURE 10.1 Menu from Cluckers, where chicken is in. (Reproduced by permission.)

restaurant was opened in Wheeling, Illinois, a suburb of Chicago, in 1988 (Figure 10.1). Both restaurants are very successful, with people waiting in line up to two hours on weekends.

The menu measures 11 by 11 inches and opens up vertically to 11 by 22 inches. It is printed in dark green type on heavy, cream-colored stock that is plastic coated for long wear. The listing begins with Appetizers and Soups. The first item is Redfish Beignets, followed by Chicken Beignets, Chicken Cluster, Skewered Chicken, Eggplant Caviar, and Peasant Picnic (Soup and a Loaf of Bread), all $5.95.

There is a Chicken Matzo Ball Soup and Gumbo Ya Ya (a New Orleans tradition, a mix of chicken and andouille sausage in a rich gumbo sauce). Then there is Chicken Chili and Clucker's Taster (a tiny portion of three soups). The appetizers range in price from $1.95 to $3.95, the soups, from $1.50 a cup to $2.25 and $2.75 a bowl.

The entrées begin with Chicken Luncheons, offered as a quarter, a half, or a whole chicken. This entrée is broiled and marinated, and served in one of five different styles—Clucker's style with honey, chutney, and curry sauce; Italian with fresh pesto; Cajun served with salsa; Bar-B-Que; and Jamaican style, hot! The other entrées are Peasant Chicken, Herb Chicken, Boneless Chicken Breast, Blackened Chicken Breast, Cajun Crispy, Chicken Fajitas, Chopped Steak, Blackened Fish, and Catch of the Day. The average price of these entrées is $7.20.

The five entrée salads are Smoked Chicken, 2350 (rows of smoked chicken, bacon, tomatoes, chopped egg, avocado, scallions, and Swiss Gruyère on a bed of mixed greens with sweet-sour poppy seed dressing), Cashew Chicken, Chinese Chicken, and Pasta Tuna Salad. The prices range from $5.75 to $6.25.

There are seven sandwiches: Chicken Salad, Crispy Sandwich, Clucker Burger (ground turkey plus vegetables), R. D. Burger, Grilled Chicken Breast, Clucker Club, and Blackened Chix. Prices range from $4.95 to $5.95.

In three boxes at the bottom of this side of the menu are three specials: Soup & Salad, Omelette of the Day, and Farmer's Pizza, for $5.95, $5.50, and $5.95.

The dessert listing at the bottom, headed The Final Touch, offers Custard Bar—two flavors of custard plus candies and fruit, Homemade Cheese Cake, Brownie à la Mode, Louisiana Bread Pudding, Fresh Fruit Plate, Chocolate Chickory Cake, and Carrot Cake. Prices range from $2.50 to $3.50.

The back of this menu describes a Clucker's Breakfast—pancakes, French toast, waffles, and a lox platter plus six omelettes, six egg entrées, and twelve extra touches (side orders).

11

Seafood

Seafood is now one of the most popular—if not the most popular—entrées on the restaurant menu. There are several reasons for this trend. First, seafood of all kinds—shellfish and saltwater as well as freshwater fish—is now available both fresh and frozen from around the world. Fresh fish can be flown from nearly every part of the globe to distribution centers in the United States. Indeed, the cargo bay of a jet flying at forty thousand feet becomes a natural freezer. The techniques of freezing and storing seafood have also made a wide variety of fish and crustaceans available. Another reason for the popularity of seafood is that nutritionists have discovered that fish and shellfish promote good health in a variety of ways. Finally, seafood has become popular because chefs in the better restaurants have learned how to prepare seafood in many new, interesting, and tasty ways.

GROWING POPULARITY

Today the annual consumption of seafood in the United States is around fifteen pounds per person. Seven years ago it was around twelve pounds per person. A major seafood supplier in Chicago, the Chicago Fish House, supplies seventy million pounds of seafood annually to its customers in various parts of the country. Of this seventy million pounds, 80 percent goes to restaurants. Fifty percent of the amount supplied is fresh, and 50 percent is frozen.

The seafood most consumed today is canned tuna: All those tiny cans on supermarket shelves add up. Fresh tuna, however, is becoming a common restaurant item. The second most popular seafood item is shrimp, and the third most popular is salmon, both fresh and canned Pacific salmon—king, sockeye, silver, and pink. Because Pacific Northwest salmon is seasonal, Atlantic salmon from Norway is imported to the United States.

Fish and shellfish are imported from the Scandinavian countries, the Mediterranean, other European countries, Asia, Africa, Australia, and New Zealand. The west and east coasts of America, the Gulf of Mexico, Alaska, and Hawaii help keep the tables supplied. Freshwater fish such as Lake Superior whitefish and coho salmon are popular not just in the Midwest but around the country.

Seafood and freshwater fish are also raised on fish farms. Shrimp is raised in farms, although not in the United States. A popular farm-raised fish is striped bass, a cross between striped sea bass and freshwater white bass. According to Nancy Abrams at the Chicago Fish House, Chicago restaurants use over one thousand pounds a week and would sell more if they could get it. Salmon is farmed in Oregon, Washington, Maine, and Alaska, and restaurants cannot keep up with the demand for farm-raised catfish.

One kind of fish—like redfish—can become so popular that the government must restrict catches of it. The availability of fish means that new seafood often appears on the menu. For example, calamari (squid) has recently become popular, though octopus and eel, which are favored in Europe and Asia, are not as well liked in America. Much seafood is seasonal, so that a fixed menu sometimes becomes difficult, but a "catch of the day" listing solves that problem.

Much can be said on the menu about the seafood served. One feature is its nutritional value. According to Nancy Abrams at the Chicago Fish House, research in the United States and other countries indicates that fish is extraordinarily healthful. The omega-3 fatty acids indigenous to fish, shellfish, and marine mammals appear to have a direct positive effect on health, especially in relation to the heart, blood, arteries, and cholesterol levels. There is also strong evidence that the omega-3 fatty acids contained in seafood oils are capable of lowering low-density lipoproteins (LDLs), which are believed to contribute to the onset of atherosclerosis. At the same time, omega-3 fatty acids apparently raise the high-density lipoproteins (HDLs) that help move cholesterol out of the system.

When cholesterol is evaluated today, it is the ratio of HDLs to total cholesterol that is relevant, as well as the total cholesterol count. It also appears that omega-3 fatty acids contribute to the thinning of the blood, aiding in the prevention of heart attacks and strokes caused by blood clots. In addition, research on the effects of omega-3 fatty acids continues in the areas of breast and prostate cancers, multiple sclerosis, asthma, certain forms of arthritis, and inflammations.

Additional health news is related to shellfish—mollusks, oysters, clams, and mussels. Originally the sterols (fatty substances) in mollusks were erroneously identified as primarily cholesterol, and heart patients and those on cholesterol-restricted diets were warned to minimize their consumption of mollusks or do without them altogether. It now has been confirmed that only about 35 percent of the original sterols designated as cholesterol are indeed cholesterol; the remaining sterols are vegetable sterols.

Shrimp, lobster, and crab are still being evaluated. It is currently believed that the cholesterol content of these shellfish is at most moderate. They are definitely very low in fat content and seem to be high in omega-3 fatty acids for the amount of fat they do contain. Moreover, shellfish contain a very high proportion of HDLs, the beneficial part of cholesterol. The picture, therefore, is bright for the healthful benefits of consuming shellfish, which also contain very large amounts of certain vitamins and minerals.

Thus far the consumption of fish-oil capsules in place of eating fish is not recommended except when dangerously high triglyceride levels are involved, according to Dr. William Castelli, director of the Framingham, Massachusetts, Heart Study, and then only under the supervision of a doctor. The Framingham program is the longest ongoing heart study in the world.

Table 11.1 shows the content of calories, omega-3, and cholesterol in various species of finfish and shellfish. The information, which is provided by the Chicago Fish House, is based on averages; even the same species of fish varies in all categories, depending on variables such as the season in which the fish was caught. You can use this data in developing menu descriptions of seafood.

Menu Strategy

In describing seafood on a menu, a long nutritional dissertation is neither required nor possible in the space available, but some mention of the benefits of seafood is in order. The cholesterol, omega-3, and calorie content can be listed in a few words. In addition, the following information should be listed for each seafood entrée:

1. Where the fish or shellfish comes from.
2. If it is fresh or frozen.
3. If it is fresh, indicate whether it was caught locally, or if it comes from a long distance and was flown in.
4. The preparation (fried, broiled, poached, baked) and the special ingredients (sauces, spices) used.

The following descriptions of seafood entrées can be used as guides.

LOBSTER THERMIDOR (IN SHELL)

Chunks of lobster meat sautéed in butter, blended in our own sherry and egg sauce, replaced in the original shell, sprinkled with Parmesan cheese, and baked.

LOBSTER SALAD

A large epicurean delight. Enticing flavor with just the right spice and herb combination. Coleslaw and crisp lettuce served with this gourmet treat.

BROILED SWORDFISH STEAK

A tender fillet of a fish found only in the waters of James Michener's South Pacific, served with drawn butter.

COLUMBIA RIVER SALMON

Only hours ago this fish was swimming in the Columbia River. Fresh, firm, delicate pink, and broiled to your taste. Only in the Pacific Northwest do you find this world-famous fish. Find out why salmon is king.

SHRIMP

Nobody prepares shrimp the way we prepare shrimp . . . let us introduce you.

DEEP-SEA SCALLOPS

Tiny, succulent balls of white meat, these scallops are like abalone, only more tender.

CRAB AU GRATIN

An interesting blend of mushrooms, delicate crabmeat, and cheddar cheese sauce that becomes ambrosia in the deft hands of our chef.

SEAFOOD PLATTER

If you'd like a little of everything listed under seafood, this is it! Shrimp, oysters, scallops, and crab legs.

JUMBO CRAB LEGS

All of our crab legs are large, but some are even larger than that! These we save to deep-fry for you, sealing in that distinctive flavor.

SHRIMP POLYNESIAN

Fresh, succulent shrimp marinated with exotic South Pacific spices and sauces. Broiled on a skewer with pineapple and bacon.

WHOLE ATLANTIC FLOUNDER

We flounder to find the right words to describe this fish feast. Perfectly seasoned and gently pampered and broiled in pure creamery butter.

TABLE 11.1 Calories, Fatty Acids, and Cholesterol in Seafood

Finfish Species per 100 gms. (3½ oz.)	Calories kcal.	Omega-3 Fatty Acids gm.	Cholesterol mg.
Bass, Striped Sea	94	.7	80
Catfish, Freshwater	115	.2	52
Cod	75	.2	42
Eel, American	223	1.2	10
Flounder	90	.3	50
Grouper	95	.3	49
Haddock	83	.2	58
Hake	87	.4	N/A
Halibut, Atlantic	115	1.3	47
Halibut, Pacific	105	.5	32
Herring, Atlantic	128	1.6	89
Herring, Pacific	100	1.7	96
Mackerel, Atlantic	176	2.5	80
Mackeral, Pacific	129	1.1	52
Mahi Mahi	89	N/A	86
Monkfish	80	N/A	35
Orange Roughy	76	0	N/A
Perch, Lake	86	.2	90
Perch, Ocean	105	.4	N/A
Pike, Northern	87	.1	49
Pollock	90	.4	N/A
Pompano	165	N/A	50
Rockfish	78	.6	42
Sablefish, Black Cod	184	1.3	49
Salmon, Atlantic	129	1.4	60
Salmon, Chinook (King)	184	1.9	N/A
Salmon, Chum	125	.6	74
Salmon, Coho (Silver)	136	1.8	N/A
Salmon, Pink	124	2.2	N/A
Salmon, Sockeye	137	2.7	35
Sea Trout	106	.5	N/A
Shark	167	1.9	46
Smelt	98	.6	70
Snapper, Red	110	.6	40
Sole	88	.1	43
Swordfish	122	.9	48
Trout, Brook	108	.3	68
Trout, Rainbow	131	1.1	56
Trout, Lake	162	1.4	36
Tuna, Albacore	172	2.1	38
Tuna, Bluefin	158	1.5	38
Tuna, Yellowfin	124	.6	45
Turbot, Greenland	147	.6	N/A
Walleye Pike	N/A	.2	34
Whitefish, Lake	162	.8	48

Shellfish Species per 100 gms. (3½ oz.)	Calories kcal.	Omega-3 Fatty Acids gm.	Cholesterol mg.
Abalone	N/A	.04	111
Clams, Softshell	62	.24	25
Clams, Hardshell	54	.24	40
Mussels, Atlantic	80	.43	63
Octopus	77	.21	122
Oysters, American	74	.51	56
Oysters, French	79	.24	N/A
Periwinkles	115	.44	N/A
Scallops, Sea	87	.18	36
Scallops, Bay or Cape	80	.13	N/A
Squid	95	.8	260
Crab, Blue or Soft	81	N/A	76
Crab, Dungeness	87	.38	N/A
Crab, Jonah	95	N/A	78
Crab, King	74	N/A	60
Crab, Snow	90	.44	N/A
Lobster, Boiled Live Maine	93	.06	72
Lobster Tails Cooked	100	.27	106
Shrimp, Mixed Species	91	.20	120

We gratefully acknowledge Seafood Nutrition (Osprey Books, 1985)—by Joyce A. Nettleton, D.Sc., R.D.—for much of the information in these charts

Source: The Chicago Fish House. (Reproduced by permission.)

OLD-FASHIONED SHORE DINNER

The works: choice of Maine chowder or lobster stew, crackers and pickles, steamed clams, bouillon, and drawn butter. Then fried clams, hot boiled lobster, chef's salad, french-fried potatoes, rolls, old-fashioned Indian pudding with whipped cream, and coffee. An adventure in good eating.

SWORDFISH STEAK

A flavored, flavorful treat from the sea. A boneless fish steak skillfully broiled to the peak of perfection and served with drawn butter and tartar sauce.

JUMBO LOBSTER LUMPS

Tender, tasty lumps of lobster meat prepared in a casserole with pure creamery butter. A delectable, palate-pleasing treat for those who like lobster but dislike the mess.

FILLET OF PERCH

From off the shores of New England. Breaded, broiled, and seasoned with tender loving care by our chefs, this is a real fish delicacy.

FROGS' LEGS

This delicacy is marinated lightly in chablis and sautéed in butter (garlic if you want it). This specialty has attracted gourmets to this restaurant from all over the country.

FRESH CATFISH

From the Missouri River, fresh catfish fried the Dixie way and served with potatoes, coleslaw, and hot hush puppies.

RAINBOW TROUT

Shipped to us daily from the cold, clear waters of nearby Ozark streams and cooked Ozark style.

LOBSTER NEWBURG

Our chef delights in cooking this delicacy to your taste: choice pieces of lobster sautéed in butter with cognac and Madeira wine and cream. Served on a bed of rice.

BOUILLABAISSE

Neptune's harvest in the form of a special fish soup consisting of fresh lobster meat, scallops, fillet of sole, shrimp (and any other good seafood that's handy) baked in a casserole with brandy.

CRABMEAT SAUTÉ ROYALE

No rich sauce, no abundance of seasoning to overpower the delicate flavor of the crabmeat. We sauté in butter only the backfin lump and added just enough zest to make this a gourmet's delight. Served with seafood pilaff rice.

RED SNAPPER STEAK PONTCHARTRAIN

One of our true seafood delicacies is this fine preparation. Fillet of red snapper sautéed in brown butter and topped with fresh crabmeat, shrimp, and lobster.

It also is good merchandising to suggest a wine to go with each seafood entrée. The standard rule is that one drinks white wine with fish and shellfish—white wine with white meat. But not all fish is white; some is red, and more and more gourmet diners are ordering red wines with their seafood entrées.

Although air transport and modern freezing techniques have made it possible for fish suppliers to guarantee a steady supply of seafood, not all finfish and shellfish are in season all year round. Oysters are a good example. To help you plan your menu, Table 11.2 is reprinted here, courtesy of the Chicago Fish House.

Some restaurants list their seafood together with their other entrées. Others have a separate seafood listing or break it down even further into two categories, fish and shellfish. Some restaurants serve only seafood. An example is Le Bernardin in New York City. It is strictly a French seafood restaurant, with only one meat dish, rack of lamb, which is always available. According to the manager, the menu stays the same, with some specials each day. In 1988, it was a *prix-fixe* menu of $40 for lunch and $65 for dinner.

SEAFOOD MENUS

Le Bernardin

Under the heading of Main Courses, Le Bernardin offers twenty-four seafood entrées (Figure 11.1). This extensive list is worth study because it shows the range of possibilities when creating a seafood listing. There is no reason to serve only cod or blackened redfish until the species become threatened. Many other fish swim in the sea. Some of the entrée examples on Le Bernardin's list are

Malelote of Monkfish with Noodles and Red Wine
Rouelle of Salmon with Fennel Julienne
Black Bass Stewed with Zucchini, Tomato, and Basil
Poached Skate with Browned Butter
Medallions of Lobster with Pasta
Lobster and Mashed Potato Pie

Other seafood listings on this menu make it out of the ordinary. Under the heading First Courses are three oyster listings, Sea Urchins, and a Selection of Raw Oysters and Shellfish. A Simply Raw listing includes Slivers of Black Bass; Pounded Tuna; Carpaccio of Tuna; Salad of Marinated Fish; Tartar of Salmon, Red Snapper, and Tuna; and Caviar-Studded Tartar of Black Bass.

Under the heading Lightly Cooked is another listing of unusual salads and other lighter items:

Salad of Poached Skate
Truffled Salad of Sea Scallops
Baked Sea Urchins
Black Bass in Coriander Bouillon
Seared Oysters with Caviar

Finally, there are three soups: Sea Urchin Soup, Clam Chowder, and Fish Soup.

Cape Cod Room

The Cape Cod Room in the Drake Hotel in the heart of Chicago and next to Lake Michigan is a much-honored seafood restaurant (Figure 11.2). It serves fresh seafood from the Atlantic and Pacific oceans as well as fish from freshwater lakes and streams and has been consistently named one of America's finest dining spots since opening in 1933. It has been a Holiday Award winner for thirty-four years. Business executives selected this restaurant as fifteenth in the nation based on a survey by *Sales and Marketing* magazine. And Zagat's consumer survey in 1987 picked the Cape Cod Room as a top hotel restaurant.

Distant harbors are evoked by the red checked tablecloths, stuffed sailfish on the walls, copper pots, exposed wooden beams, and weather vanes. The restaurant is cozy and well proportioned. At lunchtime, a master shucker opens oysters and clams by the piece or by the dozen at the oyster bar, which seats nine. The entire restaurant seats 135.

Bookbinder's red snapper soup with sherry on the side, excellent coleslaw, and wine set off classic seafood entrées. Making a choice is difficult with the many daily specials plus signature items such as Pompano en Papillote, Maryland crabcakes, six lobster dishes, five shrimp dishes, six styles of scallops, and Bouillabaisse Marseillaise.

The Cape Cod Room menu measures 13 by 11 inches. It is a horizontal menu printed in dark brown, dark green, and light tan on cream-colored stock. The cover is very heavy cover stock, uncoated, and the inside four pages are of a lighter weight cover stock, also uncoated.

TABLE 11.2 Fresh Seafood Availability Chart

Fresh Seafood Availability Chart

Lean to Fat
3 (Fat); 2 (Moderate); 1 (Lean)

Flavor
3 (Full); 2 (Moderate); 1 (Mild)

Texture
3 (Firm); 2 (Moderate); 1 (Delicate)

Availability
3 (Excellent); 2 (Good); 1 (Fair); 0 (N/A)

SPECIES	Lean To Fat	Flavor	Texture	January	February	March	April	May	June	July	August	September	October	November	December
Hawaiian															
Ahi	2	3	3	1	1	1	1	2	3	3	3	3	2	2	2
All Lepe	2	2	3	3	3	3	3	3	3	2	1	1	1	2	3
Ehu (Ula Ula)	1	2	3	2	2	2	2	1	1	1	1	2	2	2	2
Gindai	1	1	3	2	2	2	2	1	1	1	1	2	2	2	2
Hamachi	3	3	3	1	1	1	1	1	1	1	1	1	1	1	1
Hapu	3	1	3	1	1	1	1	1	3	3	3	2	2	2	1
Kajiki	2	3	3	1	1	1	2	2	3	3	3	3	2	2	2
Kaku	2	3	3	1	1	1	1	2	2	1	1	1	0	0	0
Kamanu	2	2	2	1	1	1	1	1	1	1	1	1	1	1	1
Lehi	1	1	3	2	2	2	2	1	1	1	1	2	2	2	2
Mahi Mahi	1	2	3	1	2	3	3	2	2	1	1	2	2	1	1
Onaga	1	2	3	2	2	2	2	1	1	1	1	2	2	2	2
Ono	2	2	3	1	1	1	2	3	3	3	3	3	2	1	1
Opah	2	2	3	3	3	3	3	1	1	1	1	1	1	3	3
Opakapaka	1	1	3	2	2	2	2	1	1	1	1	2	2	2	2
Papio	2	2	3	3	3	3	3	3	2	1	1	1	2	2	3
Tombo	3	3	3	1	1	1	1	2	3	3	3	3	2	2	1
Uku	1	2	3	1	1	1	2	2	2	2	2	2	2	2	1
Ulua	2	2	3	3	3	3	3	3	2	1	1	1	2	2	3
New Zealand															
Bluenose	1	1	3	3	3	3	2	2	2	2	2	3	3	3	3
Groper	1	1	3	2	2	2	2	2	3	3	3	2	2	2	2
Hoki	1	2	2	1	1	1	1	1	2	2	2	2	1	1	1
John Dory	1	1	3	3	3	3	3	2	1	1	1	2	3	3	3
Orange Roughy	1	1	2	3	3	2	2	2	2	2	2	3	3	3	3
Oreo Dory	1	1	3	3	3	2	2	2	2	2	2	3	3	3	3
Yellowtail Kingfish	1	2	3	3	3	3	3	2	1	1	1	2	3	3	3
European															
Breame	1	1	2	1	1	1	1	3	3	1	1	1	1	1	1
Brill	1	1	2	2	2	2	3	3	3	3	3	3	3	3	3
Dab	1	1	2	3	3	3	3	3	3	3	3	3	3	3	3
Eel	3	2	3	0	0	0	0	3	3	3	3	3	3	3	3
Gurnard, Red	1	1	2	2	2	3	3	3	3	3	3	3	3	3	3
John Dory	1	1	3	3	3	3	3	3	3	3	3	3	3	3	3
Mullet, Red	2	2	2	3	3	3	3	3	3	3	3	3	3	3	3
Pike, Yellow	1	1	2	3	3	3	3	0	0	0	3	3	3	3	3
Plaice	1	1	2	3	3	3	3	3	3	3	3	3	3	3	3
Ray	1	1	1	3	3	3	3	3	3	3	3	3	3	3	3
Salmon, farmed Norwegian	3	3	1	3	3	3	3	3	3	3	3	3	3	3	3
Salmon Trout	2	2	2	3	3	3	3	3	3	3	3	3	3	3	3
Sardines	3	3	2	3	3	3	3	3	3	3	3	3	3	3	3
Sea Bass	2	1	3	2	2	2	3	3	3	3	3	3	3	3	3
Sole, Dover	1	1	2	3	3	3	3	3	3	3	3	3	3	3	3
Sole, Lemon	1	1	1	3	3	3	3	3	3	3	3	3	3	3	3
Trout, Rainbow	2	2	2	3	3	3	3	3	3	3	3	3	3	3	3
Turbot	2	1	3	2	2	2	3	3	3	3	3	3	3	3	3
American—Ocean															
Amberjack	2	2	3	1	2	2	2	3	3	2	2	3	2	2	1
Bass, Black	2	1	3	3	3	2	2	1	1	1	1	1	1	1	2
Bass, Striped	2	1	3	1	1	2	1	1	1	1	2	2	0	0	0
Bluefish	3	3	1	3	2	2	3	3	2	2	1	2	3	2	2
Butterfish	3	2	1	2	2	2	2	3	3	3	3	3	2	2	2
Cod (Scrod)	1	1	1	2	2	2	3	3	3	3	3	2	2	2	1
Crevalle	2	2	3	1	1	2	3	2	2	2	2	3	3	0	1
Croaker	1	1	2	2	2	2	2	3	3	3	3	2	2	1	2
Drum, Red	1	2	3	1	1	1	1	1	1	1	1	1	1	1	1
Flounder	1	1	1	3	2	2	2	2	1	1	1	2	2	3	3
Grouper	1	1	3	1	1	2	3	3	3	3	3	2	2	2	2
Haddock	1	1	1	1	2	3	3	3	3	2	2	2	2	1	1
Halibut	1	1	3	2	2	2	3	3	3	2	3	3	2	2	2
Mackerel, King	3	3	2	3	3	3	2	2	1	1	2	1	1	1	3
Mackerel, Spanish	3	3	2	3	3	1	1	1	0	0	1	1	1	1	3
Monkfish	2	1	3	3	3	3	3	3	3	3	3	3	3	3	3
Mullet, Silver	3	2	2	3	1	2	2	2	1	2	2	3	2	3	2
Ocean Catfish	2	1	3	3	3	3	3	3	3	3	3	3	3	3	3
Ocean Perch	2	2	2	3	3	3	3	3	3	3	3	3	3	3	3
Pollock	1	1	1	3	3	3	2	2	2	3	3	3	3	3	3
Pompano	2	2	3	3	3	3	3	2	2	1	2	2	2	2	3
Porgy	2	1	2	3	2	3	3	2	2	2	2	2	3	3	1
Rockfish, West Coast	1	1	2	2	2	3	3	3	3	3	3	3	2	1	1
Salmon, farmed Baby Coho	3	2	2	2	2	2	2	2	2	2	2	2	2	2	2
Salmon, King	3	3	2	0	0	0	0	3	3	3	3	3	0	0	0
Salmon, Silver	3	3	3	0	0	0	0	0	0	3	3	3	0	0	0
Salmon, Sockeye	3	3	3	0	0	0	0	3	3	3	0	0	0	0	0
Salmon, Pink	2	3	3	0	0	0	0	0	3	3	2	0	0	0	0
Salmon, Chum	2	3	3	0	0	0	0	0	3	3	3	3	2	1	0
Salmon, Chilean	3	3	2	3	3	3	0	0	0	0	0	0	0	0	3
Seatrout	2	2	2	3	3	3	2	2	1	0	0	1	2	3	3
Shad	3	2	2	2	3	3	3	2	1	1	1	1	1	1	1
Shark	2	2	3	3	2	3	2	2	2	2	2	2	2	2	2
American—Ocean (cont.)															
Sheepshead	2	1	2	3	3	3	3	2	2	1	1	1	2	2	2
Skate Wing	1	1	1	3	3	3	2	1	1	1	1	1	2	3	3
Snapper	2	1	3	2	3	3	3	3	3	3	3	3	3	3	3
Sole, Grey	1	1	1	3	3	3	3	2	2	1	1	2	3	3	3
Sole, Lemon	1	1	1	3	3	3	3	2	2	1	1	2	3	3	3
Sole, Petrale	1	1	1	1	1	1	1	1	1	1	1	1	1	1	1
Sole, Rex	1	1	1	1	1	1	1	1	1	1	1	1	1	1	1
Sole, Yellowtail	1	1	1	3	3	3	3	2	2	1	1	2	3	3	3
Steelhead	2	2	3	0	0	0	0	0	1	2	3	3	2	1	0
Sturgeon	2	2	3	0	1	1	1	0	1	1	1	1	0	0	0
Swordfish	3	3	3	3	3	3	3	3	3	3	3	3	3	3	3
Tautog	1	1	3	2	2	2	1	1	1	1	1	2	1	1	1
Tilefish	1	1	3	1	1	2	2	2	2	2	2	3	3	3	3
Tuna	3	3	3	2	2	3	3	3	3	3	3	3	3	3	3
Whiting	2	2	1	1	1	1	2	2	2	3	3	3	3	3	2
American—Freshwater															
Bass, Rock	1	1	2	0	0	0	1	2	0	0	0	2	1	1	0
Bass, White	1	1	2	1	0	0	1	2	1	0	0	1	2	1	0
Buffalo	3	1	1	2	2	2	3	3	2	1	2	2	3	3	2
Bullhead	2	2	3	3	3	3	3	0	0	0	1	2	3	3	2
Catfish, farmed	2	3	3	3	3	3	3	3	3	3	3	3	3	3	3
Catfish, Channel	2	3	3	0	0	0	1	2	3	2	2	2	1	0	0
Crappie	1	1	2	0	0	0	1	1	1	0	0	1	1	0	0
Perch, White	1	1	2	0	0	1	1	1	0	0	0	1	1	0	0
Perch, Yellow	1	1	2	0	0	0	1	2	2	2	2	3	3	2	1
Pike, Northern	1	1	2	1	1	1	2	2	2	2	2	2	2	2	2
Sauger	1	2	3	1	1	1	2	2	2	1	1	2	3	2	2
Sheepshead	1	2	2	1	1	1	2	3	2	2	2	2	3	3	2
Smelt	2	2	2	0	0	2	3	3	3	3	3	3	3	3	2
Sunfish	1	1	2	0	0	0	1	2	0	0	0	2	1	0	0
Trout, farmed Brook	2	2	2	3	3	3	3	3	3	3	3	3	3	3	3
Trout, Lake	3	2	2	2	2	2	2	2	2	2	3	3	3	2	2
Walleye Pike	1	2	3	1	1	1	2	2	2	1	1	2	3	3	2
Whitefish, Canadian	2	2	2	2	2	2	1	1	1	1	3	3	3	3	3
Whitefish, Lake Superior	3	2	1	1	1	2	3	3	3	3	3	3	3	0	2
Shellfish, etc.															
Clams															
Cherrystone	1	3	3	3	3	3	3	3	3	3	3	3	3	3	3
Top Neck	1	3	3	3	3	3	3	3	3	3	3	3	3	3	3
Little Neck	1	3	3	3	3	3	3	3	3	3	3	3	3	3	3
Softshell	1	3	3	2	2	2	3	3	3	3	3	3	3	2	2
Shucked	1	3	3	3	3	3	3	3	3	3	3	3	3	3	3
Strips	1	3	3	3	3	3	3	3	3	3	3	3	3	3	3
Butter	1	3	3	2	2	3	3	3	1	1	1	2	3	3	3
Geoduck	1	3	3	1	2	3	3	2	1	1	1	2	3	3	2
Conch (in shell)	1	2	3	1	1	1	1	1	1	1	1	1	1	1	1
Crab, Live															
Blue	1	1	1	3	3	2	0	0	0	0	0	1	2	3	3
Dungeness	1	1	1	3	3	3	3	2	2	2	2	0	1	2	3
Softshell	1	1	2	0	0	0	0	1	2	3	3	2	1	0	0
Crab Meat	1	1	1	1	1	2	3	3	3	3	3	2	1	1	1
Claw	1	1	1	3	3	3	3	3	3	3	3	3	3	3	3
Special Body	1	1	1	3	3	3	3	3	3	3	3	3	3	3	3
Jumbo Lump	1	1	1	3	3	3	3	3	3	3	3	3	3	3	3
Stone Crab Claws	1	1	1	3	2	0	0	0	0	0	0	0	2	3	3
Crayfish															
Cooked, Fresh	1	1	1	3	3	3	3	3	3	0	0	0	0	3	3
Live	1	1	1	3	2	3	3	3	3	3	3	3	3	3	3
Tail Meat	1	1	1	3	3	3	3	3	3	3	3	3	3	3	3
Frog Legs, European	1	1	3	3	3	3	3	3	2	2	2	3	3	3	3
Langostinos, European	1	1	2	2	2	3	3	3	3	3	3	3	3	3	3
Lobster, Maine	1	1	2	2	2	3	3	3	3	2	2	3	3	3	3
Mussels															
Blue, farmed	1	3	1	3	3	3	3	3	3	3	3	3	3	3	3
Green Lipped, N.Z.	1	3	1	3	3	3	3	3	3	3	3	3	3	3	3
Oysters															
Belon	1	3	1	3	3	3	3	3	2	2	2	3	3	3	3
Blue Point	1	3	1	3	3	3	3	3	3	3	2	3	3	3	3
New Orleans	1	3	1	3	3	3	3	1	1	1	1	3	3	3	3
Malpeque	1	3	1	2	2	2	3	3	3	3	3	3	3	3	2
Shucked	1	3	1	3	3	3	3	3	2	2	2	2	3	3	3
Periwinkles	1	2	3	3	3	3	3	3	3	3	3	3	3	3	3
Prawns, Hawaiian	1	2	2	1	1	1	1	1	1	1	1	1	1	1	1
Scallops															
Bay	1	1	1	3	3	3	3	3	3	3	3	3	3	3	3
Cape	1	1	1	3	2	1	1	0	0	0	0	0	0	3	3
Sea	1	1	1	3	3	3	3	3	3	3	3	3	3	3	3
Sea with Roe	1	2	1	3	3	3	3	3	3	3	3	3	3	3	3
Shrimp	1	1	2	1	1	1	1	3	3	3	1	1	1	1	1
Squid, Cleaned	1	1	3	2	2	2	3	3	3	3	3	2	2	2	2

Chicago Fish House
1250 West Division Street
Chicago, Illinois 60622-4188
1 312 227-7000

Toll Free 1 800 367-9880
(In Illinois 1 800 367-9881)

FAX: 312 227-0451
TELEX: 858283

Source: The Chicago Fish House. (Reproduced by permission.)

Gilbert et Maguy Le Coze:
Suggestions according to the Market

	Suppl.		Suppl.
First Courses		**Main Courses**	
Oysters (nine pieces)		Sea Scallops with Sorrel and Tomatoes	
A Variety of Oysters (nine pieces)		Poached Halibut, Warm Vinaigrette	
Little Necks (dozen)		Halibut a La Nage	
Sea Urchins		Poached Halibut with Beurre Blanc	
A Selection of Raw Oysters and Shellfish	5.00	Matelote of Monkfish with Noodles and Red Wine	
		Roast Monkfish with Savoy Cabbage	
Simply Raw		Rouelle of Salmon with Fennel Julienne	
Slivers of Black Bass, Basil and Coriander Leaves		Escalope of Salmon with Sorrel (Troisgros)	
Pounded Tuna with Chives and Olive Oil		Thick Cut of Salmon, rare, mint and coarse salt	
Carpaccio of Tuna		Black Bass Stewed with Zucchini, Tomato and Basil	
Salad of Marinated Fish		Crisp Black Bass on Lobster Sauce, Potato-Fennel Purée	
Tartar of Salmon, Red Snapper and Tuna		Thinly Sliced Grouper Sautéed, on Melted Leeks	
Caviar-Studded Tartar of Black Bass	5.00	B—Liner with a Sauce of Mushroom, Tomato and Tarragon	
		Shrimps Sauteed with Thyme and Cracked Pepper, Eggplant Caviar	
Lightly Cooked		Sautéed Red Snapper in Basil-Perfumed Olive Oil	
Salad of Poached Skate		Filet of Pompano Sautéed with Italian Parsely	
Warm Lobster Salad	5.00	Poached Skate with Browned Butter	
Truffled Salad of Sea Scallops	5.00	Sautéed Codfish with an Herbed Red Wine Sauce, Fried Shallots	
Baked Sea Urchins in the Shell with their own butter		Pavé of of Codfish Covered with Caviar	5.00
Bay Scallops in the Shell with a Fondue of Tomato and Chives		Medallions of Lobster with Pasta	5.00
Fricassée of Shellfish		Lobster a La Nage	10.00
Broiled Louisiana Shrimp with Parsley-Shallot Butter		Broiled Lobster	10.00
Sea Scallops in a Chive Nage		Poached Lobster Napped with Basil Butter	10.00
Oysters with Truffle Cream	5.00	Lobster and Mashed Potato Pie	5.00
Black Bass in a Coriander Bouillon			
Seared Oysters with Caviar	5.00	**Upon Request**	
		Salad	7.50
Soups		Non-Seafood Entrées	
Sea Urchin Soup			
Clam Chowder		Roquefort with Glass of Vintage Port	15.00
Fish Soup			

Private rooms available Prix Fixe $65.00 *Please Refrain From Cigar and Pipe Smoking*

FIGURE 11.1 Menu of Le Bernardin. This expensive New York restaurant serves seafood with a French accent. (Reproduced by permission.)

The cover art is a line drawing of the bar in the restaurant with the dining area in the background. The drawing is in dark brown on a light tan background. The name Cape Cod Room appears in the upper right-hand corner in green.

This menu is organized differently from most seafood menus in that it has many more headings. The different varieties of fish and crustaceans are each given separate treatment.

The first insert page begins with appetizers, cold and hot. The cold appetizers include Smoked Salmon, Clams, Oysters, and Shrimp Cocktail. The hot appetizers include Shrimp De Jongh, Snails Bourguignonne, Clams Casino, and Oysters Rockefeller. The prices for these appetizers range from $6.95 to $9.75.

The three soups listed—The Cape Cod's Famous Bookbinder Red Snapper Soup with Sherry, Seafood Gumbo, and New England Clam Chowder—are $6.00 and $8.00 a bowl.

Entrées are also listed on this page, with the headings From Fresh Waters of the World, From the World's Oceans, and Bouillabaisse. All entrées are served with a selection of potatoes plus a salad of mixed greens or Cape Cod coleslaw. Three fresh fish are offered—Striped Bass, Broiled; Fillet of Pike, Sauté Amandine; and Fillet of Whitefish Tail, Broiled or Sautéed. These entrées are priced from $15.50 to $20.75.

Ten entrées appear under the heading of From the World's Oceans. Some of the more unusual items are Pompano Papillote—Fillet Enclosed in Parchment with Lobster and Mushrooms in Red Wine Sauce—$23.75; Imported Turbot, Broiled Maitre d'Hotel—market price; and Salmon in Potato Crust—$23.75.

The Bouillabaisse contains a Variety of Fresh and Salt Water Fish and Seafoods with Fresh Vegetable Garniture, Seasoned with Garlic, Parsley, Thyme, Saffron and Chablis Wine—Served with Garlic French Bread—$23.75.

The next page features Lobsters, Scallops, Crabmeat, and Shrimp. The six lobster offerings are Broiled or Steamed Whole Maine Lobster, Twin Lobster Tails, Lobster Thermidor, In Casserole with Rice à la Newburg & Light Lobster Cream Sauce Flavored with Sherry Wine, Lobster Creole, and Lobster Maryland Smothered in Butter with Shallots and Blended with White Wine in

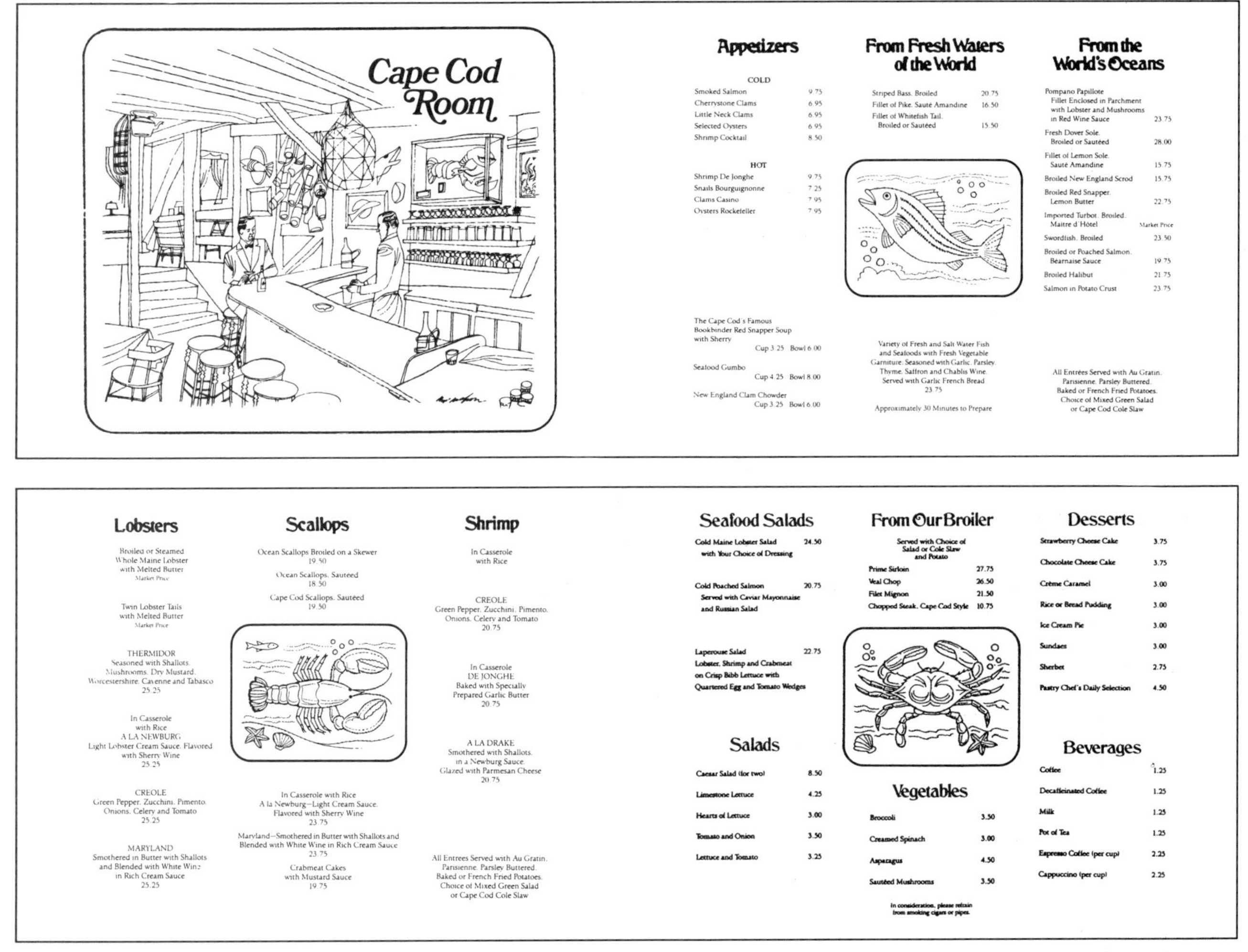

Cape Cod Room

Appetizers

COLD

Smoked Salmon 9.75
Cherrystone Clams 6.95
Little Neck Clams 6.95
Selected Oysters 6.95
Shrimp Cocktail 8.50

HOT

Shrimp De Jonghe 9.75
Snails Bourguignonne 7.25
Clams Casino 7.95
Oysters Rockefeller 7.95

The Cape Cod's Famous
Bookbinder Red Snapper Soup
with Sherry
Cup 3.25 Bowl 6.00

Seafood Gumbo
Cup 4.25 Bowl 8.00

New England Clam Chowder
Cup 3.25 Bowl 6.00

From Fresh Waters of the World

Striped Bass, Broiled 20.75
Fillet of Pike, Sauté Amandine 16.50
Fillet of Whitefish Tail,
Broiled or Sautéed 15.50

Variety of Fresh and Salt Water Fish
and Seafoods with Fresh Vegetable
Garniture; Seasoned with Garlic, Parsley,
Thyme, Saffron and Chablis Wine.
Served with Garlic French Bread
23.75

Approximately 30 Minutes to Prepare

From the World's Oceans

Pompano Papillote
Fillet Enclosed in Parchment
with Lobster and Mushrooms
in Red Wine Sauce 23.75

Fresh Dover Sole,
Broiled or Sautéed 28.00

Fillet of Lemon Sole,
Sauté Amandine 15.75

Broiled New England Scrod 15.75

Broiled Red Snapper,
Lemon Butter 22.75

Imported Turbot, Broiled,
Maitre d'Hôtel Market Price

Swordfish, Broiled 23.50

Broiled or Poached Salmon,
Béarnaise Sauce 19.75

Broiled Halibut 21.75

Salmon in Potato Crust 23.75

All Entrées Served with Au Gratin,
Parisienne, Parsley Buttered,
Baked or French Fried Potatoes.
Choice of Mixed Green Salad
or Cape Cod Cole Slaw

Lobsters

Broiled or Steamed
Whole Maine Lobster
with Melted Butter
Market Price

Twin Lobster Tails
with Melted Butter
Market Price

THERMIDOR
Seasoned with Shallots,
Mushrooms, Dry Mustard,
Worcestershire, Cayenne and Tabasco
25.25

In Casserole
with Rice
A LA NEWBURG
Light Lobster Cream Sauce, Flavored
with Sherry Wine
25.25

CREOLE
Green Pepper, Zucchini, Pimento,
Onions, Celery and Tomato
25.25

MARYLAND
Smothered in Butter with Shallots
and Blended with White Wine
in Rich Cream Sauce
25.25

Scallops

Ocean Scallops Broiled on a Skewer
19.50

Ocean Scallops, Sautéed
18.50

Cape Cod Scallops, Sautéed
19.50

In Casserole with Rice
A la Newburg—Light Cream Sauce,
Flavored with Sherry Wine
23.75

Maryland—Smothered in Butter with Shallots and
Blended with White Wine in Rich Cream Sauce
23.75

Crabmeat Cakes
with Mustard Sauce
19.75

Shrimp

In Casserole
with Rice

CREOLE
Green Pepper, Zucchini, Pimento,
Onions, Celery and Tomato
20.75

In Casserole
DE JONGHE
Baked with Specially
Prepared Garlic Butter
20.75

A LA DRAKE
Smothered with Shallots,
in a Newburg Sauce,
Glazed with Parmesan Cheese
20.75

All Entrees Served with Au Gratin,
Parisienne, Parsley Buttered,
Baked or French Fried Potatoes.
Choice of Mixed Green Salad
or Cape Cod Cole Slaw

Seafood Salads

Cold Maine Lobster Salad 24.50
with Your Choice of Dressing

Cold Poached Salmon 20.75
Served with Caviar Mayonnaise
and Russian Salad

Laperouse Salad 22.75
Lobster, Shrimp and Crabmeat
on Crisp Bibb Lettuce with
Quartered Egg and Tomato Wedges

Salads

Caesar Salad (for two) 8.50
Limestone Lettuce 4.25
Hearts of Lettuce 3.00
Tomato and Onion 3.50
Lettuce and Tomato 3.25

From Our Broiler

Served with Choice of
Salad or Cole Slaw
and Potato

Prime Sirloin 27.75
Veal Chop 26.50
Filet Mignon 21.50
Chopped Steak, Cape Cod Style 10.75

Vegetables

Broccoli 3.50
Creamed Spinach 3.00
Asparagus 4.50
Sautéed Mushrooms 3.50

In consideration, please refrain
from smoking cigars or pipes.

Desserts

Strawberry Cheese Cake 3.75
Chocolate Cheese Cake 3.75
Crème Caramel 3.00
Rice or Bread Pudding 3.00
Ice Cream Pie 3.00
Sundaes 3.00
Sherbet 2.75
Pastry Chef's Daily Selection 4.50

Beverages

Coffee 1.25
Decaffeinated Coffee 1.25
Milk 1.25
Pot of Tea 1.25
Espresso Coffee (per cup) 2.25
Cappuccino (per cup) 2.25

FIGURE 11.2 Seafood menu from the Cape Cod Room. (Courtesy of The Drake, Chicago, A Vista International Hotel. Reproduced by permission.)

Rich Cream Sauce. Prices for these lobster morsels range from $25.25 to market price.

There are three scallop entrées—$18.50 and $19.50—and three crabmeat entrées at $19.75 and $23.75. Four shrimp entrées are offered: Shrimp in Casserole with Rice, Creole Shrimp, Shrimp de Jonghe, and Shrimp à la Drake. These entrées are priced at $20.75.

The next page lists Seafood Salads, Salads, From Our Broiler (nonseafood entrées), Vegetables, Desserts, and Beverages. The three seafood salads are of special interest: Cold Maine Lobster Salad, Cold Poached Salmon served with Caviar Mayonnaise and Russian Salad, and Laperouse Salad (Lobster, Shrimp, and Crabmeat on Crisp Bibb Lettuce with Quartered Eggs and Tomato Wedges). These salads cost $24.50, $20.75, and $22.75.

The dessert listing includes Strawberry Cheese Cake, Chocolate Cheese Cake, Crème Caramel, Rice or Bread Pudding, Ice Cream Pie, Sundaes, Sherbet, and Pastry Chef's Daily Selection.

The Fishwife (Luncheon Menu)

The Fishwife's somewhat different seafood menu combines seafood and pasta (Figure 11.3). It is a three-panel menu, each panel measuring 8 by 12½ inches. It is printed in pink, green, and black on heavy, coated paper.

The first panel begins with the heading Appetizers/Bocas, including: Calamari, Fried Clam Strips, Flautas, and Chicklets (golden-fried chicken breast fillets served with mustard and honey sauce). Next come Soup and Salads. The soup is Boston Clam Chowder. The salads are Crab, Bay Shrimp, Fresh Pasta (with scallops and bay shrimp in light pesto vinaigrette), and Dinner Salad.

The next heading is The Fishwife's Sea Garden Salads: Chilled Cajun Snapper (Spicy!)*, Grilled Fillet of Sole*, Golden-Fried Calamari, and Sea Garden Salad Without Seafood*. The asterisks indicate that these items are "great plates for hungry waist-watchers—ask for dressing on the side and don't eat the garlic bread!"

FIGURE 11.3 Luncheon menu from Fishwife Restaurant. (Courtesy Fishwife Restaurant. Menu by Ibis Graphic Design. Reproduced by permission.)

The last listing on this panel is headed Egg Dishes. Omelettes are Neptune (prawns, scallops, and crab in nantua sauce), and Three Cheese Omelette. Next are Eggs Mérida, Hunter's Brunch, and Fisherman's Brunch (two scrambled eggs with tomatoes and onions, served with fresh grilled snapper Caribe [spicy], black beans, rice, and tortillas).

The center panel begins with Daily Specials from the Grill, featuring Fresh Seasonal Fish. The menu points out that "These dishes can be prepared for low salt/sugar/waist-watcher diets." Another dietary note reads: "We use only peanut and vegetable oils for all our fried items, and, in order to avoid oversaturation, we employ the use of a special process which forms an automatic seal when optimum cooking is achieved.

A sandwich list includes Golden-Fried Calamari, Golden-Fried Snapper, Golden-Fried Chicken Breast Fillet, Grilled Cheese Chontaleño Style, Shrimp Poor Boy, Golden-Fried Catfish Fillet, Crab Salad on Whole Wheat, Cajun Sausage (hot!), and Duck Sausage. An additional note points out, "The chef uses cornmeal with varied seasonings for each golden-fried dish because it aids in digestion, absorbs less oil, and tastes great!"

The bottom of this panel features pastas—Fresh Fettuccini (including Alfredo with Crab, Alfredo with Scallops, Alfredo with Prawns, Alfredo with Baby Clams, and Alfredo Seafood Combo), Al Pesto, and Portofino (rich marinara made with crab, shrimp, scallops, baby clams, and so forth).

Panel three begins with desserts: Chocolate Truffle Torte, Key Lime Pie, Lemon Chess Pie, California-Style Cheesecake, Ice Cream, and Parfaits.

Next are Coffee Specialties (see Drink Menu Chapter), Side Orders, Child's Plate, and Beverages. The side orders include Salsa Brava, Salsa Fresca, Tartar Sauce, Black Beans Nuñez with Cream, Air-Fried Potatoes, Fresh Vegetables, Rice, and Garlic Bread.

The Fishwife (Dinner Menu)

Panels one and three are the same on the dinner menu as on the luncheon menu (Figure 11.4). The different center panel begins with the same specials copy that appears on the luncheon menu and is followed by a listing of Dinner Entrées. Fifteen seafood entrées, plus one New York Steak, are listed, and prices range from \$6.95 to \$11.25. The seafood items are Golden-Fried Calamari, Pan-Fried Catfish Filet, Golden-Fried Pacific Snapper, Golden-Fried Prawns, Golden-Fried Fillet of Sole, Seafood Combination, Grilled Calamari Steak Provençal, Grilled Pacific Snapper Cancún, Grilled Snapper Lafayette, Grilled Oysters, Grilled Fillet of Sole, Sautéed Calamari Steak Abalone Style, Sautéed Prawns Jefferson, Prawns Belize, and Prawns Veneto. Information about how these items are nutritionally prepared is included on both luncheon and dinner menus.

The Fishwife, located in Pacific Grove, California, is exceptional both for combining seafood with pasta and for the amount of attention paid to the nutritional and health aspects of food preparation. This is a good menu strategy in a society that is becoming more and more health conscious.

The Fishwife's menu has an interesting and different listing of Coffee Specialties: Vienna Roast, Vienna Roast Decaffeinated, Espresso, Espresso Decaffeinated, Cappuccino (espresso and steamed milk topped with chocolate shavings), Cappuccino Decaffeinated, Caffé Latté (12-ounce glass of steamed milk and espresso topped with shaved chocolate), Caffé Reale (alcoholic—cappuccino flavored with Totara Cafe [Kahlua], or Argueso [Sherry]), Caffé Reale (nonalcoholic—cappuccino flavored with hazelnut, amaretto, or chocolate mint).

To extend your seafood menu imagination, Figure 11.5 is reprinted courtesy of the Chicago Fish House. It includes the categories of frozen, farm-raised, fresh, and smoke-cured products. A well-stocked fish and shellfish purveyor should be able to supply these items, depending, of course, on seasonal availability.

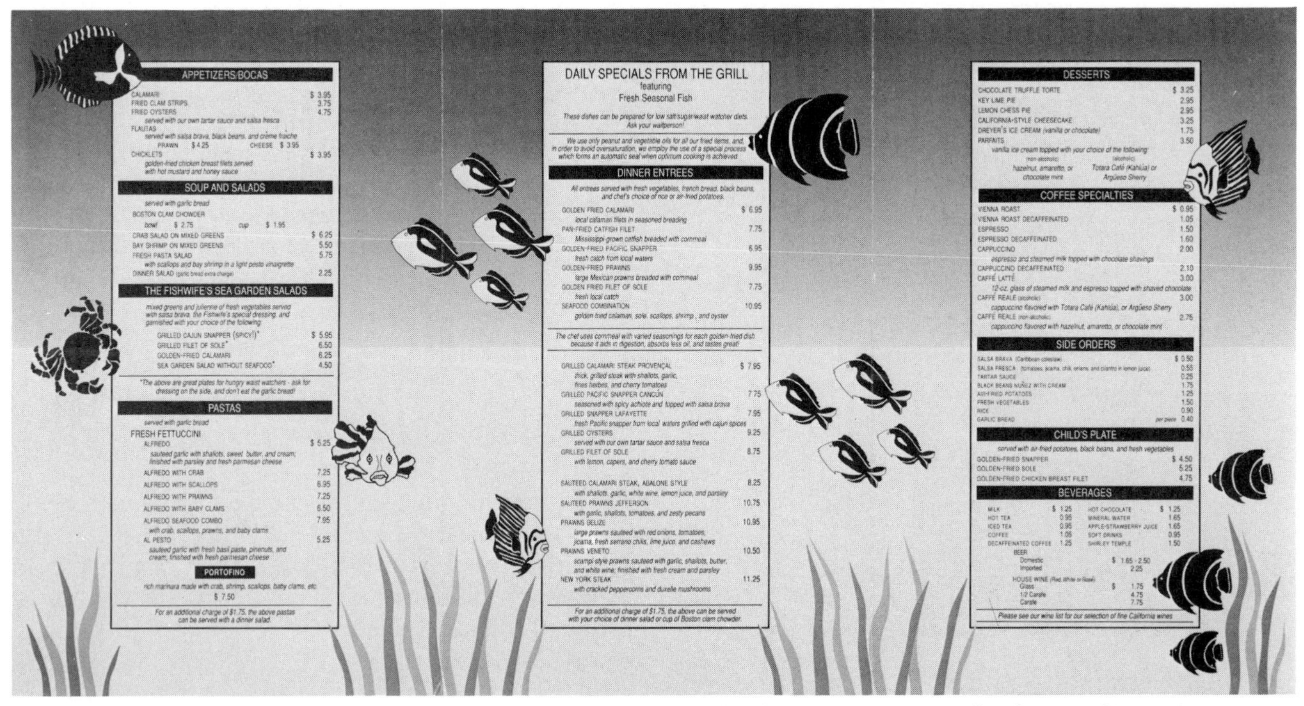

APPETIZERS/BOCAS

CALAMARI $ 3.95
FRIED CLAM STRIPS 3.75
FRIED OYSTERS 4.75
served with our own tartar sauce and salsa fresca
FLAUTAS
served with salsa brava, black beans, and crème fraiche
PRAWN $ 4.25 CHEESE $ 3.95
CHICKLETS $ 3.95
golden-fried chicken breast filets served with hot mustard and honey sauce

SOUP AND SALADS

served with garlic bread
BOSTON CLAM CHOWDER
bowl $ 2.75 cup $ 1.95
CRAB SALAD ON MIXED GREENS $ 6.25
BAY SHRIMP ON MIXED GREENS 5.50
FRESH PASTA SALAD 5.75
with scallops and bay shrimp in a light pesto vinaigrette
DINNER SALAD (garlic bread extra charge) 2.25

THE FISHWIFE'S SEA GARDEN SALADS

mixed greens and julienne of fresh vegetables served with salsa brava, the Fishwife's special dressing, and garnished with your choice of the following:
GRILLED CAJUN SNAPPER (SPICY!)* $ 5.95
GRILLED FILET OF SOLE* 6.50
GOLDEN-FRIED CALAMARI 6.25
SEA GARDEN SALAD WITHOUT SEAFOOD* 4.50

**The above are great plates for hungry waist watchers - ask for dressing on the side, and don't eat the garlic bread!*

PASTAS

served with garlic bread
FRESH FETTUCCINI
ALFREDO $ 5.25
sauteed garlic with shallots, sweet butter, and cream; finished with parsley and fresh parmesan cheese
ALFREDO WITH CRAB 7.25
ALFREDO WITH SCALLOPS 6.95
ALFREDO WITH PRAWNS 7.25
ALFREDO WITH BABY CLAMS 6.50
ALFREDO SEAFOOD COMBO 7.95
with crab, scallops, prawns, and baby clams
AL PESTO 5.25
sauteed garlic with fresh basil paste, pinenuts, and cream; finished with fresh parmesan cheese
PORTOFINO
rich marinara made with crab, shrimp, scallops, baby clams, etc.
$ 7.50

For an additional charge of $1.75, the above pastas can be served with a dinner salad.

DAILY SPECIALS FROM THE GRILL
featuring
Fresh Seasonal Fish

These dishes can be prepared for low salt/sugar/waist watcher diets. Ask your waitperson!

We use only peanut and vegetable oils for all our fried items, and, in order to avoid oversaturation, we employ the use of a special process which forms an automatic seal when optimum cooking is achieved.

DINNER ENTREES

All entrees served with fresh vegetables, french bread, black beans, and chef's choice of rice or air-fried potatoes.

GOLDEN FRIED CALAMARI $ 6.95
local calamari filets in seasoned breading
PAN-FRIED CATFISH FILET 7.75
Mississippi-grown catfish breaded with cornmeal
GOLDEN-FRIED PACIFIC SNAPPER 6.95
fresh catch from local waters
GOLDEN-FRIED PRAWNS 9.95
large Mexican prawns breaded with cornmeal
GOLDEN FRIED FILET OF SOLE 7.75
fresh local catch
SEAFOOD COMBINATION 10.95
golden-fried calamari, sole, scallops, shrimp, and oyster

The chef uses cornmeal with varied seasonings for each golden-fried dish because it aids in digestion, absorbs less oil, and tastes great!

GRILLED CALAMARI STEAK PROVENÇAL $ 7.95
thick, grilled steak with shallots, garlic, fines herbes, and cherry tomatoes
GRILLED PACIFIC SNAPPER CANCÚN 7.75
seasoned with spicy achiote and topped with salsa brava
GRILLED SNAPPER LAFAYETTE 7.95
fresh Pacific snapper from local waters grilled with cajun spices
GRILLED OYSTERS 9.25
served with our own tartar sauce and salsa fresca
GRILLED FILET OF SOLE 8.75
with lemon, capers, and cherry tomato sauce

SAUTEED CALAMARI STEAK, ABALONE STYLE 8.25
with shallots, garlic, white wine, lemon juice, and parsley
SAUTEED PRAWNS JEFFERSON 10.75
with garlic, shallots, tomatoes, and zesty pecans
PRAWNS BELIZE 10.95
large prawns sauteed with red onions, tomatoes, jicama, fresh serrano chilis, lime juice, and cashews
PRAWNS VENETO 10.50
scampi-style prawns sauteed with garlic, shallots, butter, and white wine; finished with fresh cream and parsley
NEW YORK STEAK 11.25
with cracked peppercorns and duxelle mushrooms

For an additional charge of $1.75, the above can be served with your choice of dinner salad or cup of Boston clam chowder.

DESSERTS

CHOCOLATE TRUFFLE TORTE $ 3.25
KEY LIME PIE 2.95
LEMON CHESS PIE 2.95
CALIFORNIA-STYLE CHEESECAKE 3.25
DREYER'S ICE CREAM *(vanilla or chocolate)* 1.75
PARFAITS 3.50
vanilla ice cream topped with your choice of the following:
(non-alcoholic) *hazelnut, amaretto, or chocolate mint*
(alcoholic) *Totara Café (Kahlúa) or Argüeso Sherry*

COFFEE SPECIALTIES

VIENNA ROAST $ 0.95
VIENNA ROAST DECAFFEINATED 1.05
ESPRESSO 1.50
ESPRESSO DECAFFEINATED 1.60
CAPPUCCINO 2.00
espresso and steamed milk topped with chocolate shavings
CAPPUCCINO DECAFFEINATED 2.10
CAFFÉ LATTÉ 3.00
12-oz. glass of steamed milk and espresso topped with shaved chocolate
CAFFÉ REALE (alcoholic) 3.00
cappuccino flavored with Totara Café (Kahlúa), or Argüeso Sherry
CAFFÉ REALE (non-alcoholic) 2.75
cappuccino flavored with hazelnut, amaretto, or chocolate mint

SIDE ORDERS

SALSA BRAVA (Caribbean coleslaw) $ 0.50
SALSA FRESCA (tomatoes, jicama, chili, onions, and cilantro in lemon juice) 0.55
TARTAR SAUCE 0.25
BLACK BEANS NUÑEZ WITH CREAM 1.75
AIR-FRIED POTATOES 1.25
FRESH VEGETABLES 1.50
RICE 0.90
GARLIC BREAD per piece 0.40

CHILD'S PLATE

served with air-fried potatoes, black beans, and fresh vegetables
GOLDEN-FRIED SNAPPER $ 4.50
GOLDEN-FRIED SOLE 5.25
GOLDEN-FRIED CHICKEN BREAST FILET 4.75

BEVERAGES

MILK $ 1.25
HOT TEA 0.95
ICED TEA 0.95
COFFEE 1.05
DECAFFEINATED COFFEE 1.25
HOT CHOCOLATE $ 1.25
MINERAL WATER 1.65
APPLE-STRAWBERRY JUICE 1.65
SOFT DRINKS 0.95
SHIRLEY TEMPLE 1.50
BEER
Domestic $ 1.65 - 2.50
Imported 2.25
HOUSE WINE (Red, White or Rosé)
Glass $ 1.75
1/2 Carafe 4.75
Carafe 7.75

Please see our wine list for our selection of fine California wines

FIGURE 11.4 Dinner menu from Fishwife Restaurant. (Courtesy Fishwife Restaurant. Menu by Ibis Graphic Design. Reproduced by permission.)

Product List

Chicago Fish House
1250 West Division Street
Chicago, Illinois 60622-4188
1 312 227-7000
Toll Free 1 800 367-9880
(In Illinois 1 800 367-9881)
FAX: 312 227-0451
TELEX: 858283

Frozen and Fresh Product List

FROZEN PRODUCTS

Ocean Fish

Cod
Fillets and Tails, raw
Minced Portions, raw and precooked
Breaded Portions, raw and precooked
Battered Portions
Salt Cod
Prepared Entrees

Flounder
Fillets
• Cello
• Shatterpak
• IQF
Prepared Entrees
• Whole
• Fillets

Grouper Fillets
IQF

Haddock Fillets
Cello
Breaded

Halibut
Whole
Fletches and Fillets
Steaks and Portions

Hoki Fillets
Shatterpak

Kingclip Fillets
IQF

Mahi Mahi Fillets
IQF

Monkfish Fillets
Shatterpak

Orange Roughy Fillets
Shatterpak
Breaded

Oreo Dory
Shatterpak

Ocean Catfish Fillets
Cello

Ocean Perch Fillets
Cello
Shatterpak
IQF
Breaded

Pollock Fillets
Blocks
IQF
Battered

Pompano
Whole
Fillets

Salmon
Whole, head on or off
Steaks
Fillets

Sardines
IQF

Shark
Steaks
Fillets

Snapper
Red–IQF
• Gulf
• Brazil
• Taiwan
Stuffed

Sole
North American and European
• Cello
• Shatterpak
• IQF
• Breaded
• Stuffed
Prepared Entrees
• Dover, Whole and Fillets

Sturgeon
Headless
Dressed

Swordfish
Sides
Steaks
Center-Cut Chunks

Seatrout Fillets

Greenland Turbot Fillets
Cello
Shatterpak
IQF

European Turbot
Whole

Whiting
Fillets
Headless, gutted
Arctic Queen

Freshwater Fish

Perch
North American and European
IQF
Breaded
Battered

Walleye Pike Fillets
IQF
Battered
Breaded

Smelt
IQF
Headless and Dressed
Round
Breaded
Battered
Zoo or Bait

Lake Trout
Whole or Dressed, Head On or Off

Whitefish Fillets
IQF

Farm Raised Seafood

Catfish
IQF
Whole
Steaks
Fillets
Breaded Whole
Breaded Fillets
Breaded Nuggets
Breaded Strips

Baby (Coho) Salmon
Boned

Black Tiger Shrimp
Shell on
IQF cooked, Peeled and Deveined, Tail on

Brook Trout
Dressed
Boned
Fillets
Prepared Entrees

Shellfish

Abalone

Clams
Minced Meat
Breaded Strips, Natural
Breaded Strips, Extruded
Appetizers
Zoo Meat

Conch Meat

Crab
Blue
• Whole
• Clusters
• Prepared
• Soft Shell

Crab (cont.)
Dungeness
• Whole
• Meat
• Fryleg Meat
King
• Leg
• Claw
• Split
• Meat
Snow
• Claws
• Clusters
• Meat
• Snap & Eats
Stone Claws
Imitation
• Sticks
• Chunks
• Flakes
• Claws
Appetizers

Crayfish
Whole, Cooked
Meats, Cooked

Cuttlefish (Sepia)

Langostinos
Meat, Cooked

Lobster
Tails, cold water
Tails, warm water
Meat, cold and warm water
Imitation Chunks and Tails

Mussels
Kiwi Clams (Green Lipped)

Octopus (Pulpo)
Raw, Whole
Cooked

Oysters
Breaded

Scallops
Bay
Sea
Cello
IQF
Breaded

Shrimp
Raw, white shell on
Raw, brown shell on
Cooked, shell on
Raw, freshwater shell on
Raw, peeled and deveined
Raw, broken pieces, peeled and deveined
Cooked, tail on, peeled and deveined

(continued on back)

Shrimp (cont.)
Cooked, tail off, peeled and deveined
Round, breaded
Fantail, breaded
Imitation, breaded
Battered
Stuffed
Baskets
Puffs
Appetizers

Squid (Calamari)
Whole
Cleaned
Steaks
Tubes
Rings, breaded
Steaks, breaded

Miscellaneous

Seafood Products
Alligator Meat
Frog Legs
• Raw
• Battered
Scallone
Seafood Kabobs
Seafood Platters
Escargots
• Prepared
Turtle Meat (Boneless)
Appetizers/Finger Foods

Non-Seafood Products
Cheesecakes
Mozzarella Sticks (breaded)
Seaweed Salad
Vegetables
• Cauliflower (Breaded)
• Green Pepper Rings (Breaded)
• Mushrooms (Breaded/Stuffed)
• Onion Rings (Breaded/Battered/Extruded)
• Zucchini (Breaded Rings/Sticks)

FRESH PRODUCTS

Processed to customer specifications

Ocean—North American
Amberjack
Black Sea Bass
Red Bass (Redfish)
Striped Sea Bass
White Bass
Bluefish
Bones
Butterfish
Cobia

Ocean—North American (cont.)
Cod (Scrod)
Corvina
Croaker
Eel
Flounder
Grouper
Haddock
Halibut
Mackerel
Monkfish
Mullet
Ocean Perch
Ocean White Fish
• Catfish
• Cusk
• Hake
• Pollock
• Pout
Pompano
Porgy
Pacific Rockfish
Salmon
• King (Chinook)
• Sockeye
• Silver (Coho)
• Pink
Sand Dabs
Shad
Shad Roe
Shark
Skate Wing
Red Snapper
Grey Sole
Lemon Sole
Petrale Sole
Rex Sole
Yellowtail Sole
Sturgeon
Swordfish
Tautog
Tilefish
Speckled Seatrout
Tuna
Whiting
Yellowtail

Imported
Brill
Dover Sole
Eel
Frog Legs
Grouper
John Dory
Red Mullet
Orange Roughy
Oreo Dory
Plaice
Red Gurnet
Sardines
Turbot

Hawaiian
Ahi (Tuna)
Ali Lepe (Spearfish)
Ehu (Red Snapper)
Gindai (Snapper)

Hawaiian (cont.)
Hamachi (Yellowtail Mackerel)
Hapu (Grouper)
Kajiki (Marlin)
Kaku (Barracuda)
Kamanu (Rainbow Runner)
Lehi (Long Tail Pink Snapper)
Mahi Mahi (Dolphin Fish)
Onaga (Long Tail Red Snapper)
Ono (Wahoo)
Opah (Moonfish)
Opakapaka (Pink Snapper)
Papio (Baby Pompano)
Tombo (Tuna)
Uku (Grey Snapper)
Ulua (Pompano)

Freshwater Fish
White Bass
Bluegill (Sunfish)
Buffalo
Bullhead
Carp
Channel Catfish
Crappie
White Perch
Yellow Perch
Northern Pike
Sauger Pike
Walleye Pike
Sheepshead
Smelt
Lake Trout
Whitefish (Canadian)
Whitefish (U.S.)

Farm Raised

Finfish
Striped Bass
Catfish
Baby (Coho) Salmon
Chilean Salmon
North American Salmon
Norwegian Salmon
Tilapia
Brook Trout

Shellfish
Little Neck Clams
Crayfish
Blue Mussels
Green Lipped Mussels
Hawaiian Prawns
Black Tiger Shrimp

Shellfish

Clams
Live, in shell
Shucked
Strips

Crab
Blue
• Live, Soft Shell
• Live, Hard Shell

Crab (cont.)
Dungeness
• Live
• Cooked
Stone
• Claws

Crayfish
Live, Whole
Cooked, Whole
Meat

Langostinos, Imported

Lobster
Live, Whole–All Sizes
Tails
Meat, Tail and Claw

Mussels
Live, in shell

Oysters
Live, in shell–All Sizes
Shucked–All Sizes

Scallops
Bay
Cape
Sea
Sea with Roe–Imported
Singing

Shrimp

Snails
Live, in shell

SMOKED/CURED PRODUCTS

Fresh and Frozen

Chubs
Eel
Finnan Haddie
Kippers
Mussels
Lox
Sablefish
Salmon
Domestic and Imported
• Whole
• Sliced
• Sides

Shrimp

Scallops

Sturgeon
Sides
Chunks

Brook Trout
Whole
Fillets

Lake Trout
Whole
Chunks

Tuna

Whitefish
Whole
Chunks

SPECIALTY PRODUCTS

Chicago Fish House Salads
Calamari
Crabmeat and Seafood
Shrimp
Shrimp, Crabmeat and Seafood

Caviars
Beluga Malossol
• Imported
Sevruga
• Imported
Sturgeon Malossol
• USA
Golden Whitefish
Salmon
Lumpfish
• Red
• Black

Herring
Imported
Domestic
Salted
Pickled
Cured

Canned/Packaged Goods

Anchovies

Bases
Beef
Chicken
Clam
Crab
Fish
Garlic
Lobster
Pork
Potato/Leek
Shrimp
White and Cream Sauces

Batters
Breading
Clams
Clam Juice
Escargots

FIGURE 11.5 Frozen and fresh produce list from the Chicago Fish House. (Reproduced by permission.)

12

The Multiple-Operation Menu

Fast food, chains, multiple operations, franchises—they can be giants like McDonald's, Burger King, or Wendy's, or they can be a chain of only six or twelve restaurants. What they usually have in common is specialization in certain items on the menu (burgers, pizza, or seafood) or specialization in cuisine (Mexican, Italian, and so forth) or targeting a particular market segment (the family or singles).

Specialty chains, which often began with hamburgers and french fries, have branched out with salad bars, breakfast items, and chicken nuggets. Recently Wendy's announced that its Garden Spot salad bar was to be transformed into a hot-food bar. With all these additions, there is nothing like a true burger chain anymore.

The trend is toward menu diversification. A new twist is packaged salads. Most of the new products brought out by the chains, however, originated on somebody else's menu. This product swapping is the result of intense competition. Steak houses such as Bonanza, Sizzler, and Ponderosa have adopted all-you-can-eat food bars from cafeterias and buffets—their competitors in the budget-meal category. And Rax and Wendy's fast-food chains picked up salad bars from the steak houses.

Full-service chains following the trend are picking up ideas from independent operators. Bennigan's created several short-term menus featuring foods from the Orient, Australia, and South America. T. G. I. Friday's menu of appetizer-sized foods copied the bistro—a popular concept among independent operators. Even institutional operators are creating concepts that copy the menu and style of commercial restaurants. The Army and Air Force Exchange Service, for example, has developed Anthony's Pizza as a package for Army and Air Force bases.

Besides new menu additions, some companies are developing and expanding new concepts. Winner's Corp. has opened a Mrs. Winner's Southern Cafe to lure customers who want a sit-down, country-style meal. USACafe's are franchising Ribby's, a drive-thru, walk-up, take-out rib restaurant. Full-service Italian restaurants have been opened by Jerrico, and they are considering the quick-service Italian concept. Arby's has added a dessert kiosk, which led to a franchise agreement with a cookie manufacturer.

Chains are also tailoring menus and concepts to fit available real estate. ChiChi's®, for example, has developed El Pronto, a mall-sized, quick-service version of the Mexican dining chain. Other chains are just improving their product. Pizza chains are making their product more competitive by working at the basics—new dough and new toppings. Most chains are adding seafood to the menu, but not the usual or exotic species featured in the seafood-segment leaders.

Other specialty chains, such as Steak & Ale and Grandy's, have stayed with their basic menu, hoping that by refusing to become "all things to all people" they will retain their customer base that likes beef. The theory is that too much tinkering can spoil the success base of the operations.

Foodservice marketers are now looking beyond the R&D lab and into customers' lives for direction. Health and fitness concerns dictate new menu items, and the demand for quick service has stimulated chains to increase take-out business. This includes trying new service ideas such as placing an order by phone and paying by credit card. Advertising campaigns as well as menus are being based on consumer opinion polls.

Full-service operations are also catering to quick service in the restaurant. Both Bennigan's and Red Lobster offer to serve within fifteen minutes after the order is placed.

BURGERS

Today's top burger chains are actually full-service coffee shops selling everything from hot breakfasts to late evening snacks. Hardee's breakfast menu includes a

Note: All data in this chapter come from the 1988–1989 "400" issue of *Restaurants & Institutions*.

3½-inch homemade biscuit, studded with raisins or topped with scrambled eggs and bacon or sausage. McDonald's, Burger King, Wendy's, Hardee's, and Carl's Jr. all offer entrée salads.

A new item on the menu in a burger chain can be a success or a failure. Hardee's biscuits—raisin, chicken, or sausage—account for 30 percent of sales. But even McDonald's has had failures, including hot dogs, McRibs, and the Hula Burger.

Burgers are still the basis for the success of the giant chains. McDonald's had sales of $16,100 million in 1988. Burger King was next with $5,400 million, followed by Wendy's with $2,902 million. Yet the basic burger product at these fast-food outlets, the Big Mac or the Whopper, is not where the change on the menu board is happening. Instead, that emphasis is on salads, snacks, and desserts. The big new item is packaged salads. The first to introduce this idea were Hardee's and Jack In The Box, but soon the others followed. Complete with croutons and dressing and including shrimp, these salads meet the public demand for light meals even from a fast-food restaurant.

On the other end of the menu listing, Hardee's offers soft-service ice cream, and Carl's Jr. is testing ice-cream carts and sundae bars. New ice-cream creations have also appeared, including the Sonic Blast, a mix-in ice-cream treat, and Dairy Queen's Blizzard.

Snacks as well as sweets are also appearing on the burger menu. Hardee's has Chicken Stix; Jack In The Box has Finger Foods. Mini hamburgers at Wendy's and Burger Bundles at Burger King are other snack items for the between-meal diner or lighter eater.

What do these trends mean to independent operators? If a new item is introduced by a large chain and succeeds, it tells the independent that the item is a winner with the public. The independent can then pick up the item with the knowledge that it has been tested and will be accepted by most customers.

SANDWICHES

The three top sandwich chains are Arby's (1988 sales $1,160 million), Roy Rogers ($630.2 million), and Subway ($600 million). Sales are up because sandwiches are popular. Sandwich sales increased 7 percent overall in 1987. This is 1 percent more than hamburger chain traffic and 2 percent more than the traffic average in all quick-service restaurants. In 1988, sandwiches continued to fill a niche, accounting for 6.3 percent of fast-food sales.

The Arby's chain, in its twenty-fifth year, achieved sales growth of 18 percent for 1988, two and a half times the fast-food industry average of 7 percent. One new Arby's sandwich, the Sub Deluxe, averages 7 to 12 percent of restaurant sales.

Research at International Blimpie has shown that 71 percent of the population occasionally diets. The chain, therefore, has a long-term plan to expand its menu in that direction. It has created the new Blimpie Lite line to attract the diet-conscious customer.

CHICKEN

The leading chicken chains are Kentucky Fried Chicken ($5,000 million in 1988), Church's Fried Chicken ($559.3 million), and Popeye's Famous Fried Chicken ($485 million). In spite of competition, chicken is still profitable. Kentucky Fried Chicken has the best growth record. It eliminated unsuccessful products, such as barbecued chicken, and improved others, such as biscuits. Next, the chain tried a full-sized chicken sandwich and then small sandwiches à la White Castle. Both were successful. These Chicken Littles were then copied by Popeye's and Bojangles. Several chains have gone to nonfried chicken items. Grandy's added roast chicken and also went to a diversified menu with many non-chicken items, making it more of a family restaurant chain. Chicken chains also continue to add low-fat chicken items in an effort to expand their customer base.

MEXICAN

Leading the Mexican chain operators is Taco Bell (1988 sales, $1,630 million), followed by Chi-Chi's® ($422.9 million), and El Torito ($390 million). Fajitas are the big new menu item in nearly every Mexican restaurant. In most cases steak fajitas outdistance most other offerings at the cash register, but chicken fajitas are also popular.

Combinations have also increased on the Mexican menu. Chi-Chi's®, for example, promotes a deluxe steak, chicken, pork, and shrimp fajita. Taco Bell has created a chicken fajita burrito, a flour tortilla filled with sautéed chicken, fresh vegetables, cheddar cheese, and lettuce. Taco Bueno has come up with what is probably the most original fajita—Chicken Fajita Nachos.

Enchilada dinners still sell well at El Chico, while the taco is popular nearly everywhere. At Pancho's the Mexican buffet, a twenty-item spread, continues to bring in customers, while Chi-Chi's® reports that its luncheon buffet has increased sales from 10 to 20 percent in some test units. At Garcia's, twenty-two new menu items are basically variations on existing items. For example, grilled steak strips used for fajitas are wrapped in a soft burrito and a chimichanga, then deep-fried.

Margaritas continue to be an important profit item in Mexican restaurants. At Garcia's, the upscale Margarita Royale made with premium tequila is very popular. Both Garcia's and Chi-Chi's® have extended their margarita line to include such flavors as cranberry, peach, and raspberry. El Chico's has reduced the serving size and price of their margaritas. As a result, they are selling more of them.

Although fried ice cream is the favorite dessert at Mexican restaurants, they are also planning to expand their dessert listing.

DESSERTS, SWEETS, ICE CREAM

The leading chains in the dessert/sweets/ice-cream category are: International Dairy Queen ($2,067 million), Dunkin' Donuts ($777.8 million), and Baskin-Robbins ($692.7 million). Two factors are influencing this segment of the fast-food industry. First, the customer has become nutrition-conscious, and second, the customer often wants more than just ice cream.

Low-calorie yogurt has met one demand, and bran muffins and cinnamon rolls have met the other. But premium, high-butterfat ice creams are also in demand. Super specialization in just ice cream or doughnuts has proven to be a dead end. As a result, croissant bakers are expanding with cinnamon rolls; cinnamon roll shops sell bread and muffins; muffin makers have added cookies; and cookie shops have added muffins.

Ice-cream shops are adding frozen yogurt and high-fat, liquor-laced premium ice creams with a variety of toppings. Premium ice-cream bars have also been added to compete with supermarkets. Doughnut and ice-cream shops are changing into full-service restaurants. Dairy Queen and Foster's Freeze have burgers and chicken to compete with restaurants with bigger menus. Dunkin' Donuts and Mister Donut lure post-breakfast customers with soups and sandwiches. Both of these doughnut houses have also expanded their dessert line.

SEAFOOD

The leader in seafood is Red Lobster with sales of $1,300 million in 1988. Next is Long John Silver's with $765.3 million, and then Captain D's with sales of $374.3 million. The increased popularity of seafood reflects the consumer's desire for healthful food plus variety. In 1987 Americans paid more than $28 billion for seafood in retail and foodservice outlets, a 27 percent increase over 1986.

Per-capita consumption of fish and other seafood in the United States rose from 12.3 pounds in 1982 to 15.4 pounds in 1987, according to the National Marine Fisheries Service. The gain of 5 percent in consumption from 1986 to 1987 is attributed to the increased supply of shrimp, catfish, cod, and pollock, which resulted in lower prices.

Cahner's Bureau of Food Service Research reports that between 1987 and 1988 consumer preference for broiled seafood rose 34 percent. In 1989 the National Seafood Promotional Council ran a sixteen-month, $6-million consumer magazine and television advertising program.

The Red Lobster Menu

Red Lobster, a chain of 450 restaurants, is America's largest seafood dinner house. Established in 1968, the chain has updated its menu with fresh broiled and grilled seafood items (Figure 12.1).

The menu has three panels, each panel measuring 9 by 14 inches. The entire menu is encased in heavy, clear plastic with a stitched cloth edging and is printed in full color on a cream-colored paper. The cover is a color photo of two fishing boats with the name Red Lobster in the lower right-hand corner.

The left inside panel listings begin with Appetizers. The fourteen listed range in price from $1.95 (a cup of Clam Chowder) to $4.75 (Veggie Combo—a crisp fried trio of zucchini, onion rings, and mushrooms). Six of the appetizers are seafood items.

Under the next heading, Shrimp, are seven shrimp entrées—Shrimp Louis Salad, Fried Shrimp, Shrimp Three Ways, Sizzling Shrimp, Lots of Shrimp, Popcorn Shrimp, and Shrimp Feast. Prices range from $6.95 to $13.95. The most expensive shrimp item is the Shrimp Feast—the ultimate experience for shrimp lovers! It includes chilled shrimp cocktail plus a platter of shrimp scampi broiled in a wine and garlic butter sauce, shrimp fried to a golden brown, and broiled shrimp stuffed with deviled crab.

Fish & Shellfish, at the bottom of this panel, lists six items. They range from Broiled Flounder Fillets to Fried Oysters, for prices from $7.95 to $8.95. In addition there is a Today's Fresh Catch listing with no price.

At the top of the center panel is a large color photograph. Under the heading The Great Crab Harvest of '88 are six crab specials and one child's shrimp combo. This section of the menu is framed by a border. Its position, plus the photo and the extensive descriptive copy, mean that these items are featured to sell and are probably high-profit items.

At the bottom half of the center panel Seafood Combinations are listed. Of the nine items, two—Admiral's Feast and Broiled Fisherman's Platter—are given extra emphasis in a color screen panel. Prices for these items range from $7.95 to $13.75.

Attached to the right-hand spine of the center panel is a plastic panel measuring 5 by 14 inches. Six photos plus headline, copy, and prices are inserted into this plastic holder, three on each side. The six items, all Specials, are: Fried Cheesesticks, $4.25; Shrimp & Steak

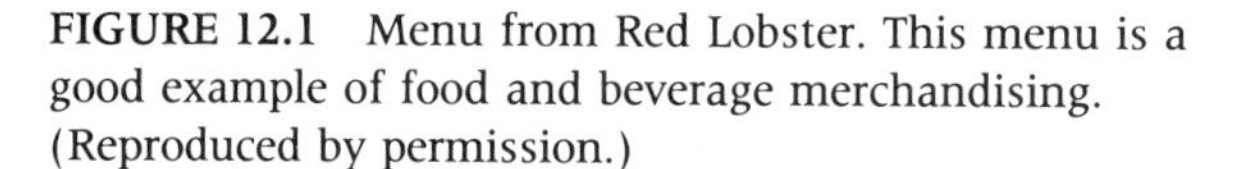

FIGURE 12.1 Menu from Red Lobster. This menu is a good example of food and beverage merchandising. (Reproduced by permission.)

APPETIZERS

Clam Chowder Cup 1.95 Bowl 2.75
Creamy New England style

Alaskan Shrimp Cocktail 3.95
Petite Alaskan shrimp topped with tangy cocktail sauce

Shrimp Cocktail 4.95
One-half dozen plump, tender shrimp

Chilled Shrimp in the Shell 5.50
Serving of 20, enough to share, fun to peel 'n eat

Calamari Rings 2.75
A unique seafood specialty. Breaded, fried and ready for dipping in our sweet & sour sauce

Cheesesticks 4.25
Delicious mozzarella cheese lightly breaded and fried, served with marinara sauce for dipping

Langostino Nachos 4.50
Crispy tortilla chips topped with langostinos, cheese, jalapeño peppers, green onions and tomatoes

Bayou Style Seafood Gumbo Cup 2.50 Bowl 3.25
A spicy Cajun gumbo, thick with seafood, garden vegetables and rice

Chicken Fingers 4.25
Tender strips of chicken breast, lightly breaded and fried

Chicken Wings 4.25
Spicy-hot Buffalo style

Fried Zucchini 2.25
Freshly breaded, fried and served with our zesty horseradish dip

Onion Rings 2.75
Batter-dipped and fried to a golden brown

Fried Mushrooms 2.25
Tender and steaming, served with our zesty horseradish dip

Veggie Combo 4.75
A crisp fried trio of zucchini, onion rings and mushrooms

SHRIMP

Entrees, except Louis Salad and Sizzling Shrimp, are served with bread and choice of two of the following: fresh vegetable of the day, rice pilaf, baked potato, fries, cole slaw, applesauce, cottage cheese, tossed salad

Shrimp Louis Salad 6.95
A fresh taste sensation! Chilled petite shrimp with fresh garden vegetables and egg slices nestled on a bed of crisp lettuce, and served with bread and our creamy Louis dressing

Fried Shrimp One Dozen 11.50 Half Dozen 8.95
Our traditional favorite! Large butterflied shrimp, freshly breaded daily in our kitchen and fried to a golden brown

Shrimp Three Ways 11.75
Three delicious shrimp tastes. Our own broiled shrimp scampi, spicy Cajun fried popcorn shrimp and fried butterflied shrimp

***Sizzling* Shrimp** 10.25
Tender shrimp and fresh garden vegetables seasoned with a wine and garlic butter sauce, served sizzling with rice pilaf, a tossed salad and bread

Lots of Shrimp 10.25
Eighteen freshly breaded fried shrimp

Popcorn Shrimp 7.95
Just pure enjoyment. Our bite size shrimp, freshly breaded and lightly fried

Shrimp Feast 13.95
The ultimate experience for shrimp lovers! Chilled shrimp cocktail plus a platter of shrimp scampi broiled in a wine and garlic butter sauce, shrimp fried to a golden brown and broiled shrimp stuffed with deviled crab

FISH & SHELLFISH

Served with bread and choice of two of the following: fresh vegetable of the day, rice pilaf, baked potato, fries, cole slaw, applesauce, cottage cheese, tossed salad

Broiled Flounder Fillets 7.95
Lightly seasoned and broiled
Also available fried

Clam Strips 7.95
An all time seafood favorite

Whole Freshwater Catfish 7.95
A tasty Southern tradition, lightly breaded and fried

Stuffed Flounder 8.50
A light combination of mild flounder and savory deviled crab

Calico Scallops 8.95
Seasoned and broiled or lightly breaded and fried

Fried Oysters 7.95
An oyster lover's treat

TODAY'S FRESH CATCH
We travel the world to bring you a tempting variety of the finest fresh fish available and take great pride in our skillful preparation of each offering. Select your favorite from our chalkboard listing and enjoy it grilled, broiled, fried or blackened.

LUNCH SERVED IN 15 MINUTES OR IT'S FREE!

LUNCH

Sailor's Platter
Shrimp Scampi, broiled fish fillet and tender fried shrimp. Choice of entree accompaniments. **$6.25**

STARTERS

Clam Chowder Cup 1.95 Bowl 2.75
Bayou Style Seafood Gumbo Cup 2.50 Bowl 3.25
Fried Zucchini 2.25
Cheesesticks 4.25
Fried Mushrooms 2.25

LUNCHEON FAVORITES

Popcorn Shrimp 4.25
Broiled Flounder 4.75
Crab in an Alfredo Sauce 5.50
Atlantic Whitefish 4.95
Fried Clam Strips 4.50
Shrimp Scampi 5.75
Langostino Marinara 4.95
Fried Shrimp 5.95
Stuffed Flounder 4.75
Fried Fish Nuggets 4.25

SEAFOOD COMBINATIONS

Seafood Broil 5.95
Oceanside Platter 7.75
Sailor's Platter 6.25
Luncheon Combo 5.50
Seaboard Platter 6.95
Calico Scallops and Shrimp 5.75
Shrimp Combo 5.95

SOUP & SANDWICH

Fish Fillet Sandwich 3.95
Chicken Breast Sandwich 3.95
Shrimp Salad Sandwich 4.95
Tuna Salad Sandwich 3.95
Grilled Hamburger 3.95

SALADS & LIGHT LUNCHES

Soup & Salad
Garden Salad 3.50
Garden Shrimp Salad 4.75
Garden Tuna Salad 3.75
Seafood Louis Salads
Petite Shrimp 4.75
Maine Lobster Meat 5.50

CREATE YOUR OWN PLATTER

Served with bread and choice of two of the following: fresh vegetable of the day, rice pilaf, baked potato, fries, cole slaw, applesauce, cottage cheese, tossed salad

Your choice! Any two of the following may be combined to create that just right seafood meal for you 10.50

Fried Shrimp
Butterflied and breaded daily in our kitchen

Broiled Flounder Fillets
Also available fried

Fried Clam Strips

Broiled Shrimp Scampi
In a wine and garlic butter sauce

Popcorn Shrimp
Petite shrimp freshly breaded

Broiled Stuffed Flounder
Filled with deviled crab

Broiled Sea Scallops
Also available fried

Fried Oysters

Broiled Stuffed Shrimp

CRAB & LOBSTER

Entrees, except Seafood Pastas, are served with bread and choice of two of the following: fresh vegetable of the day, rice pilaf, baked potato, fries, cole slaw, applesauce, cottage cheese, tossed salad

Live Maine Lobster Mkt. Price
The famous delicacy of the Northeast, flown in fresh. Steamed whole or stuffed with deviled crab and broiled

Crab in an Alfredo Sauce 8.95
Sweet snow crab meat in a creamy Parmesan cheese sauce over linguini, served with a tossed salad and bread

Alaskan Snow Crab Legs 12.95
An abundance of naturally tender and sweet snow crab legs, steamed and served with melted butter

Langostino Marinara 7.95
Petite lobsters in our Italian style tomato sauce over linguini, served with a tossed salad and bread

Broiled Rock Lobster Tail 18.50
One of the ocean's finest treasures! A 12-14 ounce lobster tail seasoned and served with melted butter
Queen Size Rock Lobster 14.50

STEAKS &

Served with bread and choice of two of the following: fresh vegetable of the day, rice pilaf, baked potato, fries, cole slaw, applesauce, cottage cheese, tossed salad

NEW! Our Steak Combination Platters now feature a juicy 9 ounce center cut Strip Steak

Steak & Rock Lobster Tail 15.95
A succulent broiled Rock lobster tail and our tender 9 ounce Strip Steak grilled to order

Steak & Snow Crab Legs 14.95
Steamed crab legs combined with our hearty 9 ounce Strip Steak grilled to order

New York Strip Steak 10.50
A juicy 9 ounce center cut grilled to your desire

Filet Mignon 12.25
8 tender ounces grilled to order

Steak & Fried Shrimp 13.25
Our freshly breaded butterflied shrimp and a hearty 9 ounce Strip Steak grilled to order

Ribeye Steak 12 ounces 11.95
A flavorful favorite grilled to order

Boneless Breasts of Chicken 7.95
Marinated and grilled also available lightly breaded & fried

All weights shown are approximate precooked weights

Trio, $11.95; Alaskan Snow Crab Legs, $3.95; Shrimp Feast, $13.95; Admiral's Feast, $12.25; and NEW! Sizzling Shrimp, $10.25.

At the top of the third, right-hand panel is the heading Create Your Own Platter. Nine items are listed, and the customer can combine any two for $10.50.

The Crab & Lobster listing that follows contains six items ranging from $7.95 to Market Price. At the bottom of this panel are Steaks &, with seven items: three steak and seafood combinations, three steaks, and one chicken entrée. These items range in price from $7.95 to $15.95.

Two of the back panels of this very functional and well-engineered menu have listings. The left-hand back panel lists Beverages—Wines, Jumbo Frozen Drinks, and Specialty Drinks. Next comes Soft Drinks and then Desserts. The five desserts range in price from $1.25 to $2.75. The featured item on this page, with a color photo, is a Strawberry Daiquiri that sells for $3.95.

The next panel is the Lunch menu. It begins with a challenge . . . *Lunch Served in 15 Minutes or It's Free!* Under the heading Starters there are five soups and appetizers. They range in price from $1.95 to $4.25.

The next listing, Luncheon Favorites, has ten items at a price spread from $4.25 to $5.95. Next, seven Seafood Combinations are listed, ranging in price from $5.50 to $7.75. At the bottom left is a Soup & Salad listing with five items for $3.95 and $4.95. At the right-hand bottom are Salads & Light Lunches. The five items listed range in price from $3.50 to $4.75.

PIZZA AND OTHER ITALIAN FOODS

America eats a lot of pizza. Pizza Hut, the pizza leader, sold $3,390 million in 1988 while Domino's was second with $2,300 million, and Little Caesar's Pizza was third with $908 million. Off-premises dining sales have increased 27.7 percent over the past five years, while on-premises dining has increased by 5.2 percent. Although emphasis has been on delivery in recent years, the issue of quality is gaining importance. At Round Table Pizza, based in San Francisco, whole-milk mozzarella cheese, dough made twice daily, and premium meats that contain no fillers are the ingredients that bring customers back.

The American Heart Association menu approval is gaining momentum today in pizza parlors. Mazzio's, for example, is launching a major campaign advertising the AHA heart emblem on its pizza.

The complete Italian concept is also gaining in popularity. The success of Olive Garden, Valentino's, Sbarro, and the Old Spaghetti Factory has caught the attention of pizza chains and other fast-food outlets that are adding pasta items to their menus.

The Olive Garden, a concept created by General Mills in 1982, now has 85 units and is expected to have 125 by 1989. At these Italian restaurants, pasta is made daily on the premises. Once seated at the umbrella-topped tables, customers are treated to an all-you-can-eat garden salad plus soft bread sticks coated with garlic butter.

Traditional Italian dishes include lasagna, spaghetti, manicotti, chicken Marsala, and Steak Tuscany. There are children's plates, soup and salad combinations, and light entrées as well as full meals. A large range of dessert offerings makes the menu even more interesting. Check averages range from $8.00 to $10.00. The success of the Olive Garden concept is proven by the 1987 sales, which reached $200 million.

STEAK AND BARBECUE

The popularity of beef is indicated by the fact that Sizzler had sales of $850 million in 1988. Additional sales of $749 million were made by Ponderosa, followed by Bonanza with sales of $571 million. Most steak houses, however, have added seafood and chicken to the menu. Others have expanded into hot-food bars. Some steak houses that expanded their menus have cut back to just beef. When Pillsbury's Steak & Ale diversified, it found the move hurt business, so it is returning to its steak identity. Stuart Anderson also tried a back-to-basics beef strategy in 1987 and experienced a 5 percent increase in beef sales. Fish and chicken are still on the menu, but they are second to steak.

Sales at Ponderosa declined by 7 percent in 1987. To meet the problem menu items were added, including a salad bar, a pasta bar, and a home-style soup bar. A Mexican-style food bar, now used as a promotion, and appetizer items such as chicken bits were added. At the Bonanza Restaurant's chain, steak now accounts for approximately 27 percent of sales.

DINNER HOUSES

This diverse group of restaurants has a common menu approach. Their customers tend to like the same things: spicy food, fresh fish, and desserts. The leaders in this category are: Bennigans (1988 sales, $458 million), TGI Fridays Inc. ($373 million), and Chili's Inc. ($350 million).

The diversity of these chains is shown by the way menus are planned and developed. At Restaurants Unlimited, new recipes are developed at the corporate level and made available to each restaurant. Recipes at The Levy Restaurants are developed at the unit level, but local chefs often consult with the *chef de cuisine* at headquarters. At the Hard Rock Cafe, the menu is standardized, with a few variations at certain outlets. Some areas get the Fresh Ahi-Tuna Sandwich, while others get the Pulled Pig.

At the Velvet Turtle group of restaurants, the four best sellers are rack of lamb, beef Wellington, prime rib, and the mixed seafood platter. For innovation the group has a "fresh sheet," which features seven to eight specials daily.

At the Charlie Brown group of restaurants, the 1988 strategy has been lower-priced and smaller portions. Guests are also given the option of combination platters that can be shared.

FAMILY DINING

For homelike dining away from home the leading chain is Denny's Restaurants, with sales of $1,300 million in 1988. Next comes the Big Boy Family Restaurants with sales of $940 million, followed by Shoney's with sales of $864 million.

Old-fashioned food, reasonably priced, is the theme of family restaurants. Emphasis has also been placed on breakfasts and more fresh and light dishes.

Bob Evans launched a new campaign—"Just a Few Smiles From Home"—with meat loaf, chicken and noodles, and beef stew. Country Kitchens and Po' Folks tested pot roast. Bill Knapp's introduced several chicken dishes and tested pasta plates.

Denny's lightened its offerings with lighter foods throughout its menu, including a chicken sandwich that sold well. Denny's is also testing variations to its popular Grand Slam breakfast. International House of Pancakes broadened its breakfast menu with a Taco Conquistador omelet. Wag's and Bill Knapp's also promoted stir-fried vegetable dishes, and Wag's and Denny's built bigger and better hamburgers, underscoring America's return to beef.

In general, family restaurants have filled in menu gaps by adding broiled and low-calorie items. At Perkins Family Restaurants a new trifold Dessert Menu was introduced. The cover has a photo of its Croissant Sundae. As a result of this menu, dessert sales went from $20,000 to $65,000 a month! Pie and sundaes are still the favorites, but high-ticket desserts such as the Croissant Sundae helped increase sales. The introduction of the melt sandwich in 1987 was also a success at Perkins. Melt sandwiches now represent 10 percent of sales at this organization. Across the board in family dining restaurant chains, home favorites such as pot roast, meat loaf, and mashed potatoes were reintroduced.

Family dining menus appeal to everyone: families, children, seniors, couples, and singles. This all-things-to-all-people menu approach is based on market analysis of customers' lifestyles and life stages.

13

Specialty Menus

Many types of foodservice operations require specialty menus. These include catering or banquet services; airlines; and restaurants that offer only certain items, such as fountain treats or pancakes. The following is an examination of these specialty menus.

THE FOUNTAIN MENU

Ice cream and frozen yogurt are popular items on the American menu list, and are big business. In 1987 Baskin-Robbins had sales of $624.7 million; Tastee-Freez had sales of $150 million; and TCBY Enterprises (frozen yogurt) had sales of $121.2 million (*Restaurants & Institutions*, "400" issue, 1988). Ice-cream sales seem to face contrasting trends. On the one hand, customers like low-calorie frozen yogurt; on the other hand, they also order high-fat, liqueur-laced premium ice creams sprinkled with a variety of toppings.

The history of ice cream is unknown, but it seems to have been more of a perfection than an invention. It began with flavored ices which were a favorite of the nobility as long ago as Alexander the Great in the fourth century B.C. Because of the difficulty of making ice cream before modern methods of refrigeration were developed, only the rich had access to this now-commonplace delicacy. Charles I of England, for example, gave "hush money" to his chef so that ice cream would be reserved for the royal table.

But the formula for ice cream could not be kept a secret, and both the popularity and the consumption of ice cream have spread. Even in early colonial America, ice cream was known. Dolly Madison, for example, gave ice cream popularity plus the presidential stamp of approval by serving it at White House receptions. The development of other fountain combinations, sodas and sundaes, came later.

In the early 1800s, carbonated soda water was introduced as a "health water." Later, flavorings were added to make soft drinks, and then flavoring, cream, and ice cream were added to create the first ice-cream soda. Strangely enough, at one time some people considered carbonated water to be intoxicating, and so they passed various blue laws outlawing the serving of sodas on Sundays. Then a creative restaurateur or fountain operator got around the law by serving ice cream and syrup flavorings, without the carbonated water, on Sunday; thus the sundae was born.

Another ice-cream development was the ice-cream cone. No statues commemorate the memory of Ernest A. Homini, but there probably should be one, because at the St. Louis World's Fair in 1904, he introduced the ice-cream cone. Another proof of ice cream's popularity is the number of flavors on the market, reputedly over two hundred. Although flavors come and go, plain vanilla is still the public's number-one choice.

In regard to menu design and merchandising, there are two basic approaches to selling ice cream and fountain items. First is the type of food operation, usually a short-order, fast-food sandwich (hamburger–hot dog) setup to which the fountain listing is as important as the featured entrées. Then there is the more conventional, usually more expensive restaurant for which ice cream is a dessert item. The two types should get different treatments.

The short-order menu should include the fountain items with the entrée listings, usually in a menu listing three basic offerings:

1. Sandwiches (hamburgers, hot dogs, and cheeseburgers).
2. Entrées (chicken, fish, a small steak selection, chili, and spaghetti).
3. Sweets (pies, cakes, ice cream, sodas, sundaes, and malts).

The usual ways to feature fountain items are through (1) bolder, larger type; (2) more descriptive copy; and (3) colored illustrations of sodas, sundaes, malts, banana splits, and so on. If fountain items are a big part of your business or if you want to make them more important, you should follow these rules:

1. List the flavors of all ice creams, sodas, sundaes, malts, shakes, and floats served.
2. Use subheadings to identify the types of fountain items, such as sodas, sundaes, and malts, especially if you have a long listing.
3. Feature some fountain items, usually special sundaes—hot fudge, strawberry, chocolate nut, or some fruit combination or banana split.

If yours is a larger, more conventional menu, you should list the ice cream and fountain items under a separate heading or mix them in with the desserts since they all function as after-dinner items (Figure 13.1).

Desserts, after-dinner drinks, and ice creams can be listed together. There are many creative ways to list and serve ice cream on a menu. One way is to allow guests to make their own sundae from a selection of ice-cream flavors, with the sauces, syrups, nuts, fruits, and the like on the side. Following are different menus featuring ice cream and fountain items.

Ghirardelli

The menu for the famous Ghirardelli Chocolate Manufactory, Soda Fountain & Candy Shop is printed in chocolate brown on cream-colored paper measuring 11 by 15 inches (Figure 13.2). One side recounts the History and Lore of Chocolate plus the story of the two families who started the business. The other side lists five special sundaes plus ice cream, sodas, beverages, hot chocolate, Bonanza Sundaes, and milk shakes.

Howard Johnson's

Howard Johnson's Ice Cream Parade menu is another example of the effective use of color photographs to sell. This menu has three panels and two folds (Figure 13.3). The panels measure 5 by 12 inches, with the tops die-cut to the outline of the ice-cream creations. Six sundae–ice-cream creations are featured, three on each side. Of

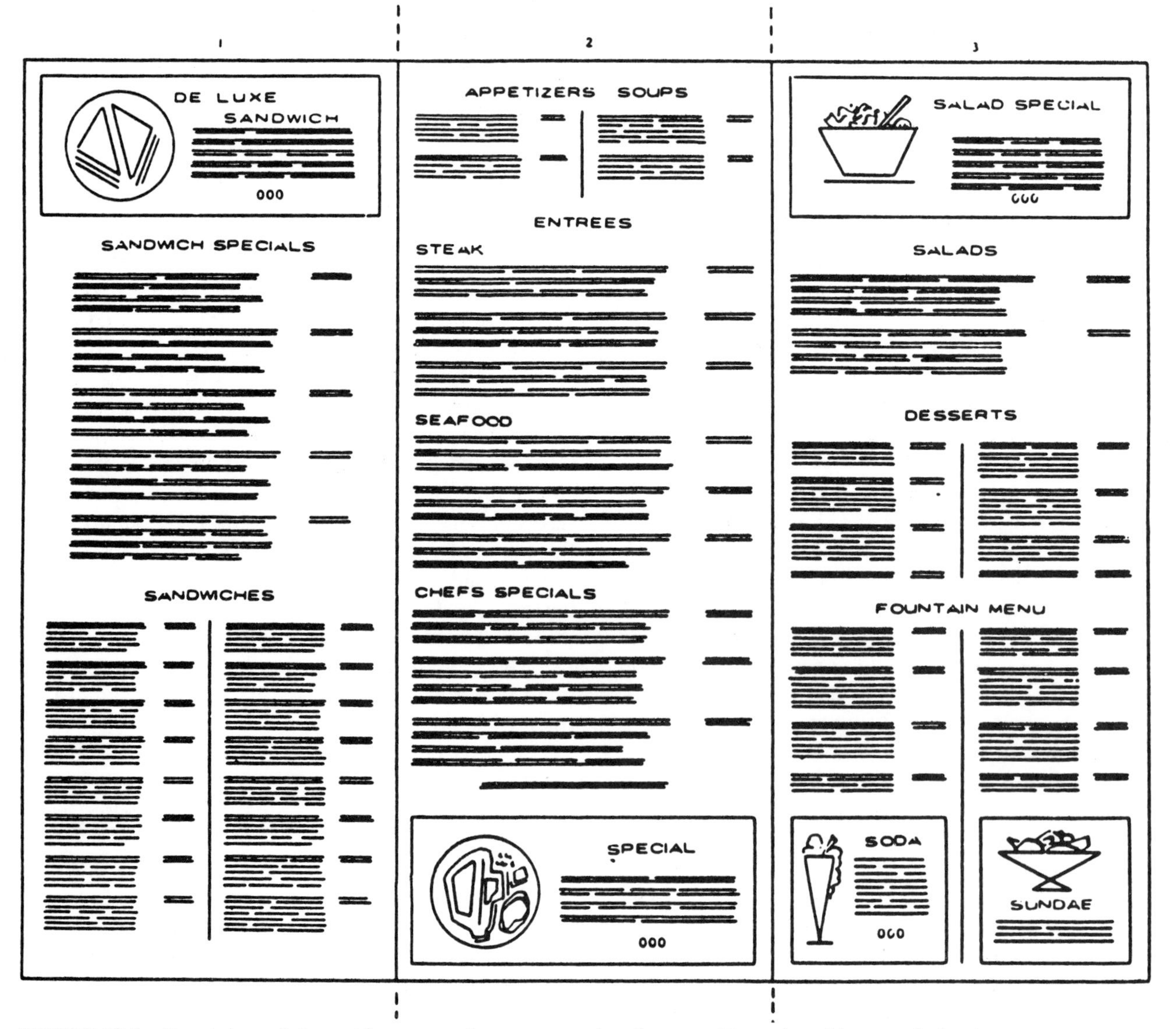

FIGURE 13.1 Fountain and dessert items on a large, conventional menu. (Reproduced by permission.)

GHIRARDELLI
Chocolate
Manufactory

Soda Fountain & Candy Shop

MENU

Ghirardelli Old Creamery Ice Cream

TWO SCOOPS OF ONE FLAVOR IN A GOBLET

Vanilla
Chocolate
Strawberry
Turkish Coffee
Toasted Almond
Chocolate Chip
Rocky Road
Mint Chocolate Chip $1.90

High Sierra Sodas

MADE THE OLD FASHIONED WAY

Chocolate (vanilla ice cream)
Chocolate (chocolate ice cream)
Strawberry (vanilla ice cream)
Strawberry (strawberry ice cream)
Vanilla Soda
Pineapple Soda $2.25

Old Favorite Beverages

Root Beer .... .50
Root Beer Float $1.75
Coca Cola .... .50
7-UP .... .50
TAB .... .50

Nob Hill Sundaes
in the best San Francisco tradition

TWIN PEAKS
A famous San Francisco landmark. Twin Peaks of chocolate and vanilla ice cream, topped with marshmallow and chocolate syrup and hidden under a blanket of whipped cream fog. Dig in and take a peek. $3.15

THE ROCK
Famous Alcatraz emerges from San Francisco Bay. Ours is a vanilla ice cream island in a whipped cream bay. It's armored with a shell of Ghirardelli chocolate. Break in ! $3.15

STRIKE IT RICH
The famous gold country of California inspired this goodie. Three marshmallow-covered chocolate ice cream mountains with a rich Ghirardelli chocolate syrup river running 'round them. Loaded with nuts and Ghirardelli chocolate nuggets. Dig for 'em. $3.25

GOLDEN GATE BANANA SPLIT
The longest span of goodness in town. Chocolate, strawberry and vanilla ice cream topped with chocolate, strawberry and pineapple syrup. A banana bridge rises above the whipped cream fog. Open up that Golden Gate ! $3.40

EMPEROR NORTON
Goblet ringed with bananas and cherries. Two big scoops of vanilla ice cream, Hot Fudge Sauce* and whipped cream. Topped with nuts. $3.40

NO SUBSTITUTIONS ON NOB HILL SUNDAES
* Ghirardelli is famous for homemade Hot Fudge Sauce.

Ghirardelli Hot Chocolate

SIP IT BY THE MUGFUL

Hot Chocolate
with Marshmallows $1.15
Hot Chocolate
with Whipped Cream $1.40

Bonanza Sundaes

CHOICE OF ICE CREAM AND TOPPING WITH WHIPPED CREAM AND NUTS

Chocolate
Strawberry
Marshmallow
Pineapple $3.00
Hot Butterscotch $3.15
HOT FUDGE SUNDAE * $3.25

Goodness Milk Shakes

MADE WITH RICH ICE CREAM

Chocolate
Strawberry
Vanilla
Pineapple $2.80
MALTS (same flavors) .... 25¢ extra

FB 8/82
GHIRARDELLI HISTORY AND LORE ON BACK OF MENU
100% Recycled Paper

FIGURE 13.2 Ghirardelli's ice-cream menu. This menu for the famous Ghirardelli Chocolate Manufactory is an effective presentation. (Reproduced by permission.)

interest are three new flavors—Waikiki Ripple, Chunky Peanut Butter Fudge, and Strawberry Almond Chip.

D. B. Kaplan's

The ice-cream menu titled Frozen Fantasies is an important part of D. B. Kaplan's Delicatessen offerings (Figure 13.4). Its four panels each measure 6 by 12 inches. The paper is white, coated stock and the printing is in three colors—red, yellow, and black. The cover has a stylized design of an ice-cream sundae plus copy and logo.

The first inside panel begins with Ice Cream Flavors Featuring: Peacock's Ice Cream. Seventeen flavors are offered. Below these flavors ten ice-cream and sundae items are listed, ranging in price from $.79 to $3.49. Next there is a listing of five shakes, floats, and malts, including Shakes Alive, The Yalta Malta, Little Miss Muffet's Curds & Whey, The Flip Flop Float, and the Transcendental Soda Jerk or Maharishi Mahesh Yogurt—yogurt filled with chunks of fresh fruit and nuts, blended with vanilla ice cream. Prices range from $1.99 to $2.99.

The next panel, Cake n' Ice Cream, lists apple pie plus the following six items, which range in price from $2.99 to $3.99.

The Chocolate Fetish Sundae—a rich, chewy brownie topped with Chocolate Almond Fetish ice cream, hot fudge, whipped cream, nuts, and streaked with chocolate syrup

The Sweet Tooth Fairy—butter pecan ice cream served atop sugar wafers and covered with caramel topping, whipped cream, and cherries

Chewy Sundae—our homemade "Blonde" brownie served hot, covered with vanilla ice cream and hot fudge

The Last Time Ever I Saw My Waist—a rich, chocolate nut brownie covered with mocha chip, chocolate chip, and chocolate ice cream, topped with hot fudge and whipped cream

The Last Straw—pound cake topped with two scoops of strawberry ice cream, crushed strawberries, and whipped cream

The Last Hurrah—pound cake topped with two scoops of chocolate chip ice cream, chocolate syrup, and whipped cream

At the bottom of this panel are Other Favorites: The Banana Splat, Pralines from Heaven, and A Berry Cool Number—blueberry ice cream and strawberry frozen yogurt topped with blueberry and strawberry toppings, whipped cream, nuts, and a cherry. These items are $4.79, $3.99, and $2.99. Specials on these two panels are accented in yellow.

The back panel starts with Sweets for My Sweet—cheesecake, cakes, cookies, and strudel from $.79 to $2.79. Next is Sensational, Delicious, Fantastic D. B. Kaplan Ice Cream Drinks, ten alcoholic and nonalcoholic ice-cream drinks for $3.59 each. Besides the Kahlua Bankhead—delicious coffee cognac ice cream, Kahlua, and strong, cool coffee, there is nonalcoholic Banana Bongo—a banana

FIGURE 13.3 Ice cream parade menu from Howard Johnson's. Color photos and good copy sell the product on this fountain menu. (Reproduced by permission.)

"Naughty!"

FROZEN FANTASIES

D.B.KAPLAN'S

WATER TOWER PLACE
280-2700

ICE CREAM FLAVORS FEATURING: PEACOCK'S ICE CREAM

VANILLA	BUTTER PECAN	PEPPERMINT STICK
BANANA	RUM RAISIN	MANDARIN ORANGE SHERBET
BLUEBERRY	MOCHA CHIP	STRAWBERRY FROZEN YOGURT
COFFEE COGNAC	ALMOND TOFFEE	PINA COLADA SHERBET
CHOCOLATE CHIP	PISTACHIO NUT	CHOCOLATE ALMOND FETISH
CHOCOLATE	STRAWBERRY	

One scoop of regular flavors 1.39
Two scoops 2.29
Three scoops 2.99
One scoop of our exclusive Chocolate Almond Fetish 1.49
One scoop sundae with topping and trim 1.99
One scoop sundae with hot fudge or caramel and trim 2.49
Two scoop sundae with topping and trim 2.99
Two scoop sundae with hot fudge or caramel and trim 3.49
Extra hot fudge or caramel .... .79
Trim - whipped cream, jimmies, nuts and cherry .... .79

SHAKES, FLOATS & MALTS

1. Shakes Alive 2.09
Our rich, creamy, thick shake with your choice of any of our flavors.

2. The Yalta Malta 2.09
Heralded as the best malt in town! Once again select your favorite flavor.

3. Little Miss Muffet's Curd & Whey 1.99
The original ole fashioned ice cream soda in your favorite flavor.

4. The Flip Flop Float 1.99
Vanilla ice cream dances to the beat of rooty root beer.

5. The Transcendental Soda Jerk or Maharishi Mahesh Yogurt 2.99
Yogurt, filled with chunks of fresh fruit and nuts, blended with vanilla ice cream. Good, and good for you, too!

CAKE N' ICE CREAM

6. Mom and 3.99
A tribute to all those lovely mothers. We take your fresh baked apple slice, melted cheddar cheese and top it with scoops of vanilla ice cream.

7. The Chocolate Fetish Sundae 3.99
A rich, chewy brownie topped with Chocolate Almond Fetish ice cream, hot fudge, whipped cream, nuts and streaked with chocolate syrup.

8. The Sweet Tooth Fairy 2.99
Butter pecan ice cream served atop sugar wafers and covered with caramel topping, whipped cream and cherries.

9. Chewy Sundae 3.49
Our homemade "Blonde" brownie served hot. Covered with vanilla ice cream and hot fudge.

10. The Last Time Ever I Saw My Waist 4.99
A rich, chocolate nut brownie covered with mocha chip, chocolate chip and chocolate ice cream. Topped with hot fudge and whipped cream.

11. The Last Straw 2.99
Pound cake topped with 2 scoops of strawberry ice cream, crushed strawberries and whipped cream. You've really had it this time!

12. The Last Hurrah 3.49
Pound cake topped with 2 scoops of chocolate chip ice cream, chocolate syrup and whipped cream. Eat it today, jog tomorrow.

OTHER FAVORITES

13. The Banana Splat 4.79
Vanilla, chocolate and strawberry ice cream on a banana. Topped by chocolate sauce, crushed pineapple and strawberries, while whipped cream and company hang overhead.

14. Pralines from Heaven 3.99
Butter pecan and almond toffee ice cream served with caramel and fudge. Topped with whipped cream. That's heaven!

15. A Berry Cool Number 2.99
Blueberry ice cream and strawberry frozen yogurt topped with blueberry and strawberry toppings, for the finish-whipped cream, nuts and a cherry

FIGURE 13.4 D. B. Kaplan's ice-cream menu. (Courtesy D. B. Kaplan's Delicatessen. A Signature of The Levy Restaurants. Reproduced by permission.)

split you can drink made with banana ice cream, real bananas, and other banana treats.

PANCAKE MENUS

Pancakes are also part of the American menu. The International House of Pancakes chain (454 units), for example, had sales of $297.5 million in 1987 (*Restaurants & Institutions*, "400" issue, 1988). Although this group of restaurants serves more than pancakes, certainly a lot of them are consumed in these restaurants. A pancake house that serves just that, pancakes, is the Walker Bros. Original Pancake House.

This franchise operation in Wilmette, Illinois, part of the Original Pancake House chain, has been in operation for twenty-eight years. The reasons are several: First, the food is excellent. Although the menu is limited, basically a breakfast menu—omelets, pancakes, waffles, egg dishes, and crepes—it evidently has items that the public likes. Second, the prices are low, ranging from $2.75 to $5.95 for entrées. Everything on the menu is à la carte, however, so the average check amounts to more than the basic entrée cost. Third, the restaurants are well designed and have attractive stained-glass windows.

BANQUET CATERING MENUS

Catering is offered by independent catering companies, some restaurants, and hotels; the last group probably caters more parties, meetings, banquets, and weddings than does any other branch of the food industry. An example of a well-designed and complete catering/banquet package is one produced by the Hilton International Taipei.

This package consists of a 9-by-12-inch folder with pockets for the individual menus and other literature, including a brochure with color photos of the hotel's banquet, meeting, and catering facilities. The left-hand pocket contains the Check List, Price List, and Floor Plan, and in the right-hand pocket are the food and drink selections: the Chinese Selection (eleven pages), Breakfast, Coffee Break, Western Lunch (four pages), Western Dinner (eight pages), Buffet (ten pages), Cocktail (six pages), and Beverage and Wine (three pages). The planning checklist is of special interest because it helps the person organizing the event ensure that nothing is left out or forgotten. It includes the date, type of function, contact person, address, inscription for signboard, room required, VIP arrivals, room setup, guest rooms, decorations (flowers), special displays, refreshment, cocktails, photographer, menu cards, music, beverages, coverage, parking, host-receptionist, security, table plan, and red carpet.

CORPORATE FOODSERVICE

Corporate foodservice has come a long way in the past thirty years. Cafeterias have evolved into food boutiques with versatile menus, inventive presentations, carving tables, specialty stations (deli, pasta, chicken, salad, ethnic foods) and even beverage bars offering everything from mineral water to wines.

Creative Gourmets®

Catering or contract foodservice includes both large and small companies. One of the larger operations is Creative Gourmets® Ltd., based in Boston. This eleven-year-old company had sales of $25 million in 1988 and has had a 40 percent growth rate for the past ten years.

The activities of Creative Gourmets® range from catering a governor's inaugural ball for six thousand guests to an engagement party for two on the Boston Common. The company also creates patient and employee foodservice for the fifty-bed Dana-Farber Cancer Institute and is exclusive caterer at the World Trade Center, Boston.

Affairs, the catering menu of Creative Gourmets®, consists of a three-panel, heavy paper folder with an eight-page listing bound inside, plus a pocket on the last panel that hold separate loose listings that can be added as required (Figure 13.5). The panels measure 8½ by 11½ inches.

The first page outlines the company's business philosophy. The next page lists ten cold and sixteen hot hors d'oeuvres under the heading Cocktail Receptions. These appetizers are priced in units of fifty, with a fifty-piece minimum. Each incremental addition is twenty-five pieces.

The next page, titled Decorative Stationary Displays, includes items such as chips, dips, cheeses, meats, marinated vegetables, and bread sticks. Next comes Food with a Flair, entrées for a hearty reception or a light dinner buffet. The fifteen items include Smoked Salmon Carved to Order, Tenderloin of Beef Carved to Order, Hot Seafood Bar, Fresh Pasta, Sushi and Sashimi, Smoked Turkey, Moo Shi, Raw Bar, Miniature Pastry Buffet, Fresh Fruits Sautéed with Brandy, and International Coffee Bar. All of these items are described in a sentence or two.

The next page sells Theme Events—packages of food, beverages, decor, and entertainment. The three described are:

A TASTE OF BOSTON

A cocktail reception featuring decorative hors d'oeuvre stations. Guests "graze" from the North End where they enjoy Scampi and Fettucine; to the Harborside for freshly shucked Clams and more on a Raw Bar. Then on to Chinatown for Peking Duck and Moo Shi; and Beacon Hill for a return to the traditional for Tenderloin of Beef and Roast Turkey.

NEW ENGLAND CLAMBAKE

No need for the beach to enjoy Lobsters and Steamers. Guests roll up their sleeves to a traditional feast beginning with Homemade Chowder and continuing with Lobsters, Steamers, Barbecued Chicken and Corn on the Cob.

NEW ORLEANS JAZZ

A Mardi Gras Masquerade sets the tone for a Gala Evening. Dramatic decor and a lively jazz ensemble might complement a menu which would include Crayfish Gumbo, Sautéed Catfish or Pan Blackened Sirloin, complete with Flaming Bananas Foster, Chocolate Whiskey Cake, or Fresh Pecan Pie.

Other theme events listed but not described are Texas Barbecue, American Bandstand, Chinese New Year, Dickens Christmas, Calypso, and Escoffier Banquet.

The liquor list has prices for both cash and open bars. The list includes beer, wine, liquor, sodas, and juices. Bar setups are also provided when the customer provides the liquor. Creative Gourmets® Ltd. carries liquor liability insurance and enforces responsible alcohol service guidelines.

Separate pocket inserts list (without prices) Continental Breakfast, Breakfast and Brunch, Accompaniments, First Courses, Salads, Entrées, Desserts, and Delivered Foods.

On another panel, the heading Policy covers deposits and payment, service, notice, decor and rental, sales tax, and room rental.

Froggy's French Café

Froggy's French Café has a much simpler catering menu (Figure 13.6). It is a small three-panel form on which to list catering requirements. Under the heading Catering, the copy reads: "Froggy's will be pleased to accommodate all your catering needs . . ."

Buffet
Sit-down party
Corporate and office catering
Cocktail parties
Picnic baskets

The inside panels are largely blank so the client may write in the food and beverage requirements. The headings (top and bottom) are Services, Wines, Spirits, Beverages, Information and Notes, Flowers and Decorations, Equipment, and Private Room.

COCKTAIL RECEPTIONS

Cold Hors d'Oeuvre

Avocado and Havarti Cheese Pinwheel	$62.50
Carrot Fritters with Creme Fraiche	$62.50
Chicken with Scallions	$75.00
Carpaccio	$75.00
Marinated Beef and Asparagus	$75.00
Cherry Tomatoes stuffed with Boursin Cheese	$75.00
Smoked Salmon Canapes	$75.00
Apricots piped with French Triple Creme Cheese	$75.00
Potato and Leek Pancakes with Sour Cream and Caviar	$75.00
Shrimp, Mediterranean or Cocktail Style	$97.50

Hot Hors d'Oeuvre

Spanikopita	$62.50
Gorgonzola and Walnuts in Phyllo Pastry	$62.50
New England Clam Profiterole	$62.50
Crab in Puff Pastry	$75.00
Mushrooms stuffed with Spinach and Gruyere Cheese	$75.00
Miniature Pizza with Fresh Tomato, Basil and Mozzarella	$75.00
Spicy Beef Turnovers	$75.00
Tenderloin Brochettes in an Herb Marinade	$75.00
Coconut Chicken Fingers with Orange Mustard Sauce	$75.00
Scallops wrapped in Bacon	$75.00
Artichoke Hearts with Parmesan Cheese in Puff Pastry	$75.00
Miniature Reuben Sandwiches	$75.00
Sundried Tomato and Mozzarella Tartlets	$75.00
Miniature Codfish Cakes with Remoulade Sauce	$87.50
Swordfish and Sweet Red Pepper Brochettes	Market Price
Oysters Rockefeller	Market Price

Hors d'Oeuvre are priced in units of 50; there is a 50 piece minimum. Each incremental addition is by 25 pieces.

Decorative Stationary Displays

Seasonal Crudites with Dips	$2.25
A selection of International and Domestic Cheeses accompanied by French Bread, Imported Biscuits and Fresh Fruit	$3.25
Festive Mexican Display with Guacamole, Red and Green Salsas, Sour Cream, Tortilla Chips and Shredded Monterey Jack Cheese	$2.95
Mediterranean Display featuring Hummus, Tabouli and Baba Ghanouj accompanied by Triangles of Toasted Pita Bread, Sweet Onions, Cucumbers, Lemons and Tomatoes	$2.75
A variety of Pates, Terrines and Mousses accompanied by Imported Crackers, Sliced Baguettes and garnished with Seasonal Herbs, Pommery Mustard and Cornichons	$4.25
Antipasto Feast featuring an assortment of Italian Meats &Cheeses, Fish, Marinated Vegetables and Bread Sticks	$4.50

FIGURE 13.5 Catering packet for Creative Gourmets® Ltd. (Courtesy Creative Gourmets® Limited. Reproduced by permission.)

FOODS WITH A FLAIR

Menu Items are prepared to order by a Professional Chef for a hearty reception or a light dinner buffet.

	Hors d'Oeuvre	Light Buffet
Peking Duck Thin Slices of Meat and Crisp Skin Rolled in a Pancake with Scallion Brushes and Hoisin Sauce	$4.25	$6.25
Smoked Salmon Carved to Order Accompanied by Sour Cream, Chopped Onions, Chopped Hard Boiled Eggs, Pumpernickel Bread, Creamed Horseradish and Capers	$7.75	$9.95
Country Baked Ham Carved to Order Accompanied by Homemade Rolls and a variety of Mustards and Chutneys	$3.25	$5.25
Tenderloin of Beef Carved to Order Accompanied by Homemade Rolls, Horseradish, Pommery Mustard and Cornichons	$5.25	$7.25
Hot Seafood Bar Bay Scallops Sauteed to Order with a Pesto Sauce or Shrimp Sauteed to Order with Garlic, White Wine and Butter	$5.75	$7.75
Fresh Pasta Tortellini with Fresh Herb Marinara Sauce and Fettucine Primavera with Alfredo Sauce	$3.25	$4.75
Thai Chicken Fingers Sauteed in a Wok with Ginger and Cashews with Dipping Sauces of Hot Curry Mustard and Indonesian Peanut Sauce	$3.75	$4.75
Sushi and Sashimi Prepared to Order with fresh Fish Selections Accompanied by Wasabi, Lemon, Rice Fingers and Pickled Red Ginger	Market Price	Market Price
Leg of Lamb Carved to Order Served with Fresh Pita Triangles, Tomatoes, Onions, Cucumbers and Tzatziki Sauce	$4.25	$6.25
Smoked Turkey Carved to Order, accompanied by a variety of Homemade Rolls, Sage Mayonnaise and Cranberry Chutney	$4.25	$6.25
Moo Shi Shrimp, Chicken, Pork or Vegetables prepared in Woks and rolled in a Pancake with Hoisin Sauce	$3.75	$5.25
Raw Bar Oysters and Littleneck Clams, Accompanied by Cocktail Sauce, Horseradish, Lemon Wedges and Wasabi	Market Price	Market Price
Miniature Pastry Buffet A selection of our own Specialty Pastries and Sweets.	$5.75	$7.75
Fresh Fruits Sauteed with Brandy and served with Heavy Cream	$4.25	$6.25
International Coffee Bar Specialty Coffees accompanied by Whipped Cream, Shaved Chocolate, Candied Orange Peel and Cinnamon	$2.75	$2.75
With Cordials	$4.50	$4.50

Foods with a Flair require an additional charge for the attending chef(s).

Any Foods with a Flair item ordered between the hours of 5 p.m. and 9 p.m., without a dinner following, will be charged the Light Buffet price.

FIGURE 13.6 Froggy's French Cafe Catering Menu. The menu is mainly blank so that the food and drink requirements can be written in. (Reproduced by permission.)

THE ROOM SERVICE MENU

Of all menus, the room service menu must work the hardest and sell the best because it stands alone. No waiter or waitress is at hand to answer questions or make suggestions, and no appetizing-looking dishes with tantalizing aromas are being served at the next table. Yet this menu can describe and sell the various foods, beverages, and services of the hotel or motel—from breakfast to cocktails. In addition, it can list the hotel services—auto rental, airline reservations, banquet and catering service, dry cleaning and laundry service, stenographer service, wake-up calls, and restaurants and shops within the hotel. Good design, good printing, the right paper, and good descriptions are as necessary here as in any good menu, and many hotels and motels create excellent room service menus that effectively sell their products.

THE AIRLINE MENU

While many airlines have cut back on foodservice, long-distance flights often have menus. Air Canada, for example, carries over eight million travelers a year and offers a variety of food and beverage items in three classes of service. The airline varies its menus about twice a year to accommodate eating trends. Of special interest is the NutriCuisine offered to first class and executive class travelers.

The drink list for first class passengers is 8 inches square with a four-color cover and a four-page listing inside (Figure 13.7). The first page lists aperitifs, cocktails, beers, and liqueurs. The center spread, in color, contains the wine list. Fine French and German wines are described in English, French, and German. The back page lists beverages and juices.

Air Canada's menus for executive class feature NutriCuisine for a Midnight Supper, plus a Ranch Breakfast for transatlantic passengers (Figure 13.8). The NutriCuisine description states:

> . . . offering our health conscious executive travellers more nutritionally balanced meals with reduced levels of salt, fat and sugar
>
> . . . has been recommended by the International Flight Catering Association
>
> . . . captured an award in IFCA's annual Mercury Award Competition in Vienna. All recipes and ingredients have been verified and approved under the nutritional specifications of Nutri-Centre Medina Inc.

The Midnight Supper consists of Salad in Season, Cold Plate of Chicken Rossini or Shrimp Brochette with Tarragon and Tomato Sauce, Green Beans, Carrot Sticks, Cheese Lychees Imperatrice, and Pan Masala. The Ranch Breakfast lists Selection of Juices; Fresh Fruit Cocktail; Akuri Stuffed Pancakes, Chicken Shashlyk, and Masala Mushrooms or Parsley Omelette, Canadian Back-Bacon, Chicken Shashlyk, and Buttered Mushrooms; and Breakfast Pastries. The menus are printed in English, French, and German.

United Airlines adds an interesting "extra" to its flight menus: a recipe for an entrée or other item on the menu, on a separate 8½-by-11-inch card. A color illustration and a general description are on one side; the recipe on the other.

CIOPPINO

"There are many versions . . . the main ingredients must come from close-by waters . . . . The thought is to be generous with seafood but to

use restraint with everything else. Use local, hard white fish, shrimp, scallops, and preferably fresh clams or mussels. You should have tomatoes, olive oil, garlic, sweet basil, and a pinch of saffron.

NEW ENGLAND SEAFOOD STEW

A creamy clam and lobster stock base with a tad of onions and thyme, chunky potatoes and pieces of lobster, whole scallops, and minced clams . . . one of the oldest culinary delights.

FIGURE 13.8 Executive class menu on Air Canada. A painting by Edgar Degas is featured on the cover. (Courtesy Air Canada. Reproduced by permission.)

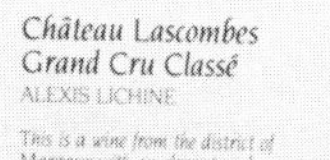

FIGURE 13.7 Air Canada's bar list for first-class travelers. (Courtesy Air Canada. Reproduced by permission.)

Château Lascombes Grand Cru Classé
ALEXIS LICHINE

This is a wine from the district of Margaux with an elegant and fruity aroma. A rich and fine structure with balance as well as an assertive finish make this Château a memorable companion to fine cuisine.

Ce vin de la commune de Margaux au bouquet élégant et fruité est séduisant et savoureux. Riche, velouté, avec des tannins équilibrés. Il présente une bonne persistence en bouche.

Dieser elegante Bordeaux mit fruchtigem Aroma, stammt von der Margaux Gegend. Seine ausgeglichene Struktur bietet einen reichen und samtartigen Geschmack.

Meursault

The dry mellow white wines of Meursault are characterized by a brilliant greenish-gold hue and a "nose" of ripe grape and hazel nut flavor. Meursault is classed as one of the most famous white wines of France.

Les vins blancs de Meursault, secs et moelleux, se reconnaissent à leur robe vert-or, à leur arôme de raisin mûr et à leur goût de noisette. Les Meursault se classent parmi les vins blancs les plus renommés de France.

Die trockenen, ausgereiften Mersaultweine zeichnen sich durch eine strahlende, grüngoldene Schattierung und einer "Blume" von reifen Trauben und Haselnussgeschmack aus. Der Mersault gilt als einer der berühmtesten Weissweine Frankreichs.

Ruedesheimer Berg Schlossberg
BALTHASAR RESS

A well known German wine. It is vinified exclusively from the Riesling, also called the Queen of the White Grapes. Slightly spicy with a touch of sweetness, this wine is very typical for the Rhine region.

Vin allemand bien connu. Il est fait exclusivement à base de riesling, considéré comme le meilleur cépage à vins blancs. Légèrement épicé et à peine sucré, ce vin est très caractéristique de la région du Rhin.

Ein sehr bekannter deutscher Wein. Er wird ausschliesslich von der Rieslingtraube gewonnen, die auch Königin der grünen Trauben genannt wird. Dieser Wein ist leicht, würzig mit einer Spur von Süsse, die für das Rheingebiet so typisch ist.

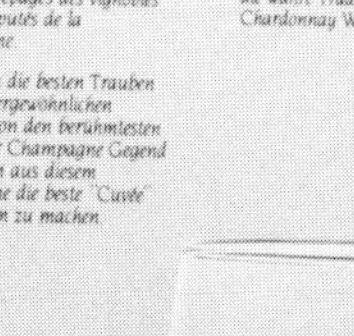

René Lalou Cuvée Prestige
G.H. MUMM CO

From the most reputable wineries of the district of Champagne, the best grapes of an exceptional harvest were assembled to make this Champagne the best "cuvée" by Mumm.

Le meilleur champagne de Mumm, produit à partir d'une vendange exceptionelle des meilleurs cépages des vignobles les plus réputés de la Champagne.

Es wurden die besten Trauben einer aussergewöhnlichen Weinlese von den berühmtesten Kellern der Champagne Gegend vereint, um aus diesem Champagne die beste "Cuvée" von Mumm zu machen.

Chardonnay
INNISKILLIN

Clean, elegant and crisp, this very dry white wine follows in the true Chardonnay wine traditions.

Vin au goût franc, élégant et limpide, très sec, dans la pure tradition des Chardonnay.

Klar, elegant und frisch, setzt dieser sehr trockene Weisswein die wahre Tradition der Chardonnay Weine fort.

Beaune Premier Cru
BOUCHARD PÈRE & FILS

This full bodied wine is generous, well balanced, lingering and brilliant. Its special character makes it sometimes close to certain wines from the Côte de Nuits.

Vin charnu, généreux, équilibré, long en bouche et harmonieux. Son caractère spécial le rapproche de certains vins des Côtes de Nuits.

Ein vitaler Wein, der sich durch seinen vollen Körper, Harmonie und strahlende Qualität auszeichnet. Sein besonderer Charakter ist bestimmten Weinen von der Côte de Nuit ähnlich.

Gamay Beaujolais
CHÂTEAU DES CHARMES

Although finished bone dry, this wine is soft, mellow and full-bodied. It carries the famous fruity taste and brilliant color traditional to the Beaujolais region wines.

Quoi que très sec, vin tendre, velouté et plein, dont le bouquet fruité et la robe éclatante rappellent les vins du Beaujolais.

Obwohl äusserst trocken, ist dieser Wein leicht, ausgereift und voll Körper. Er besitzt den berühmten Fruchtgeschmack und die strahlende Farbe - eine Tradition der Weine aus der Beaujolais Gegend.

The Stadium Club

Stadium Club Buffet

Stadium Club Buffet .... $ 8.99 Children under 10 Years .... $ 6.99

Our buffet features hot entrée items, hand-carved sandwiches, fresh pastas and sauces, gourmet salads and fresh salad greens. Served Pre-Game Only

Entrées

Brook Trout $10.99
Fresh, boneless trout, sauteed and covered with toasted almonds.

Chicken Teriyaki .... $ 9.99
Breast of chicken, grilled, basted in teriyaki sauce with brown sugar and fresh ginger.

Barbecued Baby Back Ribs........ Full Slab... $13.99 Half Slab... $10.99
Lean, meaty and tender served with our own barbecue sauce.

Fried Chicken .... $ 8.99
Crispy, golden brown chicken.

Filet Mignon $13.99
8 oz. filet grilled to your taste with sauteed mushrooms.

New York Strip........ $14.99
12 oz. center cut of choice steak grilled to perfection with sauteed mushrooms.

Each entrée is served with our House Salad or Cup of Soup and your choice of Baked Potato, Steak Fries or Seasoned Rice.

Salads

Cobb Salad........ $ 6.99
Freshly chopped vegetables, bacon, grilled chicken breast and cheddar cheese. Choice of dressing.

Shrimp & Spinach Salad .... $ 7.99
Fresh spinach, baby Alaskan shrimp, red onions and mushrooms tossed in a red wine dressing.

Sunshine Salad........ $ 6.99
Featuring the freshest and finest seasonal fruits.

Sandwiches

Half Pound Hamburger .... $ 5.99
A half pound of fresh ground beef grilled to order. Served with steak fries and cole slaw.
Onions, Mushrooms, Bacon or Cheese. Any or all, add........ $ .59

Rib-Eye Steak Sandwich........ $ 6.99
A 6 oz. marbled, flavorful rib-eye on a poppy seed roll. Served with steak fries and cole slaw.
Onions, Mushrooms, Bacon or Cheese. Any or all, add........ $ .59

Stadium Club Sandwich........ $ 6.49
Fresh breast of turkey, hickory smoked bacon, mayonnaise, lettuce and tomato slices on whole wheat bread. Served with steak fries and cole slaw.

Grilled Chicken Sandwich .... $ 6.99
Grilled, marinated chicken breast with tomato, lettuce and melted Monterey Jack cheese on a toasted onion roll. Served with steak fries and cole slaw.

Texas BBQ Beef Sandwich .... $ 5.99
Smoked brisket smothered in our own BBQ sauce on a toasted onion roll. Served with steak fries and cole slaw.

Smoked Turkey Devonshire........ $ 6.99
Smoked breast of turkey, hickory smoked bacon and tomatoes served open face on toast, thick-cut challah bread topped with melted cheddar cheese sauce. Served with steak fries and cole slaw.

Desserts

Homemade Plain or Chocolate Chip Cheesecake $ 2.99

Double Crust Apple Pie........ $ 2.49
A la mode, add........ $ .79

Cappuccino Ice Cream .... $ 2.99

Chocolate Chewy Tollhouse Sundae........ $ 3.49

Peacock's Ice Cream .... $ 1.99
Vanilla, Chocolate or Strawberry

The Levy Restaurants are pleased to cater to you and your guests at The Stadium Club. We have created an enticing menu for all of your preferences whether it be our luncheon buffet, informal dinner or a hearty weekend brunch. We pledge to use only the freshest ingredients available. We look forward to serving you and hope to enhance the excitement at Wrigley Field this season.

THE STADIUM CLUB
A signature of The Levy Restaurants

FIGURE 13.9 Menu for the Stadium Club. (Courtesy The Stadium Club. A Signature of The Levy Restaurants. Reproduced by permission.)

MENUS FOR SPORTS FACILITIES

The Stadium Club

Stadiums, ballparks, and racetracks no longer serve just hot dogs and beer in the bleachers. Many of these sports facilities have fine restaurants. The Stadium Club at the Chicago Cubs' ballpark, Wrigley Field, has a four-panel menu measuring 7 by 15 inches and printed in red and dark blue on white, uncoated stock (Figure 13.9). The cover design includes the Cubs' logo, the restaurant name, and a background of lines simulating the Cubs' striped uniform.

The food offered fits on one panel. The Stadium Club Buffet is followed by six entrées—Brook Trout, Chicken Teriyaki, Barbecued Baby Back Ribs, Fried Chicken, Filet Mignon, and New York Strip. Prices range from $8.99 to $14.99. Next are three main-course salads and six sandwiches, priced from $5.99 to $7.99. At the bottom of the panel are five desserts priced from $1.99 to $3.49.

The Paddock Room

The menu for the Paddock Room restaurant at Belmont Park measures 9 by 14 inches. The cover features a photo in sepia of a rainy day at the track in 1905 (Figure 13.10). The inside of the menu lists both food and drink.

First, five Cold Suggestions—salads and cold plates—are offered. Next is The Sandwich Board, which lists four sandwiches. Down the center of this menu in light brown panels are seven alcoholic beverage listings, including a short selection of wines, Manhattan, Man-o'-War, Bloody Mary, Tom Collins, Gin and Tonic, Saratoga Sour, and Amaretto.

The main food offerings include five appetizers, two soups, the Chef's Selections of the day (a tip-on), and four Specialties of the House. Next are three seafood entrées followed by nine desserts.

The back cover features historical information about the Belmont Stakes and the racetrack.

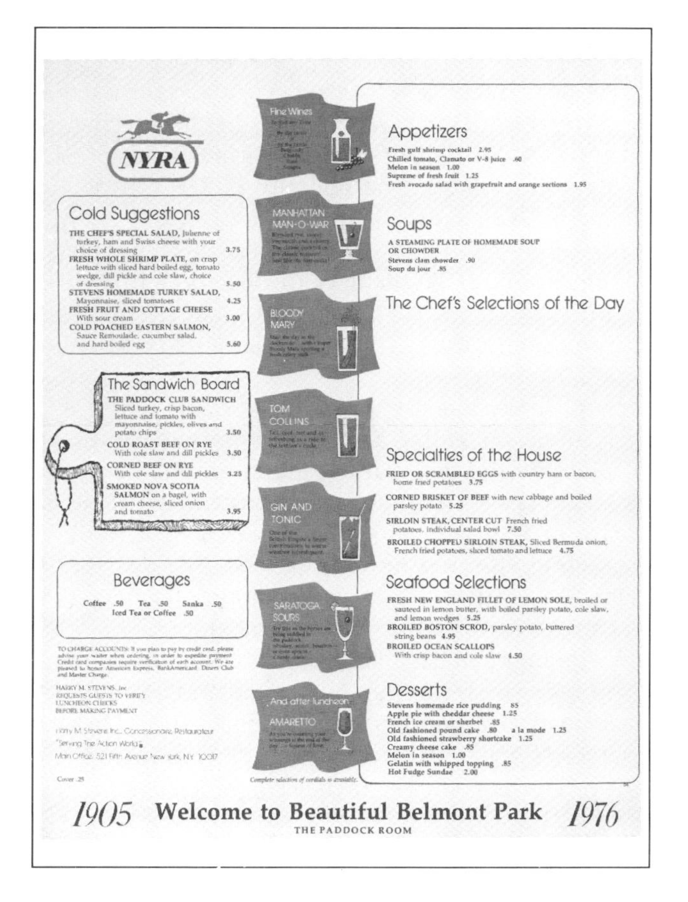

NYRA

Cold Suggestions

THE CHEF'S SPECIAL SALAD, Julienne of turkey, ham and Swiss cheese with your choice of dressing 3.75
FRESH WHOLE SHRIMP PLATE, on crisp lettuce with sliced hard boiled egg, tomato wedge, dill pickle and cole slaw, choice of dressing 5.50
STEVENS HOMEMADE TURKEY SALAD, Mayonnaise, sliced tomatoes 4.25
FRESH FRUIT AND COTTAGE CHEESE With sour cream 3.00
COLD POACHED EASTERN SALMON, Sauce Remoulade, cucumber salad, and hard boiled egg 5.60

The Sandwich Board

THE PADDOCK CLUB SANDWICH Sliced turkey, crisp bacon, lettuce and tomato with mayonnaise, pickles, olives and potato chips 3.50
COLD ROAST BEEF ON RYE With cole slaw and dill pickles 3.50
CORNED BEEF ON RYE With cole slaw and dill pickles 3.25
SMOKED NOVA SCOTIA SALMON on a bagel, with cream cheese, sliced onion and tomato 3.95

Beverages

Coffee .50 Tea .50 Sanka .50
Iced Tea or Coffee .50

TO CHARGE ACCOUNTS: If you plan to pay by credit card, please advise your waiter when ordering, in order to expedite payment. Credit card companies require verification of each account. We are pleased to honor American Express, BankAmericard, Diners Club and Master Charge.

HARRY M. STEVENS, Inc
REQUESTS GUESTS TO VERIFY
LUNCHEON CHECKS
BEFORE MAKING PAYMENT

Harry M. Stevens Inc., Concessionaire, Restaurateur
"Serving The Action World"
Main Office: 521 Fifth Avenue New York, N.Y. 10017

Cover .25

Fine Wines

MANHATTAN
MAN-O-WAR

BLOODY
MARY

TOM
COLLINS

GIN AND
TONIC

SARATOGA
SOURS

And after luncheon
AMARETTO

Complete selection of cordials is available.

Appetizers

Fresh gulf shrimp cocktail 2.95
Chilled tomato, Clamato or V-8 juice .60
Melon in season 1.00
Supreme of fresh fruit 1.25
Fresh avocado salad with grapefruit and orange sections 1.95

Soups

A STEAMING PLATE OF HOMEMADE SOUP OR CHOWDER
Stevens clam chowder .90
Soup du jour .85

The Chef's Selections of the Day

Specialties of the House

FRIED OR SCRAMBLED EGGS with country ham or bacon, home fried potatoes 3.75
CORNED BRISKET OF BEEF with new cabbage and boiled parsley potato 5.25
SIRLOIN STEAK, CENTER CUT French fried potatoes, individual salad bowl 7.50
BROILED CHOPPED SIRLOIN STEAK, Sliced Bermuda onion, French fried potatoes, sliced tomato and lettuce 4.75

Seafood Selections

FRESH NEW ENGLAND FILLET OF LEMON SOLE, broiled or sauteed in lemon butter, with boiled parsley potato, cole slaw, and lemon wedges 5.25
BROILED BOSTON SCROD, parsley potato, buttered string beans 4.95
BROILED OCEAN SCALLOPS With crisp bacon and cole slaw 4.50

Desserts

Stevens homemade rice pudding .85
Apple pie with cheddar cheese 1.25
French ice cream or sherbet .85
Old fashioned pound cake .80 a la mode 1.25
Old fashioned strawberry shortcake 1.25
Creamy cheese cake .85
Melon in season 1.00
Gelatin with whipped topping .85
Hot Fudge Sundae 2.00

1905 Welcome to Beautiful Belmont Park 1976
THE PADDOCK ROOM

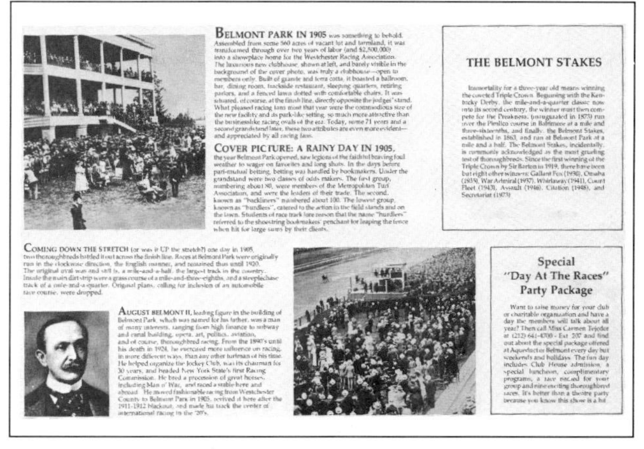

BELMONT PARK IN 1905

COVER PICTURE: A RAINY DAY IN 1905.

THE BELMONT STAKES

Special "Day At The Races" Party Package

FIGURE 13.10 Menu from the Paddock Room. (Courtesy Harry M. Stevens, Inc. Reproduced by permission.)

14

Restaurant Variety Equals Menu Variety

There are two types of multiple-restaurant operations. One is the McDonald's type—one successful operation repeated over and over in many locations across the country. Such restaurants serve basically the same foods and beverages over a long period of time. New items are tested and then introduced across the entire chain. The advantage to the public is that they can go into one of the chain restaurants in Florida, California, or Minnesota and get the same food with the same service.

The other type of multiple operation is a company with many different restaurants; in fact, there may be no two alike. One such company is the Levy Restaurants, with headquarters in Chicago. The Levy Restaurants have thirty-two restaurants in Chicago and Pittsburgh and are opening new restaurants around the country, including two in the Disney World Resort in Orlando, Florida. Because of the number and diversity of their restaurants, Levy has a corporate staff that is responsible for supporting each of the restaurant units, evaluating them from both an operational and a marketing perspective. By continually examining each restaurant from these two viewpoints, the staff is able to adapt to consumer trends and changes in the restaurant business environment.

Levy's menu and price changes vary among its restaurants and according to marketing trends. But on average, specific menu items change two to three times a year. As an example, two of Levy's restaurants, Hillary's and City Tavern, have seasonal menus that change twice a year. These seasonal menus supplement the regular menus, thereby offering variety to customers throughout the year.

In addition, most of the Levy restaurants offer specials, merchandising programs in which certain menu items vary regularly. An extreme example of this is Spaiggia, whose menu changes daily depending on the availability of imported food items. Levy's overall strategy is always to be conscious of customers' preferences.

What goes into a particular Levy restaurant menu, and how are the items selected? Menu listings are decided by a team consisting of the restaurant's general manager, regional operations manager, marketing representative, and the executive vice-president of operations. All of the Levy menus are based on the popularity and profitability of particular dishes as well as design objectives. An item's popularity is determined by a menu mix analysis which is traced through computer-generated data on a period-by-period basis. These data are evaluated regularly to ensure customer satisfaction.

The menu design varies according to objectives of each menu. Levy's marketing department has graphic artists who produce the majority of the artwork required for the menus. The staff also works closely with a marketing communications agency, which has played an important role in many of the logo designs, as well as the menu copy, layout, and artwork. The company uses outside consultants to help design a better, more profitable menu.

An important part of the Levy staff's duties is to keep abreast of eating and drinking trends. For example, despite the national decline in alcohol consumption, the Levy restaurants have experienced some increase in beer and wine consumption as a result of marketing efforts. One example of Levy's success is Randall's Rib House. Beer consumption has increased at this restaurant since the implementation of a "beer club" promotion. Beer club members are offered incentives to drink each of the sixty-six bottled beers offered at Randall's Bar, and currently, Randall's Beer Club has over six hundred members. Other solutions are the private labeling of Levy's own beer at Randall's and City Tavern, and the creation of a proprietary selection of wines for Bistro 110. Levy also has been successful at selling wine by the glass.

The Levy people noticed a movement toward blending national cuisines, and so at Eurasia, the newest Levy operation, a completely new taste has been created through the combination of continental foods and Asian flavors. Another strong trend is toward convenient, quality takeout and delivery services. Levy's has opened Chef's Express, a full-service catering and delivery service drawing food from all of their restaurants in the Sears Tower. Sales at Chef's Express have increased steadily since its opening in April 1985.

In response to the trend toward seafood, chicken, and health-oriented meals, Levy's restaurants offer a variety of chicken and fish entrées. For example, the Chestnut Street Grill introduced a "spa menu" that offers low-fat, low-cholesterol entrées to health-conscious customers. All of Levy's fast-food menus offer a variety of fresh salads, pastas, and fruits. Following are some of Levy's menu varieties.

Dos Hermanos

Dos Hermanos, a Mexican restaurant and cantina, has a large oval-shaped menu measuring 21 inches wide and 17½ inches high (Figure 14.1). The two sides fold over to form a long narrow cover 7¼ inches wide. It is printed in four colors—orange, green, and blue, with black lettering on a light tan paper. On the upper-left quadrant eight appetizers (Aperitivos) are listed, ranging in price from $2.95 to $4.95. An example is their version of nachos:

NACHOS MONTAÑA GRANDES

A mountain of hot corn tortilla chips with chorizo sausage, melted Monterey Jack and cheddar cheese topped with green sauce and guacamole *$4.95*

In the lower left quadrant are the salads (Ensaladas):

TOSTADA DEL REY

A giant tortilla basket filled with your choice of seasoned beef or chicken, shredded lettuce, onions, diced tomatoes, black olives, grated cheddar and Monterey Jack cheese, guacamole and sour cream *$5.95*

In the bottom left-hand corner is the Taco Bar:

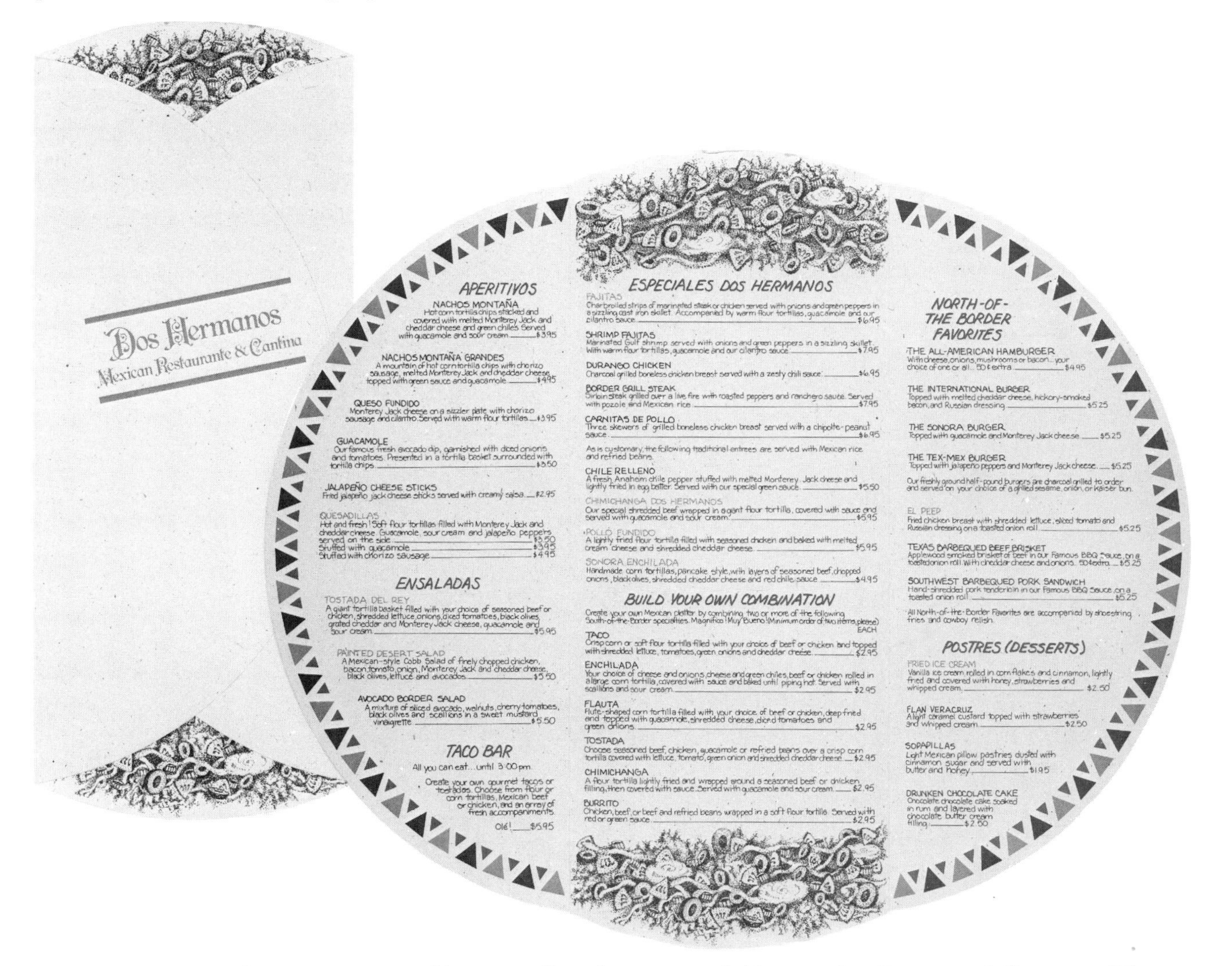

FIGURE 14.1 Menu for Dos Hermanos. This menu sells as it goes around. (Courtesy Dos Hermanos. A Signature of The Levy Restaurants. Reproduced by permission.)

TACO BAR

All you can eat . . . until 3:30 P.M.
Create your own gourmet tacos or tostadas. Choose from flour or corn tortillas, Mexican beef or chicken, and an array of fresh accompaniments. Olé! $5.95

The center panel lists the Mexican entrées. The top half is headed Especiales dos Hermanos and includes nine items: Fajitas, Shrimp Fajitas, Durango Chicken, Border Grill Steak, Carnitas de Pollo, Chile Relleno, Chimichanga dos Hermanos, Pollo Fundido, and Sonora Enchilada. Prices range from $4.95 to $7.95.

The bottom half of the entrée listing, Build Your Own Combination, includes tacos, enchiladas, flautas, tostadas, chimichangas, and burritos. Each items costs $2.95.

At the top of the right-hand panel are North-of-the-Border Favorites, basically a sandwich listing. It includes four hamburgers—the All-American, the International, the Sonora, and the Tex-Mex Burger, followed by El Peep—fried chicken breast with shredded lettuce, sliced tomato, and Russian dressing on a toasted onion roll. Last are the Texas Barbequed Beef Brisket and Southwest Barbequed Pork Sandwich. All of these items include shoestring potatoes and cowboy relish and cost $5.25 (except for one item that is $4.95).

The final food listing, Postres, has some unusual desserts listed: Fried Ice Cream, Flan Veracruz, Sopapillas, and Drunken Chocolate Cake—Chocolate chocolate cake soaked in rum and layered with chocolate butter cream filling. The desserts are priced at $2.50 and $1.95. All items are available for takeout.

The drink list on the back cover includes margaritas—plain or in five fruit flavors and in two glass sizes and two pitcher sizes. No prices are listed for the margaritas. Next comes Gulp of Mexico—a 27-ounce margarita served with Cuervo Float for $5.50. Under the heading Cerveza, eight Mexican and eight American beers are listed. House wines and sangria are also offered. During Fiesta Time, 3:00 to 8:00 P.M. Monday through Friday, complimentary appetizers are available at the Taco Bar.

Hillary's

Hillary's menu looks as through it were put together by a computer that selected the food and drink the average American likes best (Figure 14.2). Well organized and easy to read, this menu measures 8¼ by 14½ inches, folds in half, and is printed in two colors—green and gold—on cream-colored paper. The front and back covers are solid dark green, with the name and copy in white and gold.

What did the "computer" decide are America's favorites? Appetizers include Fried Onion Loaf, Chesapeake Bay Crab Cakes, Nachos, Super Nachos, Hillary's Potato Cheese Chips with Bacon and Red Peppers, Fresh

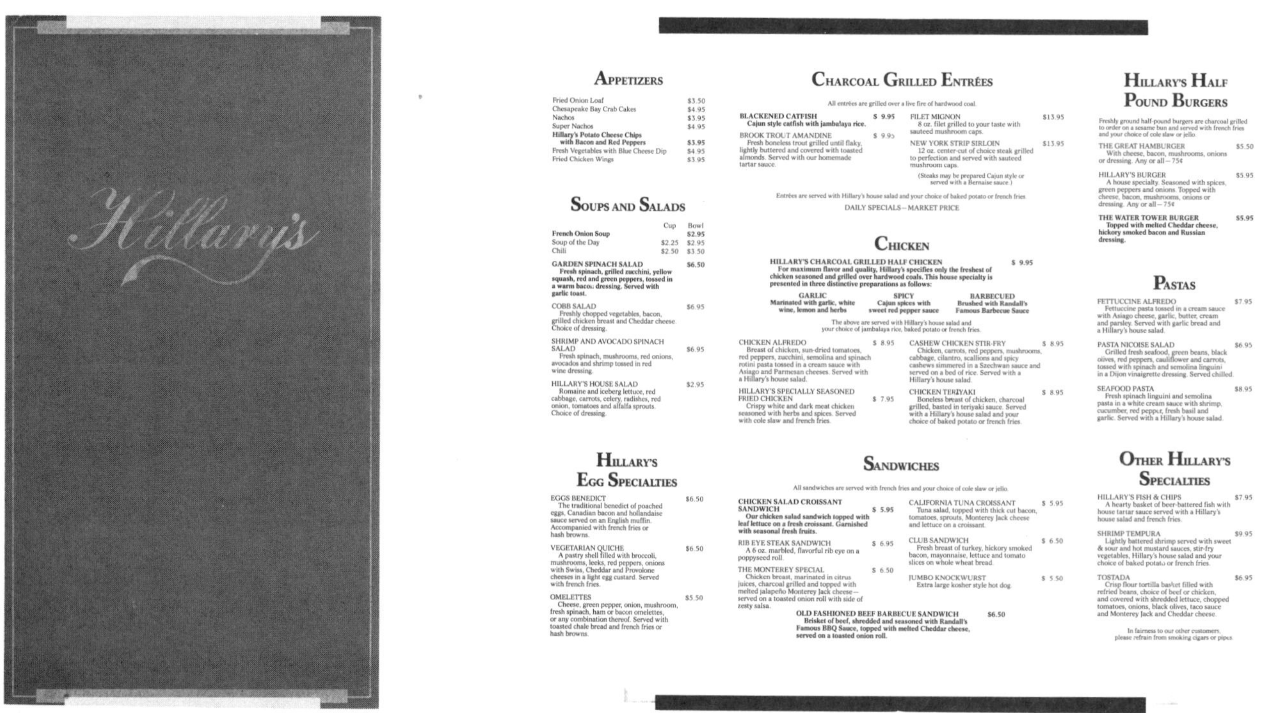

Hillary's

APPETIZERS

Fried Onion Loaf	$3.50
Chesapeake Bay Crab Cakes	$4.95
Nachos	$3.95
Super Nachos	$4.95
Hillary's Potato Cheese Chips with Bacon and Red Peppers	**$3.95**
Fresh Vegetables with Blue Cheese Dip	$4.95
Fried Chicken Wings	$3.95

SOUPS AND SALADS

	Cup	Bowl
French Onion Soup		**$2.95**
Soup of the Day	$2.25	$2.95
Chili	$2.50	$3.50

GARDEN SPINACH SALAD **$6.50**
Fresh spinach, grilled zucchini, yellow squash, red and green peppers, tossed in a warm bacon dressing. Served with garlic toast.

COBB SALAD $6.95
Freshly chopped vegetables, bacon, grilled chicken breast and Cheddar cheese. Choice of dressing.

SHRIMP AND AVOCADO SPINACH SALAD $6.95
Fresh spinach, mushrooms, red onions, avocados and shrimp tossed in red wine dressing.

HILLARY'S HOUSE SALAD $2.95
Romaine and iceberg lettuce, red cabbage, carrots, celery, radishes, red onion, tomatoes and alfalfa sprouts. Choice of dressing.

HILLARY'S EGG SPECIALTIES

EGGS BENEDICT $6.50
The traditional benedict of poached eggs, Canadian bacon and hollandaise sauce served on an English muffin. Accompanied with french fries or hash browns.

VEGETARIAN QUICHE $6.50
A pastry shell filled with broccoli, mushrooms, leeks, red peppers, onions with Swiss, Cheddar and Provolone cheeses in a light egg custard. Served with french fries.

OMELETTES $5.50
Cheese, green pepper, onion, mushroom, fresh spinach, ham or bacon omelettes, or any combination thereof. Served with toasted chale bread and french fries or hash browns.

CHARCOAL GRILLED ENTRÉES

All entrées are grilled over a live fire of hardwood coal.

BLACKENED CATFISH **$ 9.95**
Cajun style catfish with jambalaya rice.

BROOK TROUT AMANDINE $ 9.95
Fresh boneless trout grilled until flaky, lightly buttered and covered with toasted almonds. Served with our homemade tartar sauce.

FILET MIGNON $13.95
8 oz. filet grilled to your taste with sauteed mushroom caps.

NEW YORK STRIP SIRLOIN $13.95
12 oz. center-cut of choice steak grilled to perfection and served with sauteed mushroom caps.

(Steaks may be prepared Cajun style or served with a Bernaise sauce.)

Entrées are served with Hillary's house salad and your choice of baked potato or french fries.

DAILY SPECIALS—MARKET PRICE

CHICKEN

HILLARY'S CHARCOAL GRILLED HALF CHICKEN **$ 9.95**
For maximum flavor and quality, Hillary's specifies only the freshest of chicken seasoned and grilled over hardwood coals. This house specialty is presented in three distinctive preparations as follows:

GARLIC	SPICY	BARBECUED
Marinated with garlic, white wine, lemon and herbs	**Cajun spices with sweet red pepper sauce**	**Brushed with Randall's Famous Barbecue Sauce**

The above are served with Hillary's house salad and your choice of jambalaya rice, baked potato or french fries.

CHICKEN ALFREDO $ 8.95
Breast of chicken, sun-dried tomatoes, red peppers, zucchini, semolina and spinach rotini pasta tossed in a cream sauce with Asiago and Parmesan cheeses. Served with a Hillary's house salad.

HILLARY'S SPECIALLY SEASONED FRIED CHICKEN $ 7.95
Crispy white and dark meat chicken seasoned with herbs and spices. Served with cole slaw and french fries.

CASHEW CHICKEN STIR-FRY $ 8.95
Chicken, carrots, red peppers, mushrooms, cabbage, cilantro, scallions and spicy cashews simmered in a Szechwan sauce and served on a bed of rice. Served with a Hillary's house salad.

CHICKEN TERIYAKI $ 8.95
Boneless breast of chicken, charcoal grilled, basted in teriyaki sauce. Served with a Hillary's house salad and your choice of baked potato or french fries.

SANDWICHES

All sandwiches are served with french fries and your choice of cole slaw or jello.

CHICKEN SALAD CROISSANT SANDWICH **$ 5.95**
Our chicken salad sandwich topped with leaf lettuce on a fresh croissant. Garnished with seasonal fresh fruits.

RIB EYE STEAK SANDWICH $ 6.95
A 6 oz. marbled, flavorful rib eye on a poppyseed roll.

THE MONTEREY SPECIAL $ 6.50
Chicken breast, marinated in citrus juices, charcoal grilled and topped with melted jalapeño Monterey Jack cheese—served on a toasted onion roll with side of zesty salsa.

CALIFORNIA TUNA CROISSANT $ 5.95
Tuna salad, topped with thick cut bacon, tomatoes, sprouts, Monterey Jack cheese and lettuce on a croissant.

CLUB SANDWICH $ 6.50
Fresh breast of turkey, hickory smoked bacon, mayonnaise, lettuce and tomato slices on whole wheat bread.

JUMBO KNOCKWURST $ 5.50
Extra large kosher style hot dog.

OLD FASHIONED BEEF BARBECUE SANDWICH **$6.50**
Brisket of beef, shredded and seasoned with Randall's Famous BBQ Sauce, topped with melted Cheddar cheese, served on a toasted onion roll.

HILLARY'S HALF POUND BURGERS

Freshly ground half-pound burgers are charcoal grilled to order on a sesame bun and served with french fries and your choice of cole slaw or jello.

THE GREAT HAMBURGER $5.50
With cheese, bacon, mushrooms, onions or dressing. Any or all—75¢

HILLARY'S BURGER $5.95
A house specialty. Seasoned with spices, green peppers and onions. Topped with cheese, bacon, mushrooms, onions or dressing. Any or all—75¢

THE WATER TOWER BURGER **$5.95**
Topped with melted Cheddar cheese, hickory smoked bacon and Russian dressing.

PASTAS

FETTUCCINE ALFREDO $7.95
Fettuccine pasta tossed in a cream sauce with Asiago cheese, garlic, butter, cream and parsley. Served with garlic bread and a Hillary's house salad.

PASTA NICOISE SALAD $6.95
Grilled fresh seafood, green beans, black olives, red peppers, cauliflower and carrots, tossed with spinach and semolina linguini in a Dijon vinaigrette dressing. Served chilled.

SEAFOOD PASTA $8.95
Fresh spinach linguini and semolina pasta in a white cream sauce with shrimp, cucumber, red pepper, fresh basil and garlic. Served with a Hillary's house salad.

OTHER HILLARY'S SPECIALTIES

HILLARY'S FISH & CHIPS $7.95
A hearty basket of beer-battered fish with house tartar sauce served with a Hillary's house salad and french fries.

SHRIMP TEMPURA $9.95
Lightly battered shrimp served with sweet & sour and hot mustard sauces, stir-fry vegetables, Hillary's house salad and your choice of baked potato or french fries.

TOSTADA $6.95
Crisp flour tortilla basket filled with refried beans, choice of beef or chicken, and covered with shredded lettuce, chopped tomatoes, onions, black olives, taco sauce and Monterey Jack and Cheddar cheese.

In fairness to our other customers, please refrain from smoking cigars or pipes.

FIGURE 14.2 Hillary's menu. This is a menu that helps sell what is served. (Courtesy Hillary's. A Signature of The Levy Restaurants. Reproduced by permission.)

Vegetables with Blue Cheese Dip, and Fried Chicken Wings. Prices range from $3.50 to $4.95.

The Soups and Salads are next on the left-hand side of the menu. In addition to French Onion Soup and Soup of the Day, Chili is also offered by the cup or the bowl. Four salads are listed: Garden Spinach Salad, Cobb Salad, Shrimp and Avocado Spinach Salad, and Hillary's House Salad. Prices range from $2.95 to $6.95.

The last listing in the left-hand section is Hillary's Egg Specialties: Eggs Benedict, Vegetarian Quiche, and a selection of Omelettes. Prices are $5.50 and $6.50.

The center entrée section of this menu begins with Charcoal Grilled Entrées: Blackened Catfish, Brook Trout Amandine, Filet Mignon, and New York Strip Sirloin. The menu informs the customer that all entrées are grilled over a live fire of hardwood coal and that steaks may be prepared Cajun style or served with a bearnaise sauce. A house salad and baked or french-fried potatoes are included.

Under the heading Chicken are five entrées. First, listed in bold uppercase type is Hillary's Charcoal Grilled Half Chicken, a house specialty prepared in three ways:

Garlic	Spicy	Barbecued
Marinated with garlic, white wine, lemon, and herbs	Cajun spices with sweet pepper sauce	Brushed with Randall's Famous Barbecue Sauce

The other chicken entrées are Chicken Alfredo, Hillary's Specially Seasoned Fried Chicken, Cashew Chicken Stir-Fry, and Chicken Teriyaki. Prices range from $7.95 to $9.95.

At the bottom center are the seven sandwiches. Two are featured with bold type: Chicken Salad Croissant Sandwich and the Old Fashioned Beef Barbecue Sandwich. The other sandwiches are Rib Eye Steak, Monterey Special, California Tuna Croissant, Club Sandwich, and Jumbo Knockwurst. Prices range from $5.50 to $5.95.

Next comes a listing of three pastas: Fettucine Alfredo, Pasta Niçoise Salad, and Seafood Pasta. The prices are $7.95, $6.95, and $8.95.

The final listing is Other Hillary's Specials: Hillary's Fish and Chips, Shrimp Tempura, and Tostada. Prices are $7.95, $6.95, and $9.95.

An overview of this menu shows that a great number of favorites have been included: a couple of steaks, hamburgers, plenty of seafood, chicken featured sandwiches, salads, a couple of Mexican items, and Italian pastas.

In addition, Hillary's has a separate small—5 by 9 inches—Spring and Summer Menu that lists six special entrées: Good Fortune Fruit Plate, Country Smokehouse Sandwich, Chicken Niçoise Salad, Spicy Chicken and Noodles, Skillet Paella, and Pacific Coast Salmon Sandwich.

Hillary's also has a separate dessert menu offering ten desserts—some old favorites, others new creations. Prices range from $2.50 to $3.50.

Randall's Ribhouse

Randall's Ribhouse dinner menu has three panels measuring 5½ by 15 inches folded and 16½ by 15 inches open (Figure 14.3). The paper is coated with a glossy finish. The cover (front and back) is black with the name and copy reversed in white. The second color is red. As indicated by the name, ribs are the featured item. The entire menu has a Southwestern flavor, with the main emphasis on red-meat entrées, although seafood and chicken are not ignored. Even the sandwiches, soups, and salads have a spicy, Western-Southern taste.

Under the heading Barbeque Country Appetizers are soup of the day and seven appetizers—Hot Wings (chicken), Spicy Popcorn Shrimp, Smoked Shrimp in the Shell, Jumbo Shrimp Cocktail, Texas Panhandle Chili, and Fried Louisiana-Style Catfish, plus a Combination Appetizer that includes all of the above. Prices range from $2.25 for the soup to $7.95 for the Combination Appetizer.

Next on the left-hand panel is the listing Sandwiches and Salads. The sandwiches are Ribhouse Burger, Rib-Eye Steak Sandwich, and Southwestern BBQ Brisket of Beef, which is more of an entrée than a sandwich. The salads are Grilled Chicken Salad, Market Cobb Salad, and Seafood Salad. Sandwiches are $6.95 and $7.95, and salads are $7.95, $9.95, and $12.95.

The top center feature entrée listing on this menu is Ribs—Baby Back Ribs, Veal Back Ribs, Texas Beef Ribs, and Randall's Rib Mix. Prices range from $11.95 to $14.95. The rib story does not end here, however. Under the heading of Combinations are a selection of ribs combined with other entrée items—Mixed Grill, Randall's Rib Mix, Chicken and Ribs, Catfish and Ribs, Filet Mignon and Ribs, and Shrimp and Ribs. Prices on these items range from $14.95 to $17.95.

The bottom center panel entrée heading is Prime Meats: Filet Mignon, Prime New York Sirloin Strip, and Prime Kansas City Cut Strip. These steaks are served in different sizes and range in price from $13.95 to $23.95.

The Chicken and Seafood listing on the top half of the right-hand panel includes Fresh Fish Selection of the Day, Charcoal Grilled Swordfish Steak, Barbequed Salmon, Barbequed Chicken, Southern Fried Chicken, Blackened Chicken Breast, Applewood-Smoked Chicken, Catfish Filet, and Spicy Barbequed Shrimp. Prices range from $10.95 to $17.95.

The final listing on this menu, Super Sides, includes Jambalaya Rice, French Fries, Randall's House Salad, Traditional Caesar's Salad, Celery Slaw, Fried Onions, Fresh Vegetable of the Day, and Randall's Famous BBQ sauce (to go).

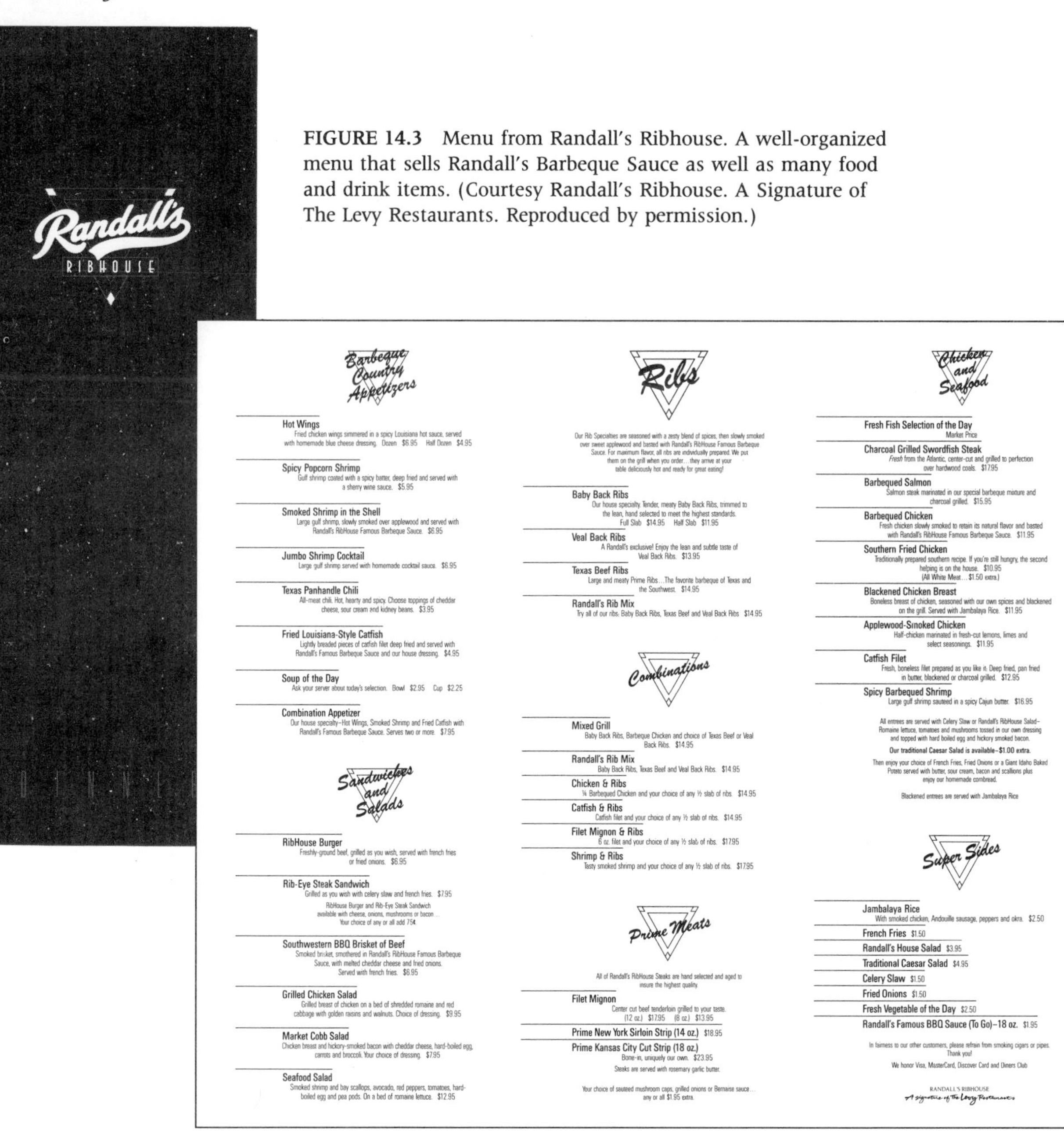

Randall's
RIBHOUSE

Barbeque Country Appetizers

Hot Wings
Fried chicken wings simmered in a spicy Louisiana hot sauce, served with homemade blue cheese dressing. Dozen $6.95 Half Dozen $4.95

Spicy Popcorn Shrimp
Gulf shrimp coated with a spicy batter, deep fried and served with a sherry wine sauce. $5.95

Smoked Shrimp in the Shell
Large gulf shrimp, slowly smoked over applewood and served with Randall's RibHouse Famous Barbeque Sauce. $6.95

Jumbo Shrimp Cocktail
Large gulf shrimp served with homemade cocktail sauce. $6.95

Texas Panhandle Chili
All-meat chili. Hot, hearty and spicy. Choose toppings of cheddar cheese, sour cream and kidney beans. $3.95

Fried Louisiana-Style Catfish
Lightly breaded pieces of catfish filet deep fried and served with Randall's Famous Barbeque Sauce and our house dressing. $4.95

Soup of the Day
Ask your server about today's selection. Bowl $2.95 Cup $2.25

Combination Appetizer
Our house specialty–Hot Wings, Smoked Shrimp and Fried Catfish with Randall's Famous Barbeque Sauce. Serves two or more. $7.95

Sandwiches and Salads

RibHouse Burger
Freshly-ground beef, grilled as you wish, served with french fries or fried onions. $6.95

Rib-Eye Steak Sandwich
Grilled as you wish with celery slaw and french fries. $7.95

RibHouse Burger and Rib-Eye Steak Sandwich available with cheese, onions, mushrooms or bacon… Your choice of any or all add 75¢

Southwestern BBQ Brisket of Beef
Smoked brisket, smothered in Randall's RibHouse Famous Barbeque Sauce, with melted cheddar cheese and fried onions. Served with french fries. $6.95

Grilled Chicken Salad
Grilled breast of chicken on a bed of shredded romaine and red cabbage with golden raisins and walnuts. Choice of dressing. $9.95

Market Cobb Salad
Chicken breast and hickory-smoked bacon with cheddar cheese, hard-boiled egg, carrots and broccoli. Your choice of dressing. $7.95

Seafood Salad
Smoked shrimp and bay scallops, avocado, red peppers, tomatoes, hard-boiled egg and pea pods. On a bed of romaine lettuce. $12.95

Ribs

Our Rib Specialties are seasoned with a zesty blend of spices, then slowly smoked over sweet applewood and basted with Randall's RibHouse Famous Barbeque Sauce. For maximum flavor, all ribs are individually prepared. We put them on the grill when you order…they arrive at your table deliciously hot and ready for great eating!

Baby Back Ribs
Our house specialty. Tender, meaty Baby Back Ribs, trimmed to the lean, hand selected to meet the highest standards. Full Slab $14.95 Half Slab $11.95

Veal Back Ribs
A Randall's exclusive! Enjoy the lean and subtle taste of Veal Back Ribs. $13.95

Texas Beef Ribs
Large and meaty Prime Ribs…The favorite barbeque of Texas and the Southwest. $14.95

Randall's Rib Mix
Try all of our ribs: Baby Back Ribs, Texas Beef and Veal Back Ribs $14.95

Combinations

Mixed Grill
Baby Back Ribs, Barbeque Chicken and choice of Texas Beef or Veal Back Ribs. $14.95

Randall's Rib Mix
Baby Back Ribs, Texas Beef and Veal Back Ribs. $14.95

Chicken & Ribs
¼ Barbequed Chicken and your choice of any ½ slab of ribs. $14.95

Catfish & Ribs
Catfish filet and your choice of any ½ slab of ribs. $14.95

Filet Mignon & Ribs
6 oz. filet and your choice of any ½ slab of ribs. $17.95

Shrimp & Ribs
Tasty smoked shrimp and your choice of any ½ slab of ribs. $17.95

Prime Meats

All of Randall's RibHouse Steaks are hand selected and aged to insure the highest quality.

Filet Mignon
Center cut beef tenderloin grilled to your taste. (12 oz.) $17.95 (8 oz.) $13.95

Prime New York Sirloin Strip (14 oz.) $18.95

Prime Kansas City Cut Strip (18 oz.)
Bone-in, uniquely our own. $23.95

Steaks are served with rosemary garlic butter.

Your choice of sauteed mushroom caps, grilled onions or Bernaise sauce… any or all $1.95 extra.

Chicken and Seafood

Fresh Fish Selection of the Day
Market Price

Charcoal Grilled Swordfish Steak
Fresh from the Atlantic, center-cut and grilled to perfection over hardwood coals. $17.95

Barbequed Salmon
Salmon steak marinated in our special barbeque mixture and charcoal grilled. $15.95

Barbequed Chicken
Fresh chicken slowly smoked to retain its natural flavor and basted with Randall's RibHouse Famous Barbeque Sauce. $11.95

Southern Fried Chicken
Traditionally prepared southern recipe. If you're still hungry, the second helping is on the house. $10.95 (All White Meat…$1.50 extra.)

Blackened Chicken Breast
Boneless breast of chicken, seasoned with our own spices and blackened on the grill. Served with Jambalaya Rice. $11.95

Applewood-Smoked Chicken
Half-chicken marinated in fresh-cut lemons, limes and select seasonings. $11.95

Catfish Filet
Fresh, boneless filet prepared as you like it: Deep fried, pan fried in butter, blackened or charcoal grilled. $12.95

Spicy Barbequed Shrimp
Large gulf shrimp sauteed in a spicy Cajun butter. $16.95

All entrees are served with Celery Slaw or Randall's RibHouse Salad–Romaine lettuce, tomatoes and mushrooms tossed in our own dressing and topped with hard boiled egg and hickory smoked bacon.

Our traditional Caesar Salad is available–$1.00 extra.

Then enjoy your choice of French Fries, Fried Onions or a Giant Idaho Baked Potato served with butter, sour cream, bacon and scallions plus enjoy our homemade cornbread.

Blackened entrees are served with Jambalaya Rice

Super Sides

Jambalaya Rice
With smoked chicken, Andouille sausage, peppers and okra. $2.50

French Fries $1.50

Randall's House Salad $3.95

Traditional Caesar Salad $4.95

Celery Slaw $1.50

Fried Onions $1.50

Fresh Vegetable of the Day $2.50

Randall's Famous BBQ Sauce (To Go)–18 oz. $1.95

In fairness to our other customers, please refrain from smoking cigars or pipes. Thank you!

We honor Visa, MasterCard, Discover Card and Diners Club

RANDALL'S RIBHOUSE
A signature of The Levy Restaurants

FIGURE 14.3 Menu from Randall's Ribhouse. A well-organized menu that sells Randall's Barbeque Sauce as well as many food and drink items. (Courtesy Randall's Ribhouse. A Signature of The Levy Restaurants. Reproduced by permission.)

On the back cover are several paragraphs of institutional copy about the ribs served at Randall's Ribhouse and Randall's Famous BBQ sauce. There is also a rib photo illustration plus a photo of the bottle of BBQ sauce. This menu is set in bold and medium condensed sans-serif type which is easy to read. The coated paper is also grease-resistant, and the menu can be easily wiped clean with a damp cloth. It should have a long life looking clean and new.

Randall's Ribhouse's luncheon menu is basically a shorter version of the dinner menu. It is a two-panel, one-fold menu with the same appearance as the dinner menu. Prices tend to be generally the same, with an occasional $1.00 reduction in similar items.

The most unusual part of Randall's offering is its beer and wine list. The beer list contains sixty-six beers and ales from around the world, each identified as to its origin. The beers are priced from $2.50 to $4.25 a bottle. The back cover contains the wine list, which is limited but covers the major categories: white wines (seven), blush wines (two), red wines (seven), and sparkling wines (five). Prices are mostly in the $13 to $18 range, with one $100 wine.

This drink list measures 5½ by 12½ inches folded and 11 by 12½ inches open and is printed on the same coated paper as are the other Randall's menus.

Randall's also has a dessert menu offering Randall's Chocolate Chewy Sundae, Peach Pecan Cobbler, Randall's Cheesecake, Homemade Pecan Pie, Double Chocolate Dream Cake, Whiskey Bread Pudding, Randall's Giant Taffy Apple, Down Home Apple Pie, and Ice Cream. Prices vary from $1.95 to $3.50.

Ravinia

Ravinia Park (Highland Park, Illinois) is the summer home of the Chicago Symphony Orchestra where classical music, pop, jazz, and blues concerts are offered in the pavilion and on the lawn where people can picnic and listen to the music. The foodservice is provided by the Levy organization. Besides catering lawn parties, a variety of restaurants and buffets are operated for the park's enjoyment.

The premier restaurant is the Cadenza, whose menu is printed in one color, dark purple, on a light cream stock. It measures 8 by 14 inches closed and 16 by 14 inches open (Figure 14.4a). Appetizers are listed on the upper left page: Seafood Chowder, Maryland Crab Cakes, Oakwood Smoked Scottish Salmon, Cajun Barbecued Shrimp, and Shrimp Cocktail. Prices are $6.50 and $6.95. The chowder is $2.95.

The next listing, Charcoal Grilled Brochettes, includes four entrées: Shrimp and Tenderloin Teriyaki, Marinated Chicken and Shrimp, Seafood Brochette, and Oriental Chicken. Prices range from $12.95 to $14.95. The entrée includes soup or salad and vegetable or potato.

This is followed by a short salad listing of three salads: Cobb Style Seafood Salad, Grilled Chicken Salad, and Grilled Lobster and Avocado Salad. Prices are $10.95, $12.95, and $13.95.

At the top of the right-hand panel are the Daily Specials. No actual specials are listed; instead, the copy states that the server will tell the customer what the daily specials are.

Next come the six Cadenza Specialties: Norwegian Salmon, Swordfish Steak, Long Island Bay Scallops, New York Strip Sirloin, Filet Mignon, and Filet Mignon and Grilled Shrimp. Prices range from $13.95 to $18.95. The next entrée listing, Other Favorites, offers Brook Trout, Cajun Barbecued Shrimp, Provimi Veal Chop, Fried Lake Perch, and Chicken Teriyaki. Prices range from $10.95 to $17.95. Soup or salad and vegetable or potato are included with all entrées on this panel.

The Levy restaurant menus often do not list nonalcoholic beverages such as coffee, tea, milk, and soft drinks, but they do usually feature wine or beer or both. The Cadenza menu has a wine list on the back cover, listing white wines, red wines, blush wines (which have taken the place of rosé wines), and sparkling wines. Wines are not offered by the glass.

Although similar in style and color to the Cadenza menu, the Rondo menu is largely a drink list (Figure 14.4b). The wines listed are the same as on the Cadenza wine list, but here they are served by the glass. A draft beer and three bottled beers are offered, and champagne is offered by the glass at $3.50.

No specific entrées are listed under the heading Rondo Fare. Instead the copy describes the buffet:

> Your choice of three nightly entrée specials served with the gourmet buffet $14.95. Our buffet features selected gourmet salads, fresh pastas and sauces, fine seasonal fruits and berries with sauces, salad greens and accompaniments, assorted cheese and fresh breads. The buffet is also available without an entrée special for $10.95.

Desserts include five items besides the Cadenza pastry cart. They range in price from $2.50 to $3.50.

Eurasia

Eurasia, an unusual restaurant and menu concept (Figure 14.5) combines European, American, and Asian cuisines. At the top of the menu is this explanation:

> At Eurasia, East meets West in a mythical selection. Here you'll taste the flavors and cuisine of Asia, married with the cooking techniques and foods of Europe and the States. Our chefs, architects, and artists have interpreted the best of the continents to create an experience remotely familiar, playfully exotic, and engagingly romantic—a cultural assimilation of delicious consequence.

Appetizers, listed under the heading First Flavors, are Spicy Ribs, Noodles Marco Polo, Peking Chicken Salad, Stir-Fried Calamari (squid) with Roasted Red Pepper and Pine Nut Nori Butter, Tuna Tartare with Sesame Crackers, Sautéed Foie Gras with Grilled Pineapple, Lamb Pot Stickers, and Duck Wontons. Prices range from $5.95 to $12.95.

The entrées, labeled Second Flavors, are Wok Charred Tuna, Peking Duck Eurasia with Crispy Scallion Crepes, Maine Lobster and Mussels, Sautéed Shrimp with Toasted Pasta, Pan-Fried Sea Scallops with Black Bean Sauce, Whole Sizzling Flounder, Sesame Grilled Lamb Chops, Wok Charred Peppered Steak, and Roasted Tandoori-spiced Chicken with Nan (a bread). Prices range from $13.95 to $21.95.

Because this menu is entirely à la carte, the entrées are followed by rice, pasta, and vegetables: Duck Fried Rice, Seasonal Greens with Ginger Aioli (dressing), Sesame Pasta, and Sweet Spiced Indian Ratatouille. Prices are $3.95 and $4.95.

Desserts include Chocolate Spike, Apricot–Lemon Tart, Ice Kacange (finely shaved ice, fresh fruit purée, and fresh fruit), Fried Banana Wontons, Ice Cream Eurasia, The Great Wall (an almond meringue box, white chocolate chip mousse, caramel mousse with dark chocolate and caramel sauces), Sweet Lemon Soup (fresh fruit, sweet almond mousse, and candied orange peel in a cool lemon soup), and Steamed Ginger Pudding Cake. Prices range from $3.50 to $5.95.

A note informs the customer that all dishes are served family style, for sharing, and are presented to the table in succession as they are completed. Items are

Cadenza

Appetizers

MARYLAND CRAB CAKES
Delicate crabmeat with peppers, onions and spices, deep fried and served with our own chili pepper mayonnaise. A Cadenza favorite. $6.50

OAKWOOD SMOKED SCOTTISH SALMON
With chopped egg, diced red onion, capers, lime wedges, our homemade dill sauce and toast points. $6.50

CAJUN BARBECUED SHRIMP
Tender shrimp sauteed in a zesty paprika and black pepper butter sauce. $6.95

SHRIMP COCKTAIL
Five jumbo shrimp on ice with cocktail sauce. $6.95

CADENZA SEAFOOD CHOWDER $2.95

Charcoal Grilled Brochettes

SHRIMP AND TENDERLOIN TERIYAKI
Skewer of shrimp and tenderloin with peppers and red onion. Basted with teriyaki sauce. $13.95

MARINATED CHICKEN AND SHRIMP
Seasoned with herbs, lemon and white wine. $12.95

SEAFOOD BROCHETTE
Swordfish, shrimp and scallops skewered with pea pods. Served with homemade tartar sauce. $14.95

ORIENTAL CHICKEN
Breast of chicken, Chinese mushrooms, pea pods and onions. Basted with sweet and sour sauce. $12.95

Each entree includes your choice of a cup of Cadenza Seafood Chowder or a house dinner salad and a choice of seasoned rice, fresh vegetables or baked potato.

Salads

COBB STYLE SEAFOOD SALAD
Bay scallops, baby shrimp, broccoli, carrots, chopped egg with tomato and lemon wedges on a bed of fresh greens. Choice of dressing. $12.95

GRILLED CHICKEN SALAD
Grilled breast of chicken on a bed of shredded romaine with red cabbage, golden raisins and walnuts. $10.95

GRILLED LOBSTER AND AVOCADO SALAD
Lobster tail charcoal grilled and sliced with red peppers, pea pods and carrots served on a bed of fresh greens. $13.95

Daily Specials

Each day, our Chef hand selects the freshest and finest seafoods, meat and poultry available. He then prepares our specials using fresh herbs and other fine products. We proudly offer these selections in addition to our regular menu.

Your server will present the specials available this evening.

Cadenza Specialties

NORWEGIAN SALMON
Flavorful Norwegian salmon, oven roasted with fresh oregano and thyme. Served with our rich white wine and butter beurre blanc sauce. $17.95

SWORDFISH STEAK
Fresh from the Atlantic, center cut and grilled over a live fire of hardwood coals. Served with our own special tartar sauce. $17.95

LONG ISLAND BAY SCALLOPS
Lightly breaded and sauteed in butter until golden brown. Served with our own special tartar sauce. $13.95

NEW YORK STRIP SIRLOIN
12 oz. specially selected center-cut steak grilled to your specifications and served with sauteed mushroom caps and herb butter. $16.95

FILET MIGNON
8 oz. center-cut beef tenderloin grilled to your taste with sauteed mushroom caps and herb butter. $15.95

FILET MIGNON & GRILLED SHRIMP
6 oz. center-cut beef tenderloin accompanied by a skewer of four large shrimp grilled in the shell. Served with drawn butter. $18.95

Other Favorites

BROOK TROUT
Fresh boneless trout, grilled until flaky, lightly buttered and served with our own special tartar sauce. $12.95

CAJUN BARBECUED SHRIMP
Tender shrimp sauteed in a zesty paprika and black pepper butter sauce. $16.95

PROVIMI VEAL CHOP
10 oz. center-cut veal chop charcoal grilled to your taste and topped with herb butter. $17.95

FRIED LAKE PERCH
Fresh lake perch, lightly breaded and deep-fried with homemade tartar sauce. $13.95

CHICKEN TERIYAKI
Boneless breast of chicken, basted in teriyaki sauce. $10.95

Each entree includes your choice of a cup of Cadenza Seafood Chowder or a house dinner salad and a choice of seasoned rice, fresh vegetables or baked potato.

Rondo

**We offer wines daily for you to try by the glass.
Your server will introduce today's selections.**

White Wines

Liberty School Chardonnay, Napa Valley
Rich and buttery. $13.00
Rodney Strong Chardonnay, Sonoma County
Crisp, medium-bodied. Nice fruit flavors. $18.00
Cuvaison Chardonnay, Napa Valley
Full-bodied, rich and full of fruit flavors. $28.00
Robert Mondavi Fume Blanc, Napa Valley
The founder of Fume Blanc! Dry, full-bodied. $23.00
Clos du Bois Riesling, Columbia Valley
Spicy, light, refreshing. $17.00
Charles Krug Chenin Blanc, Napa Valley
Refreshing, fruity, slightly sweet. $16.00

Red Wines

Beaulieu Vineyards Beautour Cabernet Sauvignon, Napa Valley
Robust, full of berry flavors. $16.00
William Hill "Silver" Cabernet Sauvignon, Napa Valley
Full-bodied, rich, with currant and cherry flavors. $20.00
Franciscan Merlot, Napa Valley
Smooth and velvety with a rich blackberry flavor. $18.00
Jaboulet-Vercherre Beaujolais-Villages,
Burgundy, light-bodied, fresh, with lots of cherry flavor. $17.00

Blush Wines

Sutter Home White Zinfandel, Napa Valley
Crisp and fruity, slightly sweet. $12.00
Robert Mondavi White Zinfandel, Napa Valley
Refreshing, medium-sweet. $14.00

Sparkling Wines

Charles LeFranc Sparkling White Zinfandel, Monterey County
A great blend of zinfandel and bubbles.
Light and refreshing with a slightly sweet finish. $15.00
Paul Cheneau Blanc de Blanc, Split, Spain
Dry and crisp, full of fruit flavor. $6.00
Korbel Extra-Dry Champagne
Crisp, medium-dry. $19.00
Piper Sonoma Brut, Sonoma
Very dry, with fruit flavors. $27.00

Rondo Fare

Your choice of three nightly entree specials served with the gourmet buffet. $14.95

Our buffet features selected gourmet salads, fresh pastas and sauces, fine seasonal fruits and berries with sauces, salad greens and accompaniments, assorted cheeses and fresh breads.

The buffet is also available without an entree special for $10.95.

Beer & Wine

Draft
Michelob $2.75

Bottled
Miller Lite $2.75
Heineken $3.00
Amstel Light $3.00

Champagne by the Glass $3.50

Wine Bar Market Price

We offer wines daily for you to try by the glass.
Your server will introduce today's selections.

Desserts

Cappuccino Ice Cream
Our signature dessert. $2.95

Cadenza Pastry Cart
A fine selection of fresh tortes, tarts and pastries.
Selection varies daily. Market Price

Turtle Pie with Caramel Sauce $3.50

Chocolate Torte $3.50

Black Raspberry Sorbet $2.50

Lemon Ice $2.50

FIGURE 14.4a, b Menus for the Cadenza and Rondo. When the Chicago Symphony Orchestra plays at Ravinia Park in the summer, Cadenza and Rondo serve the inner person. (Courtesy Ravinia Festival Dining. A Signature of The Levy Restaurants. Reproduced by permission.)

coded for spiciness with checks for mild (one check), spicy (two checks), and very spicy (three checks).

The Eurasia's drink list also combines East and West. First are five special cocktails with an Oriental flavor under the heading Kindred Spirits. They are priced at $3.75 and $4.00. A selection of two domestic and eleven imported beers is priced from $2.50 to $5.00. Three choices of Saké, at $3.25 and $3.50, are followed by the wine list, which includes two house wines, three sparkling wines, sixteen white wines, and six red wines. White wines are emphasized because they are now more popular than red wines. The house wines sell by the glass at $3.25. The other wines vary in price from $15 to $75 per bottle.

Eurasia

DINNER

Chef Stewart Parsons

At Eurasia, East meets West in a mythical setting. Here you'll taste the flavors and cuisines of Asia, married with the cooking techniques and foods of Europe and the States. Our chefs, architects and artists have interpreted the best of the continents to create an experience remotely familiar, playfully exotic, and engagingly romantic. A cultural assimilation of delicious consequence.

FIRST FLAVORS

SPICY RIBS
Grilled baby back ribs, caramelized with a sweet Thai pepper, black bean and scallion glaze $6.95

NOODLES MARCO POLO
Japanese buckwheat pasta, Manila clams, seasonal vegetables, ginger and garlic $9.95

PEKING CHICKEN SALAD
Peking roasted chicken, red leaf lettuce, frisee, sweet mango dressing with crispy fried parsnips $9.95

STIR-FRIED CALAMARI WITH ROASTED RED PEPPER AND PINE NUT NORI BUTTER
Calamari and seasonal spring vegetables stir-fried in a roasted red pepper and pine nut nori butter sauce $6.95

TUNA TARTARE WITH SESAME CRACKERS
Sashimi grade tuna, pickled ginger, Chinese parsley and tamari $8.95

SAUTEED FOIE GRAS WITH GRILLED PINEAPPLE
Goose liver sauteed with a ginger pineapple raspberry glaze served with grilled pineapple $12.95

LAMB POT STICKERS
Lamb, Napa cabbage, mushrooms and cumin filled spinach pasta crescents with sesame soy rice wine vinegar $6.95

DUCK WONTONS
Peking duck, Napa cabbage, red and yellow pepper filled fried wontons with a roasted garlic sake sauce $5.95

SECOND FLAVORS

WOK CHARRED TUNA
Sashimi grade tuna seasoned with shichimi togarashi spice mix wok-charred to medium rare with mango-papaya tear drop tomato salsa $15.95

PEKING DUCK EURASIA WITH CRISPY SCALLION CREPES
Peking roasted duck, apricot-plum chutney, cherry-ginger relish and crispy scallion crepes $21.95

MAINE LOBSTER & MUSSELS
Steamed Maine lobster and mussels with ginger and sherry butter $19.95

SAUTEED SHRIMP WITH TOASTED PASTA
Sauteed shrimp and toasted vermicelli with shiitake mushrooms, scallions and soy chili butter $15.95

PAN-FRIED SEA SCALLOPS WITH BLACK BEAN SAUCE
Sauteed sea scallops, asparagus and black bean sauce $15.95

WHOLE SIZZLING FLOUNDER
Whole flounder deep fried to crispy golden brown with garlic chips and roasted garlic sauce $16.95

SESAME GRILLED LAMB CHOPS
Grilled prime lamb loin chops, caramelized shallots and Japanese eggplant with Eurasia's sweet sesame barbecue sauce
Two Lamb Chops $14.95 Four Lamb Chops $24.95

WOK CHARRED PEPPERED STEAK
Sirloin seasoned with shichimi togarashi spice mix, grilled bok choy, oyster mushrooms, fried red onions, mirin and ginger $18.95

ROASTED TANDOORI-SPICED CHICKEN WITH NAN
Tandoori spiced half-chicken, grilled leeks, shiitake mushrooms, cucumbers, sesame mayonnaise drizzled with fresh orange and served with Nan bread $13.95

RICE, PASTA & VEGETABLES

DUCK FRIED RICE
Peking duck, seasonal vegetables, onions, peppers, scallions, bean sprouts and cilantro stir-fried with rice $4.95

SEASONAL GREENS WITH GINGER AIOLI
Mixed seasonal greens with light ginger dressing $3.95

SESAME PASTA
Cold angel hair pasta, peppers, onions and sprouts with chili sesame mayonnaise $4.95

SWEET SPICY INDIAN RATATOUILLE
Stir-fried Japanese eggplant, zucchini, onions, red and yellow peppers with tomato-ginger chutney $4.95

DESSERTS

CHOCOLATE SPIKE
Rich, dark chocolate, pine nuts, golden raisins, spikes of white and dark chocolate with seasonal fresh fruit sauce $5.95

APRICOT-LEMON TART
Light pastry with apricot-lemon custard, raisins and lemon glaze $4.95

ICE KACANGE
A Malaysian specialty of finely shaved ice, fresh seasonal fruit puree and fresh fruit $5.95

FRIED BANANA WONTONS
Bananas, white chocolate, candied walnuts, cinnamon-sugar caramel sauce and vanilla ice cream $4.95

ICE CREAM EURASIA
Eurasia's special ice creams—licorice, mango, papaya and cinnamon $3.50

THE GREAT WALL
An almond meringue box, white chocolate chip mousse and caramel mousse, dark chocolate and caramel sauces $5.95

SWEET LEMON SOUP
Fresh fruit, sweet almond mousse and candied orange peel in a cool lemon soup $4.95

STEAMED GINGER PUDDING CAKE
A moist gingery cake with orange caramel sauce and fresh whipped cream $3.95

All dishes are served family style, for sharing, and presented to the table in succession as they are completed

MILD SPICY VERY SPICY

EURASIA
A signature of The Levy Restaurants

FIGURE 14.5 Menu from Eurasia. This menu merchandizes a new restaurant concept. (Courtesy Eurasia. A Signature of the Levy Restaurants. Reproduced by permission.)

15

The Breakfast Menu

Breakfast is the least expensive restaurant meal in the United States. According to the *Gallup 1985–1986 Annual Report on Eating Out,* the average price for breakfast in a restaurant or cafeteria was $3.05, compared with averages of $4.19 for lunch and $7.10 for dinner. This report gave average breakfast prices at different types of restaurants:

Adult oriented	$4.33
Family style	3.45
Fast food	2.27
Cafeteria	2.17

Although not every restaurant serves breakfast, almost every hotel restaurant does. The breakfast menu can be a separate menu or part of the regular menu. In either case, it should be given as much attention and care as the luncheon or dinner menu.

Most breakfast menus have the following classifications:

1. Fruit and Juices
2. Cereals
   a. Dry Cereals
   b. Hot Cereals
3. Toast, Sweet Rolls
4. Eggs
5. Egg Combinations or Specials
6. Omelettes
7. Side Orders
8. Pancakes, Waffles, French Toast
9. Beverages

The special complete breakfast combinations should have the best position on the menu (center top). Putting these items in a panel or giving them bold numbers—No. 1, No. 2, No. 3—are common ways of making them stand out and catch the eye.

Breakfast menus have become more creative. In addition, some restaurants feature breakfast from early morning through the afternoon. And the price may be above average in a fine hotel in which the breakfast menu reflects the better quality and service of the establishment. The following menus show a range of price and a variety of nonstandard breakfast items.

Holiday Inn, Minneapolis

The Holiday Inn (Minneapolis) has a vertical, single-fold menu (Figure 15.1), measuring 10 by 9¾ inches folded and 10 by 18 inches open. The cover is an attractive painting of various fruits reproduced in full color. The menu begins with the heading Eggs to Omelettes, with nine items ranging in price from $3.25 to $5.25. The featured item—set in a tinted panel—is Pronto Breakfast, three scrambled eggs with diced ham, $3.95.

The next heading is From the Bakery, with six pastry and bread items, including the Continental Breakfast, $2.95. Beverages are listed last in the left column. At the top right-hand corner is the heading Hot off the Griddle, which has seven items, including french toast, pancakes, and waffles. Prices range from $2.95 to $4.25. Featured in a tinted panel is Pancakes, Bacon and Eggs, $3.95.

Under the heading Juices, Fruits and Fibers are eight items, including hot or cold cereal with bananas or strawberries. The featured item is a Breakfast Fruit and Cheese Plate, $4.95. Five items are listed under the heading A la Carte: One Egg, Two Eggs, Bacon or Sausage, Ham, and Hash Browns.

This menu is of special interest because it is a synthesis or market study of the most popular breakfast items in thirty Holiday Inns in the Midwest. Every month these Holiday Inns send computer printouts to the Chicago regional office, where they are examined and changes are made according to the items' popularity and profitability. The result is a breakfast menu that has been reduced to the basics, plus the extras that the traveling hotel guest wants.

Eggs to Omelettes

Served with golden hash browns and toast or biscuits

Pronto Breakfast Three fluffy scrambled eggs with diced ham	3.95
Two Large Fresh Eggs Cooked any style	3.25
with bacon or sausage	4.25
with ham	5.25
Three Egg Omelette	3.95
Cheese Omelette Generous helping of cheese	4.25
Ham and Cheese Omelette Diced ham and cheese	4.50
Western Omelette Diced ham, onions and green peppers	4.50
Farmers Omelette Diced ham, cheese, onions, red and green pepper, and potatoes	5.25

From the Bakery

Continental Breakfast Large juice, choice of Danish pastry, biscuits or muffins, and lots of hot coffee or tea	2.95
Danish Pastry	1.75
Blueberry or Bran Muffins	1.95
Toast, your choice	1.00
English Muffin	1.50
Country Biscuits	1.00

Beverages

Freshly Brewed Regular or Decaffeinated Coffee	.65
Hot Chocolate	.65
Tea	.65
Milk	.65

Hot off the Griddle

French Toast Four halves of extra thick bread, batter dipped and grilled	2.95
with bacon or sausage	3.95
Buttermilk Pancakes Three hearty pancakes made to order	2.95
with bacon or sausage	3.95
Belgian Waffle	3.25
with bacon or sausage	4.25
Pancakes, Bacon and Eggs Two pancakes, two eggs any style, and bacon	3.95

Juices, Fruits and Fibers

Chilled Juices: Orange, Grapefruit, Tomato, Apple, Prune	Small .85 Large 1.50
Melon in Season	1.50
Half Grapefruit	1.50
Sliced Strawberries	1.50
Sliced Banana	1.50
Hot or Cold Cereal	1.50
with banana or strawberries	2.50
Breakfast Fruit and Cheese Plate A variety of fresh fruits and three cheeses, accompanied by a muffin	4.95

A la Carte

One Egg, any style	1.25
Two Eggs, any style	1.75
Bacon or Sausage	1.95
Ham	2.95
Hash Browns	1.25

FIGURE 15.1 Breakfast menu for Holiday Inn. Holiday Inn serves this breakfast throughout the Midwest. (Courtesy Holiday Inns, Inc. Reproduced by permission.)

Country Greens Restaurant

The Country Greens Restaurant in Ronks, Pennsylvania, has a three-panel, two-fold menu that measures 14 by 17 inches when open (Figure 15.2). The two outside panels are 6½ inches wide, and the center panel is 4 inches wide. The paper is a cream-colored, uncoated cover stock. The type and illustration are dark green and purple. A well-executed, tongue-in-cheek line drawing based on Grant Wood's painting, *American Gothic,* is printed in purple.

On the far left side of this menu the words Breakfast in the Country are printed vertically in large (72-pt.) type. The listing begins in the center panel with Beverages, Fruits & Juices, and Bakery Treats. Then on the third right-hand panel are four boxes in which the featured breakfast items are listed.

Three items are featured under the heading Our Specialties: Country Breakfast, Eggs 'n Cakes, and Country-Style French Toast. This third item is described as "slices of raisin bread layered with cream cheese and strawberry preserves, then egg-dipped and grilled to perfection. Served with maple flavored syrup, $3.50."

The second box on this panel lists three pancake variations (different toppings) and three Belgian waffles (also different toppings), priced at $2.00 and $2.75.

Six different omelettes are listed next, ranging in price from $2.75 to $3.75.

Side Plates and Cereals includes the usual breakfast menu extras as well as Lancaster County pan-fried scrapple.

The Whitehall Club

The Whitehall Club, an elegant Chicago hotel that opened to the public in 1988, serves an interesting (and more expensive) breakfast selection that exceeds the national average of $3.05. The menu has two panels and a single fold, with each panel measuring 9 by 13 inches (Figure 15.3) and is printed in dark brown on heavy white uncoated paper. The type is a decorative serif face, with the descriptions set in italics.

The food and beverage selection follows the standard breakfast menu pattern, but with extra touches. For example, Chilled Fruits and Juices (eight items) includes freshly squeezed orange and grapefruit juice (for $3.50). Under the heading Specialties are listed Two Eggs Any Style (with Bacon, Sausage, Ham or Canadian Bacon), $4.50; American Breakfast (Juice, Three Eggs, Bacon, Sausage or Ham), $11.25 (with Sirloin Steak, $14.00);

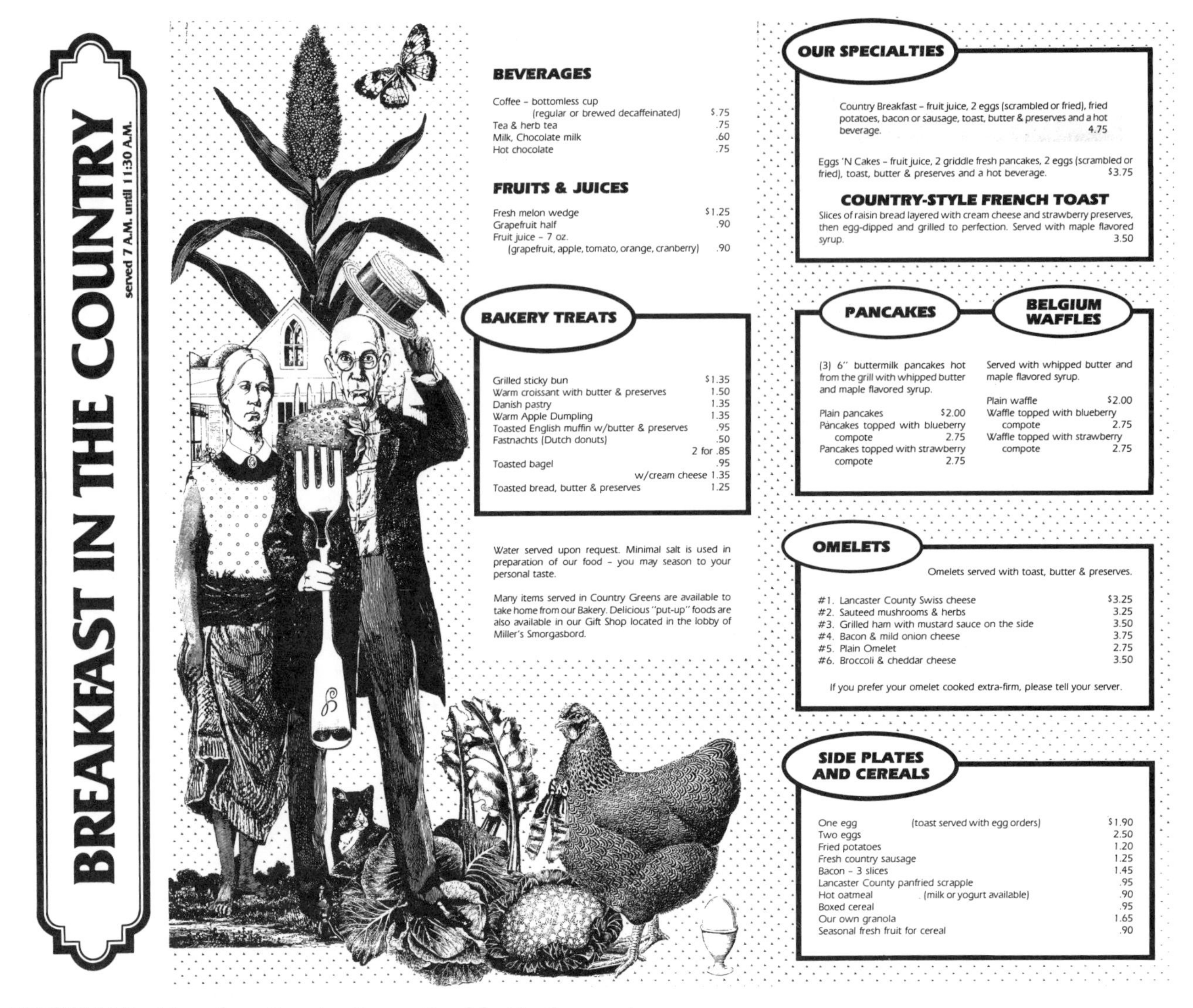

BREAKFAST IN THE COUNTRY
served 7 A.M. until 11:30 A.M.

BEVERAGES

Coffee – bottomless cup
(regular or brewed decaffeinated) $.75
Tea & herb tea .75
Milk, Chocolate milk .60
Hot chocolate .75

FRUITS & JUICES

Fresh melon wedge $1.25
Grapefruit half .90
Fruit juice – 7 oz.
(grapefruit, apple, tomato, orange, cranberry) .90

BAKERY TREATS

Grilled sticky bun $1.35
Warm croissant with butter & preserves 1.50
Danish pastry 1.35
Warm Apple Dumpling 1.35
Toasted English muffin w/butter & preserves .95
Fastnachts (Dutch donuts) .50
2 for .85
Toasted bagel .95
w/cream cheese 1.35
Toasted bread, butter & preserves 1.25

Water served upon request. Minimal salt is used in preparation of our food – you may season to your personal taste.

Many items served in Country Greens are available to take home from our Bakery. Delicious "put-up" foods are also available in our Gift Shop located in the lobby of Miller's Smorgasbord.

OUR SPECIALTIES

Country Breakfast – fruit juice, 2 eggs (scrambled or fried), fried potatoes, bacon or sausage, toast, butter & preserves and a hot beverage. 4.75

Eggs 'N Cakes – fruit juice, 2 griddle fresh pancakes, 2 eggs (scrambled or fried), toast, butter & preserves and a hot beverage. $3.75

COUNTRY-STYLE FRENCH TOAST
Slices of raisin bread layered with cream cheese and strawberry preserves, then egg-dipped and grilled to perfection. Served with maple flavored syrup. 3.50

PANCAKES

(3) 6" buttermilk pancakes hot from the grill with whipped butter and maple flavored syrup.

Plain pancakes $2.00
Pancakes topped with blueberry compote 2.75
Pancakes topped with strawberry compote 2.75

BELGIUM WAFFLES

Served with whipped butter and maple flavored syrup.

Plain waffle $2.00
Waffle topped with blueberry compote 2.75
Waffle topped with strawberry compote 2.75

OMELETS

Omelets served with toast, butter & preserves.

#1. Lancaster County Swiss cheese $3.25
#2. Sauteed mushrooms & herbs 3.25
#3. Grilled ham with mustard sauce on the side 3.50
#4. Bacon & mild onion cheese 3.75
#5. Plain Omelet 2.75
#6. Broccoli & cheddar cheese 3.50

If you prefer your omelet cooked extra-firm, please tell your server.

SIDE PLATES AND CEREALS

One egg (toast served with egg orders) $1.90
Two eggs 2.50
Fried potatoes 1.20
Fresh country sausage 1.25
Bacon – 3 slices 1.45
Lancaster County panfried scrapple .95
Hot oatmeal (milk or yogurt available) .90
Boxed cereal .95
Our own granola 1.65
Seasonal fresh fruit for cereal .90

FIGURE 15.2 Menu from Country Greens. Breakfast in the country. (Courtesy Country Greens Restaurant. Reproduced by permission.)

Omelettes, $6.75; and Corned Beef Hash with Two Poached Eggs, $9.00. From the Griddle offers four kinds of pancakes and French Toast with Whipped Orange Butter, each $8.00.

Next, The Bakery Basket is an expanded continental breakfast including breads, muffins, croissants, and Danish pastry plus preserves, juice, and coffee, for $8.00. Under the heading Continental Selections are Eggs Benedict, $9.00; Swiss Apple Pancake, $8.00; Belgian Waffle, $7.00; and Smoked Scottish Salmon Plate, Garni, $13.50. The final listings are Breakfast Breads and Pastries, Side Orders, and Beverages.

West Egg Cafe

A relatively new restaurant concept is the "breakfast all day" operation. One example is the West Egg Cafe in Chicago (Figure 15.4). The menu is printed in dark blue on white stock, and the items are listed on six long narrow columns. The food and beverage listings are comprehensive and creative.

Column 1 begins with Traditional Daystarters, the basic two-egg breakfast with accompaniments. Next come six Gourmet Pancakes, including Berried Treasures and Raisin Walnut. This is followed by Let's Talk Toast (French) and five Crepelettes: California Crepe (broccoli, cheese, avocado), Stroganoff Classic (beef, mushrooms, and sour cream), Kona Krepe (pineapple, Canadian bacon, and jack cheese), Sea Rations Deluxe (crab, seafood, mushrooms, and jack cheese), and C.C.C. (Chicago Chicken Crepe).

The final listing on this column is The Benediction: Eggs Benedict, Neptune's Benedict (with seafood), and Veggie Benedict.

The next column begins with Important Stuff: coffee, orange and grapefruit juice, followed by Eggceptional Omelettes: Cheese, Very Veggie, Ultimate Olé (with

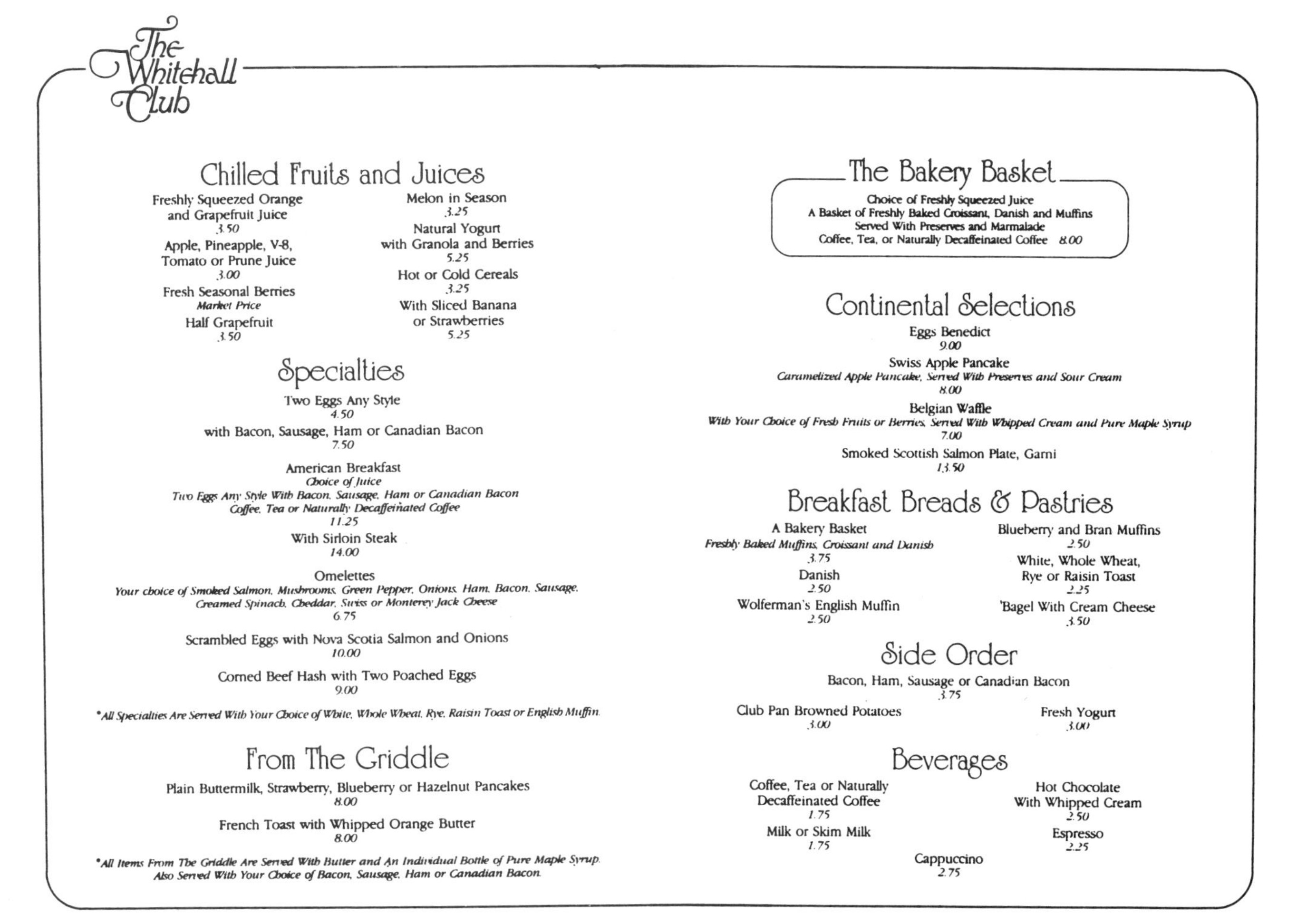

FIGURE 15.3 Breakfast menu for The Whitehall Club. Elegant early dining. (Reproduced by permission.)

chilies, onions, cheese, salsa, and sour cream), Streeterville Strogy (beef stroganoff, cheese, mushrooms, and sour cream), Bandito, Best Western, Bacado, and Lottsa Lox (lox folded into cream cheese, add onion, season, and top with tomatoes).

Column 3 is headed In Pursuit of Eggcellence. These are the bigger entrée items ranging in price from $4.95 to $5.95. All eleven entrée items are interesting and creative, as these examples show.

MAGMILE MUSHROOMS

An upscale dish of seasoned and sautéed mushroom caps, draped in bubbly cheese and served with two eggs and potatoes and an English muffin

THE GRABOWSKI

A smoked Polish sausage split and grilled, then covered with a special honey mustard, onions, and melted Swiss cheese. Extra points scored by potatoes and two eggs

THE MICHAELANGELO

An Italian frittata loaded with mushrooms, Italian sausage, green peppers, olives, pepperoni, and provolone

At the bottom of this column is a special entrée under the heading Specially Crafted Skillets, a special egg, vegetable, ham, bacon, and condiments dish.

The first segment in the next column is To Your Health, which includes Breakfast Salad, The Heartland (EggBeaters® with diced veggies, topped with cholesterol-free cheese and tomatoes, and served with whole wheat English muffin and fruit), Oatmeal, Granola, Fruit Plate, Bowl of Yogurt, and Blueberries and Cream. Next are listed soup, chili, and a variety of side orders identified as On the Side of Things.

Column 5 contains a sandwich listing plus an offering of Grilled Chicken Sandwiches. Thirteen sandwiches are listed, including:

EGGS BENJAMIN

Ham slices, tomatoes and poached eggs perched atop English muffins and covered with melted cheese, sour cream, and chives

THE DON

Italian sausage, mushrooms, green peppers, and a spicy tomato sauce served on an English muffin and topped with Italian cheeses and pepperoni

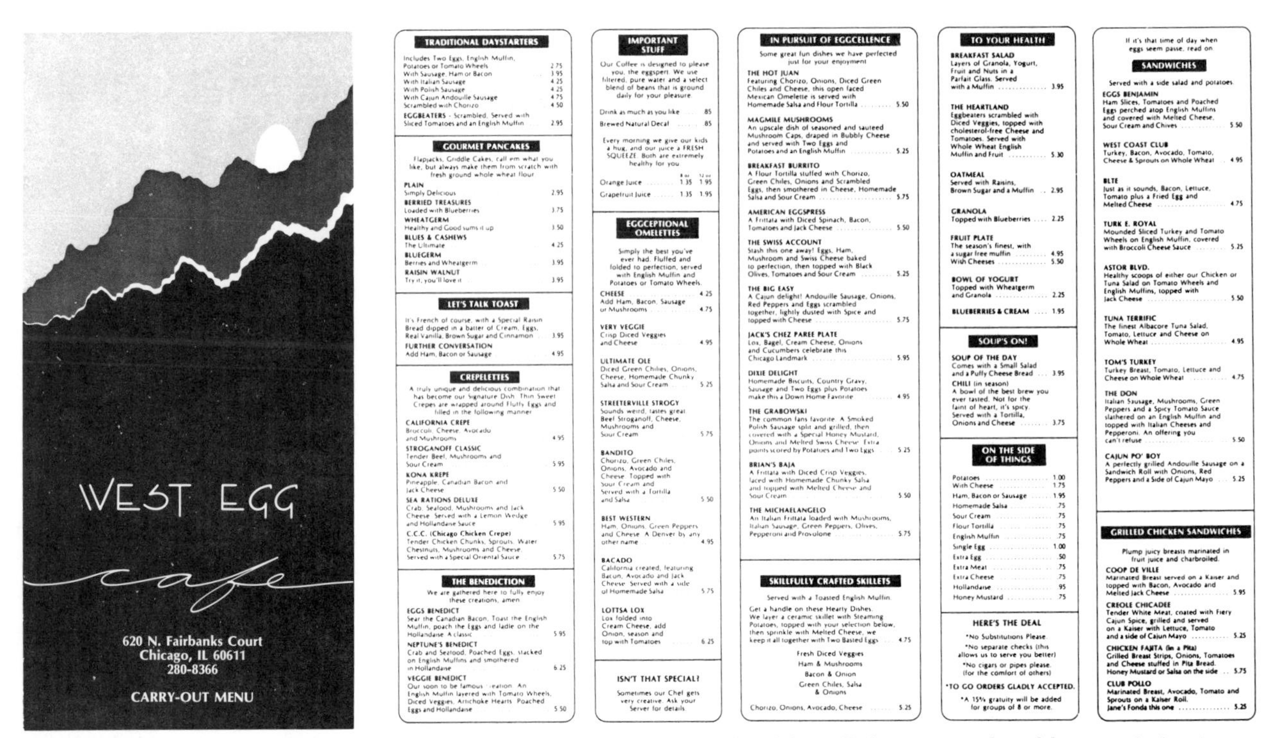

WEST EGG cafe

620 N. Fairbanks Court
Chicago, IL 60611
280-8366

CARRY-OUT MENU

TRADITIONAL DAYSTARTERS

Includes Two Eggs, English Muffin, Potatoes or Tomato Wheels 2.75
With Sausage, Ham or Bacon 3.95
With Italian Sausage 4.25
With Polish Sausage 4.25
With Cajun Andouille Sausage 4.75
Scrambled with Chorizo 4.50

EGGBEATERS - Scrambled, Served with Sliced Tomatoes and an English Muffin 2.95

GOURMET PANCAKES

Flapjacks, Griddle Cakes, call em what you like, but always make them from scratch with fresh ground whole wheat flour

PLAIN Simply Delicious 2.95
BERRIED TREASURES Loaded with Blueberries 3.75
WHEATGERM Healthy and Good sums it up 3.50
BLUES & CASHEWS The Ultimate 4.25
BLUEGERM Berries and Wheatgerm 3.95
RAISIN WALNUT Try it, you'll love it 3.95

LET'S TALK TOAST

It's French of course, with a Special Raisin Bread dipped in a batter of Cream, Eggs, Real Vanilla, Brown Sugar and Cinnamon 3.95
FURTHER CONVERSATION Add Ham, Bacon or Sausage 4.95

CREPELETTES

A truly unique and delicious combination that has become our Signature Dish. Thin Sweet Crepes are wrapped around Fluffy Eggs and filled in the following manner

CALIFORNIA CREPE Broccoli, Cheese, Avocado and Mushrooms 4.95
STROGANOFF CLASSIC Tender Beef, Mushrooms and Sour Cream 5.95
KONA KREPE Pineapple, Canadian Bacon and Jack Cheese 5.50
SEA RATIONS DELUXE Crab, Seafood, Mushrooms and Jack Cheese. Served with a Lemon Wedge and Hollandaise Sauce 5.95
C.C.C. (Chicago Chicken Crepe) Tender Chicken Chunks, Sprouts, Water Chestnuts, Mushrooms and Cheese. Served with a Special Oriental Sauce 5.75

THE BENEDICTION

We are gathered here to fully enjoy these creations, amen

EGGS BENEDICT Sear the Canadian Bacon, Toast the English Muffin, poach the Eggs and ladle on the Hollandaise. A classic 5.95
NEPTUNE'S BENEDICT Crab and Seafood, Poached Eggs, stacked on English Muffins and smothered in Hollandaise 6.25
VEGGIE BENEDICT Our soon to be famous creation. An English Muffin layered with Tomato Wheels, Diced Veggies, Artichoke Hearts, Poached Eggs and Hollandaise 5.50

IMPORTANT STUFF

Our Coffee is designed to please you, the eggspert. We use filtered, pure water and a select blend of beans that is ground daily for your pleasure.

Drink as much as you like .85
Brewed Natural Decaf .85

Every morning we give our kids a hug, and our juice a FRESH SQUEEZE. Both are extremely healthy for you.

	8 oz	12 oz
Orange Juice	1.35	1.95
Grapefruit Juice	1.35	1.95

EGGCEPTIONAL OMELETTES

Simply the best you've ever had. Fluffed and folded to perfection, served with English Muffin and Potatoes or Tomato Wheels.

CHEESE 4.25
Add Ham, Bacon, Sausage or Mushrooms 4.75
VERY VEGGIE Crisp Diced Veggies and Cheese 4.95
ULTIMATE OLE Diced Green Chilies, Onions, Cheese, Homemade Chunky Salsa and Sour Cream 5.25
STREETERVILLE STROGY Sounds weird, tastes great. Beef Stroganoff, Cheese, Mushrooms and Sour Cream 5.75
BANDITO Chorizo, Green Chiles, Onions, Avocado and Cheese. Topped with Sour Cream and Served with a Tortilla and Salsa 5.50
BEST WESTERN Ham, Onions, Green Peppers and Cheese. A Denver by any other name 4.95
BACADO California created, featuring Bacon, Avocado and Jack Cheese. Served with a side of Homemade Salsa 5.75
LOTTSA LOX Lox folded into Cream Cheese, add Onion, season and top with Tomatoes 6.25

ISN'T THAT SPECIAL?

Sometimes our Chef gets very creative. Ask your Server for details.

IN PURSUIT OF EGGCELLENCE

Some great fun dishes we have perfected just for your enjoyment

THE HOT JUAN Featuring Chorizo, Onions, Diced Green Chiles and Cheese, this open faced Mexican Omelette is served with Homemade Salsa and Flour Tortilla 5.50
MAGMILE MUSHROOMS An upscale dish of seasoned and sauteed Mushroom Caps, draped in Bubbly Cheese and served with Two Eggs and Potatoes and an English Muffin 5.25
BREAKFAST BURRITO A Flour Tortilla stuffed with Chorizo, Green Chiles, Onions and Scrambled Eggs, then smothered in Cheese, Homemade Salsa and Sour Cream 5.75
AMERICAN EGGSPRESS A Frittata with Diced Spinach, Bacon, Tomatoes and Jack Cheese 5.50
THE SWISS ACCOUNT Stash this one away! Eggs, Ham, Mushroom and Swiss Cheese baked to perfection, then topped with Black Olives, Tomatoes and Sour Cream 5.25
THE BIG EASY A Cajun delight! Andouille Sausage, Onions, Red Peppers and Eggs scrambled together, lightly dusted with Spice and topped with Cheese 5.75
JACK'S CHEZ PAREE PLATE Lox, Bagel, Cream Cheese, Onions and Cucumbers celebrate this Chicago Landmark 5.95
DIXIE DELIGHT Homemade Biscuits, Country Gravy, Sausage and Two Eggs plus Potatoes make this a Down Home Favorite 4.95
THE GRABOWSKI The common fans favorite. A Smoked Polish Sausage split and grilled, then covered with a Special Honey Mustard, Onions and Melted Swiss Cheese. Extra points scored by Potatoes and Two Eggs 5.25
BRIAN'S BAJA A Frittata with Diced Crisp Veggies, laced with Homemade Chunky Salsa and topped with Melted Cheese and Sour Cream 5.50
THE MICHAELANGELO An Italian Frittata loaded with Mushrooms, Italian Sausage, Green Peppers, Olives, Pepperoni and Provolone 5.75

SKILLFULLY CRAFTED SKILLETS

Served with a Toasted English Muffin

Get a handle on these Hearty Dishes. We layer a ceramic skillet with Steaming Potatoes, topped with your selection below, then sprinkle with Melted Cheese, we keep it all together with Two Basted Eggs 4.75

Fresh Diced Veggies
Ham & Mushrooms
Bacon & Onion
Green Chiles, Salsa & Onions
Chorizo, Onions, Avocado, Cheese 5.25

TO YOUR HEALTH

BREAKFAST SALAD Layers of Granola, Yogurt, Fruit and Nuts in a Parfait Glass. Served with a Muffin 3.95
THE HEARTLAND Eggbeaters scrambled with Diced Veggies, topped with cholesterol-free Cheese and Tomatoes. Served with Whole Wheat English Muffin and Fruit 5.30
OATMEAL Served with Raisins, Brown Sugar and a Muffin 2.95
GRANOLA Topped with Blueberries 2.25
FRUIT PLATE The season's finest, with a sugar free muffin 4.95
With Cheeses 5.50
BOWL OF YOGURT Topped with Wheatgerm and Granola 2.25
BLUEBERRIES & CREAM 1.95

SOUP'S ON!

SOUP OF THE DAY Comes with a Small Salad and a Puffy Cheese Bread 3.95
CHILI (in season) A bowl of the best brew you ever tasted. Not for the faint of heart, it's spicy. Served with a Tortilla, Onions and Cheese 3.75

ON THE SIDE OF THINGS

Potatoes 1.00
With Cheese 1.75
Ham, Bacon or Sausage 1.95
Homemade Salsa .75
Sour Cream .75
Flour Tortilla .75
English Muffin .75
Single Egg 1.00
Extra Egg .50
Extra Meat .75
Extra Cheese .75
Hollandaise .95
Honey Mustard .75

HERE'S THE DEAL

*No Substitutions Please
*No separate checks (this allows us to serve you better)
*No cigars or pipes please. (for the comfort of others)
*TO GO ORDERS GLADLY ACCEPTED.
*A 15% gratuity will be added for groups of 8 or more.

If it's that time of day when eggs seem passe, read on

SANDWICHES

Served with a side salad and potatoes

EGGS BENJAMIN Ham Slices, Tomatoes and Poached Eggs perched atop English Muffins and covered with Melted Cheese, Sour Cream and Chives 5.50
WEST COAST CLUB Turkey, Bacon, Avocado, Tomato, Cheese & Sprouts on Whole Wheat 4.95
BLTE Just as it sounds, Bacon, Lettuce, Tomato plus a Fried Egg and Melted Cheese 4.75
TURK E. ROYAL Mounded Sliced Turkey and Tomato Wheels on English Muffin, covered with Broccoli Cheese Sauce 5.25
ASTOR BLVD. Healthy scoops of either our Chicken or Tuna Salad on Tomato Wheels and English Muffins, topped with Jack Cheese 5.50
TUNA TERRIFIC The finest Albacore Tuna Salad, Tomato, Lettuce and Cheese on Whole Wheat 4.95
TOM'S TURKEY Turkey Breast, Tomato, Lettuce and Cheese on Whole Wheat 4.75
THE DON Italian Sausage, Mushrooms, Green Peppers and a Spicy Tomato Sauce slathered on an English Muffin and topped with Italian Cheeses and Pepperoni. An offering you can't refuse 5.50
CAJUN PO' BOY A perfectly grilled Andouille Sausage on a Sandwich Roll with Onions, Red Peppers and a Side of Cajun Mayo 5.25

GRILLED CHICKEN SANDWICHES

Plump juicy breasts marinated in fruit juice and charbroiled.

COOP DE VILLE Marinated Breast served on a Kaiser and topped with Bacon, Avocado and Melted Jack Cheese 5.95
CREOLE CHICADEE Tender White Meat, coated with Fiery Cajun Spice, grilled and served on a Kaiser with Lettuce, Tomato and a side of Cajun Mayo 5.25
CHICKEN FAJITA (in a Pita) Grilled Breast Strips, Onions, Tomatoes and Cheese stuffed in Pita Bread. Honey Mustard or Salsa on the side 5.75
CLUB POLLO Marinated Breast, Avocado, Tomato and Sprouts on a Kaiser Roll. Jane's Fonda this one 5.25

FIGURE 15.4 West Egg Cafe takeout menu. The restaurant features breakfast all day. (Reproduced by permission.)

CAJUN PO' BOY

A perfectly grilled Andouille sausage on a sandwich roll with onions, red peppers, and a side of Cajun mayo

The chicken sandwiches include

COOP DE VILLE

Marinated breast served on a Kaiser roll and topped with bacon, avocado, and melted jack cheese

CREOLE CHICADEE

Tender white meat coated with fiery cajun spice, grilled and served on a Kaiser with lettuce and tomato and a side of Cajun mayo

CHICKEN FAJITA

In a Pita

CLUB POLLO

Marinated breast, avocado, tomato, and sprouts on a Kaiser roll

Column 6 lists six salads and beverages: The North Pier (tuna and chicken), San Diego Spinach Salad, Chicago Sweat Shop Salad (bacon, ham, turkey, cheese, tomatoes, veggies, and lettuce), Charlie Chan Chicken Salad (charbroiled chicken strips on a nest of oriental noodles and mixed greens surrounded by Mandarin oranges, sliced water chestnuts, and cashews, accompanied with a tangy oriental dressing), Pasta Perfection, and Pacific Crab Cobb Salad.

16

The Hospital/Health Care Menu

Foodservice in a hospital or nursing home presents some special problems. The "customers" are patients, and the menu must satisfy a wide range of dietary needs and preferences. The clients cannot opt for a different "restaurant," and often their diets are restricted. These menus rarely list prices; costs are determined by the institutional budget rather than market prices. The problem for the hospital or health center, thus, is to provide nutritious and tasty food, often in large quantities, within the cost restrictions and with enough variety that long-term patients do not become bored with their meals.

It is important for the hospital to gain and keep a reputation for food "as good as in a fine restaurant." An interesting menu that offers variety and some unusual items will help. Because "room service" must be supplied three meals a day, seven days a week, this is no easy task, but many fine hospitals and health care facilities are doing just that.

Bloomington Hospital

The Bloomington Hospital in Bloomington, Indiana, has a very different and creative menu for children (Figure 16.1). The six-panel, two-fold Club Flamingo menu measures 5½ by 10½ inches folded and is printed in full color on a lightweight, cream-colored stock. Humorous, cartoon-style drawings are used throughout.

The first inside panel lists the breakfast items. The headings are: Fruits/Juices, Cereals, Entrees (bacon, ham slice, scrambled eggs, and sausage links), Breads, and Breakfast Specials—one for each of five days of the week.

The center panel is the luncheon menu. The headings are: Soups, Salads and Fruits, Breads and Veggies, Entrees (eleven) and Lunch Specials (ten). The entrées include hamburger, cheeseburger, two pizzas, Charley Tuna's sandwich, and peanut butter and jelly sandwich.

The third panel is the dinner menu. The headings are the same as the lunch menu, but the entrées include baked chicken, two pizzas, sloppy Joe on a bun, fish sticks, cheesy macaroni, spaghetti and meat balls, plus yogurt and the ubiquitous peanut butter and jelly sandwich. The daily Dinner Specials include breaded shrimp, roast pork and rosy apple sauce, Salisbury steak with oven-browned potatoes, meat loaf, and ham strips with broccoli.

On the first back panel eleven drinks are listed under the heading Milk Bar. Thirteen desserts are listed under the heading Sweet Tooth. On the back center panel is the following information:

Kids:
Want a Special Order?
Call 6254!
Parents:
Want Room Service?
Call 6310!

St. John's Regional Medical Center

St. John's is a 250-bed medical center located sixty miles northwest of Los Angeles. The facility has been operating for seventy-six years and is planning an expansion program. The menu, which is revised annually, is in three panels, each measuring 6 by 12 inches (Figure 16.2). It is printed in full color with photographs on the front and back cover and on the tops of the inside panels.

Each inside panel is used for one meal, breakfast, lunch, or dinner. The breakfast headings are Chilled Fruits and Juices (twelve); Hot or Cold Cereals (eight); Breakfast Entrees (six) plus sausage, bacon, diet syrup, and jam; Breads and Spreads (thirteen); Hot and Cold Beverages (thirteen); and Seasonings (eight).

The lunch menu headings are Appetizers, (two juices, four soups, six salads, four dressings); Lunch Entrées (three cold plates, five sandwiches, six hot entrées); Breads and Spreads (six breads, three spreads); Hot and Cold Beverages (twelve); and Seasonings (six).

FIGURE 16.1 Menu for Bloomington Hospital. A colorful and well-designed hospital menu. (Courtesy Bloomington Hospital. Reproduced by permission.)

FIGURE 16.2 Menu for St. John's Regional Medical Center. The breakfast, lunch, and dinner menus are printed together on one side and perforated so that each can be detached. (Courtesy St. John's Regional Medical Center. Reproduced by permission.)

The dinner menu headings are similar to those for lunch: Appetizers (two juices, four soups, six salads, four dressings); Dinner Entrées (three cold plates, seven hot entrées); Desserts (nine); Breads and Spreads (six breads, three spreads); Hot and Cold Beverages (twelve); Seasonings (six); and Wine—Chablis, Rosé, and Burgundy.

On the back panel that folds to the inside is the following:

To provide you with the best quality and service possible, St. John's Food Service Department has developed this menu. Each day, you will receive the menu listing the food selections for each meal. For greater variety, a daily lunch and dinner Entrée Special is designated on a separate menu insert.

Specific entrées which meet special health and dietary preferences are available. These entrées are identified by one of the following symbols:

♥ Low Cholesterol/Low Fat Entrée
○ Meatless Entrée

Please help us serve you better by doing the following:

* Write your name and room number on your menu.
* Circle all your food and seasoning choices.
* If you select a daily Entrée Special, circle TODAY'S SPECIAL.
* Keep your completed menu in your room. Our Menu Hostess will collect it from you.

The back panel of the folded menu encourages good dietary habits away from the hospital:

Good nutrition is an important part of staying healthy. With this in mind, the U.S. Dietary Goals were considered when planning your menu. These goals, which outline dietary practices in the prevention of heart disease, high blood pressure and obesity, include:

* Decrease intake of fats, sugar and salt
* Maintain normal weight
* Increase intake of fruits, vegetables and starches

You may wish to save your menus to use as guidelines when preparing meals at home. Your dietitian can discuss your diet with you in more detail.

In addition to the regular menu there is a daily special for lunch and dinner.

SPECIAL OF THE DAY

	Lunch
Monday	Fried Chicken
Tuesday	Baked Pork Chop with Apple
Wednesday	♥Oven Fried Fish
Thursday	○Cheese Manicotti
Friday	Hearty Beef Stew
Saturday	♥Orange Glazed Chicken
Sunday	♥Veal Al Limone
	Dinner
Monday	Grilled Liver and Onions
Tuesday	Chile Relleno
Wednesday	♥Chinese Pepper Steak
Thursday	Pork Chow Mein
Friday	♥Poached Salmon
Saturday	Chile Colorado
Sunday	Roast Pork

Mount Carmel East Hospital

Mount Carmel East Hospital, a 292-bed hospital in metropolitan Columbus, Ohio, has been in operation for sixteen years. It has a regular and an alternative menu.

The regular menu (Figure 16.3) has three panels, each measuring 5¾ by 12½ inches. The menu is printed in two colors, dark gray and brick red. From the left-hand panel, to the center, to the right-hand panel, the headings are Dinner Tonight, Snack Tonight, Breakfast Tomorrow, and Lunch Tomorrow.

MOUNT CARMEL EAST HOSPITAL

YOUR MENU

DINNER TONIGHT

Please Circle Selections
_____ Smaller Portions Preferred
REGULAR
THURSDAY

TO BEGIN YOUR MEAL
•Chilled Apricot Nectar
Hearty Vegetable Soup
•Mixed Green Salad with Assorted Dressings
•Italian, French, Blue Cheese, Ranch
Raspberry Applesauce Gelatin Salad

OUR SPECIALTIES
(Select One, Please)
•Italian Spaghetti with Meat Sauce
Baked Pork Chop with Spiced Apple Ring

ACCOMPANIMENTS
Bread Dressing with Gravy
Steamed Cabbage Wedge
Baby Lima Beans

FROM OUR BREAD BASKET
•Garlic Bread
White Bread | Rye Bread
Whole Wheat Bread | Crackers

A SPECIAL TREAT
Gingerbread with Whipped Topping
•Hand-Dipped Ice Cream | Gourmet Cookie
Fruit Sherbet | Homemade Custard
Fresh Fruit in Season | Creamy Pudding

BEVERAGES AND CONDIMENTS
•Coffee | •2% Milk | Margarine
Brewed Decaf Coffee | Whole Milk | Jelly
Hot Tea | Skim Milk | Honey
Decaffeinated Tea | Buttermilk | Ketchup
Iced Tea | Chocolate Milk | Mustard
Lemon | Mayonnaise
•Non-Dairy Creamer

NAME _______ ROOM _______

SNACK TONIGHT

Please Circle Selections
_____ I do not want a snack
REGULAR
THURSDAY

SOMETHING LIGHT
•Fresh Fruit in Season
Shaved Ham Sandwich
Served on croissant with lettuce and pickle

SOMETHING MUNCHY
Peanut Butter and Crackers | Popcorn
•Cheese and Crackers

SWEET ENDINGS
Chocolate Chip Cookie | Creamy Pudding
Sugar Cookie

BEVERAGES AND CONDIMENTS
2% Milk | Chocolate Milk | Margarine
Whole Milk | Buttermilk | Mayonnaise
Skim Milk | Ketchup | Mustard

NAME _______ ROOM _______

BREAKFAST TOMORROW

Please Circle Selections
REGULAR
FRIDAY

FRUITS AND JUICES
Orange Juice | •Apple Juice
Grapefruit Juice | Fresh Banana
Prune Juice | Citrus Sections

CEREALS
Corn Flakes | Rice Krispies | Bran Flakes
Granola | •Cheerios | Raisin Bran
Oatmeal

BREAKFAST BREADS
•Bran Muffin | White Toast
Sweet Roll | Whole Wheat Toast
Toasted Bagel | Bakery Donut
With cream cheese

FROM THE GRILL
•Scrambled Egg | Bacon Strips
Hard Cooked Egg
Low Cholesterol Egg Substitute

BEVERAGES AND CONDIMENTS
•Coffee | •2% Milk | •Margarine
Brewed Decaf Coffee | Whole Milk | Jelly
Hot Tea | Skim Milk | Honey
Decaffeinated Tea | Buttermilk | Lemon
Hot Cocoa | Chocolate Milk | •Non-Dairy Creamer

NAME _______ ROOM _______

LUNCH TOMORROW

Please Circle Selections
_____ Smaller Portions Preferred
REGULAR
FRIDAY

TO BEGIN YOUR MEAL
•Boston Clam Chowder
Chilled Grapefruit Juice
•Strawberry Pineapple Gelatin Salad
Mixed Green Salad with Assorted Dressings
Blue Cheese, Ranch, Italian, French

OUR SPECIALTIES
(Select One, Please)
•Baked Macaroni and Cheese
Salisbury Steak Champignon
Tuna Salad Plate
Whole fresh tomato filled with tuna salad. Served on a bed of lettuce with broccoli, cauliflower, celery, and carrots.

ACCOMPANIMENTS
Parslied Potatoes
•Peas with Pearl Onions
Whole Baby Beets

FROM OUR BREAD BASKET
•Blueberry Muffin
White Bread | Rye Bread
Whole Wheat Bread | •Crackers

A SPECIAL TREAT
•Double Fudge Chocolate Cake
Gourmet Cookie
Fruit Sherbet | Gelatin Jewels
Fresh Fruit in Season | Creamy Pudding

BEVERAGES AND CONDIMENTS
•Coffee | 2% Milk | •Margarine
Brewed Decaf Coffee | Whole Milk | Jelly
Hot Tea | Skim Milk | Honey
Decaffeinated Tea | Buttermilk | Ketchup
Iced Tea | Chocolate Milk | Mustard
Lemon | Mayonnaise
•Non-Dairy Creamer

NAME _______ ROOM _______

FIGURE 16.3 Menu for Mount Carmel East Hospital.
(Courtesy Mount Carmel East Hospital. Reproduced by permission.)

The dinner listing includes soup, two salads, two entrées, three vegetables, five breads, five desserts, ten beverages, and five condiments. The snacks include Something Light (fruit or sandwich); Something Munchy (cheese and crackers, popcorn); Sweet Endings (cookies and pudding); and Beverages and Condiments. Breakfast Tomorrow includes six fruits and juices, seven cereals, and six breakfast breads. From the Grill has three egg items (one is an egg substitute) and bacon. Ten beverages plus five condiments complete the breakfast list.

The lunch listing begins with soup, juice, and two salads. There are three entrées and three vegetables. Five breads are listed plus five desserts, eight beverages, and five condiments. The copy on the back cover describes the nutritional services of the hospital.

NUTRITIONAL SERVICES . . . HERE FOR YOU.

We know nutritious food is vitally important during your hospital stay. Nutritional Services at Mount Carmel East Hospital is committed to ensuring your continued satisfaction with meals and our service.

In keeping with today's health and lifestyle trends, we have incorporated menu items rich in fiber and essential nutrients and offer you choices of foods low in fat, cholesterol and sugar. In certain instances, your physician may have ordered a special diet for you. We will make every effort to see that your meals are tasty and enjoyable.

The alternative menu was designed for patients with special dietary needs and/or significant eating problems. The menu offers items found to be appealing to those patients with little or no appetite. The primary users of this menu are cancer patients, who are in the hospital for an extended period and are tired of the normal seven-day meal cycle or who repeatedly come in on the same day(s) each month for chemotherapy and wish a change. Many of the items on the menu are normal everyday fare but, when presented in this way, can seem more appealing to an ill patient in need of nourishment. This menu was designed to grant more choices to patients who have lost many of the choices in their lives.

The alternative menu is slightly smaller than the regular menu (Figure 16.4), measuring 5½ by 11 inches, with two large panels and one small one. The headings on this menu are Something Light, Entree Alternatives, Entree Combinations, Entrees on the Light Side, Sandwiches, Something Munchy, and Something Sweet.

Something Light is four soups plus fruit juices. Entree Alternatives are Steak, Scrambled Eggs, Baked Potato with Melted Cheese, and Pizza. Entree Combinations are Macaroni and Cheese with Green Beans, Baked Chicken Breast with Rice and Peas, Beef and Macaroni Casserole with Green Beans, and Cheese Omelet served with Canadian Bacon and French Fries. Entrees on the Light Side are Tuna, Egg, or Chicken Salad; Chef Salad; Pasta Salad; Cottage Cheese and Fruit; and Cheese and Fruit.

The Sandwiches are Ham, Roast Beef, Turkey, American or Swiss Cheese, Peanut Butter, Hamburger, Grilled Cheese, or Grilled Ham and Cheese. Something Munchy includes Potato Chips, Corn Chips, Pretzels, Peanuts, Crackers, French Fries, and Popcorn. And Something Sweet includes twelve desserts ranging from ice cream, cake and cheesecake, to yogurt and a popsicle.

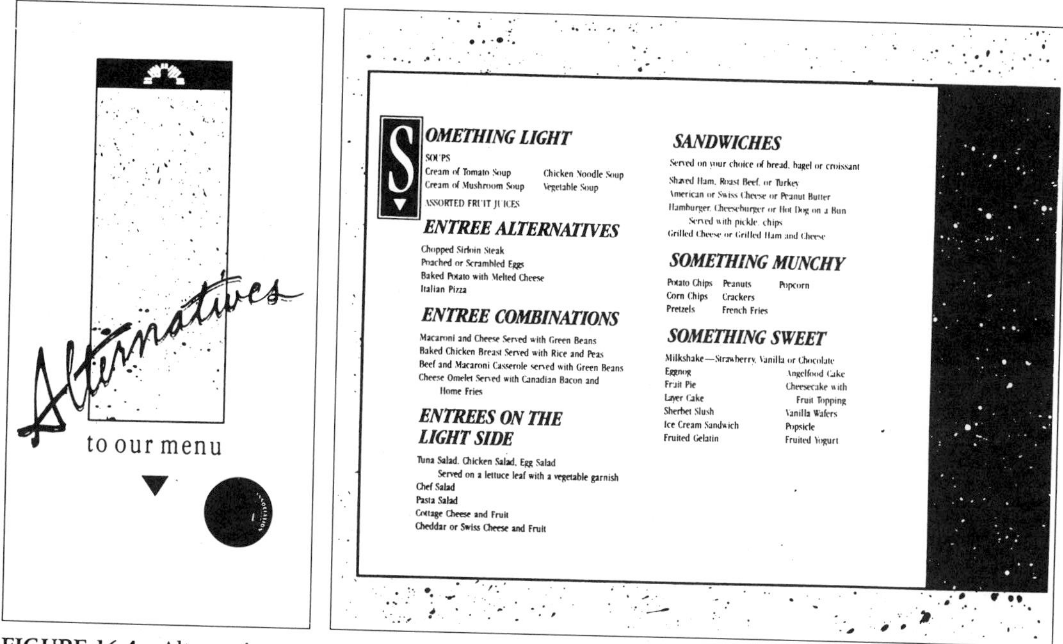
Alternatives
to our menu

SOMETHING LIGHT
SOUPS
Cream of Tomato Soup
Cream of Mushroom Soup
Chicken Noodle Soup
Vegetable Soup
ASSORTED FRUIT JUICES

ENTREE ALTERNATIVES
Chopped Sirloin Steak
Poached or Scrambled Eggs
Baked Potato with Melted Cheese
Italian Pizza

ENTREE COMBINATIONS
Macaroni and Cheese Served with Green Beans
Baked Chicken Breast Served with Rice and Peas
Beef and Macaroni Casserole served with Green Beans
Cheese Omelet Served with Canadian Bacon and Home Fries

ENTREES ON THE LIGHT SIDE
Tuna Salad, Chicken Salad, Egg Salad
Served on a lettuce leaf with a vegetable garnish
Chef Salad
Pasta Salad
Cottage Cheese and Fruit
Cheddar or Swiss Cheese and Fruit

SANDWICHES
Served on your choice of bread, bagel or croissant
Shaved Ham, Roast Beef, or Turkey
American or Swiss Cheese or Peanut Butter
Hamburger, Cheeseburger or Hot Dog on a Bun
Served with pickle, chips
Grilled Cheese or Grilled Ham and Cheese

SOMETHING MUNCHY
Potato Chips
Corn Chips
Pretzels
Peanuts
Crackers
French Fries
Popcorn

SOMETHING SWEET
Milkshake—Strawberry, Vanilla or Chocolate
Eggnog
Fruit Pie
Layer Cake
Sherbet Slush
Ice Cream Sandwich
Fruited Gelatin
Angelfood Cake
Cheesecake with Fruit Topping
Vanilla Wafers
Popsicle
Fruited Yogurt

FIGURE 16.4 Alternative menu from Mount Carmel East. (Courtesy Mount Carmel East Hospital. Reproduced by permission.)

17

The Ethnic Menu

We are a nation of immigrants. The United States has received more immigrants than any other country in history. During colonial times about one million immigrants came to America, most from England, and they brought with them the English language and other traditions that formed the basis of American life. They were followed by large numbers of Dutch, French, German, and Scotch-Irish settlers. In addition, black slaves were brought in from Africa. By 1776 about two-fifths of all Americans—except the Native Americans—were of non-English origin.

After 1776 about 10,000 immigrants a year entered the United States, but around 1830, the tide of immigration increased. During that decade, about 600,000 immigrants poured in, followed by 1.7 million in the 1840s and 2.6 million in the 1850s (U.S. Bureau of the Census). Most of these new arrivals were from Germany, Great Britain, and Ireland. The second great wave of immigration took place from 1860 to 1890, during which time more than 10 million people streamed into the United States. Most were from Germany, Great Britain, and Scandinavia. Gradually, however, the sources of immigration shifted to such countries as Austria, Hungary, Italy, and Russia.

Between 1890 and 1930 the greatest wave of immigration peaked: Nearly 23 million people came to the United States, exceeding the total from colonial times until then. Most of these new arrivals came from Greece, Hungary, Italy, Portugal, Russia, Poland, and Spain. After World War II an additional 600,000 refugees came from Germany, Hungary, Poland, the Soviet Union, and Yugoslavia.

In 1952 a new immigration law was passed setting up quotas for nations in Asia and other regions that had previously been excluded. This was later changed to one quota from the Western Hemisphere and one from the Eastern Hemisphere. As a result, immigration from India, Pakistan, Korea, the Philippines, and other Asian countries soared during the 1960s and 1970s.

From South and Central America, plus Mexico, Cuba, and Puerto Rico, has come a large Hispanic population. Since the 1960s, Mexico has sent the most immigrants to the United States. In 1987 legal immigration from all countries into the United States topped 600,000, and of this total, 72,000 came from Mexico.

The ethnic, racial, and national mix of peoples that the United States has become is reflected in its cuisine. Indeed, Americans choose from a greater variety of foods than almost anybody else in the world.

A new trend among restaurants is to mix the menu; that is, to a basic American menu serving seafood, steaks, and chicken, the restaurant adds some ethnic dishes such as Chinese Peking duck, a Mexican taco or burrito, an Italian pasta dish or pizza, and maybe a Japanese shrimp tempura. This concept is carried even further by the Eurasia restaurant in Chicago, which combines Asian and European cuisine.

THE CHINESE MENU

The Chinese have a great respect for food, possibly because they have had so many famines. As a result they have learned to cook using all edible materials. There is even a joke that the reason no dinosaurs were ever found in China was because the Chinese ate them all. The Chinese not only use a wide variety of foods but also create variety by making many by-products from one product. For example, from soybeans, the Chinese make soy sauce, a dozen fermented bean sauces, bean curd, and soybean milk.

Chinese dishes also use contrasting flavors—various blends of spicy, mild, mellow, pungent, salty, sweet, and sour—as well as contrasting textures—chewy, smooth, juicy, dry, gelatinous, spongy, and light. Different colors, aromas, and methods of cooking also add variety, such as stir-frying, red-cooking (slow stewing in soy sauce), braising, steaming, smoking, roasting, poaching, and deep-frying. Another effect is achieved by cutting. When the principal ingredient is diced, all other ingredients should be diced; when sliced, everything else is sliced. Thick pieces are matched with thick pieces, slivers with slivers. The chef must thus be an expert in precision cutting. As a result of these techniques the Chinese have created one of the great cuisines of the world, a cuisine that has developed over thousands of years.

The Han dynasty, from 207 B.C. to A.D. 220, advanced Chinese cuisine by blending the five flavors—bitter, sour, sweet, salty, and hot—in much of its cooking. The art of cutting and cooking expanded to include pickling, stewing, and baking. Over the centuries the Chinese have also incorporated various foreign foods into their diet. By the tenth and eleventh centuries they included spinach and celery from Nepal, pistachio nuts from Persia, and kohlrabi from Europe. From India the Chinese learned how to make sugar from sugarcane and wine from grapes. China, in turn, exported tea and silk to the rest of the world.

The Mongol invasion of China in 1234 brought a foreign diet that included milk, butter, and lamb. The Portuguese arrived in Canton in 1516, and subsequently they introduced potatoes and chilies. As trade with other nations increased, pineapples, papayas, tomatoes, peanuts, and maize were added. By the 1700s China's cuisine had reached its present form.

Chinese cuisine can be divided into four major categories: northern, southern, eastern, and western, regions that are distinguished in their cooking by the ingredients used, the various combinations of spices and sauces, the cooking techniques employed, and the condiments used.

Northern Cooking

China's northern regional cuisine was influenced by the Mongols and the Manchus. The former introduced the Mongolian Hot Pot: To a pot of boiling broth are added noodles, sliced bean curd, raw cabbage, and other vegetables. These are cooked briefly, and then thin slices of lamb are cooked and dipped into various condiments. The hot pot is traditionally served with sesame seed rolls, and the broth itself is the final soup course.

Lamb, rarely eaten in the rest of China, is a specialty of Peking. The northern provinces are also famous for their roasted and barbecued beef, lamb, and chicken. Classic northern dishes featuring chicken include Chicken Velvet and Mo Shu Ro, which has tree ears and golden needles for texture, with either chicken or pork as the main ingredient. This dish is served with Peking doilies, also called Mandarin pancakes. Another northern dish is Red-cooked Shoulder of Pork.

Little seafood is eaten in the North, but the Yellow River provides freshwater fish and prawns, the latter being as long as 5 inches and similar to lobster. The prawns are often deep fried or prepared with a garlic and tomato sauce.

The most famous culinary creation of the North is Peking Duck, a variation of which is Sliced Roast Duck with Scallions. The original recipe for Peking Duck took fifteen thousand words, most of which were directions for making the duck skin as crisp as possible. The ducks are roasted hanging from poles in room-sized ovens. The chefs in charge of making Peking Duck have had three months of study dedicated to the fattening, slaughtering, and cleaning of the duck, and nine months of study to master the preparation, roasting, carving, and final presentation of the dish.

The ducks are slaughtered before they are seventy days old, and during the last weeks of their lives they are artificially fed. In order to keep the meat from becoming sinewy, the ducks are given little exercise.

Peking Duck is served in a multicourse fashion, beginning with the presentation of the whole roasted duck, which is then carved at the table. The first course is the crisp, golden skin served with thin flour pancakes, or doilies. The second course is sliced duck meat folded by the diner into the pancakes, or duck meat stir fried with bean sprouts or other vegetables. The remaining courses are made with other parts of the duck.

Another northern specialty is Peking Rolls, which are finely shredded vegetables encased in an egg pancake that is dipped in batter and deep fried. The sweet-and-sour sauce made with sugar and vinegar is an invention of the northern province of Hunan. The sweet-and-sour dishes of Hunan were adopted by the Cantonese, who added fruit or tomato sauce. An example of a sweet-and-sour entrée is Sweet and Pungent Sea Bass.

Northern cooking is generally less spicy and less oily than that of the western provinces. The dishes are often lighter and milder. The vegetable most often eaten in the North is Tientsin white cabbage, which is either white-cooked (blanched in water) or red-cooked (simmered in soy sauce). A northern dessert is Peking Glazed Apples.

Southern Cooking

Southern Chinese cuisine is mainly Cantonese. The principal dishes are Lemon Squab, Roast Duck Lo Mein, Steamed Sea Bass with Fermented Black Beans, Beef Chow Fun, Barbecued Roast Pork, and numerous varieties of dim sum, including Steamed Roast Pork Buns and Shao Mai.

The province of Canton has abundant rice and a vast variety of fruits and vegetables, and the Cantonese are fond of dishes combining vegetables with meat as well as fruits. One favorite is the combination of duck with pineapple, plums, lichees, or oranges. Plums and lichees are used in many dishes. Vegetables and fruits are sometimes combined in sweet-and-sour dishes, usually fish or pork.

Cantonese cuisine also reflects its abundance of fish and seafood, provided by rivers and a coastline of more than one thousand miles. Crawfish, carp, and prawn are also pond raised. Seafood is used fresh, dried, and salted. To preserve their natural flavor, many of the fish are steamed. Also characteristic of the region are seafood sauces such as shrimp paste, made from small dried shrimp.

Ginger is a popular Cantonese seasoning and is often used for fish and seafoods. Soy sauce with chili is a popular dip for prawns. Salted black beans also are used on many seafood dishes, and vinegar is used specifically on crab dishes.

The Cantonese use exotic ingredients such as shark fins, snakes, snails, eels, frogs, turtles, and birds' nests. And the flavorful stock of Cantonese soups is often made from pigs' feet, lungs, and sweetbreads, snake, frogs' legs, fish heads, shark fins, and turtle. The Cantonese menu also includes many stir-fried dishes, including Stir-fried Lobster with Shredded Leeks.

The Cantonese like their food undercooked, which is achieved by quick stir-frying and boiling. Quick roasting, as with barbecued roast pork, is a regional favorite. They prefer steaming to other cooking processes because it is quick and leaves the food in a natural state. To the Cantonese, "well done" means not overcooked.

The South is also famous for its egg noodles, dried and fresh. Every variety of Italian pasta has its Chinese counterpart. The one thing that you will never find anywhere in China is the fortune cookie, which was created in Los Angeles by a Chinese-American named George Jung.

Eastern Cooking

Much of China's eastern cuisine is typical of Chinese cooking as a whole. The two main cities are Nanking and Hangchow, which have produced Nanking Pressed Duck and Hangchow Soya Duck. The popularity of duck is shown by the fact that Nanking alone produces forty million ducks a year. Ducks and other poultry are often steamed inside large melons and squash. Other dishes feature steamed, stuffed lotus roots, peppers, or mushrooms.

The eastern region—China's principal rice-producing area—features rice and rice-based products such as Chinese rice wine. The seasoning is usually restrained, and salt is used only lightly. The vinegars used in seasoning are produced in the region, with the most famous being a sweetened black rice vinegar. Many dishes of the region, especially fish, are flavored with this vinegar. Sugar is often used to counteract the saltiness of soy. Many sweet sauces, especially those for meat dishes, use honey or unrefined sugar. Vegetable oil is used instead of lard, and preserved foods include salted fish, seafood, dried mushrooms, and bamboo shoots.

Easterners also favor slow-cooked foods, including red-cooking, a technique in which fish, poultry, or meats are simmered for hours in a rich soy-based stock. Slow steaming as well as quick steaming is popular. Meat, poultry, and fish are marinated and wrapped in lotus leaves or paper, then folded into little envelopes and deep fried. The eastern region is also noted for its delicate noodles and cold tossed noodles.

Western Cooking

Western Chinese cuisine, especially that of Szechwan and Hunan, is hot and spicy. Szechwan cooking uses primarily chili paste, whereas Hunan dishes more commonly use raw chili peppers, although chili paste is used in some dishes. Szechwan peppercorns also create a slight numbing sensation.

The western Chinese chef believes in the harmonious blending of pungent flavors. As a result, Szechwan is famous for such dishes as Chun-Pi (orange peel) Chicken, Sesame Seed Beef, and Tea-smoked Duck, which is marinated, steamed, and then smoked above a combination of tea and camphor wood leaves over a charcoal fire. Many other western dishes, especially poultry, are smoked.

Texture is important in western Chinese cooking. Examples are Slippery Chicken and Dry Sautéed Shredded Beef. Beef is often shredded and dry-fried, which results in a chewy texture. Because the beef in this area tends to be tough, it is not only shredded and fried but also often cooked for long periods of time.

Being far from the sea, western Chinese must rely on freshwater fish. One such dish is Lake Tungting Shrimp, featuring the freshwater shrimp of Lake Tungting. Stir-fried frogs' legs and turtle soup are summertime favorites, and carp from Hunan's Yellow River is well known throughout China. One regional dish is Steamed Carp with Purple Basil.

The Szechwan cook often employs multiple cooking processes. In the case of Szechwan Crispy Duck, the duck is first steamed and then deep-fried, producing an extraordinary texture. Another multiple-cooking technique is "passing through," in which meat is fried in two or more cups of oil as a preliminary to stir-frying. Vegetables are also often dry cooked or deep fried before being stir fried and are sometimes fried with water instead of oil. The meat is then drained and stir fried with various seasonings and vegetables.

A combination of flavors is typical of Szechwan dishes. Pon Pon Chicken, for example, has a sesame seed sauce accented by chili oil and Szechwan peppercorn powder. Sesame seed paste is the predominant flavor of many Szechwan dishes, including Cold Noodles with Spicy Sesame Sauce and Vegetable Rolls with Sesame Sauce. Another Szechwan chicken specialty is Kung Pao Chicken, with garlic and chili paste.

Western Chinese chefs strive for both taste and aftertaste, using sesame seed paste, chili paste with garlic, and aromatic vinegar which is often combined with chili. Chili is also mixed with toasted ground rice, sesame seeds, peanuts, and other nuts. Dishes are highlighted with aromatic dried tangerine or orange peel. Seasoning can also be combinations of onions, garlic, ginger, star anise, peppers, and cinnamon. For example, Szechwan Crispy Duck combines scallions, ginger, star anise, peppercorns, and cinnamon. Both Hunanese and Szechwanese cooks use large quantities of sesame oil.

South of Szechwan is Yunan Province, whose cuisine has been influenced by that of India, Burma, and Tibet, resulting in more curry and dairy products than in the rest of China. Yunan specializes in goat cheese, yogurt, and fried milk curd. Its most famous food product is its ham, and as much pork is eaten in this area as is chicken. Fish from the many lakes and poultry are often cooked with walnuts, chestnuts, pine nuts, and peanuts.

Hunan Province, in the Yangtze Valley, is noted for its black tea and its glutinous rice. In Changsha, the capital of Hunan, the chefs feature smoked duck. After fattening, slaughtering, and cleaning the duck, they marinate it for seven to ten days in a brine of wine and sugar. Then the duck is hung in a smokehouse over a fire of rice husks and peanut shells.

Fukien Province, north of Kwangtung, has some special dishes. A distinct flavor in this province is red-wine sediment paste made from the lees of rice wine. It is used primarily in duck, chicken, and pork dishes and to make fermented red-wine rice. Another specialty, from the city of Amoy in Fukien, is popia, a thin pancake that diners use for wrapping a cooked filling. Another specialty of this area is dumpling skins made from meat. Ground pork and cornstarch are kneaded until a dough is formed. Called swallow skin, it is used as a wrapping for foods that are to be steamed or cooked in soups.

Szechwan Pavilion

The Szechwan Pavilion is located in a large shopping center in a suburb of Chicago. The twelve-page menu measures 9⅜ by 14 inches (Figure 17.1) and is printed in full color on a cream paper that is plastic coated to prevent soiling. Color photographs of Chinese pottery appear on the cover and each page.

On the inside front cover is a description of Szechwan cuisine, the restaurant's specialty. On the next page is information on how to order.

> Chinese meals are best enjoyed "family style" with a variety of dishes shared by all. Selections on the Szechwan Pavilion menu are offered "a la carte" to enable diners to order a variety of dishes and enjoy contrasts in flavors and textures.
>
> How many dishes?—You should order as many main dishes as the number in your party. The selection and quantity of appetizers depend upon the size and urgency of your appetite. Soup is the traditional way to begin a Chinese dinner and may be enjoyed as a beverage throughout the meal.
>
> A typical Chinese dinner would include one shellfish or fish dish and one meat and/or poultry dish, depending upon the size of the group. These may be complemented by vegetable and noodle dishes. Large groups will be able to enjoy greater variety, sampling shellfish and fish dishes and each type of meat: beef, pork, chicken and duck as well as vegetables and noodles.

On the next panel are listed thirteen appetizers, such as Spicy Szechwan Snails, Scallion Pancake, Pot Stickers, Stuffed Crab Claws, and eight "cold delicacies," including Jellyfish, Cold Noodle Salad, and Smoked Fish.

The next page lists soup, noodles, fried rice, and bread. Among the six soups priced from $1.75 to $7.95 are Shrimp Sizzling Rice, Hot and Sour Seafood, and Won Ton Soup. The noodles come fried or in soup. There are two fried rice and two bread offerings.

The following page features the Szechwan Pavilion Special Dinner (for two or more). This dinner includes

Appetizers:	Spareribs Cantonese, Spring Roll, and Fried Won Ton
Soup:	Choice of Hot and Sour or Won Ton Soup
Entrée:	Choice of one entrée per person
Beverage:	Glass of Plum Wine
	Steamed Rice, Hot Tea, and Fortune Cookie served with all entrées.
	$4.95 per person added to price of each entrée

Seven Chef's Specialties are also listed on this page: Three in a Nest, Szechwan Prawns, Phoenix and Dragon (Chicken and Lobster Cantonese), Two Flavor Lamb, Beef with Orange Peel, Three Delights (shredded chicken and abalone sautéed with bean sprouts in a delicate white sauce), and Governor's Chicken.

The next page is dedicated to lobster and shrimp, with Lobster Cantonese and Lobster Szechwan Style plus seven shrimp entrées including Sweet and Sour Shrimp, Shrimp with Cashew Nuts, and Shrimp Sizzling Rice. The next page lists nine more seafood entrées. Among the interesting items listed here are Abalone with Black Mushrooms, Ma La Frog Legs, and Kung Bao Cuttlefish.

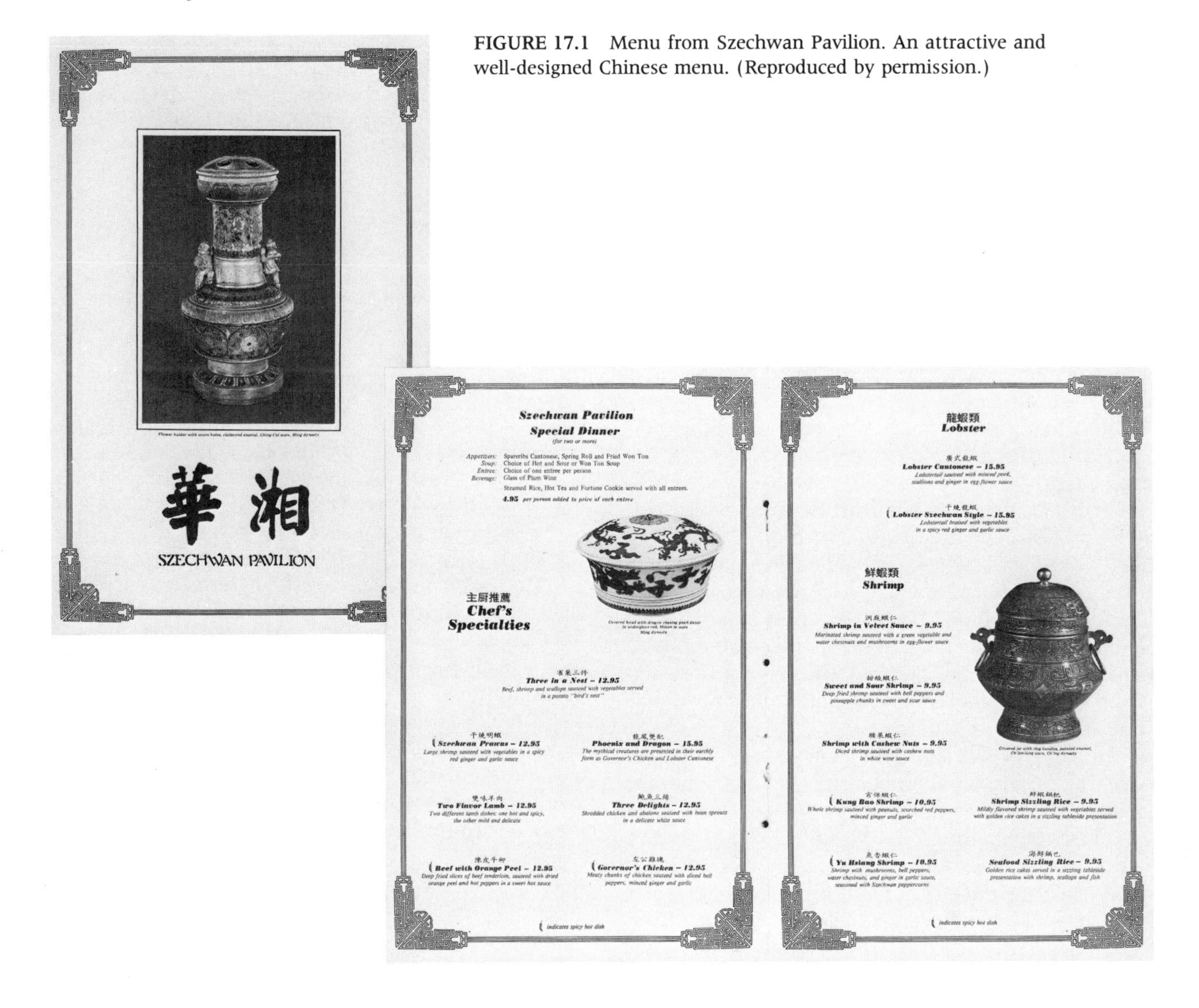

FIGURE 17.1 Menu from Szechwan Pavilion. An attractive and well-designed Chinese menu. (Reproduced by permission.)

Chicken and duck are on the following page: Lemon Chicken, Hunan Chicken, Chicken with Walnuts, and Chicken with Snow Pea Pods. The four duck entrées include the famous Peking Duck, Crispy Duck, Smoked Tea Duck, and Ginger Duck.

On page 10 are listed beef, lamb, and pork dishes. Among the beef entrées are Beef with Scallions, Mu Shu Beef (shredded beef sautéed with vegetables, served wrapped in Mandarin pancakes with scallions and hoisin sauce), Beef with Broccoli, and Kung Bao Beef (the famous Kung Bao dish with marinated sliced beef stir fried with peanuts and scorched red peppers).

There are two lamb entrées: Ma La Lamb (sliced lamb sautéed in hot sauce made of hot peppers, garlic, and ginger), and Hunan Barbecue Lamb (sliced lamb braised in a peppery Chinese barbecue sauce with essence of five spices). All hot dishes on this menu are identified by a special red symbol.

Pork is a Chinese favorite, and there are six pork entrées, including Mu Shu Pork (shredded), Twice Cooked Pork (broiled pork loin, sliced and stir fried with green peppers, black mushroom, and garlic in a spicy hot bean sauce), Sweet and Sour Pork, and Yu Hsiang Pork (shredded pork sautéed with minced black mushrooms, tree ears, bell peppers, water chestnuts, and ginger in garlic sauce seasoned with Szechwan peppercorns).

The inside back cover of this comprehensive menu features vegetables and desserts. The nine vegetables can be both entrées (for vegetarians) or side dishes. Included are Mu Shu Vegetables (shredded vegetables stir fried with vermicelli, covered with an omelet, served wrapped in a Mandarin pancake with hoisin sauce), Eggplant in Garlic Sauce, Snow Pea Pods, and Szechwan String Beans.

The six Desserts include Chinese Crepe with Dates, Banana in Flaming Rum, Fruit in Flaming Rum à la Mode, and Oriental Sundae Surprise.

THE FRENCH MENU

The number of French restaurants seems to be growing, not just in the big cities of America, but also in the more affluent suburbs, despite the average American's tendency to prefer more hearty American fare. But more Americans seem willing to pay the higher price for better-tasting food in smaller quantities.

Classical French cuisine is designed to please both the palate and the eye. Sauces are a hallmark of this cuisine and are made to complement the flavor of a dish, never overpower it. Sweet and sour flavors are seldom mixed as they are in German and Chinese cooking, and a sweet sauce is never served with fish.

Nothing, including vegetables, is overcooked or undercooked. If the dish is to be served hot, it must be served hot, and if cold, cold—not cool or lukewarm. Except for salads, which are a minor part of classical French cuisine, raw food is seldom served. Menus are carefully planned. For example, a fish course featuring a fine-textured fish, such as sole with a creamy white-wine sauce, should be followed by a meat course with more texture, such as beef, veal, lamb, or game, and its sauce should be a contrasting red-wine sauce.

No French meal is complete without wine. The regions of Burgundy and Bordeaux produce some of the world's best wines. Great care must also be taken in selecting the types and vintages of wines to be served.

The language of French cuisine is precise. If, for example, fillet of sole Adrienne is listed, the diner will expect sole fillets poached, coated with Polignac sauce, and garnished with chopped crayfish tails in nantua sauce and puffed pastry crescents. And if the menu lists fillet of sole Yvette, it should be served with chopped herbs and a garnish of small tomatoes with a fish stuffing.

French cuisine is complex. Homard à la Parisienne, for example, is basically cold poached lobster. But the lobster meat is carefully removed from the shell, and the shell is filled with salade russe—finely cut vegetables in mayonnaise. It then is decorated with medallions of lobster which are topped with truffle cutouts and glazed with aspic. The plate is then garnished with artichoke bottoms, tomatoes, hard-boiled eggs, and truffles.

Another dish, selle de veau Orloff, starts with a saddle of veal which is sliced and put back together with an onion sauce, truffle slices, and chopped mushrooms. The garnished veal is masked with mornay sauce, then gratinéed, and served with another sauce made with the reduced veal juices.

Classical French cuisine began in the palaces and chateaux of pre-Revolutionary France, and grew to its present stature in the days of the great French chefs—Marie Antoine Careme (1784–1833) and Escoffier (1846–1935). It has often been called *haute* or *grande cuisine*, but the French do not use this term. Instead, *grande cuisine* refers primarily to an extremely lavish type of cooking. Classical French cooking is a more apt term.

Why did what some consider to be the world's greatest cuisine develop in France? The answer is probably in the character of the country and its people. France has more fertile soil in temperate regions than does any other European country. It produces an unusual variety of the choicest foods and beverages, including very fine wines. Also, France borders the Mediterranean, the Atlantic, the English Channel, and the North Sea, all of which supply excellent seafood.

The French like their food fresh and in season: They eat wild strawberries in June and July and asparagus in the spring. When a fruit or vegetable is out of season, the French chef cooks something else. The menu, therefore, changes with the season, sometimes daily. The French choose their tomatoes, for example, for their taste rather than their resistance to insects or drought or ease of mechanical harvesting. They let them ripen on the vine for maximum goodness. On the other hand, they pick their string beans before they reach full size because this is when their flavor is best.

Another reason that French cuisine is so good is that the French respect and honor their chefs. The great Escoffier was made a chevalier of the legion of honor, and Alexandre Dumaine received as many medals as a field marshal. Many gourmet and wine organizations in France are devoted to the advancement of fine food and superior wines. One, the Academie Culinaire, is a group of chefs and restaurant owners who meet regularly to evaluate new recipes and cooking trends. Another group is the Club des Cents, one hundred food lovers who meet every Thursday in Paris for lunch, usually at Maxim's. Several times a year the club hires a private railroad car and travels to the provinces to dine at a top-quality restaurant. The menu is planned by club members in consultation with the chef involved. Exactly two hours is alloted to eating the meal, as prescribed by Escoffier.

Then there is the well-known *Guide Michelin*, which rates the restaurants of France and other European countries. It awards one star to a restaurant that is "good in its class," two stars to one that is "worth a detour," and three stars to a restaurant that is "worth a journey." French chefs take these ratings very seriously: When the founder of the Relais de Porquerolles restaurant retired and the guide took away its stars and dropped it from the guide, the chef committed suicide.

For the past two hundred years, restaurants have played a key role in the development of classical French cooking. Indeed, the restaurant was an eighteenth-century French invention that became popular after the revolution of 1789. The chefs of the aristocrats, who had disappeared, found employment in the new restaurants. The first restaurant, it is believed, was opened on the rue des Poulies in Paris in 1765. Its owner was

M. Boulanger; as the word *boulanger* means "baker," he may have been a baker as well as a cook. The enterprise got its name from the restoratives or "restaurants"—soups and broths—served there. Before restaurants there were inns where travelers could stay overnight and get meals, cafés where drinks were served, and caterers who sold cooked joints of meat, fowl, and stews.

But Boulanger's was the first public place where people went just to eat. His menu featured soups and dishes prepared with poultry and eggs. It must have been a good but expensive place to eat, setting a tradition that continues today. The encyclopedist Denis Diderot visited Boulanger's restaurant and reported, "I went to dine at the restaurateur's place in the rue des Poulies; one is treated well there but has to pay dearly for it."

The first real luxury restaurant in Paris was the Grande Taverne de Londres, on the rue de Richelieu. Run by a man named Beauvilliers, it opened in 1782 and reached its greatest fame in the Napoleonic era. Beauvilliers became the leading culinary authority of his time, writing a cookbook that became the standard work on French cooking. Anthelme Brillat-Savarin, who was a steady customer at the restaurant, reported that Beauvilliers had a prodigious memory, that he could recognize and greet by name, after a lapse of twenty years, people who had eaten only once or twice in his restaurant.

It was during the time of Napoleon that French restaurants came into their own. This was a time of affluence and luxury, and the number and quality of restaurants greatly increased. The culinary center of Paris then was the Palais Royal, a colonnaded, tree-lined area near the Louvre, which contained fifteen restaurants and twenty-nine cafés. The finest restaurant in the Palais Royal was the Véry Grimod de la Reyniere, with marble-topped tables and gilded candelabra. The menu offered a dozen different soups, fifteen entrées of beef, twenty of mutton, and thirty of game.

During the reign of Napoleon III (1852–1870) a famous restaurant was the Café Anglais on the rue Marivaux. The main reason for its popularity was the talented chef, Adolph Duglere, whose best-known dish was sole Duglere, a fillet of sole baked with chopped onions, tomatoes, seasoning, and white wine. With this Duglere served a sauce prepared from the cooking liquid of the fish thickened with butter and lemon juice. Another of his creations was potage Germiny, a consommé of shredded sorrel leaves enriched with egg yolks and cream.

Maxim's

The Café Anglais is gone now, but Maxim's, which opened in 1893, is still going strong. Maxim's became the dining and drinking palace of the rich and famous. Then came decline and, with World War I, the end. In 1931, however, the restaurant was revived by Octave Vaudable, who hired Albert Blaser to be his maître d'hôtel. Sole Albert became Maxim's famous dish, and Albert became Maxim's soul.

There is now a Maxim's in New York City, a re-created Maxim's of Paris. Owned by designer Pierre Cardin, the restaurant occupies 24,000 square feet in the Carlton House Hotel, and great effort has been made to ensure that it looks like the original, only newer and larger. The main dining room is at the top of a grand staircase. It seats 193 diners and is flanked by an elegant carved-wood bar and private dining rooms. On the main floor is the popular bistro L'Omnibus, which serves lunch and dinner at prices about half those in the main dining room.

The culinary staff at Maxim's consists of fifty chefs, sous chefs, sauciers, cooks, bakers, butchers, and pantrymen. The cooking and storage area occupies 7,000 square feet on three floors. According to Monty Zullo, Maxim's general manager, "Food is everything here at Maxim's." The restaurant opened officially on November 15, 1985. It was preceded by a "soft opening" of six weeks during which time the menu was refined and the kitchen was given a "shakedown" by serving forty-five private parties.

The preliminary menu was basically Maxim's of Paris, classical French cuisine built around a *prix-fixe* dinner. Since then the menu has changed several times; the *prix-fixe* dinner has been eliminated and has been replaced by a completely à la carte menu. The menu has also moved away somewhat from the classical French to more contemporary recipes created by the New York staff and to some American specialties. Have the culinary revisions on this menu produced results? "Yes," says Zullo, "we have gone from an average of 60 lunches in L'Omnibus to 200, and we started out with about 50 dinners in the main dining room and now we are serving from 125 to 150."

The menu itself measures 10 by 15 inches, 10 by 30 open with a 3-inch flap on each side that folds in to hold a loose insert that can be changed daily. The cover art is in color and in the style of Toulouse-Lautrec. The paper is white and of good quality, although not coated. The inside insert is also white but of much lighter weight. The word *Maxim's* is printed at the top in red, and the listings are in black.

The listings are computer generated and probably printed in-house, which gives the chefs the flexibility to make changes daily. The items are listed first in French in a sans serif typeface and then explained below in English in an italic typeface.

Under the heading of Petites Entrées are eight listings ranging in price from $12 to $52 (Russian caviar). Some of these "small" entrées are Lobster, Crab Meat and Truffles with Warm, Mixed Herb Dressing—$19.75; A Combination of Fresh and Smoked Salmon with Gazpacho Coulis—$15.50; Shrimps and Snails Sautéed with Sesame Seeds and Ginger—$14.50; and Thin Slices of Lamb Tenderloin on a Bed of Chilled Ratatouille—$15.00.

Under the heading of Potages is Soup du Jour—$7.50, Chicken Consommé Flavored with Lemon Grass—$8.00, and Gratinated Soup with Sweet Caramelized Onions—$7.95.

At the top right, under Poissons et Crustaces, are five seafood items, including Angler Fish Medallions and Marinated Squids with Red Peppers and Basil Sauce—$26.00, Whole Maine Lobster Braised with Saffroned Potatoes—$35.50, and Escalopines of Wild Salmon with Chervil Sauce—$30.00.

The final entrée listing is headed Viandes, which encompasses poultry, veal, lamb, beef, and venison. Some of the unusual items are Breast of Guinea Hen Baked in a Cocotte, Old Fashioned Horseradish Sauce—$29.00, Poached Fresh Duck Liver in Mushroom and Turnip Broth—$38.25, and Venison Fillets Marinated and Served with a Vegetable Cake.

Six desserts are offered at the bottom of the menu. They are ordered à la carte and include Charriot de Patisseries—$8.50; Sorbets aux Fruits Frais—$8.00; Glaces Maison—$8.00; Crêpes Suzettes—$9.50; Soufflés au Grand Marnier, au Chocolat, à la Pistache—$11.50; and La Specialité Chaude du Jour—$11.50.

Le Français

The restaurant is Le Français; the chef and former owner is Jean Banchet. The location is Wheeling, Illinois, a suburb of Chicago, and the *Mobil Guide* rating is five stars. The large menu cover, measuring 12 by 14 inches, features a color reproduction of a painting of the restaurant's interior, identified only by the names of the restaurant and the chef/owner. Inside, a two-page insert lists the various items (Figure 17.2). In addition, there is a smaller, 8½-by-11-inch insert with the daily offerings. This combination of a daily plus a permanent listing is used because a French chef will usually serve only fresh meats, fish, and vegetables—no frozen items and nothing prepared by microwave! The permanent menu listing, therefore, includes food items available year round, and the daily listing includes seasonal items.

The permanent menu begins with the heading Premiere Assiette. Two interesting cold appetizers (Le Froid) are Vegetable Pâté with Truffle Vinaigrette and Lamb and Duck Leg Confit Salad with Wild Mushrooms. Le Chaud (hot appetizers) include Snails in Phyllo Dough served with Coulis of Tomatoes, Garlic Butter, and Wild Mushrooms; and Seafood Sausage with Pistachio and Sea Urchins. Eight cold and seven hot appetizers are offered.

On the facing page of this menu at the top left are soups, or Les Potages: Duck Consommé with Ravioli, Light Lobster Bisque, and Soup du Jour. On the top right is the heading Salades, with four listed.

The entrées begin with Arrivage de Poissons du Jour (Fresh Fish from Daily Market). Fish and other Seafood are listed on the daily menu. After these come La Ferme et la Forêt (fields and forest). Some typical entrées are Grilled Guinea Hen with Fresh Thyme and Vinegar Sauce; Duck Creation of the Day; Sautéed Black Angus with Marrow, Snails, and Red Wine Sauce; and Roast Heart of Sweetbreads with Julienne of Wild Mushrooms, Truffles, and Green Beans in Cream Sauce.

In addition, the daily insert menu has eleven additional appetizers, two soups, six fresh fish entrées, twelve other entrées, and nine desserts. Some of the desserts are Gratin of Peaches with Apricot Coulis; Dark and Light Chocolate Mousse; Pôt de Crème Fernand Point; Very, Very Light Feuilleté with Raspberries and Caramel Sauce; and Jean Banchet's Special Crème Brulée.

THE GERMAN MENU

Most people think of German food as mostly sausages and sauerkraut or sauerbraten and dumplings washed down by beer. The sausages, sliced, spread, poached, or fried, however, come in hundreds of forms, from little weisswurst with veal-based stuffing to goose liver sausage with truffles. And the sauerkraut can be prepared in different ways. It may be cooked with pineapple, oranges, apples, or even oysters, or it can be cooked in beer or wine, serving as a bed for roast fowl.

Sauerbraten in the Rhenish version includes raisins, or it may be marinated in wine or buttermilk and sauced with sweet cream. The dumplings may be made from flour, grated potatoes, or bread and enriched with bacon, liver, or onions sautéed in butter and flavored with marjoram or parsley.

German cuisine, like the older American cuisine, tends to be mainly "meat and potatoes" and relatively bland when compared with the well-seasoned dishes of southern Europe; the fats used for cooking tend to be butter and lard, not olive oil. Within this framework, however, German cuisine still can be interesting.

Vorspeisen is the German word for appetizers. Some are big salads of lobster, crab, or chicken and duck which can also serve as entrées. Others are smaller, such as Champignon-Schnitte, a slice of bread topped with sauced mushrooms and browned under the broiler; or Koniginpasteten, puff-paste patties filled with meat or fish.

German soups are usually made from potatoes, dried peas, or lentils, flavored with sausage and onion, and thickened with flour. But German chefs also make clear soups, such as double consommés with tiny marrow dumplings as garnishes. And there are creamy

FIGURE 17.2 A menu from Le Français. (Reproduced by permission.)

asparagus, spinach, cauliflower, and celery soups plus crayfish bisque made with veal stock and thickened with egg yolk.

The first German fish that comes to mind is the ubiquitous herring, which may appear as rollmops (herring rolls filled with onion and pickle) and filleted Bismarck herring, or fried or marinated to be eaten with boiled new potatoes and a sauce of bacon and onions. Shellfish are also part of the German menu, including crayfish cooked with dill, lobster, and crab in ragouts and salads, and mussels cooked in white wine. From the North Sea come flounder, plaice, turbot, and sole; these can be poached or sautéed and served with butter and lemon sauce. Freshwater trout and salmon plus carp and pike also are part of the German menu.

Meat, however, is the cornerstone of German cooking. Braten, or roast, is Germany's national dish. As in America, it may be cooked in an oven or with a little liquid in a tightly covered pot. Braten may be roast pork, beef, or veal, and the beef or veal braten may be larded with bacon, stuffed with foie gras, wrapped in puff paste, cooked with wine, vegetables, or cream, basted with broth, or glazed with honey.

Chops and steaks are broiled, sautéed, or slow cooked in the German kitchen, but more often they are stuffed or garnished with mushrooms, dressing, or goose livers. Cutlets called *schnitzel* are common to the German menu. They come sauceless and unbreaded or as Rahmschnitzel (served with cream sauce) or Jagerschnitzel (with mushrooms and sour cream). Schnitzel are also served with cooked bacon or tongue and spread with fillings wrapped in pancakes, sprinkled with cheese, and baked in the oven.

The ultimate schnitzel is Schnitzel à la Holstein, which is framed by small portions of smoked salmon, caviar, mushrooms, truffles, and cooked crayfish tails. Covering the meat itself is a fried egg topped by anchovies, capers, and parsley.

The most widely used meat in German cooking is pork, fresh or cured. Fresh ham may be roasted or cured, marinated in wine, or sliced, fried in butter, and sauced with sour cream. A noteworthy cured pork is Kasseler Rippenspeer, often served with peas, white-beans, chestnuts, roast potatoes, and mushrooms or resting on a bed of sauerkraut cooked with apples.

German cooks tend to combine pork, veal, and beef in their ground meat dishes. Hamburger is a Deutsches Beefsteak, but the poached meatballs called Konigsberger Klopse are made from ground beef and pork or pork and veal bound with eggs and served with a lemon-caper sauce. Beefsteak Tartar is made of raw ground steak served with an egg yolk, chopped raw onions, anchovies, capers, and pickles.

German stews range from Wurzfleisch, made with spiced beef, to Pichelsteiner Fleisch, a combination of beef, veal, lamb, and pork. The German ragouts are sophisticated combinations of veal, tongue, sweetbreads, brains, and mushrooms cooked with wine, enriched with eggs, and often served in puff-paste shells.

The German menu lists chicken, but it favors duck and goose. Duck may be braised in beer or wine or roasted with a stuffing of apples and prunes. Goose is also a German favorite. It is stuffed with onions, apples, and herbs. The neck is stuffed with liver and pork, and the blood and giblets may be combined with dried pears, prunes, and apples in a stew called Schwarzsauer.

German foods sometimes combine sweet and sour flavors. For example, fish, meat, and vegetables are often cooked with vinegar and sweetened with sugar. Fruits may be used to get the sweet-sour effect. Dried fruits are also a major part of the German diet and are combined with pork in a dish called Silesian Heaven. In another dish apples and potatoes are combined, and in still another, prunes, barley, and bacon are simmered together in a one-dish meal.

German desserts, susse Speisen, include rice pudding, sometimes cooked with fruit, and puddings of tapioca, farina, or fruit. Apple or other fruit pancakes and fruit dumplings are served with a sweet sauce. In addition there are egg custards, almond or hazelnut creams, and fruit or wine jellies topped with whipped cream.

The German and Austrian menu is also noted for its pastries and breads. Probably the most famous German pastry is marzipan, a tasty paste of almonds and sugar flavored with rose water or orange. It has resulted in a whole German art of beautiful shapes and decoration. It is not a German invention, however, as it came from the Near East where almond trees and sugarcane have been cultivated for thousands of years.

German Beer

The Germans consume about two billion gallons of beer a year. German beers are usually distinguished as dark or light, sweet or bitter, weak or strong, and top or bottom. The latter category refers to top or bottom fermenting, which depends on the type of yeast. Among the bottom-fermented beers is lager, which is aged about six weeks to make it clear and mellow. Export is a stronger beer that is stored for two or three months.

Another German beer is the slightly bitter Pilsner. It, and other light beers, is often served with Schnapps. Bock beer is dark and strong and is brewed in the winter and consumed in the spring. Marzenbier, which is served at Oktoberfest, has a color between light and dark.

Top-fermented beers are cloudy, the result of after-fermentation in the bottle. Among these beers is the weak, foamy Weissbier (white beer), which in Munich is served with a slice of lemon. Berliner Weisse beer is delicate and champagnelike; it is brewed entirely from wheat and is usually served with a shot of syrup. Other top-fermented beers include Altbier (old beer), which is light; Kolsch, a sweet, dark, malty beer; and Malzbier, which is low in alcohol.

Hans' Bavarian Lodge

The menu for Hans' Bavarian Lodge is very attractive and professionally designed. It is printed in two colors, blue and maroon, and measures 9 by 15 inches (Figure 17.3). The cover is a heavy, white, smooth-finish paper that resists stains and wear. The logo is placed at the bottom, and at the top a die-cut window reveals part of the interior menu illustration of mountains and pine trees.

Bound inside the cover is a four-page menu. On the first page is a well-organized beer and wine list. The left column shows a wine special of the day, a tip-on that can be changed as desired. This wine is offered by both the glass and the bottle. It is followed by three house wines, premium German wines (by the glass), and California wines—Robert Mondavi, Wente Bros., and Louis M. Martini—each accompanied by a short description.

The food listing appears on the center two pages. The narrow left-hand column lists Starters and Sides. Hot Starters include Crab Cakes, Stuffed Mushrooms, Shrimp De Jonghe, Shrimp Fritters, and a Combination Platter; prices range from $4.50 to $5.95. The Cold Starters include Steak Tartar, Sülze (a head cheese), Herring in Sour Cream, and Wurst Salad (marinated cuts of cold sausage). The prices of these appetizers range from $3.95 to $5.95.

Sides includes two small salads, vegetables, and beverages.

At the top left of the large panel is the Chef's Showcase, with clips for holding two daily specials. The copy above these tip-ons states: "Your server will describe these special dishes drawn from our vast assortment of unique recipes prepared for your dining pleasure." Below the specials are two entrées, Beef Rouladen and Sauerbraten.

FIGURE 17.3 Menu for Hans' Bavarian Lodge. It is well organized and attractively designed. (Reproduced by permission.)

At the bottom of the large panel, listed under A Taste of Tradition, are Roast Duckling Berghoff, Chicken Schnitzel, Hungarian Goulash, Bavarian Medley, Roast Pork, Pork Shank, German Pot Roast, and Lamb Shank. Prices range from $8.95 to $12.95.

On the upper right, under the heading From Land and Sea, are American-style entrées—Fresh Whitefish, Beer-Battered Shrimp, and Roast Chicken. The price range is from $8.95 to $13.95 (Filet Mignon). A relish tray, soup or salad, and choice of potato, spaetzle, or vegetable are included with all entrées.

The final listing on this menu is the desserts, in the lower right-hand corner: Bavarian Apple Strudel, Black Forest Cherry Torte, Bavarian Cheesecake,

White Chocolate Raspberry Torte, and Flourless Chocolate Torte. It is left to the server to describe them.

On the back panel are descriptions of the restaurant and the menu-mix, which gives an idea of why this restaurant is popular and has lasted as long as it has. It says, "Today we serve not only Old-World favorites but also fresh seafood, veal specialties, and other daily creations which appeal to more contemporary tastes."

Another feature described here is the restaurant's annual Oktoberfest. Finally, the hours and days the restaurant is open plus credit card policy are explained.

Karl Ratzsch's

Milwaukee is a town famous for its beer and German cuisine. One of the oldest and best German restaurants there is Karl Ratzsch's (Figure 17.4). The four-panel menu measures 10½ by 16 inches. The cover is a fine color reproduction of a painting of a monk holding a basket of fresh vegetables.

The inside spread is organized into three sections. On the left, the first section features German dishes: Pork Shanks and Sauerkraut, Wiener Schnitzel, German Sauerbraten, Braised Lamb Shank, Roast Duckling, Schnitzel à la Holstein, Pork Tenderloin Cordon Bleu à la Maria Christine (Stuffed with Ham and Ementhaler Cheese and Masked with a Creamy Mushroom Sauce), Roast Goose Shank, Baked Stuffed Pork Chops, Beef Rouladen (Potato Dumpling), Schnitzel à la Ratzsch, and Roast Loin of Pork. In a box at the bottom is the Special German Dinner—Liver Dumpling Soup, Lettuce and Spinach Salad with Hot Bacon Dressing, plus a Schlacht Platte, described as a Combination of German Delicacies including a Baked Pork Shank, Bratwurst, and a juicy slice of Kassler Rippchen (Smoked Pork Chop) served with Sauerkraut, Purée of Peas, and Potato Dumpling.

The center listing consists of six daily specials, each set in its own box: Sunday—Roast Breast of Chicken; Monday—Konigsberger Klops (Veal and Pork Meatballs in a Supreme Sauce with Capers, White Wine, and Fine Herbs); Tuesday—Kassler Rippchen; Wednesday—Hungarian Goulash; Thursday—Boiled Beef Bavarian; and Friday—Salmon Steak.

The third listing is an American menu including Shrimp Sauté, Lobster and Scallop Thermidor, Stuffed Dover Sole, Broiled Red Snapper, Broiled Planked Whitefish, U.S. Prime Steer Filet Mignon, Grenadier's Beefsteak à la Ratzsch (Thick Filet Mignon with a Sauce of Mushrooms, Chicken Livers, and Madeira Wine, from a Belgian Recipe), Filet Mignon au Burgundy, U.S. Prime Ribs of Beef, Chopped Steak Viennese, and Stuffed Boneless Chicken Breasts. This listing is followed by a Chateaubriand for Two.

The German appetizers include Golden Onion Rings, Stuffed Mushroom Caps, Crisp Potato Pancakes, Hot German Potato Salad, and Caesar Salad for Two. The appetizers for the American entrées include Crab Louie, Oysters on the Half Shell, Shrimp Cocktail, Schwartzwalder Ham with Asparagus Tips Vinaigrette, Pâté Maison, and Herring Marinated in Sour Cream.

A separate dessert menu offers an assortment of German pastries as well as more conventional American desserts.

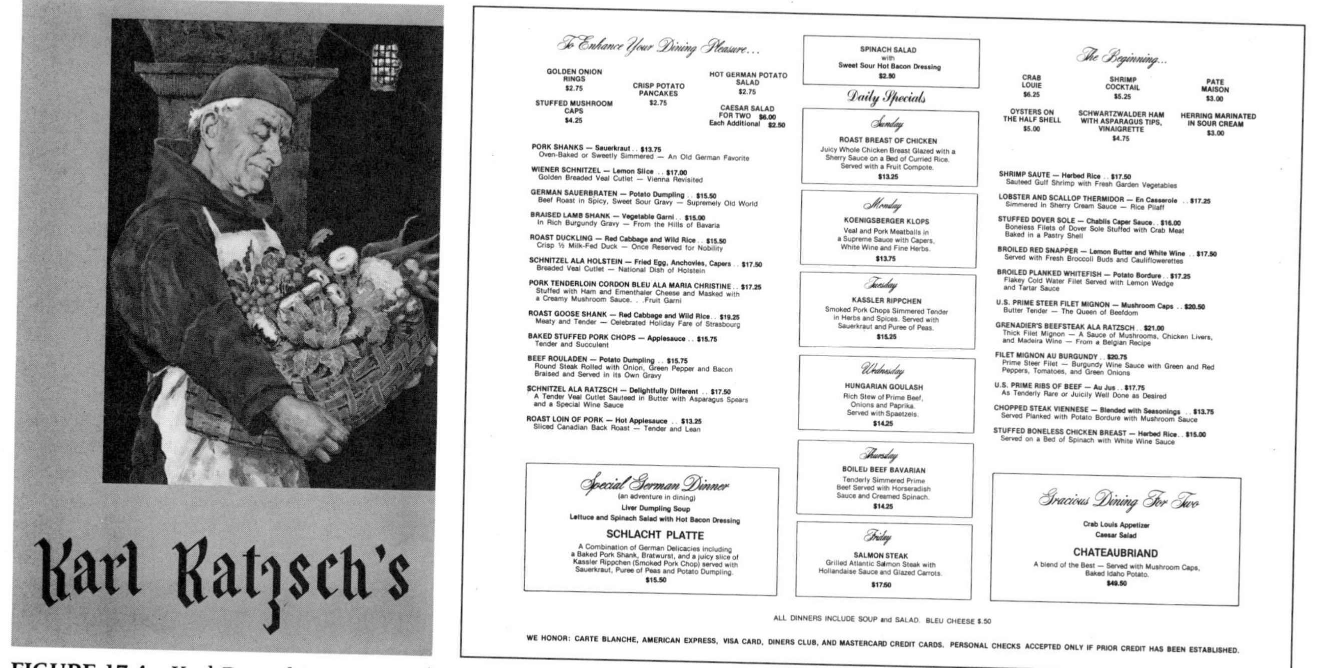

To Enhance Your Dining Pleasure...

GOLDEN ONION RINGS $2.75
STUFFED MUSHROOM CAPS $4.25
CRISP POTATO PANCAKES $2.75
HOT GERMAN POTATO SALAD $2.75
CAESAR SALAD FOR TWO $6.00 Each Additional $2.50

PORK SHANKS — Sauerkraut . . $13.75
Oven-Baked or Sweetly Simmered — An Old German Favorite

WIENER SCHNITZEL — Lemon Slice . . $17.00
Golden Breaded Veal Cutlet — Vienna Revisited

GERMAN SAUERBRATEN — Potato Dumpling . . $15.50
Beef Roast in Spicy, Sweet Sour Gravy — Supremely Old World

BRAISED LAMB SHANK — Vegetable Garni . . $15.00
In Rich Burgundy Gravy — From the Hills of Bavaria

ROAST DUCKLING — Red Cabbage and Wild Rice . . $15.50
Crisp ½ Milk-Fed Duck — Once Reserved for Nobility

SCHNITZEL ALA HOLSTEIN — Fried Egg, Anchovies, Capers . . $17.50
Breaded Veal Cutlet — National Dish of Holstein

PORK TENDERLOIN CORDON BLEU ALA MARIA CHRISTINE . . $17.25
Stuffed with Ham and Ementhaler Cheese and Masked with a Creamy Mushroom Sauce. . .Fruit Garni

ROAST GOOSE SHANK — Red Cabbage and Wild Rice . . $19.25
Meaty and Tender — Celebrated Holiday Fare of Strasbourg

BAKED STUFFED PORK CHOPS — Applesauce . . $15.75
Tender and Succulent

BEEF ROULADEN — Potato Dumpling . . $15.75
Round Steak Rolled with Onion, Green Pepper and Bacon Braised and Served in its Own Gravy

SCHNITZEL ALA RATZSCH — Delightfully Different . . $17.50
A Tender Veal Cutlet Sauteed in Butter with Asparagus Spears and a Special Wine Sauce

ROAST LOIN OF PORK — Hot Applesauce . . $13.25
Sliced Canadian Back Roast — Tender and Lean

Special German Dinner
(an adventure in dining)
Liver Dumpling Soup
Lettuce and Spinach Salad with Hot Bacon Dressing
SCHLACHT PLATTE
A Combination of German Delicacies including a Baked Pork Shank, Bratwurst, and a juicy slice of Kassler Rippchen (Smoked Pork Chop) served with Sauerkraut, Puree of Peas and Potato Dumpling.
$15.50

SPINACH SALAD
with
Sweet Sour Hot Bacon Dressing
$2.50

Daily Specials

Sunday
ROAST BREAST OF CHICKEN
Juicy Whole Chicken Breast Glazed with a Sherry Sauce on a Bed of Curried Rice. Served with a Fruit Compote.
$13.25

Monday
KOENIGSBERGER KLOPS
Veal and Pork Meatballs in a Supreme Sauce with Capers, White Wine and Fine Herbs.
$13.75

Tuesday
KASSLER RIPPCHEN
Smoked Pork Chops Simmered Tender in Herbs and Spices. Served with Sauerkraut and Puree of Peas.
$15.25

Wednesday
HUNGARIAN GOULASH
Rich Stew of Prime Beef, Onions and Paprika. Served with Spaetzels.
$14.25

Thursday
BOILED BEEF BAVARIAN
Tenderly Simmered Prime Beef Served with Horseradish Sauce and Creamed Spinach.
$14.25

Friday
SALMON STEAK
Grilled Atlantic Salmon Steak with Hollandaise Sauce and Glazed Carrots.
$17.50

The Beginning...

CRAB LOUIE $6.25
SHRIMP COCKTAIL $5.25
PATE MAISON $3.00
OYSTERS ON THE HALF SHELL $5.00
SCHWARTZWALDER HAM WITH ASPARAGUS TIPS, VINAIGRETTE $4.75
HERRING MARINATED IN SOUR CREAM $3.00

SHRIMP SAUTE — Herbed Rice . . $17.50
Sauteed Gulf Shrimp with Fresh Garden Vegetables

LOBSTER AND SCALLOP THERMIDOR — En Casserole . . $17.25
Simmered in Sherry Cream Sauce — Rice Pilaff

STUFFED DOVER SOLE — Chablis Caper Sauce . . $16.00
Boneless Filets of Dover Sole Stuffed with Crab Meat Baked in a Pastry Shell

BROILED RED SNAPPER — Lemon Butter and White Wine . . $17.50
Served with Fresh Broccoli Buds and Cauliflowerettes

BROILED PLANKED WHITEFISH — Potato Bordure . . $17.25
Flakey Cold Water Filet Served with Lemon Wedge and Tartar Sauce

U.S. PRIME STEER FILET MIGNON — Mushroom Caps . . $20.50
Butter Tender — The Queen of Beefdom

GRENADIER'S BEEFSTEAK ALA RATZSCH . . $21.00
Thick Filet Mignon — A Sauce of Mushrooms, Chicken Livers, and Madeira Wine — From a Belgian Recipe

FILET MIGNON AU BURGUNDY . . $20.75
Prime Steer Filet — Burgundy Wine Sauce with Green and Red Peppers, Tomatoes, and Green Onions

U.S. PRIME RIBS OF BEEF — Au Jus . . $17.75
As Tenderly Rare or Juicily Well Done as Desired

CHOPPED STEAK VIENNESE — Blended with Seasonings . . $13.75
Served Planked with Potato Bordure with Mushroom Sauce

STUFFED BONELESS CHICKEN BREAST — Herbed Rice . . $15.00
Served on a Bed of Spinach with White Wine Sauce

Gracious Dining For Two
Crab Louis Appetizer
Caesar Salad
CHATEAUBRIAND
A blend of the Best — Served with Mushroom Caps, Baked Idaho Potato.
$49.50

ALL DINNERS INCLUDE SOUP and SALAD. BLEU CHEESE $.50

WE HONOR: CARTE BLANCHE, AMERICAN EXPRESS, VISA CARD, DINERS CLUB, AND MASTERCARD CREDIT CARDS. PERSONAL CHECKS ACCEPTED ONLY IF PRIOR CREDIT HAS BEEN ESTABLISHED.

FIGURE 17.4 Karl Ratzsch's Menu. (Reproduced by permission.)

THE GREEK MENU

Greek cuisine is more Middle Eastern than Western. Savory lamb and baked dishes rich in olive oil are typical fare. The Greeks' most famous drink is ouzo, an anise-flavored aperitif that turns cloudy when diluted with water. Their meze, or appetizers, often are salty black and green olives and tangy white cubes of goat's-milk cheese called feta. Another appetizer is tzatziki, a cold blend of yogurt, chopped cucumber, and minced garlic.

For an entrée a Greek menu might offer veal—actually yearling beef—roasted and rubbed with lemon, or spaghetti with a sauce of ground beef cooked with onions and potatoes, but rendered aromatic with a pinch of cinnamon. A typical Greek vegetable is kolokithokorfades, zucchini tops simmered lightly in butter with scallions and tomatoes and served with grated cheese.

For a dip or a salad dressing, the Greeks have taramosalata, carp roe beaten with lemon juice, olive oil, and bits of white bread that have been soaked in water. The result is a cream-colored mixture a bit thicker than mayonnaise. Skordalia, used with fish, is a mixture of walnuts or almonds and mashed potatoes pounded together with garlic, olive oil, and lemon juice.

For Easter, the Greeks enjoy eggs dyed red, loaves of sweet bread, and mayeritsa—lamb intestines, liver, heart, lungs, and tripe, all cooked together in stock and seasoned with dill and scallions. After hours of boiling, the mixture is enlivened with an egg and lemon sauce.

Special sweets are diples, or rolls, made from thin, small sheets of dough rolled up with two forks as they are being fried. Another is loukoumades, also fried but made with yeast dough so that they puff up into feathery golden brown balls. The ingredients in these pastries are eggs, flour, and sometimes olive oil, honey, and flavorings such as cinnamon and chopped nuts.

Another Greek dish is moussaka, a casserole of fried ground meat and eggplant, potatoes, or squash. The meat can be ground beef, lamb, or mutton cooked with chopped onions, tomato paste, red wine, and parsley plus a dash of cinnamon. The meat and vegetables are combined in a casserole in alternate layers sprinkled with cheese. The crowning touch is a custard sauce made with eggs, milk, flour, and grated cheese plus a little nutmeg, which is poured over the casserole.

Tiropetes, or cheese puffs, make ideal appetizers or snacks and are made with a pastry called phyllo that comes in thin sheets that are cut into strips. The phyllo is filled with a mixture of feta cheese and beaten eggs and is rolled up.

A Greek salad is an assortment of greens, radishes, cucumbers, tomato wedges, scallions, black olives, and chunks of feta all tossed in vinaigrette sauce and sprinkled with fresh mint.

The Parthenon

The Parthenon, in Chicago, has an eight-page menu measuring 8½ by 11 inches (Figure 17.5). It is printed in black on white-enameled but not coated paper and is bound into a permanent leather cover. The first page has two paragraphs of general copy about the Parthenon, Greek culture, and the restaurant:

> Symbolizing the birthplace of Western Civilization, the Parthenon is one of Greece's proudest achievements. It is the focal point of the most famous collection of buildings in history, standing majestically on the renowned hilltop that is the acropolis of Athens.
>
> Naming our restaurant after this architectural wonder carries a deep responsibility for excellence; we will never take this responsibility lightly. We hope that in some small way our efforts will help you to know the pure enjoyment of the Greek eating experience!

The next (inside) panel contains the wine list. Five wines are offered by the bottle, carafe, or glass, and sixteen more wines by the bottle only. All are Greek wines—white, red, dry, or semisweet and the well-known Greek retsina wines. The prices per bottle are relatively low, ranging from $7.50 to $12.95 a bottle, which enables the customer to try something new in the world of wine.

Headings on the next panel are Appetizers, Cheeses, and Salads. Everything is listed in both Greek and English. Ten appetizers plus feta cheese are offered: Saganaki (cheese flambé), Eggplant Salad, Village Platter (a zestful array of gyros, pita bread cut in quarters, sliced tomatoes, and parsleyed onions), Octopus in Wine Sauce, Cheese Pies, Dolmades (meatless—vine leaves stuffed with rice and herbs), Fish Roe Salad, Tzatziki (thin slices of cucumber in yogurt with a touch of garlic), Bean Salad, and a Special Assortment.

The salad listing features a Greek Salad with hearts of lettuce, tomatoes, cucumbers, feta cheese, olives, peppers, and anchovies in olive oil.

The center two-page spread lists twenty-eight dishes under the heading Dinner Selections. Just about every Greek entrée ever created is listed here, including

GYROS

Barbecued layers of specially seasoned lamb and beef served on a bed of parsleyed onions

MELITZANOPITA

Baked eggplant and Kefalotiri cheese, wrapped in Phyllo

DOLMADES

Vine leaves stuffed with a special preparation of rice, meats and herbs in Avgolemono Sauce

MOUSSAKA

Baked layers of eggplant and meat sauce topped with Bechamel sauce and cheese

SPINACH CHEESE PIE

Special preparation of spinach, feta cheese and herbs, baked in Greek phyllo

The generous selection of lamb dishes includes Braised Lamb, Baked Lamb's Head, Lamb with Artichokes, Roast Leg of Lamb, Roast Loin of Lamb, Barbecued Lamb, Broiled Lamb Chops, and Fried Lamb's Liver. Beef, pork, and chicken dishes are also offered plus a Greek sausage, Broiled Shishkebob plus Tigania (marinated pieces of pork tenderloin, sautéed in wine sauce and served with rice pilaf and okra). A featured special included in this extensive entrée listing is Barbecued Whole Suckling Pig (for groups of twelve or more).

The entrées continue on the next page with six seafood dishes, including Pan-Fried Squid and Octopus Simmered in Tomatoes, Herbs, and Wine.

The last panel lists desserts and beverages. The six desserts include some Greek specialties such as Baklava (layers of phyllo and crushed walnuts baked in honey), Ravani (honey-almond cake topped with fresh cream), Creme Caramel, Yogurt (made by Parthenon chefs), and Yogurt with Honey and Walnuts.

THE HUNGARIAN MENU

Hungarian cuisine began with the tradition of the cauldron, the pot that was left hanging over an open fire. Today, the stews, goulashes, and soups that are meals in themselves continue this tradition. But Hungarian

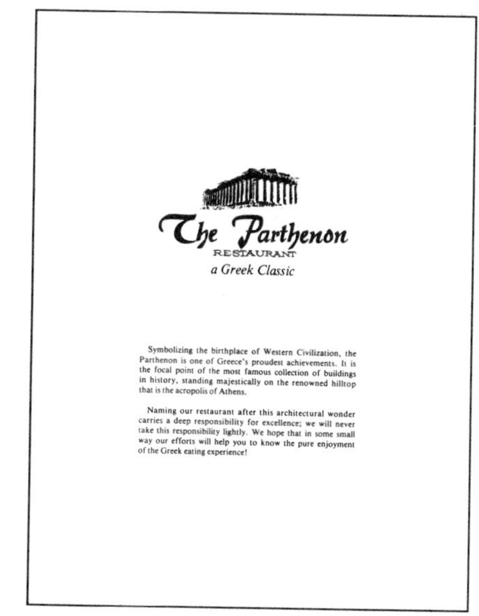

FIGURE 17.5 The Parthenon menu. (Reproduced by permission.)

WINES — ΟΙΝΟΙ

	BOTTLE ΦΟΙΑΛΗ	CARAFE ΚΑΤΟΣΤΑΡΙ	GLASS ΠΟΤΙΡΙ
RODITIS— ΡΟΔΙΤΗΣ *Dry Red*	7.50	4.10	1.50
RETSINA— ΡΕΤΣΙΝΑ *Resinated White*	7.50	4.10	1.50
FILERI (Apelia) — ΦΙΛΕΡΗ (ΑΠΕΛΙΑ) *Dry White*	7.50	4.10	1.50
COURTAKIS— ΚΟΥΡΤΑΚΗΣ *Roditis or Retsina*	7.50	4.10	1.50
CORINTH— ΚΟΡΙΝΘΟΣ *Roditis or Retsina*	7.50	4.10	1.50
CORINTH— ΚΟΡΙΝΘΟΣ *Dry White*	7.75		
MAVRODAPHNE— ΜΑΥΡΟΔΑΦΝΗ *Sweet Red*	7.50		
SANTA MARINA— ΣΑΝΤΑ ΜΑΡΙΝΑ *Semi-Sweet*	7.95		
SANTA LAURA— ΣΑΝΤΑ ΛΑΥΡΑ *Dry Red or White*	7.75		
AMBELOS— ΑΜΒΕΛΟΣ *Dry Red or White*	8.50		
DEMESTICA— ΔΕΜΕΣΤΙΚΑ *Dry Red or White*	8.95		
SANTA HELENA— ΣΑΝΤΑ ΕΛΕΝΑ *Dry White*	8.95		
SANTA ROSA— ΣΑΝΤΑ ΡΟΣΑ *Dry Red*	8.25		
CAMBAS— ΚΑΜΠΑΣ *Roditis, Retsina or Red Retsina*	8.50		
BOUTARI (Naoussa)—ΜΠΟΥΤΑΡΗ *Dry Red*	8.95		
BOUTARI BLANC *Dry White*	8.95		
ROBOLA (Komitopoulos)— ΡΟΜΠΟΛΑ *Dry White*	8.25		
BLANC DE BLANCS (Domaine Porto Carras)—ΠΟΡΤΟ ΚΑΡΡΑΣ *Dry White*	11.95		
ROBOLA CALLIGA— ΡΟΜΠΟΛΑ *Dry White*	12.50		
CHATEAU MATSA (BOUTARI) *Dry White*	12.50		
GRANDE RESERVE (BOUTARI) *Dry Red*	12.95		

APPETIZERS and CHEESES — ΟΡΕΚΤΙΚΑ ΚΑΙ ΤΥΡΙΑ

SAGANAKI— ΣΑΓΑΝΑΚΙ *Cheese flambe—a creation of The Parthenon*	2.85
EGGPLANT SALAD — ΜΕΛΙΤΖΑΝΟΣΑΛΑΤΑ *A tasty spread of eggplant flavored with garlic that is best enjoyed mounded atop thick slices of crusty bread.*	2.50
VILLAGE PLATTER *(For Two or More)*	per person 3.75
ΧΩΡΙΑΤΙΚΗ ΠΙΑΤΕΛΛΑ — Δια δύο ή περισσότερους *A zestful array of gyros, pita bread cut in quarters, tzatziki, sliced tomatoes and parsleyed onions*	κατ' άτομον 3.75
OCTOPUS in WINE SAUCE— ΟΚΤΑΠΟΔΙ ΚΡΑΣΑΤΟ *Simmered in wine and herbs, then chilled*	6.50
CHEESE PIES— ΤΥΡΟΠΙΤΑΚΙΑ *Baked delicacy of Greek Phyllo filled with special mixture of Greek Cheese*	3.50
DOLMADES *(meatless)* — ΝΤΟΛΜΑΔΕΣ ΓΙΑΛΑΝΤΖΗ *Vine Leaves stuffed with special preparation of rice and herbs*	2.95
FISH ROE SALAD—ΤΑΡΑΜΟΣΑΛΑΤΑ *Delicate dip of whipped fish roe*	2.25
TZATZIKI— ΤΖΑΤΖΙΚΙ *Thin slices of cucumber in yogurt with a touch of garlic*	2.50
BEAN SALAD— ΦΑΣΟΛΙΑ ΜΠΙΑΖΙ *Chilled beans vinaigrette*	1.95
SPECIAL ASSORTMENT— ΟΡΕΚΤΙΚΑ ΔΙΑΦΟΡΑ *Octopus, Cheese Pies, Dolmades, Fish Roe Salad, Russian Salad, Tzatziki, Bean Salad*	per person 3.95
Όκταπόδι, Τυροπιττάκια, Ντολμάδες Γιαλαντζή, Ταραμοσαλάτα, Ρωσσική, Τζατζίκι	κατ' άτομον 3.95
FETA CHEESE— ΦΕΤΑ	2.10
KASERI or KEFALOTIRI— ΚΑΣΕΡΙ ή ΚΕΦΑΛΟΤΥΡΙ	2.35

SALADS — ΣΑΛΑΤΕΣ

GREEK SALAD— ΣΑΛΑΤΑ *Hearts of lettuce, tomatoes, cucumbers, Feta cheese, olives, peppers and anchovies, in olive oil, vinegar and oregano dressing*	2.10
LARGE GREEK SALAD— ΜΕΓΑΛΗ ΣΑΛΑΤΑ	2.95
GREEK VILLAGE SALAD— ΧΩΡΙΑΤΙΚΗ ΣΑΛΑΤΑ *Tomatoes, cucumbers, Feta cheese, peppers, olives, onions and anchovies, in olive oil, vinegar and oregano dressing*	2.35
LARGE SALADS FOR TWO OR MORE	per person 2.10
ΜΕΓΑΛΕΣ ΣΑΛΑΤΕΣ ΔΙΑ ΔΥΟ Η ΠΕΡΙΣΣΟΤΕΡΟΥΣ	κατ' άτομον 2.10
RUSSIAN SALAD— ΡΩΣΣΙΚΗ ΣΑΛΑΤΑ	1.95

DINNER SELECTIONS — ΦΑΓΗΤΑ

GYROS—ΓΥΡΟΣ *Barbecued layers of specially seasoned lamb and beef served on a bed of parsleyed onions—made famous by The Parthenon*	5.50
MELITZANOPITA— ΜΕΛΙΤΖΑΝΟΠΙΤΤΑ *Baked Eggplant and Kefalotiri cheese, wrapped in Phyllo*	5.25
DOLMADES—ΝΤΟΛΜΑΔΕΣ *Vine leaves stuffed with special preparation of rice, meats and herbs in Avgolemono Sauce*	5.40
MOUSSAKA— ΜΟΥΣΑΚΑΣ *Baked layers of eggplant and meat sauce, topped with Bechamel sauce and cheese*	5.60
PASTITSIO— ΠΑΣΤΙΤΣΙΟ *Baked macaroni and meat sauce, topped with Bechamel sauce and cheese*	5.40
SPINACH-CHEESE PIE— ΣΠΑΝΑΚΟΤΥΡΟΠΙΤΤΑ *Special preparation of spinach, Feta cheese and herbs, baked in Greek phyllo*	5.10
SPECIAL COMBINATION DINNER— ΠΟΙΚΙΛΙΑ ΦΑΓΗΤΩΝ *Dolmades, Moussaka, Pastitsio, Roast Lamb, Potatoes and Vegetable* Ντολμάδες, Μουσακάς, Παστίτσιο, Άρνί Ψητό, Πατάτες καί Λαχανικό	6.65
BRAISED LAMB— ΑΡΝΙ ΚΑΠΑΜΑ *Choice of Rice Pilafi, Potatoes, Spaghetti, Okra, Eggplant, Squash or Green Beans* Μέ Πιλάφι ή Πατάτες ή Σπαγγέτο ή Μπάμιες ή Μελιτζάνες ή Κολοκυθάκια ή Φασολάκια	6.10
BEEF KAPAMA— ΜΟΣΧΑΡΑΚΙ ΚΑΠΑΜΑ *Simmered in tomatoes, herbs and wine, and served with either Rice Pilafi, Potatoes, Spaghetti, Okra, Eggplant, Squash or Green Beans* Μέ Πιλάφι ή Πατάτες ή Σπαγγέτο ή Μπάμιες ή Μελιτζάνες ή Κολοκυθάκια ή Φασολάκια	6.10
CHICKEN KAPAMA— ΚΟΤΟΠΟΥΛΟ ΚΑΠΑΜΑ *Simmered in tomatoes, herbs and wine, and served with either Rice Pilafi, Potatoes or Okra* Μέ Πιλάφι ή Πατάτες ή Μπάμιες	3.75
BAKED LAMB'S HEAD— ΚΕΦΑΛΑΚΙ ΦΟΥΡΝΟΥ *Served with Roast Potatoes*— Μέ Πατάτες Φούρνου	3.75
LAMB WITH ARTICHOKES— ΑΡΝΙ ΑΓΚΙΝΑΡΕΣ *Served with fresh hearts of artichokes in Avgolemono Sauce*	*market price*
TIGANIA— ΤΙΓΑΝΙΑ *Marinated pieces of Pork Tenderloin, sauteed in Wine Sauce and served with Rice Pilafi and Okra* Τηγανιτό χοιρινό κρασάτο μέ Πιλάφι καί Μπάμιες	6.75

DINNER SELECTIONS — ΦΑΓΗΤΑ

BARBECUED WHOLE SUCKLING PIG *Served with Rice Pilafi and Roast Potatoes* For groups of 12 or more (please call in advance)	per person 5.95
ΓΟΥΡΟΥΝΟΠΟΥΛΟ ΣΟΥΒΛΑΣ ΟΛΟΚΛΗΡΟ Μέ Πιλάφι καί Πατάτες Φούρνου — ΔΙΑ ΠΑΡΕΣ ΑΠΟ 12 ΑΤΟΜΑ ΚΑΙ ΑΝΩ — (ΠΑΡΑΚΑΛΕΙΣΘΕ ΟΠΩΣ ΤΗΛΕΦΩΝΗΣΕΤΕ ΕΝΩΡΙΤΕΡΑ)	κατ' άτομον 5.95
ROAST LEG OF LAMB— ΑΡΝΙ ΨΗΤΟ, ΜΠΟΥΤΙ *Served with Rice Pilafi and Roast Potatoes*— Μέ Πιλάφι καί Πατάτες Φούρνου	6.75
ROAST LOIN OF LAMB— ΑΡΝΙ ΨΗΤΟ, ΝΕΦΡΑΜΙΑ *Served with Rice Pilafi and Roast Potatoes*— Μέ Πιλάφι καί Πατάτες Φούρνου	7.50
ROAST YOUNG PIG— ΧΟΙΡΙΔΙΟΝ ΦΟΥΡΝΟΥ *Served with Rice Pilafi and Roast Potatoes*— Μέ Πιλάφι καί Πατάτες Φούρνου	5.95
BARBECUED LAMB— ΑΡΝΙ ΣΟΥΒΛΑΣ *Served with Rice Pilafi and Roast Potatoes*— Μέ Πιλάφι καί Πατάτες Φούρνου	7.25
BARBECUED CHICKEN— ΚΟΤΟΠΟΥΛΟ ΣΟΥΒΛΑΣ *Served with Rice Pilafi and Roast Potatoes*— Μέ Πιλάφι καί Πατάτες Φούρνου	5.75
GREEK SAUSAGE— ΛΟΥΚΑΝΙΚΑ *Made as only The Parthenon chefs can make it*	5.75
FRIED LAMB'S LIVER— ΣΥΚΟΤΑΚΙΑ ΤΗΓΑΝΙΤΑ *Served with Roast Potatoes*— Μέ Πατάτες Φούρνου	5.50
FRIED MEAT BALLS— ΚΕΦΤΕΔΑΚΙΑ ΤΗΓΑΝΙΤΑ *Served with Rice Pilafi and Roast Potatoes*— Μέ Πιλάφι καί Πατάτες Φούρνου	5.50
FRIED SWEETBREADS— ΓΛΥΚΑΔΑΚΙΑ ΤΗΓΑΝΙΤΑ *Served with Roast Potatoes*— Μέ Πατάτες Φούρνου	6.50
MEZES— ΜΕΖΕΣ *Combination of Lamb's liver, Meat Balls and Sweetbreads* Ποικιλία άπό συκωτάκια, κεφτέδες καί γλυκαδάκια	6.50
BROILED SHISHKEBOB— ΣΟΥΒΛΑΚΙ ΣΧΑΡΑΣ *Served with Rice Pilafi and Roast Potatoes*— Μέ Πιλάφι καί Πατάτες Φούρνου	7.50
BROILED DOUBLE-CUT LAMB CHOPS (TWO)— ΠΑΪΔΑΚΙΑ ΣΧΑΡΑΣ (Δύο) *Served with Rice Pilafi and Roast Potatoes*— Μέ Πιλάφι καί Πατάτες Φούρνου	12.95
BROILED T-BONE STEAK— ΜΠΡΙΤΖΟΛΑ ΜΟΣΧΑΡΙΣΙΑ *Served with Roast Potatoes*— Μέ Πιλάφι καί Πατάτες Φούρνου	11.50
BROILED CENTER-CUT PORK CHOPS— ΧΟΙΡΙΝΕΣ ΜΠΡΙΖΟΛΕΣ *Served with Rice Pilafi and Roast Potatoes*— Μέ Πιλάφι καί Πατάτες Φούρνου	6.95
CHICKEN SHISHKEBOB— ΣΟΥΒΛΑΚΙ ΑΠΟ ΚΟΤΟΠΟΥΛΟ *Served with Rice Pilafi and Roast Potatoes*— Μέ Πιλάφι καί Πατάτες Φούρνου	5.95

48D

cuisine is more than stews and goulashes. For more than a thousand years, Hungary has been the meeting place of East and West.

European merchants sailed down the Danube River to Constantinople and Asia. Crusaders passed through Hungary on their way to Jerusalem, and while the armies of France, Germany, and Italy invaded the country from the West, the Turks and Tartars invaded from the East. As a result, Hungarian cooking is characterized by variety, distinct flavors, a calculated use of color, and a combination of sophistication and simplicity. Hungarian cuisine favors pork over beef and veal, and lard is preferred to other animal or vegetable fats because grazing is limited and the raising of hogs has become a specialty. Meats are more frequently braised than broiled or roasted, and soups are always thickened with flour or a roux. Pasta dishes on the Hungarian menu are often sweetened with sugared nuts, poppy seeds, fruit, or jams and served as desserts.

Hungarian cuisine is defined by its skillful use of seasoning. The Hungarian chef believes that seasoning should not be too subtle but also not overpowering. A Hungarian kitchen contains a variety of spices, such as cinnamon, dill, poppy seeds, and caraway seeds, but the national Hungarian spice is paprika.

Paprika is what makes Hungarian cooking unlike any other. The powder is ground from dried red peppers, which were found growing in the Americas and then brought to Spain. From Spain the peppers spread across Europe to Turkey. The Turks, in turn, introduced paprika to the Hungarians during their conquest of Hungary in the sixteenth century.

While black pepper had to be imported from the Far East—and as a result was very expensive—paprika could be grown in Hungary. It thus became popular with the peasants, then the townspeople, and finally even the aristocracy. Today, the finest paprika is grown in the region surrounding the southern Hungarian town of Szeged on the Tisza River. Paprika is available in three strengths—sweet, semisweet, and hot.

Paprikas Fono

The Paprikas Fono restaurant in San Francisco is located in Ghirardelli Square, overlooking San Francisco Bay. It offers diners a stunning view and wonderful and different food and drink.

The food listings begin with From Our Gulyas Kettle. Gulyas (goulash) is one of the most famous Hungarian dishes. It is a hearty soup made with chunks of beef and diced potatoes simmered in a rich paprika broth. The name is derived from the word *gulya* meaning "cattle herd." Since ancient times Hungarian herdsmen, the *gulyas*, have prepared their meals in a *bogracs*, a thin-walled portable iron kettle suspended over an open fire.

One can also order the Kettle Gulyas Dinner, which is gulyas in an individual kettle accompanied by langos (fried peasant bread), sour cream, and chopped scallions. It is served with a dessert, either a sweet palacsinta (pastry) or strudel. The menu also offers five salads and seven pastries, fruits, and cheese, as well as ice cream—"Made at Paprikas."

Under the heading of The Hungarian Way, are nine traditional Hungarian meat and chicken dishes, ranging in price from $8.95 to $14.95. Two other entrée listings are headed Vendeglo and Csarda.

The vendeglo, or "little restaurant," is a family-type restaurant found in towns, villages, and cities throughout Hungary. Five entrées, ranging from $6.95 to $12.50, are listed under this heading, including Lazlo's Hefty Palacsintas, which is three palacsintas—a fried ham palacsinta, one light asparagus soufflé, and a third palacsinta with fresh mushroom sauce.

A csarda is a country inn, originally a haven for those on the road, from itinerant merchants and herdsmen to brigands and highwaymen. The four csarda entrées range in price from $7.50 to $8.95.

The back page of this menu has a complete wine list, including aperitifs, house wines (by the glass or decanter), red wines, white wines, rosé wines, and champagnes. Of special interest are the Hungarian wines: Egri Bikaver (a red), Badacsonyi Keknyelu (a medium-dry wine with a golden green hue), and several Tokajis (white).

Paprikas Fono's menu measures 9½ by 14 inches and has a hard, permanent, separate cover. The four-page insert is well designed with clever drawings. The paper is white (uncoated), and the listings are black and red. The type itself is large and easy to read. Hungarian items are described in enough detail to arouse the diner's curiosity, but not so completely that there is no surprise when the order is served.

THE ITALIAN MENU

Italian cooking is the source of every other Western cuisine. The first fully developed cuisine in Europe, it originated with the ancient Romans who found some of their culinary inspiration in Asia Minor and Greece. Combining all these made it possible for Italy to teach France. The *Larousse Gastronomic Encyclopedia* notes that "Italian cooking can be considered for all the countries of Latin Europe as a veritable mother cuisine."

As early as 1600, when Catherine de Medici married the future king of France and brought her expert cooks from Italy to France, Italian chefs knew the art of making modern pastry and desserts—cakes, cream puffs, and ices. These cooks prepared vegetables such as artichokes and broccoli for the first time outside Italy.

Some Roman cooking still survives in Italian cuisine, albeit in a modified form. The Romans had an early version of gnocchi, or dumplings, and made a dish similar to the modern sformato, which is a cross between a soufflé and a pudding. The Romans also introduced sweet-and-sour sauces, which were a combination of pepper, mint, pine nuts, sultana grapes, carrots, honey, vinegar, oil, wine, and musk. This sauce resembles the agrodolce sauce used in Italy today for duck, hare, zucchini, and cabbage. Another Roman contribution to Italian and eventually present-day American cuisine is cheesecake, both an unsweetened and a dessert variety called savillum.

The Arabs, who for a period of time ruled Sicily and southern Italy, contributed the technique of making ice cream and sherbet. In addition, by the late Middle Ages, interesting breads had appeared in Italy. One was sweetened with honey, flavored with spices, and dotted with bits of dried fruit and figs. This bread is the ancestor of the modern panforte of Siena. In the late thirteenth century a cookbook appeared with recipes for making vermicelli, tortelli, and tortelletti; it is the first published reference to pasta. And because this cookbook was published in 1290, years before Marco Polo returned from China, it disproves the claim that he brought back the recipe for pasta from China.

Platina's cookbook, published in 1475, suggested seasoning food with lemon juice or wine and also starting a meal with the light fresh taste of fruit. One result of this suggestion is the popular Italian appetizer of today, prosciutto—thin slices of ham—served with melon or figs.

During the Renaissance, Italy introduced sugar, coffee, and ice cream to the rest of Europe. Coffee came from Arabia by way of Venice, and by the late seventeenth century the habit of drinking coffee had become well established in both Italy and France.

The Italians also introduced foods of the New World to the Old. The first Italian mention of the tomato was in 1554; it was called a "golden apple." It took nearly two hundred years for the Italians to develop bigger, red varieties and to use tomatoes regularly in cooking. Pimentos, or red peppers, and potatoes, also followed by corn and kidney beans, came from America and became part of Italian cooking.

By the end of the sixteenth century the list of foods used in Italian cooking was complete, and the cooking techniques and eating habits had crystallized into approximately the forms known today. By the eighteenth century Italian cuisine began to be challenged by the French.

To many non-Italians, the cuisine of Italy means pasta in the form of spaghetti, macaroni, or noodles. Actually the Italian cuisine ranges from soups and interesting antipasti to meat, fish, and poultry dishes plus a profusion of delicious cheeses, cakes, and ice creams.

There is also great variety within the category of pasta, and pasta cooking varies throughout Italy. The country can be divided into two separate culinary territories. The North is the country of pasta bolognese, the flat ribbon type of noodle, usually made with eggs and often cooked to order. The South is the home of pasta napoletana, the macaroni of Naples, which is most often manufactured commercially in tubular form and frequently made without eggs. It often is dried, which makes it possible to store for a long time. Also, the North cooks with butter; the South with olive oil.

The most common forms of pasta are spaghetti, macaroni, ravioli, vermicelli, and noodles, but these are only a few of the long list of pasta varieties. The names often describe shapes, origins, or the fillings of different types of pasta. Amorini, for example, are little cupids; agnolotti, little fat lambs (rolls of pasta stuffed with meat); cannelloni, big pipes; conchiglie, conch shells; farfalle, butterflies; fusilli, spindles or twists; lingue di passeri, sparrows' tongues; mostaccioli rigati, little grooved mustaches; ricciolini, little curls; stivaletti, little boots; and vermicelli, little worms. Gnocchi, or pastalike dumplings, are also standard Italian fare. They may be made of farina, semolina, potatoes, and flour or a mixture of these.

After pasta, Italy's most important single category of food is fish and crustaceans. Italians net around 700 million pounds of fish a year, including mullet, sea bass, sole, anchovies, sardines, mackerel, tuna, and eel. The sea around Italy also provides oysters, clams, mussels, spiny lobsters, shrimp, crayfish, and the famous scampi, a relative of the shrimp. Squid, cuttlefish, and octopus are also on the Italian menu.

Italy is known for the quality of its fruits and vegetables, and its olive oil is probably the best in the world. It is also Europe's biggest producer of rice. The Italian method of cooking rice leaves each grain separate and slightly resistant to the teeth. Modern Italians, like the ancient Romans, prefer veal to beef.

Italian ice cream is probably the best in the world. It comes in two varieties, *gelati*, which resembles the milk-based ice cream in the United States, and *granita*, which is a light sherbet made with crushed ice and syrup flavored with lemon, strawberry, or coffee.

Today, Italian cooking is in tune with the requirements of the modern world. It is undemanding, adaptable, inexpensive, and flavorful. The range of Italian food is broad, but still a little narrower—more down to earth—than French food. It is democratic while still satisfying the most aristocratic taste.

Italian Wines

The Italians drink more wine than even the French, and Italy produces hundreds of different wines and exports many of them to the United States. These wines vary from dry to sweet and come from both the north and south of the country. The following describes some of them:

1. *Bardolino.* A light red wine with a dry, slightly spicy flavor. The grapes are grown on the shores of Lake Garda, near Verona.
2. *Ravello Rosato.* A sweet rosé wine from the Salerno area, it has a light fruity taste and goes well with desserts.
3. *Verdicchio dei Castelli di Jesi.* A dry white table wine from central Italy that goes well with fish.
4. *Freisa.* A red wine with a slight flinty (abrasive) taste. It is not bitter or sour; rather it combines a fruity flavor and sharpness.
5. *Frascati.* An inexpensive table wine of Rome. It is straw colored and can be dry or semisweet. Its quality varies; at its best it has a mellow, refreshing taste.
6. *Orvieto.* A pleasant, fruity white wine that is a good dessert wine. It comes from Umbria and can be either dry or semisweet.
7. *Grignolino.* A delicate red. From the vineyards of the Piedmont, its pleasant, nutty flavor goes well with meat dishes.
8. *Valpolicella.* A dark red from Verona, this strong wine can be served with highly seasoned dishes.
9. *Barbaresco.* A red from the region of Turin. Full bodied and flinty, it goes well with roasts and prime ribs.
10. *Barolo.* The greatest of the Piedmont red wines. It has a high alcohol content but is still smooth and full bodied.
11. *Brolio.* A fine Chianti classico produced in Tuscany. It has a subtle, tangy flavor.
12. *Soave.* One of the finest Italian whites, produced near Verona. Its delicate flavor and aroma are distinct.
13. *Est! Est! Est!* ("It is! It is! It is!"). A pleasant wine produced near Rome. One variety is slightly tart; the other is semisweet.
14. *Chianti.* A classic Tuscan product. It is a fresh fruity wine that goes well with pasta dishes.

Pizza

Probably Italy's most popular food import to the United States is pizza, which came from Naples. Pizza is big business. In 1988, Pizza Hut sold $2,918.4 million worth of pizza in its 5,394 outlets. Close behind was Domino's, with sales of $1,980 million from 4,279 units, and Little Caesar's, with $725 million in sales from 1,820 units (*Restaurants & Institutions*, "400" issue, 1988).

First there was plain pizza, a flat dough topped with herbs, spices, oils, cheese, and sausage and cooked in a hot oven. This new dish captured the appetites of post-World War II Americans. Today, pizza comes rolled, folded, stuffed, fried, and stacked with thirty varieties of toppings and ingredients.

Pizza first reached the United States in the early 1900s, when it was introduced by Gennarco Lombardi in New York City. His pizzeria became the model for others around the Northeast, and the dish gained some popularity in the 1920s. But not until after World War II, when its mass production helped spread pizza across America, did it become one of America's most popular foods.

Foccacia may have been the first pizza. It was a crude bread baked beneath the stones of the fire, then brushed with oil and seasoned. This flavored bread evolved into the present-day foccacia, a flat bread that can be served hot or used as a base in an open-faced sandwich.

Folded pizza has many names, depending on the size and the crust. Calzone is one; mezzaluna (half-moon) and fiadone are others. Fiadone is pizza dough that is filled with cheese, sausage, vegetables, herbs, and spices, then folded over and sealed. Panzerotti is a folded pizza made with pastry dough and often deep fried.

Stuffed pizza became popular in Chicago restaurants such as Edwardo's, Nancy's, and Giodano's. It is made in a deep pan with one layer of pizza dough covering the bottom and sides of the pan, which is then filled with combinations of meats, vegetables, cheeses, and seasonings. It is topped with a circle of dough, finished with tomato sauce, and baked in a very hot oven.

Rolled pizzas are less famous members of the family. In Sicily, bonato are filled buns or leaves, which are known in the United States as stromboli or pizza rolls. Pizza rolls look like long, crusty loaves of bread. When cut, however, they reveal spiral or solid fillings. Pizza rolls are versatile because they can be served as either appetizers or entrées.

Spiaggia

Spiaggia has a well-organized menu with plenty of items to choose from but not so many as to confuse the customer (Figure 17.6). The menu measures 9 by 9 inches folded and 9 by 18 open. The cover is mostly gray with an illustration in color. The paper is heavy white, and the listings are in black. The back cover is blank.

On the left side are Appetizers—Antipasti—including five unusual pizzas for $6.95 each. Pizza Salsiccia d'Anitra contains duck sausage, sage, and goat cheese. Pizza con Pesto has basil, garlic, pine nuts, and Romano and Provolone cheese. Seven more antipasti, ranging in price from $4.95 to $7.95, include Carpaccio—which is thinly sliced raw sirloin, olive oil, lemon, Reggiano Parmigiano cheese, and capers—and Insalata di Mare, a salad of warm shrimp, calamari, scallops, potatoes, arugula, tomatoes, basil, and extra-virgin olive oil.

At the center top is the Pasta listing of nine items ranging in price from $8.95 to $10.95. Selections include Agnolotti di Vitello—veal-filled pasta crescents with tomato, basil, and garlic sauce; Maltagliati con Anitra—assorted pasta shapes with grilled duck breast, black olives, seasonal vegetables, and duck broth; and Capelli d'Angelo del Marco Polo—Angelhair pasta with baby shrimp, broccoli, ginger, and garlic.

At the bottom center are eight entrées—fish, chicken, duck, calves liver, sirloin steak, lamb, and veal—from $13.95 to $16.95.

At the top right two soups are listed, then seven Entrée Salads which range in price from $12.95 to $18.95. These unusual salads include Gamberi, warm grilled shrimp on bibb lettuce with roasted peppers and tomato-brandy mayonnaise. D'Aragosta is a salad of fresh lobster, angelhair pasta, tomatoes, black olives, basil, caviar, and extra-virgin olive oil.

La Strada

The La Strada restaurants in Chicago and Greenwich, Connecticut, specialize in classic cuisine from selected regions of Italy. A popular spot for business lunches and intimate dinners, La Strada has been voted one of the best Italian restaurants in the country by *Gentlemen's Quarterly.*

The Chicago restaurant has a richly appointed dining room, accessible through a glass elevator, seating approximately 120. It is adjacent to the lounge area, which has a baby grand piano. Throughout the flowing layout, with its intimate cocktail lounge and two separate dining areas, soft pastels, crystal chandeliers, and deep carpeting decorate the room.

The four-page menu, which measures 10½ by 15 inches is printed on white, heavy-coated cover stock (Figure 17.7). The cover features only the name La Strada in gold plus Chicago and Greenwich.

The first panel begins with Antipasti, six cold and six hot appetizers. The hot appetizers include mussels in a light tomato, wine, and herb sauce; assorted shellfish in herb sauce; clams in a light tomato, wine, and herb sauce; baked clams; rolled eggplant, cheese, and eggs with light tomato; and scampi sautéed with wine, butter, and mushrooms.

FIGURE 17.6 The Menu from Spiaggia. It is a simple, yet elegant menu offering Italian cuisine. (Courtesy Spiaggia. A Signature of The Levy Restaurants. Reproduced by permission.)

APPETIZERS–ANTIPASTI

PIZZA CON SALSICCIA D'ANITRA Duck sausage, sage and goat cheese	$6.95
PIZZA MARGHERITA Tomatoes, basil and mozzarella cheese	6.95
PIZZA AI QUATTRO FORMAGGI Mozzarella, romano, provolone, gorgonzola cheese and sun-dried tomatoes	6.95
PIZZA SPINACI CON RICOTTA, PANCETTA E MOZZARELLA Spinach, herb ricotta cheese, pancetta and mozzarella	6.95
PIZZA COL PESTO Basil, garlic, pine nuts, romano and provolone cheese	6.95
CARPACCIO Thinly sliced raw sirloin, olive oil, lemon, reggiano parmigiano cheese, capers	5.95
MOZZARELLA, INDIVIA, POMODORI E ORIGANO Fresh mozzarella, endive, tomatoes, oregano and extra virgin olive oil	5.95
ANTIPASTO ASSORTITI Assorted antipasti of asparagus, mozzarella, roasted peppers, frittata, olives, onions	6.95
INSALATA DI CAMPO CON FORMAGGIO DI CAPRA Assorted seasonal greens, roasted goat cheese croutons, miniature tomatoes, and vinaigrette	7.95
INSALATA DI MARE Warm shrimp, calamari and scallop salad with potatoes, arugula, tomatoes, basil and extra virgin olive oil	7.95
INSALATA NORMALE Bibb lettuce, tomatoes, olives, olive oil and balsamic vinegar	4.95
INSALATA SPIAGGIA Mixed greens, quail eggs, enoki mushrooms, duck cracklings, olive oil, and balsamic vinegar	5.95

PASTA

FARFALLE ROSSE CON ASPARAGI E PISELLI MANGIATUTTO Tomato pasta butterflies with asparagus, snow peas, cream, and reggiano parmigiano cheese	$8.95
AGNOLOTTI DI VITELLO Veal filled pasta crescents with tomato, basil and garlic sauce	9.95
FETTUCCINE TRICOLORI AI QUATTRO FORMAGGI Spinach, tomato and egg pasta with cream, walnuts, mozzarella, romano, provolone and gorgonzola cheeses	9.95
MALTAGLIATI CON ANITRA Assorted pasta shapes with grilled duck breast, black olives, seasonal vegetables and duck broth	9.95
CAPELLI D'ANGELO DEL MARCO POLO Angel hair pasta with baby shrimp, broccoli, ginger and garlic	10.95
PASTICCIO DI RADICCHIO Pasta layered with grilled radicchio, cream, parmigiano cheese	$9.95
TRIANGOLI DI PESCE CON POMODORI AL FORNO E PESTO Seafood filled pasta triangles with woodburning oven roasted tomatoes and pesto	9.95
CARAMELLE AI QUATTRO FORMAGGI Four cheese filled pasta "candies" with a three tomato sauce and basil	8.95
MACCHERONCINI CON SALMONE AFFUMICATO E CAVIALE Beet pasta tubes with smoked salmon and three kinds of caviar, cream and chives	10.95

Half portions available upon request.

ENTREES–PIATTI DEL GIORNO

PESCE SPECIALE DEL GIORNO Fresh fish of the day	Market Price
PESCE CON SCAROLE Fresh seasonal fish filet grilled and served on escarole with basil garlic butter	16.95
PETTO D'ANITRA ALLA GRIGLIA Grilled sliced duck breast with juniper berries	14.95
PETTO DI POLLO AL FORNO AL LEGNO Woodburning oven roasted boneless breast of chicken with tomato rosemary sauce and grilled mushrooms	13.95
FEGATO ALLA VENEZIANA Calves liver with onions, white wine and fresh sage on grilled polenta	13.95
TAGLIATA Grilled sliced sirloin served rare with rosemary, black pepper, olive oil and lemon	15.95
SCALLOPPINE D'AGNELLO Lamb medallions grilled on sauteed spinach with pine nuts and raisins	15.95
COSTOLETTE DI VITELLO ALLA GRIGLIA CON SALVIA Grilled veal chop with fresh sage	16.95

SOUP-ZUPPE

ZUPPA D'ARAGOSTA E CALAMARI Lobster, calamari soup	$4.95
ZUPPA DI POLLO CON SCAROLE Grilled chicken, escarole and broth	3.95

ENTREE SALADS–INSALATE PIETANZE

POLLO Grilled chicken breast on arugula with pine nuts, raisins, olive oil and balsamic vinegar	12.95
GAMBERI Warm, grilled shrimp on bibb lettuce with roasted peppers and tomato-brandy mayonnaise	13.95
INSALATA DI SALTIMBOCCA Veal, fresh sage, prosciutto and white wine with assorted greens	16.95
D'ANITRA AGRO DOLCE Sliced cold duck breast with seasonal greens, grapefruit, raisins, pine nuts, olive oil and balsamic vinegar	12.95
FANTASIA DI CROSTINI Turkey and celery root salad with assorted crostini and seasonal greens	11.95
VERDURE GRIGLIATE CON MOZZARELLA Assorted grilled vegetables with fresh mozzarella and sun-dried tomato vinaigrette	12.95
D'ARAGOSTA Fresh lobster, angel hair pasta, tomatoes, black olives, basil, zucchini, caviar, extra virgin olive oil	18.95

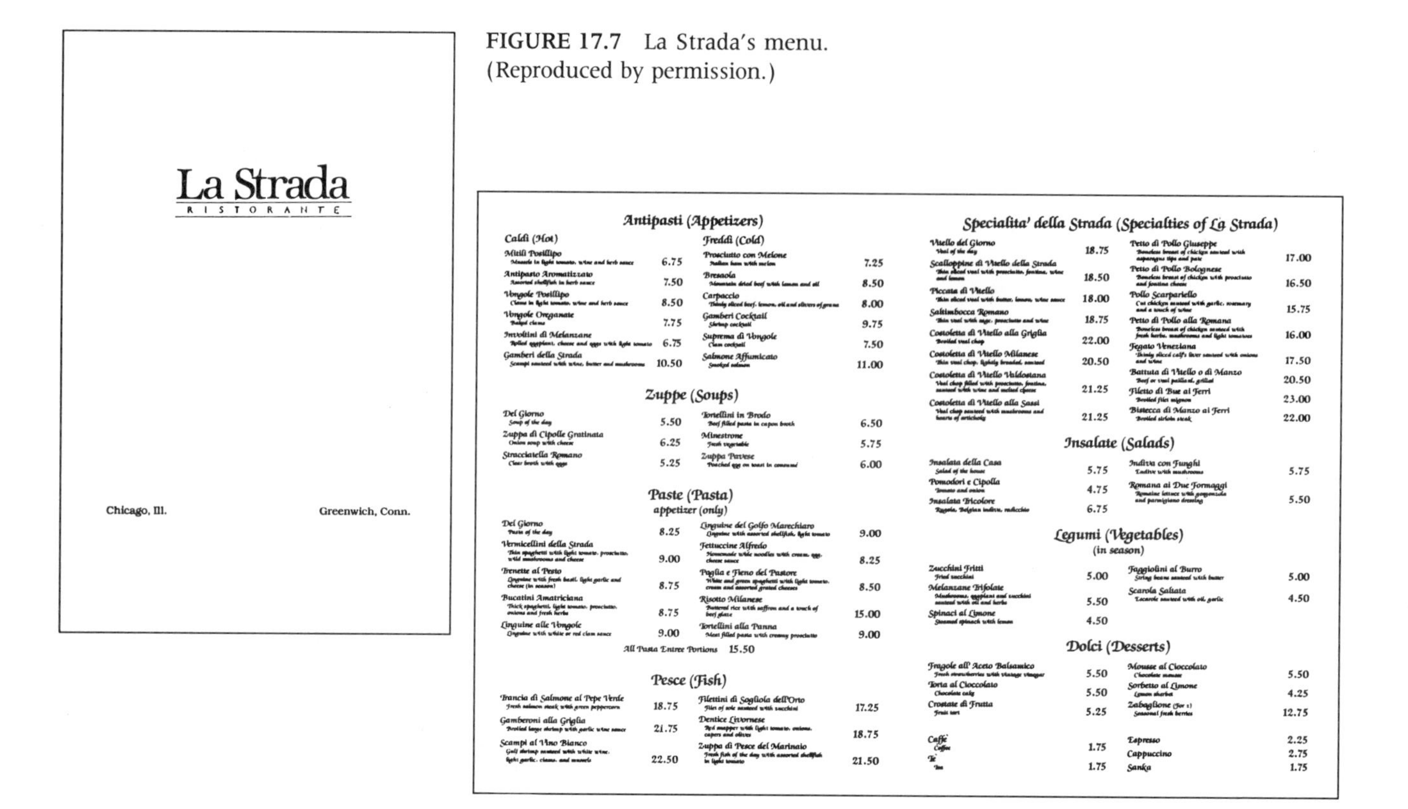

FIGURE 17.7 La Strada's menu. (Reproduced by permission.)

The cold appetizers include prosciutto (Italian ham) with melon; mountain dried beef with lemon and oil; thinly sliced beef, lemon, oil, and slivers of grana (a cooking cheese); shrimp cocktail; clam cocktail; and smoked salmon.

Among the six soups listed are the typical Italian tortellini in brodo (beef-filled pasta in capon broth), minestrone, and zuppa pavese (poached egg on toast in consommé).

Ten pasta items are offered as appetizers, although they can also be ordered as entrées. These items include thin and thick spaghetti, linguine, homemade wide noodles, white and green spaghetti, and tortellini à la panna (meat filled pasta with creamy prosciutto). The pasta comes with meat, seafood, cheese, and a variety of sauces.

The six pesce (fish) entrées include fresh salmon steak with green peppercorns; broiled large shrimp with garlic wine sauce; Gulf shrimp sautéed with white wine, light garlic, clams, and mussels; fillet of sole sautéed with zucchini; red snapper with light tomato, onions, capers, and olives; and fresh fish of the day with assorted shellfish in light tomato sauce.

On the right-hand panel of the two-page inside spread is the heart of this Italian menu—sixteen house specialties. The veal of the day is followed by seven other veal entrées: thin sliced veal; thin veal with sage prosciutto and wine; broiled veal chop; thin veal chop, lightly breaded and sautéed; veal chop filled with prosciutto and fontina and sautéed with wine and melted cheese; and veal chop sautéed with mushrooms and hearts of artichoke.

Next come four chicken entrées—boneless breast of chicken sautéed with asparagus tips and pâté; boneless breast of chicken with prosciutto and fontina cheese; cut chicken sautéed with garlic, rosemary, and a touch of wine; and boneless breast of chicken sautéed with fresh herbs, mushrooms, and light tomatoes. Beef entrées include calf's liver sautéed with onions and wine; grilled beef or veal paillard; broiled filet mignon; and broiled sirloin steak.

Following the list of six Insalate (salads) are five Legumi (vegetables) in season.

The Dolci (desserts) list features six sweets, including fresh strawberries with vintage vinegar, chocolate cake, fruit tart, chocolate mousse, lemon sherbet, and seasonal fresh berries.

The usual Italian coffees—espresso and cappuccino—are naturally on the beverage list. The price range for this menu is as follows:

Appetizers	$6.75–$10.00
Soups	$5.25–$6.50
Entrées	$15.50–$23.00
Specialties	$15.50–$22.50
Desserts	$4.25–$12.75

Cucina! Cucina!

Cucina! Cucina! restaurant is perched on the edge of Seattle's Lake Union. With a vibrant red, ochre, and teal color scheme, the airy dining room gives patrons in the 166 dining seats and 101 lounge seats unobstructed views of both the lake and one another. Stacks of plates on each table help diners share their food, adding to the convivial mood. Cucina! Cucina! serves an average of 440 dinners (as many as 700 on Saturday) and 200 lunches daily. Annual sales for this new restaurant are expected to reach $4 million.

The prices are attractive, and servers leave the menu on the table throughout the meal to encourage guests to order more. Many dishes are available in both *piccola* and *grande* sizes to make it easy to try many items. Cucina! Cucina! is a genuine Italian restaurant, so much so that it sets a half-liter can of extra-virgin olive oil on each table as a condiment. But the menu does have some slightly "foreign" items, such as Cajun calzone and an Oriental pizza.

The three-panel dinner menu measures 9½ by 14 inches and is printed in red, yellow, gray, and teal on heavy laminated white stock (Figure 17.8). The core panel is die-cut vertically in a wavy design. Except for the headings, the entire listing on the menu is hand-lettered. In addition to the restaurant's name and logo, the cover has an abstract illustration and lists the location of the two restaurants.

The first inside panel begins with six Aperitivi, which immediately gives the menu a different, continental touch. The next heading is Antipasti (six), with

FIGURE 17.8 Menu from Cucina!Cucina! (Courtesy Cucina!Cucina! Italian Cafe, a Schwartz Brothers Restaurant. Reproduced by permission.)

APERITIVI

Bellini	3.00
Campari	3.25
Negroni	3.25
Cin Cin	2.25
Punt e Mes	3.50
Cynar	3.50

ANTIPASTI

	PICCOLA	GRANDE
Fontina Marinara · fontina cheese, fried and served on marinara sauce	3.95	
Bagna Cauda · vegetables and Tuscan bread with a warm anchovy dipping sauce		3.95
Steamed Clams · steamed with capers, garlic and herbs in white wine and tomatoes		6.50
Calamari · squid deep-fried in peanut oil, garlic sauce	5.50	
Skewered Prawns · skewered with smoked mozzarella and sun dried tomatoes, deep fried, lemon sauce		5.95
Antipasto Misto · a variety of small appetizers; selection varies daily	5.95	10.75

ZUPPE

	PICCOLA	GRANDE
Minestrone · vegetables, beans, pancetta and Parmesan	1.65	2.95
Sausage and Lentil · Italian sausage, lentils, spinach, cream	1.65	2.95

INSALATE

	PICCOLA	GRANDE
Mixed Greens · with tomatoes, garlic croutons, romano, vinaigrette dressing	2.35	
Ricotta and Tomato · herbed ricotta cheese, tomatoes, basil, balsamic vinegar, virgin olive oil	3.75	
Chopped Salad · chicken, salami, lettuce, basil, chickpeas, tomatoes, scallions and provolone	4.25	6.95
Caesar · hearts of romaine, Parmesan, classic dressing	3.95	6.95
Frutti Di Mare · scallops, prawns, calamari, fennel and romaine with lemon mustard dressing		5.95

PIZZE

TRADITZIONALE

Margherita · fresh mozzarella, tomatoes, basil, extra virgin olive oil	6.75
Sausage and Peperoni · Italian sausage, hot peperoni, mozzarella, mushrooms and tomato sauce	7.95
Mushroom · cultivated and wild mushrooms, garlic, tomato and mozzarella	6.95
Quattro Formaggi · gruyere, fontina, mozzarella, Parmesan with shallots, mustard and walnuts	6.95
Schiacciata · very thin crust, fontina, extra virgin olive oil, garlic and spices	6.25
Calzone · spinach, ricotta, Italian sausage, hot peperoni, artichokes, sun dried tomatoes and mozzarella	8.25

NUOVE

Spicy Chicken · marinated chicken, green onions, sun dried tomatoes, mozzarella, rosemary and shiitake mushrooms	7.95
Canadian Bacon · with pineapple, mascarpone cheese, white pepper and mozzarella	7.95
Goat Cheese · with grilled fresh vegetables and pesto	7.95
B.B.Q. Chicken · smoked gouda, mozzarella, barbeque sauce, red onions and cilantro	7.95
Smoked Halibut · with sweet onions, capers, chives and sour cream	6.50
Indonesian Shrimp · a cheeseless pizza with black bean sauce, roasted peppers and shrimp	8.25

SPECIALITA

Chicken · boneless half chicken roasted in the wood burning oven with pancetta, butter, lemon and mushrooms	8.95
Linguine di Pescatore · prawns, squid, clams, mussels, scallops, white fish and tomato sauce	11.95
Gamberi Tradizionale · prawns sautéed with garlic, herbs, olive oil, white wine and lemon	12.50
Turkey Alla Marsala · medallions of turkey breast sautéed with mushrooms and and marsala wine	8.75

· Please see our Daily Specials sheet for additional selections ·

PASTA

	PICCOLA	GRANDE
Penne All' Arrabiata · tube shaped pasta in a fiery tomato sauce	3.95	6.95
Linguine with Clams · fresh clams, wine, garlic, butter, prosciutto and tomatoes		6.95
Linguine with Roasted Chicken · broccoli, goat cheese and pine nuts		9.75
Spaghettini Bolognese · pasta in a classic Northern Italian meat sauce	3.95	6.95
Fettuccine Alfredo · Parmesan, heavy cream and egg yolk	4.75	7.75
Spaghettini in Fresh Tomato Sauce	3.75	6.75
Fettucine Affumicate · with smoked halibut, mushrooms, peas and cream		9.50
Fettucine Guilliamo · prawns, Italian sausage, tomatoes and pesto		7.95
Ravioli · traditional veal, pork and ricotta stuffing in a light tomato sauce		7.95
Seafood Cannelloni · filled with shrimp, scallops, crab meat and ricotta, served with red and white sauces		9.95
Fregnacce · individual "lasagnes" filled with meat and cheese		8.95

GRIGLIA

Bistecca Pizzaiola · grilled sirloin steak served on garlic toasts with caper garlic tomato sauce	11.95
Grilled Prawns Marinara · skewered and chargrilled, spicy tomato sauce, with risotto and vegetables	12.50
Mixed Skewered Grill · selection varies daily	A.Q.

PANE

Toscano · hot Tuscan bread, roasted garlic and butter	2.45
Focaccia · baked in the wood burning ovens	2.65

one offered in a small or large portion. This is followed by Zuppe (two) and Insalate (five).

The center panel is dominated by the Pizze (pizza) listing. Six *traditzionale* pizzas and six *nouve* pizzas are offered. At the bottom of this panel, under the heading of Specialita, four Italian entrées are listed.

The top of the right-hand panel is headed Pasta. Eleven pastas are offered, four in large or small portions. The next heading is Griglia (the grill), which offers grilled steak, prawns, and a mixed grill. At the bottom is Pane (bread). Two breads are listed at $2.45 and $2.65. The breads are another unusual aspect of this menu, and they are served hot from the oven.

The first back panel of this menu begins with Dolce (dessert) and lists seven. Next comes Espresso, seven very special coffees, followed by Bevande (beverages). The center back panel is the wine list, Vini, divided into Italiano Bianco (white), Italiano Rosso (red), Domestico Bianco, and Domestico Rosso. Nine of these wines are offered by the glass. Besides the twenty-five Italian wines and the fourteen domestic wines listed, three sparkling wines are offered.

A feature of this restaurant not shown on the menu is the completely open kitchen. Its signature item is a two-chambered imported Italian oven that links the dining room, counter stools, and kitchen. Its wood-fired 900° heat cooks puffed, ash-bottomed pizzas in three or four minutes and lends a slightly smoky quality to whatever is roasted in it.

The Japanese Menu

Japanese cooking is not just little dishes of fish and the showmanship of the chef making the food at the table. Yes, Japanese food is served in small, carefully prepared portions, but there are enough of them to equal an average Western meal. And fish, shellfish, and seaweed do often appear on the menu, but they never become monotonous because the Japanese have devised many tasty ways of serving them.

The Japanese do pay a great deal of attention to the appearance of the meal. Dishes and bowls are selected for their harmony with particular foods. The meal should appeal to the eye as well as the taste buds.

Whereas the French and the Chinese tend to meld together many ingredients in one dish, the Japanese tend to preserve the taste and character of each, with equal attention given to each item and flavor. In a soup, for example, every ingredient is to be relished separately.

Throughout their history, the Japanese have been isolated, with periods of contact with the outside world. The first major influence was Chinese. The Japanese borrowed much from Chinese civilization, including chopsticks, but they still maintained their own characteristics. The first Westerners to be allowed into Japan were the Portuguese, who left behind their recipes for deep fat–fried foods that came to be known as *tempura*.

The origin of the word *tempura* is interesting. The Portuguese, as good Catholics, rejected meat on Ember Days, which they called by the Latin name *quatuor tempora*, or the four times of the year. During those times they ate seafood, usually shrimp. Eventually the name *tempura* became attached to the fried shrimp the Portuguese ate on these days. The Japanese, however, refined the Portuguese method of deep fat frying by using lighter batter and lighter oil, which resulted in a more delicate flavor.

Contact with the West also resulted in Japan's borrowing new foods, including meat, which had been prohibited by the Buddhist religion. Beef, pork, and poultry began to appear on the Japanese menu, and became ingredients in the Japanese sukiyaki.

Traditional dishes such as fish, seaweed, steamed rice, and tofu (soybean curd) are still popular. The Japanese tend to eat only fresh foods in season, and in the better Japanese restaurants, separate sets of dishes and serving dishes are used for each season. One seasonal food is bamboo shoots, which are eaten in the spring. In May the Japanese attention turns to tea because this is when the first new leaves of the teabush are picked. Another Japanese seasonal delicacy is the ayu, a small freshwater fish that looks like a brook trout. It is available from mid-May to the fall. Eels are also popular with the Japanese. A dish called kabayaki is an eel split, boned, and skewered on bamboo and broiled over charcoal in a sweetened soy sauce. Another food that is popular in Japan and also appears on American menus is tofu (soybean curd), which is cooked with other foods during most of the year. In the summer, however, it becomes a dish in its own right, served on ice and flavored with soy sauce and katsuobushi (dried bonito flakes), chopped scallions, and ginger. The cold, custardlike tofu makes a tasty and nonfattening-summer dinner. Another summer food is zarusoba, cold buckwheat noodles served in a special sauce.

A fall favorite is the mushroom called matsutake, which grows in red pine forests. At the peak of the season, matsutake is served in many restaurants. It may be served like a meat dish on a platter with vegetables, or it may be cooked with tofu. Another method is to marinate the mushrooms in soy sauce and sweet saké and to grill them. In the autumn a favorite Japanese fruit is the bright-orange kaki, or persimmon, which is eaten either fresh or dried, as a snack. Chestnuts are also an autumn dish, and the gingko nuts are used in soups and other dishes.

Winter is the time for white-meat fish, raw, broiled, or deep fried. It is also the season for fish stews, including a thick salmon soup with vegetables. Noodles are also served with combinations of vegetables, fish, and meat. Tangerines, or mandarin oranges, also are a winter favorite, often served with tea.

Rice is more than a staple food for the Japanese; for centuries it was the standard of wealth. The Japanese word for rice, *gohan*, also means meal. Japanese people do not feel that they have had a meal until they have had a bowl of rice. For variety the Japanese may pour sauces over their rice or cook it with other ingredients, but mostly prefer it plain.

Another important ingredient of Japanese cooking is soybeans, which can be made into the fermented soybean paste called miso, into tofu, or into soy sauce. Tofu may be fried, boiled, broiled, used to garnish soups, rolled in cornstarch and deep fried, scrambled with eggs, and mixed with sesame seed.

The two basic raw-fish dishes of Japan are sashimi and sushi. Sashimi refers to fish eaten raw by itself, usually dipped in soy sauce and horseradish. Sushi consisted of balls of vinegared rice garnished with a strip of raw fish or shellfish or with cooked shrimp, vegetables, seaweed, or egg. Sashimi may be a meal by itself, and some restaurants in Japan serve nothing else, offering a dozen or more varieties of fish for a complete dinner.

Ron of Japan

Take a circular piece of paper, 17 inches in diameter, fold it once across the center, and then fold it again. You will then have the Ron of Japan menu which is designed, when folded, to look like a fan (Figure 17.9). When the fan is opened halfway, it forms a semicircle. On the left-hand side are listed Ron's Original Cocktails, and on the facing side are the headings With Your Dinner—beers, wines, and Japanese scotch—and After Dinner—plum wine and special liqueur cocktails.

Opened to its full circle, the menu shows listings that are well organized and placed for easy ordering. On the far left are Teppan Appetizers—shrimp, chicken, scallops, and lobster tail ($16.95)—Salads (only two), and Desserts (three).

At the top left are Ron's Entrées, which are prepared at your table. There are three steaks, chicken, and omelettes plus four seafood items and five combinations of these entrées. Prices range from $5.50 (omelette) to $20.95 (lobster tail).

On the right-hand top are listed the more expensive Crown Dinners: Sirloin, Filet, Shrimp, Lobster Tail, and Chicken. These items are also prepared at the table. These dinners, which range from $13.95 to $25.95, come with a shrimp appetizer, chicken soup, salad, white rice, bean sprouts, vegetables, Japanese tea, and a choice of dessert.

A special feature, headed Ron's Favorite, is Prime Rib on a Samurai Sword, $19.95. Finally, there is the Shogun Dinner, with a fixed price of $29.95, including a lobster tail appetizer, steak, soup, salad, vegetables, white rice, and dessert.

There are also three à la carte Tea Room items and a small children's menu consisting of three items. The menu is printed in black and orange on cream-colored paper.

THE MEXICAN MENU

Mexico's culinary heritage is a combination of the foods and cooking skills of the Spanish invaders and the indigenous cuisine. In 1519 when the Spaniards arrived, they discovered native foods such as avocados, coconuts, papayas, pineapples, and prickly pears, as well as corn, tomatoes, chilies, sweet potatoes, squash, peanuts, and five kinds of beans.

The Aztecs boiled or pit-cooked turkeys, duck, venison, quail, and pigeons as well as fish and shellfish from the local waters. Cortés described the dishes at Montezuma's table as consisting of meat, fish, herbs, and fruits. Another Spaniard reported two kinds of sauces for the dishes stewed in earthenware pots: One was thickened with ground pumpkin seeds and flavored with red chilies and tomatoes; another was a tomato and chili sauce. The Aztecs ate their spicy foods with tortillas, some of which were smooth and others made from rough-ground corn, another vegetable new to the Europeans. The cooks prepared tlacoyos and gorditas, and the Aztecs ate tamales similar to the ones popular today. Among the tastes new to the Spaniards were those of chocolate and vanilla.

The Spaniards brought cinnamon, black pepper, and cloves, thyme, marjoram, and bay leaves. As early as Columbus's second voyage, the first cargo of wheat, chickpeas, melons, onions, radishes, salad greens, grapes, and sugarcane made its way to America. The Spaniards also brought horses, hogs, cattle, and chickens.

In a few decades after 1492, meat was plentiful in Mexico. Wheat bread was cheap, and rice grew where wheat and corn would not. Fruits, vegetables, and other new important food crops such as sesame seeds, almonds, and citrus flourished. But several imports did not: Olive trees would not grow in Mexico, and grapes did poorly.

Two cooking techniques give Mexican cuisine its distinctive flavor. One is asado, from the verb *asar*, meaning to broil, brown, roast, or sear. In this technique, large green chilies are flame roasted, peeled, and toasted on a griddle to deepen their flavor and release their aroma. Garlic is roasted on a dry surface, as are tomatoes and tomatillos until they blacken and blister. Meat is seared on an open fire. Corn dough, called masa—in all its forms from tortillas to boat-shaped *sopes*—is cooked on dry iron or clay surfaces, intensifying the flavors.

The second distinctive Mexican cooking technique is the initial searing of puréed sauce ingredients, often called "frying the sauce." First, a little fat goes into a hot pan. Then a chili or tomato purée is added, and as it sizzles, a thick mass is formed.

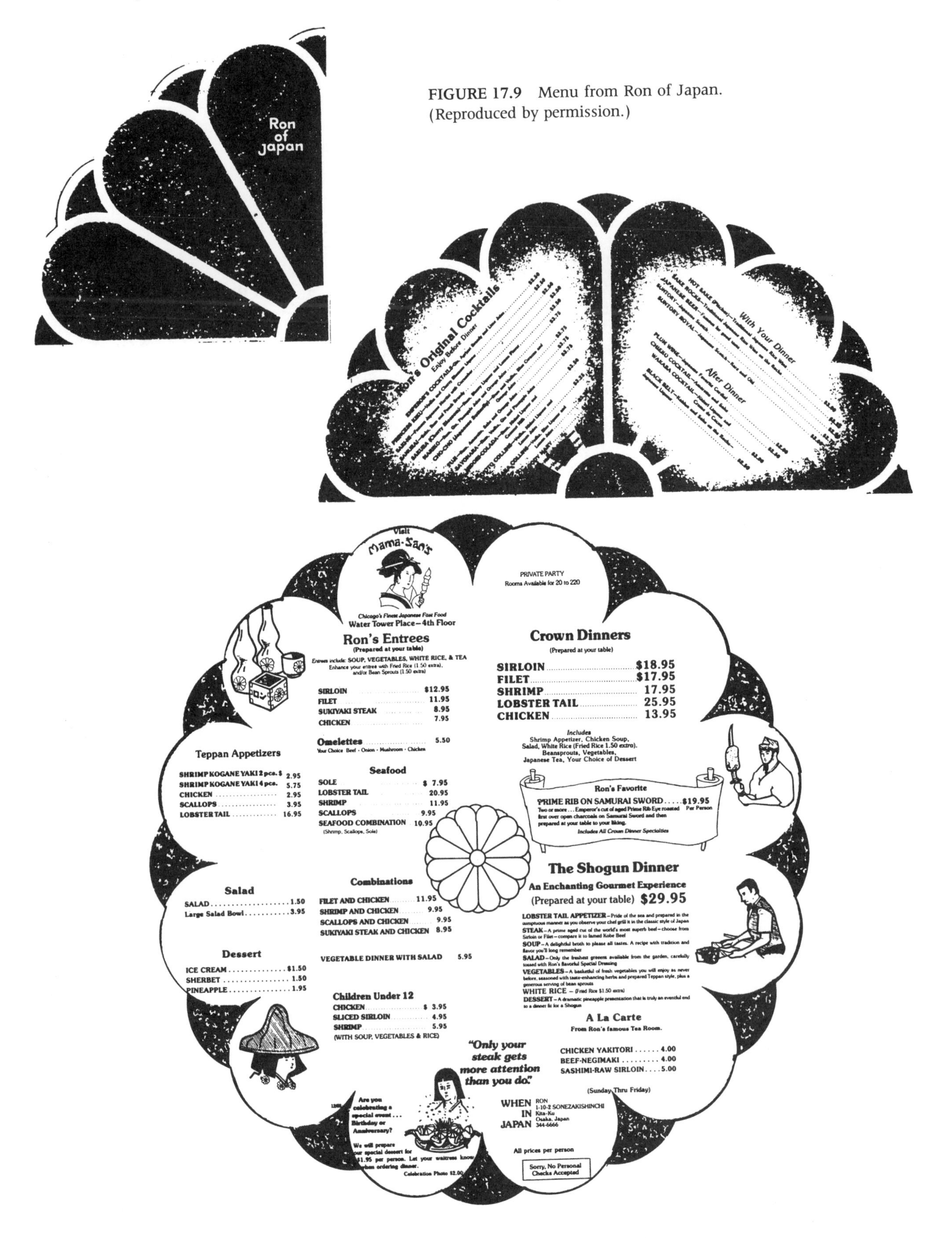

FIGURE 17.9 Menu from Ron of Japan. (Reproduced by permission.)

Another technique is grinding, which began with the crushing of corn on a rock to make the dough (masa) for tortillas. The rock slab was also used for grinding chilies, nuts, seeds, cacao beans, and even curds of fresh cheese. A bowl and mortar were used for spices and could contain the juices of tomatoes.

Salsas and encurtidos (sauces and condiments) set the scene for Mexican cooking. They are usually made from tomatoes, chilies, garlic, and onions, chopped together into a relish called salsa Mexicana. It is the ideal sauce for tacos. Salsas verdes, green sauces, are made in the same way but with small green tomatillos instead of red tomatoes. These sauces have a tartness that gives them a special distinction.

Chilies, and preparations made with them, make up the remaining Mexican sauces. Most chilies are not the hot, explosive kind, but some are hot. Picante chilies are sprinkled with lime juice and served with pickled peppers, vegetables, onions, and cheese.

Mexicans did not smoke their meats or preserve them in brine, as other people did before refrigeration. Instead, they salted long-grained slices of beef or dried beef. It is the chili peppers, however, that often preserve Mexican meat. Chilies and vinegar can be smeared on thin-sliced pork or mixed with ground pork to flavor and preserve it.

Tortillas are known everywhere in Mexico. In most places they are thin, unleavened griddle-baked cakes of fresh masa. In Juchitan, Oaxaca, however, the tortillas are nearly ¼ inch thick; they are placed on the outside wall of a hot, barrel-shaped clay oven and baked. Northern-style tortillas are made of wheat flour. Corn tortillas are also fried for tostadas and chips.

Mexicans eat a great variety of appetizers and snacks. These include bite-sized masa turnovers, served with a special relish; soft tacos made from pork; guacamole; cactus salad; and crisp pork rinds. Shredded fish and crab, melted cheese with peppers, sausages, and gratinéed crepes with black corn mushrooms are other snacks.

Mexican soups start with the flavorful broth from stewing meat, to which are added tomatoes, garlic, and onions. Cactus, wild mushrooms, vermicelli, and cheese may be used. Soups are seasoned with thyme, marjoram, and bay leaves. Lime juice, avocado, cilantro, and roasted dried chilies add to the variety.

A Mexican breakfast may consist of huevos rancheros (eggs cooked in tomato sauce, with chilies, onions, and tomatoes and served on soft corn tortillas).

The Mexican word *mole* means stew, but the word is usually used for a dark, complex sauce made with dried chilies, nuts, seeds, vegetables, spices, and a bit of chocolate. Another mole is a black, pungent chili stew/sauce.

Seafood is also part of the Mexican menu, including red snapper, crab, Gulf shrimp, bonito, yellowtail and bluefin tuna, and abalone.

Poultry—duck, turkey, and chicken—is probably the most frequently cooked meat in Mexico. In Mexico, chicken is generally simmered, steamed, or braised until tender. Served with mole it becomes a holiday dish.

Mexican pork is noted for its tenderness. It makes rich sausage, meatballs, and ground meat stuffing for chiles rellenos. It is also slowly browned in its own fat for carnitas. Beef is either sliced thin with the grain for salt preserving or drying, or it is slowly simmered to make it tender. The tripe is made into soup, and a mixture of the internal organs is made into a stew or a sauce. Liver wrapped in chitterlings, or intestines, is another delicacy.

Beans, from the large ayocotes to the smallest black ones, are essential to the Mexican table. Fried beans are the automatic accompaniment to or ingredient in most of the masa-based dishes. Nearly every Mexican dish on a menu is listed, "comes with beans and rice." Rice, however, is not native to Mexico. Rather, it came by way of the Arabs to Spain and from there to Mexico. Today it is a staple of the Mexican diet.

Mexican desserts, or *postres*, can be flan (caramel custard), a thick and gooey dessert called cajeta, or a chunk of pumpkin cooked in a dark, spicy syrup. They can be a sweet macaroonlike cocada or the soft custard of nataillas; the syrupy curds of chongas; the thick-textured, jellied guava paste (ate) with fresh cheese; rice pudding; or syrup-poached fruit.

The favorite drink in Mexican restaurants today is the margarita. This sweet-and-sour, pale green cocktail is linked to Mexico because of its tequila. The most famous Mexican drink is actually chocolate. Called the "food of the gods," it was served as a ritual drink for priests and nobles in pre-Columbian Mexico. The original Mexican alcoholic drink is pulque, made from the maguey, which must be twelve years old before the sap or "honey" can be extracted to make the drink. Pulque is a fermented drink that is slightly viscous and foamy. Some pulque is "cured" with fruits, nuts, and sugar.

Mexican beer is popular in both Mexico and the United States. Mescal, including the famous variety, tequila, is a well-known Mexican drink. Like pulque, it is made from the maguey plant: The hearts of mature magueys are roasted and shredded, and then the juice is squeezed out. Sugar is added, and it is fermented, distilled, and aged.

Guaymas

Guaymas Mexican Restaurante is located in Tiburon, California. Each panel of the four-panel menu measures 7½ by 11 inches (Figure 17.10). It is printed in brown and blue on heavy, uncoated, tan paper. The cover has a large logo plus the following copy:

> Guaymas, Mexico, is a fishing village on the Sea of Cortez, about 250 miles south of Nogales, Arizona.

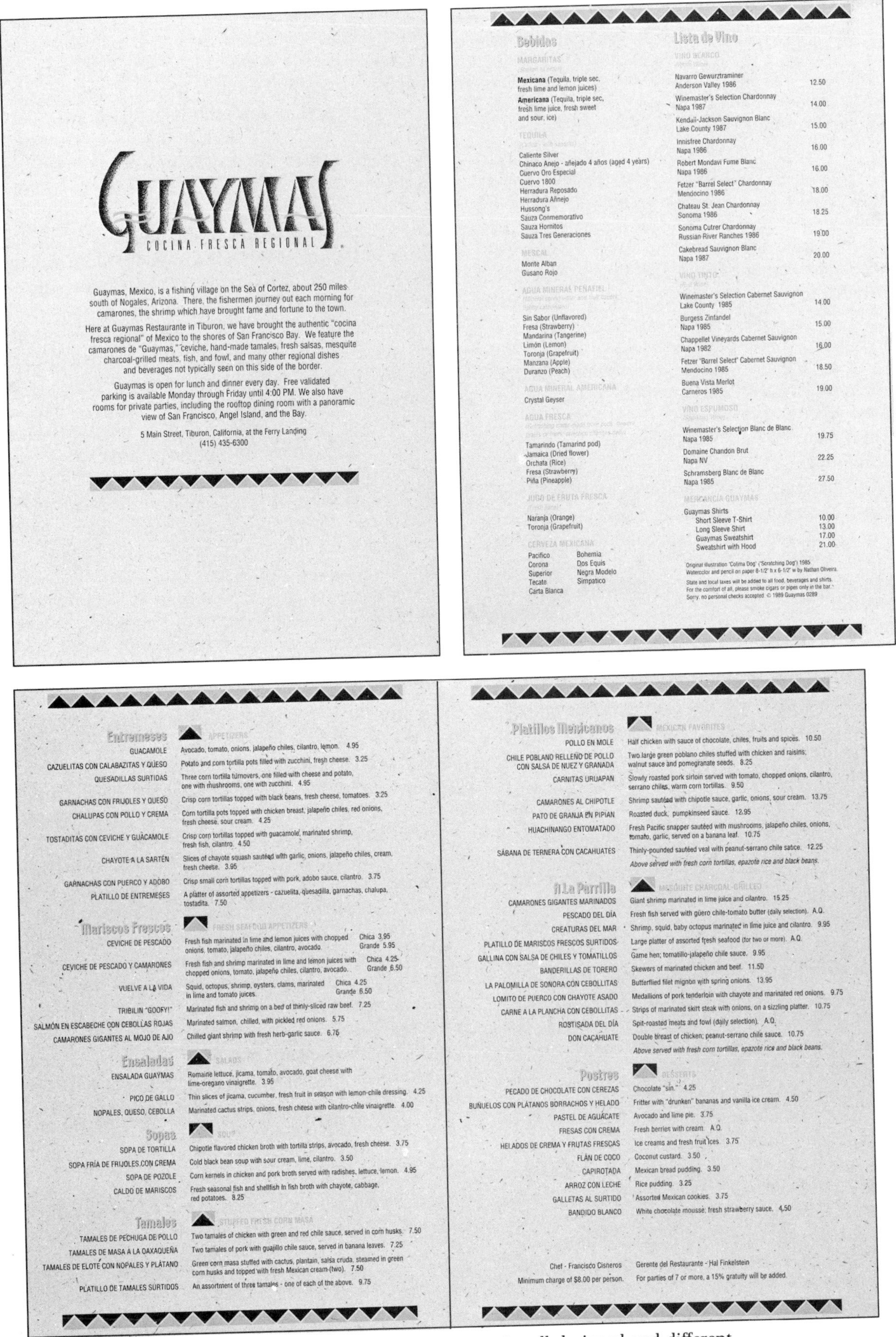

GUAYMAS
COCINA FRESCA REGIONAL

Guaymas, Mexico, is a fishing village on the Sea of Cortez, about 250 miles south of Nogales, Arizona. There, the fishermen journey out each morning for camarones, the shrimp which have brought fame and fortune to the town.

Here at Guaymas Restaurante in Tiburon, we have brought the authentic "cocina fresca regional" of Mexico to the shores of San Francisco Bay. We feature the camarones de "Guaymas," ceviche, hand-made tamales, fresh salsas, mesquite charcoal-grilled meats, fish, and fowl, and many other regional dishes and beverages not typically seen on this side of the border.

Guaymas is open for lunch and dinner every day. Free validated parking is available Monday through Friday until 4:00 PM. We also have rooms for private parties, including the rooftop dining room with a panoramic view of San Francisco, Angel Island, and the Bay.

5 Main Street, Tiburon, California, at the Ferry Landing
(415) 435-6300

Bebidas

MARGARITAS

Mexicana (Tequila, triple sec, fresh lime and lemon juices)
Americana (Tequila, triple sec, fresh lime juice, fresh sweet and sour, ice)

TEQUILA

Caliente Silver
Chinaco Anejo - añejado 4 años (aged 4 years)
Cuervo Oro Especial
Cuervo 1800
Herradura Reposado
Herradura Añejo
Hussong's
Sauza Conmemorativo
Sauza Hornitos
Sauza Tres Generaciones

MESCAL

Monte Alban
Gusano Rojo

AGUA MINERAL PEÑAFIEL

Sin Sabor (Unflavored)
Fresa (Strawberry)
Mandarina (Tangerine)
Limón (Lemon)
Toronja (Grapefruit)
Manzana (Apple)
Durazno (Peach)

AGUA MINERAL AMERICANA

Crystal Geyser

AGUA FRESCA

Tamarindo (Tamarind pod)
Jamaica (Dried flower)
Orchata (Rice)
Fresa (Strawberry)
Piña (Pineapple)

JUGO DE FRUTA FRESCA

Naranja (Orange)
Toronja (Grapefruit)

CERVEZA MEXICANA

Pacifico, Bohemia, Corona, Dos Equis, Superior, Negra Modelo, Tecate, Simpatico, Carta Blanca

Lista de Vino

VINO BLANCO

Navarro Gewurztraminer, Anderson Valley 1986	12.50
Winemaster's Selection Chardonnay, Napa 1987	14.00
Kendall-Jackson Sauvignon Blanc, Lake County 1987	15.00
Innisfree Chardonnay, Napa 1986	16.00
Robert Mondavi Fume Blanc, Napa 1986	16.00
Fetzer "Barrel Select" Chardonnay, Mendocino 1986	18.00
Chateau St. Jean Chardonnay, Sonoma 1986	18.25
Sonoma Cutrer Chardonnay, Russian River Ranches 1986	19.00
Cakebread Sauvignon Blanc, Napa 1987	20.00

VINO TINTO

Winemaster's Selection Cabernet Sauvignon, Lake County 1985	14.00
Burgess Zinfandel, Napa 1985	15.00
Chappellet Vineyards Cabernet Sauvignon, Napa 1982	16.00
Fetzer "Barrel Select" Cabernet Sauvignon, Mendocino 1985	18.50
Buena Vista Merlot, Carneros 1985	19.00

VINO ESPUMOSO

Winemaster's Selection Blanc de Blanc, Napa 1985	19.75
Domaine Chandon Brut, Napa NV	22.25
Schramsberg Blanc de Blanc, Napa 1985	27.50

MERCANCIA GUAYMAS

Guaymas Shirts	
Short Sleeve T-Shirt	10.00
Long Sleeve Shirt	13.00
Guaymas Sweatshirt	17.00
Sweatshirt with Hood	21.00

Original illustration 'Colima Dog' ('Scratching Dog') 1985. Watercolor and pencil on paper 8-1/2" h x 6-1/2" w by Nathan Oliveira.
State and local taxes will be added to all food, beverages and shirts.
For the comfort of all, please smoke cigars or pipes only in the bar.
Sorry, no personal checks accepted. © 1989 Guaymas 0289

Entremeses — APPETIZERS

GUACAMOLE	Avocado, tomato, onions, jalapeño chiles, cilantro, lemon. 4.95
CAZUELITAS CON CALABAZITAS Y QUESO	Potato and corn tortilla pots filled with zucchini, fresh cheese. 3.25
QUESADILLAS SURTIDAS	Three corn tortilla turnovers, one filled with cheese and potato, one with mushrooms, one with zucchini. 4.95
GARNACHAS CON FRIJOLES Y QUESO	Crisp corn tortillas topped with black beans, fresh cheese, tomatoes. 3.25
CHALUPAS CON POLLO Y CREMA	Corn tortilla pots topped with chicken breast, jalapeño chiles, red onions, fresh cheese, sour cream. 4.25
TOSTADITAS CON CEVICHE Y GUACAMOLE	Crisp corn tortillas topped with guacamole, marinated shrimp, fresh fish, cilantro. 4.50
CHAYOTE A LA SARTÉN	Slices of chayote squash sautéed with garlic, onions, jalapeño chiles, cream, fresh cheese. 3.95
GARNACHAS CON PUERCO Y ADOBO	Crisp small corn tortillas topped with pork, adobo sauce, cilantro. 3.75
PLATILLO DE ENTREMESES	A platter of assorted appetizers - cazuelita, quesadilla, garnachas, chalupa, tostadita. 7.50

Mariscos Frescos — FRESH SEAFOOD APPETIZERS

CEVICHE DE PESCADO	Fresh fish marinated in lime and lemon juices with chopped onions, tomato, jalapeño chiles, cilantro, avocado. Chica 3.95 Grande 5.95
CEVICHE DE PESCADO Y CAMARONES	Fresh fish and shrimp marinated in lime and lemon juices with chopped onions, tomato, jalapeño chiles, cilantro, avocado. Chica 4.25 Grande 6.50
VUELVE A LA VIDA	Squid, octopus, shrimp, oysters, clams, marinated in lime and tomato juices. Chica 4.25 Grande 6.50
TRIBILIN "GOOFY!"	Marinated fish and shrimp on a bed of thinly-sliced raw beet. 7.25
SALMÓN EN ESCABECHE CON CEBOLLAS ROJAS	Marinated salmon, chilled, with pickled red onions. 5.75
CAMARONES GIGANTES AL MOJO DE AJO	Chilled giant shrimp with fresh herb-garlic sauce. 6.75

Ensaladas — SALADS

ENSALADA GUAYMAS	Romaine lettuce, jicama, tomato, avocado, goat cheese with lime-oregano vinaigrette. 3.95
PICO DE GALLO	Thin slices of jicama, cucumber, fresh fruit in season with lemon-chile dressing. 4.25
NOPALES, QUESO, CEBOLLA	Marinated cactus strips, onions, fresh cheese with cilantro-chile vinaigrette. 4.00

Sopas — SOUP

SOPA DE TORTILLA	Chipotle flavored chicken broth with tortilla strips, avocado, fresh cheese. 3.75
SOPA FRÍA DE FRIJOLES CON CREMA	Cold black bean soup with sour cream, lime, cilantro. 3.50
SOPA DE POZOLE	Corn kernels in chicken and pork broth served with radishes, lettuce, lemon. 4.95
CALDO DE MARISCOS	Fresh seasonal fish and shellfish in fish broth with chayote, cabbage, red potatoes. 8.25

Tamales — STUFFED FRESH CORN MASA

TAMALES DE PECHUGA DE POLLO	Two tamales of chicken with green and red chile sauce, served in corn husks. 7.50
TAMALES DE MASA A LA OAXAQUEÑA	Two tamales of pork with guajillo chile sauce, served in banana leaves. 7.25
TAMALES DE ELOTE CON NOPALES Y PLÁTANO	Green corn masa stuffed with cactus, plantain, salsa cruda, steamed in green corn husks and topped with fresh Mexican cream (two). 7.50
PLATILLO DE TAMALES SURTIDOS	An assortment of three tamales - one of each of the above. 9.75

Platillos Mexicanos — MEXICAN FAVORITES

POLLO EN MOLE	Half chicken with sauce of chocolate, chiles, fruits and spices. 10.50
CHILE POBLANO RELLENO DE POLLO CON SALSA DE NUEZ Y GRANADA	Two large green poblano chiles stuffed with chicken and raisins, walnut sauce and pomegranate seeds. 8.25
CARNITAS URUAPAN	Slowly roasted pork sirloin served with tomato, chopped onions, cilantro, serrano chiles, warm corn tortillas. 9.50
CAMARONES AL CHIPOTLE	Shrimp sautéed with chipotle sauce, garlic, onions, sour cream. 13.75
PATO DE GRANJA EN PIPIAN	Roasted duck, pumpkinseed sauce. 12.95
HUACHINANGO ENTOMATADO	Fresh Pacific snapper sautéed with mushrooms, jalapeño chiles, onions, tomato, garlic, served on a banana leaf. 10.75
SÁBANA DE TERNERA CON CACAHUATES	Thinly-pounded sautéed veal with peanut-serrano chile sauce. 12.25

Above served with fresh corn tortillas, epazote rice and black beans.

A La Parrilla — MESQUITE CHARCOAL-GRILLED

CAMARONES GIGANTES MARINADOS	Giant shrimp marinated in lime juice and cilantro. 15.25
PESCADO DEL DÍA	Fresh fish served with güero chile-tomato butter (daily selection). A.Q.
CREATURAS DEL MAR	Shrimp, squid, baby octopus marinated in lime juice and cilantro. 9.95
PLATILLO DE MARISCOS FRESCOS SURTIDOS	Large platter of assorted fresh seafood (for two or more). A.Q.
GALLINA CON SALSA DE CHILES Y TOMATILLOS	Game hen; tomatillo-jalapeño chile sauce. 9.95
BANDERILLAS DE TORERO	Skewers of marinated chicken and beef. 11.50
LA PALOMILLA DE SONORA CON CEBOLLITAS	Butterflied filet mignon with spring onions. 13.95
LOMITO DE PUERCO CON CHAYOTE ASADO	Medallions of pork tenderloin with chayote and marinated red onions. 9.75
CARNE A LA PLANCHA CON CEBOLLITAS	Strips of marinated skirt steak with onions, on a sizzling platter. 10.75
ROSTISADA DEL DÍA	Spit-roasted meats and fowl (daily selection). A.Q.
DON CACAHUATE	Double breast of chicken; peanut-serrano chile sauce. 10.75

Above served with fresh corn tortillas, epazote rice and black beans.

Postres — DESSERTS

PECADO DE CHOCOLATE CON CEREZAS	Chocolate "sin." 4.25
BUÑUELOS CON PLÁTANOS BORRACHOS Y HELADO	Fritter with "drunken" bananas and vanilla ice cream. 4.50
PASTEL DE AGUACATE	Avocado and lime pie. 3.75
FRESAS CON CREMA	Fresh berries with cream. A.Q.
HELADOS DE CREMA Y FRUTAS FRESCAS	Ice creams and fresh fruit ices. 3.75
FLÁN DE COCO	Coconut custard. 3.50
CAPIROTADA	Mexican bread pudding. 3.50
ARROZ CON LECHE	Rice pudding. 3.25
GALLETAS AL SURTIDO	Assorted Mexican cookies. 3.75
BANDIDO BLANCO	White chocolate mousse; fresh strawberry sauce. 4.50

Chef - Francisco Cisneros — Gerente del Restaurante - Hal Finkelstein

Minimum charge of $8.00 per person. — For parties of 7 or more, a 15% gratuity will be added.

FIGURE 17.10 Menu from Guaymas Mexican Restaurante. A well-designed and different Mexican menu. (Courtesy Guaymas. Reproduced by permission.)

There, the fishermen journey out each morning for camarones, the shrimp which have brought fame and fortune to the town.

Here at Guaymas Restaurante in Tiburon, we have brought the authentic "cocina fresca regional" of Mexico to the shores of San Francisco Bay. We feature the camarones de "Guaymas," ceviche, hand-made tamales, fresh salsas, mesquite charcoal-grilled meats, fish, and fowl, and many other regional dishes and beverages not typically seen on this side of the border.

Guaymas is open for lunch and dinner every day. Free validated parking is available Monday through Friday until 4:00 P.M. We also have rooms for private parties, including the rooftop dining room with a panoramic view of San Francisco, Angel Island, and the Bay.

The two-column type layout inside this menu is designed to accommodate the Mexican name and English description of each item. The first listing under Mariscos Frescos (Fresh Seafood Appetizers) is written this way:

CEVICHE DE PESCADO

Fresh fish marinated in lime and lemon juices with chopped onions, tomato, jalapeño chiles, cilantro, avocado, Chica 3.95 Grande 5.95

Besides the appeal of the unusual layout, offering appetizers in two different portions and prices is a good merchandising twist. Nine appetizers are listed in addition to the six seafood appetizers. These include:

CHALUPAS CON POLLO Y CREMA

Corn tortilla pots topped with chicken breast, jalapeño chiles, red onions, fresh cheese, and sour cream, $4.25

VUELVE A LA VIDA

Squid, octopus, shrimp, oysters, clams, marinated in lime and tomato juices, Chica $4.25, Grande $6.50

Three salads and four soups are listed next. Among the different items are:

PICO DE GALLO

Thin slices of jicama, cucumber, fresh fruit in season with lemon-chile dressing, $4.25

SOPA DE TORTILLA

Chipotle-flavored chicken broth with tortilla strips, avocado, and fresh cheese, $3.75

The last listing on this panel is Tamales (Stuffed Fresh Corn Masa):

TAMALES DE PECHUGA DE POLLO

Two tamales of chicken with green and red chile sauce, served in corn husks, $7.50

TAMALES DE MASA A LA OAXAQUEÑA

Two tamales of pork with guajillo chile sauce, served in banana leaves, $7.25

TAMALES DE ELOTE CON NOPALES Y PLÁTANO

Green corn masa stuffed with cactus, plantain, and salsa cruda, steamed in green corn husks and topped with fresh Mexican cream (two), $7.50

PLATILLO DE TAMALES SURTIDOS

An assortment of three tamales—one of each of the above, $9.75

The right-hand panel begins with seven Platillos Mexicanos (Mexican Favorites) featuring chicken, pork, shrimp, roast duck, Pacific snapper, and veal—each prepared a Mexican way and served with special sauces and vegetables.

The next entrée listing is A La Parrilla (Mesquite Charcoal-Grilled), which includes shrimp, fresh fish, squid, and baby octopus, assorted seafood, game hen, chicken and beef on a skewer, filet mignon, medallions of pork tenderloin, skirt steak, spit-roasted meats and fowl, and chicken.

The entrée listings are followed by a list of ten Postres (Desserts), including some unusual ones—a fritter with "drunken" bananas and vanilla ice cream, avocado and lime pie, and coconut custard.

The drink and wine list is on the back cover of the menu. Under the heading Bebidas are listed Margaritas (Mexican and American), Tequila (ten brands), Mescal (two), Agua Mineral Peñafiel (mineral spring water and fruit flavors, lightly carbonated), Agua Mineral Americana (one), Agua Fresca (refreshing water made from pods, flowers, grains, or fruits, five), Jugo de Fruta Fresca (fresh juice, two), and Cerveza Mexicana (beer, nine). The wine list, Lista de Vin, includes nine reds, five whites, and three sparkling wines. Vintage years are included with most of these wines.

In addition, T-shirts and sweatshirts are offered for sale.

Chi-Chi's®

According to *Restaurants & Institutions*, in 1988 Chi-Chi's® had sales of $422.9 million from 192 units. This chain delivers a very high quality product. Its best sellers are the special dinners and Chajitas™, Chi-Chi's® name for fajitas. A buffet and luncheon specials are also offered.

Chi-Chi's® has a six-page, three-panel menu with each panel measuring 7½ by 16½ inches (Figure 17.11). It is printed in four colors on uncoated but slightly textured white stock and is illustrated throughout with color drawings. In addition to the logo and artwork, the cover describes some of their ingredients under Sonoran Kitchen Talk:

> Between the waters of the Gulf of California and the mountains of the Sierra Madre lie the grazing plains of Sonora, the northwest province of Mexico. Our traditional food is prepared in the contemporary style of this region and is subtly spiced. For more intense flavor and a little more heat we moved North of the Rio Grande for Tex-Mex, offering heartier portions with a taste just as big.

When the menu is opened, the first thing the customer sees is the back of the folded-in third panel, which lists the drinks served. First place is given to a large drawing of a margarita, headed Margarita Fiesta. The seven kinds of margaritas offered include Chi-Chi's® Original Margarita, Fruit Margaritas, and Gold Margarita. They are sold by the glass—$2.25 to $4.25—or by the pitcher at $6.45.

Next are listed four Special Drinks—Piña or Pepe Colada, Chi-Chi, Strawberry Daiquiri, and Las Brisas. The other headings on this page are Sangria & Wines, Cerveza, After Dinner, and Frozen Delights (nonalcoholic drinks).

The left-hand inside panel begins with a listing of nine appetizers. The one featured and illustrated is Mexican Pizza (beef, chicken, or seafood). Six kinds of nachos are listed as well as Guacamole Dip and Chile Con Queso, a Mexican cheese fondue.

The next heading, Fresh & Light, includes Taco Salad (beef or chicken), Seafood Salad, Soft Taco (beef or chicken), Mexican Dinner Salad, and San Antonio Chili. A soup of the day is also listed here. The bottom of this panel lists beverages.

The center panel, Combinations, has eight offerings. Featured first is the Special Dinner for $7.25, described as "A sampling of Chi-Chi's® favorites. Our delicious cheese and onion enchilada with seasoned ground beef, covered with Special Sauce, crispy ground beef taco and a ground beef taquito covered with guacamole. Served with sour cream."

The next heading is Chimichangas—the Humunga-Changa (beef or chicken) is featured for $6.75; the Chimichanga Combination (beef, chicken, or seafood) comes with Spanish rice and refried beans for $6.25.

The third panel is headed Char-Broiled. The subhead is Chajitas™, ranch or hacienda style. These can be ordered single, double, or deluxe with beef, chicken, shrimp, or pork. Two more Chajitas™, shrimp and combination, are offered plus Mexican T-Bone Steak, Pollo Magnifico (marinated boneless breast of chicken), and Halibut.

The next heading is Tex-Mex. The two listings are:

STEAK EL PASO

Tender juicy steak, specially seasoned, char-broiled to perfection and basted with our spicy barbecue sauce. Served with two pepper jack cheese enchiladas covered with Tex-Mex Sauce. Plus Spanish rice, barbecue sauce, and pico de gallo.

CHICKEN EL PASO

Specially seasoned boneless breast of chicken basted with our spicy barbecue sauce and char-broiled. Served with two pepper jack cheese enchiladas covered with Tex-Mex sauce. Plus Spanish rice, barbecue sauce, and pico de gallo.

Last are Desserts—Mexican "Fried" Ice Cream, Sopaipillas, and Sombrero Sundae. On all three inside panels a small Mexican flag indicates Chi-Chi's® choices.

The back center panel leads off with Create Your Own Combinations. These include Tacos, Burros, Enchiladas, and Taquitos, which come in beef, chicken, and seafood combinations. The next section is Hot and Spicy: Special Dinner Diablo™, Enchiladas Diablo™, and El Grande Diablo™. (Diablo items are made with Chi-Chi's® own pork and green chile Diablo Sauce.) Then comes North American Favorites—New York Strip Steak, Deep-fried Shrimp, Hamburger, and Cheeseburger. The menu ends with Side Orders and a short paragraph on the Banquet Facilities.

All in all, this is a well-designed and well-thought-out menu.

THE SCANDINAVIAN MENU

Scandinavia includes Norway, Sweden, and Denmark; Finland and Iceland are often considered part of Scandinavia as well. From a culinary point of view the boundaries are unimportant. The Scandinavians eat basically the same foods cooked in a similar manner and their tastes in drink, mainly beer and aquavit, are comparable.

Hroar Dege, chef, author, and director of the Norwegian Food Center in Oslo, has noted that the culinary customs of the Scandinavians can at times seem strange to people with other tastes and customs. The late Norwegian painter Edvard Munch, for example, would invite friends to his parties and serve vintage Champagne with a dish of beef and onions. And it is not unusual today to see diners drinking red wine with cod boiled in salt water!

FIGURE 17.11 Menu for Chi-Chi's®. Spectacular artwork makes this a grand Mexican menu. (Courtesy Chi-Chi's®, Inc. Reproduced by permission.)

Scandinavian cuisine is known primarily for its smörgåsbord, but it includes fish, pork, and poultry as well as beets, potatoes, cucumbers, dill, parsley, horseradish, apples, almonds, cream, and butter. The cooking tends to be simple.

Many Scandinavian recipes and foods are very old. Herring dishes, for example, have been around for centuries. Out of the North has come one of the most popular Scandinavian delicacies, cured salmon, prepared with sugar, salt, white pepper, and dill. The Swedes call it gravlax. It is served uncooked but well cured with a sweet-and-sour mustard sauce. Another Swedish dish is svartsoppa, or black soup. Sweet and spicy, it is made from a mixture of goose and pig's blood that has been stirred in a cooking pot to keep it from coagulating. Today, sherry and port are added as well.

Another staple of the Scandinavian diet is flat bread or hardtack made from potatoes, salt, barley, flour, and water. Its advantage is that it can be stored for months without spoiling.

Salt is an important ingredient in Scandinavian cooking. In Sweden the smörgåsbord would be barren without salted fish. In both Sweden and Denmark, meat and poultry are often pickled, not for preserving but to be eaten at once. For example, cooks soak a goose or a duck in brine with a little saltpeter. The bird is then boiled in fresh water with a little thyme and served in moist, thick slices with sharp mustard, dark sour rye bread, and yellow pea soup containing leeks, carrots, parsnips, onions, and celery.

Dairy products are important in the Scandinavian diet. A bowl of milk is often left on the table until it thickens. It is then sprinkled with sugar or sour rye crumbs and eaten with a spoon.

There is a saying in Scandinavia that the Danes live to eat, the Norwegians eat to live, and the Swedes live to drink. So what do the Danes eat? Meat and potatoes is the staple of their diet, and smørrebrød—open-face sandwiches—are popular. Fish is always available, but it is not as common as in the other northern countries. Generally, the Danes eat seafood as an entrée once a week.

Denmark's favorite meat is pork. The 11.5 million pigs produced annually outnumber the population of 4.8 million Danes. But meat is still expensive in Denmark, and so everyone's favorite meat-stretcher is frikadeller, made with pork and veal that have been ground and reground. The meat is mixed with chopped onions, flour or bread crumbs, eggs, and milk or soda water. The mixture is then shaped into cakes and fried in butter and oil until crusty on both sides.

Ground pork and veal have other uses in the Danish kitchen: A lid is cut off a cabbage head; the head is hollowed out and stuffed with the meat. Reassembled, the cabbage is tied up in cheesecloth and then simmered slowly and served well cooked with melted butter. The frikadeller mixture is also sometimes stuffed in a cauliflower.

Desserts are Danish favorites. Pancakes wrapped around vanilla ice cream, lemon mousse, and cream rings filled with diced pineapple or peaches are favorites. Puddings are popular, and Danish apple cake is not a cake at all but a layer of applesauce and sugared and buttered bread crumbs, topped with whipped cream and raspberry jam.

Smørrebrød, the Danish sandwich, is lunch for hundreds of thousands of Danes every day. It consists of a single thin slice of bread with paalaeg, which means "something laid on." The "something" can be slices of meat, bits of lobster or crab, rich salads, or sautéed fish fillets. At Oskar Davidson's restaurant in Copenhagen, the sandwich menu is four feet and 178 entrées long.

Norway's food is somewhat different. Breakfast often consists of herring and other salted or pickled fish plus several kinds of bread, pastries, cheese, hot and cold cereals, soft-boiled and fried eggs, bacon, potatoes, fruit juice, milk, buttermilk, and coffee.

On the Norwegian menu, soup or fish chowder may qualify as a meal in itself. It is built on a solid stock base, enriched and thickened with egg yolks. Cauliflower is also cooked and blended into a creamy soup. Spinach, caraway sprouts, and spring nettles are cooked into a thickened broth to make soup. The dessert following a meal of soup might be blueberry pancakes or waffles patterned from the hot press of a decorated iron.

The Norwegians eat more fish than the Swedes or Danes do, and lamb and mutton are served most often as the meat dish. The Norwegians also eat pork with sauerkraut, but unlike the German version that is stored in crocks, the Norwegian sauerkraut is made tart with vinegar and caraway seeds, and eaten immediately.

It is sour cream, however, that separates Norway's cooking from that of Denmark. Sour cream is used in Norway as often as sweet or whipped cream is used in Denmark. Cooks use it in soups and sauces, combine it with salt-cured meats and cold cuts, dress lettuce with it, cook fish in it, and spoon it into waffle batter.

Another item on the Norwegian table is lefse, a thin saucer-shaped holiday bread made of potatoes and cooked on an ungreased griddle. It is generally eaten buttered, sugared, and folded up like a pocket handkerchief. Norwegians also like the marrow from reindeer bones, and they have a powerful cocktail made from raw seagull eggs and aquavit.

Although Norwegians eat a great deal of fish, they do not have many ways of preparing it, and they use few sauces. Horseradish and mustard sauce seem to be the only popular flavor additions. Cod is probably the fish most often eaten, and it is usually boiled. The only seasoning is salt, although at times cut-up cod liver and seaweed may be added.

To cook cod, the Norwegians use a lot of water and so much salt that the water is briny. When the water comes to a boil, the thick slices are dropped in. Then when the water comes to a boil the second time, the pot is removed from the fire. The cod is left sitting in the water for a few minutes until the flesh loosens from the bones. It is then served on a hot platter.

The most famous Norwegian cod dish is lutefisk, made from dried cod. The cod are cleaned as soon as they are caught, tied by their tails in pairs, and hung from wooden racks in the open air. In six to twelve weeks they become hard and stiff. With their water content reduced by 84 percent, they can be stored like cordwood for long periods of time.

To make lutefisk, the dried cod must be soaked in lye for as long as two weeks, then rinsed in water several times before it is boiled, with a little salt added at the last minute. The resulting dish is an acquired Nordic taste, but surprisingly, this dried, soaked, and boiled fish is an excellent source of protein while being low in calories.

A popular Norwegian fish dish is a pudding made from ground haddock or cod, cream, cornstarch, salt, and pepper, shaped into a loaf and steamed in the oven. White in color, it can be set off by a pink shrimp sauce that also enhances its flavor.

In Sweden, a smörgåsbord can never be too big. The word means "bread-and-butter table," but it is, of course, much more than that. The restaurant smörgåsbord has cold dishes on one end of the table and hot dishes on the other end, and in between are salads, cold cuts, and meats. Besides smoked salmon and caviar, the star attraction is herring. It may come in a dozen versions, but it never tastes exactly the same twice.

The Swedes fillet herring, slice it, and cut it up into tidbits. They marinate it, pickle it, and serve it fried, jellied, layered in casseroles, stewed, and baked. They flavor it with white and red vinegars, salt and sugar, black and white pepper, powdered mustard, ginger, horseradish, crushed mustard seed, and allspice.

The smörgåsbord is not all there is to Swedish cuisine. Veal Oscar (kalvfile Oscar)—veal topped with bearnaise sauce, white asparagus, and lobster—for example, celebrates a favorite dish of King Oskar II of Sweden. The everyday food, though, is simpler. A traditional Thursday meal is yellow pea soup and crisp-edged pancakes with lingonberries for dessert.

Swedish pea soup is more of a porridge or gruel than a soup. It is cooked from dried yellow peas boiled in water with salt pork or a hambone and onions. The skins are left in the soup, which is flavored with ginger and marjoram. The custom of eating this food on Thursday dates back to the Middle Ages when Sweden was a Catholic country and Thursday and Friday were meatless days. The tiny bit of meat with the pea soup was a sort of preliminary to the totally meatless Friday.

Other Swedish dishes are pork sausage cooked or fried crisp and served with pickled beets, seaman's beef (a beer-flavored stew), and baked beans served with lean meaty bacon. For dessert a favorite is fruit soup or nyponsoppa—a soup made from the orange-red seed capsules of the rose. This "soup" is served cold with almonds and whipped cream.

Other Swedish foods are salmon pudding and potato dumplings. The salmon dish or casserole is made from salted salmon, sliced raw potatoes, and onions with an egg on top. The potato dumplings, the size of tennis balls, are stuffed with pork and are a northern Swedish dish. For eating, the dumpling is sliced and dipped in melted butter.

The potato is the "frame" around a Swedish meal. Many Swedes eat potatoes at lunch and again at supper, and in generous amounts. The veneration of the potato comes partly from the fact that its introduction into Sweden did a great deal to prevent starvation in the long cold winters.

The Swedes bake, fry, and boil potatoes in the usual way, but they also have some different preparation methods. One is Hasselback potatoes, in which the potatoes are peeled and roasted whole but scored beforehand in such a way that they fan open in the heat of the oven. As a result, each section acquires a crunchy edge. A kind of french fry is also made by peeling the potatoes, cutting them into wedges, parboiling them, and then roasting them in a lightly buttered baking dish. The result is a french fry without the fat.

To make tough beef and other meats more edible, the Swedes tend to chop it up or buy it in sausage form. Biff à la Lindstrom is an example. It looks like a hamburger on the outside, but it is different inside. It is a blend of beef, finely diced beets, chopped onions, and capers. Another variation is Färsrulader, finely chopped veal mixed with various ingredients to bind it, which is flattened out, and rolled around a core of thinly sliced leeks.

The Swedes' most interesting and different meat is reindeer. The meat is delicious, gamey but not too strong. The reindeer are raised by the Lapps in northern Sweden above the Arctic Circle. The Lapps eat not only the meat and the liver but also the marrow from the bones. A Lapp method of cooking reindeer meat is to shave it frozen into a hot frying pan to "frizzle" it.

Aquavit is the alcoholic beverage of Scandinavia. It goes with the Nordic foods just as wine goes with French food. Tipped quickly out of a glass into the mouth and swallowed, it has been compared with swallowing a flaming sword. Scandinavia has many varieties of aquavit. Denmark has nine different brands, and three dozen more can be found in Norway and Sweden. They range in taste from bland through modulations of caraway and other herbs and spices to the surprising tastes of purslane and bitter wormwood.

The beverage most often consumed in Scandinavia is coffee. It is drunk morning, noon, and night with meals, after meals, and in between as well. The Icelanders claim that they drink more of it than anyone else, and the Swedes rank themselves a close second to the Norwegians, with the Danes close behind.

Many of the baked goods of Scandinavia have been designed to go with coffee. Coffee cakes are substantial: rich with butter, and often cream filled or cream covered. The flavors include cinnamon and cardamon and, above all, almonds. The Scandinavians use almonds the way Americans use chocolate.

The Aquavit Menu

Aquavit, a Scandinavian restaurant in New York City, has a downstairs dining room and an upstairs Café Aquavit. The menu downstairs is *prix-fixe* for both lunch and dinner (Figure 17.12). Lighter meals, including open-face sandwiches that cost from $10 to $18, are available upstairs at the Café Aquavit. In keeping with its name, the restaurant offers eight different brands or variations of aquavit and a comprehensive wine list. In addition, the drink list includes Laponia, an Arctic brambleberry liqueur, and a lingonberry liqueur.

The dinner menu is organized into three courses. The first course offers ten choices and includes such items as Traditional Gravlax, Wild Mushroom Salad, Juniper Marinated Arctic Venison, and Scandinavian Shellfish Soup. The second course, the entrées, offers ten selections including One Side Sautéed Salmon, Loin of Arctic Venison, Sautéed Monkfish, and Snow Goose with a Timbale. Desserts comprise the third course and include Sorbets of Aquavit, Swedish Pancakes with Punch Raisin Ice Cream, Cheesecake with Cloudberries, Lingonberries and Whipped Cream, and Cloudberry Charlotte with Champagne Sauce.

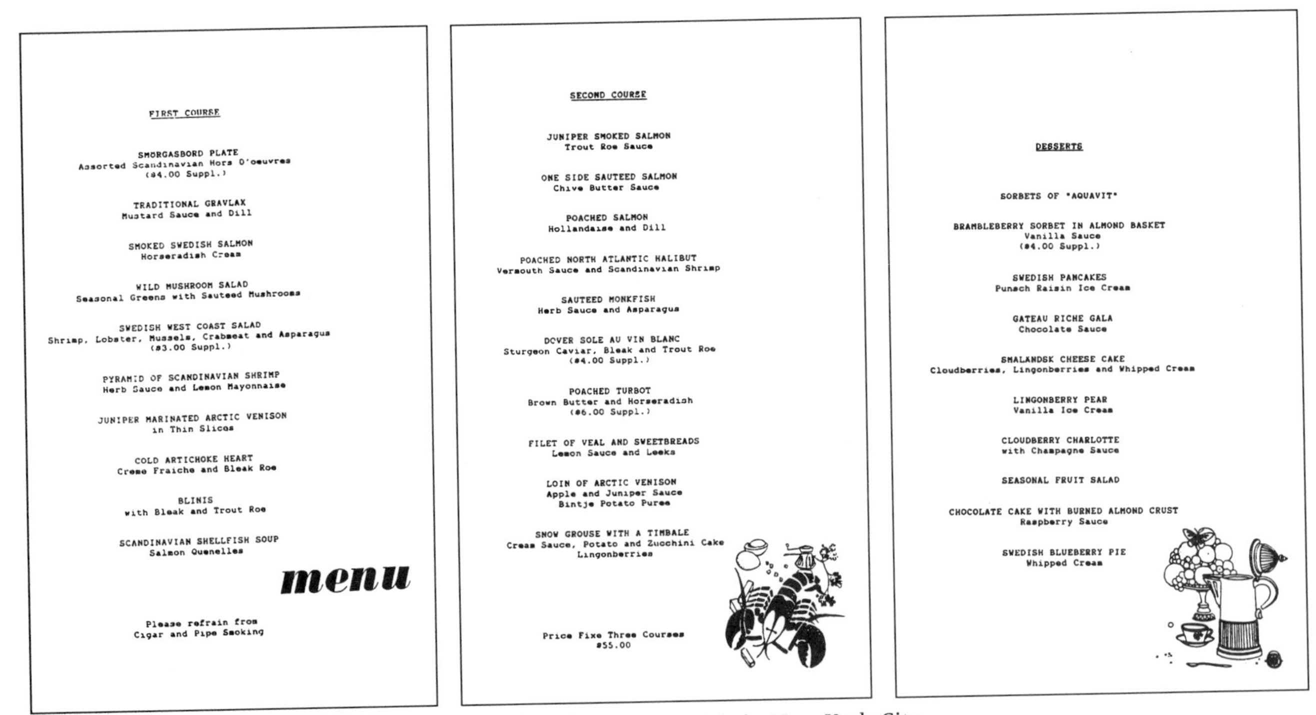

FIRST COURSE

SMÖRGASBORD PLATE
Assorted Scandinavian Hors D'oeuvres
($4.00 Suppl.)

TRADITIONAL GRAVLAX
Mustard Sauce and Dill

SMOKED SWEDISH SALMON
Horseradish Cream

WILD MUSHROOM SALAD
Seasonal Greens with Sauteed Mushrooms

SWEDISH WEST COAST SALAD
Shrimp, Lobster, Mussels, Crabmeat and Asparagus
($3.00 Suppl.)

PYRAMID OF SCANDINAVIAN SHRIMP
Herb Sauce and Lemon Mayonnaise

JUNIPER MARINATED ARCTIC VENISON
in Thin Slices

COLD ARTICHOKE HEART
Creme Fraiche and Bleak Roe

BLINIS
with Bleak and Trout Roe

SCANDINAVIAN SHELLFISH SOUP
Salmon Quenelles

menu

Please refrain from
Cigar and Pipe Smoking

SECOND COURSE

JUNIPER SMOKED SALMON
Trout Roe Sauce

ONE SIDE SAUTEED SALMON
Chive Butter Sauce

POACHED SALMON
Hollandaise and Dill

POACHED NORTH ATLANTIC HALIBUT
Vermouth Sauce and Scandinavian Shrimp

SAUTEED MONKFISH
Herb Sauce and Asparagus

DOVER SOLE AU VIN BLANC
Sturgeon Caviar, Bleak and Trout Roe
($4.00 Suppl.)

POACHED TURBOT
Brown Butter and Horseradish
($6.00 Suppl.)

FILET OF VEAL AND SWEETBREADS
Lemon Sauce and Leeks

LOIN OF ARCTIC VENISON
Apple and Juniper Sauce
Bintje Potato Puree

SNOW GROUSE WITH A TIMBALE
Cream Sauce, Potato and Zucchini Cake
Lingonberries

Price Fixe Three Courses
$55.00

DESSERTS

SORBETS OF "AQUAVIT"

BRAMBLEBERRY SORBET IN ALMOND BASKET
Vanilla Sauce
($4.00 Suppl.)

SWEDISH PANCAKES
Punsch Raisin Ice Cream

GATEAU RICHE GALA
Chocolate Sauce

SMALANDSK CHEESE CAKE
Cloudberries, Lingonberries and Whipped Cream

LINGONBERRY PEAR
Vanilla Ice Cream

CLOUDBERRY CHARLOTTE
with Champagne Sauce

SEASONAL FRUIT SALAD

CHOCOLATE CAKE WITH BURNED ALMOND CRUST
Raspberry Sauce

SWEDISH BLUEBERRY PIE
Whipped Cream

FIGURE 17.12 Menu from Aquavit. This Scandinavian restaurant is in New York City. (Courtesy Aquavit. Reproduced by permission.)

18

The Health and Fitness Menu

Your customers at table 6 have finished their entrées. After the table is cleared, your waiter or waitress approaches them with a dessert menu, a dessert cart, or just the question, "How about dessert? We have a wonderful selection." The reply is apt to be, "Oh, they sound great, but they have too many calories." At that point, the server might reply, "We have a mocha-drenched chocolate cake with only 138 calories per serving." Then the customers might very well order the cake. Furthermore, if the menu or server pointed out that the cake contained 4.1 grams protein, 2.5 grams fat, 24.8 grams carbohydrate, 103 milligrams cholesterol, 0.9 milligrams iron, 76 milligrams sodium, and 38 milligrams calcium, the customers might order the cake for the sake of health and fitness.

Many restaurants serve good, tasty food, but today there is a new concern with nutrition, cholesterol levels, calories, and such dietary elements as sodium, fiber, vitamins, and minerals. Should restaurant people be concerned with nutrition? The food processors and marketers certainly are.

Companies spend millions of dollars on commercials claiming how nutritious their products are. And if the health benefit was not there originally, it is added, or if there was a health danger, such as saturated fat, it is removed and replaced with an unsaturated fat. Do these marketers know something that restaurateurs do not or are ignoring? Some restaurant operators who are alert to trends are indeed getting on the health, fitness, and nutrition bandwagon in the kitchen and on the menu. The Hyatt Regency Hotel in Minneapolis, for example, lists the following nutritional information on the breakfast menu for The Terrace restaurant under the heading of Perfect Balance:

EGGBEATER® FRITTATA

Open-face, Eggbeater® Omelette Filled with Crisp Seasonal Vegetables Glazed with Light Cheese. Approximately: 196 Calories, 27 Grams Protein, 3 Grams Fat, 15 Grams Carbohydrates, 0 mg Cholesterol, 4 Grams Sodium

JOGGER'S BREAKFAST

Two Large Eggs, Poached or Scrambled, Served on a Bed of Freshly Sautéed Spinach and Accompanied by Plain Yogurt. Approximately: 323 Calories, 20 Grams Protein, 512 mg Cholesterol, 4 Grams Sodium

On the dinner menu for the Hyatt Regency's Terrace restaurant, the nutrition listing is also headed Perfect Balance. It lists four entrées:

NOT FOR VEGETARIANS ONLY

A Bountiful Array of Fresh Colorful Steamed Vegetables Uniquely Presented in an Oriental Steam Basket and Accompanied by a Light Lemon Margarine. Approximately: 555 Calories, 20 Grams Protein, 20 Grams Fat, 65 Grams Carbohydrates, .8 Grams Sodium

BROILED BREAST OF CHICKEN

Presented on a Bed of Poached, Shredded Zucchini, Carrots and Leeks with Herbed Tomatoes and Melted Cheese. Approximately: 427 Calories, 67 Grams Protein, 9 Grams Fat, 16 Grams Carbohydrates, 150 mg Cholesterol, .2 Grams Sodium

BROILED FRESH SEASONAL FISH

Only the Freshest Fish Available, Gently Broiled with Crushed Herbs and Spices, Garnished with a Bouquet of Poached Seasonal Vegetables. Approximately: 328 Calories, 48 Grams Protein, 2 Grams Fat, 26 Grams Carbohydrates, .3 Grams Sodium

FRESH FRUIT SUNBURST

A Fresh Apple Filled with Cottage Cheese and a Healthful Display of the Freshest Seasonal Fruit. Approximately: 452 Calories, 21 Grams Protein, 3 Grams Fat, 67 Grams Carbohydrates

Americans today are, as a whole, probably more concerned with health, fitness, and longevity than they ever have been before. A 1987 Gallup survey, for example, found that 69 percent of all Americans exercise regularly, 64 percent of the exercisers also try to eat more healthful foods, and 43 percent have lost weight.

NUTRITION MERCHANDISING

Healthful and light foods are the trend in America today, so merchandising the nutritional aspect of the menu makes good sense.

The Sheraton Plaza in Chicago, noted for its rooftop, poolside, alfresco dining, promotes healthful eating by having an Asparagus Festival each spring. At a press party Sheraton chefs demonstrate new asparagus recipes developed for the hotel's food and beverage outlets. The chefs give pointers on the selection, care, and handling of asparagus and hand out product information kits. At the hotel's ground-floor upscale restaurant, the menu is light and healthy with American Heart Association (AHA) entrées such as To Your Health Omelettes prepared with fresh vegetables and egg whites only, and skinless broiled breast of chicken with green and red bell pepper sauce.

The Thistle Lodge Restaurant at Casa Ybel resort, Sanibel Island, Florida, has a Lodge-ically Lean section on its menu that has AHA approval. One of the items on this nutrition menu is Strawberry Margarita Pie, which has only 148 calories.

Skipper's, based in Bellevue, Washington, promotes nonfried entrées as its contribution to more healthful eating. These entrées are part of a Limited Catch menu that includes such items as chilled crab with rice instead of fries. Chilled Snow Crab includes four crab legs and two claws with honey mustard dip, corn and marinated vegetable salad. Skipper's operates and franchises 204 Skipper's Seafood 'n Chowder House restaurants in fifteen states and Canada.

The award-winning fine dining Café Provençal in Evanston, Illinois, opened a lower-priced seafood and pasta restaurant. Although its menu offers steaks, steak sandwiches, and burgers, its major emphasis is on innovative chicken, seafood, and pasta appetizers and entrées.

Denny's introduced three special menus for the health- and diet-conscious customer. One, called Waist Not, Want Not, is an extended menu with calorie-counted items. All contain five hundred or fewer calories. The Salt Away! menu gives sodium content for each item—none with more than 1,100 milligrams of sodium. Dine to Your Heart's Content is a menu that follows the low-saturated-fat, low-cholesterol guidelines set by the American Heart Association.

At the Commander's Palace in New Orleans, the low- and no-alcohol drinks offered have been expanded, and the chef, Emeril Lagasse, has "lightened up" the preparation of traditional Creole and Cajun dishes. The way he fries is "airy batter and lightning fast!" Lagasse works with local hospital nutritionists and dietitians.

At Sinclair's in Chicago, owner Gordon Sinclair and chef Michael Kornick created a completely new health menu. According to Sinclair, "It's simpler to design your menu with health and nutrition in mind than to go through and make especially healthful items for customers." The restaurant also has a new policy on half-portions: Customers can order any entrée in appetizer portions for half the entrée price plus $1.00.

Can a low-calorie menu bring high profits? It did at Jack's restaurant in New York. Owned by Edward Safdie, a real estate developer and hotelier, low-calorie but highly elegant food was introduced at the restaurant in 1984. Soon 90 percent of the customers were choosing the low-calorie menu items. Next, Safdie introduced his healthful cuisine to several hotels he owns and manages, and his profits reflect the customers' approval. Safdie became so convinced of the benefits of light and healthy food that he wrote a book on the subject—*Spa Food.*

The term *spa cuisine* appeared first at the famous Four Seasons restaurant in New York. At this bastion of good taste, Chef Seppi Renggli, in collaboration with Joyce T. Leung of Columbia University's Institute of Human Nutrition, developed nutritionally balanced, calorie-counted dishes that were exquisite to both the eye and palate (see Figure 18.1). The development of Four Seasons' Spa Cuisine® has also affected the restaurant's cooking in general, according to Chef Renggli.

At Rue St. Clair in Chicago, Bistro Light luncheon and dinner selections have been introduced. The number of calories of these items does not exceed 350 and is controlled by sautéeing in nonstick pans, replacing creams and fattening sauces with herbs and spices for flavor, and using cooking methods such as roasting, broiling, and steaming.

Even meat eaters flock to Greens Restaurant at Fort Mason in San Francisco to dine on vegetarian fare. The secret? Flavor from the freshest, finest ingredients money can buy, which are then prepared by creative chefs. The restaurant was rated the number one vegetarian restaurant in San Francisco by the *San Francisco Focus* magazine.

The AHA endorsed one fast-food restaurant for its low cholesterol content—Chicken El Pollo Loco. El Pollo Loco—the crazy chicken—is a quick-service concept serving Mexican-style char-broiled chicken. At El Pollo Loco's forty-three outlets, chicken is marinated for twenty minutes in fruit juices and spiced with herbs. It is then grilled without breading or oil and served with corn or flour tortillas and a salad.

The Café at the Ritz-Carlton Hotel in Atlanta has added Fitness Cuisine to its luncheon menu. This means food with fewer calories and less salt and cholesterol. Such items include Seafood Gazpacho with Fresh Thyme, Seviche of Scallops with Cilantro and Lime, Salad of Hearts of Artichoke with Marinated Chicken and Peppers, Poached Breast of Chicken,

SPA CUISINE R

APPETIZERS		MAIN COURSES	
ARTICHOKE with Roasted Peppers	13.50	A Skewer of SHRIMP and CHICKEN	38.00
Summer FRUITS with Mango Purée	14.00	Breast of PIGEON, Wild Rice	37.00
Seviche of RED SNAPPER in Orange	14.00	Escalope of VEAL with Mustard Seeds	37.50

FIGURE 18.1 The Four Seasons' Spa Cuisine® menu. (Courtesy The Four Seasons. Reproduced by permission.)

Grilled Tuna Served on Tomato and Watercress, and Medallions of Veal with Tomato Coulis and Basil.

To stimulate business at The Rivoli restaurant in Houston, the owner, Ed Zelinsky, first redecorated it in an art nouveau style. Then he added a Lite & Lively menu giving customers some exciting (and healthy) alternatives to the standard continental fare. The menu includes Fresh Green Asparagus Vinaigrette, Soft Shell Crabs with Dill Sauce, Grilled Swordfish Steak with Capers and Lemon Butter, and Grilled Chicken Breast with Fresh Chanterelle Mushrooms and Zinfandel Butter. For dessert, Amaretto Custard Romanoff is offered.

The Levy organization's Chestnut Street Grill is one of Chicago's best places for grilled fish. The menu has a number of Spa Menu selections, all low in calories, salt, and cholesterol. These items were analyzed by a certified nutritionist at Northwestern University using the nutrient data base of the Nutrition Coding Center at the University of Minnesota. Some of the entrées on the menu are Marinated Bay Scallops, Whole Wheat Pasta Salad, Spa Antipasto, and Grilled Marinated Vegetables. In addition, in many of the other Levy restaurants, regular menu items such as brook trout, black sea bass, and Dover sole can be prepared fat free upon request. The staff at the Chestnut Street Grill is trained to give the approximate calorie content per serving of all dishes on the menu.

At R. D. Clucker's restaurant in Chicago, chicken—available whole or halved—is prepared in a healthy, low-fat manner. It is slowly marinated in fresh fruit juices and herbs and then char-broiled in view of the customers. The chicken is served mild with a honey mustard sauce, spicy hot with salsa, Italian style with fresh pesto, smoked in a salad, and "peasant style" with fresh vegetables and matzo balls in a rich broth.

At the Plaza of the Americas Hotel in Dallas, guests can now have a lighter lunch of a number of small menu items. Chef Peter Schaffrath created a Le Relais Sampler Menu from which diners can choose four appetizer-sized dishes. The thirteen selections include Smoked Atlantic Salmon and Mozzarella and Tomato Salad with Basil. This miniature menu is available in the hotel's sidewalk café, Le Relais, in addition to the regular menu.

The "doggy bag" exists because many customers are served more than they wish to eat. To solve this problem Shel Berlatsky opened a Steakhouse, H. T. Goodness, in Santa Monica, California, where diners select their own steaks from seven different cuts arranged in a display case. They specify the cut, weight, and thickness and watch while the steak is trimmed and weighed.

Large hotels were among the first to realize the importance of light and healthful foods. The Doubletree

Hotel in Orange, California, has introduced a menu featuring low-sodium and sugar-free items and ingredients approved by the American Heart Association. The management at La Regence restaurant in New York's Plaza Athenée has determined that 20 percent of lunch orders come from a special health menu, and at the Helmsley Palace's Trianon Room, a low-cholesterol, no-sodium diet menu accounts for 25 percent of all orders.

The revolving Spinnaker Lounge on the sixteenth floor of the Hyatt Regency in Cambridge, Massachusetts, affords a a spectacular view but, because of declining alcohol consumption, was not doing too well. So Karl Volker, the hotel's executive assistant manager of food and beverage, turned the room into a California-style kitchen specializing in lighter, healthier foods. The new Spinnaker now serves Shrimp Scampi with Angel Hair Pasta, Radicchio Salad with Japanese Mushrooms, Marinated Chicken with Dijon Sauce, Fresh Quiche, and a salad with diced chicken, avocado, bacon, and raspberry vinegar dressing.

19

Making the Menu Do More

A menu can be used for many things: One is creating an atmosphere or style. It can also be used to try out new items, make combination packages, and to use foreign words to add glamour to the restaurant and its cuisine.

VARIETY AND EXPERIMENTATION

A small food manufacturer created a new food product called Pizza Roll, which was offered to a large grocery chain, with the aim of getting it on the shelf. But the grocery chain demanded $25,000 just for providing shelf space. This illustrates how difficult it is to get a new food product into a supermarket.

A restaurant operator, on the other hand, can put anything on a menu, without paying a shelf fee. The only fee is the cost of changing the menu. Thus the restaurant operator who does not experiment with new products and thereby add interest and variety to the menu is missing an opportunity for more sales and greater profit.

To get the same old food, the customer can eat at home. Of course, the standard entrée, appetizer, dessert, sandwich, and salad items, perennial favorites, are necessary for a successful menu. But the unusual, exotic gourmet treat is the sign of a successful restaurant. And even if these unusual items are not ordered as often as the old standbys are, the word of mouth advertising from those who do try your exotic entrées makes them worthwhile.

The following examples show real creative menu building. Even if they do not sound like items that would fit into your menu, they should stimulate your creative thinking so that your menu will become more interesting, exciting, and salesworthy.

The Bowery restaurant in Traverse City, Michigan, for example, serves smoked Lake Michigan whitefish with dill sauce and toasted garlic rounds and a crock of BBQ meatballs as unusual appetizers. A different entrée at this eatery is Old Mission cherry duck—tender duckling roasted to a crisp golden brown and basted in a sweet cherry sauce, served on a bed of wild rice. A different dessert at The Bowery is French-fried ice cream.

On the luncheon menu at Holiday Inns in the Midwest a different food offering is headed Health Corner. Chopped steak, chicken breast, tuna salad plate, and fresh fruit and cheese plates are offered. The chicken is served without the skin, and cottage cheese goes with most of these items.

At Beall's 1860 restaurant in Macon, Georgia, a different soup is served under the heading of Extras—Beall's peanut soup. Under the heading Lively Desserts You Can Drink, this menu lists "Gentle Mint—hauntingly smooth crème de menthe with rich ice cream to help you relive chilly fall evenings on the porch of the plantation."

At the Terrace Garden Inn in Atlanta, Georgia, for a salad you can order a Pineapple Boat—one-quarter of a fresh pineapple and assorted fruits served with sherbet or cottage cheese, date nut bread, and dressing. And for a different sandwich this menu offers the Toothsome Twins—two soft Kaiser rolls, one with shrimp salad, one with chicken salad, garnished with cherry tomato and hard-boiled egg.

At Quaglino's restaurant in New York City the menu has a separate listing headed Pasta by Tino, as follows:

Sea Bass Ravioli with shrimp sauce

Rolled Salmon with champagne and tomato sauce

Green Lasagnette with crabmeat and pink sauce

Risotto with red wine and saffron

Asparagus Casserole with cheese sauce

Black Tagliolini with Lobster Sauce

The Ojai Valley Inn Country Club has a generous selection of unusual items on the menu. In the appetizer department there are Cornish hen pâté with mango relish and smoked duck sausage with warm lentil salad. The soup list includes chilled butternut squash and apple bisque plus plankton fritter. Among the salads is a half Maine lobster with green asparagus and sour cream potato salad.

The entrée listing at Ojai Valley includes golden baked fillet of lamb wrapped in spinach leaves and minted jus, veal medallions with breast of quail on carrot pancake with stewed cranberries, and Matilija Canyon steak roast with olive and herb crust. The dessert list also has unusual items, such as Pepin apple pie with wild honey ice cream, Comice pear poached in cabernet sauvignon with raspberry sauce, and mango parfait with pecan crunch.

On the lunch menu for The Whitehall Club, Chicago, are several items. One is an appetizer, Sonoma baked goat cheese with navy beans Provençal. The soups also have an extra ingredient, such as French onion soup au gratin with aged port wine and lobster bisque with sherry cream topping. The Cold Buffet offers an artichoke tulip with crab and scallops and sweet garlic vinaigrette. Among the entrées are sautéed scampi with jalapeño-papaya concasse and veal saltimbocca with prosciutto and sage.

Another way to make the menu do more is to feature a special recipe. At Antoine's restaurant in New Orleans, Oysters Rockefeller are highlighted with the following copy:

> Without a doubt the most widely imitated specialty of Antoine's is Oysters Rockefeller. Nowhere but at Antoine's, however, can you taste the authentic original recipe. Indeed, we have seen hundreds of published recipes for the dish, but none of them are even close to the real formula. It remains a family secret. (We will say that it does not include spinach.)
>
> Oysters Rockefeller were created at the turn of the century by Jules Alciatore, the son of founder Antoine Alciatore. The story which has come down is that Jules was asked at the last minute to add a hot appetizer to the menu for a private party. Jules, a master of not wasting anything, saw some surplus relish trays in the kitchen, and from them improvised a new sauce for oysters. He named it for the then-richest man in the world and its richness. It's still an Antoine's favorite.
>
> In 1938, Antoine's served its millionth order of Oysters Rockefeller. We are now getting close to Number 3,000,000. Ask your waiter for a card with the number of your order of this true American original. You are welcome to enjoy them either as a light lunch, or as the traditional first course to a grand Antione's repast.

Packages can also be sold on the menu. On the back cover of The Paddock Room menu at Belmont Park, for example, a Special "Day at the Races" Party Package is offered as follows:

> Want to raise money for your club or charitable organization and have a day the members will talk about all year? Then call (phone number) and find out about the special package offered at Aqueduct or Belmont every day but weekends and holidays. The fun includes Club House admission, a special luncheon, complimentary programs, a race named for your group and nine exciting thoroughbred races. It's better than a theater party because you know this show is a hit.

LIST IN FRENCH, EXPLAIN IN ENGLISH

French is the language of great cuisine. Listing items in French, therefore, gives the menu authenticity and panache. A French restaurant at the bottom of its ice cream and sherbet listing says: "Fabrication artisanale traditionelle," which translates as "Made in the traditional manner." The customer can be sure that there is a French chef out in the kitchen preparing special, not just ordinary, food.

When listing items in French, depending on the restaurant, it may be important to translate or explain them in English. The following is a good example of how this may be done:

FILET DE TRUITE AMANDINE

A generous fillet of rainbow trout, delicately seasoned and covered with a browned butter sauce, fresh lemon juice, and sliced toasted almonds.

SUPRÊME DE VOLAILLE, LE RUTH

A whole boneless chicken breast, stuffed with butter and lightly coated with toasted crumbs. Browned in butter and served with a light wine sauce.

EMINCE DE VEAU RÉNÉ

Thin slices of milk-fed veal sautéed in butter and covered with a wine sauce made with cream, chanterelle mushrooms, and fresh herbs.

FILET DE BOEUF AUX CHAMPIGNONS

A small tenderloin steak, selected for its rich, delicate flavor and pan broiled. Topped with sliced mushrooms in a natural sauce.

ENTRECÔTE DE BOEUF AU POIVRE

A thick sirloin strip of choice beef, seasoned with fresh, coarsely ground peppercorns, broiled and served in a sauce of burgundy and special herbs.

Following is a glossary of basic French menu words.

Glossary of French Menu Vocabulary

Agneau. Lamb
Aigre. Sour
Ail. Garlic
Aileron. Wingbone
Allumette. Matchstick potatoes
Alsacienne. Alsatian style; usually served with sauerkraut
Amandine. With almonds
Américaine. American style
Ananas. Pineapple
Anchois. Anchovy
Andalouse. With tomatoes & peppers
Anguille. Eel
Argenteuil. With asparagus
Artichaut. Artichoke
Asperges. Asparagus
Aspic. Decorated jellied piece
Aubergines. Eggplant
Béarnaise. In America, a sauce similar to hollandaise, fortified with meat glaze, and with tarragon flavor predominating
Bécasse. Woodcock
Béchamel. Cream sauce
Beignet. Fritter
Beurre. Butter
Bifteck. Beefsteak
Bisque. Thick, rich soup
Blanc. White
Blanquette. Stew with white wine
Boeuf. Beef
Boisson. Drink, beverage
Bouillabaisse. Fish stew
Bouillon. Broth
Bouquetière. With mixed vegetables
Bourguignonne. With onions and red Burgundy wine
Bouteille. Bottle
Café. Coffee
Canard. Duck
Caneton. Duckling
Carré. Rack
Cervelle. Brain
Champignon. Mushroom
Chapon. Capon
Chateaubriand. Thick filet mignon
Chaud. Warm, Hot
Chevreuil. Venison
Chou-Fleur. Cauliflower
Choux de Bruxelles. Brussel sprouts
Cochon. Suckling pig
Coeur. Heart
Compote. Stewed fruit
Concombre. Cucumber
Confiture. Jam, preserve
Consommé. Clear soup
Coquille. Shell for baking
Côte. Rib, chop
Crème. Cream
Crème Fouettée. Whipped cream
Crêpe. Pancake
Crevette. Shrimp
Croquette. Patty of meat
Déjeuner. Breakfast, lunch
Diable. Deviled
Dinde. Turkey
Du Barry. With cauliflower
Eau. Water
Ecrevisse. Crayfish
Entrecôte. Sirloin steak
Entremets. Sweet, desserts
Epinard. Spinach
Escargots. Snails
Faisan. Pheasant
Farce. Ground meat
Farci. Stuffed
Filet. Boneless ribbon
Flambé. Flamed
Foie. Liver
Foie Gras. Goose liver
Fondue. Melted cheese
Forestière. With mushroom
Four. Oven baked
Fricandeau. Braised veal morsels
Fricassée. Chicken or veal stew
Frit. Deep fat fried
Froid. Cold
Fromage. Cheese
Fumé. Smoked
Gateau. Cake
Gelée. Jelly
Gibier. Game
Gigot. Leg
Glace. Ice, ice cream
Gratin. Brown, baked with cheese
Grenouille. Frog
Grillé. Broiled
Hereng. Herring
Haricot Vert. String bean
Hollandaise. Sauce made with egg yolk, melted butter, and lemon
Homard. Lobster
Hors d'Oeuvres. Appetizers
Huitre. Oyster
Jambon. Ham
Jardinière. With vegetable
Julienne. Thin strips
Jus. Juice, gravy
Lait. Milk
Langouste. Sea crayfish or rock lobster

Lapin. Rabbit
Légume. Vegetable
Macédoine. Mixed fruits
Maître d'Hôtel. With spiced butter
Marmite. Beef consommé
Meringue. Beaten egg white
Meunière. Pan fried and served with brown butter
Mignon. Dainty
Mornay. Cheese sauce
Mousse. Whipped foam
Mouton. Mutton
Nantua. Lobster sauce
Naturel. Plain
Noir. Black
Noisette. Hazelnut
Nouille. Noodle
Oeuf. Egg
Oeufs Pochés. Poached eggs
Oie. Goose
Oignon. Onion
Pain. Bread
Pâté. Meat pie
Patisserie. Pastry
Pêche. Peach
Petit. Small
Poire. Pear
Pois. Peas
Poisson. Fish
Poitrine. Breast
Pomme. Apple
Pomme de Terre. Potato
Potage. Soup
Pot au Feu. Boiled beef with a variety of vegetables and broth served as a meal
Poulet. Chicken
Purée. Sieved food
Quenelle. Dumpling
Ragout. Stew
Ris. Sweetbread
Riz. Rice
Rognon. Kidney
Roti. Roasted
Roulade. Rolled meat
Saumon. Salmon
Sauté. Pan fry in butter
Sel. Salt
Selle. Saddle
Sorbet. Sherbet
Soufflé. Whipped pudding
Tasse. Cup
Tête. Head
Tournedos. Two small tenderloin steaks
Tranche. Slice
Truite. Trout
Veau. Veal
Velouté. White sauce made from fish, chicken, or veal stock
Vichyssoise. Hot or cold potato and leek soup
Viennoise. Vienna style, breaded
Vinaigrette. Dressing with oil, vinegar and herbs
Volaille. Poultry
Vol-au-Vent. Patty shell

SEASONING THE MENU

There is no rule that says when the menu should be changed, but a common one is to change the menu with the seasons. In the East, Northeast, Midwest, and Northwest, game dishes and fall harvest products appear in many restaurants, replacing the lighter summer fare. In the South and the Southwest where there are no great seasonal changes, the menu tends to stay the same. But in changing climates, customers seem to like a different fare. Refrigeration and modern transportation can keep the menu fairly constant, but it seems that the public changes its eating habits with the change in weather.

At Jasper's restaurant in Boston, fall is the time for New England chicken, whole baby lamb, veal, and a variety of game dishes such as venison, rabbit, and Nantucket quail. White's restaurant moves into winter with a thick New England chowder of fresh and smoked haddock, salt pork, potatoes, salt, cream, and butter. White's also serves grilled quail on a bed of slightly warmed lettuce with a mustard vinaigrette. The emphasis in these restaurants is locally produced food and fish from the Atlantic.

At Monique's, pheasant is served with cabbage and a port sauce. Elk is also part of this seasonal menu. At the Cottage restaurant in suburban Calumet City, Illinois, stuffed pheasant is served. The recipe calls for filling the bird with apples, oranges, celery and onions, marinating it in apple cider, slow-smoking it over wood and serving it with smoked garlic sauce. This restaurant also serves quail breast stuffed with dates that are in turn pitted and filled with roasted walnuts. The dates are then also marinated in apple cider.

At the Midland Hotel's Exchange restaurant in Chicago, one dish combines deer meat and beef medallions with autumn vegetables in a hunter's stew, accompanied by a dill-mustard sauce. Other fall menus in Chicago feature roast loin of pork basted with barbecue sauce and served with a corn and bean relish. At Chicago's La Strada restaurant, veal sautéed with porcini and domestic mushrooms is served with a wine sauce as a seasonal variant.

At the City Café in Manhattan, the menu is winterized with a small appetizer and large entrée plates featuring grilled quail on a salad of mâche with smoked bacon and Dijon mustard vinaigrette; grilled New York State foie gras with braised apples and sauterne; fennel-grilled red snapper with tomato and basil butter; braised saddle of rabbit with mushrooms; tomato, onions, and mashed potatoes; and veal with new potatoes, fresh rosemary, lemon, and garlic. The City Café also has a fall–winter version of an entrée staple, cassoulet. It combines sweetbreads with wild mushrooms and Madeira wine. To make veal Parmigiana, the chef at this restaurant merely adds crushed tomatoes and two kinds of cheeses to veal chops. Man Ray restaurant in Manhattan's Chelsea section adds cassoulet, stews, and other hearty dishes to the menu to make it seasonal.

In the Pacific Northwest, Atwater's changes its core menu twice a year. In October this Portland, Oregon, restaurant comes out with a fall–winter menu, and in April it presents a spring–summer version. The main items of Atwater's six-course fall–winter menu—which changes every ten days—are a variety of wild mushrooms and Chinook salmon.

In Atlanta, the weather does not change greatly in the fall, but menus still tend to reflect the season. At Bernard's and the Cajun Station, seasonal Louisiana shellfish such as oysters and crawfish appear on the menu as specials, and although rack of lamb and chateaubriand are year-round items, in the fall the game selections are expanded.

The Bowery

At The Bowery restaurant overlooking Grand Traverse Bay in Traverse City, Michigan, the core menu is reviewed each winter, as this restaurant is open seasonally—May through October. At that time, unpopular items are deleted, and new items are added. Prices are also analyzed and adjusted at this time. New cover inserts are created to promote new items and stimulate business. Figure 19.1 shows the autumn menu insert, featuring Chicken Marsala, Broiled Rainbow Trout, Tenderloin Brochette, and Cajun Chicken & Bowery Ribs. Prices are $8.95 to $10.95.

FIGURE 19.1 Menu from The Bowery. (Courtesy Schelde Enterprises, Inc. Reproduced by permission.)

SELLING OTHER THINGS ON THE MENU

Although food and drink are obviously the two main items to be sold on the menu, other items, services, information, and general promotion vary from operation to operation. Not every establishment has a decor, location, or history to sell. Not every foodservice offers takeouts, catering, or facilities for banquets, parties, and meetings. But even the operation with nothing special to sell can create some extras to add to its reputation, and often these extras can add extra income. "Extra" or "other" items that appear most often on menus are as follows:

History of foodservice operation
Story about management
Takeout or take-home service
Catering
Party-banquet-meeting facilities
Gift shop
Museum connected with establishment
Tourist attractions in the neighborhood, city, or nearby area
City, state, and national association affiliations
AAA, Mobil, and other guidebook recommendations
Credit cards honored
Map showing location

A surprising number of foodservice operations do not include merchandising possibilities such as these on their menu. In fact, most menus have several blank pages—back cover, inside back and front cover—that could be used for some of this merchandising. The following are examples of extra or other merchandising on the menu.

Froggy's

Froggy's is a fine French restaurant located in a Chicago suburb. Most French chefs like to serve fresh vegetables, fruits, meats, and fish, which often means in season. Froggy's menu uses season as a clever menu merchandising trick, by advertising next month's menu on its back cover (Figure 19.2).

Headed by the words Next Month, fifteen entrées are listed, among them: Flaky pastry shell filled with snails and baby vegetables served in a spicy red wine sauce; sliced duck and mushrooms glazed in the oven with cheese and a ginger sauce; New Zealand mussels served cold in a curry sauce with apples; chicken braised in a fresh crayfish sauce; fillet of beef served en brochette with wild rice and black peppercorn sauce; fresh salmon grilled with anchovies and olives, and served with diced tomatoes; sliced duck filled with a mousse of veal served with an olive sauce; sliced rack of lobster braised with seaweed and served with a fresh basil sauce; and flaky pastry shell filled with sweetbreads and mushrooms in red wine sauce.

The Hard Rock Cafe, with only six units, had sales of $45.2 million in 1987. Part of that income came from the sales of T-shirts and sweatshirts with the restaurant's name printed on them.

Darryl's

The Darryl's restaurant chain—thirty-seven outlets in the Southwest—sells T-shirts right on the menu, alongside the restaurant's Parmesan Chicken and Cajun-fried Catfish. Also listed on the menu are Darryl's baseball caps, sunglasses, Pilsner glasses, sun visors, barbecue sauce, and aprons. Illustrations of the merchandise vie for customer attention with food illustrations. These souvenirs are selling very well. They are arranged in a display case in each restaurant lobby, marked with a neon sign that reads Darryl's Souvenirs. When seated, the customers can order these items right off the menu from their server or bartender.

In addition to its nonfood items, Darryl's restaurant has an unusual menu with a large selection of foods and beverages aimed at a mass market (Figure 19.3). And, it merchandises both aspects of the menu very well.

It is a large menu, measuring 10 by 16 inches; the cover is die-cut in the shape of a beer mug. The entire menu is printed in full color. Inside are ten pages of listings and products for sale. Photos of foods and beverages appear on every spread. The listings and descriptions are printed in dark blue, large enough even for people with poor eyesight to read.

On the inside cover are listed twelve Specialty Drinks, with no prices. Two of the different ones are Cheap Sunglasses (a zesty blend of vodka, cranberry juice & zing!) and '57 Chevy (a nonalcoholic mix of everything fruity under the sun). Darryl's Original Premium Lager Beer is also featured on this panel.

Thirteen appetizers are listed on the next panel. An interesting item here is Santa Fe Egg Rolls (tender diced chicken, black beans, green chilis, black olives, spinach, and grated cheese deep fried in jumbo wonton wrappers with mild salsa). The nonfood items sold on this panel are baseball caps ($8.00) and Darryl's sunglasses ($4.95).

At the top of page 4 are six salads, priced from $2.45 to $5.95. The second heading is Soups, Quiche and Gumbos. The headings on page 5 are Gourmet Burgers and Sandwiches. There are five burgers, including Blackened Cajun Burger, and ten sandwiches. The Deluxe Pork Sandwich, priced at $15.95, includes a pink pig visor, which by itself sells for $10.

On pages 6 and 7 (the center spread) are two food listings, Darryl's Specialties and Sizzling Fajitas. Two nonfood items are also sold here: a T-shirt with the

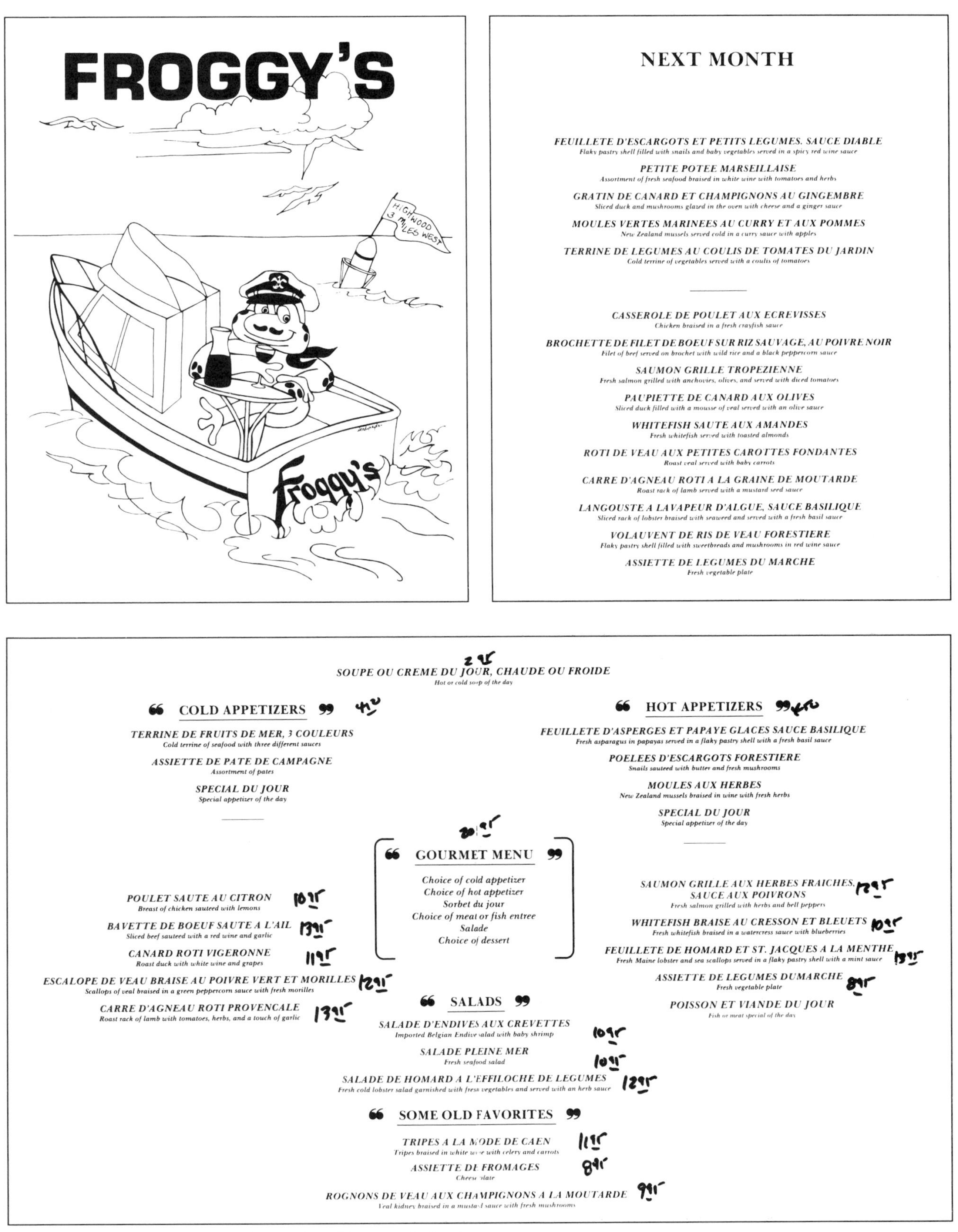

NEXT MONTH

FEUILLETE D'ESCARGOTS ET PETITS LEGUMES, SAUCE DIABLE
Flaky pastry shell filled with snails and baby vegetables served in a spicy red wine sauce

PETITE POTEE MARSEILLAISE
Assortment of fresh seafood braised in white wine with tomatoes and herbs

GRATIN DE CANARD ET CHAMPIGNONS AU GINGEMBRE
Sliced duck and mushrooms glazed in the oven with cheese and a ginger sauce

MOULES VERTES MARINEES AU CURRY ET AUX POMMES
New Zealand mussels served cold in a curry sauce with apples

TERRINE DE LEGUMES AU COULIS DE TOMATES DU JARDIN
Cold terrine of vegetables served with a coulis of tomatoes

CASSEROLE DE POULET AUX ECREVISSES
Chicken braised in a fresh crayfish sauce

BROCHETTE DE FILET DE BOEUF SUR RIZ SAUVAGE, AU POIVRE NOIR
Filet of beef served on brochet with wild rice and a black peppercorn sauce

SAUMON GRILLE TROPEZIENNE
Fresh salmon grilled with anchovies, olives, and served with dried tomatoes

PAUPIETTE DE CANARD AUX OLIVES
Sliced duck filled with a mousse of veal served with an olive sauce

WHITEFISH SAUTE AUX AMANDES
Fresh whitefish served with toasted almonds

ROTI DE VEAU AUX PETITES CAROTTES FONDANTES
Roast veal served with baby carrots

CARRE D'AGNEAU ROTI A LA GRAINE DE MOUTARDE
Roast rack of lamb served with a mustard seed sauce

LANGOUSTE A LAVAPEUR D'ALGUE, SAUCE BASILIQUE
Sliced rack of lobster braised with seaweed and served with a fresh basil sauce

VOLAUVENT DE RIS DE VEAU FORESTIERE
Flaky pastry shell filled with sweetbreads and mushrooms in red wine sauce

ASSIETTE DE LEGUMES DU MARCHE
Fresh vegetable plate

2.95
SOUPE OU CREME DU JOUR, CHAUDE OU FROIDE
Hot or cold soup of the day

" COLD APPETIZERS " 4.50

TERRINE DE FRUITS DE MER, 3 COULEURS
Cold terrine of seafood with three different sauces

ASSIETTE DE PATE DE CAMPAGNE
Assortment of pates

SPECIAL DU JOUR
Special appetizer of the day

" HOT APPETIZERS " 4.50

FEUILLETE D'ASPERGES ET PAPAYE GLACES SAUCE BASILIQUE
Fresh asparagus in papayas served in a flaky pastry shell with a fresh basil sauce

POELEES D'ESCARGOTS FORESTIERE
Snails sauteed with butter and fresh mushrooms

MOULES AUX HERBES
New Zealand mussels braised in wine with fresh herbs

SPECIAL DU JOUR
Special appetizer of the day

20.95
" GOURMET MENU "

Choice of cold appetizer
Choice of hot appetizer
Sorbet du jour
Choice of meat or fish entree
Salade
Choice of dessert

POULET SAUTE AU CITRON 10.95
Breast of chicken sauteed with lemons

BAVETTE DE BOEUF SAUTE A L'AIL 13.95
Sliced beef sauteed with a red wine and garlic

CANARD ROTI VIGERONNE 11.95
Roast duck with white wine and grapes

ESCALOPE DE VEAU BRAISE AU POIVRE VERT ET MORILLES 12.95
Scallops of veal braised in a green peppercorn sauce with fresh morilles

CARRE D'AGNEAU ROTI PROVENCALE 13.95
Roast rack of lamb with tomatoes, herbs, and a touch of garlic

SAUMON GRILLE AUX HERBES FRAICHES, SAUCE AUX POIVRONS 12.95
Fresh salmon grilled with herbs and bell peppers

WHITEFISH BRAISE AU CRESSON ET BLEUETS 10.95
Fresh whitefish braised in a watercress sauce with blueberries

FEUILLETE DE HOMARD ET ST. JACQUES A LA MENTHE 13.95
Fresh Maine lobster and sea scallops served in a flaky pastry shell with a mint sauce

ASSIETTE DE LEGUMES DUMARCHE 8.95
Fresh vegetable plate

POISSON ET VIANDE DU JOUR
Fish or meat special of the day

" SALADS "

SALADE D'ENDIVES AUX CREVETTES 10.95
Imported Belgian Endive salad with baby shrimp

SALADE PLEINE MER 10.95
Fresh seafood salad

SALADE DE HOMARD A L'EFFILOCHE DE LEGUMES 12.95
Fresh cold lobster salad garnished with fresh vegetables and served with an herb sauce

" SOME OLD FAVORITES "

TRIPES A LA MODE DE CAEN 11.95
Tripes braised in white wine with celery and carrots

ASSIETTE DE FROMAGES 8.95
Cheese plate

ROGNONS DE VEAU AUX CHAMPIGNONS A LA MOUTARDE 9.95
Veal kidneys braised in a mustard sauce with fresh mushrooms

FIGURE 19.2 Froggy's menu. (Reproduced by permission.)

FIGURE 19.3 Menu from Darryl's. Darryl's beer mug menu sells more. (Courtesy Filbert/Robinson, Inc.—Darryl's restaurant. Reproduced by permission.)

name Darryl's on it and the illustration of a head of a pig. The other is an apron also with the name Darryl's and the pig. There are sixteen specialties, mostly chicken and seafood entrées with pasta and a Giant Plank Pizza added for variety. Three fajitas are offered: chicken, beef, and combination.

Page 8 lists Ribs & Rib Combos and Steak & Steak Combos. There are five rib items. The combos are beef and pork ribs and chicken and ribs. Next to the rib listing Darryl's Barbeque Sauce (to take home) is offered. Seven items are listed under Steak & Steak Combos. The combos are steak with chicken, shrimp, or crab claws.

The meat entrées are continued at the top of page 9 with Prime Rib & Combos. The combinations offer prime rib with chicken, shrimp, or crab claws. The dessert list includes ten items. A notice is also given here of a Kid's Menu that is available for asking. The nonfood items on this panel are a children's T-shirt and gift certificates, available in any amount from $1 to $1,000.

Page 11 is a complete Sunday brunch menu. It begins with Quiche (two items) and continues with Specialties (breakfast entrées) and Omelettes. Notice the different breakfast items on this list:

FRENCH TOASTED CROISSANTS

Two extra-large croissants dipped in sweet cinnamon egg batter, fried to a delicate golden brown and served with sausage and bacon.

IRISH EGGS

Cream cheese potatoes topped with poached eggs and melted Old English cheese with fresh fruits and fresh biscuits.

Three alcoholic drinks are advertised on the Sunday brunch menu and eight nonalcoholic drinks are offered under the heading The Imposters. Cafe Gates (coffee with Grand Marnier, Tia Maria, and Crème de Cacao), Irish Coffee, and Jamaican and Bavarian coffees are also part of this menu. Selling the nonfood items directly from the menu provides Darryl's with an accurate accounting system so that the company can track souvenir sales. In addition, this merchandising method keeps the wait staff from having to alert customers to the availability of the items. This menu/catalog idea required only a slight graphic modification of the menu.

TAKEOUTS

The line between a restaurant and a supermarket is becoming blurred. Supermarkets sell cooked meals and other convenience food items that compete with restaurants, and the fast-food chains with their drive-through facilities make it possible to take out food with the greatest of ease. Certain types of restaurants such as delicatessens and bakery/restaurant combinations have always been strong in the takeout department, but, more and more, other types of restaurants are getting into the takeout business.

A takeout business is a relatively easy way to increase foodservice business without increasing table and counter space, but this kind of new business must be advertised and promoted. One of the most logical, as well as inexpensive, places to advertise a takeout business is on the menu.

Point-of-sale displays and signs will sell takeout service, but they tend to spoil the decor and appearance of a fine dining room. The takeout story can be told more completely, effectively, and in better taste right on the menu. Many operators do mention takeout service on their menus, often in a line at the bottom of a large menu: "Ask about our takeout service" or "All items listed on this menu are available for takeout." This is not good merchandising.

A more effective, creative advertising approach is to give the entire takeout story careful and complete treatment on the menu. The most logical place for this story is on the back cover. At present over 50 percent of all the back covers of menus are blank, a waste of good advertising space.

Using the back cover, however, means using it effectively. Sell your takeout foods as strongly as any other item. Start with a good heading: "Takeouts, Tops in Convenience." Use a subhead: "Enjoy Gourmet Foods at Home—Pick Up or Delivery Service." Then use illustrations. The easiest way to illustrate takeouts is to photograph your most popular items (or the items you would like to make popular) in their takeout containers or in the process of being packed in the containers. This is important because although the customers may be sold on your good cooking, quality ingredients, and varied and interesting cuisine, they may not know how the takeout items are packed. Thus by using packaging photographs you can overcome any consumer resistance concerning strength of packages, flavor loss, and carrying inconvenience.

Then, as in any good ad, use plenty of good copy. Describe each takeout item, list its price, tell how it is packed (paper box, tub, bucket, aluminum foil, or returnable metal container). Also list how many people each portion sold serves. Regardless of whether these same items are listed in the regular menu, it is good advertising to list them again. And even if the prices are the same as your regular menu, price repetition will not hurt. If you have delivery service, sell it too, and be sure to list your phone number prominently.

Obviously, your menu takeout story will reach only those customers who already patronize your operation. To sell the public outside your operation, you must use other advertising media, but you can still use the menu. Print your back cover menu ad story on light paper suitable for mailing, either in an envelope or as a self-mailer. This will save you money, as all of the preparation (copy, art, photos, typesetting) has already been done. All you have to pay for is printing and paper.

In fact, if you want to use the entire menu—regular listing plus takeout story—as a promotion piece, you can use the same method and print it on lightweight paper to be used as a direct mail piece.

Randall's Ribhouse in Chicago does a good job of promoting takeouts. On the back page of its regular menu and on a miniature menu printed on lighter paper and used as a handout, the following information is printed:

RANDALL'S PARTY-TIME SPECIAL

For groups of 10 or more you can order our Famous Barbequed Baby Back Ribs and Barbequed Smoked Chicken without the extras and enjoy party-time savings!

Barbequed Baby Back Ribs, only $9.95 per person

Barbequed Smoked Chicken, only $7.95 per person

Barbequed Baby Back Ribs & Chicken Combo, only $8.95 per person

$10.00 Minimum Order Per Delivery . . . $1.50 Delivery Charge

Monday–Thursday 4:30 P.M.–10:00 P.M.
Friday & Saturday 4:30 P.M.–11:00 P.M.
Sunday 4:00 P.M.–9:00 P.M.

Daily carryout orders available inside Randall's Ribhouse Restaurant, Monday–Friday 11:30 A.M.–5:00 P.M.

The Miniature Handout Menu

An economical and effective way to make your menu do more is to print a miniature, downsized version of the regular menu to hand out to customers and others to promote what the restaurant serves. This menu, printed on lightweight paper, can also be used as a mailer. It can be an exact replica of the regular menu or it can have some additions or deletions (see Figure 19.4).

The Red Lobster miniature handout menu, in addition to repeating the regular big menu items, features Party Platters To Go on a box in the center panel in these words:

PARTY PLATTERS TO GO

Anytime is the right time for Party Platters To Go. Just call your nearest Red Lobster and order appetizing arrangements of chilled shrimp, or tender sweet snow crab claws, plus an ample supply of cocktail sauce. Then pick up your Party Platter To Go in only one hour or less. It couldn't be easier or faster.

Along with platters, we have sensational seafood salads to go. Choose from crab, Maine lobster, tuna, langostino and shrimp salads.

To top it all off, order one of our delicious whole pies or cakes. Tangy, cool Key Lime Pie, creamy cheesecake or our Fudge Overboard.

Whenever you need great seafood fast, call your nearest Red Lobster and give us your order. Then pick up your Party Platter To Go in only one hour or less. Anytime is the right time for Party Platters To Go.

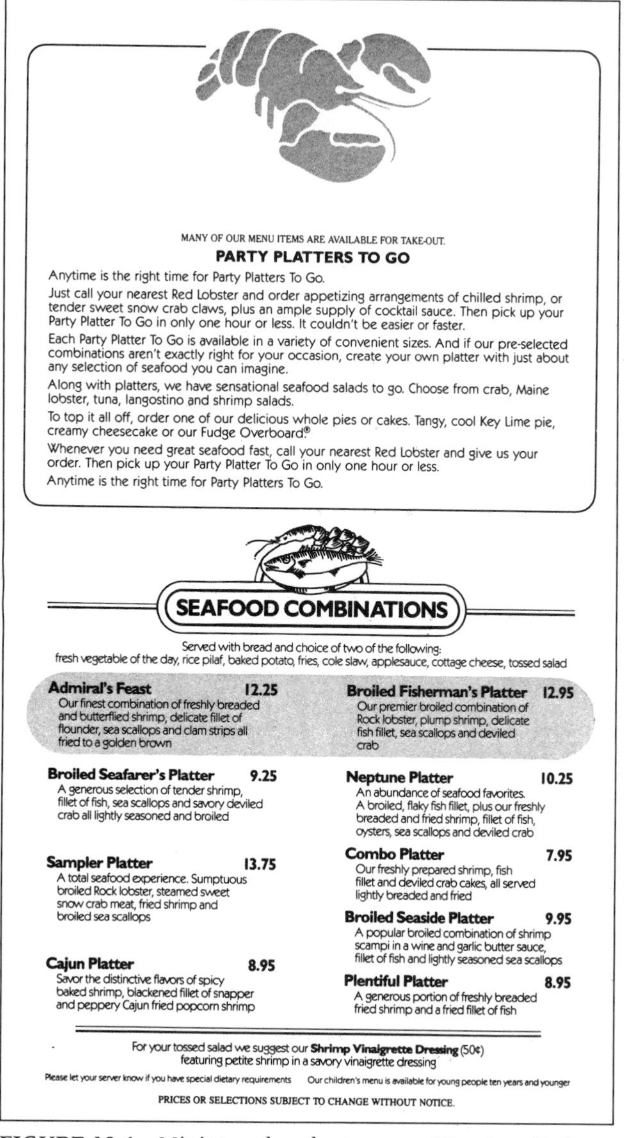
MANY OF OUR MENU ITEMS ARE AVAILABLE FOR TAKE-OUT.

PARTY PLATTERS TO GO

Anytime is the right time for Party Platters To Go.

Just call your nearest Red Lobster and order appetizing arrangements of chilled shrimp, or tender sweet snow crab claws, plus an ample supply of cocktail sauce. Then pick up your Party Platter To Go in only one hour or less. It couldn't be easier or faster.

Each Party Platter To Go is available in a variety of convenient sizes. And if our pre-selected combinations aren't exactly right for your occasion, create your own platter with just about any selection of seafood you can imagine.

Along with platters, we have sensational seafood salads to go. Choose from crab, Maine lobster, tuna, langostino and shrimp salads.

To top it all off, order one of our delicious whole pies or cakes. Tangy, cool Key Lime pie, creamy cheesecake or our Fudge Overboard®

Whenever you need great seafood fast, call your nearest Red Lobster and give us your order. Then pick up your Party Platter To Go in only one hour or less.

Anytime is the right time for Party Platters To Go.

SEAFOOD COMBINATIONS

Served with bread and choice of two of the following:
fresh vegetable of the day, rice pilaf, baked potato, fries, cole slaw, applesauce, cottage cheese, tossed salad

Admiral's Feast **12.25**
Our finest combination of freshly breaded and butterflied shrimp, delicate fillet of flounder, sea scallops and clam strips all fried to a golden brown

Broiled Fisherman's Platter **12.95**
Our premier broiled combination of Rock lobster, plump shrimp, delicate fish fillet, sea scallops and deviled crab

Broiled Seafarer's Platter **9.25**
A generous selection of tender shrimp, fillet of fish, sea scallops and savory deviled crab all lightly seasoned and broiled

Sampler Platter **13.75**
A total seafood experience. Sumptuous broiled Rock lobster, steamed sweet snow crab meat, fried shrimp and broiled sea scallops

Cajun Platter **8.95**
Savor the distinctive flavors of spicy baked shrimp, blackened fillet of snapper and peppery Cajun fried popcorn shrimp

Neptune Platter **10.25**
An abundance of seafood favorites. A broiled, flaky fish fillet, plus our freshly breaded and fried shrimp, fillet of fish, oysters, sea scallops and deviled crab

Combo Platter **7.95**
Our freshly prepared shrimp, fish fillet and deviled crab cakes, all served lightly breaded and fried

Broiled Seaside Platter **9.95**
A popular broiled combination of shrimp scampi in a wine and garlic butter sauce, fillet of fish and lightly seasoned sea scallops

Plentiful Platter **8.95**
A generous portion of freshly breaded fried shrimp and a fried fillet of fish

For your tossed salad we suggest our **Shrimp Vinaigrette Dressing** (50¢) featuring petite shrimp in a savory vinaigrette dressing

Please let your server know if you have special dietary requirements   Our children's menu is available for young people ten years and younger

PRICES OR SELECTIONS SUBJECT TO CHANGE WITHOUT NOTICE.

FIGURE 19.4 Miniature handout menu. (Courtesy Red Lobster, U.S.A. Reproduced by permission.)

20

The Drink List

For many restaurants, the bar or lounge and the wine and beverage list are important. Besides being expected by most customers, they are important contributors to the profit of the operation. Unlike food, which requires extensive preparation and a skilled chef, drinks mainly require opening a bottle or mixing various juices and alcoholic beverages. And a bartender is easier to find or train than a good chef.

But the drinking habits of Americans are changing. Restaurateurs, therefore, should be aware of these changes and respond accordingly on the drink list, at the bar, and on the menu.

Americans today are drinking less. In a North Dallas shopping center, for example, is a "beverage boutique" called High Sobriety. It serves nonalcoholic drinks such as Calistoga sparkling water from California, Chateau Yaldara (a sparking *spumonte*) from Austria, Texas Select "beer," and Carl Jung "champagne" from West Germany. It is increasingly difficult to find anyone drinking hard liquor. A fashionable watering hole in Washington, D.C., for example, now carries Moussy, a nonalcoholic beer from Switzerland. The martini, once a symbol of American drinking, is becoming an antique. The new sign of the times is the green Perrier bottle. White wine seems to be the favorite alcoholic beverage in many restaurants, and even high tea is being served in some restaurants and hotels.

A recent poll conducted for *Time* by Yankelovich, Skelly and White, Inc., showed that only 67 percent of the nation's 170 million adults over eighteen said that they drank at all. And a third of them said that they have cut back their consumption over the past few years. Only 6 percent said that they drank more.

This is a reversal of a long-standing American trend. By 1830, when we were opening the frontier and heading west, annual alcoholic consumption was seven gallons per capita—nearly three times the present level. When Prohibition ended in 1933, after a fourteen-year drinking hiatus, Americans began drinking less in bars and more in their living rooms. The cocktail party became a common social event, and the two-martini business lunch was part of entertaining clients.

Today, water snobbery is replacing wine snobbery in some eating and drinking places. Customers order water by brand name as they once did scotch. Evian is Hollywood's chic drink, and the hottest liquid refresher of all is Cit-Jet, a pressurized can of lemon juice from France. It also has become unpopular with business people to drink alcoholic beverages at lunch.

The force behind this drinking change seems to be the 76 million baby boomers of the post-World War II era. They tend to be two-income households with less time for drinking and none for hangovers, and greater awareness of the potential hazards of alcohol. Between 1974 and 1984 consumption of distilled spirits fell from 2.88 gallons per adult to 2.46 gallons. And brewers also registered a slight decline in consumption, from 36.9 gallons per person in 1957 to 35 gallons in 1984 despite the introduction of beers with lower alcoholic content.

Although they are cutting down on quantity, drinkers are more aware of quality. This is especially evident in the wine industry. Customers have become more sophisticated about wines and vintages. Even though they drink less, they drink a better, more expensive wine.

Various marketing strategies are being tried by the wineries. St. Regis, for example, has introduced a nonalcoholic vintage that has been compared with Chenin Blanc. And wine coolers have been successful, capturing about 5 to 8 percent of the wine market. They are carbonated mixtures of wine and fruit juices that have only half the alcohol content of wine, although they often contain substantial amounts of sugar.

A new wine that has appeared since 1972 is the so-called blush wine, made from red grapes such as Zinfandel or Pinot Noir but kept a pale, salmon pink by removing the skins, pulp, and seeds from the juice before they darken the liquid. The result is a wine that tastes like a white but lacks the flowery bouquet of a rosé.

As customers drink less and new laws discourage happy hours, restaurant managers are pushing food to make up for lost liquor revenues. The China Rose restaurant in Arlington, Texas, for example, replaced its happy hour with a 24-foot-long buffet stacked with Kung Pao chicken, Szechwan fish, and egg rolls to keep customers at the bar. The Long Beach Hyatt Regency Hotel features a "fruit of the month" at the juice bar. Many restaurant and hotel bars serve and list a selection of appetizers along with their drink listing. And many potent alcoholic drinks are limited to one per customer.

Many restaurant operators who depend on their beverage sales for a substantial portion of their profits must therefore increase food prices or find some other sources of income for their operation. Different drinks might be merchandised, particularly sweet dessert-type drinks. At 104 TGI Friday's restaurants around the country, for example, the most popular drink is the Pineapple Fling (lime Calistoga water and fruit juices). At the Hyatt Hotel in San Francisco the favorite is "Remember the Oreo" (crème de cacao, ice cream, and Oreo cookies).

High tea, as in England, is also beginning to catch on. Rather than gathering at the bar at the cocktail hour, business people are collecting in hotel lobbies for tea. The Breakers in Palm Beach, Florida, and the Mansion in Dallas offer decaffeinated Darjeeling tea and sandwiches. At the Ritz-Carlton in Boston, men and women discuss business deals after hours while drinking a variety of teas steeped in floral china pots. New York's Waldorf Astoria has reinstated its tea service. At San Francisco's Four Seasons Clift Hotel there is also a tea service, but some of the customers add a glass of wine to the service, to create a kind of California tea.

The catering business has also felt the impact of the decline in liquor consumption. One New York City caterer, Donald Bruce White, estimates that three-quarters of his clients now drink white wine. A San Francisco Bay caterer, Joe Toboni, who has five catering outlets, reports that hard liquor now accounts for only 10 percent of his business; five years ago it made up 70 percent. Wine and beer make up an additional 65 percent, with the rest bottled water. And out of 300 wedding guests, 250 drink wine. The other 50, mainly older people, drink hard liquor.

The trend toward light and less is also evident in other countries. In France, for example, the consumption of table wine is down, and such drinks as Diabolo Menthe (mint-flavored carbonated lemonade) and Brut de Pomme (a cider) are the latest drinks at sidewalk cafes. But even though the consumption of cheap table wines has gone down, the demand for more expensive wines and champagnes has continued strong.

A wine list is frequently part of the menu, but a beer list as large as the wine list and given the same importance is unusual. The Bowery restaurant in Traverse City, Michigan, however, does have such a beer list (Figure 20.1). It includes fifty-five different beers from Australia, Canada, China, Czechoslovakia, Denmark, England, France, Germany, Holland, Ireland, Jamaica, Japan, Mexico, New Zealand, the Philippines, Poland, Scotland, Sweden, Switzerland, and the United States. Prices for these beers (per bottle) range from $1.50 to $4.00.

Spinnaker's Restaurant's Hot Time Summer Coolers

The drink menu, roughly 9 by 9 inches (Figure 20.2), is die-cut in the form of an open ice chest. It is printed in four colors on coated stock. The chest is blue, the titles of the drinks are red, and the descriptions and prices are black. There are eight alcoholic drinks plus a selection of shakes and lemonade.

The drinks offered are imaginative and interesting. One is a Schnapps Spritz that has this description: "Cool down with your choice of Peppermint or Peach Schnapps mixed with an effervescence of fruit juices." Another is called Beach Blanket Bingo: "A taste of Kahlua and more served the old fashioned milk shake way." The Fireball is a hot Cinnamon Schnapps drink. Prices for these beverages range from $2.85 to $3.50. The shakes are $1.99, and the lemonade is 99¢.

The Spinnaker group has more than fifteen operating restaurants located at major entryways to regional shopping malls. These restaurants have about an 80/20 food-to-liquor mix. The food menu has approximately 120 items, all made from scratch. The restaurants make their own breads and desserts and squeeze their own juices.

Menu items and prices are changed every twelve to fifteen months. The Hot Time Summer Coolers drink menu alternates with a winter drink menu. The Spinnaker restaurants employ an advertising agency to design and write their menus, which also are used as table tents to merchandise the drinks to diners.

DINING AT THE BAR

At the more expensive or more stylish restaurants, the bar has been a place just to drink or simply a place to wait for a dinner partner or a table. Today, however, there is a different way to combine food and drink. It is dining at the bar.

At the bar at Aurora, an elegant restaurant in Manhattan, customers can eat smoked and marinated salmon, warm tart Provençal filled with rare tuna, onion and port wine soup, and cured chicken breasts with clusters of salad greens. Instead of a basket of pretzels or peanuts, a bowl of shaved celeryroot chips is on the marble-topped bar. According to Joseph Baum, owner

Wine

	Carafe	½ Carafe	Glass
HOUSE SELECTIONS			
DOMESTIC			
Inglenook Chablis	$ 8.50	$4.75	$2.00
Inglenook Zinfandel	$ 9.50	$5.25	$2.25
Sebastiani White Zinfandel	$10.50	$5.75	$2.75
IMPORTED			
A. Huesgen Piesporter Michelsberg	$10.50	$5.75	$2.75
Riunite Lambrusco	$ 9.50	$5.25	$2.25
Dourthe Rouge	$10.50	$5.75	$2.75
Dourthe Blanc	$10.50	$5.75	$2.75

	Bottle	½ Bottle	Split
BOTTLED WINES			
UNITED STATES			
Fetzer Zinfandel	$12.00		
Inglenook Estate Cabernet Sauvignon	$15.00	$8.00	
Beringer Estate Cabernet Sauvignon	$16.00		
Lambert Bridge Merlot	$17.00		
Robert Mondavi Red Table Wine	$11.00		
Robert Mondavi White Table Wine	$11.00		
Firestone Johannisberg Riesling	$14.00		
Foppiano Sauvignon Blanc	$14.00		
Fetzer Sundial Chardonnay	$15.00	$8.00	
Lambert Bridge Chardonnay	$18.00		
Bel Arbres White Zinfandel	$12.00		
GERMANY			
Heinrich Hilss Johannisberg Riesling	$11.00		
FRANCE			
Georges Duboeuf Beaujolais Village	$13.00		
Chateau Laroque St. Emillion	$16.00		
Chateau Mouton-Cadet Red	$14.00		
Chateau Mouton-Cadet White	$14.00		
Georges Duboeuf Saint Veran	$13.00		
MICHIGAN			
Good Harbor Johannisberg Riesling	$12.00		
Chateau Grand Traverse Chardonnay	$17.00		
Good Harbor Trillium	$11.00		
SPARKLING WINES			
Freixenet Cordon Negro Champagne	$12.00		$4.50
Sperone Asti Spumante	$12.00		$4.50

Beer

AUSTRALIA	
*Foster's Lager	$4.00
*Tooth's KB Lager	$4.00
CANADA	
Bulldog Lager	$2.50
Cinci	$1.75
Labatt's	$2.00
Labatt's Ale	$2.00
Labatt's Light	$2.00
Molson Golden Ale	$2.00
Molson Light	$2.00
Moosehead	$2.50
CHINA	
Tsing-Tao	$2.50
CZECHOSLOVAKIA	
Pilsner Urquell	$2.75
DENMARK	
Carlsberg	$2.75
Carlsberg Elephant	$2.75
ENGLAND	
Bass Pale Ale	$2.75
Newcastle Brown Ale	$2.75
Watney's	$2.75
FRANCE	
Kronenbourg	$2.50
*Fischer La Belle	$4.00
GERMANY	
Beck's	$2.50
Beck's Dark	$2.50
Dortmunder Union	$2.75
Dortmunder Union Dark	$2.75
Hacker-Pschor München	$2.50
Hacker-Pschor Weiss	$3.25
Kulmbacher	$3.75
St. Pauli Girl	$2.50
St. Pauli Girl Dark	$2.50
HOLLAND	
Brand	$2.50
Heineken	$2.50
Heineken Dark	$2.50
Grolsch	$3.75
IRELAND	
Guinness Stout	$2.50
Harp Lager	$2.50
JAMAICA	
Red Stripe	$2.75
JAPAN	
Kirin	$2.50
*Sapporo	$4.00
MEXICO	
Carta Blanca	$2.50
Corona	$2.50
Dos Equis XX	$2.50
NEW ZEALAND	
Steinlager	$2.75
PHILIPPINES	
San Miguel	$2.50
San Miguel Dark	$2.50
POLAND	
Krakus	$2.25
SCOTLAND	
McEwan's Scotch Ale	$2.75
SWEDEN	
Nordik Wolf Light	$2.50
SWITZERLAND	
Lowenbräu Zurich	$2.50
UNITED STATES	
Augsburger	$1.75
Coors	$1.50
Dempsey's Ale	$2.00
Michelob	$1.50
Michelob Light	$1.50
Miller	$1.50
Stroh's Signature	$1.50
ON TAP	
Budweiser	$1.25
Miller Light	$1.25
Molson	$1.50

*Beer for two (22-25 ounces.)

FIGURE 20.1 The Bowery's wine and beer list. (Courtesy Schelde Enterprises, Inc. Reproduced by permission.)

FIGURE 20.2 Drink list for Spinnaker's Restaurant. Hot Summer Coolers are sold on this unusual drink list. (Courtesy Spinnaker's Restaurant. Reproduced by permission.)

of the Aurora, "Eating used to be an excuse to drink. Now it's the other way around; it's fashionable to eat at a bar."

Other restaurants serve food at the bar in New York City, including the Union Square Café, Palio, Sign of the Dove, and Toscana. In San Francisco, the Washington Square Bar & Grill serves meals at the bar. Eating at the bar has advantages, one of which is price. Another is that liquor sales are sure to be stimulated. Also, it is easy and sociable for the customer to eat alone at the bar, and he or she does not take up a table for two to four.

The food offered at these bars tends to be simple. Sauces are eliminated, and spices and herbs are accented. Most of the food can be cut with a fork and is made to be eaten with one hand.

Some of the bar menu includes traditional bar fare such as salads, sandwiches, and soup. But the fare can also be more sophisticated. It can include a fresh vegetable salad or a sandwich of wine-soaked sausages on sourdough bread. Many of the items may seem like appetizers, but a meal can be assembled from small dishes of oysters, deep-fried calamari with graham cracker crumbs and anchovy mayonnaise, antipasto Toscano (a plate with melted scamorza cheese in the center, surrounded by roasted vegetables and a pear onion compote), or bruschetta (grilled bread topped with chopped tomatoes, basil, and garlic). At the Washington Square Bar & Grill a popular dish is the omelette with pesto.

Patrons eating at a bar do not always order just a cold beer but are likely to sample several wines or champagne as well as an appetizer, a main course, and a dessert.

THE DRINK LIST (BESIDE THE POINTE BAR)

The average drink list, as distinguished from a wine list, lists standard cocktails such as the Manhattan, martini, and bloody Mary, but the bar of Beside the Pointe in Phoenix, Arizona, has a much more imaginative offering. Under the heading Specialty Drinks are Peaches and Cream—peach-flavored liqueur, white crème de cacao, and cream garnished with a peach; Rangoon Ruby—pineapple, coconut, vodka, and cherry brandy; Jogger's Nog—pineapple juice, rum, yogurt, honey, and crushed ice served with a pineapple slice; and Vanishing Pointe—Salud Grande, martini, 6 ounces, garnished with three large olives, $5.95. This is the only price listed on this menu.

Some of the vanilla ice cream-blended drinks are Dreamsycle—vodka, orange sherbet, and orange juice served with orange slices; Sugar and Spice—iced coffee, nutmeg, cinnamon, and coffee liqueur with raisins; Peanut Butter and Jelly—grape jelly, smooth peanut butter, and rum or vodka blended smooth and topped with whipped cream; Root Beer Float—coffee liqueur, Galliano, and cola served in a beer mug; Lactio Grasshopper—crème de menthe and crème de cacao garnished with a mint leaf; Banana Split—banana liqueur, white crème de menthe, and crème de cacao served with banana, whipped cream, and cherry.

The Hot Drinks served in the Toucan Bar are Hot Nuts—Coffee and amaretto garnished with whipped cream; Liquid Girl Scout Cookie—white crème de menthe, white crème de cacao, brandy, and coffee topped with whipped cream and a Girl Scout Cookie (in season); Irish Tea—peach-flavored brandy, Irish whiskey, and brewed tea topped with whipped cream and peach; Orange Spice Tea—tea and rum with cinnamon stick; Orange Tea Amaretto—served with cinnamon stick; Espresso—Italy's finest; and Cappuccino—California style with eleven blended liqueurs.

This drink list measures (roughly) 7 by 12 inches. It is die-cut in the shape of a toucan (Figure 20.3). The bird itself is a colorful illustration printed on both the front and back covers. The listings inside are printed in black. The listing is headed Get a Beakful. Regarding the toucan, the following is written:

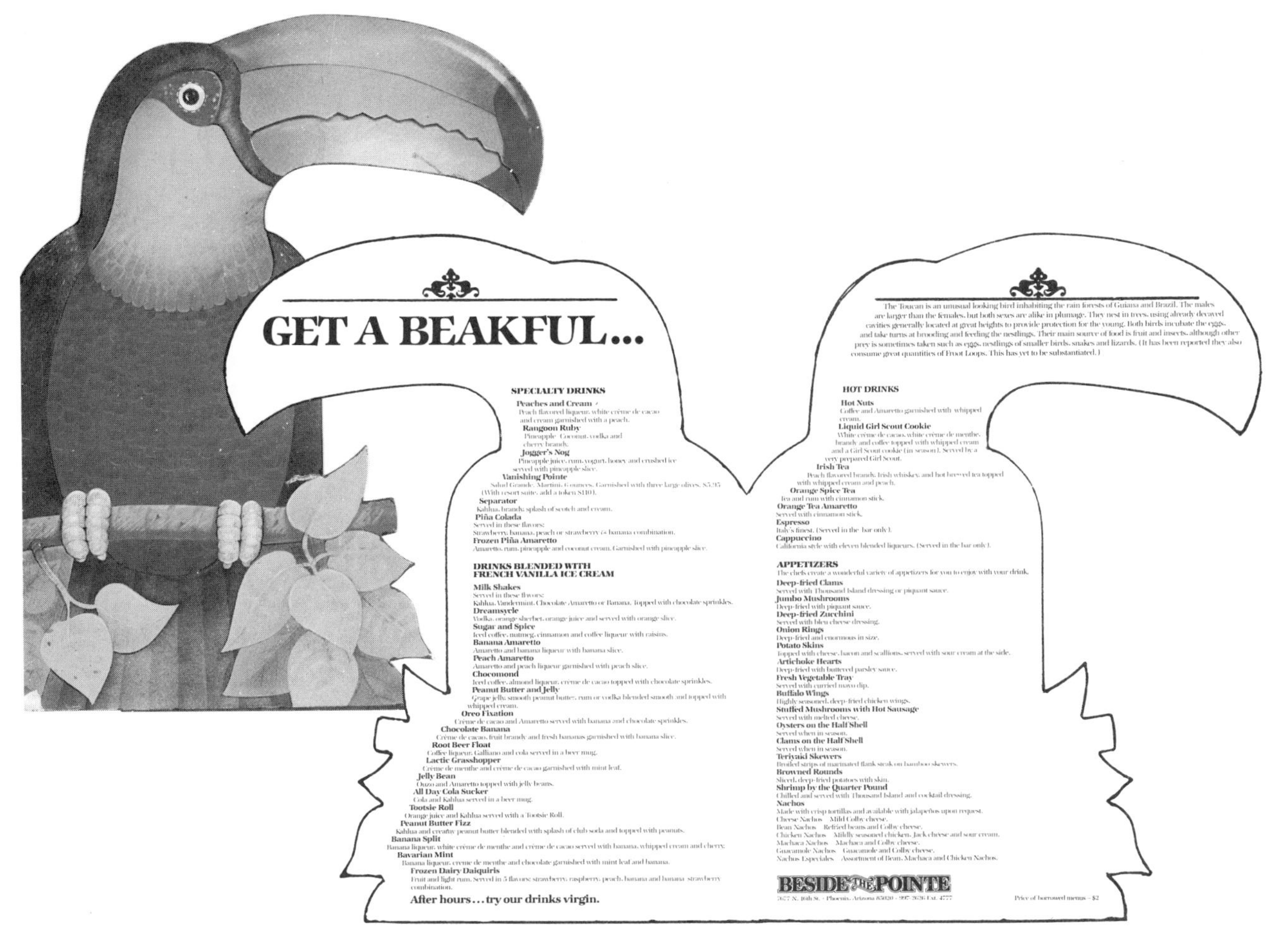

FIGURE 20.3 A clever and creative drink list from Beside the Pointe. (Courtesy Beside the Pointe. Reproduced by permission.)

The Toucan is an unusual looking bird inhabiting the rain forests of Guiana and Brazil. The males are larger than the females, but both sexes are alike in plumage. They nest in trees, using already decayed cavities generally located at great heights to provide protection for the young. Both birds incubate the eggs and take turns at brooding and feeding the nestlings. Their main source of food is fruit and insects, although prey is sometimes taken such as eggs, nestlings of smaller birds, snakes and lizards. (It has been reported they also consume great quantities of Froot Loops. This has yet to be substantiated.)

MERCHANDISING COFFEE ON THE MENU

Coffee originated in the Middle East, probably in Yemen. According to one legend, a goatherd named Kaldi noticed that his sleepy goats began to prance around excitedly after chewing certain berries. He tried the berries himself and enjoyed the stimulus they gave him. At first, coffee berries were eaten whole. Later, a kind of wine was made with the fermented pulp. The practice of roasting the beans began in the thirteenth century, and by the fourteenth century, coffee was popular throughout the Middle East.

Coffee entered Europe through Italy in the seventeenth century. At first it was opposed as a "drink of infidels," but Pope Clement VIII tried it and is reported to have said, "Why, this Satan's drink is so delicious that it would be a pity to let the infidels have exclusive use of it. We shall fool Satan by baptizing it, and making it a truly Christian beverage." Coffee reached France and England later. The first coffee house opened in England in 1650, and by 1789 there were over two thousand in London alone.

At first, the American colonies followed England in drinking tea, although coffee was served in some seventeenth-century American taverns. But after the Boston Tea Party, drinking coffee became an act of patriotism. Today, coffee consumption in the United States is about 2.4 cups per day per person, or around 25 gallons per year. This is less than the per-capita consumption of milk and soft drinks but still a considerable factor for the restaurant menu.

One way of gauging a restaurant's quality is by the coffee it serves. One of the reasons people dine out is to get something different, and a restaurant can offer coffee in many unusual ways. Some specialty coffees are described in the following list.

Café au Lait. This traditional French coffee is made by simultaneously pouring equal amounts of strong coffee and hot milk into cups or bowls. In France, café au lait is usually accompanied by croissants.

Viennese Coffee. This is extra-strong coffee with milk added to taste and served with a large dollop of sweetened whipped cream.

Spiced Coffee. Brewed with cloves, allspice, and stick cinnamon, this coffee is served in wineglasses and topped with whipped cream and nutmeg.

Espresso. Authentic espresso is brewed in an espresso machine that forces steam and boiling water through finely ground roast coffee.

Cappuccino. Espresso coffee is served with steamed, frothy milk.

Chocolaccino. Cappuccino is served in a tall cup or glass topped with whipped cream and shaved semisweet chocolate.

Caffe Fantasia. Equal quantities of hot coffee and hot chocolate are poured over a slice of orange and topped with whipped cream and cinnamon.

Coffee can be promoted, merchandised, and made into an "extra-profit" item, or it can be taken for granted. Following are some examples of how restaurants feature coffee on their menus.

Zims

Zims, a group of restaurants in San Francisco, has a separate, small coffee menu, with fourteen different coffee and alcoholic drink combinations. For example, Calipso Coffee is light rum, Tía María, and coffee; Mediterranean Coffee combines Metaxa and Galliano with mocha; and Ring-a-Ding Coffee is Christian Brothers brandy, cream, a special syrup, and a garnish of cinnamon stick, cloves, and orange.

The Golden Lion

Coffee can not only be combined with whiskey, brandy, or liqueurs, it can also be flamed for a dramatic presentation. The Golden Lion restaurant in the Olympic Hotel in Seattle lists four special coffee drinks under a Flaming Delights heading on its dessert menu: Irish Coffee with Irish Whiskey, Spanish Coffee with Brandy and Kahlua, Brazilian Coffee with Cointreau and Grand Marnier, and Wellington Coffee with Rum and Coconut Syrup.

Scottsdale Princess

La Hacienda restaurant in the Scottsdale Princess resort gives equal billing to a selection of interesting coffees on its dessert menu: Café Mexicano with Tequila, Kahlua, and whipped cream; Café Isla de Mujeres—a rich blend of dark rum and Tía María; Café Hacienda—Kahlua, Galliano, Brandy, and Grand Marnier; Acapulco Princess Café—a triple crown of Baileys, Frangelico, and Grand Marnier; Café Keoke—Brandy, Kahlua, and Crème de Cocoa; Café Español—Brandy, Tía María, and whipped cream.

BEER

Like wine, beer is beginning to be more appreciated in America. Unfortunately, in the past fifty years in the United States, the variety of locally brewed ales, beers, and stouts has largely disappeared and been replaced by industrialized beers devoid of character and identifiable less by taste than by advertising and packaging. Some regional breweries have managed to keep a few old favorites alive, and some of these deserve to be better known. But, while beer may have its aristocrats, it is basically a peasant drink, healthy and satisfying.

The origins of beer are lost in the darkness of prehistory. Possibly some ancient experimenter discovered that wild barley, when soaked, became a mush that fermented on contact with natural microorganisms. Diluted, it made a beverage that not only tasted good but made the drinker feel good.

Documents from Mesopotamia dating back to 6000 B.C. describe the preparation of a fermented beverage for sacrificial purposes. By 4000 B.C. Babylonians brewed at least sixteen varieties of beer with malted barley and spelt (a form of wheat) as the fermentable material plus honey as an important flavoring agent.

There is a relationship between baking bread and brewing beer. Both are made from grain, water, and yeast. In ancient Egypt beer was brewed from partially baked bread made from germinated barley, a method still used in Russia to make a drink known as *kvass*. The bread was soaked in water and allowed to ferment through contact with airborne yeasts. The mixture was then strained to remove the solids and was ready to drink at once.

Hops also may have been used to temper beer in ancient Egypt, and herbs were probably also used for this purpose. Date juice was used for sweetening. The Egyptians may have also known how to control yeasts.

The Greeks and Romans learned brewing from the Egyptians. Beer was particularly popular in the Roman Empire. It was described by Tacitus and praised by Julius Caesar. From the Romans the art of brewing spread to the barbarians of northern and western Europe. There beer was made from barley or wheat and sweetened with honey.

It is impossible to determine exactly when the beverage approximating modern beer appeared, but it certainly could be found in Europe in the Middle Ages. The essential element was the use of the hop as the dominant flavoring agent, which gives beer its characteristic bitterness and makes it more thirst-quenching. It is known that hops were cultivated in Germany and France by the ninth century, but British ale was drunk without the benefit of hops until Tudor times. And to this day it is possible to find beers in Scandinavia flavored with juniper berries.

Beer was brewed at home, at court, and in monasteries. Its value as a drink was enhanced by the fact that water supplies were not always pure, and fermentation destroyed many malignant microorganisms. Nearly everybody in Europe drank beer—even children.

Beer came early to America with the Pilgrims. The *Mayflower* had barrels of good English ale on board and the making of beer began soon after the Pilgrims landed. The Dutch at New Amsterdam were brewing beer by 1612. This beer or ale, like that of Germany, England, Holland, and Denmark at this time, was made with top-fermenting yeast which rises to the surface during fermentation. This method was used in America until the end of the nineteenth century.

Another yeast, however, sank to the bottom when fermenting and produced a very different beer. But more critical conditions are required for this style of brewing. The fermentation must take place at a low temperature, and to mature properly the beer must be stored for weeks or months in a cool place. Cool caves in Bavaria and Bohemia were used for this purpose. With the introduction of refrigeration this type of lager could be made anywhere.

Louis Pasteur's studies of yeast cultures and the fermentation process helped to put brewing on a scientific basis. Great brewmasters like Gabriel Sadlmeyer in Munich and Anton Dreher in Vienna placed the production of lager beers on a solid technological basis. Another great brewmaster, Frantisek Poupe, a Czech, created a very popular beer in the town of Pilsen, Czechoslovakia. Called Pilsner after the town, it was introduced in 1842. It was pale in color, well-hopped, carbonated, and refreshing. This beer is very much like Beck's or Michelob. The wave of immigration of Germans and Bohemians brought this new Pilsner to America. Excellent ales are still produced in Canada and the United States today.

The golden age of American brewing was from 1870 to 1919. American brewers rivaled their European peers in variety, quality, and even quantity. In 1890 there were ninety-four breweries in Philadelphia, seventy-seven in New York, thirty-eight in Brooklyn, forty-one in Chicago, and twenty-one in Boston. These plants produced a basic Pilsner plus a variety of other brews either top fermented or bottom fermented.

The period after the repeal of Prohibition has only one new creation to its credit—the invention of the beer can in 1935.

Willie C's Cafe

This Passport Beer List gives as much importance to beer as the best wine list gives to wine (Figure 20.4). It is a two-fold, three-panel list with each panel measuring 5 by 9 inches. It is printed in dark green, magenta, and beige on a buff, uncoated stock. The cover is an around-the-world passport to the great beers of the world at Willie C's Cafe.

Inside are listed beers from Belgium, Canada, China, Czechoslovakia, Down Under, England, France, Italy, Germany, Holland, Ireland, Japan, Kenya, the Philippines, Scandinavia, Scotland, South-of-the-Border, Switzerland, and the United States. The list for each country is not small—there are twenty-one different beers from Germany, fifteen from England, and twenty from the United States.

On the first back panel are the following definitions of "Draughty" Terms.

ALE. Brewed by the older, top-fermented process, ale is produced and aged at higher temperatures than lager (bottom-fermented) types. Its characteristic malt flavor, full palate, and vinous qualities result from the use of top-fermenting yeast. Ale is darker and more highly hopped than most lagers.

BEER. A fermented beverage made from malted cereal grain such as barley, wheat, rice, and others, in addition to hops, yeast, and water.

BOCK. This heavy, usually dark beer tastes slightly sweet and malty with a strong flavor of hops. Traditionally brewed in the winter for spring consumption, bock takes its name from the German city of Einbeck, where it was first brewed. Labels almost invariably include the figure of a billy goat—"bock" in German.

DOPPLEBOCK. The strongest, darkest beer of Germany, it is thick and rich with a long-lasting head. Brand names of dopplebock almost always end with the suffix "-ator."

DRY. Dry beers produce bold tastes that do not linger. Aftertaste is minimal or nonexistent. Dry brewing techniques usually take longer than other methods, and in the process the yeast consumes more of the natural sugars produced by the fermenting grain. Dries would never be called "sweet."

LAGER. A generic term for bottom-fermented beer, "lager" is derived from the German word for store, or age. It is produced and aged at a temperature of close to freezing, much colder than beers of the top-fermented process. The worldwide popularity of lager is due to its clarity and smoothness.

DARK LAGER. Originating in Munich, this full-bodied beer tastes sweet, malty, and slightly hoppy. It is generally more aromatic and creamier in texture than a light lager.

LIGHT LAGER. Characteristically pale gold in color and light-bodied, these lagers are fairly high in carbonation with a slight hop flavor and mellow dryness.

LIGHT BEER. For our purposes, and those of many brewers, the term "light beer" is used to designate one of lower calorie count.

MALT LIQUOR. In general, this brew is in the bottom-fermented style, tastes maltier than typical lagers, and contains a higher percentage of alcohol than other types.

PILSNER. Hailing from Pilsen, Bohemia (now known as Czechoslovakia), this lager-type beer in its true form has a slightly tannic character, with an emphasis on hops. Aged in wood, it glows with golden color and is traditionally the palest of all lagers.

PORTER. Originally brewed in England to satisfy the demand for a 50/50 mix of ale and stout, porter's dark brown hue comes from roasting the barley before the brewing process begins. It possesses a less pronounced hop flavor than ale, and is a heavier brew than most beers, with just a hint of sweetness.

STOUT. Similar to porter, but less sweet, stout is a dark, heavy, top-fermented beer with a rich, malty flavor and bitter hops taste. It is low to medium in carbonation and traditionally served at cellar temperature.

WEISS (WHEAT) BEER. This German brewing style substitutes wheat for barley, in a process that lends it a distinctive, yeasty aroma. Generally light in hops and heavy in carbonation, wheat beer's creamy appearance and texture are topped by a rich, foamy head.

On the center back panel, Willie C's Cafe merchandises beer in this way:

AROUND THE WORLD

Join Willie C's "Around the World" Club by sampling beer from eighteen of the countries represented on our beer list. Not all in one sitting, of course. When you've completed your excursion through our beer list, Willie C's will buy you dinner! What's more, we'll engrave your name on a brass plaque in a place of honor in the bar.

Thereafter, with each successive trip, you may select from any number of rewards: a free meal, a ball cap, another plaque, a souvenir, or even one of our coveted tee-shirts emblazoned with the flags of eighteen countries.

Those of you who truly love beer will want to explore our "100 Beer Club." The name says it all—an exclusive club reserved for those broad-minded people who've tried a full one hundred of Willie's worldwide beers. You'll recognize these intrepid beer-lovers by the distinctive satin jackets Willie gave them after their centennial brew.

Your server or bartender will be happy to start you toward membership in either club. There is no admission charge.

Bon Voyage!

"DRAUGHTY" TERMS

ALE A Brewed by the older, top-fermented process, ale is produced and aged at higher temperatures than lager (bottom-fermented) types. Its characteristic malt flavor, full palate and vinous qualities result from the use of top-fermenting yeast. Ale is darker and more highly hopped than most lagers.

BEER A fermented beverage made from malted cereal grain such as barley, wheat, rice and others, in addition to hops, yeast and water. Generally conceded to be the eighth wonder of the world.

BOCK B This heavy, usually dark beer tastes slightly sweet and malty with a strong flavor of hops. Traditionally brewed in the winter for spring consumption, bock takes its name from the German city of Einbeck, where it was first brewed. Labels almost invariably include the figure of a billy goat — "bock" in German.

DOPPLEBOCK DB The strongest, darkest beer of Germany, it is thick and rich with a long-lasting head. Brand names of dopplebock almost always end with the suffix "-ator."

DRY D Dry beers produce bold tastes that do not linger. Aftertaste is minimal or non-existent. Dry brewing techniques usually take longer than other methods, and in the process the yeast consumes more of the natural sugars produced by the fermenting grain. Dries would never be called "sweet."

LAGER A generic term for bottom-fermented beer, "lager" is derived from the German word for store, or age. It is produced and aged at a temperature of close to freezing, much colder than beers of the top-fermented process. The worldwide popularity of lager is due to its clarity and smoothness.

DARK LAGER DL Originating in Munich, this full-bodied beer tastes sweet, malty and slightly hoppy. It is generally more aromatic and creamier in texture than a light lager.

LIGHT LAGER LL Characteristically pale gold in color and light-bodied, these lagers are fairly high in carbonation with a slight hop flavor and mellow dryness.

LIGHT BEER LB For our purposes, and those of many brewers, the term "light beer" is used to designate one of lower calorie content.

MALT LIQUOR ML In general, this brew is in the bottom-fermented style, tastes maltier than typical lagers and contains a higher percentage of alcohol than other types.

PILSNER P Hailing from Pilsen, Bohemia (now known as Czechoslovakia), this lager-style beer in its true form has a slightly tannic character, with an emphasis on hops. Aged in wood, it glows with golden color and is traditionally the palest of all lagers.

PORTER PR Originally brewed in England to satisfy the demand for a 50/50 mix of ale and stout, porter's dark brown hue comes from roasting the barley before the brewing process begins. It possesses a less pronounced hop flavor than ale, and is a heavier brew than most, with just a hint of sweetness.

STOUT S Similar to porter, but less sweet, stout is a dark, heavy, top-fermented beer with a rich, malty flavor and bitter hops taste. It is low to medium in carbonation and traditionally served at cellar temperature.

WEISS (WHEAT) BEER W This German brewing style substitutes wheat for barley, in a process that lends it a distinctive, yeasty aroma. Generally light in hops and heavy in carbonation, wheat beer's creamy appearance and texture are topped by a rich, foamy head.

"AROUND THE WORLD"

Join Willie C's "Around the World" Club by sampling beer from eighteen of the countries represented on our beer list. Not all in one sitting, of course. When you've completed your excursion through our beer list, Willie C's will buy you dinner! What's more, we'll engrave your name on a brass plaque in a place of honor in the bar.

Thereafter, with each successive trip, you may select from any number of rewards: a free meal, a ball cap, another plaque, a souvenir, or even one of our coveted tee-shirts emblazoned with the flags of eighteen countries.

Those of you who truly love beer will want to explore our "100 Beer Club." The name says it all—an exclusive club reserved for those broad-minded people who've tried a full one hundred of Willie's worldwide beers. You'll recognize these intrepid beer-lovers by the distinctive satin jackets Willie gave them after their centennial brew.

Your server or bartender will be happy to start you toward membership in either club. There is no admission charge.

Bon Voyage!

Willie C's Cafe AND BAR

Kellogg at West St.
942-4077

Towne East Mall
686-0753

Sources: Beers of North America, Bill Yenne, 1986
The Connoisseur's Guide to Beer, Dr. James D. Robinson, 1982
The Pocket Guide to Beer, Michael Jackson, 1982
The World Guide to Beer, Michael Jackson, 1977

AROUND THE WORLD

Willie C's Cafe AND BAR

PASSPORT

The great beers of the world are at home at Willie C's Cafe and Bar, proud pourer of the largest selection of imported beers in the state.

If it's made with hops, grain, yeast, and one or the other of the world's waters, chances are excellent that we're serving it. Great beer is where you find it.

You've found yours at Willie C's.

BEER

Belgium The tradition of small breweries, many of them in Trappist monasteries, refines the top fermenting process to a level approaching art, earning Belgium its well-deserved reputation for fine, distinctive ales.

- Bios Copper Ale A
- Chimay Grande Reserve, 25 oz. A
- Chimay Red Label A
- Chimay White Label, 25 oz. A
- Duvel Ale A
- Sezoens Ale A

Canada Canada boasts North America's oldest, continuously operating brewery - Molson - and the brand that is second only to Heineken in exports to the U.S. - also Molson.

- Bulldog Lager LL
- Brown's Beer LL
- F & A LL
- Labatts Beer P
- Labatts 50 A
- Labatts Light LB
- Molson Ale A
- Molson Canadian LB
- Molson Golden LL
- Molson Light LL
- Moosehead LL in bottle or on draught
- Moosehead Light LB

China Most of the Chinese beer exported to the U.S. is of the German bottom-fermented style, being fairly dry with a "hoppy" character.

- Hua Nan LL
- Sweet China LL
- Tsingtao P

Czechoslovakia Home of the original Pilsner, Czechoslovakia has a brewing history spanning at least five hundred years. It is most noted for its crystal clear, somewhat bitter, Pilsner-style beers.

- Pilsner Urquell P

Down Under Noted more for their beer drinkers than their beers, most of the brews produced in these island nations are pale lagers with a tendency to be full-bodied and sweetish rather than malty.

- Broken Hill LB
- Coopers Big Barrel, 25 oz. LL (Australia)
- Coopers Real Ale A (Australia)
- Coopers Real Ale, 25 oz. A (Australia)
- Coopers Lager, 25 oz. LB (Australia)
- Fosters Lager, 12 oz. or 25 oz. LL (Australia)
- Old Australia Stout S (Australia)
- Steinlager, 12 oz. or 25 oz. LL (New Zealand)

England With over one-hundred-fifty breweries and more than a thousand types of beer, including four-hundred draught ales, it goes without saying that Great Britain is known as the Ale Capital of the world. But we said it anyway.

- Bass Pale Ale A in bottle or on draught
- London Light LB in bottle or on draught
- Mackeson Stout S
- Marksman Lager LL
- Samuel Smith's Imperial Stout S
- Samuel Smith's Nut Brown Ale A
- Samuel Smith's Oatmeal Stout S
- Samuel Smith's Old Brewery Pale Ale A
- Samuel Smith's Taddy Porter PR
- Watney's Red Barrel DL in bottle or on draught
- Watney's Cream Stout S
- Whitbread Ale A

France and Italy Even though noted more for their wines than beers, France and Italy have brewing histories that date back to the thirteenth century. Most of their exports to the U.S. lean to the sweet side, with just a hint of fruitiness.

- Brasseurs LL (France)
- Castello P (Italy)
- Fischer Amber, 22 oz. ML (France)
- Fischer Bitter, 22 oz. A (France)
- Fischer Labelle Strasbourgeoise, LL 12 oz. or 22 oz. (France)
- Peroni LL (Italy)

MORE BEER

Germany Without a doubt the beer center of the world, German borders encompass nearly half the breweries in the world. The home of Oktoberfest assured the continued quality of its beers with the Purity Law of 1516.

- Ayinger Altbairisch, 20 oz. DL
- Ayinger Jahrhundert, 20 oz. LL
- Beck's LL
- Beck's Dark DL
- Celebrator Dopplebock DB
- Dinkelacker LL
- Dortmunder Kronen Classic LL
- Henniger LL
- Henniger Dark DL
- Hacker-Pschorr Weiss, 20 oz. W
- Holsten LB
- Kaiserdom Rauchbier Smoked Bavarian DL
- St. Pauli Girl LL
- St. Pauli Girl Dark DL
- Spaten Club-Weisse, 16 oz. W
- Spaten Munich Light LL
- Spaten Oktoberfest DL
- Spaten Optimator DB
- Steinhauser LL
- Warsteiner P

Holland Surely one of the most widely known beers in the world is Heineken—the first beer imported by the U.S. after Prohibition, and still the largest seller. Dutch beers available in America are characteristically bitter, with an underlying hint of fruitiness.

- Amstel Light LB
- Brand Royal P
- Grolsch, 16 oz. LL
- Heineken P
- Heineken Dark DL

Ireland The Guiness Brewery in Dublin is the largest brewery in Europe and produces the single most recognized brand in the world, Guiness Stout. Seems enough to rate inclusion in *The Guiness Book of World Records*, doesn't it? What a coincidence—they publish it. Ireland is famed for the driest stouts in the world, while its lagers are rich and full bodied, almost ale-like.

- Guiness Extra Stout S
- Harp Lager LL in bottle or on draught

Japan Responding to the lightness, delicacy and freshness of Japanese cuisine, brewers in the Land of the Rising Sun have sought a similar character in their beers. Principal exports include lagers that are lightbodied and delicate in hop flavor.

- Asahi LL
- Asahi Dry D
- Kirin LL
- Kirin Dry D
- Sapporo Draft, 12 oz. or 22 oz. LL
- Sapporo Dry D

Kenya The continent of Africa might claim to be the birthplace of beer, since written accounts of the brewing process date back to at least 3000 B.C. in Egypt.

- Tusker ML

Philippines The premier brewer in the Philippines, San Miguel, is also the most well known among Asian brands worldwide. Full-bodied and strongly hopped, San Miguel's fame is due in no small part to the U.S. Armed Forces during and since World War II.

- San Miguel P
- San Miguel Dark DL

AND EVEN MORE BEER!

Scandanavia Offering a wide variety of brewing styles because of distinct local customs and laws, these Northern European countries export some pleasantly captivating products to the U.S.

- Aass Bokk B (Norway)
- Aass Pilsner P (Norway)
- Carlsberg Beer LL (Denmark)
- Carlsberg Elephant ML (Denmark)
- Nordik Wolf Light LB (Sweden)
- Ringnes Export LL (Norway)

Scotland Although better known for its whiskey, plaids and bagpipes, Scotland does produce several fine ales for export. They are characteristically fuller-bodied than their English counterparts, emphasizing malt more than hops.

- MacAndrews Scotch Ale A

South-of-the-Border Settlers from Germany, Switzerland and Austria created the style of brewing which generally dominates Central and South American beer exports, while British style is most evident in the Caribbean.

- Bohemia LL (Mexico)
- Carib LL (Trinidad)
- Caribe LL (Caribbean Islands)
- Carta Blanca LL (Mexico)
- Chihuahua LL (Mexico)
- Cordoba LL (Argentina)
- Corona Extra LL (Mexico)
- Dos Equis DL (Mexico)
- Dos Equis Special Lager LL (Mexico)
- Negra Modelo DL (Mexico)
- Pacifico LL (Mexico)
- Port Royal P (Honduras)
- Red Stripe LL (Jamaica)
- Simpatico LL (Mexico)
- Sol LL (Mexico)
- Superior P (Mexico)
- Tecate LL (Mexico)

Switzerland Swiss beer-making tradition is one of many centuries standing and closely allied to German, including adherance to the same Purity Law. Most exports are characteristically mild and dry.

- Lowenbrau Zurich Export Light LL
- Lowenbrau Zurich Export Dark DL

United States Featured here are the finer beers from some smaller, lesser known breweries right here in the good old U S of A. Individually, each is a superb specimen of a specific type of beer. As a whole, the group reflects the wide variety of high-quality domestics available regionally.

- Anchor Porter PR
- Anchor Steam Beer DL in bottle or on draught
- Augsburger P
- Augsburger Bock B
- Augsburger Dark DL
- Bolder Extra Pale Ale A
- Boulder Porter PR
- Boulder Sport LL
- Cold Springs LL
- Dixie LL
- Heilman's Special Export LL
- Heilman's Special Export Dark DL
- Heilman's Special Export Light LB
- Liberty Ale A
- Maui Lager LL
- Rolling Rock LL
- Schell Pilsner P
- Schell Weiss Beer W
- Vienna All Malt Lager LL

On tap in the Armadillo Lounge:

Anchor Steam Beer	USA
Bass Pale Ale	England
Coors Light	USA
Harp Lager	Ireland
London Light	England
Moosehead	Canada
Watney's Red Barrel	England

3/89

FIGURE 20.4 Beer list from Willie C's. (Courtesy Willie C's Cafe® and Bar. Reproduced by permission.)

21

The Wine List

Wine consumption, which showed significant growth in the 1970s, has slowed. But while drinkers are cutting down on quantity, they are going for quality. While wine consumption grew only slightly, sales jumped from $6.2 billion in 1980 to $8.2 billion in 1984 (*Time*, May 20, 1985). The probable reason for the increased sales of better quality and more expensive wines is that the wine drinker has upgraded his or her tastes. Also, there is much history and a certain "mystique" to wine drinking—comparing vintages and labels. There are wine tastings, but no beer or gin tastings.

The complexity and variety of wines present both a problem and an opportunity to the restaurant operator and staff. The proven merchandising rules, however, are not difficult to master. The important thing is to list, describe, and "romance" the wines served. A good wine-merchandising rule is to suggest food to go with the various wines—red, white, rosé, champagne, and so on. The entrée could be listed in one color, the suggested wines in another color.

Wine can also be merchandised on the menu by selling "packages," combinations such as a complete dinner plus a glass of wine or a champagne dinner with all the champagne you can drink for a fixed price.

Wine merchandising begins with a wine cellar. To build a cellar, the services of a reputable wine merchant are needed unless the buyer already has a working knowledge of wines. It is usually best to begin with a small selection and build on this base as a record of sales and customers' tastes is built up. Large wine sellers even go so far as to buy wine futures, gambling on a good year in France or California.

Eight to ten good wines are enough to make an excellent wine list. A list of twenty good wines will enhance the reputation of any quality establishment.

The wine list can be printed in the following forms:

1. Separate wine list—wines only.
2. Separate wine list with other drinks.
3. Separate section of the menu—wines only.
4. Separate section of menu—wines and other drinks.

Restaurateurs often display an extensive or unusually distinctive wine list as a separate menu. This also enables the proprietor to revise the wine and food menus separately. It is the custom in Europe to include other alcoholic drinks, such as brandy, aperitifs, whiskey, and beer, on the wine list. (These items are not usually included on the wine list in the United States.) When the wine list is a section, page, or panel of the food menu, be sure that it gets the proper billing and attention. Another effective method of selling wine is to list it alongside the food it complements. For example, the following entrée and wine could be listed together:

Rack of Loin of Spring Lamb
Baby Carrots, Pearl Onions
Garnished with Watercress
For a wine to accompany this entrée, we recommend
Red Bordeaux
Châteaux Margaux
1953

Regardless of where your wines are listed, they are usually described according to the following categories:

1. Place of origin
   a. Imported—France, Germany, Italy, Portugal, and so on
   b. American—California, the East, and so on
2. Type of wine
   a. Sparkling—Champagne, Sparkling Burgundy
   b. Still wines—all others
3. Style of wine
   a. Dry
   b. Medium
   c. Sweet
4. Color of wine
   a. Red
   b. White
   c. Rosé
   d. Blush
5. Vintage (or nonvintage)

In America especially, it is the custom to separate the imported and American wines, and it is generally considered better form to refer to American wines as American, not domestic. The reason for separating California from eastern (New York, Michigan) wines is that each is made from a different grape. California and other western grapes are grown from the *Vitis vinifera* vine imported from France. Most eastern wines are grown from the native *Vitis labrusca* vine.

The imported section of the wine list usually begins with the great wines of France—Bordeaux, Burgundy, and Champagne. This can be followed by the fine wines of Germany—Rhine, Moselle, Rhinegau, and Rhinehesse. A listing of the "special" wines of Alsace, Rhône, Loire, Italy, Portugal, Spain, and South America may follow if it is a big list.

The best California wines are produced in an area around San Francisco Bay. These valleys and counties are Napa, Sonoma, Livermore, and Santa Cruz. The best wines from these areas are the varietals, wines that take their name, characteristic flavor, and bouquet from the grape variety from which they were produced. Care must be used in selecting California wines for the wine list. For example, any red California wine can be labeled burgundy, but a varietal red wine such as Pinot Noir must be made from a minimum of 51 percent of Pinot Noir grapes, the same grape used exclusively to make the finest French red Burgundies.

Each wine should be identified by a bin number, which is written on the label of each bottle in the bin. The bin number system makes identification easy and service efficient.

The restaurant operator must decide on one of two pricing policies. One is to raise prices three or four times the wholesale price and make a large profit per bottle sold. The other policy is to make the markup smaller and thereby sell more wine by the glass or the bottle. Wine, unlike food, requires no preparation in the restaurant. It needs only to be stored in a cool, dry place, uncorked, and served. A fast-moving wine cellar means that money is not tied up in inventory; but even if wine is stored for some time, it does not lose its value because many wines improve with age.

The next question is which wines to order with which foods. For guests who have sampled many wines and know the wine-food combinations that they prefer, rules are not necessary. But there is a consensus of agreement as to what wines are best with certain foods.

First, champagne is the most versatile of all wines. It may be served with any food, or by itself; it is an elegant aperitif, an ideal dinner wine, and a perfect after-dinner wine. Pink wines (rosé) also go with almost any food.

If more than one wine is being served, the rule is to start with the lighter (usually white), proceed to the heavier, more pungent (usually red), and finish with a sweet dessert wine (sauternes—Rhine or California).

The following list is offered for reference:

Canapés: Cheese, crackers, olives	Sherry, Champagne
Soup	Sherry
Seafood	Chablis, dry Sauternes, Rhine, white Burgundy,
Fowl: Cold and roast chicken, duck, turkey, pheasant	Champagne, dry Sauternes, Rhine, white or red Burgundy
Meats: Steak, veal, lamb, roast beef, stew	Claret, Burgundy, Rosé
Italian Dishes	Chianti, Zinfandel, Barbera
Desserts	Sweet Sauternes, Champagne

The next consideration is vintage. Vintage means "gathering of the grapes," and a vintage wine is one produced from grapes of a specified year. Weather plays an important part in the quality of French and German wines. In bright, sunny weather the grapes grow to full maturity, size, and flavor, whereas bad weather results in a hard, green, small grape. A high-rated vintage year indicates that the weather was so favorable that it resulted in top-quality grapes from which extra-high-quality wine was made.

Weather conditions in the United States tend to be more stable and there is less variation between yearly productions of wine in California. Wine growers in California, however, indicate vintage years on their bottled wines, making them similar to French wines.

The Four Seasons

Many restaurants with a large wine list use a wine "book," which can be bulky and hard to handle for the customer who wants to order a special wine. In fact, a wine list containing a thousand or more wines may be excessive and lead to good wines sitting in the cellar and producing no income.

The wine list shown in Figure 21.1 from The Four Seasons restaurant solves the problem of a large offering (247 wines) by using a manageable list (11 by 17 inches) printed on both sides. On one side are listed 67 American wines, 43 Italian, 2 Hungarian, 2 Spanish, and 3 German wines, plus 15 French champagnes. The other side contains 120 French wines. First the bin number is listed, then the name of the wine and its year of vintage, followed by the price. This makes for easy selection by the server (by bin number) and does not draw attention to the price first.

The American wines are first listed under the categories of reds and whites and then by regions—Oregon, Napa, Sonoma, Monterey, Santa Cruz, and New York State. This is followed by sparkling wines. The Italian wines are also listed under the headings of red, white, and sparkling. The wines of Hungary are white, those of Spain red, and the German wines (all white) are listed under Moselle and Rhine wines.

THE FOUR SEASONS' WINE CELLAR

Paul Kovi's Selection of American Wines

Reds

OREGON
504 Pinot Noir, Bethel Heights, Bonny Doon 1985 35.00

NAPA
518 Dominus, C. Moueix 1984 72.00
515 Daniel Estate, C. Moueix 1984 36.00
511 Opus One, Mondavi-Rothschild 1984 95.00/45.00 half
513 Rubicon, Niebaum-Coppola 1980 51.00
577 Insignia, J. Phelps 1983 51.00
526 Cabernet Sauvignon, R. Mondavi Reserve 1982 65.00
509 Cabernet Sauvignon, R. Mondavi Reserve 1983 58.00
505 Cabernet Sauvignon, R. Mondavi Reserve 1978 150.00 mag
503 Cabernet Sauvignon, Mayacamas 1983 55.00
327 Cabernet Sauvignon, Diamond Creek 1982 90.00 Mag.
510 Cabernet Sauvignon, Diamond Creek 1984 60.00
520 Cabernet Sauvignon Martha's Vineyard, Heitz 1979 96.00
508 Cabernet Sauvignon, Reserve B.V. 1982 60.00
507 Cabernet Sauvignon, Reserve B.V. 1976 90.00
516 Cabernet Sauvignon, Grace Family 1982 80.00
519 Cabernet Sauvignon, Spring Mountain 1982 33.00
525 Cabernet Bosché, Freemark Abbey 1981 65.00
523 Cabernet Sauvignon, Chappellet 1979/80 33.00
514 Merlot, J. Phelps 1986 31.00
521 Merlot, Newton 1985 35.00
534 Pinot Noir, Carneros CQA 1985 51.00

SONOMA
501 Cabernet Sauvignon, Jordan 1984 38.00
522 Cabernet Sauvignon, Reserve Simi 1981 48.00
576 Cabernet Sauvignon, Ernest-Julio Gallo Reserve 1981 17.50
500 Cabernet Sauvignon, Domaine Michel 1984 42.00
528 Zinfandel Reserve, Lytton Springs 1984 31.00

MONTEREY
527 Pinot Noir, Reserve, Chalone 1983 75.00
517 Merlot, Sarah's 1984 65.00

SANTA CRUZ
502 Cabernet Sauvignon, Montebello, Ridge 1980 80.00
524 Zinfandel, York Creek, Ridge 1985 24.00
578 Le Cigare Volant, Bonny Doon 1985 27.00
530 Pinot Noir, Jensen, Calera 1985 48.00
419 Vin Gris de Cigare, Bonny Doon 1987 18.00

NEW YORK STATE
533 Reserve, Lenz 1984 21.00

Whites

NAPA
560 Chardonnay, San Giacomo, J. Phelps 1985 36.00
561 Chardonnay, Grgich Hills 1985 62.00
567 Chardonnay, Spring Mountain 1985 33.00
570 Chardonnay, Reserve, R. Mondavi 1985 46.00
586 Chardonnay, Mayacamas 1985 55.00
569 Chardonnay, Château Woltner Reserve 1986 51.00
575 Chardonnay, Long 1986 61.00
571 Chardonnay, Marina, Acacia 1986 37.00
581 Sauvignon Blanc, Long 1987 29.00
556 Sauvignon Blanc, Sterling 1986 18.00
557 Sauvignon Blanc, Mayacamas 1985 24.00
554 Johannisberg Riesling, J. Phelps 1986 18.00
553 Johann. Riesling, Late Harvest, J. Phelps 1985 47.00 half

SONOMA
582 Chardonnay, Simi 1985 29.00
562 Chardonnay, Domaine Michel 1985 36.00
559 Chardonnay, Iron Horse 1986 29.00
558 Chardonnay, Russian River, Sonoma Cutrer 1986 33.00

MONTEREY
532 Pinot Blanc, Chalone 1986 36.00
564 Chardonnay, Edna Valley 1986 30.00
555 Chardonnay, M.E.V., Mount Eden 1985 36.00
583 Chardonnay, Paul Masson 1987 18.00
572 Sauvignon Blanc, Sanford 1986 18.00
550 Muscat Canelli Vin de Glaciere, Bonny Doon 1987 42.00 half
573 Gewuztraminer Vin de Glaciere, Bonny Doon 1987 36.00 half

NEW YORK STATE
566 Chardonnay, Wiemer 1986 20.00
552 Chardonnay, Bridgehampton Reserve 1986 24.00

Sparkling

594 Beaulieu, Champagne de Chardonnay 1981 34.00
593 Iron Horse, Sonoma Brut 1983 39.00
590 Schramsberg Reserve, Napa 1981 59.00
591 Piper Sonoma, Sonoma Brut 1985 27.00
595 Chandon, Napa Valley Brut 27.00
598 Great Western Blanc de Blanc, Hammondsport 25.00

Italy

Reds

407 Barbera D'Alba, Vietti 1985 20.00
261 Barolo, Bricco Rocche, Bricco Rocche, Ceretto 1982 125.00
415 Barolo Prapo, Ceretto 1982 75.00
413 Barbaresco, S. Lorenzo, Gaja 1982 84.00
268 Barbaresco, Costa Russi, Gaja 1982 85.00
447 Barbaresco Bricco Asili, Ceretto 1982 65.00
412 Barolo Riserva, Pio Cesare 1982 60.00
403 Opera Prima, A. G. Roagna 36.00
343 Merlot, Scarpa 1986 27.00
411 Corbulino Rosso, Scarpa 1985 27.00
259 Franciacorta Rosso, Ca Del Bosco 1985 33.00
449 Recioto Amarone, Dalforno Romano 1983 42.00
309 Vigorello, San Felice 1982 33.00
334 Cabreo, Vigneto il Borgo Ruffino 1982 36.00
414 Cannaio, Monte Vertine 1983 38.00
410 Il Sodaccio, Monte Vertine 1983 38.00
417 Capannelle, R. Rossetti 1982 42.00
273 Peppoli, Chianti Classico Antinori 1985 45.00
418 Tignanello, Antinori 1982 45.00
446 Grifi, Avignonesi 1985 41.00
280 Carmignano, Tenuta Capezzana 1984 33.00
352 Brunello Di Montalcino, Biondi-Santi 1977 75.00
272 Brunello Di Montalcino, Barbi Riserva 1981 58.00
442 Rubesco, Riserva, Lungarotti 1978 45.00

Whites

596 Chardonnay, Gaja 1986 120.00 magnum
580 Chardonnay, Ca Del Bosco 1986 65.00
563 Arneis, Bruno Giacosa 1987 38.00
420 Gavi dei Gavi, La Scolca 1986 45.00
565 Soave Capitel Foscarino, Anselmi 1987 27.00
579 Prato Di Canzio, Maculan 1986 36.00
409 Tocai Friulano, M. Schioppetto 1987 27.00
568 Pinot Bianco, M. Schioppetto 1987 32.50
445 Picolit G. Dri 1986 52.00 half
423 Chardonnay, Borgo Conventi 1987 33.00
426 Chardonnay, Jermann 1987 30.00
422 Cervaro Della Sala, Antinori 1986 32.00
362 Pigato Di Albenga, Parodi 1987 30.00
366 Vin Santo Avignonesi 1981 65.00 half
574 Montecarlo Bianco, F. Mazzini 1983 23.00
424 Greco di Tufo, Mastroberardino 1986 26.00

Sparkling

472 Bruno Giacosa Extra Brut 1983 45.00
471 Nino Franco Prosecco 24.00
469 Ca Del Bosco, Brut n/v 48.00

Hungary

Whites

432 Tokaji Aszu, 5 Puttonyos 1978 24.50
430 Tokaji Essencia 1976 72.00

Spain

Reds

440 Cune Imperial Gran Riserva 1975 24.00
441 Gran Coronas, Torres, Riserva 1978 33.00

Germany

The Moselle

400 Bernkastler Badstube Kabinett, Dr. Thanisch 1985 17.00
401 Wehlener Sonnenuhr Spätlese, J. J. Prüm 1985 19.00

The Rhines

408 Hattenheim Nüssbrunnen Kabinett von Simmern 1985 12.50

The Champagnes of France

450 Bollinger, Brut n/v 48.00
475 Crémant de Cramant, Mumm n/v 85.00
467 Henriot, Cuvée Baccarat 1979 110.00
463 Jacquant Brut n/v 60.00
486 Louis Roederer, Cristal 1983 165.00
453 Moët & Chandon, Dom Pérignon 1982 135.00
455 Moët & Chandon, Imperial Brut 1982 60.00/30.00 half
457 Mumm, Cordon Rouge 1982 60.00
461 Mumm, Extra Dry n/v 42.00
476 Perrier-Jouët, Brut n/v 40.00
478 Perrier-Jouët, Rosé 1982 110.00
464 Perrier-Jouët 1982 100.00/200.00 magnum
459 Taittinger, Blanc de Blancs 1981 125.00
452 Taittinger, Comte de Champagne, Rosé 1982 150.00
487 Veuve Cliquot, Brut 1982 65.00

311 Château Haut-Brion, Graves 160.00

1975
248 Château Talbot, St. Julien 65.00
289 Château Ausone, St. Emilion 190.00
382 Château Lafite Rothschild, Pauillac 110.00 half

The Four Seasons Special Reserve

281 Château Latour, Pauillac 1971 150.00
249 Château Haut-Brion, Graves 1971 150.00
251 Château Palmer, Margaux 1970 250.00
294 Château Mouton Rothschild, Pauillac 1970 300.00
285 Château Lafite-Rothschild, Pauillac 1970 300.00
279 Château Latour, Pauillac 1970 300.00
299 Château Haut-Brion, Graves 1970 600.00 magnum
296 Château Haut-Brion, Graves 1970 270.00
602 Château Haut-Brion, Graves 1970 100.00 half
314 Château Les Ormes Des Pez, St. Estephe 1970 150.00
283 Château Gruaud-Larose, St. Julien 1967 65.00
323 Carruades de Château Lafite, Pauillac 1967 33.00 half
253 Château Mouton Rothschild, Pauillac 1966 300.00
267 Château Latour, Pauillac 1966 320.00
307 Château Lynch Bages, Pauillac 1966 300.00
262 Château Latour, Pauillac 1964 250.00
263 Château Ausone, St. Emilion 1964 220.00
264 Château Petrus, Pomerol 1964 450.00
258 Château Haut-Brion, Graves 1961 450.00
257 Château Latour, Pauillac 1961 500.00
256 Château Latour, Pauillac 1959 550.00
269 Château Cheval Blanc, St. Emilion 1955 85.00 half
246 Château Latour, Pauillac 1953 450.00
247 Château Lafite Rothschild, Pauillac 1949 600.00
244 Château Latour, Pauillac 1945 850.00

The White Wines of Bordeaux

405 Château d'Yquem, Lur-Saluce, Sauternes 1981 180.00
321 Château d'Yquem, Lur-Saluce, Sauternes 1983 120.00 half
431 Château Raymond-Lafon, Sauternes 1981 65.00
320 Château Laville Haut-Brion, Graves 1982 95.00
322 Château Smith Haut Lafitte, Graves 1986 27.00

The Red Wines of Burgundy

COTE DE NUITS
339 Chambolle Musigny D. Guyon 1985 55.00
354 Musigny, Comte de Vogüé 1979 160.00
364 Clos de la Roche, Domaine Dujac 1983 95.00
333 Nuits St. George, R. Chevillon 1983 55.00
353 Nuits St. George, Premier Cru, Faiveley 1983 65.00
332 Clos de Tart, Mommessin 1982 95.00
356 Bonne Mares, Domaine Dujac 1982 72.00
351 Volnay, Clos de Duc, D'Anguerville 1985 42.00

DOMAINE DE LA ROMANEE-CONTI
344 Romanée-Conti 1972 450.00
342 Grands Echézeaux 1978 240.00
336 Richebourg 1982 145.00
254 Richebourg 1973 250.00

COTE DE BEAUNE
345 Corton, Prince de Merode 1969 175.00
290 Corton, Prince de Merode 1971 175.00
340 Aloxe Corton, Domaine Guyon 1982 36.00

BEAUJOLAIS
338 Château de la Chaize, Brouilly 1986 14.50
355 Beaujolais-Villages, L. Jadot 1987 14.50
291 Fleurie, G. Dubeuf 1987 21.00
346 Moulin a Vent, Louis Latour 1985 18.50/10.00 half
252 Julienas, S. Fessy 1985 15.00

The White Wines of Burgundy

374 Chablis Grand Cru Moreau 1985 45.00
360 Beaune, Clos de Mouches, J. Drouhin 1986 81.00
376 Clos Blanc de Vougeot L'Heritier-Guyot 1985 75.00
367 Criot-Batard Montrachet, Fontaine-Gagnard 1985 110.00
375 Corton Charlemagne, Louis Latour 1985 120.00
372 Corton Charlemagne, Louis Jadot 1983 120.00
369 Chassagne Montrachet, Louis Latour 1986 55.00
371 Chevalier Montrachet, Louis Jadot 1984 110.00
377 Meursault Louis Jadot 1986 48.00
373 Puligny Montrachet, Domaine Leflaive 1986 85.00
383 Puligny Montrachet, L. Latour 1985 65.00
387 Batard Montrachet Domaine Leflaive 1983 135.00
363 Montrachet, Louis Jadot 1984 180.00
421 Pernand-Vergelesses, A. Guyon 1985 32.00

COUNTRY WINES
365 Pouilly-Fuissé, Louis Jadot 1986 55.00
361 Macon Lugny, "Les Charmes" 1986 19.00

The Wines of Alsace

392 Riesling, Clos Ste. Hune 1982 45.00
390 Gewurztraminer, Trimbach 1983 33.00
391 Sylvaner, Trimbach 1985 12.50

The Wines of the Loire

370 Baron de L, de Ladoucette 1985 75.00
385 Sancerre, Clos de la Perrière, Archambault 1987 18.00/10.00 half
384 Pouilly-Fumé, Domaine Coulbois 1986 30.00

The Wines of Provence

406 Cassis, Clos St. Magdleine 1985 24.00
379 Château Vignelaure, G. Brunet 1981 18.00

The Wines of the Rhone

Reds

380 Châteauneuf-du-Pape, M. Chapoutier, Cuvée. 41.00
381 St. Joseph, A. Cuilleron 1985 30.00

Whites

324 Hermitage, Chante Alouette, M. Chapoutier 1985 32.00
368 Condrieu, A. Cuilleron 1986 65.00

FIGURE 21.1 The Four Seasons' wine list. (Reproduced by permission.)

The listing of French wines begins with the Red Wines of Bordeaux, subdivided by vintage years. Next is the Four Seasons Special Reserve, twenty-five expensive wines from older vintages. This is followed by the White Wines of Bordeaux. Next come the Red Wines of Burgundy, also broken down by region.

The Water Club

Figure 21.2 shows a somewhat smaller wine list (105 selections) from The Water Club. Printed on one side of a list measuring 11 by 17 inches, it is organized into two columns, one for red and the other for white wines. There are no bin numbers but the vintage year of each wine is given after the name. The prices are listed in a column to the right. The breakdown is by countries and regions.

THE WATER CLUB

WINE LIST

WHITE WINES

CALIFORNIA	
WHITE RIESLING, TREFETHEN, NAPA 1986	16.50
CHENIN BLANC, GIRARD, NAPA 1986	17.50
GEWURZTRAMINER, MARK WEST VINEYARDS, RUSSIAN RIVER VALLEY 1986	16.50
FUMÉ BLANC, DRY CREEK, SONOMA 1986	9.75 / 19.50
SAUVIGNON BLANC, ST. CLEMENT, NAPA 1986	21.50
SAUVIGNON BLANC, MAYACAMAS, NAPA 1986	23.50
CHARDONNAY, KENDALL-JACKSON, CALIFORNIA 1987	9.75 / 19.50
CHARDONNAY, AU BON CLIMAT, SANTA BARBARA COUNTY 1986	24.50
CHARDONNAY, FREEMARK ABBEY, NAPA 1985	32.50
CHARDONNAY, PINE RIDGE, NAPA 1985	32.50
CHARDONNAY, SPRING MOUNTAIN, NAPA 1985	33.50
CHARDONNAY, TREFETHEN, NAPA 1985	33.50
CHARDONNAY, ARROWOOD, SONOMA 1986	34.50
CHARDONNAY, WILLIAM HILL, "GOLD LABEL," NAPA 1984	37.50
CHARDONNAY, SONOMA-CUTRER, LES PIERRES VINEYARD, SONOMA 1985	39.50
NEW YORK	
DRY JOHANNISBERG RIESLING, HERMANN J. WIEMER VINEYARD, FINGER LAKES 1986	15.50
CHARDONNAY, WAGNER, FINGER LAKES 1986	16.50
CHARDONNAY, LE RÊVE, NORTH FORK OF LONG ISLAND 1986	24.50
FRANCE	
LOIRE	
MUSCADET, CHATEAU DE LA RAGOTIÈRE 1986	15.50
SANCERRE, CLOS LA PERRIÈRE, ARCHAMBAULT 1986 / 1987	19.50
POUILLY FUMÉ, DOMAINE DE ST. LAURENT 1986	25.00
BURGUNDY	
MACON-CLESSÉ, JEAN BEDIN 1986	17.50
RULLY BLANC, JAFFELIN 1986	24.50
CHABLIS GRAND CRU, "BLANCHOT," ROBERT VOCORET 1986	39.50
MEURSAULT PREMIER CRU, "LES CHARMES," BOILLOT-BUTHIAU 1986	45.00
PULIGNY-MONTRACHET, ETIENNE SAUZET 1986	49.50
CHASSAGNE-MONTRACHET PREMIER CRU, "LES CAILLERETS," DOMAINE BACHELET-RAMONET 1986	49.50
CORTON CHARLEMAGNE, BONNEAU DU MARTRAY 1985	85.00
BÂTARD-MONTRACHET, DOMAINE BACHELET-RAMONET 1986	150.00
ALSACE	
PINOT BLANC, TRIMBACH 1985	16.50
RIESLING, DOMAINE WEINBACH, "RÉSERVE PERSONELLE," 1985	29.50
GEWURZTRAMINER, CHARLES SCHLERET 1985	19.50
GEWURZTRAMINER, SCHLUMBERGER, "CUVÉE CHRISTINE" (VENDAGE TARDIVE) 1983	45.00
SAUTERNES	
CHATEAU SUDUIRAUT 1983 (HALF BOTTLE)	29.50
CHATEAU D'YQUEM 1975	195.00
GERMANY	
MOSEL	
WEHLENER SONNENUHR SPÄTLESE, DR. PAULY-BERGWEILER 1985	21.00
GRAACH JOSEPHSHÖFER SPÄTLESE, VON KESSELSTATT 1985	19.50
RHINE	
SCHLOSS JOHANNISBERGER KABINETT, FÜRST VON METTERNICH 1985	26.50
AUSTRALIA	
CHARDONNAY, ROTHBURY ESTATE, HUNTER VALLEY 1987	19.50
ITALY	
VERDICCHIO "CUPRESE," COLONNARA 1987	17.50
VERNACCIA DI SAN GIMIGNANO, TERUZZI 1987	15.00
PINOT GRIGIO, TENUTA VILLANOVA 1987	18.50
SAUVIGNON, COLLIO CRU BORGO CONVENTI 1986	24.50
GAVI, "LA MERLINA," FAUSTO GEMME 1986	27.50

RED WINES

CALIFORNIA	
SYRAH, QUPÉ, CENTRAL COAST 1986	19.50
ZINFANDEL, FROG'S LEAP, NAPA 1985	18.50
MERLOT, SHAFER, NAPA 1985	24.50
PINOT NOIR, CARNEROS CREEK, CARNEROS 1984	32.50
CABERNET SAUVIGNON, ALEXANDER VALLEY VINEYARDS, ALEXANDER VALLEY 1985	19.50
CABERNET SAUVIGNON, TREFETHEN, NAPA 1984	27.50
CABERNET SAUVIGNON, ROBERT MONDAVI, NAPA 1984	14.50 / 29.00
CABERNET SAUVIGNON, CLOS DU VAL, NAPA 1983	29.50
CABERNET SAUVIGNON, CLOS PEGASE, NAPA 1985	34.50
CABERNET SAUVIGNON, HEITZ CELLAR, NAPA 1982	34.50
CABERNET SAUVIGNON, JORDAN, ALEXANDER VALLEY 1984	42.00
CABERNET SAUVIGNON, CHATEAU MONTELENA, NAPA 1982	45.00
CABERNET SAUVIGNON, FREEMARK ABBEY, BOSCHÉ VINEYARD, NAPA	
1979	48.00
1978	55.00
1976	65.00
DOMINUS ESTATE, CHRISTIAN MOUEIX, NAPA 1984	75.00
OPUS ONE, MONDAVI-ROTHSCHILD, NAPA 1983	85.00
ROSÉ	
ROSÉ OF CABERNET, SIMI, SONOMA 1986 / 1987	15.00
OREGON	
PINOT NOIR, SOKOL BLOSSER, YAMHILL COUNTY 1985	29.50
FRANCE	
BORDEAUX	
CHATEAU DE SALES, POMEROL 1983	27.50
CHATEAU PAVIE, ST. EMILION 1983	36.00
CHATEAU BRANE CANTENAC, MARGAUX 1983	38.00
CHATEAU PICHON-LALANDE, PAUILLAC 1981	75.00
CHATEAU LÉOVILLE LASCASES, ST. JULIEN 1979	75.00
CHATEAU DUCRU BEAUCAILLOU, ST. JULIEN 1979	75.00
CHATEAU MARGAUX, MARGAUX 1970	225.00
CHATEAU MOUTON-ROTHSCHILD, PAUILLAC 1970	250.00
CHATEAU LAFITE-ROTHSCHILD, PAUILLAC 1962	350.00
CHATEAU LATOUR, PAUILLAC	
1970	250.00
1966	375.00
BURGUNDY	
CÔTE DE NUITS	
MOREY-SAINT-DENIS, DOMAINE PONSOT 1982	36.00
NUITS ST. GEORGES, "LES PERDRIX," BERNARD MUGNERET 1985	36.00
CHAMBOLLE-MUSIGNY, "LES AMOUREUSES," HERVÉ ROUMIER 1985	65.00
RICHEBOURG, DOMAINE MONGEARD-MUGNERET 1984	75.00
CÔTE DE BEAUNE	
LADOIX CÔTE DE BEAUNE, PRINCE FLORENT DE MERODE 1985	32.00
POMMARD, "EPENOTS," DOMAINE DE COURCEL 1985	45.00
CORTON, "RENARDES," PRINCE FLORENT DE MERODE 1985	48.00
VOLNAY PREMIER CRU, MARQUIS D'ANGERVILLE	
CHAMPANS 1985	36.00
CLOS DES DUCS 1983 (MAGNUM)	75.00
BEAUJOLAIS	
BEAUJOLAIS VILLAGES, CHATEAU DE MONTMELAS 1987	15.50
BROUILLY, CHATEAU DE LA CHAIZE 1986	16.50
CHIROUBLES, CHATEAU DE RAOUSSET 1987	18.50
RHÔNE	
CÔTES DU RHÔNE, CHATEAU D'AIGUEVILLE 1986	15.50
CHATEAUNEUF DU PAPE, LUCIEN BARROT 1979	32.50
ITALY	
TUSCANY	
CHIANTI CLASSICO, BADIA A COLTIBUONO 1982	24.50
BRUNELLO DI MONTALCINO, LISINI 1981	32.00
PIEDMONT	
NEBBIOLO D'ALBA, BRUNO GIACOSA 1985	24.50
BAROLO, COLLINA RIONDA DI SERRALUNGA, BRUNO GIACOSA 1980	39.00
BARBARESCO, ANGELO GAJA 1983	42.00

CHAMPAGNES

FRANCE	
PERRIER-JOUËT BRUT N.V.	39.50
LOUIS ROEDERER BRUT N.V.	22.50 / 45.00
MOËT ET CHANDON BRUT IMPERIAL N.V.	49.50
VEUVE CLICQUOT YELLOW LABEL BRUT N.V.	55.00
DOM RUINART BLANC DE BLANCS 1979	95.00
KRUG, GRANDE CUVÉE	110.00
PERRIER-JOUËT, FLEUR DE CHAMPAGNE 1982	115.00
DOM PÉRIGNON 1982	140.00
CRISTAL, LOUIS ROEDERER 1983	165.00
ROSÉ CHAMPAGNES	
CHAMPAGNE DEUTZ ROSÉ 1982	75.00
TAITTINGER, COMTES DE CHAMPAGNE, ROSÉ 1981	145.00
CALIFORNIA	
ANDERSON BRUT BLANC DE BLANCS 1983	32.50
SCHRAMSBERG, BLANC DE NOIRS 1983	42.50

SAMUEL H. CORRENTI, WINE DIRECTOR

THERE IS ALSO A LIST OF DESSERT WINES, VINTAGE PORTS, RARE COGNACS, AND EAUX-DE-VIE BY THE GLASS.

FIGURE 21.2 The Water Club wine list. The club serves more wine than water with this menu. (Reproduced by permission.)

WINE MERCHANDISING

An important marketing tool for selling wine in the restaurant is an educated staff. This means that each server as well as the sommelier (if the restaurant has one) should know how to serve wine and have some basic knowledge about the wines served. Wine tastings for the staff is one way of educating and creating interest and enthusiasm among the servers. Also, outside wine consultants (including wine merchants) can be called in to educate the restaurant staff.

Computerized inventory systems linked to the cash register are used by four out of five restaurant operators today. Such systems keep track of bottle depletions and keep a large wine list up to date. A record of sales of wine by the glass can be taken from the dinner check when it is entered into a computer.

Does wine merchandising work? At Trumps in Los Angeles, 1986 wine sales were 9.39 percent of the total gross. Through the first ten months of 1987, the rate was 10 percent, and in the dining room, wine sales were greater than spirit sales. At the Angus Barn restaurant in Raleigh, North Carolina, wine sales are gradually increasing. Sales were from 12 to 13 percent of gross sales, or about $600,000 for the fiscal year 1986–1987. Sales of wine are expected to reach $1 million annually within the next four years. Wine sales at the Angus Barn average $10 to $15 per person per meal.

At the Flagstaff House restaurant in Boulder, Colorado, 95 percent of those ordering wine order bottles. Customers tend to have a glass of wine first and then order a bottle. Accordingly, the restaurant has expanded its wine list to seven hundred selections, both expensive and inexpensive. More half-bottles have been added, and there are from twenty-five to thirty offerings for wine by the glass.

The Gordon restaurant in Chicago expanded its luncheon wine sales by printing an abbreviated wine list on the back of the menu. It also used table tents to promote wine by the glass as well as ports and dessert wines, and encouraged the wait staff to sell wine during lunch. The restaurant's register-fed computer system helps update the computerized wine list twice weekly, at the time of delivery.

The New York Restaurant Group, Inc. operates four restaurants, including Smith & Wollensky and the Post House. The objective of this group has been to increase wine sales at all four restaurants. At the Post House, wine sales have grown from 9 percent to 27 percent of total sales in four years. An important aspect of the New York Restaurant Group's wine marketing is teaching the staff the correct purchasing of wines and merchandising of expensive wines. By purchasing Bordeaux and California wine futures in good vintage years, the group can list top-quality wines at prices lower than those in wine shops. The objective is turnover—selling more wine at a lower profit margin. A separate wine list, which includes port and dessert wines, is automatically presented by the server to the diner at both lunch and dinner. Wine by the glass is merchandised by table tents, on a blackboard, or by the wait staff.

A very simple but effective wine merchandising trick is to put an unopened bottle of wine on the center of the diner's table. The wine is noticed, the label is read, and the customer's interest is aroused. Organized wine-tasting events also stimulate business during the event and usually result in greater wine sales in the weeks following the formal tasting.

The 95th

The 95th is an elegant restaurant on the ninety-fifth floor of the John Hancock building in Chicago, the flagship restaurant of the ARA corporation. It was opened in 1971 and underwent a major renovation in 1981. Besides remodeling the restaurant, the cuisine was changed from Continental to American regional. Fresh ingredients and nutrition are important elements of this cuisine. Sauces do not exist except for au jus. Well-seasoned, light cooking is featured, and all of the items are made in the restaurant kitchen, including fresh baked goods, smoked items, and sausages. The menu, which is à la carte, changes seasonally, four times a year. The 95th considers itself to be a trendsetting restaurant.

The 95th's wine cellar contains 450 selections. Pricing includes a 37 to 39 percent markup, although this is smaller if the bottle costs $250 wholesale. Then the markup will be less since the gross profit is greater. The bottom price for a bottle of wine is $16.

The wine steward at The 95th says that because wine drinkers usually know the price of a particular bottle of wine in a wineshop, it is counterproductive to charge an excessive price. She also observes that "an active wine list must go with the food on the menu, and wine helps to create a fine dining environment."

The entire wine list is contained in a computer and is revised every few weeks. The pages are produced on a laser printer and held in clear plastic pages in the wine book.

A major part of the wine merchandising at The 95th is the extensive wine-by-the-glass list. The list includes five white wines priced from $4.25 to $6.00 per glass; four red wines from $6.50 to $15.00 per glass; a Johannesberg Riesling, Chateau St. Jean, at $10.00 a glass, and a Taylor Fladgate Tawney Port, thirty years old, at $18.00 a glass. All of the wines sold by the glass are completely identified and described in detail. This is the way wine by the glass should be merchandised.

Another important part of the wine-marketing programs at The 95th is the wine tastings, held every month to feature a specific group of wines (see Figure 21.3). These events include much more than wine—the restaurant organizes a dinner and speakers, and advertises the event by direct mail. Some recent wine tastings at The 95th were "The American View of France," and "The American View of Italy." Chefs and wine growers were flown in from each country to give demonstrations and describe their wines.

Educating the staff as well as the customer is an important component of the wine program at The 95th. According to the wine steward, "The biggest problem in the wine industry is an unqualified salesman talking to an unqualified buyer. By making the entire staff qualified and enthusiastic, wine sales are certain to increase."

Monterey Cannery

The Monterey Cannery fresh seafood restaurants in California and Hawaii feature fresh seafood and mesquite and kiawi charcoal broiling. The wine list, in keeping with the restaurant name, is in the form of a large coffee can measuring 7 inches high and 6 inches in diameter (Figure 21.4). The can is painted white, and the list is printed in color on a white paper wrap-around with an illustration of the restaurant and the heading Wine List in bold, red letters.

The listing itself consists of nine domestic white wines, three blush wines, three red wines, two sparkling wines, four imported white wines, four California white wines, house wines, five California premium house wines, and premium wines by the glass. Prices range from $11.50 to $23.00 per bottle. Wines by the glass or carafe range from $1.95 per glass to $12.50 for a carafe.

The Monterey Cannery carries the idea of placing an unopened bottle of wine on the table one step further. The bottle is put in the coffee can, which serves as the wine list, and the list is sure to be noticed and read.

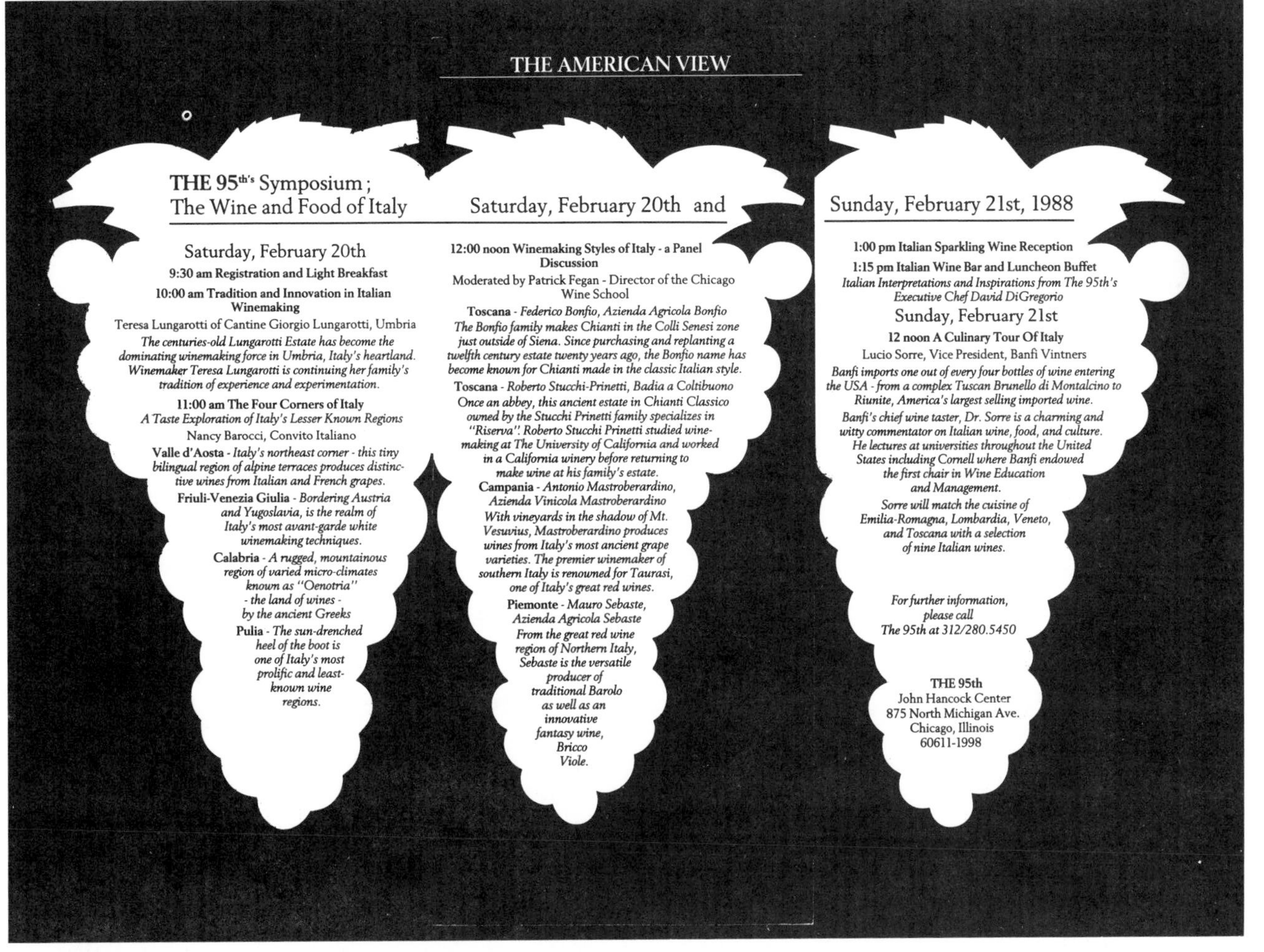

THE AMERICAN VIEW

THE 95th's Symposium;
The Wine and Food of Italy

Saturday, February 20th and

Sunday, February 21st, 1988

Saturday, February 20th

9:30 am Registration and Light Breakfast

10:00 am Tradition and Innovation in Italian Winemaking

Teresa Lungarotti of Cantine Giorgio Lungarotti, Umbria

The centuries-old Lungarotti Estate has become the dominating winemaking force in Umbria, Italy's heartland. Winemaker Teresa Lungarotti is continuing her family's tradition of experience and experimentation.

11:00 am The Four Corners of Italy

A Taste Exploration of Italy's Lesser Known Regions

Nancy Barocci, Convito Italiano

Valle d'Aosta - *Italy's northeast corner - this tiny bilingual region of alpine terraces produces distinctive wines from Italian and French grapes.*

Friuli-Venezia Giulia - *Bordering Austria and Yugoslavia, is the realm of Italy's most avant-garde white winemaking techniques.*

Calabria - *A rugged, mountainous region of varied micro-climates known as "Oenotria" - the land of wines - by the ancient Greeks*

Pulia - *The sun-drenched heel of the boot is one of Italy's most prolific and least-known wine regions.*

12:00 noon Winemaking Styles of Italy - a Panel Discussion

Moderated by Patrick Fegan - Director of the Chicago Wine School

Toscana - *Federico Bonfio, Azienda Agricola Bonfio*

The Bonfio family makes Chianti in the Colli Senesi zone just outside of Siena. Since purchasing and replanting a twelfth century estate twenty years ago, the Bonfio name has become known for Chianti made in the classic Italian style.

Toscana - *Roberto Stucchi-Prinetti, Badia a Coltibuono*

Once an abbey, this ancient estate in Chianti Classico owned by the Stucchi Prinetti family specializes in "Riserva". Roberto Stucchi Prinetti studied winemaking at The University of California and worked in a California winery before returning to make wine at his family's estate.

Campania - *Antonio Mastroberardino, Azienda Vinicola Mastroberardino*

With vineyards in the shadow of Mt. Vesuvius, Mastroberardino produces wines from Italy's most ancient grape varieties. The premier winemaker of southern Italy is renowned for Taurasi, one of Italy's great red wines.

Piemonte - *Mauro Sebaste, Azienda Agricola Sebaste*

From the great red wine region of Northern Italy, Sebaste is the versatile producer of traditional Barolo as well as an innovative fantasy wine, Bricco Viole.

1:00 pm Italian Sparkling Wine Reception

1:15 pm Italian Wine Bar and Luncheon Buffet

Italian Interpretations and Inspirations from The 95th's Executive Chef David DiGregorio

Sunday, February 21st

12 noon A Culinary Tour Of Italy

Lucio Sorre, Vice President, Banfi Vintners

Banfi imports one out of every four bottles of wine entering the USA - from a complex Tuscan Brunello di Montalcino to Riunite, America's largest selling imported wine.

Banfi's chief wine taster, Dr. Sorre is a charming and witty commentator on Italian wine, food, and culture. He lectures at universities throughout the United States including Cornell where Banfi endowed the first chair in Wine Education and Management.

Sorre will match the cuisine of Emilia-Romagna, Lombardia, Veneto, and Toscana with a selection of nine Italian wines.

For further information, please call The 95th at 312/280.5450

THE 95th
John Hancock Center
875 North Michigan Ave.
Chicago, Illinois
60611-1998

FIGURE 21.3 Notice of a wine tasting. This mailer went to the patrons of The 95th restaurant. (Courtesy The 95th. Operated by the Dining Division of ARA Services. Reproduced by permission.)

FIGURE 21.4 The Monterey Cannery restaurant puts its wine list on a can. (Reproduced by permission.)

22

Creative Menus

A restaurant can display creativity in many ways—for example, through decor, menu design, and, of course, the food itself. The restaurants featured here are noted for their creative menu copy and design or for their unusual and original cuisine.

The Cajun Kitchen

Want to make your entire menu takeout? Print it on one side of a brown paper bag, as the Cajun Kitchen does. This menu offers entrées (steak and seafood), sandwiches, and breakfast plus beer, wine, and spirits on one side of a 10½-by-14½-inch brown paper bag. Printed in dark green and red, the listings are separated by boxes.

This limited menu offers steaks, ribs, and seafood as well as "Po-Boy" and hamburger sandwiches. Most items feature a Cajun or Creole accent. For instance, the Delta Queen is a burger topped with sliced mushrooms, artichoke hearts, and "plantation sauce."

The Ivy Barn and the Greenhouse

The Ivy Barn and the Greenhouse in West Palm Beach, Florida, and San Diego, California, have clever, attractive, and effective food and beverage menus. The drink menu and the food menu (Figure 22.1) are envelopes that look like a seed package with a color illustration of sweet peas. On the back of the envelopes is a description of how to plant and grow the flowers. The envelopes measure 6 by 9 inches.

Inside the drink list envelope are three die-cut cards with tabs entitled Fruit Drinks, Fun Drinks, and A Change of Pace. The Fruit Drinks panel is light blue with dark blue type. The next card, Fun Drinks, is a light green with dark green type, and the third card, a Change of Pace, is pink with purple type. In addition to the drinks, this menu advertises hors d'oeuvre plates.

The three food menu sections are headed Home Cookin'—Depending on where your home is, Beef Specialties, and Refreshingly Different . . . Sandwiches, Salads and Crepes. The Home Cookin' panel is light blue with dark blue type. This is a six-day menu with a different entrée offered each day.

The second food menu panel—Beef Specialties—is a pastel green with the listing of four sandwiches printed in dark green. The third menu card—pink paper with purple type—lists more sandwiches, salads, and crepes.

Boston Subway

The Boston Subway restaurant is in Hopkins, Minnesota, a suburb of Minneapolis. The menu has two panels and one fold and resembles a large subway ticket torn in half (Figure 22.2). The front panel, which measures 7½ by 11 inches, says Boston Subway, Admit One, and One Way. The menu color is orange with the listings in black. The paper is heavy, uncoated cover stock.

San Simeon

The San Simeon restaurant in Dallas has an attractive menu, but what makes it stand out is that through seasoning, preparation, or special ingredients, every item on the menu is unusual and creative (Figure 22.3). The complete listing is duplicated here to show the variety and creativity.

APPETIZERS

Smoked Gulf Shrimp rolled in Blue Corn Pancake with Sun Dried Tomato Salsa 8.50

Lobster and Pumpkin Pan Roast with Herb Brioche 11.00

Smoked Wild Mushroom Lasagna with Sauce of Yellow Tomatoes and Lemon Vodka 8.00

FIGURE 22.1 These "seed packet" menus from the Greenhouse and the Ivy Barn feature pull-out food and drink inserts. (Courtesy The Ivy Barn Restaurant. Reproduced by permission.)

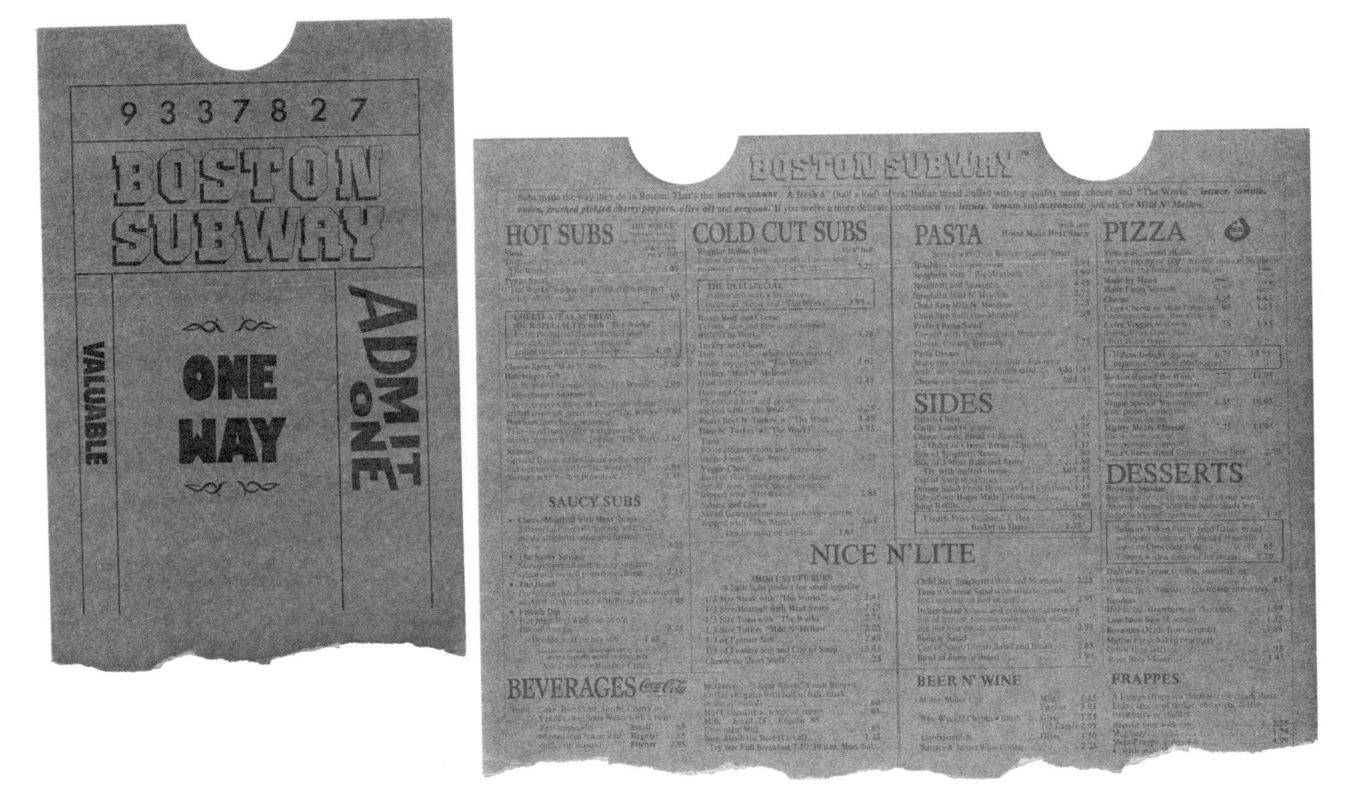

FIGURE 22.2 This menu for The Boston Subway is just the ticket. (Courtesy The Boston Subway Restaurant. Reproduced by permission.)

Escargot and Crescenza Cheese Ravioli with Chianti Thyme Sauce 7.50

Scottish Smoked Salmon and Mascarpone Cream with Lemon Mint Vinaigrette 9.50

Pan Seared Venison served on Sweet Potato Cake with Virginia Ham Sauce 9.00

SOUPS

White Bean and Roasted Garlic Soup with Red Bell Pepper Cream 5.00

Chowder of Venison Sausage, Sweet Corn and Wild Rice 5.50

Soup Du Jour 4.50

SALADS

Pan Fried Bobwhite Quail, Granny Smith Apple and Wild Rice Salad with Blackberry Mustard Dressing 8.75

Carpaccio of Tuna and Louisiana Crabmeat with Tomato Ginger Relish 8.00

Mozzarella and Tomato Salad with Marinated Shiitake Mushrooms and Roma Tomato Coulis 7.50

San Simeon Salad 6.00

ENTRÉES

Roast Breast of Pheasant with Gewurztraminer Pear Sauce and Walnut Barley Timbale 22.00

Caribbean Snapper Steamed in Coconut Milk with Key Lime Lobster Sauce 21.00

Pan Seared Breast of Duck with Sun Dried Cherry Sauce and Star Anise Sweet Potatoes 20.00

Rack of Lamb with Pumpernickel Goat Cheese Crust and Zinfandel Rosemary Sauce 24.00

Alaskan Salmon with Crisp Potato Crust and Fennel Mustard Sauce 21.00

Smoked Tenderloin of Beef with Cabernet Horseradish Sauce and Sweet Corn Grit Cake 23.00

Grilled Swordfish with White Clam Ginger Sauce and Tomato Chutney 22.50

Roast Breast of Chicken with Sauce of Sweet Peppers, Tasso Ham and Mustard 18.50

Grilled Veal T-Bone with Orange Thyme Butter and Spaghetti Squash 23.50

Sauteed Dover Sole with Sauce of Papaya, Cucumber and Mint 24.00

VEGETABLES AND POTATOES

Stir Fried Spinach 4.00

Cream Corn Casserole 3.25

Steamed Asparagus Spears 6.00

Three Cheese Potatoes 3.00

FIGURE 22.3 The menu from the San Simeon is an unusually creative presentation. (Courtesy San Simeon restaurant. Reproduced by permission.)

·APPETIZERS·

Smoked Gulf Shrimp rolled in Blue Corn Pancake with Sun Dried Tomato Salsa 8.50

Lobster and Pumpkin Pan Roast with Herb Brioche 11.00

Smoked Wild Mushroom Lasagna with Sauce of Yellow Tomatoes and Lemon Vodka 8.00

Escargot and Crescenza Cheese Ravioli with Chianti Thyme Sauce 7.50

Scottish Smoked Salmon and Mascarpone Cream with Lemon Mint Vinaigrette 9.50

Pan Seared Venison served on Sweet Potato Cake with Virginia Ham Sauce 9.00

·SOUPS·

White Bean and Roasted Garlic Soup with Red Bell Pepper Cream 5.00

Chowder of Venison Sausage, Sweet Corn and Wild Rice 5.50

Soup Du Jour 4.50

·SALADS·

Pan Fried Bobwhite Quail, Granny Smith Apple and Wild Rice Salad with Blackberry Mustard Dressing 8.75

Carpaccio of Tuna and Louisiana Crabmeat with Tomato Ginger Relish 8.00

Mozzarella and Tomato Salad with Marinated Shiitake Mushrooms and Roma Tomato Coulis 7.50

San Simeon Salad 6.00

The Club is Available for Private Parties

·ENTREES·

Roast Breast of Pheasant with Gewurztraminer Pear Sauce and Walnut Barley Timbale 22.00

Caribbean Snapper Steamed in Coconut Milk with Key Lime Lobster Sauce 21.00

Pan Seared Breast of Duck with Sun Dried Cherry Sauce and Star Anise Sweet Potatoes 20.00

Rack of Lamb with Pumpernickle Goat Cheese Crust and Zinfandel Rosemary Sauce 24.00

Alaskan Salmon with Crisp Potato Crust and Fennel Mustard Sauce 21.00

Smoked Tenderloin of Beef with Cabernet Horseradish Sauce and Sweet Corn Grit Cake 23.00

Grilled Swordfish with White Clam Ginger Sauce and Tomato Chutney 22.50

Roast Breast of Chicken with Sauce of Sweet Peppers, Tasso Ham and Mustard 18.50

Grilled Veal T-Bone with Orange Thyme Butter and Spaghetti Squash 23.50

Sauteed Dover Sole with Sauce of Papaya, Cucumber and Mint 24.00

·VEGETABLES AND POTATOES·

Stir Fried Spinach 4.00

Cream Corn Casserole 3.25

Steamed Asparagus Spears 6.00

Three Cheese Potatoes 3.00

Wild Mushroom Ratatouille 5.00

Assorted Pastries and Berries of the Season are Available for Your Dining Pleasure

A Selection of Cigars may be Purchased at the Humidor

Wild Mushroom Ratatouille 5.00

Assorted Pastries and Berries of the Season are Available for Your Dining Pleasure

A selection of Cigars may be Purchased at the Humidor

Country Greens

Country Greens on Route 30 East in Ronks, Pennsylvania, has an unusual menu designed by Jan Yatsko (Figure 22.4). It is printed in two colors, purple and dark green, on a light tan paper that is crisp and textured and not coated. It is a three-panel, two-fold menu, but each panel is a different width. The menu is 14 inches deep; the first panel is 6½ inches wide, the second is 4¼ inches, and the third is 6¼ inches wide.

When folded, panel 3 faces the customer, and the words Good Eatin' in the Country in large letters are visible from panel 1 running vertically up the side of the menu. When opened there is a line drawing on the bottom of panel 1, a take-off on Grant Wood's famous painting "American Gothic." The items listed on this panel are soups, salads, and beverages.

The listings on the center panel are headed Deli-Style Sandwiches and Desserts. The dessert listing refers the customer to the dessert menu while giving an overview of the dessert selections. Eleven sandwiches are listed. Two of these are under the heading of Croissant Sandwiches. The two featured sandwiches are Sliced Breast of Turkey (Lancaster County Swiss cheese, tomatoes, greens, mayonnaise, pumpernickel bread) and Cashew Chicken Salad on Croissant (white meat chicken, abundant cashews, and our own cooked dressing. Served with sprouts).

Panel 3 has four sections, headed Chicken Every Which Way, Beef, Seafood, and Country Eggs. Under the chicken listing are Chicken Grille, Chicken Tenders, Chicken Pot Pie, and Chicken and Waffles. Under Beef are Braised Beef Burgundy and five burgers. Under Seafood are listed Crabcake Sandwich, Peel-and-Eat Shrimp, and Breaded Butterfly Shrimp. The Country Eggs listing is an abbreviated breakfast listing for late risers.

This menu also has a separate entrée insert titled Country Evenings, which is inserted after 4 P.M. It measures 5½ by 13 inches and is printed on the same paper and in the same colors as the rest of the menu. It lists five entrées, four Combination Dinners (Italian, Chicken & Waffles, Chicken Pot Pie, and Braised Beef Burgundy), plus a Spaghetti listing that includes seven offerings. This add-on, which looks like part of the permanent menu, gives flexibility to the menu.

Red Robin International

Red Robin International's colorful and interesting menu is designed for summer business (Figure 22.5). It is die-cut in the shape of a pineapple and measures roughly 9 by 17 inches. The smiling pineapple face on the cover sports colorful sunglasses, and the copy reads "Summer Red Robin Shades." The entire menu is in bright summer hues. The menu items are set in black type and centered on the inside two panels. They are surrounded by vivid color illustrations of fruits and vegetables. On the left panel are listed Appetizers—Seashell Pasta Salad and Buzzard Wings; Chilled Summer Soup—Southwestern Gazpacho; and Signature Salads—Tropical Extravaganza and Seashell Pasta Supreme.

The right-hand panel lists Chilled Salad Plates—Caribbean Chicken, BBQ Chicken, and Stir-Fry Chicken Salad; and Summer Sandwiches—Robin's Deluxe Clubhouse and Caribbean Chicken. All items are described in detail.

The back cover displays the dessert and drink listings. Here too the listings, in black type, are surrounded by colorful fruit illustrations. Under the heading Desserts in Summer Shades are Strawberry Tall Cake, New York Cheesecake, and Frozen Strawberry Yogurt. Under the heading Exotic Summer Drinks are Tropical Fruit Nectars, New York Seltzers, and The Soda Fountain. Iced Tea, Iced Coffee, Frozen Mai Tai, Peach Schnappsicle, Caribbean Breeze, and Tropical Margaritas are listed under the heading Cool and Refreshing. Margaritas include Guavarita, Cocopinerita, and Passionorangerita (fever remedies created by Master Mixologist Tim O'Brien).

Checkers Cafe

Checkers Cafe's Hot Platters menu is a brightly colored record album, complete with record (Figure 22.6). It is designed with the latest computer graphic techniques. In most cases, foods are grouped by category and described with phrases drawn from popular rock and roll tunes; for example, the Hefty and the Eaters section includes Sargeant Peppered Shrimp and Rockin Chicken. Other items are All American Burger and the Hot Doggers, Shake Cattle and Roll, and Eggcetera.

One side of the actual record features seven popular desserts such as Checkered Chip Monk Ice Cream Sandwich, America's Apple Pie, and Bananamation. The pizza selection is on the flip side. Six pizza slices are illustrated by color photographs.

The record jacket and menu measure 12 by 12 inches. The entire menu is printed in full color on heavy,

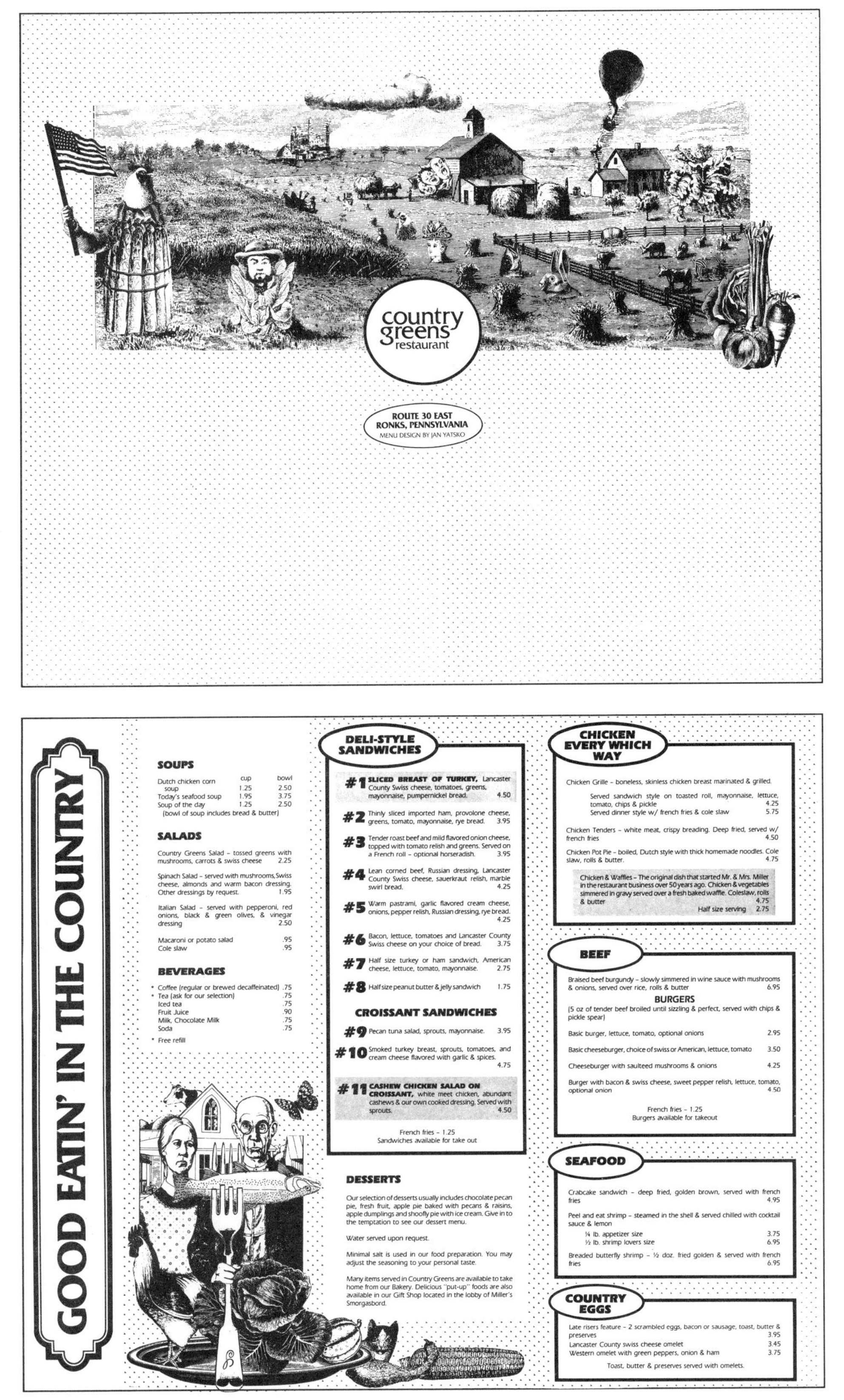

country greens restaurant

ROUTE 30 EAST
RONKS, PENNSYLVANIA
MENU DESIGN BY JAN YATSKO

GOOD EATIN' IN THE COUNTRY

SOUPS

	cup	bowl
Dutch chicken corn soup	1.25	2.50
Today's seafood soup	1.95	3.75
Soup of the day	1.25	2.50

(bowl of soup includes bread & butter)

SALADS

Country Greens Salad – tossed greens with mushrooms, carrots & swiss cheese 2.25

Spinach Salad – served with mushrooms, Swiss cheese, almonds and warm bacon dressing. Other dressings by request. 1.95

Italian Salad – served with pepperoni, red onions, black & green olives, & vinegar dressing 2.50

Macaroni or potato salad .95
Cole slaw .95

BEVERAGES

* Coffee (regular or brewed decaffeinated) .75
* Tea (ask for our selection) .75
Iced tea .75
Fruit Juice .90
Milk, Chocolate Milk .75
Soda .75

* Free refill

DELI-STYLE SANDWICHES

#1 SLICED BREAST OF TURKEY, Lancaster County Swiss cheese, tomatoes, greens, mayonnaise, pumpernickel bread. 4.50

#2 Thinly sliced imported ham, provolone cheese, greens, tomato, mayonnaise, rye bread. 3.95

#3 Tender roast beef and mild flavored onion cheese, topped with tomato relish and greens. Served on a French roll – optional horseradish. 3.95

#4 Lean corned beef, Russian dressing, Lancaster County Swiss cheese, sauerkraut relish, marble swirl bread. 4.25

#5 Warm pastrami, garlic flavored cream cheese, onions, pepper relish, Russian dressing, rye bread. 4.25

#6 Bacon, lettuce, tomatoes and Lancaster County Swiss cheese on your choice of bread. 3.75

#7 Half size turkey or ham sandwich, American cheese, lettuce, tomato, mayonnaise. 2.75

#8 Half size peanut butter & jelly sandwich 1.75

CROISSANT SANDWICHES

#9 Pecan tuna salad, sprouts, mayonnaise. 3.95

#10 Smoked turkey breast, sprouts, tomatoes, and cream cheese flavored with garlic & spices. 4.75

#11 CASHEW CHICKEN SALAD ON CROISSANT, white meet chicken, abundant cashews & our own cooked dressing. Served with sprouts. 4.50

French fries – 1.25
Sandwiches available for take out

DESSERTS

Our selection of desserts usually includes chocolate pecan pie, fresh fruit, apple pie baked with pecans & raisins, apple dumplings and shoofly pie with ice cream. Give in to the temptation to see our dessert menu.

Water served upon request.

Minimal salt is used in our food preparation. You may adjust the seasoning to your personal taste.

Many items served in Country Greens are available to take home from our Bakery. Delicious "put-up" foods are also available in our Gift Shop located in the lobby of Miller's Smorgasbord.

CHICKEN EVERY WHICH WAY

Chicken Grille – boneless, skinless chicken breast marinated & grilled.

Served sandwich style on toasted roll, mayonnaise, lettuce, tomato, chips & pickle 4.25
Served dinner style w/ french fries & cole slaw 5.75

Chicken Tenders – white meat, crispy breading. Deep fried, served w/ french fries 4.50

Chicken Pot Pie – boiled, Dutch style with thick homemade noodles. Cole slaw, rolls & butter. 4.75

Chicken & Waffles – The original dish that started Mr. & Mrs. Miller in the restaurant business over 50 years ago. Chicken & vegetables simmered in gravy served over a fresh baked waffle. Coleslaw, rolls & butter 4.75
Half size serving 2.75

BEEF

Braised beef burgundy – slowly simmered in wine sauce with mushrooms & onions, served over rice, rolls & butter 6.95

BURGERS

(5 oz of tender beef broiled until sizzling & perfect, served with chips & pickle spear)

Basic burger, lettuce, tomato, optional onions 2.95

Basic cheeseburger, choice of swiss or American, lettuce, tomato 3.50

Cheeseburger with saulteed mushrooms & onions 4.25

Burger with bacon & swiss cheese, sweet pepper relish, lettuce, tomato, optional onion 4.50

French fries – 1.25
Burgers available for takeout

SEAFOOD

Crabcake sandwich – deep fried, golden brown, served with french fries 4.95

Peel and eat shrimp – steamed in the shell & served chilled with cocktail sauce & lemon
¼ lb. appetizer size 3.75
½ lb. shrimp lovers size 6.95

Breaded butterfly shrimp – ½ doz. fried golden & served with french fries 6.95

COUNTRY EGGS

Late risers feature – 2 scrambled eggs, bacon or sausage, toast, butter & preserves 3.95
Lancaster County swiss cheese omelet 3.45
Western omelet with green peppers, onion & ham 3.75

Toast, butter & preserves served with omelets.

FIGURE 22.4 Creative menu from Country Greens. (Courtesy Country Greens restaurant. Reproduced by permission.)

FIGURE 22.5 This menu from Red Robin is worthy of Pineapple Pol. (Courtesy Red Robin International. Reproduced by permission.)

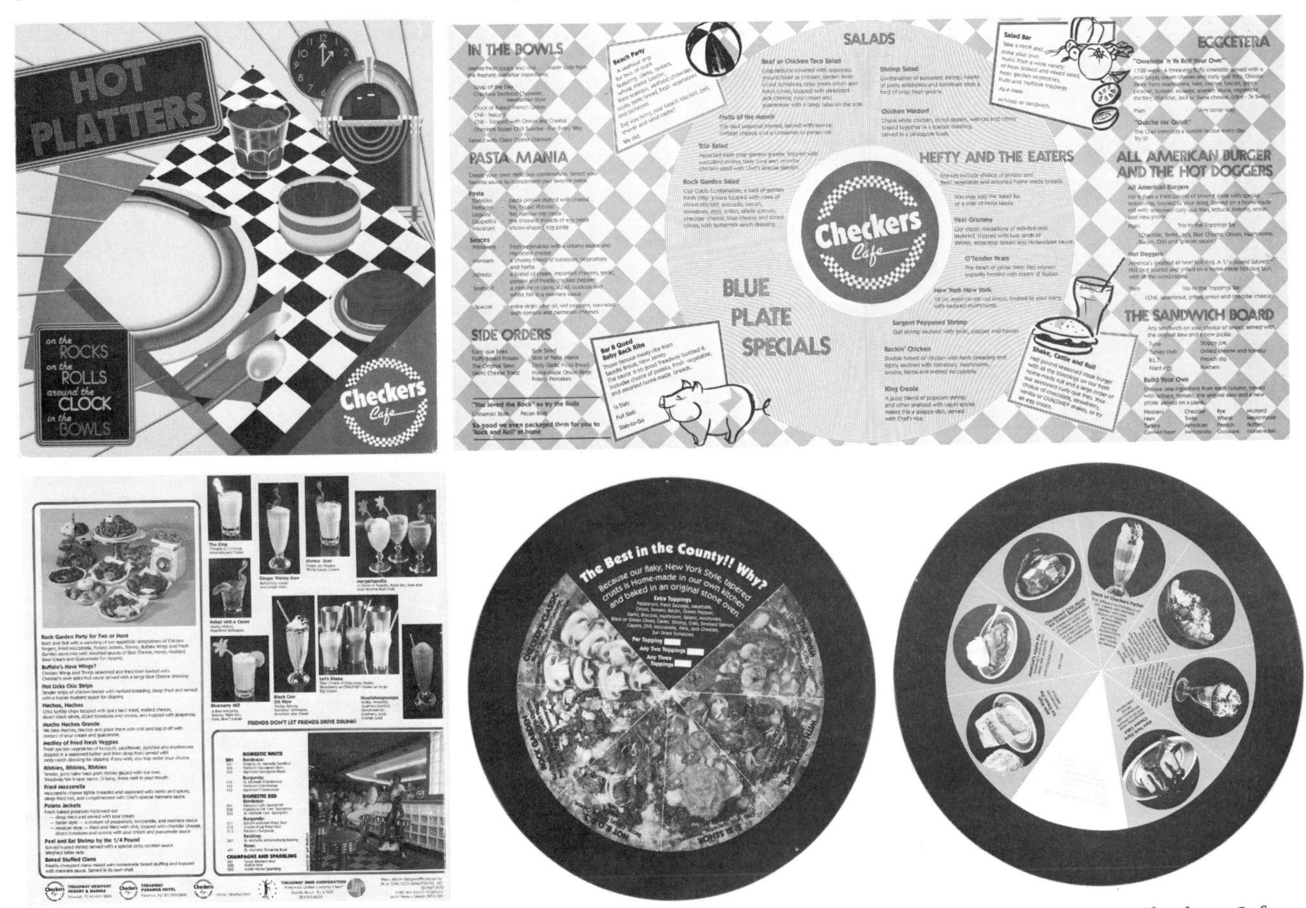

FIGURE 22.6 Menu from Checkers Cafe. A record jacket (plus records) makes this a creative menu. (Courtesy Checkers Cafe. Treadway Inns Corporation. Menu album designed/produced by Ron Carlucci Advertising, Inc. Reproduced by permission.)

coated paper, just like an album jacket. The cover shows a checkerboard with "on the ROCKS, on the ROLLS, around the CLOCK and in the BOWLS," written on the board.

For changes to the menu, a daily blue plate special card is placed in the album. Prices can easily be changed on this menu, as they are written on the menu with a special permanent pen that can be removed by lacquer.

Trader's Grill

If you are staying at the Taipei Hilton in Taiwan and decide to eat at the Trader's Grill, you will receive a sophisticated, illustrated menu of appetizers, soups, and entrées (Figure 22.7). This eight-page menu measures 10 by 14 inches. Each page of listings on the right-hand side has an illustration facing it on the left-hand side. The illustrations are "antique" pick-up color drawings that complement the unusual food listings. The listing pages are framed by ornaments, and they and the type are dark brown on a yellow background. The paper is heavy, glossy, cover stock lightly coated for extended wear.

The appetizers are listed under the heading To Begin With. The five unusual items include Truffled Goose Liver—a sherried parfait presented in its terrine plus melba toast; Escargots Madagascar—sautéed snails in fresh green pepper buds and cream chablis; The Golden Coins—the Chinese name for a delicacy of prawn and crabs; Poseidon's Treasure—gravlax, prawn salad, marinated herring, and smoked pomfret, each served with their particular sauce; Sashimi—Oluanpi tuna from the local waters served with green horseradish, soya, and shredded turnip.

Five soups are offered: Essence of Oxtail—refined with old sherry and served with ginger straw; Potage Bourguignon—snail soup, prepared and flamed at your table (for two); Consommé Double with Beef Marrow; Velouté of Fresh Tomatoes—garnished with whipped cream and golden croutons; and Taiwanese Oyster Soup—with ginger, Chinese parsley, black mushrooms, and sesame oil.

The next entrée listing is headed From the Rotisserie. For lunch the offering is Crisp Pork Knuckle—with caraway seed, served with a cabbage salad and roesti potatoes. For dinner, the offering is Spit Roasted Lamb Leg "Provençale" with glaced shallots.

The next entrée heading is Trader's Choice: Goose Liver "Berlin"—slices of fresh goose liver sautéed in butter and garnished with apple rings and crisp fried onions; Veal Escalope "Oscar"—tender baby veal topped with medallions of lobster and glazed with an

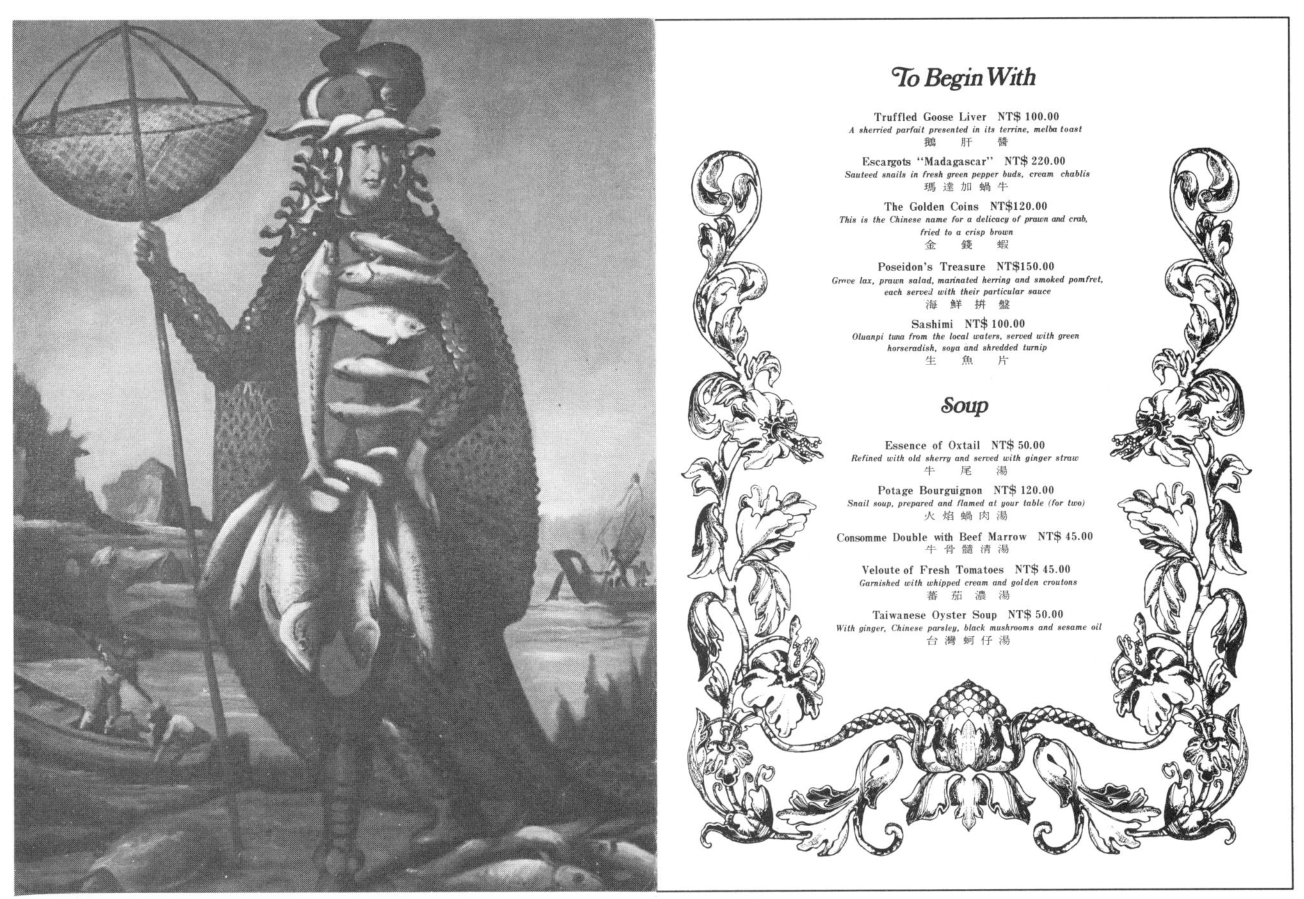
To Begin With

Truffled Goose Liver NT$ 100.00
A sherried parfait presented in its terrine, melba toast
鵝 肝 醬

Escargots "Madagascar" NT$ 220.00
Sauteed snails in fresh green pepper buds, cream chablis
瑪 達 加 蝸 牛

The Golden Coins NT$120.00
This is the Chinese name for a delicacy of prawn and crab, fried to a crisp brown
金 錢 蝦

Poseidon's Treasure NT$150.00
Grave lax, prawn salad, marinated herring and smoked pomfret, each served with their particular sauce
海 鮮 拼 盤

Sashimi NT$ 100.00
Oluanpi tuna from the local waters, served with green horseradish, soya and shredded turnip
生 魚 片

Soup

Essence of Oxtail NT$ 50.00
Refined with old sherry and served with ginger straw
牛 尾 湯

Potage Bourguignon NT$ 120.00
Snail soup, prepared and flamed at your table (for two)
火 焰 蝸 肉 湯

Consomme Double with Beef Marrow NT$ 45.00
牛 骨 髓 清 湯

Veloute of Fresh Tomatoes NT$ 45.00
Garnished with whipped cream and golden croutons
蕃 茄 濃 湯

Taiwanese Oyster Soup NT$ 50.00
With ginger, Chinese parsley, black mushrooms and sesame oil
台 灣 蚵 仔 湯

FIGURE 22.7 A creative menu from the Taipei Hilton. (Courtesy Hilton International, Taipei. Reproduced by permission.)

herb sauce; Ginger Fillet—fillet tips on ginger cream sauce with herbs and a touch of garlic; Pork Cutlet "Alsacienne"—served with sauerkraut and snow potatoes; and Cherry Duck—a crisp roasted duck, complemented with glazed dark cherries.

Under the heading of Flaming and Fancy are seven entrées: Steak Tartar, Black Pepper Steak, Veal Kidney "Dijon," King Prawn "Au Sherry," Pork Fillet "Woronoff," Spring Chicken with Black Mushrooms, and Fillet of Beef Svegedi.

The fourth listing of entrées is under the heading From the Glowing Coals: Trader's Delight—a tenderloin and a freshly caught lobster tail served with bearnaise sauce; Shish Kebab; Mixed Grill; Colorado Prime Choice Sirloin; Charbroiled Rib of Beef—for two persons, carved tableside and offered with corn pancakes and bacon.

Bleachers Restaurant

The menu of Bleachers restaurant in the Village East Resort and Conference Center at Lake Okoboji, Spirit Lake, Iowa, is creative in design, copy, and cuisine. A horizontal eight-page menu, it measures 14 by 8½ inches and is designed and die-cut to look like a sports event ticket (Figure 22.8). It is printed in red, blue, and black on heavy but uncoated stock.

The cover has a large Bleachers logo plus copy reading "Admit One" and "Your Ticket to Good Eating." Pages 2 and 3 are dominated by an illustration of assorted "bleacher bums." Panel one has a listing of beverages headed The Pre-Game Show—House Features (unusual cocktails such as Goombay Smash, Lemon Lush, and Long Island Tea). The other categories are By the Glass California House Wines, Non Alcoholic Specialties (some different items here, such as Clausthaler malt beverage from Germany and Chamay Sparkling French Cider), and Best of Beers.

Appetizers, snacks, soup, and chili are listed on page 3 under the heading Starters and Sidelines. Page 4 contains the salad listing plus a drawing and a paragraph of copy about Babe Ruth. Seven salads are listed, including Curry Bird Salad (creamy chicken salad lightly seasoned with curry spices in a fresh pineapple shell) and Fisherman Salad in a Pastry Shell (crabmeat, shrimp, and other ocean fare along with bits of celery, bell peppers, and scallions folded into a mayonnaise dressing).

Page 5 lists a Varsity Sandwich Board and includes a drawing plus a paragraph of copy about Wilt Chamberlain. Eleven sandwiches are listed. Featured in a box is Slim & Trim, only 530 calories (grilled chicken breast seasoned with lemon pepper, fresh fruit, cottage cheese, and muffins).

Page 6 Features at Bleachers is the entrée listing. To the left is a drawing and copy about Billie Jean King. Seven beef, pork, and seafood entrées are featured. A Friday and Saturday Night Special (roast prime rib of beef) is featured in a box, and four stir-fry selections—shrimp, chicken, scallops, and steak—complete the entrée offerings.

FIGURE 22.8 Menu from Bleachers. (Courtesy Bleachers® Restaurant. Village East Resort and Conference Center. Reproduced by permission.)

Just Desserts, Things To Drink, and Jr. Varsity (children's menu) are listed on page 7. Desserts include New York Pinstripe Cheesecake (with three toppings), Double Rich Carrot Cake with cream cheese icing, Ice Cream, Sherbet, Pie, A Dessert Tray, and Ice Cream Drinks.

The children's Jr. Varsity menu includes Chicken Strips and French Fries, P.B. & J. Sandwich, and Grilled Cheese and French Fries. The famous athlete featured on this panel is Jack Nicklaus.

The back cover has a drawing and copy about Johnny Unitas as well as suggestions for after-dinner drinks (Happy Endings) and party planning (the party, banquet, and meeting capabilities of Village East Resort, Okoboji).

Ginsberg + Wong

Located in the colorful Village by the Grange in Toronto, Ontario, Canada, Ginsberg + Wong offers its clientele oversized portions of deli and Chinese cuisine with an oversized menu listing more than seventy-five items (Figure 22.9). The food is presented in Chinese steam baskets and sizzling platters. The restaurant features a cast of cooks in an open kitchen, a roving magician, and an energetic wait staff. Constructed of light wood and used brick with stained-glass windows, the restaurant presents a sunny atmosphere. Children are delighted with the presentation of a giant fortune cookie on birthdays or special occasions.

Ginsberg + Wong has a large, three-panel menu. Two panels measure 12 by 20 inches and one panel measures 6 by 20 inches. The cover is illustrated by a comic strip with the story of how Ginsberg and Wong met and opened a combined deli and Chinese restaurant. The artwork plus the rest of the menu is printed in full color on heavy, white, plastic-coated paper.

The first inside column begins with On Your Mark! Get Set! GO! (appetizers and extras). There are nine of these items, some Chinese, some deli. Next, five hot soups are offered, among them Bubbie Ginsberg's Jewish Chicken Soup and Grandma Wong's Hot & Sour Power Soup. Soups are followed by The Garden Party—seven listed salads.

At the top right of this panel the heading is Papa Ginsberg's Deli Delights with an offering of nine traditional deli sandwiches, including lox and bagels. This is followed by Zuper Duper Sandwiches (three)—Chicken a la Zing, the Ike and Tina Tuna Review, and the Veal Thing.

The center panel begins with five more traditional entrées that are neither Chinese nor deli fare: a salmon-trout fillet, pepper steak, BBQ'd spare ribs, chicken, and T-bone steak. These are followed by twenty Chinese Treasures (entrées), giving the customer plenty to choose from.

At the top right of the second center panel is listed From the Grill of Your Dreams—a hamburger and a hot dog. Thirteen extras are listed under the heading Topper Uppers.

On the third narrow panel the inside top listing is Quenchers—Beer, Wine, Sangria, and Cocktails. This is followed by Other Crazy Concoctions—Long Island Iced Tea, Gumbay Smash, Beautiful, Bountiful Bloody Mary, Margarita Magnifica, The Hammer, and Ugly, Ungainly Bloody Caesar. Next come five Ice Cream Dreams, Shots (vodka, gin, scotch, rye, and rum), and Shooters.

The back side of the smaller panel begins with Oasis of Dessert, offering six desserts—cakes, pies, cheesecake, and chocolate mousse. This is followed by Sundae Shopping (six sundaes). Next, under the heading of Cafe International, are six coffees (Dubliner's Dream Irish Coffee, El Café Madrid, Brazilian Bombshell, Bailey's Brew, Count Cristo, and Jamaica Farewell). Finally, under the heading Wet, But Not Too Wild, is a soft drink listing.

The combination of deli and Chinese cuisine plus the colorful cartoon artwork and the sprightly copy combine to make this an exceptionally creative menu.

Prairie

The Prairie restaurant in Chicago is unusual in its cuisine, which might be called "heartland" American (Figure 22.10). According to Chef Stephen Langlois, "The Prairie's whole tradition rests on the idea of ripe and fresh Midwestern foods." The menu, therefore, is changed seasonally to present Midwestern products in the best way.

There are eight Starters (appetizers), all unusual: Corn Chowder with Tarragon Leaves and Paprika Bacon; Sauté of Regional Mushrooms in a Corn Muffin with a Light Mushroom Cream; Warm Apple Sausage and Sage Turnover, Apple Cider Glaze; Smoked Turkey–Yam Fritters in a Sweet and Sour Cranberry Custard Sauce; Mild Brandied Gameloaf of Duck, Pheasant, and Rabbit served with Wild Plum Ketchup; Grilled Smoked Trout Terrine with Horseradish–Dill Mayonnaise; Fresh Breast of Turkey Sandwich on Wheat Millet Bread; and Paper Thin Smoked Ham Grilled with Smoked Gouda on Wheat Millet Bread.

Next are five salads offered either in a small plate version or as an entrée: Warm Spinach Salad with Thinly Sliced Grilled Pork Loin and Apple Caraway Kraut; Assorted Baby Lettuces with Fried Coho Salmon and Toasted Pumpkin Seeds; A Prairie Chef's Salad with Local Meats, Cheeses and Greens, served with choice of dressing; Sliced Grilled Duck Breast Salad with Marinated Root Vegetables and Honey Thyme Dressing; and Roasted Lamb Rack Salad with Boneless Lamb Slices, Blue Cheese, Pickled Pumpkin, and Bibb Lettuce. A Prairie Field Salad is also offered. As entrées, these salads vary in price from $9 to $13. As small-plate items to accompany an entrée, they run from $6 to $9.

FIGURE 22.9 Menu from Ginsberg + Wong. (Reproduced by permission.)

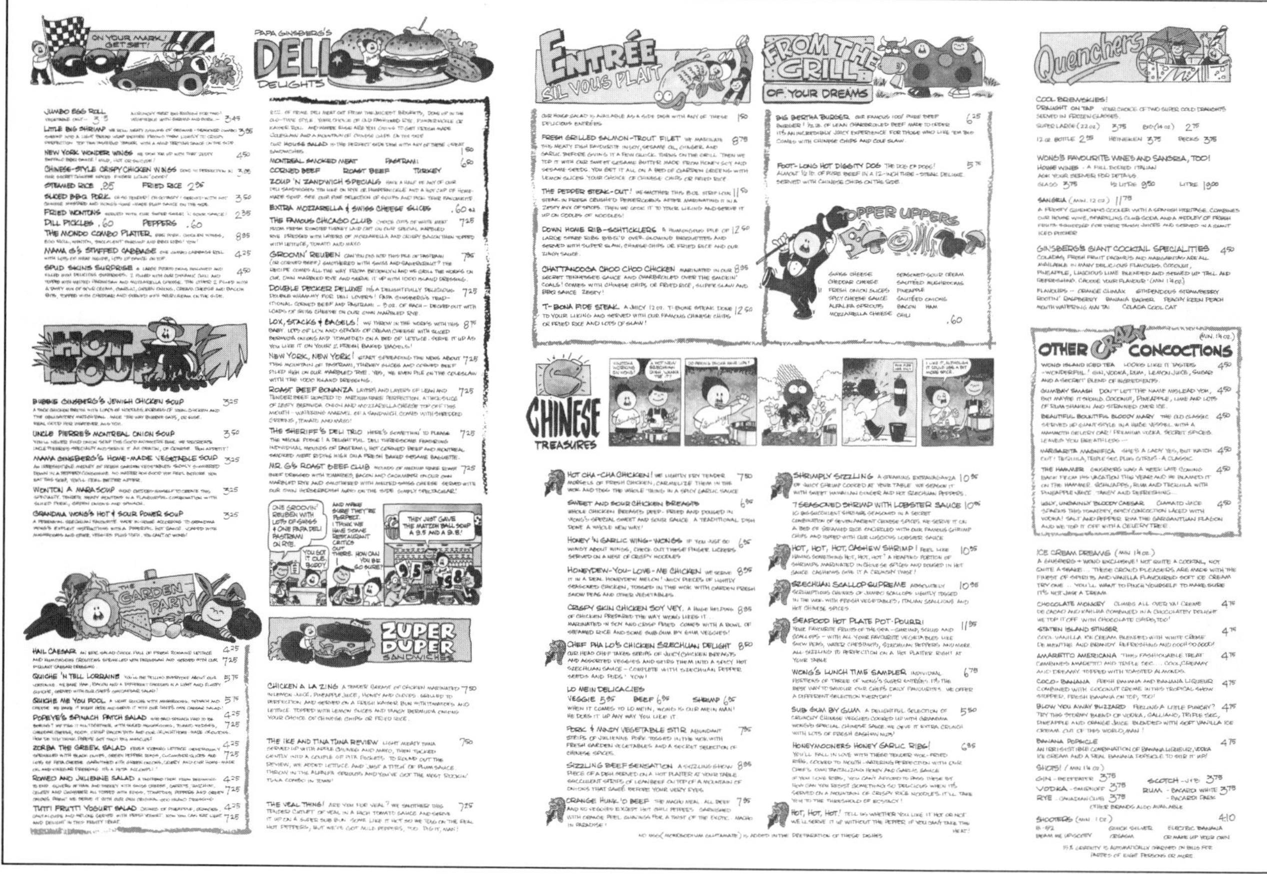

WINE LIST

Sparkling Wine

Bin		
700	Domaine Chandon Blanc de Noir	$27.00
701	Iron Horse Brut	35.00
702	Mount Pleasant Brut Reserve	25.00
703	Piper-Sonoma Brut	26.00
704	Scharffenberger Brut Blanc de Blancs	35.00
705	Michel Tribaut Brut Rose	26.00

White Wine

706	Acacia Chardonnay Carneros	32.00
707	Chateau Grand Traverse Chardonnay	25.00
708	Chateau St. Jean Chardonnay Belle Terre Vineyard	28.00
709	Crosswoods Chardonnay	25.00
710	DeLoach Sonoma Valley Chardonnay	30.00
711	Edna Valley Chardonnay "Edna Valley"	30.00
712	Far Niente Chardonnay	45.00
713	Kalin Chardonnay	40.00
714	Kendall-Jackson Proprietors Reserve Chardonnay	30.00
715	Kistler Dutton Ranch Chardonnay	30.00
716	Le Crema Chardonnay	21.00
717	Sonoma-Cutrer Chardonnay "Russian River"	26.00
718	William Hill Chardonnay "Reserve Gold Label"	31.00
719	Dry Creek Fume Blanc	25.00
720	Husch Sauvignon Blanc "La Ribera"	18.00
721	Matanzas Creek Sauvignon Blanc	25.00
722	Morgan Sauvignon Blanc	19.00
723	Pine Ridge Chenin Blanc	17.00
724	Congress Spring Pinot Blanc	19.00
725	Eyrie Pinot Gris	19.00
726	Chateau Grand Traverse Riesling	21.00
727	Lynfred Vidal Blanc	18.00

Red Wine

728	Arrowwood Cabernet Sauvignon	31.00
729	Alexander Valley Cabernet Sauvignon	21.00
730	Caymus Napa Cuvee Cabernet Sauvignon	23.00
731	Chateau Montelena Cabernet Sauvignon	36.00
732	R. B. Cohen Cabernet Sauvignon	28.00
733	Girard Cabernet Sauvignon	30.00
734	Far Niente Cabernet Sauvignon	47.00
735	J. Phelps Insignia	45.00
736	Pine Ridge Cabernet Sauvignon "Rutherford Ranch"	23.00
737	Silverado Cabernet Sauvignon	26.00
738	Stags Leap Wine Cellars Napa Valley Cabernet Sauvignon	33.00
739	Adelsheim Pinot Noir	30.00
740	Calera Pinot Noir "Reed"	40.00
741	Ricciohli Pinot Noir	31.00
742	Mondavi Reserve Pinot Noir	35.00
743	Clos du Bois Merlot	21.00
744	Buena Vista Merlot	20.00
745	Alexis Baily Marshal Foch	16.00
746	Mount Pleasant Emigra Red	17.00
747	Wollersheim Du Sac	16.00
748	Lynton Springs Zinfandel	21.00

PRAIRIE

A restaurant of the heartland

•

Located in the Landmark Omni Morton Hotel

500 S. Dearborn, Chicago, IL 60605

312.663.1143

A Fall and Winter Menu

STARTERS

Corn Chowder with Tarragon Leaves and Paprika Bacon	3.50
Saute of Regional Mushrooms in a Corn Muffin with a Light Mushroom Cream	6.50
Warm Apple Sausage and Sage Turnover, Apple Cider Glaze	6.50
Smoked Turkey-Yam Fritters in a Sweet and Sour Cranberry Custard Sauce	6.50
Mild Brandied Gameloaf of Duck, Pheasant and Rabbit, served with Wild Plum Ketchup	6.50
Chilled Smoked Trout Terrine with Horseradish-Dill Mayonnaise	6.50
Fresh Breast of Turkey Sandwich on Wheat Millet Bread *(Available Lunch Only)*	7.00
Paper Thin Smoked Ham Grilled with Smoked Gouda on Wheat Millet Bread *(Available Lunch Only)*	7.00

SALADS

Warm Spinach Salad with Thinly Sliced Grilled Pork Loin and Apple Caraway Kraut	10.00
Small Plate with Entree	7.00
Assorted Baby Lettuces with Fried Coho Salmon and Toasted Pumpkin Seeds	12.00
Small Plate with Entree	9.00
A Prairie Chef's Salad with Local Meats, Cheeses and Greens, Served with Your Choice of Dressing	9.00
Small Plate with Entree	6.00
Sliced Grilled Duck Breast Salad with Marinated Root Vegetables and Honey Thyme Dressing	11.00
Small Plate with Entree	8.00
Roasted Lamb Rack Salad with Boneless Lamb Slices, Blue Cheese, Pickled Pumpkin and Bibb Lettuce	13.00
Prairie Field Salad, with Your Choice of Dressings	4.00

Stephen Langlois, Executive Chef
A Chicago Dining Authority, Inc. Restaurant

FROM THE WOOD BURNING GRILL

Boneless Dubuque Pork Chop with Bar-B-Que Butter	15.00
Grilled Provimi Veal Chop with Apples, Chestnuts and Cranberries	22.00
Planked Lake Superior Whitefish with Door County Accompaniments and Scallion Flavored Fish Broth	16.00
One Pound Chargrilled Kansas City Strip Steak	21.00
A Prairie Buffalo Sirloin Steak, Reduced Natural Juices	21.00
A Smaller Steak	16.00

MAIN COURSES

Boneless Duck Breast Pan Roasted Medium Rare, Served with a Dried Cherry and Port Wine Sauce	17.00
Smaller Portion *(Available Lunch Only)*	12.00
Panned Baby Coho Salmon with Bacon, Leeks and Black Walnuts	17.00
Herb Roasted Rack of Wisconsin Lamb, Natural Juices	21.00
Baked Walleye Pike Stuffed with Vegetables and Wild Rice Served with a Four Parsley Sauce	17.00
Roasted Chicken with Corn and Sage Dressing in a Chive Cream Gravy	14.00
Our Favorite Winter Burgoo; a Traditional Prairie Stew of Buffalo, Rabbit Sausage and Winter Vegetables	16.00
A Smaller Stew	13.00

All Entrees are Served with a Selection of Relishes and Side Dishes.

DESSERTS

Walnut and Caramel Schaum Torte	4.00
Homemade Sweet Potato Praline Cheesecake	4.00
Butterscotch Raisin Meringue Pie	4.00
Chocolate Cake with Chocolate Maple Mousse and Dutch Honey	4.00
Warm Indian Persimmon Pudding with Dried Blueberries	4.50
Fresh Homemade Apple Pie	4.00
Bittersweet Hot Fudge Sundae	4.00
Homer's Old-Fashioned Ice Cream: Chocolate, Vanilla, PrairieBerry, Apple Cinnamon	3.00

Please refrain from smoking pipes or cigars.

FIGURE 22.10 The Prairie restaurant menu. (Courtesy A Chicago Dining Authority, Inc. Restaurant. Reproduced by permission.)

An ample selection of entrées is listed under the headings From the Wood Burning Grill and Main Courses. The five grilled entrées include Boneless Dubuque Pork Chop with Bar-B-Que Butter; Grilled Provimi Veal Chop with Apples, Chestnuts and Cranberries; Planked Lake Superior Whitefish with Door County Accompaniments and Scallion Flavored Fish Broth; One Pound Chargrilled Kansas City Strip Steak; and a Prairie Buffalo Sirloin Steak, Reduced Natural Juices.

Six items are listed under Main Courses: Boneless Duck Breast Pan Roasted Medium Rare, Served with a Dried Cherry and Port Wine Sauce; Panned Baby Coho Salmon with Bacon, Leeks and Black Walnuts; Herb Roasted Rack of Wisconsin Lamb, Natural Juices; Baked Walleye Pike Stuffed with Vegetables and Wild Rice; Chicken with Corn and Sage Dressing in a Chive Cream Gravy; and Our Favorite Winter Burgoo, a Traditional Prairie Stew of Buffalo,

Rabbit Sausage and Winter Vegetables. (This is a winter and fall menu.)

Some new midwestern desserts are listed on this menu: Walnut and Caramel Schaum Torte; Homemade Sweet Potato Praline Cheesecake; Butterscotch Raisin Meringue Pie; Chocolate Cake with Chocolate Maple Mousse and Dutch Honey; Warm Indian Persimmon Pudding with Dried Blueberries; Fresh Homemade Apple Pie; Bittersweet Hot Fudge Sundae; and Homer's Old Fashioned Ice Cream.

Prairie's wine list includes some unusual American wines not usually served in restaurants. Six sparkling wines include Iron Horse Brut; twenty-two white wines include Crosswoods Chardonnay, Dry Creek Fumé Blanc, and Pine Ridge Chenin Blanc. Among the twenty-one red wines listed are Arrowwood Cabernet Sauvignon, Mount Pleasant Emigra Red, and Lynton Springs Zinfandel.

Prairie's menu brings together the finest regional foodstuffs, retaining the best old American recipes but updating them with new creative touches.

23

Two Decades of Menu Change and Continuity

Four restaurant menus, from 1965 to 1988, are compared here: the Scandia restaurant menu from Los Angeles, the Whitehall Club menu from Chicago, the Gage & Tollner's restaurant menu from Brooklyn, and the Four Seasons restaurant menu from Manhattan.

As might be expected, the 1988 menus show much higher prices than those of the 1965 menus. This increase is the result of inflation. There are other changes. In nearly every case, the 1988 menu lists fewer items in all categories than does the 1965 menu. In many instances this reduction in the number of items has been accompanied by upscaling of the items offered.

Other menu patterns are constant. Sirloin and filet mignon steaks, seafood, and chicken are steady favorites. Special dishes such as the ethnic ones on the Scandia menu and Steak Diane on the Whitehall Club menu remain popular.

This comparison over a twenty-three-year period is not a scientific survey. The restaurants compared are upscale, expensive establishments. But they have stayed in business—in the case of Gage & Tollner's, over one hundred years!

Scandia

In 1988 the Scandia restaurant, now known as Petersen's Scandia, was still serving food similar, if not identical, to that served in 1965. The prices have changed drastically, but good food, well prepared, is still the requirement for a top-quality restaurant.

The 1965 Scandia menu listed twenty cold appetizers (Figure 23.1), ranging in price from $.85 for Danish Liver Pâté to $2.75 for Fresh Smoked Baltic Salmon. In addition, a Cold Cabaret for two or more, a miniature smörgåsbord served at the table, was offered at $4.75 per person. The 1988 Scandia lists twelve appetizers (Figure 23.2) ranging in price from $4.75 to $14.75, plus Imported Beluga Caviar at $42.00 per ounce. A Smörgås Bricka similar to the Cold Cabaret (for two or more) is offered at $8.75 per person.

Two different and interesting appetizers on the current menu are Viking Blinis—Miniature Pancakes flavored with Aquavit and Served with Sour Cream and Danish Caviar; and the Great Hamlet's Dagger—Tiny Lobster Tails Deviled and Broiled on the Skewer, Flambéed with Aquavit and Served with Caviar Sauce.

The 1965 menu also had a listing of eight hot appetizers, including the Great Hamlet's Dagger. Prices were $1.85 and $2.00.

Five soups were offered on the 1965 menu, at $.65 and $.85. These included Swedish Pea Soup and Curried Turtle Soup. The 1988 menu also has four soups, but the Swedish Pea Soup sells for $3.50.

Eleven salads were offered on the old menu, for prices ranging from $.85 to $2.00. The 1988 menu lists seven salads, ranging in price from $3.50 to $17.75 for Broiled Seafood Salad—Swordfish, Shrimp, Salmon, Scallops, Tortellini, Raddicchio, Butter Lettuce, Dill, Broccoli, and Bell Peppers with a Basil Tomato Dressing.

On the 1965 menu, but not on the 1988 menu, was the heading Aquavit—served ice cold—with imported beer for $.85 each. Vegetables were listed à la carte on the old menu but not on the new one.

Both menus list entrées under the heading Scandia Specialties. The 1965 menu had nine entrees, ranging in price from $3.00 to $6.00 for the Viking Sword. The 1988 menu also lists nine entrées, six of which are on both menus: Veal Oskar ($4.85 and $22.50); Böf Med Lög—Tenderloin steak with onions ($4.85 and $20.50); Biff Lindström—Chopped sirloin steak mixed with chopped beets, onions and capers, topped with fried egg ($3.25 and $13.75); and Kålldolmar—Cabbage filled with veal and pork stuffing with rice ($3.75 and $13.50).

Two specials appeared on both menus: Lammesaddel (for two or more)—Young fillet of lamb ($4.50 and

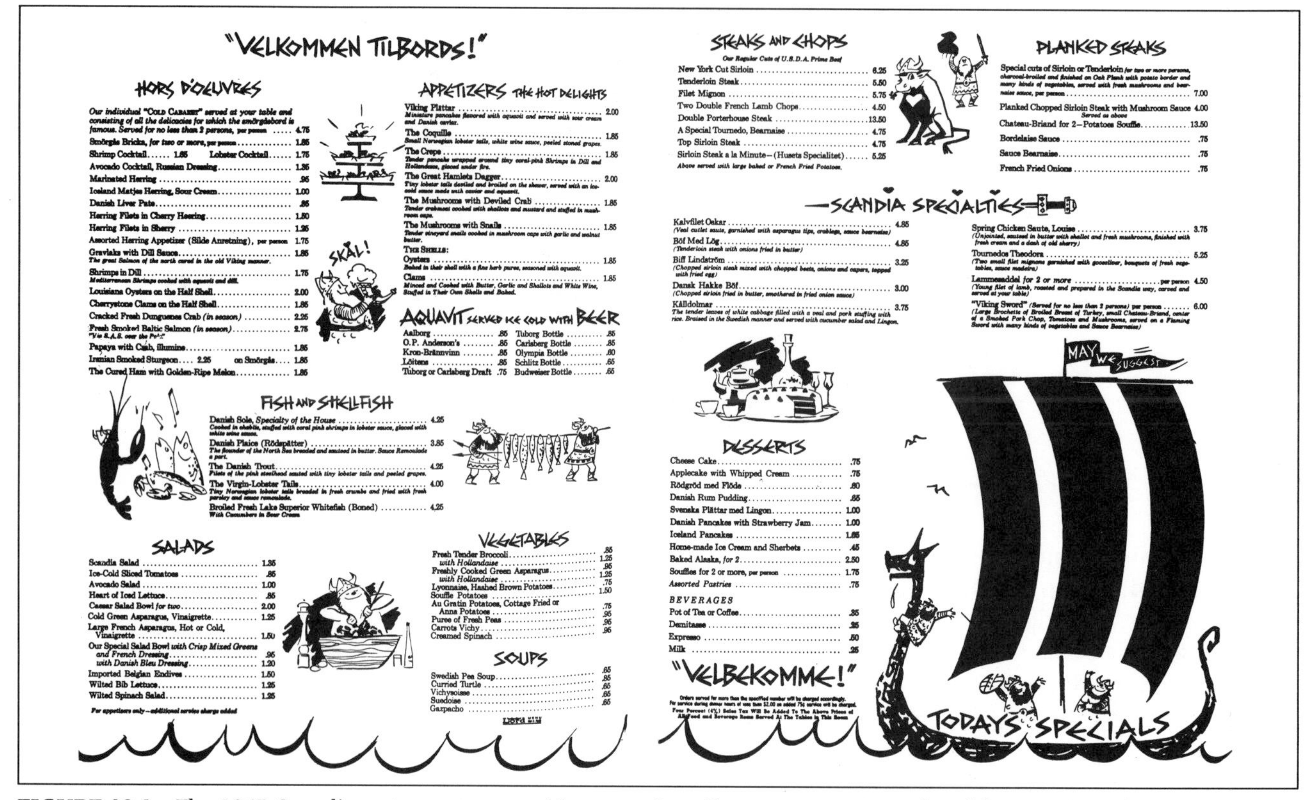

"VELKOMMEN TILBORDS!"

HORS D'OEUVRES

Our individual "Cold Cabaret" served at your table and consisting of all the delicacies for which the smörgåsbord is famous. Served for no less than 2 persons, per person 4.75
Smörgås Bricka, *for two or more,* per person 1.85
Shrimp Cocktail ..... 1.85 Lobster Cocktail 1.75
Avocado Cocktail, Russian Dressing 1.35
Marinated Herring ..... .95
Iceland Matjes Herring, Sour Cream 1.00
Danish Liver Pate ..... .85
Herring Filets in Cherry Heering 1.50
Herring Filets in Sherry 1.25
Assorted Herring Appetizer (Silde Anretning), per person 1.75
Gravlaks with Dill Sauce 1.85
The great Salmon of the north cured in the old Viking manner.
Shrimps in Dill 1.75
Mediterranean Shrimps cooked with aquavit and dill.
Louisiana Oysters on the Half Shell 2.00
Cherrystone Clams on the Half Shell 1.85
Cracked Fresh Dunguenes Crab *(in season)* 2.25
Fresh Smoked Baltic Salmon *(in season)* 2.75
Papaya with Crab, Illumine 1.85
Iranian Smoked Sturgeon ..... 2.25 on Smörgås 1.85
The Cured Ham with Golden-Ripe Melon 1.85

APPETIZERS THE HOT DELIGHTS

Viking Plattar 2.00
Miniature pancakes flavored with aquavit and served with sour cream and Danish caviar.
The Coquille 1.85
Small Norwegian lobster tails, white wine sauce, peeled stoned grapes.
The Crepe 1.85
Tender pancake wrapped around tiny coral-pink Shrimps in Dill and Hollandaise, glazed under fire.
The Great Hamlets Dagger 2.00
Tiny lobster tails deviled and broiled on the skewer, served with an ice-cold sauce made with caviar and aquavit.
The Mushrooms with Deviled Crab 1.85
Tender crabmeat cooked with shallots and mustard and stuffed in mushroom caps.
The Mushrooms with Snails 1.85
Tender vineyard snails cooked in mushroom caps with garlic and walnut butter.
The Shells:
Oysters 1.85
Baked in their shell with a fine herb puree, seasoned with aquavit.
Clams 1.85
Minced and Cooked with Butter, Garlic and Shallots and White Wine, Stuffed in Their Own Shells and Baked.

AQUAVIT SERVED ICE COLD WITH BEER

Aalborg	.85	Tuborg Bottle	.85
O.P. Anderson's	.85	Carlsberg Bottle	.85
Kron-Brännvinn	.85	Olympia Bottle	.80
Löitens	.85	Schlitz Bottle	.65
Tuborg or Carlsberg Draft	.75	Budweiser Bottle	.65

FISH AND SHELLFISH

Danish Sole, *Specialty of the House* 4.25
Cooked in chablis, stuffed with coral pink shrimps in lobster sauce, glazed with white wine sauce.
Danish Plaice (Rödspätter) 3.85
The flounder of the North Sea breaded and sauteed in butter. Sauce Remoulade a part.
The Danish Trout 4.25
Filets of the pink steelhead sauted with tiny lobster tails and peeled grapes.
The Virgin-Lobster Tails 4.00
Tiny Norwegian lobster tails breaded in fresh crumbs and fried with fresh parsley and sauce remoulade.
Broiled Fresh Lake Superior Whitefish (Boned) 4.25
With Cucumbers in Sour Cream

SALADS

Scandia Salad 1.35
Ice-Cold Sliced Tomatoes ..... .85
Avocado Salad 1.00
Heart of Iced Lettuce ..... .85
Caesar Salad Bowl *for two* 2.00
Cold Green Asparagus, Vinaigrette 1.25
Large French Asparagus, Hot or Cold, Vinaigrette 1.50
Our Special Salad Bowl *with Crisp Mixed Greens and French Dressing* ..... .95
with Danish Bleu Dressing 1.20
Imported Belgian Endives 1.50
Wilted Bib Lettuce 1.25
Wilted Spinach Salad 1.25
For appetizers only—additional service charge added

VEGETABLES

Fresh Tender Broccoli ..... .85
with Hollandaise 1.25
Freshly Cooked Green Asparagus ..... .95
with Hollandaise 1.25
Lyonnaise, Hashed Brown Potatoes ..... .75
Souffle Potatoes 1.50
Au Gratin Potatoes, Cottage Fried or Anna Potatoes ..... .75
Puree of Fresh Peas ..... .95
Carrots Vichy ..... .95
Creamed Spinach ..... .95

SOUPS

Swedish Pea Soup ..... .65
Curried Turtle ..... .85
Vichysoisse ..... .65
Suedoise ..... .65
Gazpacho ..... .65

STEAKS AND CHOPS

Our Regular Cuts of U.S.D.A. Prime Beef
New York Cut Sirloin 6.25
Tenderloin Steak 5.50
Filet Mignon 5.75
Two Double French Lamb Chops 4.50
Double Porterhouse Steak 13.50
A Special Tournedo, Bearnaise 4.75
Top Sirloin Steak 4.75
Sirloin Steak a la Minute—(Husets Specialitet) 5.25
Above served with large baked or French Fried Potatoes.

PLANKED STEAKS

Special cuts of Sirloin or Tenderloin *for two or more persons, charcoal-broiled and finished on Oak Plank with potato border and many kinds of vegetables, served with fresh mushrooms and bearnaise sauce,* per person 7.00
Planked Chopped Sirloin Steak with Mushroom Sauce 4.00
Served as above
Chateau-Briand for 2—Potatoes Souffle 13.50
Bordelaise Sauce ..... .75
Sauce Bearnaise ..... .75
French Fried Onions ..... .75

—SCANDIA SPECIALTIES—

Kalvfilet Oskar 4.85
(Veal cutlet saute, garnished with asparagus tips, crablegs, sauce bearnaise)
Böf Med Lög 4.85
(Tenderloin steak with onions fried in butter)
Biff Lindström 3.25
(Chopped sirloin steak mixed with chopped beets, onions and capers, topped with fried egg)
Dansk Hakke Böf 3.00
(Chopped sirloin fried in butter, smothered in fried onion sauce)
Kålldolmar 3.75
The tender leaves of white cabbage filled with a veal and pork stuffing with rice. Braised in the Swedish manner and served with cucumber salad and Lingon.
Spring Chicken Saute, Louise 3.75
(Unjointed, sauteed in butter with shallot and fresh mushrooms, finished with fresh cream and a dash of old sherry)
Tournedos Theodora 5.25
(Two small filet mignons garnished with gooseliver, bouquets of fresh vegetables, sauce madeira)
Lammesaddel *for 2 or more* ..... per person 4.50
(Young filet of lamb, roasted and prepared in the Scandia way, carved and served at your table)
"Viking Sword" *(Served for no less than 2 persons)* per person 6.00
(Large Brochette of Broiled Breast of Turkey, small Chateau-Briand, center of a Smoked Pork Chop, Tomatoes and Mushrooms, served on a Flaming Sword with many kinds of vegetables and Sauce Bearnaise)

DESSERTS

Cheese Cake ..... .75
Applecake with Whipped Cream ..... .75
Rödgröd med Flöde ..... .80
Danish Rum Pudding ..... .65
Svenska Plättar med Lingon 1.00
Danish Pancakes with Strawberry Jam 1.00
Iceland Pancakes 1.65
Home-made Ice Cream and Sherbets ..... .45
Baked Alaska, *for 2* 2.50
Souffles for 2 or more, per person 1.75
Assorted Pastries ..... .75

BEVERAGES

Pot of Tea or Coffee ..... .35
Demitasse ..... .25
Expresso ..... .50
Milk ..... .25

"VELBEKOMME!"

Orders served for more than the specified number will be charged accordingly.
For service during dinner hours of less than $2.00 an added 75¢ service will be charged.
Four Percent (4%) Sales Tax Will Be Added To The Above Prices of All Food and Beverage Items Served At The Tables In This Room

FIGURE 23.1 The 1965 Scandia restaurant menu. (Courtesy Scandia restaurant. Reproduced by permission.)

$22.50); and Viking Sword (for two or more)—Large brochette of broiled breast of turkey, small chateaubriand, center of a smoked pork chop, tomatoes and mushrooms, served on a flaming sword with many kinds of vegetables and sauce bearnaise ($6.00 and $19.50 per person).

Under the heading Steaks and Chops eight entrées were listed on the 1965 menu, at prices ranging from $4.50 to $13.50 for Double Porterhouse Steak. The 1988 menu lists only five entrées, with a price range from $20.50 to $23.00. Duplications on the two menus are Filet Mignon ($5.75 and $21.50) and Two Double French Lamb Chops ($4.50 and $22.00).

Both menus have a Fish and Shellfish heading. The 1965 menu listed five items, with prices from $3.85 to $4.25. On the 1988 menu are three seafood entrées. Two of them appear on both menus—Fresh Lake Superior Whitefish ($4.25 and $27.75) and Scandia Sole ($4.25 and $22.00).

The 1965 menu listed eleven desserts, with prices ranging from $.60 to $1.65 (Iceland Pancakes) and Baked Alaska for two for $2.50. The 1988 menu has only four dessert offerings, with prices from $3.00 to $5.00.

This menu has remained remarkably stable for twenty-three years except for price increases. The special ethnic entrées have evidently kept their popularity over the years.

Gage & Tollner's

This venerable chop-and-chowder house is Brooklyn's most famous landmark restaurant. It was established in 1879 and still has its original Gay Nineties atmosphere. The rows of cut-glass chandeliers, mirrored walls lined with dark red brocade, and hat hooks large enough to accommodate the "stove-pipe" hats of the horse-and-buggy era all are there, preserved today just as they were one hundred years ago.

This restaurant, now run by Edward and Thomas Dewey, who inherited it from their father, provides steaks and chops broiled to perfection and some of the finest seafood on the eastern seaboard. The secret of their distinctive broilings is that they have a special anthracite broiler, having found that hard coal burns without fumes and consequently does not obscure the real flavor of meat or seafood.

The Gage & Tollner's 1965 menu listed nine appetizers (Figure 23.3), ranging in price from $.40 to $2.75 (Lobster Cocktail). The 1988 menu has fifteen appetizers, and the Lobster Cocktail costs $8.50. Under Soups and Bisques, the old menu listed ten items with a price range from $.60 to $3.25 (bowl) for Lobster Bisque. The new menu lists only four items under this heading, and Lobster Bisque costs $7.00 a bowl (Figure 23.4).

DINNER

Appetizers

SMORGAS BRICKA (for two or more) . . . . . . per person 8.75

SHRIMP COCKTAIL 10.75

LOBSTER COCKTAIL 14.75

GRAVAD LAKS 10.00
With Dill Sauce

Viking Blinis 6.75
Miniature Pancakes Flavored with Akvavit and Served with Sour Cream and Danish Caviar

The Great Hamlet's Dagger . . 14.75
Tiny Lobster Tails Deviled and Broiled on the Skewer, Flambeed with Akvavit and Served with Caviar Sauce

SCANDIA MATJES HERRING 5.75
Sour Cream

MARINATED HERRING . . . 4.75

CRACKED DUNGENESS CRAB (in season) 12.75

IMPORTED BELUGA CAVIAR . . . . (Per Ounce) 42.00

Escargots Bourguignonne . . 7.75
Marinated in Red Wine, Shallots, Garlic and Herb Butter with a Dash of Pernod

Shrimp Scandia 13.50
Shrimp, Marinated and Broiled, with Roasted Bell Peppers, Butter Lettuce and Tarragon Vinaigrette

Soups

French Onion Soup 4.95
Baked in the Traditional Manner

Swedish Pea Soup 3.50

Suedoise 3.50

Soup du Jour 3.50

Salads

Broiled Seafood Salad 17.75
Swordfish, Shrimp, Salmon, Scallops, Tortellini, Raddicchio, Butter Lettuce, Dill, Broccoli, Bell Peppers with a Basil Tomato Dressing

Mixed Green Salad 3.50

Scandia Salad 4.50

Cucumber Salad 3.00

Caesar Salad 4.50

Rosenberg Salad 16.00
Lobster, Crab, Shrimp, Chicken Breast

Swanson Salad 9.50
Chopped Lettuce, Tomato, Eggs, Avocado, Crisp Bacon and French Dressing

Scandia Specialties

VEAL OSKAR 22.50
Veal Cutlet Saute, Garnished with Asparagus, Crab Legs, Sauce Bearnaise

BOF MED LOG 20.50
Tenderloin Steak, with Onions Fried in Butter

BIFF LINDSTROM 13.75
Chopped Steak Mixed with Chopped Beets, Onions and Capers, Topped with Fried Egg

FRIKADELLER 12.50
With Red Cabbage, Cucumber Salad and Lingon

WIENERSCHNITZEL 19.50
With Cucumber Salad

KALLDOLMAR 13.50
The Tender Leaves of White Cabbage Filled with a Veal and Pork Stuffing with Rice. Braised in the Swedish Manner and Served with Cucumber Salad and Lingon

BREAST OF CHICKEN MARGIE 14.25
Boneless Breast of Chicken sauteed with Shallots and Fresh Mushrooms, Finished with Cream and a Dash of Old Sherry, Served with Rice and Vegetable

LAMMESADDEL (for two or more) . . . . per person 22.50
Young Saddle of Lamb, Roasted and Prepared in the Scandia way, Carved and Served at Your Table

VIKING SWORD (for two or more) . . . per person 19.50
Large Brochette of Broiled Breast of Turkey, Small Chateaubriand, Center of a Smoked Pork Chop, Tomatoes and Mushrooms, Served on a Flaming Sword with Many Kinds of Vegetables and Sauce Bearnaise

Steaks & Chops

Prime New York Cut 21.50

Filet Mignon 21.50

Two Double French Lamb Chops 22.00

A Special Tournedo, Bearnaise 20.50

Chateaubriand (for two or more) . . per person 23.00
Bouquetiere of Vegetables with Bearnaise Sauce

Desserts

Cakes and Pastries 3.75

Ice Cream and Sherbet 3.00

Fresh Berries 5.00

Fresh Fruits 4.00

Fish & Shellfish

Fresh Lake Superior Whitefish (Boned) 17.75
Broiled, Served with Cucumbers in Sour Cream

Imported Dover Sole 22.00
Sauteed or Broiled

Scandia Sole:
Specialty of the House 22.00
Poached Dover Sole in White Wine, Coral Pink Shrimp, Glazed in Lobster and White Wine Sauces

All Orders Split will be Charged a 2.00 Supplement

(Luncheon Menu see over)

FIGURE 23.2 The 1988 Scandia restaurant menu. (Courtesy Scandia restaurant. Reproduced by permission.)

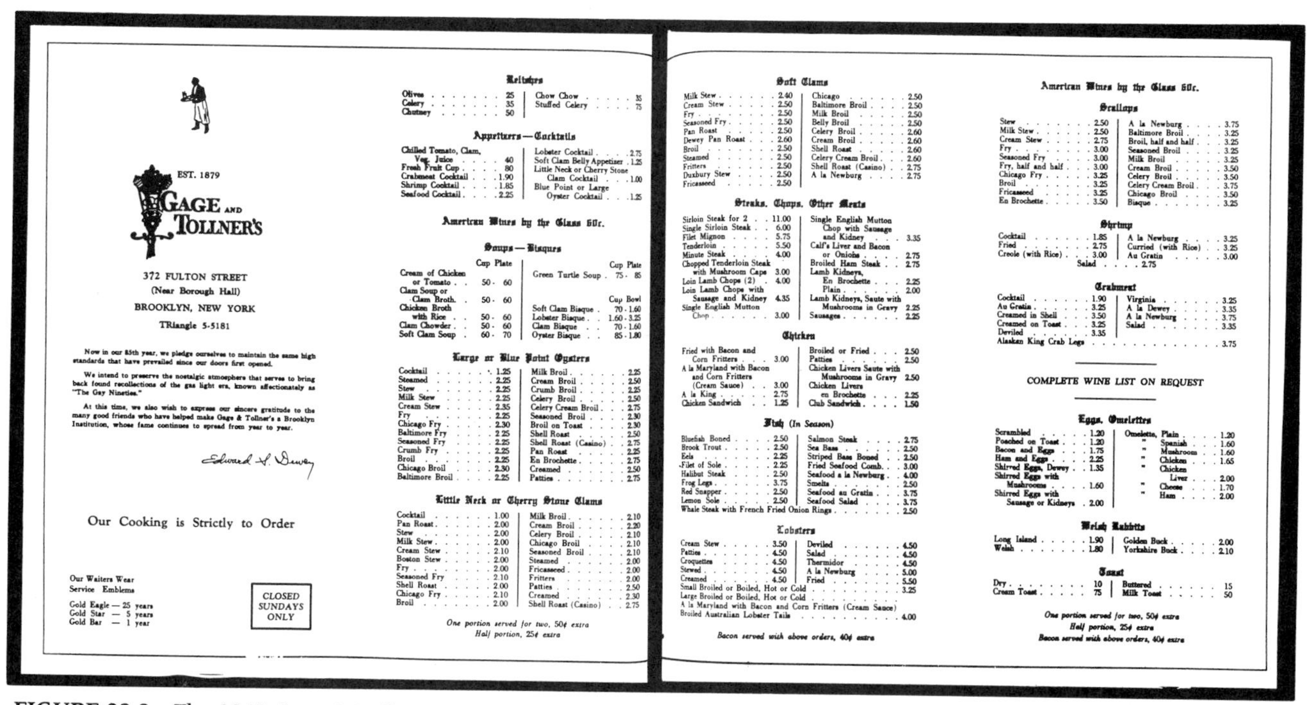

EST. 1879

GAGE AND TOLLNER'S

372 FULTON STREET
(Near Borough Hall)
BROOKLYN, NEW YORK
TRiangle 5-5181

Now in our 85th year, we pledge ourselves to maintain the same high standards that have prevailed since our doors first opened.

We intend to preserve the nostalgic atmosphere that serves to bring back found recollections of the gas light era, known affectionately as "The Gay Nineties."

At this time, we also wish to express our sincere gratitude to the many good friends who have helped make Gage & Tollner's a Brooklyn Institution, whose fame continues to spread from year to year.

Edward S. Dewey

Our Cooking is Strictly to Order

Our Waiters Wear Service Emblems

Gold Eagle — 25 years
Gold Star — 5 years
Gold Bar — 1 year

CLOSED SUNDAYS ONLY

Relishes

Olives . . . 25; Celery . . . 35; Chutney . . . 50; Chow Chow . . . 35; Stuffed Celery . . . 75

Appetizers—Cocktails

Chilled Tomato, Clam, Veg. Juice . . . 40
Fresh Fruit Cup . . . 80
Crabmeat Cocktail . . . 1.90
Shrimp Cocktail . . . 1.85
Seafood Cocktail . . . 2.25
Lobster Cocktail . . . 2.75
Soft Clam Belly Appetizer . 1.25
Little Neck or Cherry Stone Clam Cocktail . . . 1.00
Blue Point or Large Oyster Cocktail . . . 1.25

American Wines by the Glass 60c.

Soups—Bisques

	Cup	Plate
Cream of Chicken or Tomato	50	60
Clam Soup or Clam Broth	50	60
Chicken Broth with Rice	50	60
Clam Chowder	50	60
Soft Clam Soup	60	70
Green Turtle Soup	75	85

	Cup	Bowl
Soft Clam Bisque	70	1.60
Lobster Bisque	1.60	3.25
Clam Bisque	70	1.60
Oyster Bisque	85	1.80

Large or Blue Point Oysters

Cocktail . . . 1.25
Steamed . . . 2.25
Stew . . . 2.25
Milk Stew . . . 2.25
Cream Stew . . . 2.35
Fry . . . 2.25
Chicago Fry . . . 2.30
Baltimore Fry . . . 2.25
Seasoned Fry . . . 2.25
Crumb Fry . . . 2.25
Broil . . . 2.25
Chicago Broil . . . 2.30
Baltimore Broil . . . 2.25
Milk Broil . . . 2.25
Cream Broil . . . 2.50
Crumb Broil . . . 2.25
Celery Broil . . . 2.50
Celery Cream Broil . . . 2.75
Seasoned Broil . . . 2.30
Broil on Toast . . . 2.30
Shell Roast . . . 2.50
Shell Roast (Casino) . . . 2.75
Pan Roast . . . 2.25
En Brochette . . . 2.75
Creamed . . . 2.50
Patties . . . 2.75

Little Neck or Cherry Stone Clams

Cocktail . . . 1.00
Pan Roast . . . 2.00
Stew . . . 2.00
Milk Stew . . . 2.00
Cream Stew . . . 2.10
Boston Stew . . . 2.00
Fry . . . 2.00
Seasoned Fry . . . 2.10
Shell Roast . . . 2.00
Chicago Fry . . . 2.10
Broil . . . 2.00
Milk Broil . . . 2.10
Cream Broil . . . 2.20
Celery Broil . . . 2.10
Chicago Broil . . . 2.10
Seasoned Broil . . . 2.10
Steamed . . . 2.00
Fricasseed . . . 2.00
Fritters . . . 2.00
Patties . . . 2.50
Creamed . . . 2.30
Shell Roast (Casino) . . . 2.75

One portion served for two, 50¢ extra
Half portion, 25¢ extra

Soft Clams

Milk Stew . . . 2.40
Cream Stew . . . 2.50
Fry . . . 2.50
Seasoned Fry . . . 2.50
Pan Roast . . . 2.50
Dewey Pan Roast . . . 2.60
Broil . . . 2.50
Steamed . . . 2.50
Fritters . . . 2.50
Duxbury Stew . . . 2.50
Fricasseed . . . 2.50
Chicago . . . 2.50
Baltimore Broil . . . 2.50
Milk Broil . . . 2.50
Belly Broil . . . 2.50
Celery Broil . . . 2.60
Cream Broil . . . 2.60
Shell Roast . . . 2.60
Celery Cream Broil . . . 2.60
Shell Roast (Casino) . . . 2.75
A la Newburg . . . 2.75

Steaks, Chops, Other Meats

Sirloin Steak for 2 . . . 11.00
Single Sirloin Steak . . . 6.00
Filet Mignon . . . 5.75
Tenderloin . . . 5.50
Minute Steak . . . 4.00
Chopped Tenderloin Steak with Mushroom Caps . . . 3.00
Loin Lamb Chops (2) . . . 4.00
Loin Lamb Chops with Sausage and Kidney . . . 4.35
Single English Mutton Chop . . . 3.00
Single English Mutton Chop with Sausage and Kidney . . . 3.35
Calf's Liver and Bacon or Onions . . . 2.75
Broiled Ham Steak . . . 2.75
Lamb Kidneys, En Brochette . . . 2.25
Plain . . . 2.00
Lamb Kidneys, Saute with Mushrooms in Gravy . . . 2.25
Sausages . . . 2.25

Chicken

Fried with Bacon and Corn Fritters . . . 3.00
A la Maryland with Bacon and Corn Fritters (Cream Sauce) . . . 3.00
A la King . . . 2.75
Chicken Sandwich . . . 1.25
Broiled or Fried . . . 2.50
Patties . . . 2.50
Chicken Livers Saute with Mushrooms in Gravy . . . 2.50
Chicken Livers en Brochette . . . 2.25
Club Sandwich . . . 1.50

Fish (In Season)

Bluefish Boned . . . 2.50
Brook Trout . . . 2.50
Eels . . . 2.25
Filet of Sole . . . 2.25
Halibut Steak . . . 2.50
Frog Legs . . . 3.75
Red Snapper . . . 2.50
Lemon Sole . . . 2.50
Salmon Steak . . . 2.75
Sea Bass . . . 2.50
Striped Bass Boned . . . 2.50
Fried Seafood Comb. . . . 3.00
Seafood a la Newburg . . . 4.00
Smelts . . . 2.50
Seafood au Gratin . . . 3.75
Seafood Salad . . . 3.75
Whale Steak with French Fried Onion Rings . . . 2.50

Lobsters

Cream Stew . . . 3.50
Patties . . . 4.50
Croquettes . . . 4.50
Stewed . . . 4.50
Creamed . . . 4.50
Deviled . . . 4.50
Salad . . . 4.50
Thermidor . . . 4.50
A la Newburg . . . 5.00
Fried . . . 5.50
Small Broiled or Boiled, Hot or Cold . . . 3.25
Large Broiled or Boiled, Hot or Cold . . .
A la Maryland with Bacon and Corn Fritters (Cream Sauce)
Broiled Australian Lobster Tails . . . 4.00

Bacon served with above orders, 40¢ extra

American Wines by the Glass 60c.

Scallops

Stew . . . 2.50
Milk Stew . . . 2.50
Cream Stew . . . 2.75
Fry . . . 3.00
Seasoned Fry . . . 3.00
Fry, half and half . . . 3.00
Chicago Fry . . . 3.25
Broil . . . 3.25
Fricasseed . . . 3.25
En Brochette . . . 3.50
A la Newburg . . . 3.75
Baltimore Broil . . . 3.25
Broil, half and half . . . 3.25
Seasoned Broil . . . 3.25
Milk Broil . . . 3.25
Cream Broil . . . 3.50
Celery Broil . . . 3.50
Celery Cream Broil . . . 3.75
Chicago Broil . . . 3.50
Bisque . . . 3.25

Shrimp

Cocktail . . . 1.85
Fried . . . 2.75
Creole (with Rice) . . . 3.00
A la Newburg . . . 3.25
Curried (with Rice) . . . 3.25
Au Gratin . . . 3.00
Salad . . . 2.75

Crabmeat

Cocktail . . . 1.90
Au Gratin . . . 3.25
Creamed in Shell . . . 3.50
Creamed on Toast . . . 3.25
Deviled . . . 3.35
Virginia . . . 3.25
A la Dewey . . . 3.35
A la Newburg . . . 3.75
Salad . . . 3.35
Alaskan King Crab Legs . . . 3.75

COMPLETE WINE LIST ON REQUEST

Eggs, Omelettes

Scrambled . . . 1.20
Poached on Toast . . . 1.20
Bacon and Eggs . . . 1.75
Ham and Eggs . . . 2.25
Shirred Eggs, Dewey . . . 1.35
Shirred Eggs with Mushrooms . . . 1.60
Shirred Eggs with Sausage or Kidneys . . . 2.00
Omelette, Plain . . . 1.20
" Spanish . . . 1.60
" Mushroom . . . 1.60
" Chicken . . . 1.65
" Chicken Liver . . . 2.00
" Cheese . . . 1.70
" Ham . . . 2.00

Welsh Rabbits

Long Island . . . 1.90
Welsh . . . 1.80
Golden Buck . . . 2.00
Yorkshire Buck . . . 2.10

Toast

Dry . . . 10
Cream Toast . . . 75
Buttered . . . 15
Milk Toast . . . 50

One portion served for two, 50¢ extra
Half portion, 25¢ extra
Bacon served with above orders, 40¢ extra

FIGURE 23.3 The 1965 Gage & Tollner's menu. (Courtesy Gage & Tollner's. Reproduced by permission.)

Appetizers—Cocktails

Crabmeat Virginia App.	8.00	Soft Clam Belly Broil Appetizer	6.00
Seafood Cocktail	8.00	Little Neck or Cherry Stone Clams on ½ Shell	5.00
Shrimp Cocktail	7.00	Oyster Cocktail	7.00
Crabmeat Cocktail	8.50	Clams Casino	6.00
Chilled Tomato, V8 Juice	1.00	3 Clams & 3 Oysters	6.00
Oysters Casino	7.50	Oysters Rockefeller	7.50
Steamer Appetizer	6.00	Stuffed Mushrooms	5.50
Lobster Cocktail	8.50		

Soups—Bisques

	Cup	Plate		Cup	Plate
Chicken Broth & Rice	2.00	2.50	Clam Chowder	2.50	3.00
Fish Chowder	2.50	3.00	Lobster Bisque	6.00	7.00

Choice of Mixed Green Salad or Slaw or Hashed Browned or French Fried Potatoes with entree

Soft Clam Bellies

Belly Broil	12.00	Chicago	12.00
Stew	12.00	Baltimore Fry	12.00
Fry	12.00	Celery Broil	12.00
Seasoned Fry	12.00	Cream Broil	12.50
Pan Roast	12.00	Celery Cream Broil	12.50
Dewey Pan Roast	12.00	Shell Roast	12.00
Fritters	12.50	Shell Roast Casino	12.00
Duxbury Stew	12.00	A la Newburg	12.50

Oysters

Steamed	12.50	Broil	12.50
Cream Stew	13.00	Celery Cream Broil	13.00
Fry	12.50	Seasoned Broil	12.50
Baltimore Fry	12.50	Shell Roast Casino	13.00
Seasoned Fry	12.50		

Bay Scallops

Fry	12.00	Seasoned Broil	12.00
Seasoned Fry	12.00	A la Newburg	12.50
½ Oyster ½ Scallops	12.00	Celery Cream Broil	12.50
Broil	12.00	Coquilles St. Jacques	12.50
Baltimore	12.00		

Shrimp

Fried	15.50	Curried with Rice and Chutney	15.50
Creole (with Rice)	15.50	Au Gratin	16.50
A la Newburg	16.50	Salad	15.50
Scampi	15.50		

Crabmeat

Au Gratin	15.50	A la Newburg	16.50
Deviled	15.50	Salad	16.50
Virginia	15.50	Soft Shell Crabs	___
A la Dewey	16.50		

Fresh Fish (In Season)

Bluefish Boned	10.00	Fried Seafood Combination	15.00
Filet of Sole	12.00	Seafood a la Newburg	18.00
Red Snapper	20.00	Seafood au Gratin	18.00
Lemon Sole	12.50	Seafood Salad	18.00
Boned Shad	___	Seafood Virginia	18.00
Shad Roe	___	Swordfish	___
Shad & Roe Combination	___	Coho Salmon	13.50
Dover Sole	___		

Lobsters

Cream Stew	16.50	Thermidor	17.00
Deviled	16.50	A la Newburg	17.00
Salad	16.50	Fried	16.50

Broiled or Steamed—according to size

A la Maryland with Bacon and Corn Fritters (Cream Sauce) 18.00

Steaks, Chops, Other Meats

Sirloin Steak for 2	35.00	Single Lamb Chop	10.00
Single Sirloin Steak	18.00	Single English Mutton Chop	18.00
Filet Mignon	22.00	Single English Mutton Chop with Sausage, Bacon and Kidney	19.00
Petit Filet Mignon, Bearnaise Sauce	12.50	Calf's Liver and Bacon or Onions	14.00
Chopped Steak with Mushroom Caps	8.50		
Loin Lamb Chops (2)	19.00		
Loin Lamb Chops with Bacon, Sausage and Kidney	20.00		

Choice of Mixed Green Salad or Slaw or Hashed Browned or French Fried Potatoes with any entree above

Chicken

Fried with Bacon and Corn Fritters	9.00	Broiled or Fried	8.00
A la Maryland with Bacon, Corn Fritters and Cream Sauce	9.50	Chicken Sandwich	3.50
		Club Sandwich	5.00
		Salad	7.50

Omelettes and Welsh Rabbits (Cheese)

Plain Omelet	4.00	Welsh Rabbit	4.50
Spanish Omelet	4.50	Long Island Rabbit	5.00
Mushroom Omelet	4.50	Golden Buck	5.50
Chicken Omelet	4.50	Yorkshire Buck	6.00

Vegetables

Fresh Seasonal	___	Corn Fritters	2.50
Tomatoes, Stewed	1.50	French Fried Onions	2.50
Fried	2.50	Mushrooms, Sauteed	4.00
Grilled	2.50	Rice	1.50
Spaghetti au Gratin	2.50	Lemon Rice	1.75
Fried Eggplant	2.50		

Potatoes

Boiled	1.50	Hashed Browned in Cream	2.50
French Fried	1.75	Au Gratin	2.50
Baked Idaho, Sour Cream	2.25	O'Brien	2.00
Lyonnaise	2.00	Sweets, Fried	2.00
Julienne	1.75	Grilled	2.00
Hashed Browned	2.00	Candied	2.50

Salads

Coleslaw, Spicy	1.50	Dilled Cucumber	2.50
Creamy	1.50	Mixed Green	2.50
Georgia	2.00	Hearts of Lettuce	2.50
Onion & Tomato	2.50	Lettuce & Tomato	2.50
Combination	3.00	Sliced Tomatoes	2.50

Served with Gage & Tollner French, Mayonnaise or Russian Dressing
Blue Cheese Dressing—1.00

IRISH COFFEE 4.00

Beverages

Coffee, per person	1.50	Espresso	2.00
Milk	1.00	Tea	1.50
Brewed Decaf	1.50	Iced Tea or Coffee	1.50

Only Pure Cream Served

FIGURE 23.4 The 1988 Gage & Tollner's menu. (Courtesy Gage & Tollner's. Reproduced by permission.)

The oyster listing on the 1965 menu offered twenty-six different oyster entrées, costing from $1.25 to $2.75 (Shell Roast Casino). The 1988 menu has only nine oyster selections, and Shell Roast Casino now costs $13.00. Twenty-two different cherrystone clam dishes were listed on the 1965 menu in addition to twenty-one soft clam entrées. Neither of these clam listings appears on the 1988 menu.

The shrimp listing on the 1965 menu offered seven items with prices from $1.85 to $3.25 (Shrimp Newburg). The newer menu also offers seven shrimp dishes, and Shrimp Newburg costs $16.50. The scallop listing on the 1965 menu offered twenty entrées, with prices from $2.50 to $3.75. Only nine scallop dishes remain on the 1988 menu. Seasoned Broil was $3.25 in 1965; in 1988 it cost $12.00. In 1965 there were twelve Lobster offerings, with Lobster Thermidor costing $4.50; in 1988 it cost $17.00. Ten crabmeat entrées were listed on the old menu, while the new menu lists seven. Au Gratin Crabmeat that used to cost $3.25 cost $15.50 in 1988.

The fresh fish (in season) listing appears on both menus, with seventeen items on the 1965 menu and fifteen on the 1988 menu. Prices for fish entrées in 1965 varied from $2.50 to $3.75. By 1988 fish entrées cost from $10.00 to $20.00. Under the heading Steaks, Chops, Other Meats, the old menu listed sixteen entrées with prices from $2.00 to $11.00 (sirloin steak for two). On the 1988 menu there are eleven meat entrées, and sirloin steak for two costs $35.00.

The chicken listing in 1965 had nine items, with prices from $1.25 to $3.00. The 1988 menu has six chicken entrées, priced from $3.50 to $9.50. Both menus list omelettes and Welsh rabbits, but a major addition to the 1988 menu is the listing of vegetables and potatoes à la carte, as well as ten salads à la carte.

The Whitehall Club

One of the best Chicago restaurants is the Whitehall Club; it is one of the few American restaurants mentioned in the *Guide Michelin*.

The dining room is elegantly paneled and decorated with an antique wallpaper like the one used in Sacher's in Vienna. The staff at the Whitehall Club, which is now a hotel open to the public, has a recipe for good cooking: "Two cups care, one heaping teaspoonful of imagination and generous dashes of subtlety." The result is some of the most delicious food served anywhere.

The Whitehall Club 1965 menu listed twenty-one appetizers (Figure 23.5). Prices ranged from $.75 to $6.50 (Beluga caviar). The 1988 appetizer list is much shorter, with only six items (Figure 23.6). The price range is from $6.50 to $11.00, and Jumbo Shrimp on Ice with Soy and Ginger Cocktail Sauce now costs $10.00. In 1965 a Shrimp Cocktail went for $1.50. The old menu listed nine soups; the 1988 menu lists only three. French Onion Soup au Gratin with Aged Port Wine cost $4.50 in 1988. In 1965 Baked Onion Soup Parisienne was $.75.

The 1965 menu listed fifteen salads, with prices ranging from $.75 to $4.00. The 1988 menu lists three salads, with prices from $4.50 to $7.00. A Caesar Salad on the old menu cost $1.75; in 1988 it was $7.00.

The 1965 menu had three main-dish listings: Sea & Stream, Entrées, and From the Charcoal Broiler, with a total of thirty-five entrées. On the 1988 menu only twelve entrées are listed under the headings Entrées and Specialties. On the old menu the prices ranged from $3.75 to $12.50 for a Chateaubriand (for two) or a Prime Double Sirloin. The 1988 price range is $17.00 to $25.00.

Some of the items that survived the decades are Steak Diane, Prepared Table Side ($6.50 and $24.00), Sirloin Steak ($6.25 and $21.00), Filet Mignon ($6.25 and $22.00), and Breast of Chicken ($4.00 and $17.00). Three seafood items—Grilled Ahi Tuna, Sautéed Norwegian Salmon, and Grilled Florida Swordfish—are on the 1988 menu. The 1965 menu had ten Sea & Stream entrées.

The old menu offered fifteen vegetables à la carte. The 1988 menu has no à la carte vegetable listing. The 1965 dessert listing offered eighteen items, with prices from $4.70 to $2.25. The menu for 1988 offers only two categories—a Pastry Cart ($4.00) and Today's Hot Soufflés ($5.50).

The Whitehall Club menu has obviously changed over the years. Prices have increased as one would expect because of inflation, but the other big change is the offering of fewer items in every category. Some items, however, such as Steak Diane have stayed popular and on the menu for twenty-three years!

The Four Seasons

This Manhattan restaurant is a mainstay of powerful people with company credit cards. According to a *Wall Street Journal* survey in 1987, it is the favorite restaurant anywhere of chief executives of big corporations. In 1988 the owners spent more than $500,000 redecorating the establishment. The objective was to give the restaurant a slightly warmer look without changing its appearance to any significant degree. According to the customers, the project was a great success.

The Four Seasons was designed three decades ago at a cost of $4.5 million by the eminent architect Philip Johnson and is considered by some to be a paragon of modern architecture. The restaurant, however, has had some hard times in the past, and fifteen years ago it was actually losing money. In the early 1970s, the new owners, Tom Margittai and Paul Kovi, took it over from Restaurant Associates and hit on a winning formula: They gave customers what they seem most to want—comfort, attention, and fine cuisine. Good food is available in New York, but comfort, personal attention, and consideration are not so common. When Margittai and Kovi bought the restaurant, they began training the staff members to study carefully their customers' desires and habits. If the customer ordered Bombay Gin, for example, the next time he came in the captain was able to ask him, "Bombay Gin straight up, sir?"

When a customer calls the Four Seasons for a reservation, a card is prepared with his or her name on it. When the customer shows up, the host discreetly passes the card to the captain. Thus, both are able to address the customer by name.

The Four Seasons is not inexpensive. Not counting tax and tip, the average customer runs up a bill per person of $55 for a Grill Room lunch to $68 for a Pool Room lunch. A full dinner with appetizer, dessert, and a couple of drinks can total $100 per person including tax and tip, but there is a pretheater *prix-fixe* dinner for $41.50.

Regarding the food served, most food writers in New York find dishes to praise, and the influential food critic of the *New York Times*, Bryan Miller, gave the restaurant three coveted stars (of a possible four) in a 1985 review.

To many people who dine at the Four Seasons, however, the company counts as much as the food and service. On a recent day, lunch guests included Gerald Ford, Henry Kissinger, Bill Blass, investment banker Peter G. Peterson, and financier Sanford I. Weill. "It is lunch as theater," says Art Cooper, the editor-in-chief of *Gentleman's Quarterly*.

DINNER

THE WHITEHALL CLUB

Appetizers Cocktails

Grey Perles of Fresh Beluga Caviar (when available) 6.50
Foie Gras Strasburgeois 5.00 — Canelloni, Quo Vadis 1.25
Pate de foie Maison 1.75 — Our Own Marinated Herrings 1.00
Imported Prosciutto with Melon in Season 2.25 — Broiled Grapefruit .75
Alaskan King Crab Legs, Mustard Mayonnaise 2.00
Scampi Meuniere 2.00 — *Fresh Fruit Cocktail 1.50*
Shrimp Cocktail, Sauce Maison 1.50 — Fresh Lump Crab Meat Cocktail 1.75
Baked Crabmeat, Deauville 2.00 — Cherrystone Clams 1.00
Escargots Bourguignonne 2.00
Baked Crabmeat, Hampton 2.00 — Shrimps Provencale 2.00
Blue Points in Half Shell 1.50 — *Escargots Saute Bordelaise 2.00*
Broiled Langoustines, Sauce Choron 2.00
Baked Oysters, Rockefeller or Bourguignonne 2.00

Soups

Consomme Double .65 — Chicken Broth .65 — *Petite Marmite, Henry IV 1.00* — *Baked Onion Soup Parisienne .75* — Green Turtle Xeres 1.50
Vichyssoise, Cold .65 — Madrilene (Jelly) .65 — *French Crayfish Bisque 1.25*
Chicken and Crab Gumbo WHITEHALL 1.50

Sea & Stream

Whole Dover Sole, Grilled Hoteliere 4.00 — Turbot, Saute Belle Meuniere 4.00 — Grilled Lake Superior Jumbo Whitefish 3.75
Whole Broiled Maine Lobster 6.50 — *Crab Meat Louise 4.25* — Frog Legs Meuniere or Provencale 4.25
Baked Lobster, Thermidor or Mornay 6.50 — *Shrimps Curry, Madras 4.00* — *Split and Boned Colorado Brook Trout Amandine 3.75*
Long Island Pearl Scallops, Saute Meuniere 4.25

Entrees

Veal Kidney Saute, Bruxelloise 3.75 — Scaloppine of Veal, Au Marsala 3.75 — *Rock Cornish Game Hen, WHITEHALL 4.00*
Sliced Beef Tenderloin Pepper Steak, Cantonese 5.50 — Steak Diane (prepared at table) 6.50 — Tournedos of Beef Rossini 6.25
Saute Calf's Liver and Bacon 4.00 — *Calf's Sweetbreads, Perigourdine 3.75* — Long Island Duckling Bigarade, Wild Rice 4.50
Our Special Corned Beef Hash WHITEHALL with Poached Egg 3.75 — Rack of Spring Lamb Persillade (for two, 45 minutes) 9.00
Supreme of Chicken, A La Kiev 3.75 — Royal Squab, Wild Rice 4.00 — Double Breast of Chicken, Saute Mascotte 4.00

From the Charcoal Broiler

Prime Sirloin 6.25 — Prime Double Sirloin 12.50 — Minute Steak 5.25 — Filet Mignon 6.25
Steak Au Poivre Flambe, Au Cognac 7.00 — Chateaubriand (for two) 12.50 — French Lamb Chops 4.25
Chopped Sirloin 3.75 — Calf's Liver Steak 4.00 — Calf's Sweetbreads 3.75 — *Half Spring Chicken 3.50*
At your request the above grillades will be accompanied by Perigourdine or Mushroom Sauce
(Bearnaise Sauce .75 Extra)

Vegetables

French String Beans .75 — *Petit Pois Bonne Femme .75* — *Baby Carrots .75* — Golden Kernel Corn .75
Spinach, Leaf or Creamed .75 — Broccoli Hollandaise 1.50 — Fried Onion Rings .75
Braised Belgian Endives 1.50 — *Large, White French Asparagus, Melted Butter or Hollandaise 2.00*
POTATOES: Hashed Brown .60 — French Fried .60 — Lyonnaise .60 — Baked Idaho .50 — Au Gratin .60 — Cottage Fried .75

Salads

Chicken 3.25; White Meat 3.75 — *Shrimp 3.75* — *Fresh Crab Meat 4.00*
WHITEHALL Salad 1.50 — Chef 1.50 — Belgian Endive 1.50 — Hearts of Lettuce .75 — Romaine .75
Kentucky Limestone Lettuce 1.25 — Avocado 1.25 — Mixed Green .75
Large White French Asparagus, Vinaigrette 2.00 — Hearts of Palm 1.50 — Sliced Tomato .75 — Caesar Salad 1.75
At your request Salads will be served with French Club, Sour Cream, Thousand Island or Lorenzo Dressing
Russian Dressing .75 — *Roquefort Dressing .75*

Desserts

Strawberries, Romanoff 2.25 — Assorted Ice Creams .70 — Fresh Pineapple au Kirsch 1.25 — Snowball 1.00
Sherbets .70 — Parfaits .75 — Coupe Angele 1.00 — Peach Melba 1.00 — *Cherries Jubilee 2.00*
Profiterolles au Famous WHITEHALL Chocolat 1.00 — Crepe Suzette 2.25 — Gateau du Jour .75 — Pear Helene 1.00 — Zabaglione 1.75
Whitehall Special Hot Caramel or Chocolate Fudge Sundae 1.00 — *Whitehall Special Chocolate Ice Cream .70*
Fruits Frais Au Porto 1.50
CHEESE: Liederkranz, Camembert, Swiss Gruyere, Roquefort, Cream Cheese, Tilsiter with Toasted Crackers, per portion .75

Patience is a virtue—So is culinary art—Please, your indulgence!

Special Blend Whitehall Coffee Pot .50 — Demi Tasse .25 — Sanka .40 — Postum .40 — Expresso .60
Orange Pekoe Tea .40 — Coffee Diable 2.25 — Grade "A" Milk .35 — Cocoa or Chocolate .60

FIGURE 23.5 The 1965 Whitehall Club dinner menu.
(Reproduced by permission.)

The Whitehall Club

Appetizers

Grilled Baby Lamb Chops with Prickly Pear Cactus Relish
ten dollars and fifty cents

Selection of Pates and Terrines, Raspberry Cumberland Sauce
seven dollars

Ragout of Escargot with Sweet Garlic and Morels
six dollars and fifty cents

Gravlax and Salmon Tartare with a Trio of Sauces
ten dollars

Jumbo Shrimps on Ice with Soy and Ginger Cocktail Sauce
ten dollars

Belon Oysters on Ice, Red Wine Vinegar, Chives and Shallot Sauce
eleven dollars

Soups

Soup Du Jour
four dollars

French Onion Soup Au Gratin with Aged Port Wine
four dollars and fifty cents

Lobster Bisque en Croute
five dollars

Salads

Whitehall Bibb Salad, choice of dressing
four dollars and fifty cents

Mixed Field Greens, Balsamic Vinaigrette
five dollars

Caesar Salad (Table Side)
seven dollars

Entrees

Grilled Ahi Tuna on Navy Beans Provencale
twenty one dollars

Sauteed Norwegian Salmon, Fresh Basil-Chardonnay Beurre Blanc
eighteen dollars

Grilled Florida Swordfish, Sundried Tomato-Saffron Sauce
nineteen dollars

Sauteed Breast of Duckling, Jalapeño-Papaya Relish
nineteen dollars

Sauteed Medallions of Veal Loin, Pear-Onion Compote
twenty two dollars and fifty cents

Braised Veal Chop, Fresh Rosemary Glace
twenty three dollars

Sauteed Breast of Free-Range Chicken
with Wild Mushrooms and Roasted Red Pepper Sauce
seventeen dollars

Specialties

Pepper Steak or Steak Diane Prepared Table Side
twenty four dollars

Dover Sole Meuniere
twenty five dollars

Roast Rack of Lamb, Ratatouille Timbale
twenty four dollars

Dry Aged Sirloin of Beef, with Herb Butter
twenty one dollars

Filet Mignon, Blue Cheese-Chive Butter
twenty two dollars

Dessert

Choose from our Pastry Cart
four dollars

Today's Hot Souffles
five dollars and fifty cents

Charles W. Hayes
Chef de Cuisine

Driss Idrissi
Maitre d' Hotel

FIGURE 23.6 The 1988 Whitehall Club dinner menu. (Reproduced by permission.)

Located at street level in the Seagram Building in Manhattan, the Four Seasons is in a high-rent neighborhood, which probably explains its high prices, but the operation is very successful. The restaurant's revenues have risen to about $14 million a year, from $2 million fifteen years ago.

Both the 1965 and 1988 Four Seasons menus list Hot and Cold Appetizers (Figures 23.7 and 23.8). The 1965 menu listed eighteen items with prices from $.95 to $7.50 (caviar). The 1988 menu lists thirteen Cold Appetizers ranging from $10.50 to $48.00 (Beluga caviar). The old Hot Appetizer listing included six items priced from $1.85 to $2.50.

The soup listing on the 1965 menu had ten items, while the 1988 menu lists only five. The prices in 1965 ranged from $.95 to $1.35; on the 1988 menu the soups cost $8.00 and $8.50.

The 1965 menu had three subheadings for its entrées under the heading This Evening's Entrées: Sea and Fresh Water Fish; A Variety of Seasonals; and Steaks, Chops, and Birds. Thirty-eight entrées were listed under these headings. Three French Lamb Chops sold for $5.95, and a Filet Mignon cost $7.50. A typical seafood was Salmon Steak for $5.50.

On the 1988 menu under the heading This Evening's Entrées twenty-two are listed, about half the number listed in 1965. Two of these items are prepared tableside, and five items are prepared for two people. A filet mignon on this menu costs $38.00; double lamb chops are $38.00; and filet of salmon is $37.50. The old menu listed four salads as a main course and seven salads as accompaniments, for prices ranging from $.85 to $5.85. Twelve selections were listed under the Vegetables and Potatoes (à la carte) listing, priced from $.95 to $3.85 for a spinach soufflé for two.

The 1988 menu lists twelve items under the heading of Salads, Vegetables and Potatoes, with prices ranging from $5.50 to $8.50. This menu also lists four dessert options: Flamed Peaches, $9.50; a Selection from the Dessert Wagon, $7.50; Sherbets and Ice Creams, $6.50; and a Choice of Soufflés (Cappuccino or Grand Marnier), $8.50.

A new section on the 1988 menu is the Spa Cuisine® listing, consisting of three appetizers ($13.50

Dinner at The Four Seasons

ICED BROCHETTE OF SHRIMP 2.25   PERIWINKLES Mignonette 1.65
Small Clams with Green Onions and TRUFFLES 1.65
YOUNG SALMON OR STURGEON, Our Smokehouse 2.95
SUMMER Hors d'Oeuvre, A Sampling 2.50
LOBSTER CHUNKS with Sorrel 3.25   A TUREEN OF AUGUST Fruit .95
Ham Mousse in Whole Peach, VIRGINIA 1.50

Hot Appetizers

Crisped Shrimp Filled with MUSTARD FRUITS 1.95
CALF'S BRAINS en Brioche 1.85   BEEF MARROW in Bouillon or Cream 1.85
Field Mushrooms and PROSCIUTTO EN CROUSTADE 2.25
THE FOUR SEASONS Mousse of Trout 2.50
SNAILS in Their Shells, BURGUNDIAN STYLE 1.85

Cream Cressonière 1.10   AN AUGUST Vegetable Potage 1.10
Consommé Royale 1.25
COLD: Beet and Onion Madrilène .95   Gazpacho 1.25

Sea and Fresh Water Fish

Planked Silver SALMON STEAK 5.50   RED CURRY OF ROCKFISH, Mango Rice 4.85
Broiled MAINE LOBSTER 6.50; Filled with CRABMEAT 7.85   The CLASSIC Truite au Bleu 5.50
Poached LOBSTER in Court-Boullion 6.75   Summer Sole, FOUR SEASONS 4.95

SOFT SHELL CRABS, Amandine 5.50   VEAL CHOPS Sautéed, Grand'mère 5.75
WHOLE BABY CHICKEN, Smitane Sauce, Wild Rice 5.50

A Variety of Seasonals

CALF'S LIVER AND PROSCIUTTO, Venetian Style 5.25   RARE FILET STROGONOFF 6.50
ROAST RACK OF LAMB Persillé with Robust Herbs, for Two 14.00
Braised SQUAB, Farci Suprême 6.50   Atelier of TWO QUAIL 6.75

BROILED OVER CHARCOAL *
Amish Ham Steak, Apricot Dumpling 4.85   Calf's Liver-THICK, Sage Butter 5.25
* * * * * * *
Sirloin VINTNERS STYLE 7.75   SKILLET STEAK with Smothered Onions 7.50
Beefsteak SCANDINAVIAN 7.75   Filet of Beef POIVRE, Flambé 8.00
Butterfly Steak Paillard, FOUR SEASONS 6.75
SPIT ROASTED WITH HERBS *
FARMHOUSE DUCKLING, Brandied Apricots, for Two 13.00
BROCHETTE OF MARINATED LAMB, Turkish Pilaff 5.25

Summer Salads

* * * * * * *
Bouillabaisse Salad 4.75   Mousse of Gaspé Salmon 5.65
JULEP OF CRABMEAT in Sweet Pepperoni 5.50   Buffet of Sliced Meats, DUTCH POTATO SALAD 5.85
AS A DINNER ACCOMPANIMENT *
COOKED CARROTS, Sweet and Sour 1.25   Beefsteak Tomato, CARVED AT TABLE 1.25
Beets and RIPE OLIVE .85   Early Summer Greens 1.25
OUR FIELD GREENS ARE SELECTED EACH MORNING AND WILL VARY DAILY

SEASONAL GATHERINGS MAY BE VIEWED IN THEIR BASKETS   ZUCCHINI with Walnuts .95
Leaf Spinach, ELIZABETH .95   BOUQUET PLATTER, per Person 1.50
MANGETOUTS 1.25   Cracked Wheat, Forestiére .95

Cold Appetizers

THE NEW AMSTERDAM HERRING, Pommes Vapeur 2.25   Todays Melon .95
Tidewater BLUE CRAB Lump 2.95   SMOKED NATIVE BROOK TROUT, Spiced Cream 2.65
SUMMER COUNTRY TERRINE 2.25   Cherrystones in PEPPER VINAIGRETTE 1.50
PROSCIUTTO with Ripe Figs or Melon 2.75   Caviar, per Serving 7.50
Little Neck or Cherrystone Clams 1.50   MOUSSE of Chicken Livers 2.25
Egg in TARRAGON ASPIC, Strasbourg Toast 1.75   VITTELLO TONNATO — PICCOLO 1.75

LOBSTER QUICHE, Savory 1.50
Smoked SALMON SOUFFLÉ, Onion Sauce 2.65
Mussels in POTS 2.25   Tiny Shrimps in Shoyu — French Fried 2.50
CRÊPES OF CRABMEAT, Imperial 2.45
Our Coquille Saint-Jacques 2.25

Soups and Broths

Chicken Cream with NEW OATS 1.35   Double Consommé with Sorrel 1.25
Onion Soup with PORT, Gratinée 1.25
Black Cherry Soup 1.25   Watercress VICHYSSOISE 1.10

BARQUETTE OF FLOUNDER with Glazed Fruits 4.95   Crabmeat Casanova FLAMBÉ 5.75
Sea Bass—GRILLED 4.65   LOBSTER AROMATIC Prepared Tableside 6.50
Frog's Legs PROVENÇALE or Sautéed with Moselle 5.25

This Evening's Entrees

ROAST SIRLOIN OF BEEF, Tomato Provençale 6.50
LAMB STEAK IN SUSU CURRY, Mango Rice 5.85

CRISPED DUCKLING with Peaches, Sauce Cassis 5.95   MEADOW VEAL CUTLET with Morels 5.75
Baby Pheasant in Golden Sauce—NUTTED WILD RICE 6.25
Sweetbreads in Mustard Crumbs, DIABLOTINE 5.50

Steaks, Chops, and Birds

* * * * * * *
Jersey Poularde 4.50   Three French Lamb Chops 5.95
* * * * * * *
SIRLOIN STEAK or FILET MIGNON Served for One 7.50; for Two 15.00
Côte de Boeuf, Bordelaise, for Two 18.00   Entrecôte à la Moëlle 7.75
Twin Tournedos with WOODLAND MUSHROOMS 7.00
* * * * * * *
Baby Lamb: ROASTED EPAULET, for Two 11.00; OREGANO ROASTED LEG, for Three 17.00
THE HEART OF THE PRIME RIB 5.50

* AS A MAIN COURSE
LOBSTER AND SHRIMP in Zucchini, Sauce Vincent 6.00   AVOCADO with Scallops Seviche 5.25
ROAST CHICKEN, Green Bean Salad 5.75   BEEF IN BURGUNDY ASPIC 4.75
* * * * * * *
NASTURTIUM Leaves 1.50   WILTED SPINACH and Bacon 1.35
Raw Mushrooms, MALABAR DRESSING 1.75
Salad Dressing with Roquefort or Feta Cheese .50 additional

Vegetables and Potatoes

The YOUNGEST CARROTS in Butter 1.25   BEIGNETS VARIES 1.35   ONIONS in Onions .95
BROCCOLI FLOWERS, Hollandaise 1.95   LANCASTER Corn Kernels, Tableside 1.50
Wild Rice 1.65   SOUFFLÉ OF SPINACH, for Two 3.85

FIGURE 23.7 The 1965 Four Seasons dinner menu. (Courtesy The Four Seasons restaurant. Reproduced by permission.)

and $14.00) and three main courses ($38.00, $37.00, and $37.50). The appetizers are Artichoke with Roasted Peppers, Summer Fruits with Mango Purée, and Seviche of Red Snapper in Orange. The main courses are A Skewer of Shrimp and Chicken, Breast of Pigeon with Wild Rice, and Escalope of Veal with Mustard Seeds.

Both the dinner and luncheon menus are printed and dated daily. The Four Seasons also changes its menu with the seasons, four times a year. The 1988 menu discussed here was a summer menu for Monday, August 22. The restaurant also has a Grill Room and a Bar Room menu plus a Theater Dinner menu.

The Theater Dinner menu lists eight appetizers, four entrées, and a Spa Cuisine® offering of one appetizer and one entrée. Four desserts are included in this package, which has a fixed price of $41.50. The Bar

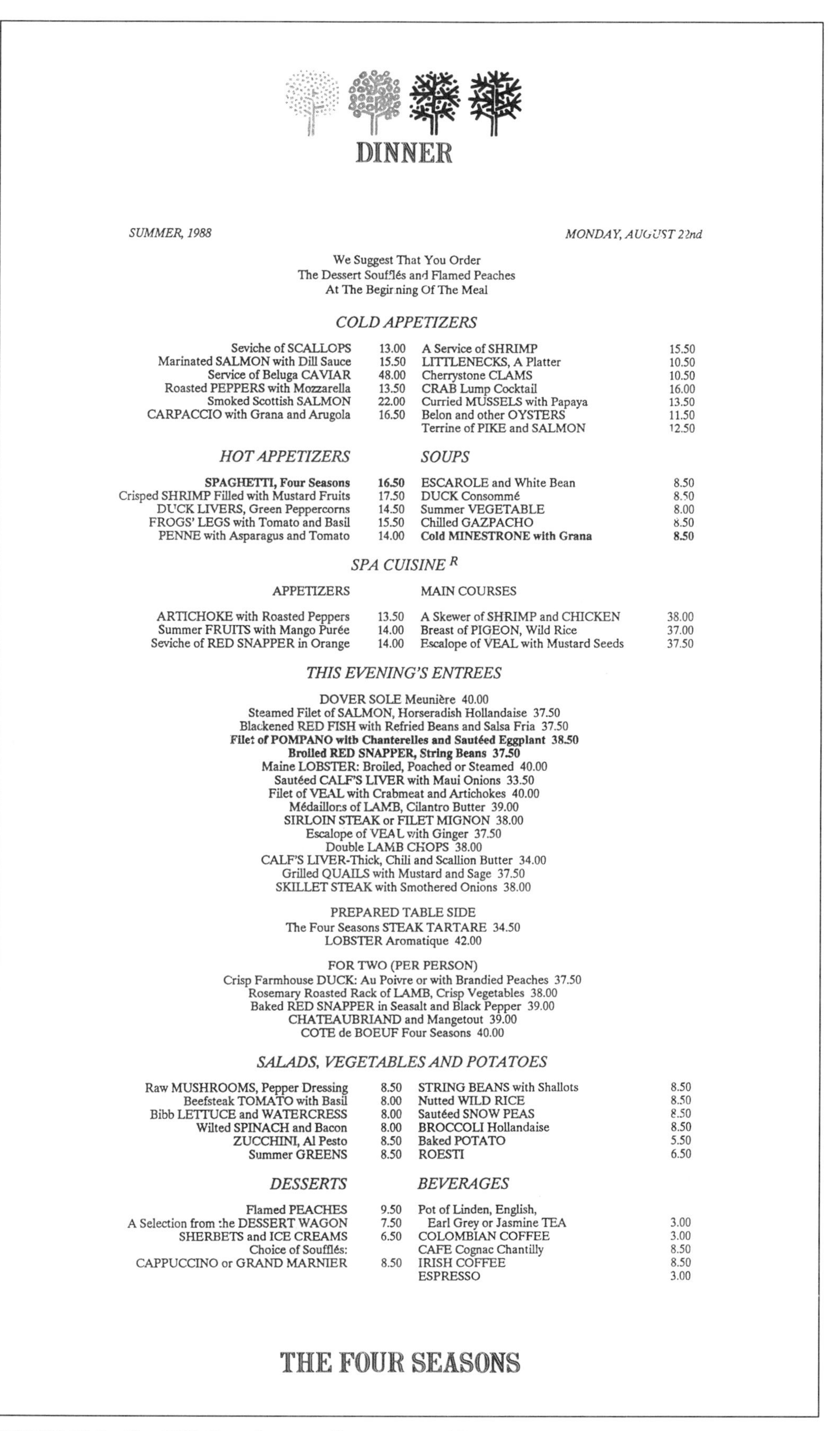

DINNER

SUMMER, 1988 *MONDAY, AUGUST 22nd*

We Suggest That You Order
The Dessert Soufflés and Flamed Peaches
At The Beginning Of The Meal

COLD APPETIZERS

Seviche of SCALLOPS	13.00	A Service of SHRIMP	15.50
Marinated SALMON with Dill Sauce	15.50	LITTLENECKS, A Platter	10.50
Service of Beluga CAVIAR	48.00	Cherrystone CLAMS	10.50
Roasted PEPPERS with Mozzarella	13.50	CRAB Lump Cocktail	16.00
Smoked Scottish SALMON	22.00	Curried MUSSELS with Papaya	13.50
CARPACCIO with Grana and Arugola	16.50	Belon and other OYSTERS	11.50
		Terrine of PIKE and SALMON	12.50

HOT APPETIZERS		*SOUPS*	
SPAGHETTI, Four Seasons	**16.50**	ESCAROLE and White Bean	8.50
Crisped SHRIMP Filled with Mustard Fruits	17.50	DUCK Consommé	8.50
DUCK LIVERS, Green Peppercorns	14.50	Summer VEGETABLE	8.00
FROGS' LEGS with Tomato and Basil	15.50	Chilled GAZPACHO	8.50
PENNE with Asparagus and Tomato	14.00	**Cold MINESTRONE with Grana**	**8.50**

SPA CUISINE [R]

APPETIZERS		MAIN COURSES	
ARTICHOKE with Roasted Peppers	13.50	A Skewer of SHRIMP and CHICKEN	38.00
Summer FRUITS with Mango Purée	14.00	Breast of PIGEON, Wild Rice	37.00
Seviche of RED SNAPPER in Orange	14.00	Escalope of VEAL with Mustard Seeds	37.50

THIS EVENING'S ENTREES

DOVER SOLE Meunière 40.00
Steamed Filet of SALMON, Horseradish Hollandaise 37.50
Blackened RED FISH with Refried Beans and Salsa Fria 37.50
Filet of POMPANO with Chanterelles and Sautéed Eggplant 38.50
Broiled RED SNAPPER, String Beans 37.50
Maine LOBSTER: Broiled, Poached or Steamed 40.00
Sautéed CALF'S LIVER with Maui Onions 33.50
Filet of VEAL with Crabmeat and Artichokes 40.00
Médaillons of LAMB, Cilantro Butter 39.00
SIRLOIN STEAK or FILET MIGNON 38.00
Escalope of VEAL with Ginger 37.50
Double LAMB CHOPS 38.00
CALF'S LIVER-Thick, Chili and Scallion Butter 34.00
Grilled QUAILS with Mustard and Sage 37.50
SKILLET STEAK with Smothered Onions 38.00

PREPARED TABLE SIDE
The Four Seasons STEAK TARTARE 34.50
LOBSTER Aromatique 42.00

FOR TWO (PER PERSON)
Crisp Farmhouse DUCK: Au Poivre or with Brandied Peaches 37.50
Rosemary Roasted Rack of LAMB, Crisp Vegetables 38.00
Baked RED SNAPPER in Seasalt and Black Pepper 39.00
CHATEAUBRIAND and Mangetout 39.00
COTE de BOEUF Four Seasons 40.00

SALADS, VEGETABLES AND POTATOES

Raw MUSHROOMS, Pepper Dressing	8.50	STRING BEANS with Shallots	8.50
Beefsteak TOMATO with Basil	8.00	Nutted WILD RICE	8.50
Bibb LETTUCE and WATERCRESS	8.00	Sautéed SNOW PEAS	8.50
Wilted SPINACH and Bacon	8.00	BROCCOLI Hollandaise	8.50
ZUCCHINI, Al Pesto	8.50	Baked POTATO	5.50
Summer GREENS	8.50	ROESTI	6.50

DESSERTS		*BEVERAGES*	
Flamed PEACHES	9.50	Pot of Linden, English,	
A Selection from the DESSERT WAGON	7.50	Earl Grey or Jasmine TEA	3.00
SHERBETS and ICE CREAMS	6.50	COLOMBIAN COFFEE	3.00
Choice of Soufflés:		CAFE Cognac Chantilly	8.50
CAPPUCCINO or GRAND MARNIER	8.50	IRISH COFFEE	8.50
		ESPRESSO	3.00

THE FOUR SEASONS

FIGURE 23.8 The 1988 Four Seasons dinner menu. (Courtesy The Four Seasons restaurant. Reproduced by permission.)

Room menu is à la carte, with fourteen appetizers, thirteen entrées, and three desserts. The Grill Room menu lists eight appetizers, nine main courses, and three Grill Room curries. This menu also lists four wines by the glass for $5.75.

Chardonnay, Groth, Napa 1985
Chardonnay, Sonoma Cutter 1986
Merlot, J. Phelps 1986
Moulin à Vent, L. Latour 1985

The wine list offers a very good selection of American, Italian, and French reds, whites, and champagnes, and sparkling wines. Prices for a bottle of wine range from $12.00 to $150.00 for a Taittinger Comte de Champagne Rosé 1982.

The changes in this menu (or menus) are significant. The number of items in all categories was reduced. The Theater Dinner menu and Spa Cuisine® were added, and more menus were created for the Bar and Grill Rooms.

24

The Most Common Menu Mistakes

A study of thousands of menus over many years shows a pattern of mistakes in design, listing, copy, and marketing. These are not just errors of omission and commission but also a failure of attitude. The menu is not taken seriously enough. Although it has been proved many times that changing and improving the menu alone can raise profits, restaurant operators just do not believe it.

First, some restaurateurs do not "know" their menu. That is, they do not know which items are the most popular, least popular, and in-between. And they may not know which items are the most profitable. Next, even if they do know the items' popularity and profitability, they do nothing to make profitable items more popular, or they do not know how to accomplish this.

What is needed is a menu strategy to build the check and move profitable items, make the unpopular items more popular, and keep the customer coming back. This means that the restaurant operator makes the major decisions as to what to sell and what to feature on the menu. These decisions should not be left to the printer, artist, or copywriter. They are important to an effective menu, but they cannot determine the importance of the items. They cannot determine the menu strategy; they can only implement it.

One common mistake is a menu too small in size or number of pages to accommodate the foods and beverages served. The result is crowding, type too small to read easily, no room for descriptions, and no room for specials in larger, bolder type. The size or number of pages should be the end result of the number of items listed—in easy-to-read type—with enough room allowed to give special attention in the form of copy, artwork, and bolder type to those items that should be featured to increase profits. Often too many items are listed on the menu. Menus vary considerably in this regard, but the general trend is toward a shorter listing. Thirty or forty items should be the maximum. The problem with an overly large menu is twofold. First, it often means that the customer takes a much longer time to order, which reduces turnover and therefore profit. In a restaurant in which the average check is $20 or $50, this is not a problem, but if the check is much less, the time spent by each customer does become important. Second, a very large menu can confuse the diner: There is so much to choose from that choosing becomes difficult.

Another common menu mistake is printing the listings in too-small type. Not everybody has 20/20 vision even with eyeglasses or contact lenses. And with the aging of the population, more and more diners may have vision problems. Also, the lighting in the restaurant may be designed for atmosphere, not for easy reading. The menu should be tested to see whether it can be read easily by everybody.

Printing the items in any color other than black is usually a mistake. Unless the type is a very dark brown or blue, it is hard to read. The safest practice is to print the words on the menu in black. This is especially true if colored paper is used.

Another common menu mistake is a lack of descriptions. Strangely enough, if asked, a restaurant manager or owner would probably speak eloquently about the food served, how it is prepared, the originality of the recipes, the quality of the ingredients, and so on. But none of this information may appear on the menu. This does not mean that a menu must be a literary masterpiece but, rather, that basic information should be included with some sell copy. A professional writer will provide the best menu copy if given adequate information. But the chef in the kitchen and the manager up front usually know more about the food and drink served. Answers to the following questions will provide most of the essential information:

1. What is it?
2. How is it prepared?
3. How is it served?
4. Does it have unusual taste and quality properties?
5. Where do the ingredients come from? (Norwegian Salmon, for example.)

Another menu mistake is to assume that one menu is enough. In some cases it is, but often the addition of extra menus can increase sales. Large hotels know that they need not only several different types of restaurants in the hotel but also several different menus—breakfast, luncheon, dinner, coffee shop, dining room, room service, and, in many cases, a poolside menu and a bar menu. A dessert menu can build the check, and a bar food menu can increase sales in the liquor department. A good wine list can increase wine sales. And having separate breakfast, luncheon, and dinner menus usually makes more sense than trying to combine them on one menu.

Given the relative decline in liquor consumption in restaurants, it is a mistake not to list and merchandise all of the drinks served. This means featuring imaginative mixed drinks (alcoholic and nonalcoholic) and providing a wine list, either separate or as part of the menu. Also, it is a good idea to recommend a specific wine for each entrée along with the copy describing the dish. Aperitifs should be part of the wine list, and after-dinner drinks should be part of the dessert menu.

Descriptions of house wines should include the vineyard or bottler and the vintage year. Some smart restaurant merchandisers have created beer lists of twenty or thirty different beers, and sometimes they give a bonus to drinkers who have tried ten or more of the different beers over a certain period of time.

A new mistake is appearing on computer-produced menus. Although the computer can print type in many different sizes and faces, most menus produced in this way look as though they were done on an ordinary typewriter. The answer is to get a designer to produce a sample menu that makes the best use of the type sizes and styles available on the computer.

The menu also should not be too "rigid," that is, it should allow for the addition of daily or weekly specials. These can be tip-ons or pages of the menu that can be replaced. This flexibility makes it possible for the kitchen to take advantage of seasonal foods as they become available, and it also gives variety to the repeat customer.

It almost goes without saying that the menu should be clean and not torn or soiled, but some restaurants still make a bad impression by using tired and worn-out menus. For those menus encased in plastic, wiping them with a damp cloth can clean them, but for those menus that are not coated, varnished, or covered with clear plastic, the answer is new, crisp, clean menus, every day.

In addition, the menu should offer basic information, including the restaurant's address, phone number, days and hours open, reservation policy, credit cards honored, and dress code (if any), as well as catering and takeout information. If miniature menus are handed out, this information is even more important.

Index